THE CHRONICLES OF NEWGATE

ARTHUR GRIFFITHS

CONTENTS

PREFACE   v

VOLUME 1

INTRODUCTORY CHAPTER (1)	3
MEDIÆVAL NEWGATE	19
NEWGATE IN THE SIXTEENTH CENTURY.	45
NEWGATE IN THE SEVENTEENTH CENTURY (DOWN TO THE GREAT FIRE).	71
NEWGATE IN THE SEVENTEENTH CENTURY (AFTER THE GREAT FIRE).	107
IN THE PRESS-YARD	148
EXECUTIONS	173
ESCAPES	213
THE GAOL CALENDAR	236
THE GAOL CALENDAR (CONTINUED)	279
THE GAOL FEVER	316
THE NEW GAOL	338
FOOTNOTES TO VOLUME 1	361

VOLUME 2

CRIMES AND CRIMINALS	381
NEWGATE DOWN TO 1818	429
PHILANTHROPY IN NEWGATE	464
THE BEGINNINGS OF PRISON REFORM	489
THE FIRST REPORT OF THE INSPECTORS OF PRISONS	519
EXECUTIONS (continued).	551
NEWGATE NOTORIETIES	583

NEWGATE NOTORIETIES (continued)	630
LATER RECORDS	677
NEWGATE NOTORIETIES	701
NEWGATE REFORMED	735
FOOTNOTES TO VOLUME 2	757

PREFACE

WHEN I undertook the work of which these two volumes are the result, I scarcely realized the extent of the task before me. Now at the termination of my labours, which have extended over a period of nearly five years, I cannot give my work to the public without regret that it has not been accompanied by deeper study and more widespread research. But I have, in truth, been almost overwhelmed by the mass of materials at hand. These always increased enormously with every digression, and I found at length that I *must* be satisfied with what I had instead of seeking for more. Even with this restriction I have often been compelled to reject much, to epitomize and perhaps unduly abbreviate what I have used. A really copious and detailed history of Newgate would be a most voluminous affair. This well-known prison, which has stood for centuries upon the same site, is in itself an epitome of the criminal history of England; to have traced its chronicles down from epoch to epoch, closely and minutely, would have been wearisome to the reader. There is a family resemblance in crimes in all ages;

when, therefore, the more prominent cases have been selected for description, a general impression will have been conveyed of the whole. I have followed this principle throughout, and have endeavoured to present a general, but not too detailed, picture of the various criminal periods through which Newgate has passed.

But the claims of Newgate on the public interest are not limited to the melancholy histories of those whom it has held in durance. Newgate, as the annexe of the Old Bailey, or great criminal law court of this city, has ever been closely connected with the administration of justice in this country. In its records are to be read the variations of our Statute Book. We may trace at Newgate the gradual amelioration of the penal code, from the days of its pitiless ferocity, to the time when, thanks to the incessant protests of humanitarian and philanthropist, a milder system of punishment became the rule. All this has found more than a passing mention in my pages. Again, Newgate, the city jail, the chief prison of the chief town in the kingdom, might have been expected to lead the van in prison reform; that it remained constantly, from the first and almost to the last, one of the worst-kept prisons in the kingdom, reflects but little credit upon those responsible for its management. The fact, however, that crying evils were constantly present in the great jail, brings Newgate at once into close connection with the whole subject of prison reform. To represent Newgate as it existed even before Howard commenced his crusade, and long afterwards, has naturally, therefore, fallen within the scope of my work. Nor have I confined myself strictly to this prison, but I have endeavoured to trace the slow progress of improvement throughout the whole country from first to last.

I cannot conclude these brief remarks without adding a few words of thanks to those who have assisted me in my undertaking. I have received much valuable information from Sidney

Smith, Esq., the last Governor of Newgate; from Mr. Mapperson, its last chief warder; and from many other officials of the prison. But most of all am I indebted to my friend, William Linton, Esq., formerly Governor of Petworth and Nottingham prisons, who has long rendered me the most cordial assistance and co-operation.

November, 1883.

VOLUME 1

INTRODUCTORY CHAPTER (1)

Brief survey of Newgate—The first gaol—Its antiquity—Its inmates and general condition—Whittington's prison—Rebuilt after the Fire—Misgovernment, neglect, and injustice—Capital convicts and executions—First dawn of reform—A new Newgate built by Dance—State of interior continues deplorable—Mrs. Fry—The first inspectors of prisons—Amelioration long insisted upon introduced at last—Newgate closed in 1880.

IN antiquity and varied interest Newgate prison yields to no place of durance in the world. A gaol has stood on this same site for almost a thousand years. The first prison was nearly as old as the Tower of London, and much older than the Bastille. Hundreds of thousands of "felons and trespassers" have from first to last been incarcerated within. To many it must have been an abode of sorrow, suffering, and unspeakable woe, a kind of terrestrial inferno, to enter which was to abandon every hope. Imprisonment was often lightly and capriciously inflicted in days before our liberties were fully won, and innumerable victims of tyranny and oppression have been lodged in Newgate.

Political troubles also sent their quota. The gaol was the half-way-house to the scaffold or the gallows for turbulent or short-sighted persons who espoused the losing side; it was the starting-place for that painful pilgrimage to the pillory or whipping-post which was too frequently the punishment for rashly uttered libels and philippics against constituted power. Newgate, again, was on the high road to Smithfield; in times of intolerance and fierce religious dissensions numbers of devoted martyrs went thence to suffer for conscience' sake at the stake. For centuries a large section of the permanent population of Newgate, as of all gaols, consisted of offenders against commercial laws. While fraudulent bankrupts were hanged, others more unfortunate than criminal were clapped into gaol to linger out their lives without the chance of earning the funds by which alone freedom could be recovered. Debtors of all degrees were condemned to languish for years in prison, often for the most paltry sums. The perfectly innocent were also detained. Gaol deliveries were rare, and the boon of arraignment and fair trial was strangely and unjustly withheld, while even those acquitted in open court were often haled back to prison because they were unable to discharge the gaoler's illegal fees. The condition of the prisoners in Newgate was long most deplorable. They were but scantily supplied with the commonest necessaries of life. Light scarcely penetrated their dark and loathsome dungeons; no breath of fresh air sweetened the fetid atmosphere they breathed; that they enjoyed the luxury of water was due to the munificence of a Lord Mayor. Their daily subsistence was most precarious. Food, clothing, fuel were doled out in limited quantities as charitable gifts; occasionally prosperous citizens bequeathed small legacies to be expended in the same articles of supply. These bare prison allowances were further eked out by the chance seizures in the markets; by bread forfeited as inferior or of light weight, and meat declared unfit to be publicly sold.

All classes and categories of prisoners were herded indiscriminately together: men and women, tried and untried, upright but misguided zealots with hardened habitual offenders. The only principle of classification was a prisoner's ability or otherwise to pay certain fees; money could purchase the squalid comfort of the master's side, but no immunity from the baleful companionship of felons equally well furnished with funds and no less anxious to escape the awful horror of the common side of the gaol. The weight of the chains, again, which, till quite recently, innocent and guilty alike wore, depended upon the price a prisoner could pay for "easement of irons," and it was a common practice to overload a new-comer with enormous fetters and so terrify him into lavish disbursement. The gaol at all times was so hideously overcrowded that plague and pestilence perpetually ravaged it, and the deadly infection often spread into the neighbouring courts of law.

The foregoing is an imperfect but by no means overcoloured picture of Newgate as it existed for hundreds of years, from the twelfth century, indeed, to the nineteenth. The description is supported by historical records, somewhat meagre at first, perhaps, but becoming more and more ample and better substantiated as the period grows less remote. We have but scant information as to the first gate-house gaol. Being part and parcel of the city fortifications, it was intended mainly for defence, and the prison accommodation which the fate afforded with its dungeons beneath, and garrets above, must have been of the most limited description. More pains were no doubt taken to keep the exterior strong and safe against attack, than to render the interior habitable, and we may conclude that the moneys willed by Whittington for the re-edification of Newgate were principally expended on the restoration and improvements of the prison. "Whit's palace," as rebuilt by Whittington's executors, lasted for a couple of centuries, and was throughout that period the principal gaol for the metropolis. Reference is constantly made to it in the history of the times. It was the natural receptacle for rogues, roysterers, and masterless men. It is described as a hot-bed of vice, a nursery of crime. Drunkenness, gaming, profligacy of the vilest sort, went forward in the prison without let or hindrance. Contemporary petitions, preserved in the State papers, penned by inmates of Newgate pining for liberty, call their prison-house a foul and noisome den. The gaoler for the time being was certain to be a brutal partisan of the party in power, especially bitter to religious or political opponents who fell into his hands. But too frequently also he was a rapacious, extortionate, over-reaching despot, whose first and only thought was to turn the prisoners into profit, and make all the money he could out of those whom the law put completely in his power.

With occasional, but not always sufficient, repairs, but without structural alterations, Whittington's Newgate continued to serve down to the seventeenth century. About 1629 it was in a state of utter ruin, and such extensive works were undertaken to re-edify it that the security of the gaol was said to be endangered, and it was thought better to pardon most of the prisoners before they set themselves free. Lupton, in his 'London Carbonadoed,' speaks of Newgate as "new-fronted and new-faced" in 1638. Its accommodations must have been sorely tried in the troublous years which followed. It seems to have been in the time of the Commonwealth when "our churches were made into prisons," and demands for space had greatly multiplied, that Newgate was increased by the addition of the buildings belonging to the Phœnix Inn in Newgate Street. The great fire of 1666 gutted, if not completely destroyed, Newgate, and its reconstruction became imperative. Some say Wren was the architect of the new prison, but the fact is not fully substantiated. Authentic and detailed information has, however, been preserved concerning it; it is figured in a familiar woodcut which may be seen in every modern history of London, while a full description of the interior, both plan and appropriation, has been left by an anonymous writer, who was himself an inmate of the gaol[2]. The prison was still subordinated to the gate, which was an ornate structure, with great architectural pretensions. But as a writer in the 'Gentleman's Magazine' well put it about a century ago, "The sumptuousness of the outside but aggravated the misery of the wretches within." Some effort was made to classify, and the Newgate of that day contained five principal divisions or sides: there was the master's side, for debtors and felons respectively; the common side, for those same two classes of prisoners; and lastly the press yard, for prisoners of note. The right to occupy the master's side was a luxury dearly purchased, but the accommodation obtained, albeit indifferent, was palatial to that provided for the impecunious on the common side. The only inmates of the Newgate prison I am now describing who were comparatively well off, were those admitted to the press yard; a division composed of "large and spacious rooms" on all the three floors of the prison, and deemed by a legal fiction to be part of the governor's house.

How desperate was the case of the bulk of the inmates of Newgate will be amply set forth as my narrative proceeds. A few brief facts will suffice here to give a general idea of this foul prison house. The whole place except the press yard was so dark that candles, "links or burners," were used all day long; the air was so inconceivably disgusting, that the ventilator on the top of the prison could exercise no remedial effect. That malignant disease, the gaol fever, was chronic, and deaths from it of frequent occurrence. Doctors could be got with difficulty to attend the sick in Newgate, and it was long before any regular medical officer was appointed to the prison. Evil was in the ascendant throughout; wickedness and profligacy prospered; the weakest always went to the wall. Tyranny and oppression were widely practised: not only were the gaolers extortionate, but their subordinates, the inferior turnkeys, even the bed-makers, and the gate-keeper's wife levied black mail on the pretence of affording relief, and with threats or actual ill-usage when payment was withheld. Certain favoured prisoners wielded recognized authority over their fellows. Unwritten but accepted customs suffered the general body to exact "garnish," or "chummage," from new comers, fees for the privilege of approaching the fire, and generally for immunity from persecution, the sums thus raised being forthwith expended in strong drink. The "cellarmen" were selected prisoners who could sell candles at their own prices, and got a percentage upon the liquors consumed, with other advantages. Other prisoners were employed in the distribution of food; in the riveting and removing of shackles; even in the maintenance of discipline, and when so acting were armed with a flexible weapon, "to the great terror and smart of those who dispute their authority." Into these filthy dens, where misery stalked rampant and corruption festered, unhappy prisoners brought their families, and the population was greatly increased by numbers of innocent persons, women, and even children, to be speedily demoralized and utterly lost. Lunatics raving mad ranged up and down the wards, a terror to all they encountered. Common women were freely admitted; mock marriages were of constant occurrence, and children were frequently born within the precincts of the gaol. There was but little restriction upon the entrance of visitors. When any great personage was confined in Newgate, he held daily levees and received numbers of fashionable folk. Thus Count Konigsmark, when arrested for complicity in the murder of Mr. Thynne, "lived nobly" in the keeper's house, and was daily visited by persons of quality. When political prisoners, Jacobite rebels, or others were incarcerated, their sympathizers and supporters came to "comfort them" by sharing their potations. Even a notorious highwayman like Maclane, according to Horace Walpole, entertained great guests, and it was the "mode" for half the world to drive to Newgate and gaze on him in the "condemned hold."

In sharp contrast with the privations and terrible discomforts of the poorer sort was the wild revelry of these aristocratic prisoners of the press yard. They had every luxury to be bought with money, freedom alone excepted, and that was often to be compassed by bribing dishonest officials to suffer them to escape. They kept late hours, collecting in one another's rooms to roar out seditious songs over innumerable bowls of punch. At times they exhibited much turbulence, and refused to be locked up in the separate chambers allotted to them. No attempt was made to coerce them, or oblige them to observe due decorum and submit to the discipline of the prison. Yet while they thus experienced ill-placed and unjust leniency, others far less culpable were ground down till they were "slowly murdered there by the intolerable horrors of the place."

As a general rule the movement of offenders through Newgate was pretty rapid. The period of imprisonment for debtors might be often indefinitely prolonged, and there was the well-known case of Major Bernardi and his companions, who were detained for forty years in Newgate without trial or the chance of it. Some, too, languished awaiting transfer to the West Indian or American plantations by the contractors to whom they were legally sold. But for the bulk of the criminal prisoners there was one speedy and effectual system of removal, that of capital punishment. Executions were wholesale in those times. The code was sanguinary in the extreme. The gallows tree was always heavily laden. There was every element of callous brutality in the manner of inflicting the extreme penalty of the law. From the time of sentence to the last dread moment the convict was exhibited as a show, or held up to public contempt and execration. Heartless creatures flocked to the gaol chapel to curiously examine the aspect of condemned malefactors. Men who had but a short time to live mingled freely with their fellow-prisoners, recklessly carousing, and often making a boast that they laughed to scorn and rejected the well-meant ministrations of the ordinary.

The actual ceremony was to the last degree cold-blooded and wanting in all the solemn attributes fitting the awful scene. The doomed was carried in an open cart to Tyburn or other appointed place; the halter already encircled his neck, his coffin was at his feet, by his side the chaplain or some devoted amateur philanthropist and preacher striving earnestly to improve the occasion. For the mob it was a high day and holiday; they lined the route taken by the ghastly procession, encouraging or flouting the convict according as he happened to be a popular hero or unknown to criminal fame. In the first case they cheered him to the echo, offered him bouquets of flowers, or pressed him to drink deep from St. Giles's Bowl; in the latter they pelted him with filth and overwhelmed him with abuse. The most scandalous scenes occurred on the gallows. The hangman often quarrelled with his victim over the garments, which the former looked upon as a lawful perquisite, and which the latter was disposed to distribute among his friends; now and again the rope broke, or the drop was insufficient, and Jack Ketch had to add his weight to the hanging body to assist strangulation. Occasionally there was a personal conflict, and the hangman was obliged to do his office by sheer force. The convicts were permitted to make dying speeches, and these orations were elaborated and discussed in Newgate weeks before the great day; while down in the yelling crowd beneath the gallows spurious versions were hawked about and rapidly sold. It was a distinct gain to the decency and good order of the metropolis when Tyburn and other distant points ceased to be the places of execution, and hangings were exclusively carried out in front of Newgate, just over the debtors' door. But some of the worst features of the old system survived. There was still the melodramatic sermon, in the chapel hung with black, before a large congregation collected simply to stare at the convicts squeezed into one pew, who in their turn stared with mixed feelings at the coffin on the table just before their eyes. There was still the same tumultuous gathering to view the last act in tragedy, the same bloodthirsty mob swaying to and fro before the gates, the same blue-blooded spectators, George Selwyn or my Lord Tom Noddy, who breakfasted in state with the gaoler, and so got a box seat or rented window opposite at an exorbitant rate. The populace were like degenerate Romans in the amphitheatre waiting for the butchery to begin. They fought and struggled desperately for front places: people fell and were trampled to death, hoarse roars came from thousands of brazen throats, which swelled into a terrible chorus as the black figures of the performers on the gallows stood out against the sky. "Hats off!" "Down in front!" these cries echoed and re-echoed in increasing volume, and all at once abruptly came to an end—the bolt had been drawn, the drop had fallen, and the miserable wretch had gone to his long home.

The policy which had brought about the substitution of Newgate for Tyburn no doubt halted halfway, but it was enlightened, and a considerable move towards the private executions of our own times. It was dictated by the more humane principles which were gradually making head in regard to criminals and crime. Many more years were to elapse, however, before the eloquence of Romilly was to bear fruit in the softening of our sanguinary penal code. But already John Howard had commenced his labours, and his revelations were letting in a flood of light upon the black recesses of prison life. It is to the credit of the authorities of the City of London that they recognized the necessity for rebuilding Newgate on a larger and more improved plan before the publication of Howard's reports. The great philanthropist made his first journey of inspection towards the end of 1773; in the following year he laid the information he had obtained before the House of Commons, and in 1777 published the first edition of his celebrated 'State of Prisons.' As early as 1755 the Common Council had condemned Newgate in no measured terms; declared it to be habitually overcrowded with "victims of public justice, under the complicated distresses of poverty, nastiness, and disease," who had neither water, nor air, nor light in sufficient quantities; the buildings were old and ruinous, and incapable of any "improvement or tolerable repairs." It was plainly admitted that the gaol ought to be at once pulled down. But as usual the difficulty of providing funds cropped up, and the work, though urgent, was postponed for some years. The inadequacy of the prison was so obvious, however, that the matter was presently brought before a committee of the House of Commons, and the necessity for rebuilding clearly proved. A committee of the Corporation next met in 1767 to consider ways and means, and they were fortified in their decision to rebuild by convincing evidence of the horrible condition of the existing prison. A letter addressed to the committee by Sir Stephen Jansen stigmatizes it as "an abominable sink of beastliness and corruption." He spoke from full knowledge, having been sheriff when the prison was decimated by gaol fever. In the same year Parliamentary powers were obtained to raise money to rebuild the place, and the new Newgate was actually commenced in 1770, when Lord Mayor Beckford, father of "Vathek" Beckford, laid the first stone. Its architect was George Dance, and the prison building, which still stands to speak for itself, has been counted one of his finest works. Howard, who gives this historic prison the first place in his list, must have visited it while the new buildings were in progress. The plan did not find favour with him, but he enters into no particulars, and limits his criticisms to remarking, "that without more than ordinary care the prisoners in it will be in great danger of gaol fever." According to modern notions the plan was no doubt faulty in the extreme. Safe custody, a leading principle in all prison construction, was compassed at the expense of most others. The prison façade is a marvel of strength and solidity, but until reappropriated in recent years its interior was a limited confined space, still darkened, and deprived of ventilation, by being parcelled out into courts, upon which looked the narrow windows of the various wards.

The erection of the "new and commodious gaol," as it is described in an Act of the period, proceeded rapidly, but three or four years after Howard's visit it was still uncompleted. This Act recites what had been done, referring to the valuable, extensive areas, which had been taken in for the construction of this great prison, and provides additional funds. In 1780, however, an unexpected catastrophe happened, and the new buildings were set on fire by the Lord George Gordon rioters, and so much damaged that the most comprehensive repairs were indispensable. These were executed in 1782. Many years were to elapse before any further alterations or improvements were made.

It was soon evident that Dance's Newgate, imposing and appropriate as were its outlines and façade, by no means satisfied all needs. The progress of enlightenment was continuous, while complaints that would have been stifled or ignored previously were now occasionally heard. Yet the wretched prisoners continued to be closely packed together. Transportation had now been adopted as a secondary punishment, and numbers who escaped the halter were congregated in Newgate waiting removal beyond the seas. The population of the prison had amounted to nearly six hundred at one time in 1785. According to a presentment made by the Grand Jury in 1813, in the debtors' side, built for one hundred, no less than three hundred and forty were lodged; in the female felons' ward there were one hundred and twenty in space intended for only sixty. These females were destitute and in rags, without bedding, many without shoes. In later years the figures rose still higher, and it is authoritatively stated that there were as many as eight, nine, even twelve hundred souls immured within an area about three-quarters of an acre in extent. We have the evidence of trustworthy persons that grievous abuses still continued unchecked. All prisoners were still heavily ironed until large bribed had been paid to obtain relief. All manner of unfair dealing was practised towards the prisoners. The daily allowance of food was unequally divided. Bread and beef were issued in the lump, and each individual had to scramble and fight for his share. Prisoners had no bedding beyond a couple of dirty rugs. Exorbitant gaol fees were still demanded on all sides; the Governor eked out his income by what he could extort, and his subordinates took bribes wherever they could get them. It was customary to sell the place of wardsman, with its greater ease and power of oppression, to the highest bidder among the prisoners. Unlimited drinking was allowed within the walls; the prison tap, with the profits on sales of ale and spirits, was a part of the Governor's perquisites. All this time there was unrestrained intercommunication between the prisoners; the most depraved were free to contaminate and demoralize their more innocent fellows. Newgate was then, and long continued, a school and nursery for crime. It was established beyond doubt that burglaries and robberies were frequently planned in the gaol, while forged notes and false money were often fabricated within the walls and passed out into the town.

The disclosure of these frightful evils led to a Parliamentary inquiry in 1814, and the worst facts were fully substantiated.[3] The prison was not water-tight, rain came in through the roof;

broken windows were left unglazed; it was generally very dirty; the gaoler admitted that with its smoked ceilings and floors of oak, caulked with pitch, it never could look clean. The prisoners were not compelled to wash, and cleanliness was only enforced by a general threat to shut out visitors. Sometimes a more than usually filthy person was stripped, put under the pump, and forced to go naked out into the yard. The poor debtors were in terrible straits, herded together, and dependent upon the casual charities for supplies. Birch, the well-known tavern-keeper, and others, sent in broken victuals, generally the stock meat which had helped to make the turtle-soup for civic feasts. The chaplain took life very easy, and, beyond preaching to those who cared to attend chapel, ministered but little to the spiritual wants of his charge. His indifference was strongly condemned in the report of the Commons Committee. The chapel congregation was generally disorderly: prisoners yawned, and coughed, and talked enough to interrupt the service; women were in full view of the men, and many greetings, such as "How do you do, Sall?" often passed from pew to pew. No attempt was made to keep condemned convicts, male or female, separate from other prisoners; they mixed freely with the rest, saw daily any number of visitors, and had unlimited drink.

It was a little before the publication of the Committee's Report that that noble woman, Mrs. Fry, first visited Newgate. The awful state of the female prison, as she found it, is described in her memoirs. Three years elapsed between her first visit and her second. In the interval, the report last quoted had borne some fruit. An Act had been brought in for the abolition of gaol fees; gaol committees had been appointed to visit and check abuses, and something had been done to ameliorate the condition of the neglected female outcasts. Yet the scene within was still dreadful, and permanent amelioration seemed altogether beyond hope. What Mrs. Fry quickly accomplished against tremendous difficulties, is one of the brightest facts in the whole history of philanthropy. How she persevered in spite of prediction of certain failure; how she won the co-operation of lukewarm officials; how she provided the manual labour for which these poor idle hands were eager, and presently transformed a filthy den of corruption into a clean and whitewashed workroom, in which sat rows of women, recently so desperate and degraded, stitching and sewing orderly and silent: these extraordinary results with the most unpromising materials will be found detailed in a subsequent page.[4]

There was no one, unfortunately, to undertake the same great work upon the male side. "The mismanagement of Newgate had been for years notorious," says the Hon. H. G. Bennet, in a letter addressed to the Common Council, "yet there is no real reform. The occasional humanity of a sheriff may remedy an abuse, redress a wrong, cleanse a sewer, or whitewash a wall, but the main evils of want of food, air, clothing, bedding, classification, moral discipline remain as before." But appeals, however eloquent, were of small avail. Time passed, and at last there was a general impetus towards prison reform. The question became cosmopolitan. Close inquiry was made into the relative value of systems of punishment at home and abroad. Millbank Penitentiary was erected at the cost of half a million, to give full scope to the experiment of reformation. Public attention was daily more and more called to prison management. Yet through it all Newgate remained almost unchanged. It was less crowded, perhaps, since having been relieved by the opening of the Giltspur Street Compter, and that was all that could be said. In 1836, when the newly-appointed Government inspectors made their first report, the internal arrangements of Newgate were as bad as ever. These inspectors were earnest men, who had made prisons and prison management a study. One was the Rev. Whitworth Russell, for many years chaplain of Millbank; the other Mr. Crawford, who had written an admirable State paper upon the prisons of the United States, the result of long personal investigation.

The report framed a strong indictment against the Corporation, who were mainly responsible. Well might the inspectors close it with an expression of poignant regret, not unmixed with indignation, at the frightful picture presented of the existing state of Newgate.[5] The charges were unanswerable, the only remedy immediate and searching reform. As a matter of fact various abuses and irregularities were put an end to the following year, but the alterations, so said the inspectors in a later report, only introduced the outward semblance of order. "The master evil, that of gaol association, and consequent contamination, remained in full activity." Year after year the inspectors repeated their condemnatory criticisms, but were unable to effect any radical change. For quite another decade, Newgate continued a by-word with prison reformers. In 1850, Colonel, afterwards Sir Joshua Jebb, told the select committee on prison discipline, that he considered Newgate, from its defective construction, one of the worst prisons in England. Captain Williams, a prison inspector, was of the same opinion, and called Newgate quite the worst prison in his district. The fact was, limitation of area rendered it quite impossible to reconstitute Newgate and bring it up to the standard of modern prison requirements. Either great additions must be made to the site, an operation likely to be exceedingly costly, or a new building must be erected elsewhere. These points had already been discussed repeatedly and at length by gaol committees and the Court of Aldermen, and a decision finally arrived at, to erect a new prison on the Tufnell Park Estate, in the north of London. And this, now known as Holloway Prison, was opened in 1852.

Newgate, relieved of the unnatural demands upon its accommodation, was easily and rapidly reformed. It became now simply a place of detention for city prisoners, an annexe of the Old Bailey, filled and emptied before and after the sessions. Considerable sums were expended in reconstructing the interior and providing the largest possible number of separate cells for the confinement of the limited number of prisoners who now required to be accommodated. As such it continued to serve until the year 1880, when, under the principles of concentration which formed the basis of the Prison Act of 1877, it was closed. It was found the House of Detention at Clerkenwell had sufficient space to accommodate all prisoners awaiting trial at the Central Criminal Court, and that Newgate prison was not wanted except when the sessions were actually sitting. It ceased, therefore, to be used except as a temporary receptacle at such times, but it is also still the metropolitan place of execution.

MEDIÆVAL NEWGATE

Earliest accounts of Newgate prison—The New Gate, when built and why—Classes of prisoners incarcerated—Of high degree, as well as all categories of common criminals—Brawlers, vagabonds, and 'roarers' committed to Newgate; also those who sold adulterated food—Exposure in pillory and sometimes mutilation preceded imprisonment—The gradual concession of privileges to the Corporation—Lord Mayor constituted perpetual justice of the peace—Corporation obtains complete jurisdiction over Newgate—The sheriffs responsible for the good government of prisons on appointment—Counted prisoners held keys, and the cocket or seal of Newgate—Forbidden to farm the prison or sell the post of keeper—The rule in course of time contravened, and keepership became purchaseable—Conflict of authority between sheriffs and Corporation as to appointment of keeper—Condition of the prisoners in mediæval times—Dependent on charity for commonest necessaries; food, clothing, and water—A breviary bequeathed—Gaol falls into ruin and is rebuilt by Whittington's executors in 1422—This edifice two centuries later is restored, but destroyed in the great Fire of 1666.

THE earliest authentic mention of Newgate as a gaol or prison for felons and trespassers occurs in the records of the reign of King John. In the following reign, A.D. 1218, Henry III. expressly commands the sheriffs of London to repair it, and promises to reimburse them for their outlay from his own exchequer. This shows that at that time the place was under the direct control of the king, and maintained at his charges. The prison was above the gate, or in the gate-house, as was the general practice in ancient times. Thus Ludgate was long used for the incarceration of city debtors. To the gate-house of Westminster were committed all offenders taken within that city; and the same rule obtained in the great provincial towns, as at Newcastle, Chester, Carlisle, York, and elsewhere. Concerning the gate itself, the New Gate and its antiquity, opinions somewhat differ. Maitland declares it to be "demonstrable" that Newgate was one of the four original gates of the city; "for after the fire of London in 1666," he goes on to say, "in digging a foundation for the present Holborn bridge, the vestigia of the Roman military way called Watling Street were discovered pointing directly to this gate; and this I take to be an incontestable proof of an original gate built over the said way in this place." Maitland in this conjecture altogether departs from the account related by Stowe. The latter gives a precise and circumstantial description of the building of Newgate, which he calls the fifth principal gate of the city. There is, however, every reason to suppose that a gate had existed previously hereabouts in the city wall, and the site of the new gate is identical with one which was long called Chamberlain's Gate, because that official had his court in the Old Bailey hard by. According to Stowe, Newgate was erected about the time of Stephen or the first Henry under the following circumstances. After the destruction of the old cathedral church of St. Paul in 1086, Mauritius, Bishop of London, resolved to build an entirely new edifice upon the site, intending to construct a work so grand that "men judged it would never be performed, it was so wonderful to them for height."[6] In pursuance of his great scheme the Bishop enclosed a large space of ground for cemetery and churchyard, and in doing so stopped up and obstructed the great thoroughfare from Aldgate in the east to Ludgate in the west. The traffic now was driven to choose between two long detours: one passing to the northward of the new cemetery wall, and so by Paternoster Row, Ave Maria Lane, and Bowyer Row, to Ludgate; the other, still more circuitous, by Cheape and Watling Street, thence southward through Old Change, west through Carter Lane, up Creadlam north, and finally westward again to Ludgate. These routes, as Stowe observes, were "very cumbersome and dangerous both for horse and man. For remedy whereof a new gate was made and so called, by which men and cattle, with all manner of carriages, might pass more directly (as before) from Aldgate through West Cheape to St. Paul's on the north side, through St. Nicholas Shambles and Newgate market to Newgate, and from thence to any part westward over Holborn Bridge, or turning without the gate into Smithfield and through Iseldon (Islington) to any part north and by west."

Of that ancient Newgate, city portal and general prison-house combined, but scant records remain. A word or two in the old chroniclers, a passing reference in the history of those troublous times, a few brief and formal entries in the city archives—these are all that have been handed down to us. But we may read between the lines and get some notion of mediæval Newgate. Foul, noisome, terrible are the epithets applied to this densely-crowded place of durance.[7] It was a dark, pestiferous den, then, and for centuries later, perpetually ravaged by deadly diseases.

Its inmates were of all categories. Prisoners of State and the most abandoned criminals were alike committed to it. Howel, quoted by Pennant, states that Newgate was used for the imprisonment of persons of rank long before the Tower was applied to that purpose. Thus Robert de Baldock, Chancellor of the realm in the reign of Edward II., to whom most of the miseries of the kingdom were imputed, was dragged to Newgate by the mob. He had been first committed to the Bishop's prison, but was taken thence to Newgate as a place of more security; "but the unmerciful treatment he met with on the way occasioned him to die there within a few days in great torment from the blows which had been inflicted on him." Again, Sir Thomas Percie, Lord Egremond, and other people of distinction, are recorded as inmates in 1457. But the bulk of the prisoners were of meaner condition, relegated for all manner of crimes. Some were parlous offenders. There was but little security for life or property in that old London, yet the law made constant war against the turbulent and reckless roughs. Stowe draws a lively picture of the state of the city at the close of the twelfth century. One night a brother of Earl Ferrers was slain privately in London. The king (Edward I.) on hearing this "swore that he would be avenged on the citizens." It was then a common practice in the city for "an hundred or more in company of young and old to make nightly invasions upon the houses of the wealthy, to the intent to rob them, and if they found any man stirring in the city they would presently murder him, insomuch that when night was come no man durst adventure to walk in the streets." Matters at length came to a crisis. A party of citizens young and wealthy, not mere rogues, attacked the "storehouse of a certain rich man," and broke through the wall. The "good man of the house" was prepared and lay in wait for them "in a corner," and saw that they were led by one Andrew Bucquinte, who carried a burning brand in one hand and a pot of coals in the other, which he essayed to kindle with the brand. Upon this the master, crying "Thieves!" rushed at Bucquinte and smote off his right hand. All took to flight "saving he that had lost his hand," whom the good man in the next morning delivered to Richard de Lucy, the king's justice. The thief turned informer, and "appeached his confederates, of whom many were taken and many were fled." One, however, was apprehended, a citizen "of great countenance, credit, and wealth, named John Senex, or John the Old, who, when he could not acquit himself by the water dome, offered the king 500 marks for his acquittal; but the king commanded that he should be hanged, which was done, and the city became more quiet."

Long before this, however, Edward I. had dealt very sharply with evil-doers. By the suspension of corporation government following that king's conflict with the city authority, "all kinds of licentiousness had got leave to go forward without control." At length the frequency of robberies and murders produced the great penal statute of the 13 Edward I. (1287). By this Act it was decreed that no stranger should wear any weapon, or be seen in the streets after the ringing of the couvre-feu bell at St. Martin's-le-Grand; that no vintners and victuallers should keep open house after the ringing of the said bell under heavy fines and penalties; that "whereas it was customary for profligates to learn the art of fencing, who were thereby emboldened to commit the most unheard-of villanies, no such school should be kept in the city for the future upon the penalty of forty marks for every offence." Most of the aforesaid villanies were said to be committed by foreigners who from all parts incessantly crowded to London; it was therefore ordered that no person not free of the city should be suffered to reside therein; and even many of those that were were obliged to give security for their good behaviour.[8]

The 'Liber Albus,' as translated by Riley, gives the penalties for brawling and breaking the peace about this date. It was ordained that any person who should draw a sword, *misericorde* (a dagger with a thin blade used for mercifully despatching a wounded enemy), or knife, or any arm, even though he did not strike, should pay a fine to the city of half a mark, or be imprisoned in Newgate for fifteen days. If he drew blood the fine was twenty shillings, or forty days in Newgate; in striking with the fist two shillings, or eight days' imprisonment, and if blood was drawn forty pence, or twelve days. Moreover, the offenders were to find good sureties before release, and those on whom the offence was committed had still "recovery by process of law."

Nor were these empty threats. The laws and ordinances against prowlers and vagabonds, or "night-walkers," as they were officially styled, were continually enforced by the attachment of offenders. Many cases are given in the memorials of London. Thus, 4 Edw. II. A.D. 1311: Elmer de Multone was attached on indictment as a common night-walker in the ward of Chepe; "in the day," it was charged, "he was wont to entice persons and strangers unknown to a tavern and there deceive them by using false dice." He was furthermore indicted "in Tower ward for being a cruiser and night-walker against the peace, as also for being a common 'rorere.'"[9] Multone was committed to prison. Others met with similar treatment. John de Rokeslee was attached as being held suspected of evil and of beating men coming into the city;" "Peter le Taverner, called Holer," the same, and for going with sword and buckler and other arms; John Blome was indicted "as a common vagabond[10] for committing batteries and other mischiefs in the ward of Aldresgate and divers other wards." "A chaplain," our modern curate, Richard Heryng, was attached on similar charges, but was acquitted. Not only were the "roarers" themselves indicted when taken in this act, but also those who harboured them, like John Baronu mentioned in the same document as attached "for keeping open house at night, and receiving night-walkers and players at dice." The prohibition against fencing-masters was also rigorously enforced, as appears by the indictment of "Master Roger le Skirmisour, for keeping a fencing school for divers men, and for enticing thither the sons of respectable persons so as to waste and spend the property of their fathers and mothers upon bad practices, the result being that they themselves become bad men. Master Roger, upon proof of a jury that he was guilty of the trespasses aforesaid, was committed to Newgate."

Incarceration in Newgate, however, was meted out promptly for other offences than those against which the last-mentioned legislation was directed. Priests guilty of loose living, Jews accused rightly or wrongly, now of infanticide, of crucifying children, now of coining and clipping, found themselves in the gaol for indefinite periods. People, again, who adulterated or sold bad food were incontinently clapped into gaol. Thus William Cokke of Hesse (or Hayes) was charged with carrying a sample of wheat in his hand in the market within Newgate, and following one William, the servant of Robert de la Launde Goldmsith, about from sack to sack, as the latter was seeking to buy wheat, telling him that such wheat as the sample could not be got for less than twenty-one pence per bushel, whereas on the same day and at the same hour the same servant could have bought the same wheat for eighteen pence. Cokke, when questioned before the Mayor, Recorder, and certain aldermen, acknowledged that he had done this to enhance the price of wheat to the prejudice of all the people. He was in consequence committed to gaol, and sentenced also to have the punishment of the pillory. The same fate overtook Alan de Lyndeseye and Thomas de Patemere, bakers, who were brought before the bench at Guildhall, and with them "bread they had made of false, putrid, and rotten materials, through which persons who bought such bread were deceived and might be killed." The fear of imprisonment, again, was before the eyes of all who sought to interfere with the freedom of the markets. Thus it is recorded in the ordinances of the cheesemongers, that "whereas the hokesters (hucksters) and other who sell such wares by retail do come and regrate such cheese and butter before prime rung, and before that the commonalty had been served, may it be ordained that no such hokesters shall buy of any foreigner before the hour of prime on pain of imprisonment at the will of the Mayor." Similar penalties were decreed against "regrating" fish and other comestibles for the London markets.

In 1316 Gilbert Peny was bound in the third time in default for selling bread deficient in weight. He had been twice drawn on the hurdle, and it was therefore now adjudged that he should be drawn once more, and should then forswear the trade of a baker in the city for ever. One of many similar cases is that of William Spalyng, who, for selling putrid beef at "les Stokkes," the stocks market near Walbrook, was put upon the pillory, and the carcases were burnt beneath. Another who made shoes of unlawful material had them forfeited. Bakers who stole dough from the moulding-boards of other bakers were exposed on the pillory with the dough hung about their necks[11].

Richard le Forester, for attempting to defraud with a false garland or metal chaplet for the head, was sentenced to stand in the pillory, and afterwards to forswear the city for a year and a day. Traders convicted of having blankets vamped in foreign parts with the hair of oxen and of cows were punished, and the blankets were burnt under the pillory on Cornhill. Similarly, false gloves, braces, and pouches were burnt in the High Street of Chepe near the stone cross there. John Penrose, a taverner, convicted of selling unsound wine, was adjudged to drink a draught of the said wine, and the remainder was then poured out on his head. Alice, wife of Robert de Cranstom, was put in the thew, or pillory for women, for selling ale by short measure; and so was Margery Hore for selling putrid soles, the fish being burnt, and the cause of her punishment proclaimed. Two servants of John Naylere were placed in the stocks upon Cornhill for one hour, and their sacks burnt beside them, for selling a deficient measure of charcoal, while their master's three horses were seized and detained by the Mayor's sergeant until he (Naylere) came and answered for the aforesaid falsity and deceit. William Avecroft, having unsound wine, the sheriffs were ordered to pour all the wine in the street and wholly make away with it, according to the custom of the city.

The 'Liber Albus' contains other ordinances against brawlers and loose livers. The former, whether male or female, were taken to the thew, a form of pillory, carrying a distaff dressed with flax and preceded by minstrels. The latter, whether male, female, or clerics, were marched behind music to Newgate, and into the Tun in Cornhill.[12] Repeated offences were visited with expulsion, and the culprits were compelled to forswear the city for ever. The men on exposure had their heads and beards shaved, except a fringe on their heads two inches in breadth; women who made the penance in a hood of "rag" or striped cloth had their hair cut round about their heads. Worse cases of both sexes were shaved like "an appealer," or false informer. The crime of riotous assembling was very sharply dealt with, as appears from the proclamation made in the King's (Edward III.) departure for France. It was then ordained that "no one of the city, of whatsoever condition he shall be, shall go out of the city to maintain parties, such as taking leisure, or holding days of love (days of reconciliation between persons at variance), or making other congregations within the city or without in disturbance of the peace of our lord the king, or in affray of the people, and to the scandal of the city." Any found guilty thereof were to be taken and put into the prison of Newgate, and there retained for a year and day; and if he was a freeman of the city, he lost his freedom for ever.

The city authorities appear to have been very jealous of their good name, and to have readily availed themselves of Newgate as a place of punishment for any who impugned it. A certain John de Hakford, about the middle of the fourteenth century, was charged with perjury in falsely accusing the chief men in the city of conspiracy. For this he was, presumably upon proof, remanded by the Mayor and aldermen to Newgate, there to remain until they shall be better advised as to their judgment. A little later on, Saturday the morrow of St. Nicholas (6 Dec., 1364), this judgment was delivered, to the effect that the said John shall remain in prison for one whole year and a day, and the said John within such year shall four times have the punishment of the pillory, that is to say, one day in each quarter of the year, beginning on the Saturday aforesaid, and in this manner: "The said John shall come out of Newgate without hood or girdle, barefoot and unshod, with a whetstone hung by a chain from his neck and lying on his breast, it being marked with the words 'a false liar,' and there shall be a pair of trumpets trumpeting before him in his way to the pillory, and there the cause of this punishment shall be solemnly proclaimed, and the said John shall remain in the pillory for three hours of the day, and from thence shall be taken back to Newgate in the same manner, there to remain until his punishment be completed in manner aforesaid." This investiture of the whetstone was commonly used as a punishment for misstatement;[13] for it is recorded in 1371 that one Nicholas Mollere, servant of John Toppesfield, smith, had the punishment of the pillory and whetstone for "circulating lies," amongst others that the prisoners at Newgate were to be taken to the Tower of London, and that there was to be no longer a prison at Newgate.

Again in 1383, William Berham for slandering the Mayor was adjudged to be put upon the pillory on the same day, there to stand for one hour of the day with one large whetstone hung from his neck in token of the lie he told against the Mayor, and another smaller whetstone in token of a lie told against a lesser personage. After that he was to be taken back to Newgate, and thence for the five following days to be taken to the pillory, before noon on one day and after noon on the next, and there exposed with the whetstone as before. A few years later one Robert Stafferstone for slandering an alderman was adjudged to be imprisoned in Newgate for the next forty days, "unless he should find increased favour." This favour he did subsequently find, and "upon his humiliation he was committed to prison until the morrow, namely, Palm Sunday, and on the same Sunday should be taken from the prison to his house, and from thence proceed between the eighth and ninth hour, before dinner, with his head uncovered, and attended by an officer of the city, carrying a lighted wax candle weighing two pounds through Walbrook Bokelersbury, and so by Conduit and Chepe to St. Lawrence Lane in the Old Jewry, and on to the chapel of the Guildhall, where he was to make offering of the candle. That done, all further imprisonment was to be remitted and forgiven."

A sharper sentence was meted out about the same date to William Hughlot, who for a murderous assault upon an alderman was sentenced to lose his hand, and precept was given to the sheriffs of London to do execution of the judgment aforesaid. Upon this an axe was brought into court by an officer of sheriffs, and the hand of the said William was laid upon the block there to be cut off. Whereupon John Rove (the alderman aggrieved), in reverence of our lord the king, and at the request of divers lords, who entreated for the said William, begged of the Mayor and aldermen that the judgment might be remitted, which was granted accordingly. The culprit was, however, punished by imprisonment, with exposure on the pillory, wearing a whetstone, and he was also ordered to carry a lighted wax candle weighing three pounds through Chepe and Fleet

Streets to St. Dunstan's church, where he was to make offering of the same.

But, however sensitive of their good name, the Mayor and aldermen of those times seem to have been fairly upright in their administration of the law. The following case shows this. A man named Hugh De Beone, arraigned before the city coroner and sheriff for the death of his wife, stood mute, and refused to plead, so as to save his goods after sentence. For thus "refusing his law of England," the justiciary of our lord the king for the delivery of the gaol of Newgate, committed him back to prison, "there in penance to remain until he should be dead."[14]

The punishment inflicted, the goods thus saved were handed over to the defunct criminal's executor as appears from the following. "Be it remembered that on Saturday next before the Feast of the Apostles Simon and Jude (28 October), in the eleventh year of King Edward, after the conquest, the third, came John Fox, citizen and vintner of London, before Gregory de Nortone, Recorder, and Thomas de Margus, chamberlain of the Guildhall of London, into the chamber of the Guildhall aforesaid, and acknowledged that he had received of Walter de Moedone and Ralph de Uptone, late sheriffs of London, the goods and chattels underwritten in the presence of John de Shirborne, coroner, and the Sheriff of London aforesaid, on the oath of Edward de Mohaut, pellifer,[15] and others." The inventory of goods is curious, and is perhaps worth quoting at length. There were—

One mattress, value 4s.; six blankets and one serge, 13s. 6d.; one green carpet, 20s.; one torn coverlet, with shields of cendale, 4s.; one coat, and one surcoat, of *worstede*, 40d.; one robe perset, furred, 20s.; one robe of medly, furred, one mask, one old fur, almost consumed by moths, 6d.; one robe of scarlet, furred, 16s.; one robe of perset, 7s.; one surcoat, with a hood of ray, 2s. 6d.; one coat, with a hood of perset, 1s. 6d.; one surcoat, and one coat of ray, 6s. 1d.; one green hood of cendale, with edging, 6d.; seven linen sheets, 5s.; one table-cloth, 2s.; three table-cloths, 1s. 6d.; and a great many other articles, including "brass pots," "aundirons," "tonour," "iron herce," "savenapes," bringing the total value to £12 18s. 4d.

Long years elapsed between the building of Newgate and the date when the city gained complete jurisdiction over the prison. King Henry III.'s orders to repair the gaol at his own charge has been mentioned already. Forty years later the same monarch pretended to be keenly concerned in the good government of Newgate. Returning from Bordeaux when his son Edward had married the King of Spain's sister, Henry had passed through Dover and reached London on St. John's day. The city sent to congratulate him on his safe arrival, the messengers taking with them a humble offering of one hundred pounds. The avaricious king was dissatisfied, and instead of thanking them, intimated that if they would win his thanks they must enlarge their present; whereupon they gave him "a valuable piece of plate of exquisite workmanship, which pacified him for the present." But Henry was resolved to squeeze more out of the wealthy burgesses of London. An opportunity soon offered when a clerk convict, one John Frome, or Offrem,[16] charged with murdering a prior, and committed for safe custody to Newgate, escaped therefrom. The murdered man was a cousin of Henry's queen, and the king, affecting to be gravely displeased at this gross failure in prison administration, summoned the mayor and sheriffs to appear before him and answer the matter. The mayor laid the fault from him to the sheriffs, forasmuch as to them belonged the keeping of all prisoners within the city. The mayor was therefore allowed to return home, but the sheriffs remained prisoners in the Tower "by the space of a month or more"; and yet they excused themselves in that the fault rested chiefly with the bishop's officers, the latter having, at their lord's request, sent the prisoner to Newgate, but being still themselves responsible with the bishop for his safe keeping. These excuses did not satisfy the king, who, "according to his usual justice," says Noorthouck, "demanded of the city, as an atonement of the pretended crime, no less than the sum of three thousand marks." The fine was not immediately forthcoming, whereupon he degraded both the sheriffs, and until the citizens paid up the enormous sum demanded, he caused the chief of them to be seized and clapped into prison.

The city was ready enough, however, to purchase substantial privileges in hard cash. Many of its early charters were thus obtained from necessitous kings. In this way the Corporation ransomed, so to speak, its ancient freedom and the right of independent government.

In 1327 a further point was gained. The support of the citizens had been freely given to Queen Isabella and her young son in the struggle against Edward II. On the accession of Edward III. a new charter, dated in the first year of his reign, was granted to the city of London. After confirming the ancient liberties, it granted many new privileges; chief among them was the concession that the Mayor of London should be one of the justices for gaol delivery of Newgate, and named in every commission for that purpose. The king's marshal might in future hold no court within the boundary of the city, nor were citizens to be called upon to plead beyond them for anything done within the liberties. No market might be kept within seven miles of London, while the citizens were permitted to hold fairs and a court of "pye powder" therein; in other words, a court for the summary disposal of all offences committed by hawkers or pedlers, or perambulating merchants, who have *les pieds poudrés*, or are "dusty-footed."[17] Other privileges were obtained from the king during his reign. A second charter granted them the bailiwick of Southwark, a village which openly harboured "felons, thieves, and other malefactors," who committed crimes in the city and fled to Southwark for sanctuary; and a third guaranteed them against the competition of foreign merchants, who were forbidden to sell by retail in the city, to keep any house, or act as broker therein. Again, the election of the mayor was established on a more settled plan, and vested in the mayor and aldermen for the time being. Another charter conceded to the Corporation the honour of having gold and silver maces borne before the chief functionary, who about this period became first entitled to take rank as Lord Mayor. The vast wealth and importance of this great civic dignitary was to be seen in the state he kept up. The Lord Mayor even then dispensed a princely hospitality, and one eminent citizen in this reign, Henry Picard by name, had the honour of entertaining four sovereigns at his table, viz. the kings of England, France, Scotland, and Cyprus, with the Prince of Wales and many more notables. This Picard was one of the Guild of Merchant Vintners of Gascony, a Bordeaux wine merchant, in fact, and a Gascon by birth, although a naturalized subject of the English king. The Vintners gave the city several lord mayors.

Richard II. was not so well disposed towards the city. Recklessly extravagant, wasteful and profuse in his way of living, he was always in straits for cash. The money needed for his frivolous amusements and ostentatious display he wrung from the Corporation by seizing its charters, which were only redeemed by the payment of heavy fines. The sympathies of the city were therefore with Henry Bolingbroke in the struggle which followed. It was able to do him good service by warning him of a plot against his life, and Henry, now upon the throne, to show his gratitude, and "cultivate the good understanding thus commenced with the city, granted it a new charter." The most important clause of Henry's charter was that which entrusted the citizens, their heirs and successors, with the custody "as well of the gates of Newgate and Ludgate, as all other gates and posterns in the same city." The same clause gave them the office of gathering the tolls and customs in Cheap, Billingsgate, and Smithfield there rightfully to be taken and accustomed;[18] "and also the tronage, that is to say, the weighing of lead, wax, pepper, allom, madder, and other like wares, within the said city for ever." The great concession was, however, in the reign of Edward IV., whose charter was the fullest and most explicit of any previously granted. By this the mayor, recorder, and aldermen who had been Lord Mayor were constituted perpetual justices of the peace of the city; they were also appointed justices of *oyer* and *terminer*; their customs were to be accepted as established beyond controversy by the declaration of the mayor through the recorder; they were exempted from serving as jurors, and so forth, beyond the city. The borough of Southwark was once more clearly placed under the jurisdiction of the city; the citizens were entitled to the goods and chattels of traitors and felons, and the privilege of the annual Southwark Fair, with the pie powder court, was confirmed.

By this time the gate and prison must have passed under the control of the civic authorities. They had, however, already enjoyed the privilege of contributing to its charges. This appears from an entry as far back as September 1339, in the account of expenditure of Thomas de Maryus, chamberlain. The item is for "moneys delivered to William Simond, Sergeant of the Chamber, by precept of the mayor and aldermen, for making the pavement within Newgate, £7 6s. 8d." How complete became the power and responsibility of the Corporation and its officers is to be seen in the account given in the 'Liber Albus' of the procedure when new sheriffs were appointed.[19] They were sworn on appointment, and with them their officers, among whom were the governor of Newgate and his clerk. After dinner on the same day of appointment the old and new sheriffs repaired to

Newgate, where the new officials took over all the prisoners "by indenture" made between them and the old.[20] They were also bound to "place one safeguard there at their own peril," and were forbidden to "let the gaol to fenn or farm." Other restrictions were placed upon them. It was the sheriffs' duty also, upon the vigil of St. Michael, on vacating their office, to resign into the hands of the mayor for the time being the keys of Newgate, the Cocket or Seal of Newgate, and all other things pertaining unto the said sheriffwick.[21] All the civic authorities, mayor, sheriffs, aldermen, and their servants, including the gaoler of Newgate, were forbidden to brew for sale, keep an oven, or let carts for hire; "nor shall they be regrators of provisions, or hucksters of ale, or in partnership with such." Penalties were attached to the breach of these regulations. It was laid down that any who took the oath and afterwards contravened it, or any who would not agree to abide by the ordinance, should be forthwith "ousted from his office for ever." It was also incumbent upon the sheriffs to put "a man sufficient, and of good repute, to keep the gaol of Newgate in due manner, without taking anything of him for such keeping thereof, by covenant made in private or openly." Moreover, the gaoler so appointed swore before the Lord Mayor and aldermen that "neither he nor any of them shall take fine or extortionate charge from any prisoner by putting on or taking off his irons, or shall receive moneys extorted from such prisoners." He was permitted to levy fourpence from each upon release, "as from ancient time has been the usage, but he shall take fees from no person at his entrance there;" indeed, he was warned that if he practised extortion he would be "ousted from his office," and punished at the discretion of the mayor, aldermen, and common council of the city.

It will be made pretty plain, I think, in subsequent pages, that these wise and righteous regulations were both flagrantly ignored and systematically contravened. The rule against farming out the prison may have been observed, and it may not be clearly proved that the sheriffs ever took toll from the gaoler. But the spirit of the law, if not its letter, was broken by the custom which presently grew general of making the gaolership a purchaseable appointment. The buying and selling of offices, of army commissions, for instance, as we have seen practised within recent years, at one time extended also to the keeperships of gaols. It is recorded in the Calendar of State papers that one Captain Richardson agreed for his place as keeper of Newgate for £3000. A larger sum, viz. £5000, was paid by John Huggins to Lord Clarendon, who "did by his interest" obtain a grant of the office of keeper of the Fleet prison for the life of Huggins and his son. One James Whiston, in a book entitled 'England's Calamities Discovered, or Serious Advice to the Common Council of London,'[22] strongly remonstrates against this practice, which he stigmatizes as "bartering justice for gold." His language is plain and forcible. "Shall the public houses built at the city charges [it appears that at that time Ludgate, Newgate, the Fleet, and the Compters were all put up to the highest bidder] be sold for private lucre?... He that sells a gaoler's place sells the liberty, the estate, the person, nay, the very lives of the prisoners under his jurisdiction." "Purchased cruelty," the right to oppress the prisoners, that is to say, in order to recover the sums spent in buying the place, "is now grown so bold that if a poor man pay not extortionary fees and ruinous chamber-rent, he shall be thrown into holes and common sides to be devoured by famine, lice, and disease. I would fain know," he asks, "by what surmise of common sense a keeper of a prison can demand a recompense or fee from a prisoner for keeping him in prison?... Can he believe that any person can deserve a recompense for opening the door of misery and destruction?... But now such is the confidence of a purchaser, that to regain his sum expended he sells his tap-house at prodigious rates, ... he farms his sheets to mere harpies, and his great key to such a piece of imperious cruelty (presumably his chief turnkey) as is the worst of mankind." Following the same line of argument, he says "it will perhaps be thought impertinent to dispute a gaoler's demands for admitting us into his loathsome den, when even the common hangman, no doubt encouraged by such examples, will scarce give a malefactor a cast of his office without a bribe, demands very formally his fees, forsooth, of the person to be executed, and higgles with him as nicely as if he were going to do him some mighty kindness." Eventually an act was passed specifically forbidding the sale of such places. This statute affirms that "none shall buy, sell, let, or take to farm, the office of under-sheriff, gaoler, bailiff, under pain of £500, half to the king and half to him that shall sue."

Before leaving the subject of the sheriffs' jurisdiction in regard to Newgate, it may be interesting to refer to a conflict between them and the Corporation as to the right to appoint the gaoler. It is recorded in the State papers, under date March 1, 1638, that Isaac Pennington and John Wollaston were elected and sworn sheriffs for the ensuing year. They went, according to ancient custom, to Newgate, where, having received the keys and the charge of the prisoners from the former sheriffs, they substituted for the actual keeper one James Francklin, who about the 15th of the following October died. Accordingly the sheriffs appointed and settled Henry Wollaston as keeper of the gaol, who peaceably executed the duties of that place for six weeks. The rest of the story is best told in the language of the record. After that time "the Lord Mayor and aldermen, never charging Wollaston with any miscarriage, sent for him to their court at Guildhall, and demanded of him the keys of the said prison, who refusing to deliver them to any without the consent of the sheriffs, was then detained until some officers were sent from the said court, who forcibly brought the officer's servants intrusted with the said keys and prisoners by the said Wollaston, and, without the knowledge or consent of the said sheriffs, delivered them to Richard Johnson, a young man not free of the city, clerk to the recorder, whom they (the sheriffs, from whom this protest comes) consider to be very unfit for such a trust. For redress, the sheriffs by all fair means have applied themselves divers times to the Lord Mayor and court of aldermen, who refuse to restore the said Wollaston. The sheriffs conceive that the trust and keeping of the said gaol, both by law and reason, ought to be in their disposition, and that it is inseparable, incident to, and of common right belonging to their office, they being liable to punishments for any escapes, and amerciaments for non-appearance of prisoners in Her Majesty's courts of justice, with many other such like damages and fears."

How the case was finally settled does not appear. But the matter was one in which the king (Charles I.) would probably claim to have a voice. The appointment might be in the gift and actually made by the Corporation, but the city authorities were often invited by the Court to put in some royal nominee, a request which might easily be interpreted into a command. Thus in April 1594, the Lords of the Council addressed the mayor, aldermen, and sheriffs, soliciting them to appoint Richard Hutchman, one of Her Majesty's sergeants-at-arms, keeper of Newgate, *vice* Dios, deceased. In June the Corporation reply that they regret they cannot appoint Hutchman. The Lords' Council now issue a peremptory order to place him in office, which was done, but the Corporation was not to be beaten. Next year a fresh representation is made to the Lords in Council, stating the reasons why the city authorities had dismissed Mr. Hutchman from his place.

Another State paper, dated 1633, gives a draft of a letter recommending one A. B. for the appointment of keeper, vacant by the "nomination of one not deemed to have been legally put in." Some seventy years later, according to another authority, the question was definitely settled. In this (dated 1708) it is set forth that "the keeper of the prison holds that place of great trust under the queen (Anne), giving about £8000 security, and the prison is turned over to each of the new sheriffs when sworn in by delivering them a key. The place is in the gift of the Lord Mayor and aldermen."

Let us return to Mediæval Newgate. Whatever the authority, whether royal or civic, the condition of the inmates must have been wretched in the extreme, as the few brief references to them in the various records will sufficiently prove. The place was full of horrors; the gaolers rapacious and cruel. In 1334 an official inquiry was made into the state of the gaol, and some of the atrocities practised were brought to light. Prisoners detained on minor charges were cast into deep dungeons, and there associated with the worst criminals. All were alike threatened, nay tortured, till they yielded to the keepers' extortions, or consented to turn approvers and swear away the lives of innocent men. These poor prisoners were dependent upon the charity and good-will of the benevolent for food and raiment. As far back as 1237 it is stated that Sir John Pulteney gave four marks by the year to the relief of prisoners in Newgate. In the year 1385 William Walworth, the stalwart mayor whose name is well remembered in connection with Wat Tyler's rebellion, gave "somewhat" with the same good object. "So have many others since," says the record. The water supply of the prison, Stowe tells, was also a charitable gift. "Thomas Knowles, grocer, sometime Mayor of London, by license of Reynold, prior of St. Bartholomew's in Smithfield, and also of John Wakering, master of the hospital of St. Bartholomew, and his brethren, conveyed the waste of water at the cistern near unto the common fountain and Chapel of St. Nicholas (situate by the said hospital) to the gaols of Ludgate and Newgate, for the relief of the prisoners."

In 1451, by the will of Phillip Malpas, who had been a sheriff some twelve years previous, the sum of £125 was bequeathed to "the relief of poor prisoners." This Malpas, it may be mentioned here, was a courageous official, ready to act promptly in defence of city rights. In 1439 a prisoner under escort from Newgate to Guildhall was rescued from the officer's hands by five companions, after which all took sanctuary at the college of St. Martin's-le-Grand.[23] "But Phillip Malpas and Robert Marshal, the sheriffs of London, were no sooner acquainted with the violence offered to their officer and the rescue of their prisoner, than they, at the head of a great number citizens, repaired to the said college, and forcibly took from thence the criminal and his rescuers, whom they carried in fetters to the Compter, and thence, chained by the necks, to Newgate."

For food the prisoners were dependent upon alms or upon articles declared forfeit by the law. Thus some bread of light weight, seized on the 10th August 1298, was ordered to be given to the prisoners in Newgate. Again, the halfpenny loaf of light bread of Agnes Foting of Stratford was found wanting 7 shillings (or 4⅕ oz.) in weight; therefore it was adjudged that her bread should be forfeited, and it also was sent unto the gaol. All food sold contrary to the statutes of the various guilds was similarly forfeited to the prisoners. The practice of giving food was continued through succeeding years, and to a very recent date. A long list of charitable donations and bequests might be made out, bestowed either in money or in kind. A customary present was a number of stones of beef. Some gave penny loaves, some oatmeal, some coals. Without this benevolence it would have gone hard with the poor population of the Gatehouse gaol. It was not strange that the prison should be wasted by epidemics, as when in 1414 "the gaoler died and prisoners to the number of sixty-four;" or that the inmates should at times exhibit a desperate turbulence, taking up arms and giving constituted authority much trouble to subdue them, as in 1457 when they broke out of their several wards in Newgate, and got upon the leads, where they defended themselves with great obstinacy against the sheriffs and their officers, insomuch that they, the sheriffs, were obliged to call the citizens to their assistance, whereby the prisoners were soon reduced to their former state.

The evil effects of incarceration in Newgate may be further judged by the fate which overtook the city debtors who were temporarily removed thither from Ludgate. An effort had been made in 1419 to put pressure upon them as a class. An ordinance was issued by Henry V. closing the Ludgate prison for debtors. It had been found that "many false men of bad disposition and purpose have been more willing to take up their abode there, so as to waste and spend their goods upon the ease and license that there is within, than pay their debts." Wherefore it was ordained that "all prisoners therein shall be removed and safely carried to Newgate, there to remain each in such keeping as his own deserts shall demand." The order was, however, very speedily rescinded. A later ordinance in the same year sets forth that "whereas, through the abolition and doing away with the prison of Ludgate, which was formerly ordained for the good and comfort of citizens and other reputable persons, and also by reason of the fœtid and corrupt atmosphere that is in the hateful gaol of Newgate, many persons who lately were in the said prison of Ludgate, who in the time of William Sevenoke, late mayor, for divers great offences which they had there compassed were committed to the said gaol (of Newgate), are now dead, who might have been living, it is said, if they had remained at Ludgate abiding in peace there; and seeing that every person is sovereignly bound to support and be tender to the lives of men, the which God hath bought so dearly with His precious blood; therefore Richard Whittington, now mayor (1419), and the aldermen, on Saturday the 2nd November, have ordained and established that the gaol of Ludgate shall be a prison from henceforth to keep therein all citizens and other reputable persons whom the mayor, aldermen, sheriffs, or chamberlain of the city shall think proper to commit and send to the same, provided always that the warder shall be a good and loyal man, giving sufficient surety," &c. Ten or twelve years later a similar exodus from Ludgate to Newgate and back again took place. "On the Tuesday next after Palm Sunday 1431, all the prisoners of Ludgate were conveyed into Newgate by Walter Chartsey and Robert Large, sheriffs of London, and on the 13th April the same sheriffs (through the false suggestion of John Kingesell, gaoler of Newgate) did fetch from thence eighteen persons, freemen, and these were led to the Counters pinioned as if they had been felons. But on the 16th June Ludgate was again appointed for freemen, prisoners for debt, and the same day the same freemen entered by ordinance of the mayor, aldermen, and commons; and by them Henry Deane, tailor, was made keeper of Ludgate."

One other charitable bequest must be referred to here, as proving that the moral no less than the physical well-being of the prisoners was occasionally an object of solicitude. In the reign of Richard II. a prayer-book was specially bequeathed to Newgate in the following terms:—

"Be it remembered that on the 10th day of June, in the 5th year (1382), Henry Bever, parson of the church of St. Peter in Brad Street (St. Peter the Poor, Broad Street), executor of Hugh Tracy, Chaplain, came here before the mayor and aldermen and produced a certain book called a 'Porte hors,'[24] which the same Hugh had left to the gaol of Newgate, in order that priests and clerks there imprisoned might say their service from the same, there to remain so long as it might last. And so in form aforesaid the book was delivered unto David Bertelike, keeper of the gate aforesaid, to keep it in such manner so long as he should hold that office; who was also then charged to be answerable for it. And it was to be fully allowable for the said Henry to enter the gaol aforesaid twice in the year at such times as he should please, these times being suitable times, for the purpose of seeing how the book was kept."[25]

We are without any very precise information as to the state of the prison building throughout these dark ages. But it was before everything a gate-house, part and parcel of the city fortifications, and therefore more care and attention would be paid to its external than its internal condition. It was subject, moreover, to the violence of such disturbers of the peace as the followers of Wat Tyler, of whom it is written that, having spoiled strangers "in most outrageous manner, entered churches, abbeys, and houses of men of law, which in semblable sort they ransacked, they also brake up the prisons of Newgate and of both the Compters, destroyed the books, and set the prisoners at liberty." This was in 1381. Whether the gaol was immediately repaired after the rebellion was crushed does not appear; but if so, the work was only partially performed, and the process of dilapidation and decay must soon have recommenced, for in Whittington's time it was almost in ruins. That eminent citizen and mercer, who was three times mayor, and whose charitable bequests were numerous and liberal, left moneys in his will for the purpose of rebuilding the place, and accordingly license was granted in 1422, the first year of Henry VI.'s reign, to his executors, John Coventre, Jenken Carpenter, and William Grove, "to re-edify the gaol of Newgate, which they did with his goods." This building, such as it was, continued to serve until the commencement of the seventeenth century.

In 1629 a petition from the gaoler to the king sets forth[26] that "by reason of the great ruins of the gaol it is now in hand to be repaired." The gaoler further states that there is great danger lest in time of repair some of the prisoners should escape, and prays directions to the Lord Mayor and Recorder to certify how many prisoners are capable of His Majesty's mercy, and to the Attorney General to prepare pardons. This document is underwritten, "Reference to Recorder to certify, and to the Attorney General to prepare, a pardon;" following which is a recommendation from Sir Heneage Finch (the first-named official) to release forty-four. Subsequently the east side of Newgate was "begun to be repaired, Sir James Campbell being mayor, and finished the year following, Sir Robert Drury, Baronet, being mayor." The expense was borne wholly or partly by the locality, as the records show in 1632 an account of the assessment of the parish of St. Stephen Walbrook, in which "two fifteenths were to be gathered for repairing Newgate." It is this re-edification which is referred to in Lupton's 'London Carbonadoed,' 1638, who speaks of Newgate as new fronted and new faced.

I have been unable to ascertain any exact figure of this old Newgate, either in its ancient or improved aspect. The structure, such as it was, suffered so severely in the great fire of 1666 that it became necessary to rebuild it upon new and more imposing lines.

This may be described as the third edifice: that of the twelfth century being the first, and Richard Whittington's the second. Of this third prison details are still extant, and I propose to describe it fully on a later page.[27]

NEWGATE IN THE SIXTEENTH CENTURY.

Prison records meagre—Administration of justice and state of crime—Lenity alternates with great severity—Disturbances in London—The 'Black Waggon'—A 'prentice riot—Criminal inmates of Newgate—Masterless men—Slandering the Corporation—Robbery with violence—Debtors—Conscience prisoners—Martyrs in reign of Henry VIII.—Religious dissidents: Porter, Anne Askew—Maryan persecutions—Rogers—Bishop Hooper—Philpot—Alexander the cruel gaoler of Newgate—Underhill the hot gospeller in Newgate—Crime in Elizabeth's reign—The training of young thieves—Elizabethan persecutions: both puritans and papists suffered—The seminary priests—Political prisoners—Condition of gaol—Oppression of the inmates and their disorderly conduct—Gaolers of that period generally tyrants—Crowder, keeper of Newgate, called to account.

THE prison records of the sixteenth century are very meagre. No elaborate system of incarceration as we understand it existed. The only idea of punishment was the infliction of physical pain. There were prisons, but these receptacles, except for debtors, were only the ante chambers of the pillory and the scaffold. The penalties inflicted were purely personal, and so to speak final; such as chastisement, degradation, or death. England had no galleys, no scheme of enforced labour at the oar, such as was known to the nations of the Mediterranean seaboard, no method of compelling perpetual toil in quarry or mine. The germ of transportation no doubt was to be found in the practice which suffered offenders who had taken sanctuary to escape punishment by voluntary exile,[28] but it was long before the plan of deporting criminals beyond seas became the rule. In Henry VIII.'s time, says Froude, "there was but one step to the gallows from the lash and the branding-iron." Criminals did not always get their deserts, however. Although historians have gravely asserted that seventy-two thousand executions took place in this single reign, the statement will not bear examination, and has been utterly demolished by Froude.[29] As a matter of fact offenders far too often escaped scot free through the multiplication of sanctuaries, which refuges, like that of St. Martin's-le-Grand, existed under the very walls of Newgate, the negligence of pursuers, and not seldom the stout opposition of the inculpated.[30] Benefit of clergy claimed and conceded on the most shadowy grounds was another easy and frequent means of evading the law. Some judges certainly had held that the tonsure was an indispensable proof; but all were not so strict, and "putting on the book," in other words, the simple act of reading aloud, was deemed sufficient. So flagrant was the evasion of the law, that gaolers for a certain fee would assist accused persons to obtain a smattering of letters, whereby they might plead their "clergy" in court. It may be added that although the abuse of the privilege was presently greatly checked, it was not until the reign of William and Mary that benefit of clergy was absolutely denied to burglars, pickpockets, and other heinous offenders.

Yet there were occasional spasmodic intervals of

extraordinary severity. Twenty thieves, says Sir Thomas More in his 'Utopia,' might then be seen hanging on a single gibbet. Special legislation was introduced to deal with special crimes. Although there was an appropriateness in the retribution which overtook him, the sentence inflicted upon the Bishop of Rochester's cook in 1531, under a new act passed on purpose, was ferociously cruel. This man, one Richard Rose or Rouse, was convicted of having poisoned sixteen persons with porridge specially prepared to put an end to his master. The crime had been previously almost unknown in England, and special statutory powers were taken to cope with it. An act was at once passed defining the offence to be high treason, and prescribing boiling to death as the penalty. Rose was accordingly, after conviction, boiled alive in Smithfield. It may be added that this cruel statute, which may be read *in extenso* in Froude, was soon afterwards repealed, but not before another culprit, Margaret Davy by name, had suffered under its provisions for a similar offence.

Newgate, like all other gaols, was at times scandalously overcrowded, not only with the felons and trespassers who long languished waiting trial, but with far less guilty offenders. There were also the debtors and the conscience prisoners: the delinquents whose crime was impecuniosity or commercial failure, and the independent thinkers who stoutly maintained their right to profess forms of belief at variance with the government creed of the hour. It is only a passing glimpse that we get of the meaner sort of criminal committed to Newgate in these times. The gaol, as I have said, was but the ante-chamber to something worse. It was the starting-point for the painful promenade to the pillory. The jurors who were forsworn "for rewards or favour of parties were judged to ride from Newgate to the pillory in Cornhill with paper mitres on their heads, there to stand, and from thence again to Newgate."[31] Again, the ringleaders of false inquests, Darby, Smith, and Simson by name, were, in the first year of Henry's reign (1509), condemned to ride about the city with their faces to the horses' tails, and paper on their heads, and were set on the pillory at Cornhill. After that they were brought back to Newgate, where they died for very shame.[32]

A longer story and a heavier doom was that of the 'prentice lads who upon 'Evil May-day,' as it was afterwards called, raised a tumult in the city against the competition of foreign workmen, who were about this time established in great numbers in the suburbs. One John Lincoln, a meddlesome city broker, was so much exercised at this foreign interference that he went about seeking a parson who would declaim against it from the pulpit. One Dr. Bell or Bele, who was to preach at the Spital Church, agreed to read from the pulpit a bill which this Lincoln had drawn up, and which set forth the wrongs suffered by native artificers and merchants. Dr. Bell followed the reading by an inflammatory sermon upon the text *Pugna pro Patria*, by which "many a light-headed person took courage and openly spoke against" the foreigners. As divers ill things had been done of late by these strangers, the people's rancour was kindled most furiously against them. Conflicts took place in the streets between "the young men of the city" and the strangers, so that several of the former were committed to Newgate. Among others Stephen Studley, skinner, and Stephenson Betts. Then arose "a secret rumour that on May-day following the city would slay all the aliens." News thereof reached Cardinal Wolsey, who summoned the Lord Mayor, and desired him to take all due precautions. It was settled by agreement between the Corporation and the cardinal that every citizen should be commanded to shut up his doors after nine at night, and keep his servants within. It so chanced that Alderman Sir John Mundy the same night, coming from his ward, found two young men playing at the bucklers, and many others looking on. The order for early closing had not indeed been fully circulated as yet. Sir John Mundy ordered the combatants to desist, and on their hesitation was for sending them to the Compter. But the apprentices rose against the alderman, crying, "'Prentices! clubs! clubs!" A crowd soon collected, the alderman took to flight, and by eleven at night there were in Cheap six or seven hundred "serving-men, watermen, courtiers, and others," and out of St. Paul's Churchyard came some three hundred more. The mob, growing riotous, attacked the Compter and released all prisoners confined therein for "hurting the strangers"; thence they went to Newgate and set free Studley and Betts. Gaining courage by these excesses, they ranged the streets, throwing sticks and stones, spoiling all they found. The strangers were the principal victims. The house of one Mewtas, a Picard, and those of other Frenchmen residing at the Greengate, Leadenhall, were broken open and plundered. The riot continued till three in the morning, "at which time they began to withdraw, but by the way were taken by the mayor and others, and sent to the Tower, Newgate and the Compters to the number of three hundred."

The king took very summary measures for the punishment of the rioters. Bell the preacher was arrested and sent to the Tower. A commission of *oyer* and *terminer* was forthwith opened at the Guildhall, and the whole of the prisoners, to the number of two hundred and seventy-eight, were marched through the streets, tied with ropes, and put upon their trial. Lincoln the ringleader and other thirteen were sentenced to be hanged, drawn, and quartered; for execution whereof ten pairs of gallows were put up in divers parts of the city: "before each of the Compters, at Newgate, St. Martin's, Aldersgate, and Bishopgate, which gallows were set on wheels, to be removed from street to street and door to door as the prisoners were to be executed." Lincoln suffered death, but the rest were reprieved pending the king's pleasure. He lay at his manor of Greenwich just then, and thither the mayor, recorder, and divers aldermen repaired to beg mercy for the city. But Henry VIII. was not to be easily appeased. He still blamed the city authorities for not checking these disorders in a more determined fashion, and referred them for answer to his chancellor the cardinal. Wolsey granted them his favour for a consideration, and counselled them to again petition the king. They came to him, therefore, at his palace of Westminster, to the number of four hundred men, in their shirts, bound together with ropes, and with halters about their necks, and were at first sharply rebuked by the cardinal, who told them they deserved death. But at the earnest entreaty of the attendant lords, who were much moved by the humiliating sight, they were pardoned and dismissed. The gallows in the city were taken down, and all in durance were set free. Thus ended the "black waggon," as the procession of citizens was called, but "not, as it is thought, without paying a considerable sum of money to the cardinal to stand their friend, for at that time he was in such power he did all with the king."[33]

A few further extracts will serve to describe some other criminal inmates of Newgate in those times. The quotations are from the 'Remembrancia,' 1579-1664. Searches appear to have been regularly made for suspected persons, who when caught were committed to ward. Thus, 1519, a search was made in the house of William Solcocke in Holborne, and it was found that one Christopher Tyllesley had lain there two nights. "He has no master, and is committed to Newgate." Again, "in the house of Christopher Arundell one Robert Bayley: has no master, and is committed to Newgate." To Newgate were also committed any who were bold enough to malign the great Cardinal Wolsey, in the plenitude of his power, as was Adam Greene in June 1523, a prisoner in Ludgate, who repeated to the keeper what he had heard from a "bocher" (butcher), to the effect that Wolsey had told the king that all London were traitors to his Grace. Greene was warned to keep silent, but he said "he would abide by it, for he had it from a substantial man who would also abide by it."

It was not less dangerous to let the tongue wag too freely against the city authorities. Articles are exhibited (April, 1524) against "John Sampye, tailor, for saying (1) that he had been wrongfully imprisoned in the Compter by the Mayor of London and Nicholas Partriche, alderman; (2) that they had no power to send any man to ward; (3) that many were cast away by lying in the Compter and Newgate at the command of the Corporation." The Corporation appear also to have dealt in a very high-handed fashion with the city bakers, possibly to break down their monopoly, but a little on personal private grounds. In 1526 the bakers petition Wolsey for redress, setting forth that they have always been accustomed to "occupy the making and selling of bread for the city, and since the time of Edward II. have been used to take up wheat arriving in London at the price given them by the mayor; but within the last five years certain persons, aldermen and others, out of malice to the mystery and under colour of common weal, have procured that all the wheat coming to the city should be garnered at the Bridge House, and the bakers suffered to buy no other.... Lately the mayor and aldermen tried to compel the bakers to buy two thousand quarters of musty wheat at 12s. when sweet wheat may be bought for 7s. or 8s." When some bakers refused the mayor sent them to Newgate for eleven days, and shut up their houses and shops, not allowing their wives or families to visit them or buy their bread.

Now and again more serious crimes are recorded. In March 1528, Stephen reports to Thomas Cromwell that between the hours of six and seven, "five thieves knocked at the door of Roderigo the Spaniard, which dwelleth next the goldsmith against your door.[34] Being asked who was there, they answered one from the Court, to speak with Roderigo. When the door was opened three of them rushed in and found the said Roderigo sitting by the fire with a poor woman dwelling next to Mrs. Wynsor. Two tarried and kept the door, and strangled the poor woman that she should not cry. They then took Roderigo's purse, and killed him by stabbing him in the belly, but had not fled far before two of them were taken and brought to Newgate."

Debtors were too small fry to be often referred to in the chronicles of the times. Now and again they are mentioned as fitting objects for charity, royal and private. In the king's book of payments is the following entry, under date May 1515. "Master Almoner redeeming prisoners in Newgate, Ludgate, and the Compter, £20." The State Papers, 1581, contain a commission to the Lord Mayor, recorder, and sheriffs of London, and many others, all charitable folk, and some sixty in number, to compound with the creditors of poor debtors, at that time prisoners in Newgate, Ludgate, and the two Compters of the city. Although debtors in gaol who volunteered for service on shipboard were discharged by proclamation from the demands of their creditors, as a general rule committal to Newgate on account of monetary mismanagement appears to have been more easily compassed than subsequent release. The same volume of State Papers contains a petition from Richard Case to Lord Burghley, to the effect that he had been committed to Newgate "upon the unjust complaint of Mr. Benedict Spinola, relative to the lease of certain lands and tenements in London." The petitioner further "desires to be discharged from prison, and to have the queen's pardon," but there is no allusion to his enlargement.[35] The impolicy of confining debtors was not to be fully realized till three more centuries had passed away. But as early as 1700 a pamphlet preserved in the 'Harleian Miscellany,' and entitled 'Labour in Vain,' anticipates modern feeling and modern legislation. The writer protests against the imprisonment of debtors, which he compares to shutting up a cow from herbage when she gives no milk. "In England we confine people to starve, contrary to humanity, mercy, or policy. One may as reasonably expect his dog," he says, "when chained to a post should catch a hare, as that poor debtors when in gaol should get wherewithal to pay their debts."

Details of the incarceration and sufferings of prisoners for conscience sake, in an age when polemics were backed up by the strong arm of the law, are naturally to be met with more frequently in the partisan writings of the time. Throughout the reigns of Henry VIII., Mary, and even in that of Elizabeth, intolerance stalked rampant through the land, filling the prisons and keeping Smithfield in a blaze. Henry was by turns severe on all creeds. Now Protestants, now Catholics suffered. He began as an ardent champion of Romish doctrines, and ended by denying the supremacy of the Pope. In the first stage he persecuted so-called heretics, in the second he despoiled Church property, and sent monks and priors to gaol and to the gallows. Foxe gives a long and detailed list of the Protestant martyrs from first to last. One of the most prominent was Richard Bayfield, a monk of Bury, who became an inmate of Newgate. Foxe relates[36] that a letter of inquiry was issued by the Bishop of London to the Lord Mayor and sheriffs to be present at St. Paul's on the 20th November 1531, to receive the said Richard Bayfield, alias Soundesam, "a relapsed heretic after sentence." The sheriffs carried him to Newgate, whence they were commanded again to bring him into Paul's upper choir, there to give attendance upon the bishop. Later on they are ordered to have him into the vestry, and then to bring him forth again in Antichrist's apparel to be degraded before them. "When the bishop had degraded him," says old Foxe, "kneeling upon the highest step of the altar, he took his crosier staff and smote him on the breast that he threw him down backwards and brake his head, and that he swooned; and when he came to himself again he thanked God that he was delivered from the malignant Church of Antichrist, and that he was come into the true sincere Church of Jesus Christ militant here on earth; ... and so was he led forth through the choir to Newgate, and there rested about an hour in prayer, and so went to the fire in his apparel manfully and joyfully, and there for lack of a speedy fire was two quarters of an hour alive."

Henry was, however, impartial in his severity. In 1533 he suffered John Frith, Andrew Hewett, and other Protestants, to the number of twenty-seven, to be burned for heresy. The years immediately following he hunted to death all who refused to acknowledge him as the head of the Church. Besides such imposing victims as Sir Thomas More, and Fisher, Bishop of Rochester, many priests suffered. In 1534 the prior of the London Carthusians, the prior of Hexham, Benase, a monk of Sion College, and John Haite, vicar of Isleworth, together with others, [37] were sentenced to be hanged and quartered at Tyburn. In 1538 a friar, by name Forrest, was hanged in Smithfield upon a gallows, quick, by the middle and armholes, "and burnt to death for denying the king's supremacy and teaching the same in confession to many of the king's subjects." Upon the pile by which Forrest was consumed was also a wooden image, brought out of Wales, called "Darvell Gatheren," which the Welshmen "much worshipped, and had a prophecy amongst them that this image would set a whole forest on fire, which prophecy took effect."[38]

The greatest trials were reserved for the religious dissidents who dared to differ with the king. Henry was vain of his learning and of his polemical powers. No true follower of Luther, he was a Protestant by policy rather than conviction, and he still held many tenets of the Church he had disavowed. These were embodied and promulgated in the notorious Six Articles, otherwise "the whip with six tails," or the Bloody Statute, so called from its sanguinary results. The doctrines enunciated were such that many could not possibly subscribe to them; the penalties were "strait and bloody," and very soon they were widely inflicted. Foxe, in a dozen or more pages, recounts the various presentments against individuals, lay and clerical, for transgressing one or more of the principles of the Six Articles; and adds to "the aforesaid, Dr. Taylor, parson of St. Peter's, in Cornhill; South, parish priest of Allhallows, in Lombard Street; Some, a priest; Giles, the king's beerbrewer, at the Red Lion, in St. Katherine's; Thomas Lancaster, priest; all which were imprisoned likewise for the Six Articles." "To be short," he adds, "such a number out of all parishes in London, and out of Calais, and divers other quarters, were then apprehended through the said inquisition, that all prisons in London, including Newgate, were too little to hold them, insomuch that they were fain to lay them in the halls. At last, by the means of good Lord Audeley, such pardon was obtained of the king that the said Lord Audeley, then Lord Chancellor, being content that one should be bound for another, they were all discharged, being bound only to appear in the Star Chamber the next day after All Souls, there to answer if they were called; but neither was there any person called, neither did any appear."[39]

Bonner, then Bishop of London, and afterwards one of the queen's principal advisers, had power to persecute even under Henry. The Bible had been set up by the king's command in St. Paul's, that the public might read the sacred word. "Much people used to resort thither," says Foxe, to hear the reading of the Bible, and especially attended the reading of one John Porter, "a fresh young man, and of a big stature," who was very expert. It displeased Bonner that this Porter should draw such congregations, and sending for him, rebuked him very sharply for his reading. Porter defended himself, but Bonner charged him with making expositions on the text, and gathering "great multitudes about him to make tumults." Nothing was proved against Porter, but "in fine Bonner sent him to Newgate, where he was miserably fettered in irons, both legs and arms, with a collar of iron about his neck, fastened to the wall in the dungeon; being there so cruelly handled that he was compelled to send for a kinsman of his, whose name is also Porter, a man yet alive, and can testify that it is true, and dwelleth yet without Newgate. He, seeing his kinsman in this miserable case, entreated Jewet, the keeper of Newgate, that he might be released out of those cruel irons, and so, through friendship and money, had him up among other prisoners, who lay there for felony and murder." Porter made the most of the occasion, and after hearing and seeing their wickedness and blasphemy, exhorted them to amendment of life, and "gave unto them such instructions as he had learned of in the Scriptures; for which his so doing he was complained, and so carried down and laid in the lower dungeon of all, oppressed with bolts and irons, where, within six or eight days, he was found dead."

But the most prominent victim to the Six Articles was Anne Askew, the daughter of Sir William Askew, knight, of Lincolnshire. She was married to one Kyme, but is best known under her maiden name. She was persecuted for denying the Real Presence, but the proceedings against her were pushed to extremity, it was said, because she was befriended in high quarters. Her story is a melancholy one. First one Christopher Dene examined her as to her faith and belief in a very subtle manner, and upon her answers had her before the Lord Mayor, who committed her to the Compter. There, for eleven days, none but a priest was allowed to visit her, his object being to ensnare her further. Presently she was released upon finding sureties to surrender if required, but was again brought before the king's council at Greenwich. Her opinions in matters of belief proving unsatisfactory, she was remanded to Newgate. Thence she petitioned the king, also the Lord Chancellor Wriottesley, "to aid her in obtaining just consideration." Nevertheless, she was taken to the Tower, and there tortured. Foxe puts the following words into her mouth: "On Tuesday I was sent from Newgate to the sign of the Crown, where Master Rich and the Bishop of London, with all their power and flattering words, went about to persuade me from God, but I did not esteem their glosing pretences.... Then Master Rich sent me to the Tower, where I remained till three o'clock." At the Tower strenuous efforts were made to get her to accuse others. They pressed her to say how she was maintained in prison; whether divers gentlewomen had not sent her money. But she replied that her maid had "gone abroad in the streets and made moan to the 'prentices," who had sent her alms. When further urged, she admitted that a man in a blue coat had delivered her ten shillings, saying it came from my Lady Hertford, and that another in a violet coat had given her eight shillings from my Lady Denny—"whether it is true or not I cannot tell." "Then they said three men of the council did maintain me, and I said no. Then they did put me on the rack because I confessed no ladies or gentlemen to be of my opinion, and thereon they kept me a long time; and because I lay still, and did not cry, my Lord Chancellor and Master Rich took pains to rack me with their own hands till I was nigh dead. Then the lieutenant (Sir Anthony Knevet) caused me to be loosed from the rack. Incontinently I swooned, and then they recovered me again. After that I sat two long hours, reasoning with my Lord Chancellor, on the bare floor." At last she was "brought to a house and laid in a bed with as weary and painful bones as ever had patient Job; I thank my Lord God there-for. Then my Lord Chancellor sent me word, if I would leave my opinion, I should want nothing; if I did not, I should forthwith to Newgate, and so be burned...."

Foxe gives full details of her torture in the Tower. At first she was let down into a dungeon, and the gaoler, by command of Sir

Anthony Knevet, pinched her with the rack. After this, deeming he had done enough, he was about to take her down, but Wriottesley, the Lord Chancellor, "commanded the lieutenant to strain her on the rack again; which, because he denied to do, tendering the weakness of the woman, he was threatened therefore grievously of the said Wriottesley, saying he would signify his disobedience to the king. And so consequently upon the same, he (Wriottesley) and Master Rich, throwing off their gowns, would needs play the tormentors themselves.... And so, quietly and patiently praying unto the Lord, she abode their tyranny till her bones and joints were almost plucked asunder, in such sort as she was carried away in a chair." Then the chancellor galloped off to report the lieutenant to the king; but Sir Anthony Knevet forestalled by going by water, and obtained the king's pardon before the complaint was made. "King Henry," says Foxe, "seemed not very well to like of their so extreme handling of the woman."

Soon after this Mistress Askew was again committed to Newgate, whence she was carried in a chair to Smithfield, "because she could not walk on her feet by means of her great torments. When called upon to recant she refused, as did the martyrs with her." Whereupon the Lord Mayor, commanding fire to be put under them, cried, "Fiat Justitia," and they were burned.

The Maryan persecutions naturally filled Newgate. It would weary the reader to give lengthened descriptions of the many martyrs who passed through that prison to Smithfield. But a few of the victims stand prominently forward. Two of the earliest were John Rogers, vicar of St. Sepulchre and prebendary of St. Paul's, and Hooper, Bishop of Gloucester. Rogers was the protomartyr—the first sacrificed to the religious intolerance of Mary and her advisers. Foxe says that after being a prisoner in his own house for a long time, Rogers was "removed to the prison called

Newgate, where he was lodged among thieves and murderers for a great space." He was kept in Newgate "a full year," Rogers tells us himself, "at great costs and charges, having a wife and ten children to find; and I had never a penny of my livings, which was against the law." He made "many supplications" out of Newgate, and sent his wife to implore fairer treatment; but in Newgate he lay, till at length he was brought to the Compter in Southwark, with Master Hooper, for examination. Finally, after having been "very uncharitably entreated," he was "unjustly, and most cruelly, by wicked Winchester condemned." The 4th February, 1555, he was warned suddenly by the keeper's wife of Newgate to prepare himself for the fire, "who being then found asleep, scarce with much shogging could be awakened." Being bidden to make haste, he remarked, "If it be so, I need not tie my points." "So was he had down first to Bonner to be degraded, whom he petitioned to be allowed to talk a few words with his wife before his burning"—a reasonable request, which was refused. "Then the sheriffs, Master Chester and Master Woodroove, took him to Smithfield; and his wife and children, eleven in number, ten able to go, and one at the breast, met him as he passed. This sorrowful sight of his own flesh and blood could nothing move him, but that he constantly and cheerfully took his death with wonderful patience in the defence and quarrel of Christ's gospel."[40]

While detained in Newgate, Master Rogers devoted himself to the service of the ordinary prisoners, to whom he was "beneficial and liberal," having thus devised "that he with his fellows should have but one meal a day, they paying, notwithstanding, the charges of the whole; the other meal should be given to them that lacked on the other (or common) side of the prison. But Alexander their keeper, a strait man and a right Alexander, a coppersmith indeed, ... would in no case suffer that."

This Alexander Andrew, or Alexander, as he is simply called, figures in contemporary records, more especially in the writings of Foxe, as a perfect type of the brutal gaoler. "Of gaolers," says Foxe, "Alexander, keeper of Newgate, exceeded all others." He is described as "a cruel enemy of those that lay there (Newgate) for religion. The cruel wretch, to hasten the poor lambs to the slaughter, would go to Bonner, Story, Cholmley, and others, crying out,

'Rid my prison! rid my prison! I am too much pestered by these heretics." Alexander's reception of an old friend of his, Master Philpot, committed to Newgate,[41] is graphically told by the old chronicler. "'Ah, thou hast well done to bring thyself hither,' he says to Philpot. 'I must be content,' replied Philpot, 'for it is God's appointment, and I shall desire you to let me have some gentle favour, for you and I have been of old acquaintance.' 'Well,' said Alexander, 'I will show you great gentleness and favour, so thou wilt be ruled by me.' Then said Master Philpot, 'I pray you show me what you would have me to do.' He said, 'If you will recant I will show you any pleasure I can.' 'Nay,' said Master Philpot, 'I will never recant whilst I have my life, for it is most certain truth, and in witness thereof I will seal it with my blood.' Then Alexander said, 'This is the saying of the whole pack of you heretics.' Whereupon he commanded him to be set upon the block, and as many irons upon his legs as he could bear, for that he would not follow his wicked mind.... 'But, good Master Alexander, be so much my friend that these irons may be taken off.' 'Well,' said Alexander, 'give me my fees, and I will take them off; if not, thou shalt wear them still.' Then Master Philpot said, 'Sir, what is your fee?' He said four pounds was his fee. 'Ah,' said Master Philpot, 'I have not so much; I am but a poor man, and I have been long in prison.' 'What wilt thou give me, then?' said Alexander. 'Sir,' said he, 'I will give you twenty shillings, and that I will send my man for, or else I will lay my gown to gage. For the time is not long, I am sure, that I shall be with you, for the bishop said I should be soon despatched.' Then said Alexander unto him, 'What is that to me?' and with that he departed for a time, and commanded him to be had into limbo. And so his commandment was fulfilled; but before he could be taken from the block the clerk would have a groat. Then one Willerence, steward of the house, took him on his back and carried him down his man knew not whither. Wherefore Master Philpot said to his man, 'Go to Master Sheriff, and show him how I am used, and desire Master Sheriff to be good unto me;' and so his servant went straightway, and took an honest man with him.

"And when they came to Master Sheriff, which was Master Ascham, and showed him how Master Philpot was handled in Newgate, the sheriff, hearing this, took his ring off his finger and delivered it unto that honest man that came with Master Philpot's man, and bade him go unto Alexander the keeper and command him to take off his irons and handle him more gently, and give his man again that which he had taken from him. And when they came to the said Alexander and told their message from the sheriff, Alexander took the ring, and said, 'Ah, I perceive that Master Sheriff is a bearer with him and all such heretics as he is, therefore to-morrow I will show it to his betters;' yet at ten by the clock he went to Master Philpot where he lay and took off his irons, and gave him such things as he had taken before from his servant."

Alexander's zeal must have been very active. In 1558 it is recorded that twenty-two men and women were committed to Newgate for praying together in the fields about Islington. They were two and twenty weeks in the prison before they were examined, during which Alexander sent them word that if they would hear a mass they should be delivered. According to Foxe a terrible vengeance overtook this hard-hearted man. He died very miserably, being so swollen that he was more like a monster than a man. The same authority relates that other persecutors came to a bad end.

Bishop Hooper soon followed Rogers to the stake. The same Monday night, Feb. 4, 1555, the keeper of Newgate gave him an inkling that he should be sent to Gloucester to suffer death, "and the next day following, about four o'clock in the morning before day, the keeper with others came to him and searched him and the bed wherein he lay, to see if he had written anything, and then he was led to the sheriffs of London and other their officers forth of Newgate, to a place appointed not far from Dunstan's Church, Fleet Street, where six of the Queen's Guards were appointed to receive him and to carry him to Gloucester, ..." where execution was to be done.

We obtain a curious insight into the gaol at Newgate during Mary's reign from the narrative of the 'Hot Gospeller.' Edward Underhill, a yeoman of the Guard, was arrested in 1553 for "putting out" a ballad which attacked the Queen's title. Underhill was carried before the Council, and there got into dispute with Bourne, a fanatic priest whom he called a papist. "Sir John Mason asked what he meant by that, and he replied, 'If you look among the priests of Paul's you will find some mumpsimusses there. This caused much heat, and he was committed to Newgate." At the door of the prison he wrote to his wife, asking her to send his night-gown, Bible, and lute, and then he goes on to describe Newgate as follows:[42]—

"In the centre of Newgate was a great open hall; as soon as it was supper-time the board was covered in the same hall. The keeper, whose name was Alexander, with his wife came and sat down, and half a dozen prisoners that were there for felony. Underhill being the first that for religion was sent into that prison. One of the felons had served with him in France. After supper this good fellow, whose name was Bristow, procured one to have a bed in his (Underhill's) chamber who could play well upon a rebeck. He was a tall fellow, and after one of Queen Mary's guard, yet a Protestant, which he kept secret, or else he should not have found such favour as he did at the keeper's hands and his wife's, for to such as loved the gospel they were very cruel. 'Well,' said Underhill, 'I have sent for my Bible, and, by God's grace, therein shall be my daily exercise; I will not hide it from them.' 'Sir,' said he, 'I am poor; but they will bear with you, for they see your estate is to pay well; and I will show you the nature and manner of them, for I have been here a good while. They both do love music very well; wherefore, you with your lute, and I to play with you on my rebeck, will please them greatly. He loveth to be merry and to drink wine, and she also. If you will bestow upon them, every dinner and supper, a quart of wine and some music, you shall be their white son, and have all the favour they can show you.'

"The honour of being 'white son' to the governor and governess of Newgate was worth aspiring after. Underhill duly provided the desired entertainment. The governor gave him the best room in the prison, with all other admissible indulgences.

"At last, however, the evil savours, great unquietness, with over many draughts of air, threw the poor gentleman into a burning ague. He shifted his lodgings, but to no purpose; the evil savours followed him. The keeper offered him his own parlour, where he escaped from the noise of the prison; but it was near the kitchen, and the smell of the meat was disagreeable. Finally the wife put him away in her store closet, amidst her best plate, crockery, and clothes, and there he continued to survive till the middle of September, when he was released on bail through the interference of the Earl of Bedford."

There was a truce to religious persecution for some years after Mary's death. Throughout Edward's reign and the better part of Elizabeth's it was only the ordinary sort of criminal who was committed to the gaol of Newgate. The offences were mostly coining, horse-stealing, and other kinds of thefts. "One named Ditche was apprehended at the sessions holden at Newgate on 4th December, 1583, nineteen times indicted, whereof he confessed eighteen, who also between the time of his apprehension and the said sessions impeached many for stealing horses, whereof (divers being apprehended) ten were condemned and hanged in Smithfield on the 11th December, being Friday and horse-market there."[43] The 'Remembrancia' gives a letter from Mr. Valentine Dale, one of the masters of the Court of Requests, to the Lord Mayor, stating that the wife of John Hollingshead had petitioned the Queen to grant a reprieve and pardon to her husband, a condemned felon, and directing the execution to be stayed, and a full account of his behaviour and offence forwarded to Her Majesty. The Lord Mayor in reply says that he had called before him the officers of Newgate, who stated that Hollingshead had been for a long time a common and notorious thief. This was the fourth time he had been in Newgate for felonies, and upon the last occasion he had been branded with the letter T (thief). Coiners were very severely dealt with. The offence was treason, and punished as such. There are many cases on record, such as—"On the 27th of January Phillip Meshel, a Frenchman, and two Englishmen were drawn from Newgate to Tyburn, and there hanged. The Frenchman quartered who had coined gold counterfeit; of the Englishmen, the one had clipped silver, and the other cast testers of tin." "The 30th of May Thomas Green, goldsmith, was drawn from Newgate to Tyburn, and there hanged, headed, and quartered, for clipping of coin, both gold and silver."

Towards the end of the reign, in spite of the stringent acts against vagrancy, the country swarmed with rogues and beggars —vagabonds who laid the farmers under contribution, and terrified all honest folk out of their lives. In London crime was rampant. Even then it had its organization; there were houses which harboured thieves, in which schools were maintained for the education of young pickpockets. Maitland tells us that in the spring of 1585, Fleetwood the recorder with several other magistrates searched the town and discovered seven houses of entertainment for felons. They found also that one Walton, a gentleman born, once a prosperous merchant, "but fallen into decay," who had kept an alehouse which had been put down, had begun a "new business." He opened his house for the reception of all the cut-purses in and about the city. In this house was a room to learn young boys to cut purses. Two devices were hung up; one was a pocket, the other was a purse. The pocket had in it certain counters, and was hung round with hawk's bells, and over them hung a little sacring[44] bell. The purse had silver in it, and he that could take out a counter without any noise was allowed to be a public *foyster*; and he that could take a piece of silver out of the purse without noise of any of the bells was adjudged a clever *nypper*. These places gave great encouragement to evil-doers in these times, but were soon after suppressed.

In 1581 a fresh religious persecution began, happily without the sanguinary accessories of that of Mary's reign. Elizabeth had no love for the puritans; she also began now to hate and fear the papists. Orthodoxy was insisted upon. People who would not go to church were sent first to prison, then haled before sessions and fined a matter of twenty pounds each. Still worse fared the adherents or emissaries of Rome. Years before (1569) a man, John Felton, had been drawn from Newgate into Paul's Churchyard, and there hanged and quartered as a traitor for affixing a bull of Pope Pius V. on the gate of the Bishop of London's palace. In 1578 it is recorded that "the papists are stubborn." So also must have been the puritans. "One Sherwood brought before the Bishop of London behaved so stubbornly that the bishop will show no more favour to those miscalled puritans." Next began a fierce crusade against the "seminary" priests, who swarmed into England like missionaries, despatched *in partibus infidelium* to minister to the faithful few and bring back all whom they could to the fold. Newgate was now for ever full of these priests. They adopted all manner of disguises, and went now as soldiers, now as private gentlemen, now openly as divines. They were harboured and hidden by faithful Roman Catholics, and managed thus to glide unperceived from point to point intent upon their dangerous business. But they did not always escape observation, and when caught they were invariably laid by the heels and hardly dealt with. Gerard Dance, alias Ducket, a seminary priest, was arraigned (1581) at the Old Bailey before the Queen's justices, and affirmed that although he was in England, he was subject to the Pope in ecclesiastical causes, and that the Pope had now the same authority in England that he had a hundred years past, and which he had at Rome, "with other traitorous speeches, for the which he was condemned to be hanged, drawn, and quartered." The same year William Dios (a Spaniard?), keeper of Newgate, sends a certificate of the names of the recusants now in Newgate, "viz. Lawrence Wakeman and others, ... the two last being of the precise sort." April 20, 1586, Robert Rowley, taken upon seas by Captain Burrows going to Scotland, is committed first to the Marshalsea, and from thence to Newgate. Next year, August 26, Richard Young reports to Secretary Walsyngham that he has talked with sundry priests remaining in the prisons about London. "Some," he says, "are very evil affected, and unworthy to live in England. Simpson, alias Heygate, and Flower, priests, have justly deserved death, and in no wise merit Her Majesty's mercy. William Wigges, Leonard Hide, and George Collinson, priests in Newgate, are dangerous fellows, as are also Morris Williams and Thomas Pounde, the latter committed as a layman, but in reality a professed Jesuit. Francis Tirrell is an obstinate papist, and is doubted to be a spy."

We read as follows in an intercepted letter from Cardinal John Allen, Rector of the English College at Rheims, to Mr. White, seminary priest in the Clink,[45] and the rest of the priests in Newgate, the Fleet, and the Marshalsea. "Pope Sextus sends them his blessing, and will send them over for their comfort Dr. Reynolds, chief Jesuit of the college at Rheims, who must be carefully concealed," ... with others, ... "whose discourses would be a great joy to all heretics. They will bring some consecrated crucifixes, late consecrated by his Holiness, and some books to be given to the chiefest Catholics, their greatest benefactors." This letter was taken upon a young man, Robert Weston, travelling to seek service, "who seems to have had considerable dealings with recusants, and to have made very full confessions."

It was easier for all such to get into Newgate just then—than to obtain release. Henry Ash and Michael Genison, being prisoners in Newgate, petition Lord Keeper Pickering for a warrant for their enlargement upon putting in good security for their appearance; "they were long since committed by Justice Young and the now Bishop of London for recusancy, where they remain, to their great shame and utter undoing, and are likely to continue, unless he extend his mercy." In 1598 George Barkworth petitions Secretary Cecil "that he was committed to Newgate six months ago on suspicion of being a seminary priest, which he is not; has been examined nine times, and brought up at sessions four times; begs the same liberty of the house at Bridewell which was granted him at Newgate."

Political prisoners were not wanting in Newgate in the Elizabethan period. In 1585 instructions are given[46] to the recorder to examine one Hall, a prisoner in Newgate, charged with a design for conveying away the Queen of Scots. This was a part of

Babington's conspiracy, for which Throgmorton also suffered. Other victims, besides the unfortunate Queen herself, were Babington, Tichbourne, and many more, who after trial at the Old Bailey, and incarceration in Newgate, were hanged in St. Giles's Fields. The execution was carried out with great barbarity; seven of the conspirators were cut down before they were dead and disembowelled. Another plot against Elizabeth's life was discovered in 1587, the actors in which were "one Moody, an idle, profligate fellow, then prisoner in Newgate, and one Stafford, brother to Sir Edward Stafford." The great Queen Bess in these last days of her reign went in constant terror of her life; and a third conspiracy to poison her, originating with her own physician and Lopez, a Jew, led to their execution as traitors. Again, Squires, a disbanded soldier, was charged with putting poison on the pommel of her saddle, and although he admitted his guilt upon the rack, he declared when dying that he was really innocent.

All this time within Newgate there was turbulence, rioting, disorders, accompanied seemingly by constant oppression. The prisoners were ready to brave anything to get out. General gaol deliveries were made otherwise than in due course of law. Those that were fit to serve in the sea or land forces were frequently pardoned and set free. A petition to the Lord Admiral (1589) is preserved in which certain prisoners, shut out from pardon because they are not "by law bailable," beg that the words maybe struck out of the order for release, and state that they will gladly enter Her Majesty's service. Many made determined efforts to escape. "The 16th December, 1556," says Hollinshed, "Gregory, Carpenter, Smith, and a Frenchman born were arraigned for making counterfeit keys wherewith to have opened the locks of Newgate, to have slain the keeper and let forth the prisoners; at which time of his arraignment, having conveyed a knife into his sleeve, he thrust it into the side of

William Whiteguts, his fellow-prisoner, who had given evidence against him, so that he was in great peril of death thereby; for the which fact he was immediately taken from the bar into the street before the justice hall, when, his hand being first stricken off, he was hanged on a gibbet set up for the purpose.

"The keeper of Newgate was arraigned and indicted for that the said prisoner had a weapon about him and his hands loose, which should have been bound."

Yet the keeper of Newgate and other gaolers were by no means irresponsible agents. Two cases may be quoted in which these officials were promptly brought to book. In 1555 the keeper of the Bread Street Compter, by name Richard Husband, pasteler, "being a wilful and headstrong man," who, with servants like himself, had dealt hardly with the prisoners in his charge, was sent to the gaol of Newgate by Sir Rowland Hill, mayor, with the assent of a court of aldermen. "It was commanded to the keeper to set those irons on his legs which were called widows' alms; these he wore from Thursday till Sunday in the afternoon." On the Tuesday he was released, but not before he was bound over in an hundred marks to act in conformity with the rules for the managing of the Compters. "All which notwithstanding, he continued as before: ... the prisoners were ill-treated, the prison was made a common lodging-house at fourpence the night for thieves and night-walkers, whereby they might be safe from searches that were made abroad." He was indicted for these, and other enormities, "but did rub it out, and could not be reformed, till the prisoners were removed; for the house in Bread Street was his own by lease or otherwise, and he could not be put from it."[47] A searching inquiry was also made into the conduct of Crowder, the keeper of Newgate in 1580,[48] or thereabouts. The State Papers contain an information of the disorders practiced by the officers of Newgate prison, levying fines and taking bribes, by old and young Crowders, the gaolers. "Crowder and his wife," says the report, "be most horrible blasphemers and swearers." The matter is taken up by the lords of the council, who write to the Lord Mayor, desiring to be fully informed of all disorders committed, and by whom. "They are sending gentlemen to repair to the prison to inquire into the case, and requesting the Lord Mayor to appoint two persons to assist them." Sir Christopher Hatton also writes to the Lord Mayor, drawing attention to the charges against Crowder. The Lord Mayor replies that certain persons had been appointed to inquire, but had not yet made their report. The Court of Enquiry are willing to receive Crowder, but he persists in refusing (to explain). "He would not come to their meeting, but stood upon his reputation." The result, so far as can be guessed, was that Crowder was pensioned off. But he found powerful friends in his adversity. His cause was espoused by Sir Thomas Bromley, Lord Chancellor, who informs the Lord Mayor that he thinks Crowder has been dealt with very hardly, and that his accusers were persons unworthy of credit. Apparently Crowder had no chance of being reinstated, for his friend the Lord Chancellor tries next to get his pension raised. The exact amount is not stated, but Sir Thomas Bromley suggests that it should be made up to £40, twenty nobles of which should be paid by his successor. There is no mention of any such increase having been conceded.

NEWGATE IN THE SEVENTEENTH CENTURY (DOWN TO THE GREAT FIRE).

More Jesuit emissaries in Newgate—Richardson and others—Their fate—Some escape—Greater favour shown them under Charles I. through intercession of Henrietta Maria—But freedom not easily procured—Case of Thomas Coo—Of John Williams—The Mayor of Sudbury in Newgate—Also an alderman—Pardons and release still given on condition of military service—Troubles with King fill Newgate—Ship-money—Speaking ill of King's sister entails imprisonment in Newgate for life—Parliament growing more powerful insists of execution of six Jesuits suffered to linger on in Newgate—Irish rebels taken on high seas, in Newgate—Also offenders against plague ordinances, and against religion or morality—Strange news from Newgate—Interior of gaol—Condition of prisoners—Fanatical conduct of keeper—Nefarious practices of turnkeys—They levy black mail—"Coney catching" described—Several cases of such swindling —Civil war reflected in prison records—More Irish arrested at Devonshire—Sent to London and lodged in Newgate for examination —Arbitrary imprisonment imposed by House of Lords on Richard Overton—Case of Colonel Lilburne—"Free born John"—Newgate annals record transfer of power to Commonwealth—Royalists in gaol —Also prisoners of mark—The Portuguese ambassadors' brother in Newgate charged with murder, and executed—Also Lord Buckhurst and others.

THE disturbing elements of society continued much the same in the early part of the seventeenth century as in the years immediately preceding. There were the same offences against law and order, dealt with in the same summary fashion. Newgate was perpetually crowded with prisoners charged with the same sort of crimes. Bigotry and intolerance continued to breed persecution. All sects which differed from that professed by those in power were in turn under the ban of the law. The Romish priest still ventured into the hostile heretic land where his life was not worth a minute's purchase; Puritans and Nonconformists were committed to gaol for refusing to surrender their heterodox opinions: these last coming into power were ruthlessly strict towards the openly irreligious backslider. Side by side with these sufferers in the cause of independent thought swarmed the depredators, the wrong-doers, whose criminal instincts and the actions they produced were much the same as they had been before and as they are now.

The devoted courage of the Jesuit emissaries in those days of extreme peril for all priests who dared to cross the channel claims for them a full measure of respect. They were for ever in trouble. When caught they met hard words, scant mercy, often only a short shrift. Repeated references are made to them. In the State Papers July 1602 is a list of priests and recusants in prison, viz. "Newgate—Pound (already mentioned), desperate and obstinate; ... in the Clink, Marshalsea, King's Bench, are others; among them Douce, a forward intelligence, Tichborne, Webster, perverter of youth," &c. They were ever the victims of treachery and espionage.[49] "William Richardson, a priest of Seville College (the date is 1603), was discovered to the Chief Justice by one whom he trusted, and arraigned and condemned at Newgate for being a priest and coming to England. When examined he answered stoutly, yet with great modesty and discretion, moving many to compassionate him and speak against the Chief Justice, on whom he laid the guilt of his blood." He was executed at Tyburn, hanged and quartered, but his head and quarters were buried. "Such spectacles," says the writer, Ant. Rivers, to Giacomo Creleto, Venice, "do nothing increase the gospel...." A further account says that William Richardson, alias Anderson, was betrayed by a false brother, sent to Newgate, and kept close prisoner over a week, no one being allowed to see him. The Chief Justice, interrupting other trials, called for him, and caused him to be indicted of high treason for being a priest and coming to England. All of which he confessed, and there being no evidence against him, the Chief Justice gave his confession in writing to the jury, who found him guilty. "He thanked God and told the Chief Justice he was a bloody man, and sought the blood of the Catholics. He denied that he was a Jesuit or knew Garnet[50]...."

These priests were not very rigorously guarded. On the 27th November 1612 seven escaped from Newgate. They must also have been very indifferently lodged. When a number of them were transferred for greater security to Wisbeach Castle, they petitioned that they were unable to provide themselves with bedding and other necessaries for their removal, and begged that orders might be taken for their providing. The keeper was closely watched lest he should be too easy with his prisoners. Questions are suggested to be put to him, examining him as to his connivance with recusants, and allowing them to escape or enjoy great liberty. In 1611 Sir Thomas Lake writes to Lord Salisbury to the effect that the king is resolved the keeper of Newgate shall be very severely punished for allowing reverence to priests and masses to be said in the prison.[51] It was evident they were permitted some license, although contraband, for Secretary Conway issues instructions on May 13, 1626, to the provost marshal of Middlesex directing him to search for popish books, massing stuff, and reliques of popery in Newgate. Even in Elizabeth's time it appears that mass was said in Newgate, and one John Harrison, when charged in 1595 with being in possession of certain popish relics and papers, admitted that he had been married in Newgate by an old priest then in prison with his (H.'s) wife and himself.

Somewhat better times dawned for the Roman Catholic ministers after the accession of Charles I. His queen, Henrietta Maria, was able to help them. Her favouring of papists was indeed one of the many causes of the discontent which culminated in civil war. The king himself addresses the keeper of Newgate to the effect that "at the instance of the queen we have granted Pulteney Morse, lately indicted upon suspicion of being a priest, and still prisoner at Newgate, to be enlarged upon security to appear before the council when he shall be thereunto called. He has given security to that purpose; we therefore command you to set him at liberty." The queen herself at times personally applied for the release of prisoners confined in Newgate for matters of religion. Often priests committed escaped incarceration, and were found to be at liberty after arrest. But it was not always easy to obtain enlargement when once laid by the heels. Here is the petition to the queen (State Papers, May 1634) of Thomas Reynolds, a secular priest, who has been more than five years in Newgate, "where by the unwholesomeness of the air, the strictness of the imprisonment, and his great age he is fallen into many dangerous infirmities. He now prays the queen to move the king to release him. His application is backed up by a medical certificate signed by three doctors that petitioner is affected with sciatica, colic, defluxion of rheum, and the stone. He is fifty-eight years of age." The result of the petition is not given.

It was not only in the case of the religious prisoners that freedom was difficult to compass. A very hard case is that of Thomas Coo, committed to Newgate on grounds that are not traceable. He states, October 1618, to Sir Julius Cæsar and Sir Fulk Greville that his loyal service in preserving the life of his sovereign by discovering the London insurrection has been rewarded with famine and a dungeon. He is resolved to live no longer, leaving his son "to conceal his mystical designs."[52] Fifteen years later, but still in Newgate, he makes his "submission from Newgate dungeon dunghill, almost famished; acknowledging his contrition of heart, and stating his readiness to do any penance the council may command, beseeches to know what his punishment may be." His long imprisonments in Newgate and elsewhere have "stript petitioner, even of clothes from his back, and from that of the bearer of the letter, his lame child." He prays that he may be forthwith either banished according to their order of the 28th October of the 5th King Charles (1630), or be allowed close prisoner in some other place where he may have some allowance to preserve him from starving. Six years more pass, and again (1639) he petitions the council, stating that there was neither legal warrant for his commitment to the Fleet eight years, nor for his six years' detention in Newgate, whither he was thence removed. There were sent with him certain transcribed papers, importing some orders and rules issuing out of the Star Chamber, Chancery, and King's Bench, in which courts the prisoner was never defendant, convented, nor convicted. The only paper against him was a supposed Inner Star Chamber order of voluntary banishment, to the effect that the petitioner was to depart the kingdom within twenty days, dated 1629. "Gaolers," says the poor prisoner, "are made his judges, and jurors only give their verdict to whom his carcase belongs to be interred."

A light matter sufficed to secure committal to Newgate. John Williams in a petition states that he was committed to Newgate for being one at the depopulation of the forest of Dean. There he has remained for five years, and now prays enlargement, not having wherewith to maintain himself in prison with his wife and poor children, who were seemingly incarcerated with him. The coachmen of even great people were committed to Newgate for contravening the Star Chamber order as to the route they should take to and from the playhouse in Blackfriars. Frequenters were invited to go to and fro by water, but if they drove they were to be set down by the west end of St. Paul's Churchyard or Fleet Conduit. Again Robert Coleman (1631), having found certain writings of the secretary and other noble personages, and thinking they belonged to the Earl of Dorset, went to the Old Bailey, where Lord Dorset was sitting on the bench, to deliver them up. "One Barnes was to be tried," states Coleman subsequently in a petition, "and there was some one there to beg his estate, whereupon the Earl of Dorset committed the prisoner (Coleman) to Newgate, where he has been ever since detained, and could not bring the writings to the secretary;" "prays that he may be allowed to come to him for that purpose." Christopher Crowe, a prisoner in Newgate, and another victim to the oppression of a great noble, about the same date (1632) petitions the council: "I am in great misery," he says, "having no friends nor means." For six weeks he has had for his allowance but a halfpenny in bread one day and a farthing's worth the next. "Is heartily sorry for his words spoken against the Marquis of Hamilton, and prays enlargement." Others in Newgate sought noble protection, and petitioned the great peers to procure release. John Meredith petitions Henry Earl of Holland, Captain of the Guard, reminding him that when he (Meredith) and his wife were committed to Newgate, his lordship on their appeal had sent an order for their discharge, which had been disregarded, and now, "having lain in prison a fortnight, he prays that he and his wife may forthwith be enlarged." This has no effect, so Meredith and his wife Joan petition the Earl of Manchester, Lord President. "They had now remained in prison three weeks; pray for an enlargement from Newgate gratis,[53] and that the sergeants who arrested them may be committed."

Prisoners of still greater consequence languished often hopelessly in Newgate Gaol. Now it is the wardens of divers city companies for not making up their proportion towards the previous year's provision of corn; now a respectable freeman and stationer, William Cooke, who had built a shed of timber in the open street in High Holborn adjoining Furnival's Inn. He was committed to Newgate till he should demolish the same. But, as Inigo Jones and others represent to the council, "he lies in prison, and the shed continues," and they suggest an order to the principals of Furnival's Inn, or to the sheriffs of London, to take the shed away. Next comes a greater personage, John Andrews, the Mayor of Sudbury, who has unhappily fallen foul of a messenger of the Star Chamber named Potter. This messenger came to Andrews with a warrant claiming his assistance for the apprehension of certain unlicensed dealers in tobacco in Sudbury, to which warrant he "gave due obedience." Potter was presently himself brought before the mayor, "accused of many blasphemies and oaths," and for compounding for money with the culprit who had unlawfully trafficked in tobacco. Upon this the mayor told Potter that he thought him worthy to be committed to prison. Potter then fell to abusing the mayor in scoffs and threatening speeches, telling him that he would have him set in the stocks, and that he cared not a pin for the mayor's authority. The exasperated Andrews committed

Potter to prison. But Potter's threats were not without substantial foundation, for Andrews' action is deemed improper, and he is himself committed to Newgate. From thence he humbly submits himself, and prays discharge from that loathsome prison.

Even an alderman was not safe. Thomas Middleton in 1603, having been duly elected alderman, refused to be sworn, whereupon he was committed to Newgate by the Lord Mayor and court of aldermen, "according to their oaths and the custom of the city." For this they were sharply reproved by the king, and ordered to release him immediately, "as he was employed in important state service which privileged him from arrest."

These were days of widespread oppression, when Strafford, Laud, the Star Chamber, and ecclesiastical courts gave effect to the king's eager longings for arbitrary power. The following is from a half-mad fanatic who has offended the relentless archbishop. "The petition of Richard Farnham, a prophet of the most high God, a true subject to my king, and a prisoner of my saviour Christ, in Newgate, to Archbishop Laud and the rest of the high commissioners, whom he prays to excuse his plainness, being no scholar.... Desires to know the cause of his being detained so long in prison, where he has been kept a year next April without coming to his answer. Thinks they have forgotten him. If he be a false prophet and a blasphemer and a seducer, as most people report that he is, the high commissioners would do well to bring him to trial. What he wrote before he came into prison and what he has written since he will stand to.... If he does not get his answer this summer he intends to complain to the king, believing that it is not his pleasure his subjects should suffer false imprisonment to satisfy the archbishop's mind." Of the same year and the same character is this other petition from William King, a prisoner in Newgate "for a little treatise delivered to Lord Leppington." Has remained in thraldom twenty-seven months; expresses contrition and prays enlargement on bail, or that he may be called to answer. Forty years more were to elapse before the passing of the Habeas Corpus Act; but the forgoing will show how grievously this so-called palladium of an Englishman's liberties was required.

Pardons free or more or less conditional were, however, vouchsafed at times. Release from prison was still, as before, and for long after, frequently accompanied by the penalty of military service. This had long been the custom. On declaration of war in the earlier reigns, it was usual to issue a proclamation offering a general pardon to those guilty of homicides and felonies on condition of service for a year and a day. Even without this obligation prisoners in durance might sue out a pardon by intercession of some nobleman serving abroad with the king. But later on the release was distinctly conditional on personal service. The Lord Mayor certifies to the king (1619) that certain prisoners in Newgate, whose names and offences are given, are not committed for murder; so they are reprieved, as being able-bodied and fit to do service in foreign parts. Another certificate states that William Dominic, condemned to death for stealing a purse value £4, is reprieved, "this being his first offence, and he an excellent drummer, fit to do the king service." Again, the king requires the keeper of Newgate to deliver certain reprieved prisoners to Sir Edward Conway, junior, to be employed in His Majesty's service in the Low Countries. Recorder Finch reports that he has furnished "Conway's son with seven prisoners fit for service; sends a list of prisoners now in Newgate, but reprieved. Some have been long in gaol, and were saved from execution by the prince's return [with Buckingham from Spain?] on that day. They pester the gaol, which is already reported crowded, this hot weather, and would do better service as soldiers if pardoned, 'for they would not dare to run away.'" A warrant is made out June 5, 1629, to the sheriffs of London to deliver to such persons as the Swedish ambassador shall appoint forty-seven persons, of whom one was Elizabeth Leech—was she to be employed as a sutler or *vivandière*?—being prisoners condemned of felonies, and remaining in the gaols of Newgate and Bridewell, who are released "to the end that they may be employed in the service of the King of Sweden"—Gustavus Adolphus, at that time our ally. There are numerous entries of this kind in the State papers. Sometimes the prisoners volunteer for service. "John Tapps, by the displeasure of the late Lord Chief Justice and the persecution of James the clerk and one of the keepers,[54] has been kept from the benefit of the pardon which has been stayed at the Great Seal. Begs Lord Conway to perfect his work by moving the Lord Keeper in his behalf, and in the mean time sending some powerful warrant for his employment as a soldier." Certain other convicted prisoners in Newgate, who had been pardoned in respect of the birth of Prince Charles (Charles II.), petition that they are altogether impoverished, and unable to sue out their pardons. They pray that by warrant they may be transported into the State of Venice under the command of Captain Ludovic Hamilton. This document is endorsed with a reference to the Lord Chief Justice of the Common Pleas to certify concerning these delinquents and their crimes. George Gardener, a prisoner in Newgate, also petitions the king in March 1630, stating that he was committed by the council on the information of James Ingram, deputy warden of the Fleet, to prevent petitioner prosecuting the said Ingram for his notorious extortions. He has remained in Newgate since April previous, and by Ingram's procurement was shut up amongst felons in the common gaol, whereby he might have been murdered. "Prays that he may be allowed to go abroad on security." Here is another petition, that of Bridget Gray to the council. She states (July 19, 1618) that her grandson, John Throckmorton, is a prisoner in Newgate for felony, and prays that he may be discharged, this being his first offence, and Sir Thomas Smythe being ready to convey him beyond seas. Upon this is endorsed an order that if the mayor or recorder will certify that Throckmorton was not convicted of murder, burglary, highway robbery, rape, or witchcraft, a warrant may be made for his banishment. The certificate is forthcoming, and is to the effect that Throckmorton's crime was aiding in stealing a hat, value 6s., for which the principal, Robert Whisson, an old thief, was hanged.

The gaol calendar reflects the vicissitudes of these changing, troublous times. There were many London citizens who, sharing the patriotic spirit of Hampden and Pym, found themselves clapped into prison for refusing to submit to the illegal taxations of Charles I. In a long statement, 16th April, 1639, from Edward Rossingham to Lord Conway he says that the Lord Mayor labours hard to get in the ship-money. "Some pay and many refuse; but such as do refuse he requires to enter into a recognizance of so much money to attend the council. Three citizens stand committed to Newgate, not because they refuse to pay ship-money, but because they refuse to enter into bond to attend the Board to answer their not paying the same. Divers others refused, and were sent to Newgate; but upon better consideration they paid their money, and were released again." The temper of the Government as regards ship-money is further shown by the arrest and trial of the keeper of Newgate for permitting a prisoner committed for non-payment of this unlawful tax to go at large. It appears that the offender, Richard Chambers, had been several times remanded to the same custody, and had been allowed to escape.

It was highly dangerous to speak lightly of dignities in these ticklish times. The State trials give an account of the hard measure meted out to one Edward Floyde for scandalizing the princess palatine, Elizabeth, James I.'s daughter, and titular Queen of Bohemia. Floyde was charged with having said, while a prisoner in the Fleet, "I have heard that Prague is taken, and goodman Palsgrave and goodwife Palsgrave (Elizabeth) have taken to their heels and run away." This puerile, gossip seriously occupied both houses of Parliament, and eventually the Lords awarded and adjudged that Edward Floyde be deemed an infamous person, incapable of bearing arms as a gentleman, whose testimony was not to be taken in any court or cause. He was also sentenced to ride with his head to his horse's tail from Westminster to the pillory in Cheapside; after this to be whipped from the Fleet to Westminster, there again to stand on the pillory. He was to pay a fine of £5000 to the king, and imprisoned in Newgate during his life.

In 1642, according to a published document,[55] Newgate "hath not been more replenished with prisoners these many years than now, there being very nigh three hundred prisoners committed to that infamous castle of misery." It was still the mere gatehouse prison, and its accommodation must have been of the most limited description. Chief among these inmates were six Jesuit priests who had been condemned to die, but had, no doubt through the powerful advocacy of Henrietta Maria, obtained a reprieve. "Whereupon did arise a tumultuous mutiny among the other prisoners, who refused to die without the Jesuits; but afterwards they (the mutineers) were mitigated in a kind of pacified tranquillity." Parliament had also petitioned that "execution might be imposed upon" these priests; but the king would not condescend thereunto till his further pleasure, "whereupon they (the Jesuits) have continued secure in Newgate ever since, one man being solely excepted, viz. Goodman, who died last Good Friday, and at once deceived both Gregory[56] and Tyburn." But the Parliament was at this date too near its rupture with the king to submit to be thus put off, and re-petitioned, stating "these Jesuits were an obstacle to their assiduous proceedings;" and His Majesty replied that if they were "the obstruction and hindrance of reformation in the Church they might be forthwith executed without further delay." Henrietta Maria's strong attachment to the Roman Catholic faith is satirized in the old German print, which I have taken from the Crowle 'Pennant's London', and which represents the Queen doing penance at Tyburn over the grave of some recently executed priests. It is said that "the pore queen" walked afoot—some say barefoot—from St. James to Tyburn in the dead of night. A state coach followed with attendants, and her father confessor. The whole story is probably apocryphal, but the print is interesting as one of the earliest representations of Tyburn tree. The pilgrimage took place in 1628, but the print is of a later date.

Other prisoners at this time were certain Irishmen suspected to be rebels who had apparently been captured on the high seas, and eventually committed to Newgate. When formally examined before the Parliament, the servants, seamen, and soldiers were remitted; only the master of the ship, the captain, lieutenants, and ancients were detained, "and still continue in prison." The court was to examine them further; but as this did not come off, the Parliament would, it was thought, censure them. These, found to be ten in number, five of them friars, four soldiers, and one a pilgrim, were at length examined "before a committee in the court of wards, who demanded of them their intents in coming over to Ireland, and to what effect: four of which very peremptorily denied, and said they came over with occasions of merchandize, but one of them betrayed the rest, and affirmed that they were friars, and came over into England to save souls for heaven." The other five were carried down unto Westminster before the same committee. The master of the ship, being called first, "did show a commission unto them for his going; they then asked him whether he would take the oath of allegiance, which he was willing to take. When asked as to the oath of supremacy, he replied that he was an ignorant man, and did not understand what it meant." Three of the others could not speak a word of English, whereupon the master did interpret what they spake. "It seems by the exposition of the master of the ship that they have been in service under the Prince of Orange half a year; they were taken captives at Flanders; they served in France two years, and a half-year in Spain, and now come into their own country."

Neglect of the stringent ordinances passed to protect life during the constant visitations of that fearful scourge the plague brought down the one universal penalty, committal to Newgate, upon offenders. Here is a long story about Stephen Smith, a fishmonger, whose door was by the sufferance of the warder broken open, and William Fenn, servant to Smith, who had already been indicted for offences committed during the several infections of that house, entered the house and brought a quantity of salted fish to the door for sale. Yet all the time Susan Wheelyer, a maid-servant of Smith's, was shut up in the house infected with the plague. Smith had unlawfully abandoned his house. Fenn was apprehended and shut up with the late infected servant under a better guard. "I have committed the warder," says Sir William Slingsby, who makes the report, "and commanded the fish to be carried in again, and the doors locked and guarded.... These proceedings I suspect to be done by the private directions of Smith." The orders of the council on the above were prompt and severe. Stephen Smith was at once committed to Newgate, "there to be kept under strong bolts until further orders," while William Fenn was sent to the pest-house, and a weight of iron placed on his heels to keep him safe and quiet there. It was ordered further, that the warders for their great neglect be put in the stocks before Smith's house.

Newgate, during the last great plague epidemic, received all offenders against the sanitary rules. These were enforced by the Middlesex justices, who were directed to be most careful for the relief of the citizens and for the prevention of the spreading of infection. Diligent circumspection was to be used to prevent the removal of goods or persons from London or Westminster to other towns and villages, or up and down the Thames; also to put pressure upon those belonging to infected families who refused to shut themselves up. Refusal to obey or neglect of these orders was to be visited with committal to Newgate and indictment at the next sessions.

Offences against morality and religion were met with the same penalty of imprisonment. Incontinence and loose living were high misdemeanours. In an extract from the register of the High Court of Commission we find that Nicholas Slater of Royden, Essex, a married man, had run off with Blanche Cowper, another man's wife. Defendants lived together in various places. "Slater, like a vagabond, without license had wandered up and down the kingdom professing physic and surgery, and carried Blanche about with him from place to place." Slater was committed close prisoner to Newgate, there to remain during pleasure, and Blanche to Bridewell. There was added penance in Ware and Stepney, while Slater was fined £1000 and Blanche £100 to His Majesty. The last part of the sentence points to Charles's shifts to raise money. This was in 1638. Another story of the same kind, but with a different issue, is of the same date. George Harrison in Newgate petitions the Archbishop of Canterbury and the Lords of the High Commission Court for enlargement. A certain John Cock had, it appears, discovered the incontinent life of John Thierry and Ursula Baythorpe. The latter offered Cock £27 to be silent, which he was willing to accept, and went with the petitioner Harrison to a tavern, the place appointed for the handing over of the money. But they fell into a trap, and were arrested at the tavern; thence they were carried to the Compter and committed to Newgate. Afterwards at a sessions they were indicted, and, on the testimonies of the merchant and the said Ursula's sister and her husband, were whipped three times to the pillory, where they stood eleven hours. They were not suffered to come down till they had asked Thierry's and Ursula's forgiveness before all the spectators, and so were three times whipped back again. "By the extremity of which execution petitioner lost his speech and almost his understanding, and Cock was carried home dead in the cart. By which cruelty and disgrace petitioner, who was formerly well respected, is now utterly undone." Thierry must have had good friends at court. But the informer seems to have been right in his denunciation, for both the accused were subsequently "detected to the court," and it was proved that the said poor men had only suffered for "meddling with the truth." Petitioner now prays that the merchant (Thierry) may be ordered to give him and his poor children relief and restitution for their sufferings.

A quaint pamphlet entitled 'Strange News from Newgate,' dated 1647, states that on the 10th January, "being the blessed sabbath, at Botolph's Church near Bishopgate, in sermon time, there arose a great disturbance by one Evan Price, a tailor, who stood up and declared himself to be Christ, which words much amazed the people, and divers timorous spirits into a great fear.... Whereupon he was immediately apprehended and carried before the Right Honourable the Lord Mayor, where he was examined seriously and at length, although no doubt a religious lunatic." He was asked whether he had worked miracles, whether he was married, ... "with divers other arguments objected against him, which he was not able to answer, but remained obstinate in his devilish and satanical opinion." But after some time spent upon his examination, "as he still remained in his hell-bred opinion, not hearkening to any advice or counsel whatsoever," it was ordered that he should be committed to Newgate, which was accordingly performed. "Five days later he was arraigned at the Old Bailey, and coming to the bar, was examined by the judges, but seemed resolute not to make any confession." The pamphlet ends abruptly, and does not give the result of his trial.

It must have been consequent on some conflict with the ecclesiastical authority that Edward Powell, alias Anderson, was sent from Ely as a prisoner to Newgate. The story rests on a report from Bishop Wren of Ely to the council, dated 5th June 1638. Powell had been apprehended upon a riot committed by an assemblage which went by the name of Anderson's Camp, but was not imprisoned for his share therein, but for his misdemeanours and foul speeches at the time of arrest. He was accused of being an abettor of the riot, although not present at it. When he had been at Newmarket the previous Lent, Powell paid the town-crier twopence to proclaim a gathering of the people to go to the king with a petition about their fens; "for the losing of the fens would be the losing of their livelihood." Upon this Powell was summoned before Mr. Justice Goodrick, but denied the charge. Next day Mr. Goodrick, going into the market-place, found a crowd there with cudgels in their hands, and Powell with them. Powell, interrogated, asked whether the king's market was not open to all, and rejoined his company. As the result of these disturbances, Powell was arraigned and sentenced to a fine of £200, and to be imprisoned, and "now lies in execution for the same. Since his removal from the prison at Ely to Newgate, the poor people are very quiet and in good order." Powell from his captivity addresses his "loving friends and neighbours in the city of Ely, and others," in letters which were seized. In these he expresses a hope of deliverance when the king comes to London, and that he has refused to give up his friends' names, whereby they might be fined and imprisoned, although daily urged to do so by fair offers and large promises, and also by threatening language, terrible speech, and protestation of perpetual imprisonment. He then asks these friends to make a collection for him and his family, and gives a dark picture of his prison—"this loathsome gaol, in which we are accompanied with noisome stinks, cold, lousy to dying, and almost all other miseries."

There is nothing especially remarkable in the purely criminal cases of this period; offences have a strong family likeness to those of our own day. Culprits are "cast" for "taking a chest of plate out of a house;" for "taking £100 from a gentleman," and so forth. Now and again appears a case of abduction, a common crime in those and later days. Sarah Cox prays the king's pardon for Roger Fulwood, who was convicted of felony for forcibly marrying her against her will. But she begs at the same time her protection for person and estate from any claims in regard to the pretended marriage. Knights of the road have already begun to operate; they have already the brevet rank of captain, and even lads of tender years are beguiled into adopting the profession of highway robber. Counterfeiting the king's or other great seals was an offence not unknown. A Captain Farrar is lodged in Newgate (1639), accused of counterfeiting His Majesty's signature and privy signet. His method of procedure was simple. Having received a document bearing His Majesty's privy seal for the payment of a sum of £190, he removed the seal and affixed it to a paper purporting to be a license from the king to levy and transport two hundred men beyond seas. This he published as a royal license. When arraigned he admitted that the charge was true, but pleaded that he had done the same according to the king's commands. He was reprieved until further orders.

The condition of the prisoners within Newgate continued very deplorable. This is apparent from the occasional references to their treatment. They were heavily ironed, lodged in loathsome dungeons, and all but starved to death. Poor Stephen Smith, the fishmonger,[57] who had contravened the precautionary rules against the plague, petitions the council that he has been very heavily laden with such intolerable bolts and shackles that he is lamed, and being a weak and aged man, is like to perish in the gaol. "Having always lived in good reputation and been a liberal benefactor where he has long dwelt, he prays enlargement on security." The prison is so constantly overcrowded that the prisoners have "an infectious malignant fever which sends many to their long home. The magistrates who think them unfit to breathe their native air when living bury them as brethren when dead." All kinds of robbery and oppression were practised within the precincts of the gaol. Inside, apart from personal discomfort, the inmates do much as they please. "There are seditious preachings by fifth monarchy men at Newgate," say the records, "and prayers for all righteous blood." Some time previous, when the Puritans were nominally the weakest, they also held their services in the prison. Samuel Eaton, a prisoner committed to Newgate as a dangerous schismatic, is charged with having conventicles in the gaol, some to the number of seventy persons. He was, moreover, permitted by the keeper to preach openly. The keeper was petitioned by one of the inmates to remove Eaton and send him to some other part of the prison, but he replied disdainfully, threatening to remove the petitioner to a worse place. He, the keeper himself, attended the conventicles, "calling it a very fair and goodly company, and staying there some season." Besides this, he gave license to Eaton to go abroad, to preach, contrary to the charge of the High Commission (1638). Another complaint made by the petitioner is that the keeper caused petitioner's sister to be removed out of the prison contrary to the opinion of a doctor, and that she died the very next day. Her chamber after her removal was assigned to Eaton, it being the most convenient place in the prison for holding his conventicles.

This keeper may be condemned as a fanatical partizan at

worst. But he had predecessors who were active oppressors, eager to squeeze the uttermost farthing out of their involuntary lodgers. The bar kept within the prison must have been a cause of continued extortion, although those who pandered to the cupidity of the bar-keepers occasionally got into trouble. Sir Francis Mitchell, we read, was sent on foot and bareheaded to the Tower on account of his patent for ale-houses. "He is a justice of Middlesex, and had a salary of £40 a year from Newgate prison on condition of sending all his prisoners there," ... no doubt to drink the liquor supplied to the prison bar.

But still worse was the conduct of the under-strappers. An instruction to the Lord Mayor and sheriffs in the State Papers (Dec. 1649) directs them to examine the miscarriages of the under officers of Newgate who were favourers of the felons and robbers there committed, and to remove such as appear faulty. The nefarious practices of the Newgate officers were nothing new. They are set forth with much quaintness of diction and many curious details in a pamphlet of the period, entitled the 'Black Dogge of Newgate.' There was a tavern entitled the 'Dogge Tavern in Newgate,' as appears by the State Papers, where the place is indicted by an informer for improper practices. The author of the pamphlet pretends that the dog has got out of prison and leapt into a sign-board. "'What the devil's here?' quoth a mad fellow going by, seeing the black cur ringed about the nose with a golden hoop, having two saucer-like eyes, and an iron chain about his neck. The public-house must be a well-customed house where such a porter keeps the door and calls in company." The writer enters it and describes the scene. He finds "English, Scottish, Welsh, Irish, Dutch, and French in several rooms; some drinking the neat wine of Orleans, some the Gascony, some the Bordeaux. There wanted neither sherry sack nor charnico, paligo nor Peter Seeme, amber-coloured canary or liquorish Ipocras, brown beloved Bastard, fat Alicant, or any quick-spirited liquor that might draw their will into a circle...." Not desiring to mix with such company, the writer sat himself and called for his "whole pint" alone. Presently he was joined by a "poor thin-gut fellow with a face as red as the gilded knobs of an alderman's horse-bridle, who as it seemed had newly come out of limbo." The two treated each other, and then exchanged opinions as to the sign of the tavern, wondering how it came first to be called the Black Dog of Newgate; and the writer maintained that he had read in an old chronicle "that it was a walking spirit in the likeness of a black dog, gliding up and down the streets a little before the time of execution, and in the night while the sessions continued." From this archæological exercise they pass on to discuss the prison and its officers. This part of the pamphlet sheds a strong light upon the evil-doings of the turnkeys, who appear to have been guilty of the grossest extortion, taking advantage of their position as officers of the law to levy black-mail alike on criminals and their victims. Of these swindling turnkeys or bailiffs, whom the writer designates "coney-catchers," he tells many discreditable tales, one or two of which may be worth transcribing.

The term coney-catching had long been in use to define a species of fraud akin to our modern "confidence trick," or, as the French call it, the *vol à l'Americain*. Shakespeare, in the 'Merry Wives of Windsor,' makes Falstaff call Bardolph, Nym, and Pistol "coney-catching rascals." The fraud was then of but recent introduction. It is detailed at length by Robert Greene in his 'Notable Discovery of Cozenage,' published in 1591. He characterizes it as a new art. Three parties were needed to practise it, called respectively the setter, the verser, and the barnacle; their game, or victim, was the coney. The first was the decoy, the second was a confederate who plied the coney with drink, the third came in by accident should the efforts of the others to beguile the coney into "a deceit at cards have failed." In the end the countryman was completely despoiled. Later on there was a new nomenclature: the setter became the beater, the tavern to which the rogues adjourned was the "bush," and the quarry was the bird. The verser was the retriever, the barnacle was the pot-hunter, and the game was called bat-fowling. Greene's exposure was supposed to have deprived the coney-catchers of a "collop of their living." But they still prospered at their nefarious practices, according to the author of the 'Black Dogge,' to whom I will now return.

This was their plan of procedure. Two coney-catchers enter a tavern together, and there find a gentleman drinking wine. They note his appearance, his weapons, his good cloak and his neat apparel, and are clear that he has a good store of money; so they make up to him. The three become friendly, and the gentleman stands treat. After two or three pottles of wine are disposed of one of the rogues says to their entertainer, "I pray you heark in your ear. Thus it is; my fellow hath a warrant to take you, therefore in kindness I pray you draw your purse and give him an angel to spend in drink, and I will undertake we will not see you at this time." The stranger, however, would not be imposed upon, and said they were coney-catching knaves, and that they should not wrong him in any respect. "Whereupon the two sent for a constable, and charged the other with felony. The constable, recognizing the two as officials, took the stranger into custody and deprived him of his weapons. Then the two told the constable they would be answerable for his prisoner, and took charge of him. Now mark what followed. As these two knaves were bringing the party charged with felony to Newgate, one of them offered yet xx shillings to set him free, of which, when the party had considered, knowing though he was clear of that he was charged, yet if he lay in prison till the Sessions it would be greater charges. When he was on Newgate stairs ready to go into the gaol, he was content to leave his cloak, what money he had in his purse, and his weapons, which were in the constable's hand, in pawn for the xx shillings, which the coney-catchers took, and discharged the prisoner without any more to do."

A little later the same victim is again encountered, with a companion, in a tavern without Bishopgate, where he "had spoke for supper." In came the swindling turnkeys, whereat the other set on the best face he could, and bade them welcome. The coney-catchers accepted the invitation, and ate and drank merrily. Supper being ended, the reckoning was called for, the shot paid, and, all things discharged, the coneys would fain have been gone. "But one of the knaves said nay: ... thus it is, such a man was robbed within this week, and hath got out a warrant for you by name. He hath lost £10; now, if you will restore the money, and bestow xx shillings on us two to drink for our pains, we will undertake to satisfy the party and be your discharge. If not, we have a warrant, and you must answer it at Newgate. This back reckoning is something sharp, but there is no remedy; either pay so much money, or else must a constable be sent for, and so to Newgate as round as a hoop."

"To be short, this was the conclusion: the coney put down £10, every penny whereof was to be paid to the man in the moon, for I dare take it upon my death neither of these coneys did offend any such man in manner these knaves had charged them."

A favourite hunting-ground for these swindlers was at Westminster Hall during term time. Their method was to send confederates in among the thickest of the crowd, where the cut-purses were likely to be busiest, and there "listen if any purse were cut that day." The coney-catchers themselves were posted, one by the water stairs, the other at the gate, where they could not fail to intercept the cut-purse who had committed the theft. Presently they recognize him, accost and stop him. The cut-purse, anxious to curry favour, offers to stand both wine and a breakfast, but the coney-catcher will not tarry. He declares with an oath that he is really sorry to have met the cut-purse that day, "for there is a mischief done, and he fears some one will smoke for it." At this time the cut-purse is afraid, but for that time he scapeth their fingers. After this the swindler makes it his business to seek out the victim of the robbery, and on discovering him, promises that if he will only be guided by him he will help him to most of his money again. The honest fellow, a countryman, delighted, offers "at first word" one half to get other half back, the whole amount being ten pounds. "Then away goeth the coney-catcher to a justice," from whom he obtains a warrant to take up all suspected persons. The warrant obtained, the coney-catcher is as "pleasant as a pie," and with his countryman spend some time drinking a pottle of wine, after which the turnkey takes leave of his client, who goes to his lodging, and "the coney-catcher about his faculty." Now, woe to the cut-purses we may meet, for they must to Newgate on his warrant; but although he apprehends twelve or sixteen, the real culprit is certainly not among them. "The honest company of cut-purses being all in Newgate, H. (the coney-catcher) goes presently and certifies the justice what a set of notable thieves he has taken, and desiring the justice to examine them about the theft, warning him that they will confess nothing, which indeed the justice findeth true." They are remanded to Newgate, and *en route* beg H. to stand their friend, "assuring him of their innocency; yet rather than be in prison one offereth ten shillings, some more, some less, as they are of ability, with promise of more if H.'s good words gain them their release."

"Now the coney-catcher hath the matter as he would wish it, and taking their money, first he goeth presently to the justice and certifieth him that these which he had apprehended did none of them cut the purse, and for that he hath gotten knowledge who did, he desireth that they may be bailed." The justice, glad to hear the culprit is known, yields ready assent, and the captive cut-purses are set free.

H.'s next business is to hunt up the real thief, and meeting him, "spareth not to tell him how sore the justice is against him, and how earnestly the countryman will pursue the law; and further, he sweareth that some of those that were in Newgate told the justice plainly that he cut the purse. This peal ringeth nothing well in the cut-purse's ears, who can find no favour but to Newgate." So he entreats the coney-catcher to stand his friend, who promises at length to do any good he can, at the same time cautioning the cut-purse to confess nothing, "what proof soever come against him," assuring him further, that the man who lost the money, although sore bent against, "yet he will partly be ruled by him, H." But the arrest is made; the thief is conveyed to Newgate, and there, by way of welcome, a good pair of bolts and shackles are clapped upon his legs. Then H. sends for the countryman, telling him the good news that the thief is taken and in limbo; and together they go before the justice, to whom H. "signifieth how the case standeth, railing mightily against the cut-purse," whose guilt can easily be proved, and begging his worship to summon the thief. The cut-purse is sent for, and "having taken out his lesson," doggedly refuses to confess, upon which the justice returneth him to Newgate, there to abide till the next sessions. The countryman is bound over to give evidence, but he, "dwelling far from London, and it being long to next Law Day, allegeth he cannot be in the city at that time, for he is a poor man, and hath great occasion of business."

On leaving the justice H. returns to Newgate, and assures the cut-purse that he has laboured hard "with him who had his purse cut to take his money again, and not to give evidence against him; that if he may have his money again he will presently go out of town." The cut-purse, taking H.'s hand (as witness) that no man shall give evidence against him at the sessions, doth presently send abroad to his friends for the money; which as soon as it cometh he delivereth to H., and withal a large overplus, because he will be thus sure of H.'s favour.

"This done, H. goes to the countryman and tells him he got no more but six or seven pounds, of which, if he will accept, and proceed no further against the party, he hath it to pay him; marry he will not be known to the countryman, but that he had that money of some friend of the cut-purse's, who upon the former condition is willing it should be paid, if not, to have his money again.

"The countryman, having haste out of the city, is glad to take it, out of which sum, if it be seven pounds, H. must have half; so that the poor man, of ten pounds hath but three pounds ten shillings, whereas the coney-catcher by this account hath got at one hand and another very near forty marks. The money shared, the countryman takes horse and away he rides. Again H.'s mouth is stopt, and the next sessions the cut-purse is quit by proclamation, no man being there to give evidence against him."

Plain symptoms of the approaching struggle between the king and the commons are to be met with in the prison records. Immediately after the meeting of the Long Parliament, orders were issued for the enlargement of many victims of Star Chamber oppression. Among them was the celebrated Prynne, author of the 'Histriomatrix,'[58] who had lost his ears in the pillory; Burton a clergyman, and Bastwick a physician, who had suffered the same penalties, all came out of prison triumphant, wearing ivy and rosemary in their hats. Now Strafford was impeached and presently beheaded; Laud also was condemned. The active interference of Parliament in all affairs of State extended to the arrest of persons suspected of treasonable practices. A curious document issues from Newgate in 1642, where several supposed rebels and others have been imprisoned. It is a petition[59] which was presented to Parliament by Colonel Goret, who had commanded some of them in France. The petition sets forth that Daniel Dalley, master of a small barque, of "Kinsaile in Ireland," had been freighted, about the 10th November, 1641, out by two gentlemen, merchants of Kingsale, with beef, tallow, and hides for "St. Mallowes in France." There these commodities had been "vended," and the same merchants laid out their money in wine and fruits to freight the vessel home again. "All being done, and they ready to set sail, the governor (of St. Mallowes) sent a command to Daniel Dalley the master, that he should take nine gentlemen with him, which should pay for their passage." "By reason of the troubles,"[60] the master refused; but Dalley was obliged to take them on board, under threat of committal to gaol, and by the governor's warrant and command. He then set sail, and two days after he had gone to sea a storm rose at south and S. S. W., which drove them into Saltcombe in the west country, "where the passengers went ashore and took lodging till it would please God to send fair weather." However, notice of their landing came to Captain Foskew, "one that had command of a fort of his majesty's there," who summoned them before him and examined them. Finding they could not give a good account of their designs, he committed them, with the merchants and the ship's company, until he communicated with Parliament. In reply the Parliament sent for them to London, and lodged them in Newgate. There they lay from day to day expecting to be called up by Parliament, but this being so long delayed, they petitioned for enlargement.

On the Parliament side it appeared that information had been given the House of Commons that certain mariners and commanders were proceeding from France to Ireland to take part in the rebellion, they having a commission about them for the purpose. Also that one Captain Foskew had taken and stayed the said mariners and sea captains. "The honourable assembly," therefore, as well out of their pious and grave consideration for the better satisfaction of the kingdom, as for the prevention of such dangers as might follow from their landing in Ireland, made an order to bring the prisoners to London for examination. This was done with all proper precaution. Each sheriff saw to their safe conduct in his own county, "not suffering them to go together, but the commanders to be kept away from the rest." By virtue of the Speaker's (Lenthall) warrant, they were delivered by the sheriff of Devon to the next sheriff, and so from county to county, until they came to Middlesex, where they were received by the sheriffs of Middlesex, and committed to Newgate, the county gaol, "where they were with much care imprisoned and strictly kept, some of them being placed in the master's, others in the common side."

The petition already mentioned set forth that the said captains, "being all strangers and destitute of acquaintance, except with a few persons of this town. They declared that they were his majesty's true and loyal subjects, most of them born within the king's realm of Ireland, all strictly obliged and most ready to defend his rights and privileges to the utmost of their power. Being 'necessitated in their native country,' they repaired three years previously to France, where they served in martial affairs under Colonel Goret, till they were disbanded, and resolved to return home. They were, however, detained at Saltcombe, in the county of Devon, where they were imprisoned and their goods seized. Since then they had lain in Newgate, 'where they are liable to remain in great misery, to their loss of time, and utter destruction and ruin.' They begged, therefore, that they might be 'forthwith convented before the honourable assembly to answer their charge,' and having proved their loyalty, might be restored to their former liberty and fortunes." The answer to this petition is not recorded, except that the prisoners hoped daily to be sent for, a committee of the House having been appointed to examine them. Meantime they carried themselves civilly in the gaol, and with patience looked for the time when they should be called for their answer. They were conscious of innocence; they denied "all intentions of assisting the rebels in Ireland, or any act which might tend to their disloyalty," the true cause of their return home being a want of employment in France.

There are other cases of imprisonment more or less arbitrary in these troubled times. Another petition may be quoted, that of Richard Overton, "a prisoner in the most contemptible gaol of Newgate," under an order of the House of Lords. Overton tells us how he was brought before that House "in a warlike manner, under pretence of a criminal fact, and called upon to answer interrogations concerning himself which he conceived to be illegal and contrary to the national rights, freedoms, and properties of the free commoners of England, confirmed to them by Magna Charta, the Petition of Right, and the Act for the Abolishment of the Star Chamber." Overton was therefore emboldened to refuse subjection to the said House. He was adjudged guilty of contempt, and committed to Newgate, where he was seemingly doomed to lie until their lordships' pleasure shall be further signified, which "may be perpetual if they please, and may have their wills, for your petitioner humbly conceiveth that he is made a prisoner to their wills, not to the law, except their wills may be a law." On this account he appealed to the Commons "as the most sovereign Court of Judicature in the land," claiming from them "repossession of his just liberty and freedom, or else that he may undergo the penalty prescribed by the law if he be found a transgressor." Whether Overton was supported by the Commons against the Lords does not appear, but within three years the Lower House abolished the House of Peers.

Here is yet another petition from a better known inmate of Newgate, the obstinately independent Colonel Lilburne, commonly called "Freeborn John." Lilburne was always at loggerheads with the government of the city. In 1637, when following the trade of bookseller, he was convicted by the Star Chamber for publishing seditious libels, and sentenced to the pillory, imprisonment, and a fine of £5000. In 1645 he falls foul of the Parliament, and writes a new treatise, calling in question their power. For this, although he had already done good service to the Parliamentary cause and had earned the grade of Lieutenant-Colonel in the field, he is first questioned, then sent to Newgate. He dates from thence, in 1646, a letter to Mr. Wollaston, the keeper of Newgate, or his deputy. He states that he has seen a warrant commanding the keeper to produce him before the House of Lords, but that the warrant expresses no reason why he should "dance attendance before them," nor does he know any reason why he should, or any law that compels him thereto. The Lords had already endeavoured illegally to try him, a commoner, before their bar, for which, under hand and seal, he protested to their faces against them as violent and illegal encroachers upon his rights and liberties, and appealed to the proper tribunal, the Commons, for which appeal he was arbitrarily committed to gaol. Lilburne goes on to say,—

"Sir, I am a freeman of England, and therefore I am not to be used as a slave or vassal by the Lords, which they have already done, and would further do; I also am a man of peace and quietness, and desire not to molest any, if I be not forced thereunto, therefore I desire you, as you tender my good and your own, take this for an answer, that I cannot, without turning traitor to my liberty, dance attendance to their lordships' bar, being bound in conscience, duty to God, myself, thine, and my country, to oppose their encroachments to the death, which, by the strength of God, I am resolved to do. Sir, you may, or cause to be exercised upon me some force or violence to pull and drag

me out of my chamber, which I am resolved to maintain as long as I can, before I will be compelled to go before them; and therefore I desire you, in a friendly way, to be wise and considerate before you do that which, it may be, you can never undo.

"*Sir, I am your true and fair-conditioned prisoner, if you will be so to me,*

"*John Lilburne.*

"*From my cock-loft in the press-yard of Newgate, 23rd June, 1646.*"

Lilburne was eventually banished by the Rump Parliament; but in 1653 he returned to England, and threw himself upon the tender mercies of the Protector. Cromwell would do nothing, and left him to the law. Lilburne was then arrested, and committed to Newgate. At the next sessions he was arraigned, but refused to plead unless furnished with a copy of his indictment. He managed to put off his trial by various expedients till the next sessions, when he was acquitted by the jury. In Thurloe's State papers it is stated that "John Lilburne was five times at his trial at the Sessions House, where he most courageously defended himself from Mr. Stale, the recorder's, violent assaults with his old buckler, Magna Charta, so that they have let him alone." "Freeborn John" was so popular with malcontents of all shades of opinion, that the authorities, from Oliver Cromwell downward, were really afraid of him. Oliver professed to be enraged against him, and anxious for his punishment, yet he privately paid him a pension equal to the pay of a Lieutenant-Colonel, and, as Thurloe says, "thought the fellow so considerable, that during the time of his trial he kept three regiments continually under arms at St. James'." The jury which acquitted Lilburne were summoned to answer for their conduct before the

Council of State. Yet there is little doubt that the court was overawed by the mob. For Thurloe says there were six or seven hundred men at the trial, with swords, pistols, bills, daggers, and other instruments, that, in case they had not cleared him, they would have employed in his defence. The joy and acclamation was so great after he was acquitted, that the shout was heard an English mile.

The mob had been turbulent enough to give cause for alarm on a previous occasion. Four or five years previously the puritanical zeal of the Lords had produced a stringent ordinance against tippling and gaming on the Lord's Day. This occasioned a great tumult, which originated in Moorfields, and agitated the metropolis for a couple of days. It is said that, but for the vigorous action of Fairfax, the Government would have been overthrown. The people mastered a part of the trainbands, seized their drums and colours, beat up for recruits, then forming into something like military order, they surprised Newgate and Ludgate in the night, and seized the keys. The rioters divided into two parties: one marched upon Whitehall, but were discomfited *en route*; the other ranged the city, possessing themselves of ordnance, arms, and ammunition. Prompt measures were, however, taken at a council of war, and Fairfax, entering the city at the head of two regiments, put several to the sword, took many prisoners, and dispersed the rest.

The transfer of power to the Commonwealth is significantly recorded in the annals of Newgate. A whole batch of warrants are to be found in the State papers about 1649, ordering the committal of persons charged with being in arms against the Parliament—the offenders are mostly military officers. Thus the keeper of Newgate, Richard Dicke by name, is commanded to receive Lieutenant-Colonel Clarke, Major Wright, and Captain Wescott; also Lieutenant Gage, Robert Wood, pilot, and Robert

Parker, taken in a man of war, all charged with levying war. Again, the Commonwealth directs W. Roberts to be sent to Newgate for being an agent of the proclaimed King of Scotland. Later on, Colonel Clarke, already mentioned, was released on his signing the test, and finding securities for good behaviour. Captain Matthew Harrison is committed for bearing arms against the Parliament, and "drinking a health to Charles, the late king's son, by name King Charles II." The recorder is directed to examine Colonel Jones concerning Captain Harrison, and to see that he be proceeded against according to law. A declaration is made before the Council of State as to Charles Pullen, "lately a prisoner in Newgate," committed there for being found in the Hart frigate. Pullen had escaped from prison, and was liable to the penalty of death if recaptured; but the council remit the penalty in order to exchange Pullen for Ensign Wright, a prisoner at Jersey. In Nov. 1650 John Jolfe is committed to Newgate for carrying the Roebuck out of the Commonwealth. Royalist sympathizers find but scant comfort. The keeper of Newgate is ordered to receive and imprison one Pate, and hold him in safe custody, for aiding Lieutenant-General Middleton to escape from the Tower; and a similar warrant is made out against Mitchell for being accessory to the escape of Colonel Edward Massey from the same place.

All this time prisoners of great mark were at times confined in Newgate. That noted royalist, Judge Jenkins, was among the number. His crime was publishing seditious books, and sentencing to death people who had assisted against the Parliament. He was indeed attainted of high treason under an ordinance which started in the House of Commons, and was ultimately passed, and sent to the House of Lords. A committee was sent from "the Commons' House to Newgate, which was to interview Judge Jenkins, and make the following offer to him— viz. that if he would own the power of the Parliament to be lawful, they would not only take off the sequestrations from his estates, amounting to £500 per annum, but they would also settle a pension on him of £1000 a year." His reply was to the following effect: "Far be it from me to own rebellion, although it was lawful and successful." As the judge refused to come to terms with them, he remained in Newgate till the Restoration.

People of still higher rank found themselves in gaol. The brother of the Portugal ambassador, Don Pantaleon Sa, is sent, with others, to Newgate for a murder committed by them near the Exchange. It was a bad case. They had quarrelled with an English officer, Gerard, who, hearing the Portuguese discoursing in French upon English affairs, told them they did not represent certain passages aright. "One of the foreigners gave him the lie, and all three fell upon him, and stabbed him with a dagger; but Colonel Gerard being rescued out of their hands by one Mr. Anthuser, they retired home, and within one hour returned with twenty more, armed with breastplate and head-pieces; but after two or three turns, not finding Mr. Anthuser, they returned home that night."[61] Don Pantaleon made his escape from prison a few days later, but he was retaken. Strenuous efforts were then made to obtain his release. His trial was postponed on the petition of "the Portugal merchants." The Portugal ambassador himself had an audience of Cromwell, the Lord Protector. But the law took its course. Don Pantaleon pleaded his relationship, and that he had a commission to act as ambassador in his brother's absence; this was disallowed, and after much argument the prisoners pleaded guilty, and desired "to be tried by God and the country." A jury was called, half-denizens, half-aliens, six of each, who, after a full hearing, found the ambassador's brother and four more guilty of murder and felony. Lord Chief Justice Rolles then sentenced them to be hanged, and fixed the day of execution; "but by the desire of the prisoners it was respited two days." This was the 6th July, 1654. On the 8th, Don Pantaleon Sa was reprieved, or more exactly, his sentence was commuted to beheading. On the 10th he tried to escape, without success, and on the same day he was conveyed from Newgate to Tower Hill in a coach and six horses in mourning, with divers of his brother's retinue with him. There he laid his head on the block, and "it was chopt off at two blows." The rest although condemned were all reprieved, except one, an English boy concerned in the murder, who was hanged at Tyburn.[62]

Other distinguished inmates, a few years later, were Charles Lord Buckhurst, Edward Sackville, and Sir Henry Bellayse, K.B., who, being prisoners in Newgate, petitioned the Lord Chief Justice, March 10th, to be admitted to bail, one of them being ill of the small-pox. They were charged seemingly with murder. Their petition sets forth that "while returning from Waltham to London, on the 8th February, they aided some persons, who complained that they had been robbed and wounded in pursuit of the thieves, and in attacking the robbers wounded one who has since died." Sir Thomas Towris, Baronet, petitions the king (Charles II.) "not to suffer him to lie in that infamous place, where he has not an hour of health, nor the necessaries of life. He states that he has been four months in the Tower, and five weeks in Newgate, charged with counterfeiting His Majesty's hand, by the malice of an infamous person who, when Registrar Accountant at Worcester House, sold false debentures." Sir Thomas "wished to lay his case before His Majesty at his first coming from Oxford, but was deceived, and the way to bounty stopped."

NEWGATE IN THE SEVENTEENTH CENTURY (AFTER THE GREAT FIRE).

Newgate refronted in 1638—Destroyed in Great Fire of 1666—How rebuilt—Façade described—Account of interior by B. L. of Twickenham—Various parts or sides—The lodge and condemned hold—The master debtors' side—The master felons' side—The common debtors' side—The common felons' side—The press-yard and castle—The chapel—Miserable condition of inmates—Some few pleaded unhealthiness as an excuse for release—Suicides frequent—Mr. Norton—Newgate called by Recorder a nursery of rogues—Negligence of keepers—The gaoler Fells indicted for permitting escapes—Crimes of the period—Clipping and coining greatly increased—Enormous profits of the fraud—Coining within the gaol itself deemed high treason—Heavy penalties—Highway robbery very prevalent—Instances—Officers and paymasters with the king's gold robbed—Stage coaches stopped—All manner of men took to the road, including persons of good position—Their effrontery—Whitney—His capture, and attempts to escape—His execution—Efforts to check highway robbery—A few types of notorious highwaymen—"Mulled sack"—Claude Duval—Nevison—Abduction of heiresses—Mrs.

Synderfin—Miss Rawlins—Miss Wharton—Count Konigsmark—The German princess—Other criminal names—Titus Oates—Dangerfield—The Fifth Monarchy men—William Penn—The two Bishops, Ellis and Leyburn.

NEWGATE was refronted and refaced in 1638 in the manner already described.[63] No further change or improvement was made in the building until a total re-edification became inevitable, after the great fire in 1666. Of the exact effect of that conflagration upon the prison gate-house I can discover no authentic records. Knight, in his 'London,' gives a woodcut of the burning of Newgate, designed by Fussel, which many dismissed as imaginative rather than historically accurate. The gate as represented is altogether larger than it could possibly have been, and the aspect of the structure is very much what a nineteenth century artist would conceive a mediæval prison would be. According to a writer in the 'Gentleman's Magazine' for April, 1764, Newgate was only damaged, not destroyed, in the great fire. He goes on to speak of the "present beautiful structure," an edifice so inadequate for prison purposes, it may be remarked that it had already been condemned at this date, and schemes for its entire reconstruction propounded. This beautiful structure as represented in the woodcut is thus described by the above-mentioned writer:—

"The west side is adorned with three ranges of Tuscan pilasters with their entablatures, and in the inter columniations are four niches, in one of which is a figure representing Liberty; the word 'libertas' is inscribed on her cap, and at her feet lies a cat in allusion to Sir Richard Whittington, a benefactor to the prison, who is said to have made the first step to his advancement and good fortune by a cat. The inside of the gate is also adorned with a range of pilasters, with their entablatures, and in their niches are the figures of Justice, Mercy, and Truth.... Newgate," he continues, "considered as a prison is a structure of more cost and beauty than was necessary, because the sumptuousness of the outside but aggravates the misery of the wretches within; but as a gate to such a city as London, it might have received considerable additions both of design and execution, and abundantly answered the cost in the reputation of the building. The gate of a city, erected rather for ornament than use, ought to be in the style of the triumphal arches.... If Newgate be considered as a prison, it is indeed a very dismal one. It is the county gaol for Middlesex both for debtors and malefactors, as well as the city prison for criminals. The debtor, rendered unfortunate by the vicissitudes of trade or unforeseen losses, has the reproach of being confined in the same prison with the greatest villains, and too often his being in Newgate is imputed by the ignorant to crimes which he abhors. On the other hand, those confined as criminals are, even before they are found guilty by the laws of their country, packed so close together that the air being corrupted, ... occasions a dismal, contagious disease called the gaol distemper, which has frequently carried off great numbers, and even spread its contagion to the Court of Justice, where they take their trials. But to prevent these dreadful effects the city has introduced a ventilator on the top of Newgate to expel the foul air, and make room for the admission of such as is fresh; and during the sessions herbs are also spread in the Justice Hall and the passages to it to prevent infection. However, as these precautions, with some others, have often proved ineffectual, and as the prison in its present state is far from being commodious, it was lately resolved by the Common Council of the city of London to petition Parliament for leave to build a new prison in a more commodious place."

An accurate and detailed account of the interior of the 1667 prison has been preserved in a small work published in 1724, and written by "B. L. of Twickenham." This book purports to be "an accurate description of Newgate, with the rights, privileges, allowances, fees, dues, and customs thereof, together with a parallel between the master debtors' side and the several spunging houses in the county of Middlesex, 1724." The author's short historical preface contains no new facts. It is when he proceeds to describe the inside of the building, such as he evidently knew it from personal inspection, that his account becomes interesting. He gives no illustrations, but I have constructed plans of each floor from the descriptions in the letter-press, which may assist the reader in understanding the text.

Newgate, as is plain from the woodcut, spanned the roadway, which passed beneath by the arch, and seemingly, as in Temple Bar in our time, without gate or obstruction. This roadway outside the gate, or to the westward, was Holborn; within, or to the eastward, it was Newgate Street. The prison proper seems to have consisted of all the upper stories of the gatehouse; but so far as I can deduce from "B. L.," only the rooms or apartments to the south of the arch or gateway, upon the ground-floor. Behind the gate front the prison building extended some way back parallel with Newgate Street, an increase of accommodation dating from the time of the Commonwealth, when "our very churches were made prisons, so great was the demand for room." This extension was accomplished by taking in the buildings belonging to the Phœnix Inn in Newgate Street.

Before proceeding to a detailed description of the various chambers and cellars into which the interior was divided, it will be well to recount briefly the general divisions to be found within Newgate. These were—

PARTS OR SIDES.

I. The Master Debtors' Side.
II. The Master Felons' Side.

III. The Common Side for Debtors.
IV. The Common Side for Felons.
V. The Press-Yard and Castle.

   I. The Master Debtors' Side comprised—

THE HALL WARD
 The King's Bench ward
 The Stone ward

   II. The Master Felons' Side comprised—

THE DRINKING-CELLAR and Hall
 The Gigger, or Visiting-room
 First Ward
 Second and Third wards

   III. The Common Side for Debtors comprised—

THE STONE HALL
 High hall
 Tangier
 Debtors' hall
 Women's ward

   IV. The Common Side for Felons comprised—

THE STONE HOLD
  Lower ward
  Middle ward
  Waterman's hall (for women)
  Women's second ward

V. The Press-Yard and Castle comprised several rooms on ground and three upper floors, as well as an exercising ground.

BESIDES THE FOREGOING there was a chapel at the topmost story and a number of independent rooms, such as the Bilbows, Press-room, Condemned holds, and Jack Ketch's kitchen.

At the entrance, on the threshold of the prison, was the lodge, "where prisoners were first received, and where they were generally fettered if the cause of their imprisonment require it." Other writers less favourably disposed than B. L. affirm that almost all prisoners without exception were in those days ironed upon reception, whatever their condition. This, in effect, was one of the many acts of extortion practised without let or hindrance by the gaolers of the past. Debtors and unconvicted persons were clapped into manacles for a time, and until they were terrified into purchasing release; the most heinous offenders were also heavily weighted until they chose to purchase "easement," and choice of a lighter set of chains. There was no reception ward in Newgate such as we understand it, but hard by the lodge was a chamber which served as a first resting-place for most male prisoners, as well as the last for not a few. The condemned hold for males, says B. L., is situated "adjacent to the lodge." Another writer, the author of 'The History of the Press-Yard,' states more precisely that the men's condemned hold, "falsely supposed a noisome vault underground, lies between the top and bottom of the arch under Newgate." It was only imperfectly lighted, a "dark opace wild room," entered by a hatch, about twenty feet in length and fifteen in breadth. The floor was of stone, but on it was a wooden barrack bed raised, "whereon you may repose yourself if your nose suffers you to rest." Along and above this bed-place are "divers ring bolts, wherein such prisoners are locked as are disorderly. There is only one window, which is so very small that very little light comes thereby, so that the room is very dark. It is customary," adds B. L., "when any felons are brought to the lodge in Newgate, to put them first in this condemned hold, where they remain till they have paid two-and-sixpence, after which they are admitted to the masters' or common felons' side." This is a mild way of describing the custom already referred to.

I. From the lodge admission was gained at once to the Master Debtors' Side. The principal room, in dimensions twenty-five feet by fifteen, was the Hall Ward (I), which lay to the southern side of the prison, and owned one window, five feet by six, with two casements for air. In the midst of the west side of this ward was a fire-place and good chimney, in which burnt constantly a fire of sea-coal for the general benefit. It had also wooden benches and a good common table; and in the north-west corner was a bench and shelf of wood, on which scullery work was performed. Six and a half feet above the floor, on the north and east sides, was a gallery, supported by fir-posts, wherein were five partitions for beds, one at the end of the other. These beds were made of flock, and were "of their kind very good;" the charge was half-a-crown per week per bed, and for sheets two shillings per month, "paid at the time of receiving them." Doors on the debtors' side were locked at 9 P.M. and opened at 8 A.M. The last arrival had to keep all clean, or pay two pence daily to have it done. "Underneath the gallery in this Hall ward is a very good place for the prisoners therein to walk at their pleasure, which advantage the other wards are deficient of."

The King's Bench Ward (2) lay over the Hall Ward. Its dimensions were twenty-one feet by fifteen, and it was ten feet high. It had one window six feet by four, with a southern aspect probably like that of the Hall ward. The bed partitions were the same, but on the floor, which was of oak plank. The fees too were similar. The Stone Ward (3), alongside, is described as the very best, and pleasantly situated over the gateway towards Holborn, and therefore facing west. But the beds were all on the floor, which was of stone, with fire-place fees and so forth, as in the other rooms. At the head of the stairs, between the King's Bench Ward and the Stone Ward, was a small apartment called "my Lady's Hold," in which were only two beds, for the accommodation of any female debtors who came to the master's side. "This small apartment," says one author (B. L.), "is the very worst part of the master's side."

II. The lowermost apartment in the Master Felons' Side was a large cellar (4), some four feet below the level of the street, comprising a central drinking-room or hall, with three wards alongside, two of which were appropriated to men and one to women. Prices ruled as follows in this underground tavern: wine was sold at 2s. a bottle, strong drink at 4d. per quart, and brandy at 4d. per quartern. A "cellar-man," so called, was selected by the turnkeys from among the prisoners for the regulation and government of his fellows, who was allowed to make what profit he could on the sale of candles, as well as a penny upon every quart of beer or bottle of wine sold, "with other advantages." Immediately over the drinking vaults was "a spacious hall," named the "Gigger" (5), after the small grate or gigger in the door, at which prisoners in the various wards on this side were permitted to have interviews with their friends from outside. The privilege of entrance to this hall, or to the cellar below, was conceded only on payment of a fee of 1s. 6d. per diem. The same sum was charged to any felon's friend who was admitted to the gigger, and desired to see his friends in the tap-room; besides which they paid the cellar-man for a candle to light them down, and the price of a quart of beer, or 5d. Above the gigger again stairs led to the first ward (6), in which was "a good light, a good fire-place, and convenient lodging-rooms, as also very good flock beds, for the use of which each felon pays 3s. 6d. per week. Over this ward are the other two (7 and 8), which are both of the same magnitude and light, with the like appurtenances belonging thereto." B. L. further tells us that the prisoners were generally utilized for all prison services. Not only did they perform all menial offices, and distribute the allowance of food, such as it was, but they were also employed to rivet on and remove the irons of their fellows. Discipline even was entrusted to them; and B. L. speaks of certain prisoners who maintained order "with a flexible weapon, to the great terror and smart of those who dispute their authority. Every felon at his coming in pays 14s. 10d. for fees and garnish money only, 1s. 6d. for coals, and 1s. to be spent amongst the prisoners of the ward."

III. The Common Side for Debtors comprised four apartments, all situate towards Newgate Street, in other words, facing north. The ground-floor apartment was named the "Stone Hall" (9); its dimensions are not given, but it owned a cistern for water, and on the north side a chimney, "in which no fires are made except at Christmas, when there is a quantity of beef boiled there to be given to the felons." This Stone Hall led to some subordinate chambers; in the north-east angle was the iron hold for fetters, and in the south-east a chamber for the confinement of refractory prisoners, styled "the Partner's room," where four men could lie at a time. In the south-west of the room was a large place called the "tap-house," in which were sold beer, ale, brandy, wine, tobacco, and pipes, at the customary prices, "which of their kind are absolutely good." Of the tap-house itself B. L. speaks in less complimentary terms. "It is great pity," he says, "that greater decorum is not maintained among the prisoners of the common side, especially in the tap-house, for therein, by connivance, the felons are permitted to converse and drink with the debtors; by which means such wretchedness abounds therein, that the place has the exact aspect of hell itself, and by this means 'tis much to be questioned whether one debtor in ten who enters therein an honest man comes out the same, the wickedness of the place is so great."

At the west side of the Stone Hall was a staircase, leading to a large room called "High Hall" (10), wherein felons alone were admitted to walk. I have placed this High Hall in the plan on that part of the gate-house which lay to the north side of Holborn. There is no precise evidence that it was exactly so situated, but as all other rooms on this first floor can be pretty accurately placed, I think the conclusion is just that High Hall was approximately where I have put it. High Hall was large, being thirty-three feet by twenty-eight, and in altitude twelve. In the midst of the place was a stone anvil, whereon the irons were knocked off the unhappy persons sentenced to death, when they came down from the chapel (on the third floor), on their way to the cart which was to carry them to Tyburn.

Opposite the entrance to the tap-house was a passage leading to a second common-side debtors room. This came to be called "Tangier" (11) in due course, no doubt from the stifling atmosphere. "The air in this ward is very bad," says B. L., "occasioned by the multitude of the prisoners in it, and the filthiness of their lodging." The room was large, but "dark and stinking," and it only contained "divers barracks for the prisoners to lie on." Debtors' Hall (12), a third room for common-side debtors, was on the floor above. It also faced Newgate Street, and being higher up, enjoyed very good air and light. It had a very large window, which was, however, unglazed, and subjected the prisoners not only to the weather, but also to all kinds of rain, snow, sleet, &c., which the north-eastern winds produce. Unlike those in Tangier, the prisoners in Debtors' Hall had no barrack-beds to lie on, and were obliged therefore to sleep upon the boarded floor. Close by Debtors' Hall was a kind of kitchen, containing a large fire-place and grate, and known in B. L.'s time as the Hangman's, or Jack Ketch's kitchen, "because it is the place in which that honest fellow boils the quarters of such men as have been executed for treason."[64] Over this kitchen again, on the third floor, that is to say, was "an indifferent good ward," called the Women's Ward (13), and devoted to common debtors of that sex.

These poor debtors were but ill lodged and provided for. They had no firing save what they themselves found. They had to provide their own beds or sleep on the boards supplied by the sheriffs. But every debtor on the common side was allowed "each day one coarse household wheaten loaf, almost the bigness of a common penny white loaf; and there is also given a certain quantity of beef every week, in proportion to the number of debtors. Every debtor at his entrance paid 11s. 6d. garnish money, which was expended among the prisoners of the ward, and on discharge or removal a further fee of 7s. 10d. as on the master's side. 'The conversation of these debtors,' says B. L., 'was generally very profligate, being, as before mentioned, perpetually drinking and conversing with the felons.'"

IV. The Common Felons' Side, which was adjacent to that for the common debtors, was evidently a foul disgrace to the prison and to those charged with the administration of the law. B. L. describes it as "a most terrible, wicked, and dreadful place." In this side were five wards. The first, known as the Stone Hold (14), was an underground dungeon lying beneath the "middle ward," which I fix somewhere near the Tangier Ward of the debtors' common side. "The Stone Hold," says the authority already quoted, "was a terrible, stinking, dark, and dismal place, situate underground, into which no daylight can come. It was paved with stone; the prisoners had no beds, and lay on the pavement, whereby they endured great misery and hardship. The unhappy persons imprisoned therein are such as at their unfortunate entrance cannot pay the customary fees of the gaol." Alongside the Stone Hold was the "Lower Ward" (15), another large dungeon, in which were confined felons for non-payment of fines. The Middle Ward (16), on the floor above, was for those who had paid their bare fees, no more. Here also they had no beds, but the floor on which they lay was of oak, not stone. There were two wards for common female felons. The first, on this second floor, was called "Waterman's Hall" (17), a very dark and stinking place; the floor is of oaken planks, which is all the bed allotted to its miserable inhabitants. Water was, however, well supplied to this ward. Close by it were other rooms applied to ghastly uses. One was the "press-room," still used in the writer's time for the execution of the frightful sentence of pressing to death culprits arraigned who refused to plead; another the Bilbows,[65] adjacent to the press room, also very dark, "and used as a refractory cell for such as occasioned quarrel or disturbance." Near this again was the women's condemned hold, "a small, dark, dismal dungeon, wherein is a barrack for the prisoners to lie on, but no fire-place, and it is therefore cold at all times. A second ward (18) for common side females existed on the third, or floor above all, "the highest part of the whole gaol in the north part thereof, and is of large extent, in which is one window only, and that very small." Barracks were fixed on the walls on each side, but without any kind of bed whatsoever. "The persons imprisoned therein were generally those that lie for transportation, and they, knowing their time to be short here, rather than bestow one minute towards cleaning the same, suffer themselves to live far worse than swine, and, to speak the truth, the Augean Stable would bear no comparison to it, for they are almost poisoned by their own filth, and their conversation is nothing but one continued course of swearing, cursing, and debauchery, insomuch that it passes all description and belief.... It is with no small concern," he adds, "that I am obliged to observe that the women in every ward of this prison are exceedingly worse than the worst of the men, not only in respect to nastiness and indecency of living, but more especially as to their conversation, which, to their great shame, is as profane and wicked as hell itself can be."

These remarks, unhappily, are fully borne out by more modern experience. Female prisoners are, as a rule, far worse than the male.

V. The one division remaining, and commonly called the Press-Yard and Castle, was quite the best part of the prison. The entrance was at the base of the stairs between the common debtors' and the common felons' sides. It was composed of "divers large spacious rooms," on all three floors: those on the ground and first floor faced towards east and south; those on the second—the Castle so called—to the west. These rooms were all well supplied with light and air, free from all ill smells, and possessed all necessary appurtenances. A yard or place for walking in the open air was attached to this side, and was situate between the door or postern which entered from Newgate Street and the fabric itself. This yard, which was fifty-four feet long by seven feet wide, and was handsomely paved with Purbeck stone, could have been little better than a narrow passage running the whole north side of the prison between the building and its boundary wall. The Press-Yard was for State prisoners, or great and opulent criminals who could afford to pay such high premium at entrance as they and the gaoler might agree upon, and also the weekly rent of their wards. This premium was fixed according to the quality of the individual, and ranged from £20 to £500. The weekly rent of tenancy of the rooms was 11s. 6d. per head, 1s. of which was paid to a woman called the laundress, who made the fires and cleaned the rooms; the remainder went into the gaoler's pocket. The prisoners themselves provided their fires and candles, as also all other necessaries, "save the beds, which were very good of their kind, and which the gaoler found, sheets being always excepted." A less aristocratic section of this very select part of the prison was the Castle, which comprised two wards above the Stone ward and King's Bench ward of the master debtors' sides, and of the same dimensions, with the same air and light, as the wards immediately beneath. In the Castle wards were divers partitions for beds, for each of which a prisoner paid 2s. 6d. per week.

The remainder of this top floor, with the exception of the high hall, and the second ward for common female felons, was taken up by the prison chapel, which looked towards the south-east. The chapel was partitioned on the north side into large apartments called pens, which were all strongly built, as they contained every Sunday the common debtors and the felons of both kinds. The pulpit stood in the north-west angle of the chapel, against it were the pens of the male common debtors, next to them those of the male and female felons, but in separate divisions, and in the pens were gratings through which the occupants could be observed from the chapel pews. On the south side, opposite the felons' pens, were two very handsome enclosures for the master debtors; adjoining the pulpit was another large pew, wherein were placed such prisoners as were under sentence of death, and here in this same apartment "the blessed sacrament was administered to them at proper times, more particularly on the morning before execution." Besides these were a number of other handsome open pews, free to all persons who choose to come and sit in them. They were generally well filled on the Sundays when the condemned sermon was preached to prisoners about to die.[66]

A few corroborative facts may be quoted from other authorities as to the horrors of Newgate, the mismanagement, tyranny, and lax discipline which prevailed. Its insanitary condition was chronic, which at times, but only for influential inmates, was pleaded as an excuse for release. Lord Montgomery, a prisoner there in 1697, was brought, Luttrell tells, out of Newgate to the King's Bench Court, there to be bailed, upon two affidavits, which showed that there was an infectious fever in Newgate, of which several were sick and some dead. He was accordingly admitted to bail, himself in £10,000, and four sureties—the Duke of Norfolk, the Earl of Yarmouth, Lord Carington, and Lord Jeffereys—in £5000 each. An effort to secure release was made some years later in regard to Jacobite prisoners of note, less successfully, although the grounds alleged were the same and equally valid.

If a prisoner was hopelessly despondent, he could generally compass the means of committing suicide. A Mr. Norton, natural son of Sir George Norton, condemned for killing a dancing-master (because the latter would not suffer him to take his wife away from him in the street), poisoned himself the night before his reprieve expired. The drug was conveyed to him by his aunt without difficulty, "who participated in the same dose, but she is likely to recover." Nor were prisoners driven to this last desperate extremity to escape from durance. Pepys tells us in 1667, August 1, that the gates of the city were shut, "and at Newgate we find them in trouble, some thieves having this night broken open prison."

Within the gaol all manner of evil communication went forward unchecked among the prisoners. That same year Sir Richard Ford, the recorder, states that it has been made appear to the court of aldermen "that the keeper of Newgate hath at this day made his house the only nursery of rogues, prostitutes, pickpockets, and thieves in the world, where they were held and entertained and the whole society met, and that for the sake of the sheriffs[67] they durst not this day commit him for fear of making him let out the prisoners, but are fain to go by artifice to deal with him." The keeper at this time was one Walter Cowday, as appears from a State pardon "for seven prisoners ordered to be transported by their own consent," which he endorses. Sharper measure was dealt out to his successor, Mr. Fells, the keeper in 1696, who was summoned to appear before the Lords Justices for conniving at the escape of Birkenhead, alias Fish, alias South, East, West, &c., one of the conspirators in Sir John Fenwick's business, and who lay in prison "to be speedily tried." On examination of Fells, it was stated that Birkenhead's escape had been effected by a bribe, whereupon the sheriffs were instructed to find out the truth in order to displace Fells. Fells was furthermore charged with showing favour to Sir John Fenwick by suffering him to have pens, ink, and paper alone; a little later he was convicted on two indictments before Lord Chief Justice Holt at Guildhall, viz. for the escape of Birkenhead already mentioned, and of another prisoner imprisoned for non-payment of fine. Fell's sentence was postponed till the next term at the King's Bench Bar; but he moved the court in arrest of judgment, a motion which the King's Bench took time to consider, but which must have been ultimately decided in his favour, as two years later Fells still held the office of gaoler of Newgate.

The crimes of the latter half of the seventeenth century are of the same character as those of previous epochs. Many had, however, developed in degree, and were more widely practised. The offence of clipping and coining had greatly increased. The extent to which it was carried seems almost astounding. The culprits were often of high standing. A clipper, by name White, under sentence of death, was reprieved by the king upon the petition of the House of Commons in order that a committee of the House might examine him in Newgate as to his accomplices and their proceedings. Accordingly, White made "a large discovery" to the committee, both of clippers and coiners, and particularly of Esquire Strode, who had been a witness at the trial of the Earl of Bath (1697). Luttrell says (1696), among twenty persons convicted of coining was Atkinson, the beau "that made such a figure in town about eight years before, and spent an estate of £500 per annum in Yorkshire." In the lodgings of a parson, by name Salisbury, who was arrested for counterfeiting stamped paper, several instruments for clipping and coining were found. University men were beguiled into the crime of clipping; so were seemingly respectable London tradesmen. Goldsmiths and refiners were repeatedly taken up for these malpractices. "A goldsmith in Leicester Fields and his servants committed to Newgate for receiving large quantities of broad money from Exeter to clip it."[68] "A refiner's wife and two servants committed to Newgate for clipping; the husband escaped." Bird, a laceman, in custody for coining, escaped; but surrendered and impeached others. Certain gilders committed to Newgate petitioned therefrom, that if released they would merit the same by a discovery of a hundred persons concerned in the trade. Such are the entries which appear time after time in contemporary chronicles.

The numbers engaged in these nefarious practices were very great. In 1692 information was given of three hundred coiners and clippers dispersed in various parts of the city, for several of whom warrants were issued, some by the Treasury, others by the Lord Chief Justice. The profits were enormous. Of three clippers executed at Tyburn in 1696, one, John Moore, the tripeman, was said to have got a good estate by clipping, and to have offered £6000 for his pardon. Three other clippers arrested in St. James'

St., and committed to Newgate, were found to be in possession of £400 in clippings, with a pair of shears and other implements. The information of one Gregory, a butcher, who "discovered" near a hundred persons concerned in the trade, went to prove that they made as much as £6000 a month in counterfeit money. "All their utensils and moulds were shown in court, the latter being in very fine clay, which performed with great dexterity." The extent of the practice is shown by the ingenuity of the machinery used. "All sort of material for coining was found in a house in Kentish town, with stamps for all coins from James I." The work was performed "with that exactness no banker could detect the counterfeit." So bold were the coiners, that the manufacture went forward even within the walls of Newgate. Three prisoners were taken in the very act of coining in that prison. One of the medals or tokens struck in Newgate as a monetary medium among the prisoners is still to be seen in the Beaufoy Collection at Guildhall. Upon the obverse of the coin the legend is inscribed: "Belonging to the cellar on the master's side, 1669;" on the reverse side is a view of Newgate and the debtors' prison.

The heaviest penalties did not check this crime. The offence was high treason; men sentenced for it were handed, drawn, and quartered, and women were burnt. In 1683 Elizabeth Hare was burnt alive for coining in Bunhill Fields. Special legislation could not cope with this crime, and to hinder it the Lords of the Treasury petitioned the Queen (Mary in the absence of William III.) to grant no pardon to any sentenced for clipping unless before their conviction they discovered their accomplices.

Highway robbery had greatly increased. The roads were infested with banditti. Innkeepers harboured and assisted the highwaymen, sympathizing with them, and frequently sharing in the plunder. None of the great roads were safe: the mails, high officials, foreigners of distinction, noblemen, merchants, all alike were stopped and laid under contribution. The following are a few of the cases which were of constant occurrence. "His Majesty's mails from Holland robbed near Ilford in Essex, and £5000 taken, belonging to some Jews in London." The Worcester waggon, wherein was £4000 of the king's money, was set upon and robbed at Gerard's Gross, near Uxbridge, by sixteen highwaymen. The convoy, being near their inn, went on ahead, thinking all secure, and leaving only two persons on foot to guard it, who, having laid their blunderbusses in the waggon, were on a sudden surprised by the sixteen highwaymen, who took away £2,500. and left the rest for want of conveniences to carry it." Two French officers (on their way to the coast) were robbed by nine highwaymen of one hundred and ten guineas, and bidden to go home to their own country. Another batch of French officers was similarly dealt with on the Portsmouth road. Fifteen butchers going to market were robbed by highwaymen, who carried them over a hedge and made them drink King James' health. The Portsmouth mail was robbed, but only of private letters; and the same men robbed a captain going to Portsmouth with £5000 to pay his regiment with. Three highwaymen robbed the Receiver-General of Bucks of a thousand guineas, which he was sending up by the carrier in a pack; the thieves acted on excellent information, for although there were seventeen packhorses, they went directly to that which was laden with the gold. Seven on the St. Alban's Road near Pinner robbed the Manchester carrier of £15,000 king's money, and killed and wounded eighteen horses to prevent pursuit. The purser of a ship landed at Plymouth and rode to London on horseback, with £6000 worth of rough diamonds belonging to some London merchants which had been saved out of a shipwreck. Crossing Hounslow Heath, the purser was robbed by highwaymen. "Oath was thereupon made before a justice of the peace," says Luttrell, in "order to sue the Hundred for the same." The Bath coach was stopped in Maidenhead thicket, and a footman who had fired at them was shot through the head. The Dover stage coach, with foreign passengers, was robbed near Shooter's Hill, but making resistance, one was killed. The western mail was robbed by the two Arthurs, who were captured and committed to Newgate. They soon escaped therefrom, but were again arrested at a tavern by Doctors' Commons, being betrayed by a companion. They confessed that they had gone publicly about the streets disguised in Grecian habits, and that one Ellis, a tobacconist, assisted them in their escape, for which he was himself committed to Newgate. John Arthur was soon afterwards condemned and executed. Henry Arthur was acquitted, but soon after quarrelling about a tavern bill in Covent Garden, he was killed in the *mêlée*.

All manner of men took To the road. Some of the Royal guards were apprehended for robbing on the highway. Lifeguardsmen followed the same gentlemanly occupation when on duty. "Thompson, a lifeguardsman, committed on suspicion of robbing Welsh drovers, is refused bail, there being fresh evidence against him."[69] Captain Beau, or Bew, formerly of the Guards, was seized at Knightsbridge as a highwayman, and afterwards poisoned himself. Seven of his gang were committed to Newgate. Harris, 'the lifeguardsman' tried at the Old Bailey for robbing on the black mare and acquitted, was again tried a month later, and condemned. He was then reprieved, and Sir William Penn obtained the Queen's pardon for him, and a commission as lieutenant in the Pennsylvania Militia, to which colony he was to transport himself. Persons of good social status engaged in the perilous trade. One Smith, a parson and a lecturer at Chelsea, when brought up at Westminster for perjury, was found to be a confederate with two highwaymen, with whom he had shared a gold watch, and planned to rob Chelsea Church of its plate. Smith when arraigned appeared in Court in his gown, but he was "sent to Newgate, and is like to be hanged." Disguised highwaymen were often found in reputable citizens and quiet tradesmen, who upon the surface seemed honest folk. A mercer of Lombard Street was taken out of his bed and charged by a cheesemonger as being the man that rubbed him two years previously. Another mercer was taken up near Ludgate on suspicion of being a highwayman, and committed. Saunders, a butcher of St. James' market, was charged with robbing the Hampton coach, and discovered three confederates, who were captured on Sunday at Westminster Abbey. "Two highwaymen taken near Highgate, one of whom was said to be a broken mercer, the other a fishmonger." Two of Whitney's gang were said to be tradesmen in the Strand—one a goldsmith and one a milliner.

Nothing could exceed the cool impudence with which reputed robbers showed themselves in public places. They did not always escape capture, however. "A noted highwayman in a scarlet cloak," says Luttrell, "and coat laced with gold taken in Covent Garden." Another was taken in the Strand and sent to Newgate. Five more were captured at the Rummer, Charing Cross; three others, notorious highwaymen, taken at the 'Cheshire Cheeze.' At times they fought hard for liberty. "One Wake, a highwayman, pursued to Red Lion Fields, set his back against the wall and faced the constables and mob. He shot the former, and wounded others, but was at last taken and sent to Newgate." Whitney, the famous highwayman, was taken without Bishopsgate, being "discovered by one Hill, as he (Whitney) walked the street. Hill observed where the robber 'housed' and calling for assistance, went to the door." Whitney defended himself for about an hour, but the people increasing, and the officers of Newgate being sent for, he surrendered himself, but not before he had stabbed Hill with a bayonet, "not mortal." He was cuffed and shackled with irons, and committed to Newgate.

Whitney had done business on a large scale. He had been

arrested before by a party of horse despatched by William III., which had come up with him lurking between St. Alban's and Barnet. He was attacked, but made a stout defence, killing some and wounding others before he was secured. He must have got free again very soon afterwards. His second arrest, which has just been detailed, was followed by that of many others of his gang. "Three were seized near Chelsea College by some soldiers; two more were in company, but escaped." On Sunday two others were taken; one kept a livery stable at Moorfield's. Soon after his committal there was a strong rumour that he had escaped from Newgate, but "he continues closely confined there, and has forty pounds weight of irons on his legs. He had his tailor to make him a rich embroidered suit with peruke and hat, worth £100; but the keeper refused to let him wear them, because they would disguise him from being known."[70] Whitney made many attempts to purchase pardon. He offered to discover his associates, and those that give notice when and where the money is conveyed on the roads in coaches and waggons. He was, however, put upon his trial, and eventually convicted and sentenced to death. He went in the cart to the place of execution, but was reprieved and brought back to Newgate with a rope round his neck, followed by a "vast" crowd. Next night he was carried to Whitehall and examined as to the persons who hired the highwaymen to rob the mails. But he was again ordered for execution, and once more sought to gain a reprieve by writing a letter in which he offered, if he might have his pardon, to betray a conspiracy to kill the king. His last appeal was refused, and he suffered at Porter's Block, near Cow Cross, Smithfield.

Determined efforts were made from time to time to put down these robberies, which were often so disgracefully prevalent that people hardly dared to travel along the roads. Parties of horse were quartered in most of the towns along the great highways. Handsome rewards were offered for the apprehension of offenders. A proclamation promised £10 for every highwayman taken, and this was ere long increased to £40, to be given to any who might supply information leading to an arrest. Horses standing at livery in and about London, whose ownership was at all doubtful, were seized on suspicion, and often never claimed. It was customary to parade before Newgate persons in custody who were thought to be highwaymen. They were shown in their riding-dresses with their horses, and all gentlemen who had been robbed were invited to inspect this singular exhibition.[71] But the practice flourished in spite of all attempts at repression.

One or two types of the highwaymen of the seventeenth century may here be fitly introduced. One of the earliest and most celebrated was Jack Cottington, alias Mulled Sack, who had been a depredator throughout the Commonwealth epoch, and who enjoyed the credit of having robbed Oliver Cromwell himself on Hounslow Heath. His confederate in this, Horne, once a captain in Downe's foot regiment, was overtaken, captured, and hanged, but Cottington escaped. Jack Cottington began as a chimney-sweep, first as an apprentice, then on his own account, when he gained his soubriquet from his powers in drinking mulled sack. From this he graduated, and soon gained a high reputation as a pickpocket, his chief hunting-ground being churches and puritan meeting-houses, which he frequented demurely dressed in black with a black *roquelaire*. He succeeded in robbing Lady Fairfax of a gold watch set with diamonds and a gold chain as she was on her way to Dr. Jacomb's lecture at Ludgate; and a second time by removing the lynch-pin from her Ladyship's carriage when on her way to the same church, he upset the coach, and giving her his arm, relieved her of another gold watch and seals. After this he became the captain of a gang of thieves and night prowlers, whom he organized and led to so much purpose that they alarmed the whole town. His impudence was so great that he was always ready to show off his skill as a thief in any public-house if he was paid for it, in a performance he styled "moving the bung." He was not content to operate in the city, but visited the Parliament House and Courts of Law at Westminster, and was actually caught in the act of picking the Protector's pocket. He narrowly escaped hanging for this, and on coming out of gaol took permanently to the highway, where he soon achieved a still greater notoriety. With half-a-dozen comrades he robbed a government waggon conveying money to the army, and dispersed the twenty troopers who escorted it, by attacking them as they were watering their horses. The waggon contained £4000, intended to pay the troops quartered at Oxford and Gloucester. Another account states that near Wheatley, Cottington put a pistol to the carrier's head and bade him stand, at which both carter and guard rode off for their lives, fearing an ambuscade. The town of Reading he laid under frequent contribution, breaking into a jeweller's shop in that town and carrying off the contents, which he sported on his person in London. Again at Reading, hearing that the Receiver-General was about to send £6000 to London in an ammunition waggon, he entered the receiver's house, bound the family, and decamped with the money. Being by this time so notorious a character, he was arrested on suspicion, and committed for trial at Abingdon Assizes. There, however, being flush of cash, he found means to corrupt the jury and secure acquittal, although Judge Jermyn exerted all his skill to hang him. His fame was now at its zenith. He became the burthen of street songs—a criminal hero who laughed the gallows to scorn. But about this time he was compelled to fly the country for the murder of Sir John Bridges, with whose wife he had had an intrigue. He made his way to Cologne, to the Court of Charles II., whom he robbed of plate worth £1500. Then he returned to England, after making overtures to Cromwell, to whom he offered certain secret papers if he might be allowed to go scot free. But he was brought to the gallows, and nobly deserved his fate.

Claude Duval is another hero whose name is familiar to all readers of criminal chronology. A certain halo of romance surrounds this notorious and most successful highwayman. Gallant and chivalrous in his bearing towards the fair sex, he would spare a victim's pockets for the pleasure of dancing a "corranto" with the gentleman's wife. The money he levied so recklessly he lavished as freely in intrigue. His success with the sex is said to have been extraordinary, both in London and in Paris. "Maids, widows, and wives," says a contemporary account, "the rich, the poor, the noble, the vulgar, all submitted to the powerful Duval." When justice at length overtook him, and he was cast for death, crowds of ladies visited him in the condemned hold; many more in masks were present at his execution. After hanging he lay in state in the Tangier Tavern at St. Giles, in a room draped with black and covered with escutcheons; eight wax tapers surrounded his bier, and "as many tall gentlemen in long cloaks." Duval was a Frenchman by birth —a native of Domfront in Normandy, once a village of evil reputation. Its curé was greatly surprised, it is said, at finding that he baptized as many as a hundred children and yet buried nobody. At first he congratulated himself in residing in an air producing such longevity; but on closer inquiry he found that all who were born at Domfront were hanged at Rouen.

Duval did not long honour his native country with his presence. On the restoration of Charles II. he came to London as footman to a person of quality; but soon took to the road. Numerous stories are told of his boldness, his address, and fertility of resource. One of the most amusing is that in which he got an accomplice to dress up a mastiff in a cow's-hide, put horns on his head, and let him down a chimney into a room where a bridal merry-making was in progress. Duval, who was one of the guests, dexterously profited by the general dismay to lighten the pockets of an old farmer whom he had seen secreting a hundred pounds. When the money was missed it was supposed that the devil had flown away with it. On another occasion, having revisited France, he ingratiated himself with a wealthy priest by pretending to possess the secret of the philosopher's stone. This he effected by stirring up a potful of molten inferior metal with a stick, within which were enclosed a number of sprigs of pure gold, as black lead is in a pencil. When the baser metals were consumed by the fire, the pure gold remained at the bottom of the pot. Overjoyed at Duval's skill as an alchemist, the priest made him his confidant and bosom friend, revealing him his secret hoards, and how they were bestowed. One day, when the priest was asleep after dinner, Duval gagged and bound him, removed his keys, unlocked his strong boxes, and went off with all the valuables he could carry. Duval was also an adroit cardsharper, and won considerable sums at play by "slipping a card"; and he was most astute in laying and winning wagers on matters he had previously fully mastered. His career was abruptly terminated by his capture when drunk at a tavern in Chandos St., and he was executed, after ten years of triumph, at the early age of twenty-seven.

William Nevison, a native-born member of the same fraternity, may be called, says Raine, "the Claude Duval of the north. The chroniclers of his deeds have told us of his daring and his charities, for he gave away to the poor much of the money he took from the rich." Nevison was born at Pontefract in 1639, and began as a boy by stealing his father's spoons. When chastised by the schoolmaster for this offence, he bolted with his master's horse, having first robbed his father's strong box. After spending some time in London thieving, he went to Flanders and served, not without distinction, in a regiment of English volunteers commanded by the Duke of York. He returned presently to

England, and took to the road. Stories are told of him similar to those which made Duval famous. Nevison was on the king's side, and never robbed Royalists. He was especially hard on usurers. On one occasion he eased a Jew of his ready money, then made him sign a note of hand for five hundred pounds, which by hard riding he cashed before the usurer could stop payment. Again, he robbed a bailiff who had just distrained a poor farmer for rent. The proceeds of the sale, which the bailiff thus lost, Nevison restored to the farmer. In the midst of his career, having made one grand *coup*, he retired from business and spent eight years virtuously with his father. At the old man's death he resumed his evil courses, and was presently arrested and thrown into Leicester Gaol. From this he escaped by a clever stratagem. A friendly doctor having declared he had the plague, gave him a sleeping draught, and saw him consigned to a coffin as dead. His friend demanded the body, and Nevison passed the gates in the coffin. Once outside, he was speedily restored to life, and resumed his old ways. He now extended his operations to the capital, and it was soon after this that he gained the soubriquet, given by Charles II., it is said, of "Swift Nick." There seems to be very little doubt that Nevison was actually the hero of the great ride to York, commonly credited to Turpin. The story goes that he robbed a gentleman at Gadshill, then riding to Gravesend, crossed the Thames and galloped across Essex to Chelmsford. After baiting he rode on to Cambridge, and Godmanchester, thence to Huntingdon, where he baited his mare and slept for an hour; after that, holding to the north road, and not galloping his horse all the way, reached York the same afternoon. Having changed his clothes, he went to the bowling-green, where he made himself noticeable to the Lord Mayor. By and by, when recognized and charged with the robbery at Gadshill, Nevison called upon the mayor to prove that he had seen him at York; whereupon he was acquitted, "on the bare supposition that it was impossible for a man to be at two places so remote on one and the same day."

Nevison appears to have been arrested and in custody in 1676. He was tried for his life, but reprieved and drafted into a regiment at Tangier. He soon deserted, and returning to England, again took to the road. He was next captured at Wakefield, tried, and sentenced to death; but escaped from prison, to be finally taken up for a trifling robbery, for which he suffered at York. The depositions preserved by the Surtees' Society show that he was the life and centre of a gang of highway robbers who worked in association. They levied black mail upon the whole country side; attended fairs, race meetings, and public gatherings, and had spies and accomplices, inn-keepers and ostlers, who kept them informed of the movements of travellers, and put them in the way of "likely jobs" to be done. Drovers and farmers who paid a tax to them escaped spoliation; but all others were very roughly handled. The gang had its head-quarters at the Talbot Inn, Newark, where they kept a room by the year, and met at regular intervals to divide the proceeds of their robberies.

Many instances are recorded of another crime somewhat akin to highway robbery. The forcible abduction of heiresses was nothing new; but it was now prosecuted with more impudence and daring than heretofore. Luttrell tells us, under date 1st June, 1683, that one Mrs. Synderfin, a rich widow, was taken out of her carriage on Hounslow Heath, by a Captain Clifford and his comrades. They carried her into France to "Calice" against her will, and with much barbarous ill-usage made her marry Clifford. Mrs. Synderfin or Clifford was, however, rescued, and brought back to England. Clifford escaped, but presently returning to London was seized and committed to custody. He pleaded in defence his great passion for the lady, and his "seeing no other way to win her." It was not mere fortune-hunting, he declared, as he possessed a better estate than hers. But the Lord

Chief Justice charged the jury that they must find the prisoners guilty, which they did, and all were sentenced to imprisonment in Newgate for one year. Captain Clifford was also to pay a fine of £1000, two of his confederates £500 each, and two more £100. In the same authority is an account how—"Yesterday a gentleman was committed to Newgate for stealing a young lady worth £10,000, by the help of bailiffs, who arrested her and her maid in a false action, and had got them into a coach, but they were rescued." Again, a year or two later, "one Swanson, a Dane, who pretends to be a Deal merchant, is committed to Newgate for stealing one Miss Rawlins, a young lady of Leicestershire, with a fortune of £4000. Three bailiffs and a woman, Swanson's pretended sister, who assisted, are also committed, they having forced her to marry him. Swanson and Mrs. Bainton were convicted of this felony at the King's Bench Bar; but the bailiffs who arrested her on a sham action were acquitted, with which the court was not well pleased. Swanson was sentenced to death, and executed. As also the woman; but she being found with child, her execution was respited." A more flagrant case was the abduction of Miss Mary Wharton in 1690, the daughter and heiress of Sir George Wharton, by Captain James Campbell, brother to the Earl of Argyll, assisted by Sir John Johnson. Miss Wharton, who was only thirteen years of age, had a fortune of £50,000. She was carried away from her relations in Great Queen Street, on the 14th Nov., 1690, and married against her will. A royal proclamation was forthwith issued for the apprehension of Captain Campbell and his abettors. Sir John Johnson was taken, committed to Newgate, and presently tried and cast for death. "Great application was made to the king and to the relations of the bride to save his life," but to no purpose, "which was thought the harder, as it appeared upon his trial that Miss Wharton had given evident proof that the violence Captain Campbell used was not so much against her will as her lawyers endeavoured to make it." Luttrell says, "Sir John refused pardon unless requested by the friends of Mrs. Wharton. On the 23rd December he went in a mourning coach to Tyburn, and there was hanged." No mention is made of the arrest of Captain Campbell, whom we may conclude got off to the continent. But he benefited little by his violence, for a bill was brought into the House of Commons within three weeks of the abduction to render the marriage void, and this, although the Earl of Argyll on behalf of his brother petitioned against it, speedily passed both Houses.

The affair of Count Konigsmark may be classed with the foregoing, as another notorious instance of an attempt to bring about marriage with an heiress by violent means. The lady in this case was the last of the Percies, the only child and heiress to the vast fortune of Jocelyn, the Earl of Northumberland. Married when still of tender years to the Earl of Ogle, eldest son of the Duke of Newcastle, she was a virgin widow at fifteen, and again married against her consent, it was said, to Thomas Thynne, Esq., of Longleat;[72] "Tom of Ten Thousand," as he was called on account of his income. This second marriage was not consummated; Lady Ogle either "repented herself of the match and fled into Holland,"[73] or her relatives wished to postpone her entry into the matrimonial state, and she was sent to live abroad. Previous to her second marriage, a young Swedish nobleman, Count Konigsmark, when on a visit to England, had paid his addresses to her, but he had failed in his suit. After his rejection he had conceived a violent hatred against Mr. Thynne. The Count was "a fine person of a man, with the longest hair I ever saw,[74] and very quick of parts. He was also possessed of great wealth and influence;" "one of the greatest men," Sir John Reresby tells us, "in the kingdom of Sweden; his uncle being at that time governor of Pomerania, and near upon marrying the King's (of Sweden) aunt." Konigsmark could command the devoted service of reckless men, and among his followers he counted one Captain Vratz, to whom he seems to have entrusted the task of dealing with Mr. Thynne. Vratz, although a brave soldier, who had won his promotion at the siege of Mons, under the Prince of Orange, and to whom the King of Sweden had given a troop of horse, was willing to act as an assassin. The Count came to London, living secretly in various lodgings, as he declared to hide a distemper from which he suffered, but no doubt to direct privately the operations of his bravoes. Vratz associated with himself one Stern, a Swedish lieutenant, and Boroski, "a Polander," who had arrived in England destitute, and whom, it was subsequently proved, the Count had furnished with clothes and arms. The murderers, having set a watch for their victim, attacked him at the corner of Pall Mall, about the spot where Her Majesty's Theatre now stands, as he was riding on Sunday night the 21st February, 1681, in his carriage from the Countess of Northumberland's house. One of them cried to the coachman, "Stop, you dog!" and a second, Boroski, immediately fired a blunderbuss charged with bullets into the carriage. Four bullets entered Mr. Thynne's body, each of which inflicted a mortal wound. The murderers then made off.

The unfortunate gentleman was carried dying to his own house, where he was presently joined by the Duke of Monmouth, his intimate friend, Lord Mordaunt, and Sir John Reresby, specially sent by King Charles, who feared that some political construction would be put upon the transaction, and was anxious that the perpetrators of the crime should be apprehended. Reresby, who was an active magistrate, granted warrants at once against several suspected persons, and he himself, accompanied by the Duke of Monmouth and others, made a close search, which ended in the arrest of Vratz in the house of a Swedish doctor, in Leicester Fields. His accomplices were also soon taken, and all three were examined by the King in Council, when they confessed that they had done the deed at the instigation of Count Konigsmark, "who was lately in England."[75] At the same time a Monsieur Foubert, who kept an "Academy" in London, which a younger brother of Count Konigsmark attended, was arrested as being privy to the murder, admitted that the elder brother had "arrived incognito ten days before the said murder, and lay disguised till it was committed, which gave great cause to suspect that the Count was at the bottom of the whole bloody affair."[76] The King despatched Sir John Reresby to seize Konigsmark, "but the bird had flown; he went away betimes, on the morning of the day after the deed was perpetrated."[77] He went down the river to Deptford, then to Greenwich, and the day after to Gravesend, where he was taken by two King's messengers, accompanied by "Mr. Gibbons, servant to the Duke of Monmouth, and Mr. Kidd, gentleman to Mr. Thynne." He was dressed "in a very mean habit, under which he carried a naked sword." When seized he gave a sudden start, so that his wig fell off, and the fact that he wore a wig, instead of his own hair as usual, was remembered against him at his trial, as an attempt at disguise. The Count was carried to an inn in Gravesend, where he expressed very great concern when he heard that his men had confessed; declaring that it (the murder) was a stain upon his blood, "although one good action in the wars, or lodging on a counterscarp, would wash all that away." His captors received the £200 reward, promised in the *Gazette*, and in addition the £500 offered by Sir Thomas Thynne, Mr. Thynne's heir.

 They carried him at once to London, before the King in Council, where he was examined, but the Council being unwilling to meddle on account of his quality, as connected with the kingdom of Sweden, he was then taken before Chief Justice Pemberton, who could, if he thought fit, send him to gaol. He was examined again till eleven at night, and at last, "much against the Count's desire," committed him to Newgate. He stood upon his innocency, and confessed nothing, yet "people are well satisfied that he is taken."[78] While in Newgate, Count Konigsmark was lodged in the governor's house, and was daily visited by persons of quality. Great efforts were now made to obtain his release. The M. Foubert, already mentioned, came to Sir John Reresby, and offered him any money to withdraw from the prosecution, but the overtures were stoutly rejected, and his emissary was warned to be cautious "how he made any offers to pervert justice." A more effectual attempt at bribery was probably made on the jury, of whom the prisoner challenged eighteen. He had their names on a list, and knew beforehand whom he could or could not trust. The Judge, Lord Chief Justice Pemberton, was also clearly in his favour. The defence set up was that Vratz had taken upon himself to avenge an affront offered by Mr. Thynne to his master, and Count Konigsmark denied all knowledge of his follower's action. The Count tried to explain the privacy in which he lived, and his sudden flight. But the counsel for the prosecution laid great stress on the intimacy between him and the murderers; the absence of any object on the part of the latter, unless instigated by the former. The Chief Justice, however, summed up for the Count, assuring the jury that a master could not be held responsible for the acts of his servants, if ignorant of them, and that if they thought the Count knew nothing of the murder till after it was done, they must acquit him. Which they did, "to the no small wonder of the auditory," as Luttrell says, "as more than probable good store of guineas went amongst them." Konigsmark was set at liberty at the end of the trial, but before his discharge he was bound in heavy securities, in £2000 himself, and £2000 from two friends, to appear at the King's Bench bar the first day of the following term. "Yet notwithstanding, the Count is gone into France, and it is much doubted whether he will return to save his bail."[79]

After his departure he was challenged by Lord Cavendish and Lord Mordaunt, but no duel came off, Konigsmark declaring that he never received the cartel till too late. His agents or accomplices, or whatever they may be called, were convicted and executed.[80]

Count Konigsmark did not long survive Mr. Thynne, nor did he succeed in winning Lady Ogle's hand. That doubly widowed yet virgin wife presently married the Duke of Somerset, by whom she had two sons. As for Konigsmark, according to the 'Amsterdam Historical Dictionary,' quoted in Chambers' 'Book of Days,' he resumed the career of arms, and was wounded at Cambray in 1683. He afterwards went to Spain with his regiment, and distinguished himself on several occasions; after that he accompanied an uncle Otto William to the Morea, where he was present at the battle of Argas. In this action he so overheated himself that he was seized with pleurisy, and died at the early age of twenty-seven, within little more than four years of the murder of Mr. Thynne. It was another Count Konigsmark, near relative of this, Count Philip, whose guilty intrigue with Sophia Dorothea, wife of George I., when Elector of Hanover, led to his assassination in the Electoral palace.

In the foregoing the softer sex were either victims or the innocent incentives to crime. In the case of that clever and unscrupulous impostor Mary Moders, otherwise Carelton, commonly called the German Princess, it was exactly the opposite. The daughter of a chorister in Canterbury Cathedral, she married first a shoemaker; then, dissatisfied with her lot, ran off to Dover and committed bigamy with a doctor. She was apprehended for this, tried, and acquitted for want of evidence. She next passed over into Holland, and went the round of the German spas, at one of which she encountered a foolish old gentleman of large estate, who fell in love with her and offered marriage. She accepted his proposals and presents; but having cajoled him into intrusting her with a large sum to make preparations for the wedding, she absconded to Amsterdam and Rotterdam, where she took ship and came over to London. Alighting at the Exchange Tavern, kept by a Mr. King, she assumed the state and title of a princess, giving herself out as the ill-used child of Count Henry Van Wolway, a sovereign prince of the empire. John Carelton, a brother-in-law of her landlord's, at once, "in the most dutiful and submissive manner," paid his addresses to her, and she at last condescended to marry him. Carelton was presently undeceived by an anonymous letter, which proved his wife to be a cheat and impostor. The princess was arrested, committed to Newgate, and tried for polygamy at the Old Bailey, but was a second time acquitted. On her release, deserted by Carelton, she took to the stage, and gained some reputation, especially in a piece written for her entitled the 'German Princess.' Her fame spread through the town, and she was courted by numberless admirers, two of whom she played off against each other; and having fleeced both of several hundred pounds, flouted them for presuming to make love to a princess. Another victim to her wiles was an elderly man, "worth about £400 per annum," who loaded her with gifts; he was "continually gratifying her with some costly present or another, which she took care to receive with an appearance of being ashamed he should heap so many obligations on her, telling him she was not worthy of so many favours."[81] One night when her lover came home in liquor, she got him to bed, and when he was asleep rifled his pockets, securing his keys and a bill on a goldsmith for a hundred pounds. Opening all his escritoires and drawers, she stole everything, gold pieces, watches, seals, and several pieces of plate, and then made off. After this she led a life of vagabondage, moving her lodgings constantly, and laying her hands on all she could steal. She was adroit in deceiving tradesmen, and swindled first one and then another out of goods. At last she was arrested for stealing a silver tankard in Covent Garden, and committed again to Newgate. This time she was found guilty and cast for death, but the sentence was commuted to transportation. She was sent in due course to Jamaica, but within a couple of years escaped from the plantations, and reappeared in England. By some means she managed to pass off as a rich heiress, and inveigled a rich apothecary into marriage, but presently robbed him of above £300 and left him. Her next trick was to take a lodging in the same house with a watchmaker. One night she invited the landlady and the watchmaker to go to the play, leaving her maid, who was a confederate, alone in the house. The maid lost no time in breaking open the watchmaker's coffers, and stole therefrom thirty watches, with about two hundred pounds in cash, which she carried off to a secure place in another part of the town. Meanwhile the "princess" had invited her dupes to supper at the Green Dragon Tavern in Fleet Street, where she managed to give them the slip and joined her maid. This was one of the last of her robberies. Soon afterwards fate overtook her quite by accident. The keeper of the Marshalsea, in search of some stolen property, came to the house where she lodged, in New Spring Gardens, and saw her "walking in the two-pair-of-stairs room in a night-gown." He went in, and continuing his search, came upon three letters, which he proceeded to examine. "Madam seemed offended with him, and their dispute caused him to look at her so steadfastly that he knew her, called her by her name, and carried away both her and her letters."[82] She was committed and kept a prisoner till 16th January, 1673, when she was arraigned at the Old Bailey, as the woman Mary Carelton, for returning from transportation. On the last day of the sessions she received sentence of death, "which she received with a great deal of intrepidity."

She appeared more gay and brisk than ever on the day of her

execution. When the irons were removed from her on her starting for Tyburn, she pinned the picture of her husband Carelton to her sleeve, and carried it with her to the gallows. She discovered herself to a gentleman in the crowd as a Roman Catholic, and having conversed with him for some time in French, on parting said, *Mon ami, le bon Dieu vous benisse.* At the gallows she harangued the crowd at some length, and died as she had lived, a reckless although undoubtedly gifted and intelligent woman.

Prominent among the criminal names of this epoch is that of the informer, Titus Oates, no less on account of the infamy of his conduct than from the severe retribution which overtook him in the reign of James II. The arraignment of Green, Berry, and Laurence Hill for the trial of Sir Edmundbury Godfrey, who were brought for the purpose "from Newgate to the King's Bench Bar," is a well-known judicial episode of the year 1678. Oates was the principal witness against them; but he was followed by Praunce, an approver, and others. After much evidence for and against, and much equivocation, the Lord Chief Justice Scroggs summed up the evidence strongly for conviction. When the jury soon returned a verdict of guilty, the Lord Chief Justice commended them, and said if it were the last word he had to speak he would have pronounced them guilty. Sentence was then given, and within a fortnight they were executed. These victims of the so-called Popish Plot were, however, amply and ruthlessly avenged. Macaulay tells the story. Oates had been arrested before Charles II.'s death for defamatory words, and cast in damages of £100,000. He was then, after the accession of James II., tried on two indictments of perjury, and it was proved beyond doubt that he had by false testimony deliberately murdered several guiltless persons. "His offence, though in a moral light murder of the most aggravated kind, was in the eye of the law merely a misdemeanour." But the tribunal which convicted made its punishment proportionate to the real offence. Brutal Judge Jeffries was its mouthpiece, and he sentenced him to be unfrocked and pilloried in Palace yard, to be led round Westminster Hall, with an inscription declaring his infamy over his head; to be pilloried in front of the Royal Exchange, to be whipped from Aldgate to Newgate, and after an interval of two days to be whipped from Newgate to Tyburn. He was to be imprisoned for life, and every year to be brought from his dungeon and exposed in different parts of the capital. When on the pillory he was mercilessly pelted, and nearly torn to pieces. His first flogging was executed rigorously in the presence of a vast crowd, and Oates, a man of strong frame, long stood the lash without a murmur. "But at last his stubborn fortitude gave way. His bellowings were frightful to hear. He swooned several times; but the scourge still continued to descend. When he was unbound it seemed he had borne as much as the human frame could bear without dissolution.... After an interval of forty-eight hours Oates was again brought out from his dungeon. He seemed unable to stand, and it was necessary to drag him to Tyburn on a sledge." He was again flogged, although insensible, and a person present counted the stripes as seventeen hundred. "The doors of the prison closed upon him. During many months he remained ironed in the darkest hole in Newgate." A contemporary account written by one of his own side declares he received "upwards of two thousand lashes—such a thing was never inflicted by any Jew, Turk, or heathen but Jeffries.... Had they hanged him they had been more merciful; had they flayed him alive it is a question whether it would have been so much torture."[83]

Dangerfield, another informer of the Oates type, but of lesser guilt, was also convicted and sentenced to be similarly flogged from Aldgate to Newgate, and from Newgate to Tyburn. "When he heard his doom he went into agonies of despair, gave himself up for dead, and chose a text for his funeral. His forebodings were just. He was not indeed scourged quite so severely as Oates had been; but he had not Oates's iron strength of body and mind." On his way back to prison he was assaulted by Mr. Francis, a Tory gentleman of Gray's Inn, who struck him across the face with a cane and injured his eye. "Dangerfield was carried dying into Newgate. This dastardly outrage roused the indignation of the bystanders. They seized Francis, and were with difficulty restrained from tearing him in pieces. The appearance of Dangerfield's body, which had been frightfully lacerated by the whip, inclined many to believe that his death was chiefly if not wholly caused by the stripes which he had received." The Government laid all the blame on Francis, who was tried and executed for murder.

Religion and politics still continued to supply their quota of inmates. The law was still cruelly harsh to Roman Catholics, Quakers, and all Nonconformists.

The Fifth Monarchy men in 1661, when discomfited and captured, were lodged in Newgate, to the number of twenty or more. Venner, the ringleader, was amongst them. The State Trials give the trial of one John James, who was arraigned at the King's Bench for high treason. He was found guilty of compassing the death of the king, and suffered the cruel sentence then in force for the crime. James has left some details of the usage he received in Newgate, especially in the matter of extortion. Fees to a large amount were exacted of him, although a poor and needy wretch, "originally a small coal-man." In the press-yard he paid 16s. to the keeper Hicks for the use of his chamber, although he only remained there three or four days. The hangman also came to demand money, that "he might be favourable to him at his death," demanding twenty pounds, then falling to ten, at last threatening, unless he got five, "to torture him exceedingly. To which James said he must leave himself to his mercy, for he had nothing to give him." Yet at the execution, the report says the sheriff and the hangman were so civil to him as to suffer him to be dead before he was cut down. After that he was dismembered; some of them were burnt, the head and quarters brought back to Newgate in a basket, and exposed upon the gates of the city. Venner and several others suffered in the same way.

Many Quakers were kept in Newgate, imprisoned during the king's pleasure for refusing to take the oaths of allegiance and supremacy. Thus John Crook, Isaac Grey, and John Bolton were so confined, and incurred a præmunire or forfeiture of their estates. But the must notable of the Quakers were Penn and Mead. In its way this is a most remarkable trial, on account of the overbearing conduct of the Bench towards the prisoners. In 1670 these two, the first described as gentleman, the second as linen-draper, were indicted at the Old Bailey for having caused a tumultuous assembly in Gracechurch Street. The people collected, it was charged, to hear Penn preach. The demeanour of the prisoners in the court was so bold, that it drew down on them the anger of the recorder, who called Penn troublesome, saucy, and so forth. The jury were clearly in their favour, and brought in a verdict of not guilty, but the court tried to menace them. The Lord Mayor, Sir Samuel Stirling, was especially furious with Penn, crying, "Stop his mouth; gaoler, bring fetters and stake him to the ground." At last the jury, having refused to reconsider their verdict, were locked up; while Penn and Mead were remanded to Newgate. Next day the jury came up, and adhered to their verdict. Whereupon the recorder fined them forty marks apiece for not following his "good and wholesome advice," adding, "God keep my life out of your hands."[84] The prisoners demanded their liberty, "being freed by the jury," but were detained for their fines imposed by the judge for alleged contempt of court. Penn protested violently, but the recorder cried, "Take him away!" and the prisoners were once more haled to Newgate. Edward Bushell, one of the above-mentioned jurors, who was committed to Newgate in default of payment of fine, subsequently sued out a Habeas Corpus, and was brought before Lord Chief Justice Vaughan, who decided in his favour, whereon he and the other jurymen were discharged from gaol.

There were Roman Catholics too in Newgate, convicted of participation in the Popish plot. Samuel Smith the ordinary publishes in 1679 an account of the behaviour of fourteen of them, "late Popish malefactors, whilst in Newgate." Among them were Whitehead, provincial, and Fenwick, procurator, of the Jesuits in England, and William Harcourt, pretended rector of London. The account contains a description of Mr. Smith's efforts at conversion and ghostly comfort, which were better meant than successful.

After the revolution of 1688 there was an active search after Romish priests, and many were arrested; among them two bishops, Ellis and Leyburn, were sent to Newgate. They were visited in gaol by Bishop Burnet, who found them in a wretched plight, and humanely ordered their situation to be improved. Other inmates of Newgate at this troublous period were the Ex-Lord Chief Justice Wright and several judges. It was Wright who had tried the seven bishops. Jeffries had had him made a judge, although the Lord Keeper styled him the most unfit person in the kingdom for that office. Macaulay says very few lawyers of the time surpassed him in turpitude and effrontery. He died miserably in Newgate about 1690, where he remained under a charge of attempting to subvert the Government.

IN THE PRESS-YARD

Press-yard described—Charges for admission—Extortionate fees paid to turnkeys and governor—The latter's perquisites—Night carousing in Press-yard—Penalty for excess—Days how spent—Arrival of Jacobite prisoners—Discussed by lower officials—Preparations for them—Their appearance and demeanour—High prices charged for gaol lodgings—They live royally—First executions abate their gaiety—Escapes—Keeper superseded by officials specially appointed by Lord Mayor—Strictness of new régime—A military guard mounts—Rioting and revels among the Jacobites once more checked by execution of members of the party—Rumours of an amnesty—Mr. Freeman, who fired a pistol in theatre when Prince of Wales was present, committed to Press-yard—Freeman's violent conduct—Prisoners suffer from overcrowding and heat—Pardons—Rob Roy in Newgate—Other prisoners in Press-yard—Major Bernardi—His history and long detentions—Dies in gaol after forty years' imprisonment.

THE situation of this section of the prison has been already indicated. It was intended more especially for State prisoners, or those incarcerated on "commitments of State," and was deemed to be part and parcel of the governor's house, not actually within the precincts of the prison. This was a pious fiction, put forth as an excuse for exacting fees in excess of the amounts prescribed by Art of Parliament. A sum of twenty guineas was charged for admission to this favoured spot; in other words, "for liberty of having room enough to walk two or three of a breadth."[85] "The gentlemen admitted here are moreover under a necessity of paying 11s. each per week, although two and sometimes three lie in a bed, and some chambers have three or four beds in them."[86] The act referred to specially provided that keepers might not charge more than half-a-crown per week as rent for every chamber. This rule the governor of Newgate—"for this haughty commander-in-chief over defenceless men is styled by the same name as the constable of the Tower"—entirely ignored, and the prisoner committed to his custody had to decide between submitting to the extortion, "or take up his abode in the common gaol," where he had thieves and villains for his associates, and was "perpetually tormented and eaten up by distempers and vermin."

The extortion practised is graphically described by one who endured it. The author of the 'History of the Press-yard,' after having been mulcted on first arrival at the lodge for drink and "garnish,"[87] was, although presumably a State prisoner, and entitled to better treatment, at once cast in the condemned hold. In this gruesome place, which has been already described, he lay "seized with a panic dread" at the survey of his new tenement, and willing to change it for another on almost any terms. "As this was the design of my being brought hither, so was I made apprized of it by an expected method; for I had not bewailed my condition more than half-an-hour, before I heard a voice from above crying out from a board taken out of my ceiling, which was the speaker's floor, 'Sir, I understand your name is ——, and that you are a gentleman too well educated to take up your abode in a vault set apart only for thieves, parricides, and murderers. From hence criminals after sentence of death are carried to the place of execution, and from hence you may be removed to a chamber equal to one in any private house, where you may be furnished with the best conversation and entertainment, on a valuable consideration.'" The speaker went on to protest that he acted solely from good will; that he was himself a prisoner, and had suffered at first in the same manner, but had paid a sum to be removed to better quarters, "which he thanked God he enjoyed then to his heart's content, wanting for nothing that a gaol could afford him." The victim begged to know the terms, and to be put in communication with the proper officer to make a contract for release. The other promised accordingly, and a quarter of an hour afterwards "clang went the chain of my door and bolts, and in comes a gentleman-like man of very smiling aspect," who apologized profusely, swearing that those who had ill-used a gentleman in such an unhandsome manner should be well trounced for it. "He moreover excused the want of suitable entertainment for persons of condition in prison-houses, and assured me that I should be immediately conducted to the governor's house, who would take all imaginable care of my reception. After this he very kindly took me by the hand to lead me down into the lodge, which I rightly apprehended as a motive to feel my pulse, and therefore made use of the opportunity to clap two pieces, which he let my hand go to have a fast grip of, in his."

His deliverer was the head turnkey, by name Bodenham Rouse, whom he accompanied to the Lodge, and there again stood drink. "We gave our service to one another in a glass of wine, drawn by Dame Spurling, the fat hostess who kept the tap in the Lodge." Over the friendly glass terms were propounded and accepted, and having paid down his twenty guineas—a large sum, excused on the grounds that Mr. Pitt the governor had paid £1000 for his place—the prisoner followed his guide through Phœnix court into the governor's house, where he had the honour of saluting and taking a dram of arrack with the great Mr. Pitt, who "as a mark of his favourable intentions to me, gave order for furnishing me a bed with clean sheets, after I had paid the woman that brought them to my barrack of a chamber in the press-yard, whither I was soon conveyed through a door with a great iron chain to it, five shillings."

The new-comer was cordially welcomed and introduced by "George, the cobbler of Highgate,"[88] apparently a prison official, to a congenial companion, who explained to him the ways of the place. It was in the first place incumbent on every arrival to pay his footing. About seven or eight o'clock the entrance fee was demanded. It had previously been only six bottles of wine, and tobacco in proportion. This was now raised to ten or twelve bottles, which, if a prisoner was straitened for money, "could be scored at the bar of the honest tapster, who, though he lost several hundred pounds by that method of proceeding, was not discouraged from going on with it in favour of unhappy gentlemen." This talk lasted over pipes and a pot of stout, until notice was brought by "a person in gray hairs, who had then the keys of the press-yard, that all things were ready for an evening refreshment, and that honest Tom the butler had carried the bottles, pipes, and tobacco into our refectory, called the tap-room." Here the giver of the entertainment seated himself at the head of the table, and the guests on each side of him. Among them was a major who had been in the army[89] so long that he was of the same standing as the Duke of Marlborough, and "commanded over General Mallow, now a great officer in Spain, when he was an ensign on the Irish establishment." Another was "a gentleman, who being of the late King James's Horse Guards, had adhered to that exiled monarch's fortunes till he was driven out of Ireland." Both these gentlemen had married since their confinement, the one, though near seventy,[90] "to a young woman not much above twenty ... the other, of less advanced years, to a widow gentlewoman of a like age, who lived very comfortably with him—" of course in the prison.

They met the new-comer with "all possible civility, and indeed made the hours pass over more agreeably than he could have expected in that place." They drank deep and late. "I continued whipping out sixpences to advance more bottles, till our cheerfulness was turned into drowsiness, and merriment became the subject of dispute with some of my fellow-prisoners, so it was thought high time by the most sober of us to break up and retire to our chambers, with the ceremony of the turnkeys locking each of the two staircase-doors after us." The new prisoner, furnished with a clay candlestick, "because he had not yet equipped himself with one of earthenware," found his way up three pairs of stairs to a large room, which had its entrance through the chapel. The bars were as thick as his wrist, and very numerous. The stone walls, which had borne the same hue for above half a century, were bedaubed with texts of Scripture written in charcoal, such as "Man is born to trouble, as the sparks fly upward," "Before I was afflicted I went astray, but now I have kept Thy word." There were bedsteads made of boards for the bedding, but neither "flocks nor feathers to make one." The tables and chairs were of like antiquity and use. "And Potiphar's wife's chambermaid's hat at the coffee-house in Chelsea had as fair a claim to any modern fashion as any one thing in the room." Our author is disgusted at the accommodation provided for the price, twelve shillings a week, and another twelve pence for the woman or nurse who cleaned the place. But he is consoled by being told what he had escaped by not being locked up on the master's side, "where, besides a thousand other inconveniences, I must have paid one and sixpence per diem for leave to associate myself with pickpockets in a dark and stinking cellar."

The following morning he was admitted into other mysteries of the place. All who had exceeded the previous night had to pay the usual forfeit, a groat in drink for the turnkeys, which the latter collect very punctually, and at the payment of the forfeit, "as many persons as think fit may be present." The names of the offenders having been called over with all ceremony, all pleaded guilty and promptly paid the fine, which was forthwith spent in liquor, to be consumed by the cobbler of Highgate and his fellows. From this time forward the novice was free of the place, and was looked upon by the other prisoners as one of themselves. The morning passed with the ordinary diversions. Talk over the persons of distinction who had gone to Tyburn out of such and such a room, was varied by the perusal of newspapers hired out by the turnkeys, and the discussion of the literary merits of the last dying speech composed by a condemned prisoner, who was on the brink of the gallows. One is given by the author of 'The Press-yard' in extenso, the oration of one J—— B—ggs, an "orange merchant," sentenced to die for outwitting the Bank of England, a flowery piece of rhetoric, hardly worth transcribing, which wound up with these words,—

"So much by way of oration. Here, Jack (Ketch), do your office decently and with despatch; these clothes, hat, and wig are yours; you will find fifteen shillings and some grocery in my pocket. Now, Mr. Ordinary, you may sing the psalm if you please, and I'll endeavour as well as it is possible to bear a bob with you, but let it be none of your penitential ones."

Thus passed the day. Towards evening visitors began to flock in from outside to take their bottle and comfort "the distressed inhabitants" of Newgate press-yard in the only way possible, by inordinate drinking. Of the visitors some were friends and relatives, others came from sheer predilection for criminal society.

Among them was an alderman's son, "who, not having so much prudence as his father, rendered himself suspected by keeping suspicious company." Political affinities attracted more: the eminent merchant, "who would have done much better to relieve the Militia officer (? Bernardi), he came to carouse with, at a distance, than to appear so publicly in support of a person obnoxious to the Government;" or the clergyman, "who had made himself famous at Whitechapel, or in Saint Laurence's Church, whom it behoved in a particular manner to take heed of his ways, since his zeal had already gained him the opposite party's displeasure." All of these came and went as they pleased. Conviviality was general, liquor was freely called for, potations were deep, and the press-yard of Newgate at night time was like the tap-room of a common inn.

The moment was one of considerable political excitement. The Pretender's first attempt had collapsed in the north, and the press-yard was about to be crowded with more eminent guests. Our author is aroused one fine morning by loud joy-bells pealing from the churches, and he learns from his Jacobite companion that the "king's (Pretender's) affairs were ruined, and that the generals Willis and Carpenter had attacked the Jacobite forces in Preston, and taken all prisoners at discretion." Newgate is convulsed by the news. Its officers are wild with delight, "calling for liquor after an extravagant manner, and drinking to their good luck, which was to arise from the ruin and loss of lives and fortunes in many good families." A dialogue is overheard between the hangman, the deputy bed-maker, and a turnkey's understrapper to the following effect:—

Executioner. Come, Doll, here's to you. Good days to us once more. If this news be true I am made a man for ever.

Bed-maker. What news, Mr. Marvell?[91] Has the Parliament lengthened out the suspension of the Habeas Corpus Act?

Deputy Turnkey. No, you fool; something better than that.

Exec. Two or three hundred prisoners for high treason. Drink a bumper to their sudden arrival. They'll be your tenants very speedily.

Bedm. How! Two or three hundred! Where shall we stow them?

Dep. T. Never heed that we shall find room for them, provided they have wherewithal to pay for it.

Exec. Pay for it! Most of them have very great estates, and are topping gentry, so there is no question we shall all of us make a penny by them.

Dep. T. I for fees to lighten their irons.

Bedm. I for keeping their chambers sweet and clean.

Exec. I for civility money in placing their halters' knot right under their left ear, and separating their quarters at the place of execution with all imaginable decency.

Bedm. But with fine gentlemen such as these are said to be, what is their crime?

Dep. T. She's so stupid as not to remember that we are talking of the defeated rebels.

Bedm. True; now I understand you. And those sort of gentry are to be brought hither?

Dep. T. Yes, you fool. Tom, t'other quarter of Geneva; we shall call for our bottle of port in a few days. I'll e'en think of conning my new lesson against the prisoners come to town. "May it please your honour, this pair of derbys is as bright as silver, and weigh two guineas lighter than those such a gentleman has on."

Bedm. And I, these sheets are made of the finest holland, and are never used but when persons of the first rank are to lie in them. Sir, such an one gave me a guinea the first night he hand-selled them.

Exec. I shall not be behindhand with this, though it will come last to my turn to finger any of their money. For you are to remember, that besides £3 per head I shall have from the sheriff for the execution of every peer, their clothes and the money in their pockets will likewise be my perquisites. And for every gentleman hanged and quartered I am to have the like sum, with the respective gratifications they shall make me for a quick and easy despatch; so that in all likelihood, provided the king does not unseasonably spoil my market by reprieves and pardons, which I hope he will never consent to, I shall not only purchase the title of an esquire, but the estate too, and be in a condition of yet taking an apprentice (? as hangman) under the same that are usually given to a Turkey merchant, which may make my wife hold up her head one day or other to the level of an alderman's wife.

This conversation was presently interrupted by the approach of Mr. Pitt, the governor, who came, accompanied by other officials, to survey the rooms, and estimate the number of new tenants that could be accommodated therein. All due preparations made, a few days more brought to Newgate the unfortunate noblemen and gentlemen who had surrendered at discretion, hoping thus, although vainly, to save both life and estate. On their arrival in London they were led in triumph through the streets to their respective places of durance—viz. the Tower, the Marshalsea, Newgate, and the Fleet. The prisoners on arrival at Highgate were met by Major-General Tarlton with two battalions of Royal Foot Guards, completely armed. Cords were also brought sufficient to pinion each prisoner after the manner of condemned criminals, and to lead their horses with, "for each, from the lord to the footman, was accommodated with a Grenadier to that end." Thus under safe conduct they marched from the Hill of Highgate to their several places of confinement. The Major-General led the way, being "preceded by several citizens of more loyalty than compassion, who made repeated huzzas to excite the mob to do the like." After the

General commanding came a company of the first regiment of Guards, "who made a very fine appearance." Then came the division for the Tower, two and two, the Earl of Derwentwater and Lord Widdrington in the first rank, the other lords and noblemen following with haltered horses, bound like common malefactors, and reviled and hooted.

Those for Newgate brought up the rear. They were civilly and humanely treated on arrival there. The officers received them under the gateway, and no sooner were the prisoners alighted from their horses and their names called over, than their cords were immediately cut from their arms and shoulders, and refreshment of wine brought to them. "Their number was about seventy," says our author.[92] "And amongst them in particular I could not but cast my eye upon one Mr. Archibald Bolair, who in the sixteenth year of his age was said to have signalized his courage, and have displayed as much skill and dexterity in feats of arms in the battle of Preston as the oldest commander of them, Brigadier Macintosh himself, though trained up in warlike affairs, not excepted. What induced me to distinguish him from the rest was the fearless way of expression he made use of when the clerk of the prison cut his cords. 'By my soul, man,' said he, 'you should not have done that, but kept it whole that I might either have been hanged with it, or have it to show, if I escaped the gallows, how I had been led like a dog in a string for twice two miles together.' Mr. Bolair then enquired feelingly for his followers, who had been brought so many miles from home out of observance of his orders, and he was anxious that they should not want." Young Mr. Bolair was told off to the same room as our author, into which two additional beds were placed, for the convenience of the keeper, who by four beds in one room, filled each with three tenants, got £6 per week, besides the sums paid as entrance money.

The prisoners included many persons of note. Two of them

—Mr. Forster, who thought himself slighted and ill-used because, in consideration of his seat in Parliament, he had not been imprisoned in the Tower; and Francis Anderson, esquire, commonly called Sir Francis, a gentleman of £2000 per annum —had apartments in the governor's house at £5 per head per week. There were also Colonel Oxborough, Brigadier Macintosh, the two Talbots, the Shaftos, Mr. Wogan, and Captain Menzies, who with their adherents and servants were thrust into the worst dungeons,—such as "the lion's den" and the "middle dark,"—till for better lodgment they had advanced more money than would have rented one of the best houses in Piccadilly or St. James's Square. The fee or premium paid by Mr. Forster and Sir Francis Anderson for being accommodated in the governor's house was £60, and it cost the latter twenty-five guineas more to keep off his irons. Mr. Widdrington, Mr. Ratcliffe, and others paid twenty guineas apiece for the like favour at their first coming in; and every one that would not be turned to the common side, ten guineas, beside two guineas, one guinea and ten shillings per man for every week's lodging, although in some rooms the men lay four in a bed. As the result of these extortions it was computed that Mr. Pitt cleared some £3000 or £4000 in three or four months, "besides valuable presents given in private, and among others a stone (entire) horse."

Money was, however, plentiful among the incarcerated Jacobites, and so far as was consistent with their situation, they lived right royally. Sympathetic friends from without plied them with wines and luxurious diet. They had every day a variety of the choicest eatables in season, "and that too as early as the greatest and nicest ladies."[93] Forty shillings for a dish of peas was nothing to their pockets, nor 13s. for a dish of fish. These, "with the best French wine, was an ordinary regale." They "lived in this profuse manner, and fared so sumptuously through the means of daily visitants and helps from abroad." Money circulated plentifully within the prison. While it was difficult to change a guinea at any house in the street, nothing was more easy than to have silver for gold in any quantity in Newgate. Nor did many of them lack female sympathy. Ladies of the first rank and quality, even tradesmen's wives and daughters, "made a sacrifice of their husbands' and parents' rings and precious movables for the use of those whom the law had appointed to be so many sacrifices themselves."[94] "It is not to be supposed that a champion so noted for the cause as Captain Silk was neglected; for he had his full share of those treats which soon made his clothes too little for his corpse." When not feasting and chambering, the prisoners found diversion in playing shuttlecock, "at which noble game the valiant Forster beat all who engaged him, so that he triumphed with his feather in the prison though he could not do it in the field."[95]

For long there was nothing among them but "flaunting apparel, venison pasties, hams, chickens, and other costly meats." But soon all their jollity came abruptly to an end. The news of the sad fate of the two peers Derwentwater and Kenmure, who had been brought to trial and executed upon Tower Hill, "abated their gaiety." They were yet more unmistakably reminded of their perilous position by the notice which now came to them to provide themselves with counsel and witnesses for their own defence. Fresh committals too were made to Newgate; prisoners were sent in from the Tower and the Fleet. Among them were Mr. Howard, brother to the Duke of Norfolk, the Master of Nairn, Mr. Baird Hamilton, "a gentleman who behaved with wonderful gallantry at the action of Preston;" Mr. Charles Radcliffe, Lord Derwentwater's brother, "a youth of extraordinary courage;" Mr. Charles and Mr. Peregrine Widdington, "two gentlemen of diversion and pleasure, both papists;" the two Mr. Cottons, father and son, "nonjurant protestants, and of great estate in Huntingdonshire;" Mr. Thomas Errington, "a gentleman that had been in the French service, ... with the laird of Macintosh, Colonel McIntosh, and Major McIntosh, together with other Scotch gentlemen."

Brought thus face to face with their very pressing danger, all more or less cast about them for some means of escape. Several desperate attempts were made to break prison. Thus on the 14th March it was discovered that several had tried to get out by breaking through the press-yard wall, "from which they were to be let down by a rope, instead of being tucked up by one at Tyburn." For this several were placed in irons. Some time later Mr. Forster got clean away,[96] as did Brigadier Macintosh and eight others. Mr. George Budden, formerly an upholsterer near Fleet bridge, also effected his escape; and last, but not least, Mr. Charles Radcliffe, Lord Derwentwater's brother. After Mr. Forster's escape the Government took greater precautions, and a lieutenant with thirty men of the Foot Guards was ordered to do constant duty at Newgate. Mr. Pitt, the keeper, was strongly suspected of collusion, and was attached on a charge of high treason, being after arrest committed to the custody of one Wilcox, a messenger, "who used him in a barbarous manner, contrary no doubt to the instruction of the noble lord that issued the warrant for his confinement." The city authorities, no doubt exercised at the insecurity of their gaol, also roused themselves "to look better after their prison of Newgate," and instead of leaving Mr. Rouse chief turnkey in charge of the whole place, specially appointed Mr. Carleton Smith, an officer of the Lord Mayor's, and with him Mr. Russell, to take care of the rebels in the press-yard. These new officials "performed their part so well," it is said, "by examining all the visitors, debarring entrance to all riding hoods, cloaks, and arms, and by sitting up all night in the prison, each in his turn, that not one man escaped from thence during their time."

The new keepers appear to have stirred up much animosity from their punctual discharge of their duties. Mr. Russell, we read, shortly after his appointment was very much abused and threatened by Captain Silk and some of the rebels, who surrounded him in the press-yard, but he made his retreat without any harm. There must have been some in the reigning monarch's service with secret sympathies for the Pretender; for it is recorded, May 14th, that "an officer of the guards with two others conversed with the rebels all day." They were, moreover, humoursome and abusive to the new keepers because of their care in looking after their prisoners; whereof Messrs. Carleton Smith and Russell complained to the Lord Mayor, who thereupon ordered that no officer should be permitted to visit the prisoners without the express permission of the Secretary of State; and next day it is stated the officer in fault was "submissive and sorry for his offence." This was not the first offence of the kind. A few days before the officer of the guard went in (even then), "contrary to custom," with his sword on to see the prisoners. He continued with them for some hours, and whether heated with wine or otherwise, beat one of the turnkeys as he brought in a rebel from trial. This officer was placed in arrest, and another mounted guard in his place, who "prevented the drunkenness and other irregularities of the soldiers which might have given the prisoners an opportunity to escape."

Matters were not too comfortable for the military guard. The men at the gate were liable to insults as on the 19th May, when they were reviled by a Tory constable. They were also open to efforts to wean them from their allegiance. One day Mr. Carleton Smith detected a prisoner, Isaac Dalton,[97] in durance for libel, endeavouring to corrupt the sentinels by giving them money to drink the Pretender's health with. "But he missed his aim." The soldiers heartily drank to King George in wine supplied by Mr. Smith, and declared they would oppose the

Pretender to the last drop of their blood. All the guards were not equally loyal, however. On another occasion the soldiers of the guard "had the impudence to sing Captain Silk's dearly beloved tune, 'The king shall have his own again,' for which their officer, Captain Reeve, a very loyal gentleman, threatened them with imprisonment."

The peril of the prisoners bred a certain reckless turbulence among them. On the 29th May a mob collected in great numbers outside, carrying oaken boughs on pretence of commemorating the restoration. The guard was reinforced, lest the mob should attempt to break open the gaol. Inside the rebels were very noisy, and insulted their keepers; "but they were soon put out of a capacity of doing much harm, for by way of precaution they were all locked up before ten o'clock." This hour of early closing was continued, and greatly resented by them. A few days later they made a great disturbance at the sound of a bell set up by order of the Lord Mayor to ring them to their apartments at the regular hour. They asked for the order. It was read to them, to their manifest dissatisfaction, for it referred the recent escapes to the unaccountable liberty of indulgence permitted them, and insisted that upon the ringing of the bell in question all should betake themselves to their apartments. Ten was the hour of retiring "at farthest"; any infringement of the rule would be followed by the deprivation of all freedom, and double irons for the offenders. Except Captain Silk, however, all acquiesced in the order. He alone, "with his usual impudence, bullied the keeper, and made many unbecoming reflections upon the Lord Mayor and sheriffs." Nor did insubordination end here. A day or two later the Lord Mayor's notice, which had been posted up in the various press-yard rooms, was torn down by the rebels in contempt of authority.

A fresh and more serious riot soon occurred in the streets, on the occasion of the thanksgiving on the anniversary of

Preston fight. Several visitors came to the rebels with rue and thyme in their hats and bosoms in contempt of the day; but the new keepers made bold to strip them of their badges and strew the floors with them, "as more worthy to be trodden underfoot than be worn by way of insult on that glorious day." About midnight brickbats were thrown from the neighbouring houses upon the soldiers on guard; and the guard in retaliation fired up at the places whence came the attack. Mr. Carleton Smith, whose turn it was to sit up, feared some attempt was being made to break the gaol, and "leaping out to know the occasion of the firing, searched several of the houses; in doing which he was like to have been shot by a ball which came up to the room where he was." But the loyalty of the rebels to their cause was not to be checked. It broke out again on the 10th June, the anniversary of the Pretender's birth. "Captain Booth, whose window looked into Phœnix Court, was so insolent as to put out a great bunch of white roses at his window," and several visitors of both sexes came wearing the same rebellious badges. But again the keepers pulled them out and threw them on the floor.

In all these disturbances Captain Silk was a ringleader. He is continually ready to make a noise. Now he swears revenge upon the keeper for not allowing supper to be carried in to him and his "conrogues" after 10 P.M.; now he incites other prisoners to riot. "They are for the most part very drunk and rude, so that it was with great difficulty that they were got to their rooms by one o'clock in the morning." Next day Captain Silk continues his insolence. He threatens Mr. Smith for refusing to pass in visitors after regulated hours. Again he and his companions are drunk and insolent, and cannot be got to their rooms till the same late hour. A night or two later they crowded about the doors when they were opened, cursing and assaulting the person who rang the night-bell. Captain Silk, as before, encouraged them, and to provoke them further, when the bell sounded cried out, "Get up, ye slaves, and go."

Sadder moments soon supervened. The trials were proceeding, and already the law had condemned several. Among the first to suffer were Colonel Oxborough and Mr. Gascoigne: the latter was offered his pardon on conditions which he rejected, and both began to make great preparations for "their great change." Colonel Oxborough, who lay in the condemned hold, behaved with an astonishing serenity of mind; and when his friends expressed their concern in tears, he gravely rebuked them, showing an easiness very unaccustomed in the bravest minds under such a sentence. Next an order of the court came down for the execution of twenty-four more who had been condemned, and "universal sorrow" prevailed in the gaol. Parson Paul,[98] one of the number, was "so dejected he could not eat;" most of the other prisoners retired to their apartments to vent their grief, and a vast number of their friends in tears came to condole with them. After this all were busy with petitions to the court. Some were immediately successful. Handsome young Archibald Bolair was discharged, "at which Lady Faulconbridge, his supposed benefactress, went out with a smiling countenance." Next night he returned in his kilt to visit his friends, but was denied entrance. That same midnight there were great shouts of joy in the prison: a reprieve had come down for all but Parson Paul and Justice Hall,[99] both of whom were led next day to Tyburn. Neither would admit the ministrations of the Ordinary, to whom they "behaved rudely," and they were attended at the place of execution by priests of their own stamp in a lay habit. They (the condemned) were hardened to the highest degree, says their implacable opponent, and gave free vent to their treason in seditious speeches at the gallows.

Great consternation prevailed after these executions. It was greatly increased by the known displeasure of the Government at the demeanour of some of the condemned at Tyburn. But the king (George I.) was now gone on a visit to Hanover; and the Prince of Wales, as regent, was pleased to put an end to the further effusion of blood. Rumours of an Act of Indemnity were spread abroad, and abundance of visitors came to congratulate the prisoners on their approaching release. But the happy day being still postponed, the Jacobites became turbulent once more; Mr. Pitt, the old governor, who had been tried for neglect in allowing Mr. Forster and others to escape, had been acquitted, upon which the Lord Mayor and sheriffs recalled Messrs. Carleton Smith and Russell. The latter delivered up their charge, "having performed it so well that not one prisoner had escaped." But Mr. Pitt was again unfortunate; and suffering another man (Flint) to escape, the court of aldermen resolved to reinstate Smith and Russell. This gave great dudgeon to the rebels in the press-yard, who soon proved very refractory, refusing to be locked up at the proper time. Then they made bitter reflections on the advice given to the new keepers in the 'Flying Post,' a Whiggish organ, who were, as the author of the 'Secret History' observes sarcastically, "so inhuman, that they would let none of the rebels make their escape, either in the habits of women, footmen, or parsons." It was difficult for the keepers not to give cause of offence. Their prisoners were angry with them because they would not sit down and drink with them, "as the old ones used to do;" even upon the bribe, offered when the indemnity loomed large, of swallowing a bumper to King George. Captain Silk was troublesome as ever. One Sunday he cursed and swore prodigiously because the doors had been shut during divine service, and his roaring companions could not have access to him. Another time the prisoners insulted the keepers, asking them why they carried arms? The Jacobites declared they could not endure the sight since the battle of Preston. Just about now the keepers were informed that the rebels intended to do them a mischief—a threat which did not deter them, however, from strictly performing their duty.

Another prisoner added greatly to the trials of the keepers about this period. This was Mr. Freeman, who was committed for firing a pistol in the playhouse when the prince was there. Freeman was continually intoxicated when in gaol. He was also very mischievous, and kept a burning candle by him most part of the night, to the great danger of the prison, especially when in his mad freaks. "He is a lusty, strong, raw-boned man, has a stern, dogged look, as of an obstinate temper when vexed, but fawning and treacherous when pleased." In a day or two Freeman showed the cloven foot. He flew into a violent passion, and beat one of the female servants of the prison, "shutting the door against the keepers, after he had wounded one of them with a fork which he held in one hand, having a knife and pistol in the other." He was overpowered, and carried to the condemned hold, where he was put in irons. His villainous designs there appeared by his setting his handkerchief on fire, and concealing it in his hat near his bed, and it was suspected that he wished to set the gaol on fire, so that the prisoners might have the opportunity to escape. A day later Mr. Freeman "regretted that he had not murdered his keeper in the last scuffle;" and the same day Mr. Menzies and Mr. Nairn did honestly tell the keepers that the prisoners meant to injure them, Freeman's disturbance having been raised "chiefly to that end, and that the female servant he only pretended to assault, so as to make her cry out murder before she was in the least hurt."

Royal clemency was still delayed, and the advancing summer was intensely hot. The close confinement of so many persons in a limited space began to tell seriously on the prisoners. A spotted fever,[100] which had before shown itself with evil effects, reappeared. It had proved fatal to Mr. Pitcairn the previous August, and in the winter Mr. Butler had died of the same. Now it carried off Mr. Kellet, Sir Francis Anderson's man. Mr. Thornton was also attacked, but through the care of his doctors recovered. Next month (June) Mr. David Drummond died, and Mr. Ratcliffe was indisposed. It was generally feared that the distemper would become contagious; whereupon some of the principal inmates, among them Mr. Ratcliffe, the two Mr. Widdingtons, Mr. Murray, and Mr. Seaton, "who is styled by them the Earl of Dumferline," petitioned the Prince Regent and council for enlargement to more commodious prisons. The king's physicians were accordingly despatched to the prison to inquire into its sanitary condition. Their report was that no contagious distemper existed. The matter was therefore ordered to stand until his Majesty's pleasure should be known at his arrival from Hanover. George I. soon afterwards returned, and signified his orders for an Act of Grace, which duly passed both Houses of Parliament.

The news of an amnesty was joyfully received in the press-yard. One of the first acts of the prisoners so soon to be set free was to get in a poor fiddler, "whom they set to play tunes adapted to their treasonable ballads;.... but this was so shocking to the keepers that they turned the fiddler out." Next the prisoners had a badger brought in, and baited him with dogs. Other already pardoned rebels came and paid ceremonious visits, such as Mr. Townley, who appeared with much pomp and splendour after his discharge from the Marshalsea. Several clergymen also visited; and a noted common council man, whose friends stood a bowl of punch that night in Captain Silk's room. The State prisoners were soon "very busy in getting new rigging, and sending away their boxes and trunks; so that they looked like so many people removing from their lodgings and houses on quarter-day." On July 4th a member of Parliament came to assure Mr. Grierson that the Act of Indemnity would surely pass in a few days. This occasioned great joy. A fortnight later the pardon was promulgated, and all the prisoners remaining were taken to Westminster to plead the Act, "where many were so very ungrateful that they refused to kneel or speak out in asking the king's pardon till they were forced to it."[101]

According to this last-quoted writer, the rebels in Newgate were not of exemplary character. "Their daily practice in prison was profane swearing, drunkenness, gluttony, gaming, and lasciviousness." That such was permitted speaks volumes as to the shameful negligence of prison rule in those unsettled times.

There were other rebel prisoners, who do not seem to have benefited by this act of grace, and who remained much longer in prison. It is recorded in the 'Weekly Journal' of January 24th, 1727, that the King (George I.) had pardoned another batch of Jacobites, who had been capitally convicted in the first year of his reign for levying war against him. The pardoned traitors were Robert Stuart, of Appin; Alexander Macdonald, of Glencoe; Grant, of Glenmorrison; Maclimmin, of that Ilk; Mackenzie, of Fairburn; Mackenzie, of Dachmalnack; Chisholm, of Shatglass; Mackenzie, of Ballumakie; MacDougal, of Lorne; and two others, more notable than all the rest, "James, commonly called Lord, Ogilvie," and "Robert Campbell, *alias* Macgregor, commonly called Rob Roy." They had been under durance in London, for it is added that "on Tuesday last they were carried from *Newgate* to *Gravesend*, to be put on ship-board for transportation to Barbadoes." Rob Roy marching handcuffed to Lord Ogilvie through the London streets from Newgate to the prison barge at Blackfriars, and thence to Gravesend, is an incident that has escaped the notice of Walter Scott, and all of Rob's biographers. The barge-load of Highland chiefs, and of some thieves, seems, however, to have been pardoned, and allowed to return home.

Before leaving the press-yard some reference must be made to certain political "suspects" who were lodged therein for terms varying from nineteen to forty years. Their case is remarkable, as being the last instance of the suspension of the Habeas Corpus Act in England, with the full knowledge and sanction of Parliament, and in spite of repeated strongly-urged petitions from the prisoners for release. Their names were John Bernardi, Robert Cassilis, Robert Meldrum, Robert Blackburne, and James Chambers. Of these, the first-named, Major Bernardi, is the old officer referred to by the writer of the 'History of the Press-Yard.'[102] Bernardi has told his own story in a volume penned in Newgate, and "printed by J. Newcomb, in the Strand, for the benefit of the author, 1729." Macaulay is disposed to discredit the version given by Bernardi, although there is a certain air of truthfulness in the prisoner's narrative. Bernardi begins at the beginning. He was of Italian extraction, he tells us. His ancestors had been in the diplomatic service. Count Philip de Bernardi, his great-grandfather, came to England with a Genoese embassy. Francis Bernardi, son of the former, and father of Major John, was also accredited to Charles II. on the restoration, but when replaced as resident, being English born, he preferred to live and die in the land of his birth. According to his son, he was a stern parent, ready to award him penal treatment, with imprisonment for trifles, "in a little dark room or dungeon allowing him only bread and small beer when so confined." By-and-by John ran away from home, and through the favour of Lady Fisher was employed as a "listed soldier" in a company at Portsmouth when barely fifteen years of age. A year or two later his god-father, Colonel Anselme, took him to the Low Countries, where by gallant conduct in the wars he gained an ensigncy from the Prince of Orange. At the siege of Maestrict he lost an eye, and was badly wounded in the arm. When scarcely twenty he was promoted to a lieutenancy, and eight years later obtained a company in Colonel Monk's regiment. He was now, by his own account, arrived "at a high pitch of fortune."

He was a captain at twenty-seven in an established service, was personally well known to the Prince of Orange (afterwards William III.), had married well, and was, with his wife's fortune, in the receipt of "a considerable income."

James II., on coming to the throne, summoned home all English officers in the service of the States. Among the few who obeyed was Major Bernardi, and he then gave up, as he says, a certainty for an uncertainty. Very soon his former chief, the Prince of Orange, replaced James upon the throne, and Bernardi, unfortunately for himself, thereafter espoused the wrong side. He refused to sign the "association put about by General Kirk," under which all officers bound themselves to stand by William "against all persons whomsoever," and proceeded to France to throw in his lot with the exiled king. When James embarked for Ireland, Bernardi followed in command of a party of newly-organized adherents. He was at several of the engagements in that island, and was presently commissioned Major. After that he went to the Highlands with Seaforth Mackenzie on a special mission, and on his return had the honour of dining at the same table with the king. A second mission to Scotland followed, after which Bernardi made his way south, and escaping great perils by the way, reached London, meaning, when he had disposed of horses and effect, to cross over to Flanders. At Colchester, however, from which he hoped to reach easily a port of embarkation, he was seized and committed on suspicion, first to the town gaol, then to that of Chelmsford. After being much harassed he at length obtained his release, only to be soon involved in still greater trouble.

To his great misfortune he now fell in with one Captain Rookwood. It was about the time of the discovery of the assassination plot, of which Major Bernardi declares that he was in absolute ignorance till he heard of it like the rest of the world. He was by chance in the company of Captain Rookwood at a tavern, and was with him arrested on suspicion of being "evil-minded men." While in the Compter Rookwood incautiously revealed his own identity, and was lost. Rookwood seems at the same time to have unintentionally betrayed Bernardi, whose name had, it appears, and in spite of his protestations of perfect innocence, been included in a proclamation. The inference is that the Government was in the possession of certain information that Bernardi was mixed up in the plot.[103] Both men were carried before the Council, and committed close prisoners to Newgate, "loaded with heavy irons, and put into separate dismal, dark, and stinking apartments." Rookwood was speedily condemned and executed at Tyburn. Bernardi remained in prison without trial, until after Sir John Fenwick had suffered. Then with his fellow-prisoners he was taken to the Old Bailey to be bailed out, but at the instance of the Treasury solicitor, who "whispered the Judges upon the Bench," they were relegated to Newgate, and a special Act passed rapidly through the House to keep them for another twelve-month on the plea of waiting for further evidence against them. A second Act was passed prolonging the imprisonment for another year; then a third, to confine them during the king's pleasure. On the death of the king (William III.), a fresh Act extended the imprisonment during the reign of Queen Anne. During this long lapse of time repeated applications were made to Judges, but the release of the prisoners was always bitterly opposed by the law officers. Bernardi's doctors certified that imprisonment was killing him; he suffered from fits and the constant trouble of an old wound. Nevertheless he lived on; and when in his sixty-eighth year he married, in Newgate, a second, virtuous, kind, and loving wife, who proved "a true help-meet," supporting him by her good management, and keeping his heart from breaking in the "English Bastille." Bernardi had ten children born in Newgate of this second wife. The imprisonment continued through the reigns of

George I. and II. Frequent petitions were unheeded, and finally Bernardi died in Newgate in 1736, the last survivor, after forty years' incarceration, and aged eighty-two.

EXECUTIONS

Reasons for legal punishments—Early forms: branding, mutilation, whipping, the pillory, and stocks—Penalties for females: the ducking-stool, branks, and scourge—Capital punishment universal—Methods of inflicting death—Awful cruelties—The English custom—Pressing to death—Major Strangways—Spiggot and Burnworth—Abolition of this punishment—Decapitation and strangulation—The guillotine and gallows—Places of execution in London: Smithfield, St. Giles, Tower Hill, Tyburn—Derivation of Tyburn—Site of Tyburn gallows—Tyburn a generic title—An execution in 1662: that of Colonel Turner—Crowds at executions—Fashionable folk attend—George Selwyn—Breakfast party at Newgate—Ribald conduct of the mob at executions—That of Earl Ferrers and of Sheppard—Demeanour of condemned: effrontery, or abject terror—Improper customs long retained—St. Giles' Bowl—Saddler of Bawtry—Smoking at Tyburn—Spiritual attentions of Ordinary not always devoted—Amateur preachers and others assist—Richard Dove's bequest—The hangman and his office—Resuscitation—Early cases—Sir William Petty's operation—Tyburn proces-

sion continues—Supported by Dr. Johnson—Sheriffs suggest discontinuance—Their reasons—The front of Newgate substituted as the scene of execution.

THE universal instinct of self-preservation underlies the whole theory of legal punishments. Society, since men congregated together, has claimed through its rulers to inflict penalties upon those who have broken the laws framed for the protection of all. These penalties have varied greatly in all ages and in all times. They have been based on different principles. Many, especially in ruder and earlier times, have been conceived in a vindictive spirit; others, notably those of the Mosaic law, were retaliatory, or aimed at restitution. All, more or less, were intended also to deter from crime. The criminal had generally to pay in his person or his goods. He was either subjected to physical pain applied in degrading, often ferociously cruel ways, and endured mutilation, or was branded, tortured, put to death; he was mulcted in fines, deprived of liberty, or adjudged as a slave to indemnify by manual labour those whom he had wronged. Imprisonment as practised in modern times has followed from the last-named class of punishments. Although affecting the individual, and in many of its phases with brutal and reckless disregard for human suffering, it can hardly be styled a purely personal punishment, upon which I propose now more particularly to treat, and the present chapter will deal only with penalties corporeal.

Taking first the punishments which fell short of death, those most common in this country until comparatively recent times, were branding, mutilation, dismemberment, whipping, and degrading public exposure. Branding was often carried out with circumstances of atrocious barbarity. Vagabonds were marked with the letter V, idlers and masterless men with the letter S, betokening a condemnation to slavery; any church brawler lost his ears, and for a second offence might be branded with the letter F, as a fraymaker and fighter. Sometimes the penalty was to bore a hole of the compass of an inch through the gristle of the right ear. Branding was the commutation of a capital sentence on clerk convicts, or persons allowed benefit of clergy, and it was inflicted upon the brawn of the left thumb, the letter M being used in murder cases, the letter T in others. In the reign of William and Mary, when the privilege of benefit of clergy was found to be greatly abused, an Act was passed, by which the culprit was branded or "burnt in the most visible part of the left cheek nearest the nose." Mutilation was an ancient Saxon punishment, no doubt perpetuating the Mosaic law of retaliation which claimed an eye for an eye, a tooth for a tooth, a limb for a limb. William the Conqueror adopted it in his penal code. It was long put in force against those who broke the forestry laws, coiners, thieves, and such as failed to prove their innocence by ordeal. Although almost abandoned by the end of the sixteenth century, the penalty of mutilation, extending to the loss of the right hand, still continued to be punishment for murder and bloodshed within the limits of a royal residence. The most elaborate ceremonial was observed. All the hierarchy of court officials attended; there was the sergeant of the woodyard, the master cook to hand the dressing-knife, the sergeant of the poultry, the yeoman of the scullery with a fire of coals, the sergeant farrier who heated and delivered the searing irons, which were applied by the chief surgeon after the dismemberment had been effected. Vinegar, basin, and cloths were handed to the operator by the groom of the salcery, the sergeant of the ewry, and the yeoman of the chandrey. "After the hand had been struck off and the stump seared, the sergeant of the pantry offered bread, and the sergeant of the cellar a pot of red wine, of which the sufferer was to partake with what appetite he might."[104] Readers of Sir Walter Scott will remember how Nigel Olifaunt, in the 'Fortunes of Nigel,' was threatened with the loss of his hand for having committed a breach of privilege in the palace of Greenwich and its precincts. Pistols are found on his person when he accidentally meets and accosts James I. For the offence he may be prosecuted; so Sir Mungo Malagrowther complacently informs him, *usque ad mutilationem* even to dismemberation. The occasion serves the garrulous knight to refer to a recent performance, "a pretty pageant when Stubbs the Puritan was sentenced to mutilation for writing and publishing a seditious pamphlet against Elizabeth. With Stubbs, Page the publisher also suffered. They lost their right hands," the wrist being divided by a cleaver driven through the joint by the force of a mallet. "I remember," says the historian Camden, [105] "being then present, that Stubbs, when his right hand was cut off, plucked off his hat with his left, and said with a loud voice, 'God save the Queen.' The multitude standing about was deeply silent, either out of horror of this new and unwonted kind of punishment, or out of commiseration towards the man...." The process of mutilation was at times left to the agonized action of the culprit: as in the brutal case of one Penedo, who in 1570, for counterfeiting the seal of the Court of Queen's Bench, was twice put in the pillory on market-day in Cheapside. The first day one of his ears was to be nailed to the pillory in such a manner that he should be compelled "by his own proper motion" to tear it away; and on the second day he was to lose his other ear in the same cruel fashion. William Prynne, it will be remembered, also lost his ears on the pillory, but at the hands of the executioner. The Earl of Dorset, in giving the sentence of the Star Chamber Court, asked his fellow-judges "whether he should burn him in the forehead, or slit him in the nose?... I should be loth he should escape with his ears; ... therefore I would have him branded in the forehead, slit in the nose, and his ears cropt too." Having suffered all this on the pillory, he was again punished three years later, when he lost the remainder of his ears, and was branded with the letters S. L. (seditious libeller) on each cheek. Dr. Bastwick and others were similarly treated.[106] Prynne was a voluminous writer, and is said to have produced some two hundred volumes in all. A contemporary, who saw him in the pillory at Cheapside, says "they burnt his huge volumes under his nose, which almost suffocated him."

Although mutilations and floggings were frequently carried out at the pillory, that well-known machine was primarily intended as a means of painful and degrading exposure, and not for the infliction of physical torture. The pillory is said to have existed in this country before the Norman Conquest, and it probably dates from times much more remote. The ετηλη of the Greeks, the pillar on which offenders were publicly exhibited, seems to have been akin to the pillory, just as the κυφων, or wooden collar, was the prototype of the French *carcan* or iron circlet which was riveted around the culprit's neck, and attached by a chain to the post or pillory. With us the pillory or "stretch neck" was at first applied only to fraudulent traders, perjurers, forgers, and so forth; but as years passed it came to be more exclusively the punishment of those guilty of infamous crimes, amongst whom were long included rash writers who dared to express their opinions too freely before the days of freedom of the press. Besides Prynne, Leighton, Burton, Warton, and Bastwick, intrepid John Lilburne so suffered, under the Star Chamber decree, which prohibited the printing of any book without a license from the Archbishop of Canterbury, the Bishop of London, or the authorities of the two universities. Daniel Defoe again, who was pilloried in 1703 for his pamphlet. 'The Shortest Way with the Dissenters.' Defoe gave himself up, and was pilloried first in Cheapside, and afterwards in the Temple. The mob so completely sympathized with him, that they covered him with flowers, drank his health, and sang his

'Ode to the Pillory' in chorus. Dr. Shebbeare was pilloried in 1759, for his 'Letters to the People of England.' But he found a friend in the under-sheriff, Mr. Beardmore, who took him to the place of penitence, in a state-coach, and allowed a footman in rich livery to hold an umbrella over the doctor's head, as he stood in the pillory. Beardmore was afterwards arraigned for neglect of duty, found guilty, and sentenced to fine and imprisonment.

In 1765, Williams the publisher, who reprinted Wilkes' 'North Briton,' stood in the pillory in Palace Yard for an hour. For the moment he became popular. He arrived in a hackney-coach numbered 45,[107] attended by a vast crowd. He was cheered vociferously as he mounted the pillory with a sprig of laurel in each hand; and a gentleman present made a collection of two hundred guineas for him in a purple purse adorned with orange ribbons. In front of the pillory the mob erected a gallows, and hung on it a boot, with other emblems, intended to gibbet the unpopular minister Lord Bute. Williams was conducted from the pillory amid renewed acclamations, and the excitement lasted for some days. Lampoons and caricatures were widely circulated. Several street ballads were also composed, one of which began:

"Ye sons of Wilkes and Liberty,
Who hate despotic sway,
The glorious Forty-Five now crowns
This memorable day.
And to New Palace Yard let us go, let us go."

Lord Dundonald in 1814 was actually sentenced to the pillory, but the Government shrank from inflicting the punishment upon that much wronged naval hero. The pillory ceased to be a punishment, except for perjury, in 1815, but was not finally abolished until 1837, and as late as 1830 one Dr. Bossy suffered on it for perjury.

The earliest form of pillory was simply a post erected in a cross-road by the lord of the manor, as a mark of his seigneury. [108] It bore his arms, and on it was a collar, the *carcan* already mentioned, by which culprits were secured. This was in course of time developed, and the pillory became a cross-piece of wood fixed like a sign-board at the top of a pole, and placed upon an elevated platform. In this cross were three holes, one for the head, the other two for the wrists. The cross-piece was in two halves, the upper turning on a hinge to admit the culprit's head and hands, and closed with a padlock when the operation of insertion was completed. A more elaborate affair, capable of accommodating a number of persons, is figured in mediæval woodcuts, but this sort of pillory does not appear to have been very generally used. The curious observer may still see specimens in England of this well-known instrument of penal discipline, one is preserved in the parish church of Rye, Sussex, another is in the museum at Brighton.

The stocks served like the pillory to hold up offenders to public infamy. The first authentic mention of them is in a statute of Edward III., by which they were to be applied to unruly labourers. Soon after this they were established by law in every village, often near the parish church. They were the punishment for brawling, drunkenness, vagrancy, and all disorderly conduct. Wood-stealers or "hedge-tearers" were set in the stocks about the year 1584 for a couple of days with the stolen wood in front of them. The story goes that Cardinal Wolsey, when a young parish priest, was put in the stocks at Lymington by Sir Amyas Poulett, for having exceeded at a village feast. The old chap's books contain numerous references to the stocks of course. Welch Taffy, "the unfortunate traveller," was put into the stocks for calling a justice of the peace a "boobie;" and "Simple Simon," when he interfered in a butter-woman's quarrel, was adjudged to be drunk and put into the stocks between the two viragoes, who scolded him all the time. The story of Lord Camden when a young barrister having a desire to try the stocks, and his being left in them by an absent-minded friend for the part of the day, is probably well known. The stocks were not wholly abolished till a few years ago.[109] The Stokesley stocks were used within thirty years of the present time, and as late as 1860 one John Gambles of Stanningly was sentenced to sit in the stocks for six hours for Sunday gambling, and actually endured his punishment.[110] Stocks are still to be seen at Heath near Wakefield, Painswick in Gloucestershire, and other places. In all cases the physical discomfort of the stocks no less than that of the pillory, was generally aggravated by the rude horseplay of a jeering and actively offensive mob. A reference to the inconvenient attentions of the bystanders at such an exhibition will be found in an old chapbook, entitled 'The True Trial of the Understanding,' in which among other riddles the following is given:

Promotion lately was bestowed
Upon a person mean and small:
Then many persons to him flowed,
Yet he returned no thanks at all.
But yet their hands were ready still
To help him with their kind good will.

The answer is, a man pelted in the pillory.

Worse sometimes happened, and in several cases death ensued from ill-usage in the pillory. Thus when John Waller, *alias* Trevor, was pilloried in 1732, in Seven Dials, for falsely accusing innocent men, so as to obtain the reward given on the conviction of highwaymen, so great was the indignation of the populace that they pelted him to death. The coroner's inquest returned a verdict of wilful murder, but against persons unknown. In 1763 a man who stood in the pillory at Bow, for an unnatural crime, was killed by the mob. Ann Marrow, who had been guilty of the strange offence of disguising herself as a man, and as such marrying three different women, was sentenced to three months' imprisonment, and exposure on the pillory, at Charing Cross. So great was the resentment on the populace, principally those of the female sex, that they pelted her till they put out both her eyes.[111]

No account of the minor physical punishments formerly inflicted would be complete without reference to the methods of coercing ill-conditioned females. These were mostly of the same character as the pillory and stocks. Chief among them was the Ducking or Cucking-stool, "a scourge for scolds," and once as common in every parish as the stocks. Other varieties of it were known under the names of Tumbrell, the Gumstole, the Triback, the Trebucket, and the Reive. It may be described briefly as consisting of a chair or seat fixed at the end of a long plank, which revolved on a pivot, and by some simple application of leverage upset the occupant of the chair into a pond or stream. Mr. Cole, 1782, describes one which was hung to a beam in the middle of a bridge; the Leominster stool which is still preserved is a plank upon a low substantial framework, having the seat at one end, and working like an ordinary see-saw. That at Wooton Basset was of the tumbrell order, and was a framework on a pair of wheels, with shafts at one end, the stool being at the other. In this, as in the Leicester "scolding cart," and other forms of tumbrels, the culprit was paraded through the town before immersion. The punishment was primarily intended for scolds, shrews, and "curst queens," but it was also applied to female brewers and bakers who brewed bad ale, and sold bad bread. It was inflicted pursuant to sentence in open court, but in some parts the bailiffs had the power within their own jurisdictions, and the right of gallows, tumbrell, and pillory was often claimed by lords of the Manor. The greatest antiquity is claimed for this sort of punishment. Bowine declares that it was used by the Saxons, by whom it was called "Cathedra in qua rixosæ mulieres sedentes aquæ demergebantur." No doubt the ducking was often roughly and cruelly carried out. We have in the frontispiece of an old chapbook, which relates how "an old woman was drowned in Ratcliffe highway," a pictorial representation of the ceremony of ducking, and it is stated that she met her death by being dipped too often or too long. That the instrument was in general use through the kingdom is proved by numerous entries in ancient records. Thus Lysons, in his 'Environs of London,' states that at a court of the Manor of Edgware in 1552 the inhabitants were presented for not having a tumbril and a ducking-stool as laid down by law. In the Leominster town records the bailiff and chamberlains are repeatedly brought up and fined either for not providing "gumstoles" or not properly repairing them, while in the same and other records are numerous statements of bills paid to carpenters for making or mending these instruments. The use of them moreover was continued to very recent times. A women was ducked under Kingston Bridge for scolding in 1745. At Manchester, Liverpool, and other Lancashire towns the stool was in use till the commencement of this century. So it was at Scarborough, where the offender was dipped into the water from the end of the old pier. But the latest inflictions seemingly were at Leominster, where in 1809 a woman named Jenny Pipes was paraded and ducked near Kerwater Bridge, while another Sarah Leeke was wheeled round the town in 1817, but not ducked, the water being too low.

The ducking-stool was not always an effectual punishment. It appears from the records of the King's Bench that in the year 1681 Mrs. Finch, a notorious scold, who had been thrice ducked for scolding, was a fourth time sentenced for the same offence, and sentenced to be fined and imprisoned. Other measures were occasionally taken which were deemed safer, but which were hardly less cruel. The "branks," or bridle, for gossips and scolds, was often preferred to the ducking-stool, which endangered the health, and moreover gave the culprit's tongue free play between each dip. The branks was a species of iron mask, with a gag so contrived as to enter the mouth and forcibly hold down the unruly member. "It consisted of a kind of crown or framework of iron, which was locked upon the head and was armed in front with a gag,—a plate or a sharp-cutting knife or point."[112] Various specimens of this barbarous instrument are still extant in local museums, that in the Ashmolean at Oxford being especially noticeable, as well as that preserved in Doddington Park, Lincolnshire. The branks are said to have been the invention of agents of the Spanish Inquisition, and to have been imported into this country from the Low Countries, whither it had travelled from Spain.

The brutality of the stronger and governing to the weaker and subject sex was not limited to the ducking-stool and branks. It must be remembered with shame in this more humane age[113] that little more than a hundred years ago women were publicly whipped at the whipping-post by the stocks, or at any cart's tail. The fierce statute against vagrants of Henry VIII.'s and Elizabeth's reign made no distinction of sex, and their ferocious provisions to the effect that offenders "should be stripped naked from the middle upwards, and whipped till the body should be bloody," long continued in force. Men with their wives and children were flogged publicly, and sometimes by the order of the clergyman of the parish. Girls of twelve and thirteen, aged women of sixty, all suffered alike; women "distracted," in other words out of their minds, were arrested and lashed; so were those that had the small pox, and all who walked about the country and begged.[114] The constable's charge for whipping was fourpence, but the sum was increased latterly to a shilling. The whipping-post was often erected in combination with the stocks. A couple of iron clasps were fixed to the upright which supported the stocks, to take the culprit's hands and hold him securely while he was being lashed. A modification of this plan has long been used at Newgate for the infliction of corporal punishment, and it may still be seen in the old ward at the back of the middle yard.

Ferocious as were most of the methods I have detailed of dealing with offenders against the law, they generally, except by accident, fell short of death. Yet were there innumerable cases in those uncompromising and unenlightened ages in which death alone would be deemed equal to the offences. Rulers might be excused perhaps if they were satisfied with nothing less than a criminal's blood. As Maine says,[115] "The punishment of death is a necessity of society in certain stages of the civilizing process. There is a time when an attempt to dispense with it baulks two of the great instincts which lie at the root of all penal law. Without it the community neither feels that it is sufficiently revenged on the criminal, nor thinks that the example of his punishment is adequate to deter others from imitating him." Hence all penal legislation in the past included some form of inflicting the death sentence. These have differed in all ages and in all climes: about some there was a brutal simplicity; others have been marked by great inventiveness, great ingenuity, much refinement of cruelty. Offenders have been stoned, beaten, starved to death; they have been flayed alive, buried alive, cast headlong from heights, torn to pieces by wild animals, broken on the wheel, crucified, impaled, burnt, boiled, beheaded, strangled, drowned. They have been killed outright or by inches, enduring horrible agonies;[116] after death their bodies have been dismembered and disembowelled, as a mark of degradation. Irresponsible tyrants went further than lawgivers in devising pains. The Sultan Mechmed cut men in the middle, through the diaphragm, thus causing them to die two deaths at once. It is told of Crœsus that he caused a person who had offended him to be scratched to death by a friller's carding-combs. What the Vaivod of Transylvania did to the Polish leader, George Jechel, may be read in the pages of Montaigne. The frightful barbarity to which he and his followers were subjected need not be repeated here.

The tender mercies of continental nations towards criminals may be realized by a reference to one or two of their contrivances for the infliction of death. The Iron Coffin of Lissa, for example, wherein the convicted person lay for days awaiting death from the fell pressure of the heavily-weighted lid, which slid down slowly, almost imperceptibly, upon his helpless frame; or the Virgin of Baden Baden, the brazen statue whose kiss meant death with frightful tortures, the unhappy culprit being commanded to prostrate himself and kiss the statue, but as he raised his lips a trap door opened at his feet, and he fell through on to a spiked wheel, which was set in motion by his fall. There was the *chambre à crucer*, a short hollow chest lined with sharp stones, in which the victim was packed and buried alive; or the "bernicles," a mattrass which clutched the sufferer tight, while his legs were broken by heavy logs of wood; or the long lingering death in the iron cages of Louis XI., the occupant of which could neither sit, stand, or lie down. Again, the devilish tortures inflicted upon the murderers Ravaillac and Damiens caused a shudder throughout Europe. Ravaillac was burnt piecemeal, flesh was torn from him by red-hot pincers, scalding oil and molten lead were poured upon his bleeding wounds, he was drawn and dismembered by horses while still alive, and only received his *coup de grace* from the sticks and knives of the hellish bystanders, who rushed in to finish more savagely what the executioner had been unable to complete. As for Damiens, the process followed was identical, but the details preserved of an event nearer our own time are more precise and revolting. He was fastened down upon a platform by iron gyves, one across his breast, the other just above his thighs; his right hand was then burnt with brimstone, he was pinched with red-hot pincers, after which boiling oil, molten wax, rosin, and lead were poured upon his wounds. His limbs were next tightly tied with cords, a long and protracted operation, during which he must have suffered renewed and exquisite torture; four stout, young, and vigorous horses were attached to the cords, and an attempt made to tear his limbs asunder, but only with the result of "extending his joints to a prodigious length," and it was necessary to second the efforts of the horses by cutting the principal sinews of the sufferer. Soon after this the victim expired. Then his body was burnt and the ashes scattered to the winds.

In this country the simpler firms of executions have generally obtained. The stake was no doubt in frequent use at certain periods for particular offences, but the axe and the rope were long the most common instruments of despatch. Death was otherwise inflicted, however. Drowning is mentioned by Stowe as the fate of pirates, and a horrible method of carrying out capital punishment remained in force until 1772. Pressing to death, or the *peine forte et dure*, was a development of the ancient prison *forte et dure* the punishment of those who refused "to stand to the law;" in other words, stood mute, and refused to plead to a charge. Until the reign of Henry IV. such persons were condemned to penance and perpetual imprisonment, but the penance meant confinement in a narrow cell and absolute starvation.[117] Some evaded the dread consequences, and therefore a more awful form of torture was introduced with the object of compelling the silent to speak. An accused person who persistently stood mute was solemnly warned three times of the penalty that waited on his obstinacy, and given a few hours for consideration. If the prisoner continued contumacious, the following sentence was passed upon him, or her:

"That you be taken back to the prison whence you came to a low dungeon, into which no light can enter; that you be laid on your back on the bare floor with a cloth round your loins, but elsewhere naked; that there be set upon your body a weight of iron as great as you can bear—and greater; that you have no sustenance, save on the first day three morsels of the coarsest bread, on the second day three draughts of stagnant water from the pool nearest to the prison door, on the third day again three morsels of bread as before, and such bread and such water alternately from day to day till you die."

The press was a form of torture with this difference that, when once applied, there was seldom any escape from it. The practice of tying the thumbs with whipcord was another form of torture inflicted to oblige an accused person to plead, and in force as late as the reign of Queen Anne.

Regarding the *peine forte et dure* Holinshed says, that when accused felons stood mute of malice on arraignment they were pressed to death "by heavy weights laid upon a board that lieth over their breasts and a sharp stone under their backs, and these commonly hold their peace thereby to save their goods unto their wives and children, which if they were condemned should be confiscated to the prince." There are continual references to the *peine forte et dure* in the legal records throughout the fifteenth to the seventeenth centuries. In 1605 Walter Calverly, Esq., of Calverly in Yorkshire, who was arraigned for the murder of his wife and two children, stood mute, and was pressed to death in York Castle. Another notable instance of the application of this fearful punishment was in the case of Major Strangways, who was arraigned in February 1657-8 for the murder of his brother-in-law Mr. Fussell. He refused to plead unless he was assured that if condemned he might be shot as his brother-in-law had been. In addition he said that he wished to preserve his estate from confiscation. Chief Justice Glyn reasoned with him at length, but could not alter his decision, and he was duly sentenced to the *peine forte et dure*. The sentence ran that he was to be put into a mean room where no light could enter, and where he was to be laid upon his back with his body bare; his legs and arms were to be stretched out with cords, and then iron and stone were to be laid upon him "as much as he could bear—and more;" his food the first day was to be three morsels of barley bread, and on the second day he was "to drink thrice of water in the channel next to the prison, but no spring or fountain water—and this shall be his punishment till he dies."

Strangways suffered in Newgate. He was attended to the last by five pious divines, and spent much of his time in prayer. On the day of execution he appeared all in white "waistcoat, stockings, drawers, and cap, over which was cast a long mourning-cloak," and so was "guarded down to a dungeon in the press-yard, the dismal place of execution." On his giving the appointed signal, "his mournful attendants performed their dreadful task. They soon perceived that the weight they laid on was not sufficient to put him suddenly out of pain, so several of them added their own weight, that they might sooner release his soul." He endured great agonies. His groans were "loud and doleful," and it was eight or ten minutes before he died. After death his body was exposed to view, and it was seen that an angle of the press had been purposely placed over his heart, so that he might the sooner be deprived of life, "though he was denied what is usual in these cases, to have a sharp piece of timber under his back to hasten execution."

In 1721, Nathaniel Hawes, who had come to be what we should call now-a-days an habitual criminal, and who had been frequently in Newgate, took to the road. After various successful adventures, he stopped a gentleman on Finchley Common, who was more than his match and made him prisoner. He was conveyed to London and committed to Newgate. When brought to the bar of the Old Bailey he refused to plead, giving as his reason that he meant to die as he had lived, like a gentleman.

When he was seized, he said he had on a fine suit of clothes, which he intended to have gone to the gallows in, but they had been taken from him. "Unless they are returned, I will not plead," he went on, "for no one shall say that I was hanged in a dirty shirt and a ragged coat." He was warned what would be the consequences of his contempt of the law, but he obstinately persevered, and was accordingly sentenced to the press. He bore a weight of 250 lbs. for about seven minutes, and then gave in, being unable any longer to bear the pain. On return to Court he pleaded "Not Guilty," but was convicted and sentenced to death. Hawes declared to the last that he was one of Jonathan Wild's victims.

Two years later, William Spiggot and Thomas Phillips, arraigned for highway robbery, refused to plead, and were also sentenced to the press. Phillips, on coming into the press-yard, was affrighted by the apparatus, and begged that he might be taken back to Court to plead, "a favour that was granted him; it might have been denied to him." Spiggot, however, remained obdurate, and was put under the press, where he continued half an hour with a weight to the amount of 350 lbs. on his body; "but, on addition of the 50 lbs. more, he likewise begged to plead." Both were then convicted and hanged in the ordinary course of law. Again, Edward Burnworth, the captain of a gang of murderers and robbers which rose into notoriety on the downfall of Wild, was sentenced to the press at Kingston in 1726, by Lord Chief Justice Raymond and Judge Denton. He bore the weight of 1 cwt. 3 qrs. 2 lbs. on his breast for the space of an hour and three minutes, during which time the High-Sheriff who attended him used every argument to induce him to plead, but in vain. Burnworth, all the time, was trying to kill himself by striking his head against the floor. At last he was prevailed on to promise to plead, was brought back to Court, and duly sentenced to death.

The last instance in which the press was inflicted was at Kilkenny in Ireland. A man named Matthew Ryan stood mute at his trial for highway robbery, and was adjudged by the jury to be guilty of "wilful and affected dumbness and lunacy." He was given some days' grace, but still remaining dumb, he was pressed to death in the public market of Kilkenny. As the weights were put upon him the wretched man broke silence and implored that he might be hanged, but the Sheriff could not grant his request.

In 1741 a new press was made and fixed in the press-yard, for the punishment of a highwayman named Cook, but it was not used. The 12th Geo. III. (1772) at length altered the law on this head, and judgment was awarded against mutes as though convicted or they had confessed. In 1778 one so suffered at the Old Bailey. Finally, it was provided by the 7 and 8 Geo. IV., cap. 28, that the Court should enter a plea of "Not Guilty" when the prisoner will not plead.

The principal forms of capital punishment, however, as the derivation of the expression implies, have dealt with the head as the most vulnerable part of the body. Death has been and still is most generally inflicted by decapitation and strangulation. The former, except in France, where it came to be universal, was the most aristocratic method; the latter was long applied only to criminals of the baser sort. Until the invention of the guillotine, culprits were beheaded by sword or axe, and were often cruelly mangled by a bungling executioner. It is asserted by the historian that the executioner pursued the Countess of Salisbury about the scaffold, aiming repeated blows at her, before he succeeded in striking off her head. This uncertainty in result was only ended by the ingenious invention of Dr. Guillotin, the rude germ of which existed long previously in the Scotch "maiden." The regent Morton, who introduced this instrument into Scotland, and who himself suffered by it, is said to have taken it from the Halifax Gibbet.[118] Guillotin's machine was not altogether original, but it owed more to the Italian "Mannaïa" than to the "maiden." Nor, according to Sanson the French headsman, was he the actual inventor of the notorious instrument guillotine, which bears his name. The guillotine was designed by one Schmidt, a German engineer and artificer of musical instruments. Guillotin enthusiastically adopted Schmidt's design, which he strongly recommended in the assembly, declaring that by it a culprit could not suffer, but would only feel a slight freshness on the neck. Louis XVI. was decapitated by the guillotine, as was the doctor, its sponsor and introducer.

Strangulation, whether applied by the bowstring, cord, handkerchief, or drop, is as old as the hills. It was inflicted by the Greeks as an especially ignominious punishment. The "sus per coll." was not unknown in the penal law of the Romans, who were in the habit also of exposing the dead convict upon the gibbet, "as a comfortable sight to his friends and relations."

In London various places have been used for the scene of execution. The spot where a murder had been committed was often appropriately selected as the place of retribution. Execution Dock was reserved for pirates and sea-robbers, Tower Hill for persons of rank who were beheaded. Gallows for meaner malefactors were sometimes erected on the latter place, the right to do so being claimed by the city. In the reign of Edward IV., however, there was a conflict of authority between the king and the corporation on this point. The king's officer set up a scaffold and gallows on Tower Hill, whereupon the Mayor and his brethren complained to the king, who replied, that he had not acted in derogation of the city liberties, and caused public proclamation to be made that the city exercised certain rights on Tower Hill. Executions also took place, according to Pennant, at the Standard in Chepe. Three men were beheaded there for rescuing a prisoner, and in 1351 two fishmongers for some unknown crime. Smithfield had long the dismal honour of witnessing the death-throes of offenders. Between Hozier and Cow Lanes was anciently a large pool called Smithfield Pond or Horse Pool, "from the watering of horses there;" to the southwest lay St. John's Court, and close to it the public gallows on the Town Green. There was a clump of trees in the centre of the green, elms, from which the place of execution was long euphemistically called "The Elms." It was used as such early in the thirteenth century, and distinguished persons, William Fitzosbert, Mortimer, and Sir William Wallace suffered here. About 1413 the gibbet was removed from Smithfield and put up at the north end of a garden wall belonging to St. Giles' Leper Hospital, "opposite the Pound where the Crown Tavern is at present situate, between the end of St. Giles High Street and Hog Lane." But Smithfield must have been still used after the transfer of the gallows to St. Giles. In 1580 another conflict of jurisdiction, this time between the city and the Lieutenant of the Tower. A gibbet was erected in that year in East Smithfield, at Hog Lane, for the execution of one R. Dod, who had murdered a woman in those parts. "But when the sheriff brought the malefactor there to be hanged Sir Owen Hopton, the Lieutenant of the Tower, commanded the sheriff's officers back again to the west side of a cross that stood there," and which probably marked the extent of the liberties of the Tower. Discussion followed. The sheriffs with their prisoner accompanied the Lieutenant into a house to talk it over, "whence after a good stay they all departed." The city gave way—the gibbet was taken down, and the malefactor carried to Tyburn in the same afternoon, where he was executed.

The gallows were no doubt all ready for the business, for Tyburn had been used for executions as long as Smithfield. There were elms also at Tyburn, hence a not uncommon confusion between the two places of execution. Tyebourne has been ingeniously derived from the two words "Tye" and "Bourne," the last a bourne or resting-place to prisoners who were taken bound. Pennant gives the derivation "Tye," the name of a brook or "bourne" which flowed through it. In Mr. Loftie's 'History of London'[119] he points out that the Tyburn of earliest times was a bleak heath situated at the end of the Marylebone Lane as we know it, and which, as it approached the town, had two branches. He suggests that the brook or "Bourne" also divided into two, hence the name "Teo burne" or two streams. Mr. Waller[120] gives the same derivation, and in one of the earliest mention of the Tyburn, an ancient chapter at Westminster, dated 951, it is called Teoburne. There were many Tyburns, however, and as in London the gallows were moved further and further westward of the building of houses, so the name of Tyburn travelled from Marylebone Lane to Edgeware Road. As time passed on it came to be the generic name for all places of execution, and was used at York, Liverpool, Dublin, and elsewhere. Tyburn was a kind of Golgotha, a place of infamy and disgrace. Here certain zealous Protestant gentlemen from the Temple in 1585 hung in chains an image, a Popish image, although styled Robin Hood. When Colonel Blood seized the Duke of Ormond in St. James' Street it was with the avowed intention of carrying him to Tyburn, there to be hanged like a common criminal. The exact position of the Tyburn gallows has been a matter of some controversy. Mr. Robins[121] places the Elms Lane as the first turning to the right in the Uxbridge Road after getting into it from the Grand Junction Road opposite the Serpentine. In Smith's 'History of Marylebone,' he states that the gallows stood on a small eminence at the corner of the Edgeware Road near the turnpike. Other authorities fix the place in Connaught Square; because in a lease of one of the houses, No. 49, granted by the Bishop of London, the fact that the gallows once stood on the site is expressly mentioned in the parchment.

It was commonly reported that many human bones were exhumed between Nos. 6 and 12, Connaught Place, as well as in the garden of Arklow House, which stands at the south-west angle of the Edgeware Road. But Mr. Loftie states as a matter of fact that no such discovery was ever made. A careful but fruitless search at the time Connaught Place was built produced a single bone, probably part of a human jaw-bone, but nothing more. As to Arklow House, the report is distinctly denied by the owner himself. It is, however, pretty certain that at a later date the gallows were kept at a house at the corner of Upper Bryanston Street and the Edgeware Road, in front of which they were erected when required.

A detailed account has been preserved of the execution of Colonel John Turner in 1662, which presents a strange picture of the way in which the extreme penalty of the law was carried out in those days. The scene of the execution was not Tyburn, however, but a place in Leadenhall Street at Lime Street end, a spot near where the deed for which Turner suffered was perpetrated. An immense crowd had gathered, as usual, to witness the convict's death. Pepys was there of course—"up," he tells us; "and after sending my wife to my Aunt Wright's, to get a place to see Turner hanged, I to Change." On his way he met people flocking to the place of execution, and mingling with the crowd, "got," somewhere about St. Mary Axe, "to stand upon the wheel of a cart for a shilling in great pain above an hour before the execution was done. He delaying the time by long discourses and prayers one after another in hopes of a reprieve, but none came." κυφωνTurner was drawn in a cart from Newgate at eleven in the morning, accompanied by the ordinary and another minister, with the sheriffs, keeper of the gaol, and other officials in attendance. On coming to the gibbet he called the executioner to him, and presented him with money in lieu of his clothes, which his friends desired to keep. Then standing in the cart, he addressed the crowd with great prolixity. He dwelt on the cardinal sins; he gave a circumstantial account of his birth, parentage, family history; he detailed his war services as a loyal cavalier, with his promotions and various military rewards. With much proper feeling he sought to lessen the blame attached to his accomplices in the murder, and to exonerate the innocent accused. At intervals in this long discourse he was interrupted now by the sheriffs with broad hints to despatch, now by the ordinary as to the irrelevance and impropriety of such remarks from a man about to die. Again the keeper of Newgate taxed him with other crimes, saying, for example, "Pray, Colonel Turner, do you know nothing of a glass jewel delivered to the Countess of Devonshire in room of another?" or "How about the fire in Lothbury, or the mysterious death of your namesake Turner, who died in your house?"

The condemned man discoursed at great length upon these various points, and was again and again reminded that it would be better for him to prepare for his approaching end. Still he continued his harangue and took a new departure when he remembered the condition of the condemned hold of Newgate, into which he had been cast after coming from the sessions. This hole, as it was called, he characterizes as "a most fearful, sad, deplorable place. Hell itself in comparison cannot be such a place. There is neither bench, stool, nor stick for any person there; they lie like swine upon the ground, one upon another, howling and roaring—it was more terrible to me than this death. I would humbly beg that hole may be provided with some kind of boards, like a court of guard, that a man may lie down upon them in ease; for when they should be best prepared for their ends they are most tormented; they had better take them and hang them as soon as they have their sentence." This aspersion, however, on this part of his gaol the keeper tried to refute by stating that seventeen out of the nineteen poor wretches confined in the hole managed to escape from it, bad as it might be.

But the reprieve for which Turner looked in vain still tarried. He was obliged now to fall to his prayers. These, by the Christian charity of the officials, he was permitted to spin out as long as he pleased. Then he went through the ceremony of distributing alms money for the poor, money for his wife, to be passed on to his young son's schoolmaster. At last he directed the executioner to take the halter off his shoulders, and afterwards, "taking it in his hands, he kissed it, and put it on his neck himself; then after he had fitted the cap and put it on, he went out of the cart up the ladder." The executioner fastened the noose, and "pulling the rope a little, says Turner, What, dost thou mean to choke me? Pray, fellow, give me more rope—what a simple fellow is this! How long have you been executioner, that you know not how to put the knot?" At the very last moment, in the midst of some private ejaculations, espying a gentlewoman at a window nigh, he kissed his hand, saying, "Your servant, mistress," and so he was "turned off," as Pepys says of him, "a comely-looking man he was, and kept his countenance to the last. I was sorry to see him. It was believed there were at least twelve or fourteen thousand people in the street."

There was nothing new in this desire to gloat over the dying agonies of one's fellow-creatures. The Roman matron cried "habet," and turned down her thumb when the gladiator despatched his prostrate foe. Great dignitaries and high-born dames have witnessed without a shudder the tortures of an *auto da fé*; to this day it is the fashion for delicately-nurtured ladies to flock to the Law Courts, and note the varying emotions, from keenest anguish to most brutal *sangfroid*, of notorious murderers on trial.[122] It is not strange, then, that in uncultivated and comparatively demoralized ages the concourse about the gallows should be great, or the conduct of the spectators riotous, brutal, often heartless in the extreme. There was always a rush to see an execution. The crowd was extraordinary when the sufferers were persons of note or had been concerned in any much-talked-of case. Thus at the hanging of Vratz, Borosky, and Stern, convicted of that same murder of Mr. Thynne of which Count Konigsmark was acquitted,[123] an execution which took place in 1682, all London turned out to stare. The gallows had been set up in Pall Mall, the scene of the crime. "Many hundreds of standings were taken up by persons of quality and others." The Duke of Monmouth, one of the most intimate friends of the murdered man, was among the spectators in a balcony close by the gallows, and was the cynosure of every eye, fixing the glance of even one of the convicts, Captain Vratz, who "stared at him fixedly till the drop fell."

The fashion of gazing at these painful exhibitions grew more and more popular. Horace Walpole satirizes the vile practice of thus glorifying criminals. "You cannot conceive," he says to Sir Horace Mann, "the ridiculous rage there is of going to Newgate, the prints that are published of the malefactors, and the memoirs of their lives set forth with as much parade as Marshal Turrenne's" (Boswell). George Selwyn, chief among the wits and beaux of his time, was also conspicuous for his craving for such horrid sights. He was characterized by Walpole as a friend whose passion it was to see coffins, corpses, and executions. Judges going on assize wrote to Selwyn, promising him a good place at all the executions which might take place on their circuits. Other friends kept him informed of approaching events, and bespoke a seat for him, or gave full details of the demeanour of those whose sufferings he had not been privileged to see. Thus Henry St. John writes to tell him of the execution of Waistcott, Lord Harrington's butler, for burglary, which he had attended, with his brother, at the risk of breaking their necks "by climbing up an old rotten scaffolding, which I feared would tumble before the cart drove off with the six malefactors." St. John goes on to say that he had a full view of Waistcott, "who went to the gallows with a white cockade in his hat as an emblem of his innocence, and died with some hardness, as appeared through his trial." Another correspondent, Gilly Williams, gives additional particulars. "The dog died game: went in the cart in a blue and white frock ... and the white cockade. He ate several oranges on his passage, inquired if his hearse was ready, and then, as old Rowe would say, was launched into eternity." Again George Townshend, writing to Selwyn from Scotland of the Jacobites, promises him plenty more entertainment on Tower Hill. The joke went round that Selwyn at the dentist's gave the signal for drawing a tooth by dropping his handkerchief, just as people did to the executioner on the scaffold. He would go anywhere to see men turned off. He was present when Lord Lovat was decapitated, and justified himself by saying that he had made amends in going to the undertaker's to see the head sewn on again. So eager was he to miss no sight worth seeing, that he went purposely to Paris to witness the torture of the unhappy Damiens. "On the day of the execution," Jesse tells us,[124] "he mingled with the crowd in a plain undress suit and bob wig; when a French nobleman, observing the deep interest he took in the scene, and imagining from the plainness of his attire that he must be a person in the humbler ranks of life, resolved that he must infallibly be a hangman. 'Eh bien, monsieur,' he said, 'Êtes vous arrivé pour voir ce spectacle?' 'Oui, monsieur.' 'Vous êtes bourreau?' 'Non, monsieur,' replied Selwyn, 'je n'ai pas l'honneur; je ne suis qu'un amateur.'"

It was in these days, or a little later, when Newgate became the scene of action, that an execution was made the occasion of a small festivity at the prison. The governor gave a breakfast after the ceremony to some thirteen or fourteen people of distinction, and his daughter, a very pretty girl, did the honours of the table. According to her account, few did much justice to the viands: the first call of the inexperienced was for brandy, and the only person with a good appetite for her broiled kidneys, a celebrated dish of hers, was the ordinary. After breakfast was over the whole party adjourned to see the cutting down.

That which was a morbid curiosity among a certain section of the upper classes became a fierce hungry passion with the lower. The scenes upon execution days almost baffle description. Dense crowds thronged the approaches to Newgate and the streets leading to Tyburn or other places of execution. It was a ribald, reckless, brutal mob, violently combative, fighting and struggling for foremost places, fiercely aggressive, distinctly abusive. Spectators often had their limbs broken, their teeth knocked out, sometimes they were crushed to death. Barriers could not always restrain the crowd, and were often borne down and trampled underfoot. All along the route taken by the procession people vented their feelings upon the doomed convicts: cheering a popular criminal to the echo, offering him nosegays or unlimited drink; railing and storming, on the other hand at those they hated or, worse still, despised. When Earl Ferrers was hanged in 1760 the concourse was so great that the procession took three hours to travel from Newgate to Tyburn. Lord Ferrers told the sheriffs that passing through such a multitude was ten times worse than death itself. The same brutality was carried to the foot of the gallows. The mob surged around the cart conversing with the condemned: now encouraging, now upbraiding, anon making him a target for all manner of missiles, and this even at the last awful moment, when the convict was on his knees wrapped in prayer. A woman named Barbara Spencer was beaten down by a stone when actually in supplication upon her knees. When Jack Sheppard, that most popular but most depraved young criminal, was executed, an incredible number of persons was present. The crowd was unruly enough even before execution, but afterwards it grew perfectly frantic. When the body had hung the appointed time, an undertaker ventured to appear with a hearse to carry it off, but being taken for a surgeon's man about to remove Jack Sheppard to the dissecting-room, he incurred the fierce displeasure of the mob. They demolished the hearse, then fell upon the undertaker, who with difficulty escaped with life. After that they seized the body and carried it off, throwing it from hand to hand, until it was covered with bruises and dirt. It was taken as far as the Barley Mow in Long Acre, where it lay some hours, and until it was discovered that the whole thing was a trick devised by a bailiff in the pay of the surgeons, and that the body had been forcibly taken from a person who really intended to bury it. The mob was now excited to frenzy, and a serious riot followed. The police being quite inadequate to quell it, the military were called in, and with the aid of several detachments of Guards the ringleaders were secured. The body was given over to a friend of Sheppard's to bury, the mob dispersed to attend it to St. Martin's Fields, where it was deposited under a guard of soldiers and eventually buried.

While these wild revels were kept up both before and after the execution the demeanour of the doomed partook too often of the general recklessness. The calendars are full of particulars of the manner in which condemned convicts met their fate. Many awaited the extreme penalty, and endured it with callous indifference or flippant effrontery. Only now and again did their courage break down at the eleventh hour, and so prove that it was assumed. A few notable examples may be cited as exhibiting their various moods. Paul Lewis, once a lieutenant in the Royal Navy, but an irreclaimable scoundrel, who took eventually to the road, and was sentenced to death for highway robbery, was boldly unconcerned after sentence. In Newgate he was the leader of the revels: they dubbed him captain, like Macheath; he sat at the head of the table, swore at the parson, and sang obscene songs. It was not until the warrant of execution arrived at the prison, when all bravado evaporated, and he became as abject as he had before appeared hardened. John Rann the highwayman, better known as Sixteen String Jack, had a farewell dinner-party after he was convicted, and while awaiting execution: the company included seven girls; "all were remarkable cheerful, nor was Rann less joyous than his companions." Dick Turpin made elaborate preparations for his execution; purchased a new suit of fustian and a pair of pumps to wear at the gallows, and hired five poor men at ten shillings per head, to follow his cart as mourners, providing them with hat-bands and mourning-bands. Nathaniel Parkhurst who, when in the Fleet for debtors, murdered a fellow-prisoner, demolished a roast fowl at breakfast on the morning of his execution, and drank a pint of liquor with it. Jerry Abershaw was persistently callous from first to last. Returning from court across Kennington Common, he asked his conductors whether that was the spot on which he was to be twisted? His last days in the condemned cell he spent in drawing upon the walls with the juice of black cherries designs of the various robberies he had committed on the road. Abershaw's *sangfroid* did not desert him on the last day. He appeared with his shirt thrown open, a flower in his mouth, and all the way to the gallows carried on an incessant conversation with friends who rode by his side, nodding to others he recognized in the crowd, which was immense.[125] Still more awful was the conduct of Hannah Dagoe, a herculanean Irish woman, who plied the trade of porter at Covent Garden. In Newgate while under sentence she was most defiant. She was the terror of her fellow-prisoners, and actually stabbed a man who had given evidence against her. When the cart was drawn in under the gallows she got her arms loose, seized the executioner, struggled with him, and gave him so violent a blow on the chest that she nearly knocked him down. She dared him to hang her, and tearing off her hat, cloak, and other garments, the hangman's perquisites, distributed them among the crowd in spite of him. After a long struggle he got the rope around her neck. This accomplished, she drew her neckerchief from round her head over her face, and threw herself out of the cart before the signal was given with such violence that she broke her neck and died instantly. Many ancient customs long retained tended to make them more hardened. Chief among these was the offer of strong drink by the way. When the gallows stood at St. Giles it was the rule to offer malefactors about to be hanged a great bowl of ale, "as the last refreshment they were to receive in this life." This drink was long known as the "St. Giles' Bowl." The practice of giving drink was pretty general for years later and in many parts of the country. In Yorkshire at Bawtry, so the story runs, a saddler was on his way to be hanged. The bowl was brought out, but he refused it and went on to his death. Meanwhile his reprieve was actually on the road, and had he lingered to drink time sufficient would have been gained to save him. Hence came the saying that "the saddler of Bawtry was hanged for leaving his ale." Other convicts are mentioned in an uncomplimentary manner because they dared to smoke on their road to the gallows. "Some mad knaves took tobacco all the way as they went to be hanged at Tyburn." This was in 1598, when the use of the weed introduced by Sir Walter Raleigh was still somewhat rare. A hundred years later the misbehaviour was in "impudently calling for sack" and drinking King James' health; after which the convicts affronted the Ordinary at the gallows, and refused his assistance.

There were few who behaved with the decency and self-possession of Lord Ferrers, who went to his shameful death in a suit of white and silver, that, it was said, in which he had been married. He himself provided the white cap to be pulled over his face, and the black silk handkerchief with which his arms were to be bound. His last words were, "Am I right?" and immediately the drop fell. In his case there had been an unseemly wrangle upon the gallows between the executioner and his assistant. Lord Ferrers had given the latter, in mistake for his chief, a fee of five guineas, which the head executioner claimed, and the assistant would not readily surrender. Some were in abject terror till the last act commenced. Thus John Ayliffe, a forger, was in the utmost agonies the night preceding his execution; his agitation producing an intolerable thirst, which he vainly sought to allay by copious draughts of water. Yet his composure quite returned on his road to Tyburn, and he "behaved with decency at the fatal tree." It was just the reverse with Mrs. Meteyard, who with her daughter murdered a parish apprentice. She was in a fit when put into the cart, and she continued insensible all the way to Tyburn. Great efforts were made to restore her, but without avail, and she was in an unconscious state when hanged.

It may be questioned whether that close attention was paid to the spiritual needs of the condemned which is considered indispensable in these more humane days. No doubt many rejected the offers of the ordinary, refusing to attend chapel, pretending to belong to out-of-the-way persuasions, and still declining the ministrations of clergymen of any creed; others pretended, like Dean Swift's Tom Clinch, that they went off with a clear conscience and a calm spirit,

"Without prayer-book or psalm."

But very probably this indifference to the ordinary and his ghostly counsels arose from a suspicion that he was not very earnest in what he said. The Newgate ordinary, although a sound protestant, was a father confessor to all criminals. Not the least profitable part of his emoluments came from the sale of his account of the execution of convicts, a species of gaol calendar which he compiled from information the condemned men themselves supplied. That the ordinary attached great value to this production is clear from the petition made by one of them, the Reverend Paul Lorraine, to the House of Commons, that his pamphlet might be exempted from the tax levied upon paper. Several of these accounts have been preserved, and I have referred to them in my chapter, "The gaol calendar." But it is easy to understand that the ordinary might have been better employed than in compiling these accounts, however interesting they may be, as illustrating the crime of the last century. It is also pretty certain that, although, doubtless, blameless and exemplary men, Newgate chaplains were not always over-zealous in the discharge of their sacred office in regard to the condemned. There were many grim jokes among the prisoners themselves as to the value of the parson's preaching. Thus in the Reverend Mr. Cotton's time as ordinary, convicts were said to go out of the world with their ears stuffed full of cotton; and his interpretation of any particular passage in Scripture was said to go in at one ear and out at the other.[126] Hence the intrusion, which must have seemed to them unwarrantable, of dissenting and other amateur preachers, of well-meaning enthusiasts, who devoted themselves with unremitting vigour to the spiritual consolation of all prisoners who would listen to them. It is impossible to speak otherwise than most approvingly of the single-minded, self-sacrificing devotion of such men as Silas Told, the forerunner of Howard, Mrs. Fry, the Gurneys, and other estimable philanthropists. Nevertheless unseemly polemical wrangles appeared to have been the result of this interference, which was better meant than appreciated by the authorized clerical officer. Dr. Doran, referring to the execution of James Sheppard (Jacobite Sheppard, not Jack), gives an account of a conflict of this kind. "Sheppard's dignity," he says, "was not even ruffled by the renewed combat in the cart of the Newgate chaplain and the nonjuror. Each sought to comfort and confound the culprit according to his way of thinking. Once more the messengers of peace got to fisticuffs, but as they neared Tyburn the nonjuror kicked Paul[127] (the ordinary) out of the cart, and kept by the side of Sheppard till the rope was adjusted. There he boldly, as those Jacobite nonjurors were wont, gave the passive lad absolution for the crime for which he was about to pay the penalty; after which he jumped down to have a better view of the sorry spectacle from the foremost ranks of spectators."

It was no doubt on account of the insufficiency of the spiritual consolations offered to the condemned that led old Richard Dove, or Dow, to make his endowment for tolling the prisoner's bell. He bequeathed fifty pounds a year for ever, so Stowe tells us, with this philanthropic purpose. When condemned prisoners were being "drawn to their executions at Tyburn," a man with a bell stood in the churchyard by St. Sepulchre's, by the wall next the street, "and so to put them in mind of their death approaching." Later on these verses took the form of exhortation, of which the following is the substance—

"You prisoners that are within, who for wickedness and sin, after many mercies shown you, you are now appointed to die to-morrow in the forenoon: give ear and understand that to-morrow morning the greatest bell of St. Sepulchre's shall toll for you, in form and manner of a passing bell, as used to be tolled for those who are at the point of death, to the end that all godly people hearing that bell, and knowing it is for you going to your death, may be stirred up heartily to pray to God to bestow His grace and mercy upon you whilst you live. I beseech you, for Jesus Christ his sake, to keep this night in watching and prayer for the salvation of your own souls, whilst there is yet time and place for mercy: as knowing to-morrow you must appear before the judgment-seat of your Creator, there to give an account of all things done in this life, and to suffer eternal torments for your sins, committed against Him, unless upon your hearty and unfeigned repentance you find mercy, through the merits, death, and passion of your only Mediator and Advocate, Jesus Christ, who now sits at the right hand of God, to make intercession for as many of you as penitently return to Him." In addition to the foregoing there was an admonition pronounced to the condemned criminals as they passed St. Sepulchre's church wall on their way to execution, which was to the following effect:—

"All good people pray heartily unto God for those poor sinners who are now going to their death, for whom this great bell doth toll.

"You that are condemned to die, repent with lamentable tears; ask mercy of the Lord for the salvation of your own souls, through the merits, death, and passion of Jesus Christ, who now sits at the right hand of God, to make intercession for as many of you as penitently return unto Him.

"Lord have mercy upon you,

Christ have mercy upon you.

Lord have mercy upon you,

Christ have mercy upon you."

In times when scaffold and gallows were perpetually crowded, the executioner was a prominent if not exactly a distinguished personage. The office might not be honourable, but it was not without its uses, and the man who filled it was an object of both interest and dread. In some countries the dismal paraphernalia—axe, gibbet, or rack—have been carried by aristocratic families on their arms:[128] in France the post of executioner was long hereditary, regularly transmitted from father to son, for many generations, and enjoyed eventually something of the credit vouchsafed to all hereditary offices. With us the law's finisher has never been held in great esteem. He was on a par rather with the Roman *carnifex*, an odious official, who was not suffered to live within the precincts of the city. The only man who would condescend to the work was usually a condemned criminal, pardoned for the very purpose. Derrick, one of the first names mentioned, was sentenced to death, but pardoned by Lord Essex, whom he afterwards executed. Next to him I find that one Bull acted as executioner about 1593. Then came Gregory Brandon, the man who is generally supposed to have decapitated Charles I., and who was commonly addressed by his Christian name only. Through an error Brandon was advanced to the dignity of a squire by Garter, king at arms, and succeeding executioners were generally honoured with the same title. Brandon was followed by his son; young Brandon by Squire Dun, who gave place in his turn to John Ketch, the godfather of all modern hangmen.[129] Jack Ketch did not give entire satisfaction. It is recorded in Luttrell that Ketch was dispossessed in favour of Pascha Roose, a butcher, who served only a few months, when Ketch was restored. After Ketch, John Price was the man, a pardoned malefactor, who could not resist temptation, and was himself executed for murder by some one else. Dennis, the hangman at the Lord George Gordon riots, had also been sentenced to death for complicity, but obtained forgiveness on condition that he should string up his former associates.

They did their work roughly, these early practitioners. Sometimes the rope slipped, or the drop was insufficient, and the hangman had to add his weight, assisted by that of zealous spectators, to the sufferer's legs to effect strangulation. Now and again the rope broke, and the convict had to be tied up a second time. This happened with Captain Kidd, the notorious pirate, who was perfectly conscious during the time which elapsed before he was again tied up. The friends of another pirate, John Gow, were anxious to put him out of his pain, and pulled his legs so hard, that the rope broke before he was dead, necessitating the repetition of the whole ceremony. Even when the operation had been successfully performed, the hanged man sometimes cheated the gallows. There are several well-authenticated cases of resuscitation after hanging, due doubtless to the rude and clumsy plan of killing. To slide off a ladder or drop from a cart might and generally did produce asphyxia, but there was no instantaneous fracture of the vertebral column as in most executions of modern times. The earliest case on record is that of Tiretta de Balsham, whom Henry III. pardoned in 1264 because she had survived hanging. As she is said to have been suspended from one morning till sunrise the following day, it is difficult to believe the story, which was probably one of many mediæval impostures. Females, however, appear to have had more such escapes than males. Dr. Plot[130] gives several instances, one that of Anne Green, who in 1650 came to when in the hands of the doctors for dissection; another of Mrs. Cope, hanged at Oxford in 1658, who was suspended for an unusually long period, and afterwards let fall violently, yet she recovered, only to be more effectually hanged next day. A third substantiated case was that of half-hanged Maggie Dickson, who was hanged at Edinburgh in 1728, and whom the jolting of the cart in which her body was removed from the gallows recovered. The jolting was considered so infallible a recipe for bringing to, that it was generally practised by an executed man's friends in Ireland, where also the friends were in the habit of holding up the convict by his waistband after he had dropped, "so that the rope should not press upon his throat," the sheriff philanthropically pretending not to see.

Sir William Petty, the eminent surgeon in Queen Anne's time, owed his scientific fame to his having resuscitated a woman who had been hanged. The body had been begged, as was the custom, for the anatomical lecture; Petty finding symptoms of life, bled her, put her to bed with another woman, and gave her spirits and other restoratives. She recovered, whereupon the students subscribed to endow her with a small portion, and she soon after married and lived for fifteen years. The case of half-hanged Smith was about the date 1705. He was reprieved, but the reprieve arrived after he had been strung up; he was taken down, bled, and brought to. Smith afterwards described his sensations minutely. The weight of his body when he first dropped caused him great pain; his "spirits" forced their way up to his head and seemed to go out at his eyes with a great blaze of light, and then all pain left him. But on his resuscitation the blood and "spirits" forcing themselves into their proper channels gave him such intolerable suffering "that he could have wished those hanged who cut him down." William Duell, hanged in 1740, was carried to Surgeon's Hall, to be anatomized; but as his body was being laid out, one of the servants who was washing him perceived that he was still alive. A surgeon bled him, and in two hours he was able to sit up in his chair. Later in the evening he was sent back to Newgate, and his sentence changed to transportation. In 1767, a man who had hanged for 28 minutes was operated on by a surgeon, who made an incision into the wind-pipe. In less than six hours the hanged man revived. It became a constant practice for a condemned man's friends to carry off the body directly it was cut down to the nearest surgeon's, who at once operated on it by bleeding, and so forth. The plan was occasionally but rarely successful. It was tried with Dr. Dodd, who was promptly carried to an undertaker's in Tottenham Court Road and placed in a hot bath; but he had been too well handed for recovery. A report was long current that Fauntleroy the banker, who was executed for forgery, had been resuscitated, but it was quite without foundation.

 The Tyburn procession survived till towards the end of the eighteenth century. It had many supporters, Dr. Johnson among the number. "Sir," he told Boswell, when Tyburn had been discontinued, "executions are intended to draw spectators. If they do not draw spectators they do not answer their purpose. The old method was most satisfactory to all parties: the public was gratified by a procession, the criminal is supported by it. Why is all this to be swept away?" The reason is given by the sheriffs for the year 1784, and is convincing. In a pamphlet published that year it is set forth that the procession to Tyburn was a hideous mockery on the law; the final scene had lost its terrors; it taught no lesson of morality to the beholders, but tended to the encouragement of vice. The day of execution was deemed a public holiday, to which thousands thronged, many to gratify an unaccountable curiosity, more to seize an opportunity for committing fresh crimes. "If we take a view of the supposed solemnity from the time at which the criminal leaves the prison to the last moment of his existence, it will be found to be a period full of the most shocking and disgraceful circumstances. If the only defect were the want of ceremony the minds of the spectators might be supposed to be left in a state of indifference; but when they view the meanness of the apparatus, the dirty cart and ragged harness, surrounded by a sordid assemblage of the lowest among the vulgar, their sentiments are inclined more to ridicule than pity. The whole progress is attended with the same effect. Numbers soon thicken into a crowd of followers, and then an indecent levity is heard." The crowd gathered as it went, the levity increased, "till on reaching the fatal tree it became a riotous mob, and their wantonness of speech broke forth in profane jokes, swearing, and blasphemy." The officers of the law were powerless to check the tumult; no attention was paid to the convict's dying speech—"an exhortation to shun a vicious life, addressed to thieves actually engaged in picking pockets." The culprit's prayers were interrupted, his demeanour if resigned was sneered at, and only applauded when he went with brazen effrontery to his death. "Thus," says the pamphlet, "are all the ends of public justice defeated; all the effects of example, the terrors of death, the shame of punishment, are all lost."

The evils it was hoped might be obviated "were public executions conducted with becoming form and solemnity, if order were preserved and every tendency to disturb it suppressed." Hence the place of execution was changed in 1784 from "Tyburn to the great area that has lately been opened before Newgate." The sheriffs were doubtful of their power to make alterations, and consulted the judges, who gave it as their opinion that it was within the sheriffs competence. "With this sanction, therefore," the sheriffs go on to say, "we have proceeded, and instead of carting the criminals through the streets to Tyburn, the sentence of death is executed in the front of Newgate, where upwards of five thousand persons may easily assemble; here a temporary scaffold hung with black is erected, and no other persons are permitted to ascend it than the necessary officers of justice, the clergyman, and the criminal, and the crowd is kept at a proper distance. During the whole time of the execution a funeral bell is tolled in Newgate, and the prisoners are kept in the strictest order.

"We hope this alteration will produce many good effects to the public, to the criminal, and to the prisoners in the gaol. The crowd of spectators will probably be more orderly, because less numerous, and more subject to control by being more confined; and also it will be free from the accession of stragglers, whom a Tyburn procession usually gathers on its passage, and who make the most wanton part of it. Add to this the sentiments which the sight must naturally raise in the breast of every man when exhibited with due solemnity; when the mind is allowed to fix its whole attention upon this scene of awful ceremony, it will feel with becoming dread the pain of disobedience and the terror of example. Nor will the effect of this change be lost upon the criminal: his spirits will be composed by the decorum of the place, and he may prepare his soul for its dissolution by calm meditation, which he could not have exercised under the former noise and disorder; the fearful may gather strength and the hardened yield to remorse from the awe and reverence with which they view their fate. To those in confinement, who feel the heavy hand of justice so near the walls, it must necessarily become a useful lesson of duty and obedience, and a strong admonition to repentance. Example ought from its very nature to be directed principally to the wicked, that they who have most offended may feel most sensibly the certain consequence of offending; in the present instance the application of it is conformable to its original design and to the first principles of justice. It will be administered so as to amend the lives of those prisoners who may escape the fate of their lost companion, and to make those fitter for it who are doomed to suffer."

I shall return to the subject of executions in the second volume, and shall have to show that the horrors of executions were but little diminished by the substitution of the Old Bailey as the scene. Seventy-four years were to elapse before the wisdom of legislators and the good sense of the public insisted that the extreme penalty of the law should be carried out in strictest privacy within the walls of the gaol.

ESCAPES

E*scapes from Newgate mostly commonplace—Causes of escapes—Mediæval prison breaking—Scheme of escape in a coffin—Other methods—Changing clothes—Setting fire to prison—Connivance of keepers—Ordinary devices—Quarrying walls, taking up floors, cutting their fetters, &c.—Jack Sheppard—His escapes from Newgate—His capture—Special instructions from Secretary of State for his speedy trial and execution—Burnworth's attempt—Joshua Dean—Daniel Malden's two escapes—His personal narrative and account of his recapture—Stratagem and disguise—Female clothing—Mr. Barlow the Jacobite detected in a woman's dress and taken to the Old Bailey—General Forster's escape—Mr. Pitt the governor suspended and suspected of complicity—Brigadier Macintosh and fifteen other Jacobites escape—Some retaken—Mr. Ratcliffe gets away—Again in trouble in the '45 and executed.*

ESCAPES from Newgate have been numerous enough, but except in a few cases not particularly remarkable. They miss the extraordinary features of celebrated evasions, such as those of Casanova Von Trenck and Latude. The heroes of Newgate, too, were mostly commonplace criminals. There was but little romance about their misdeeds, and they scarcely excite the sympathy which we cannot deny to victims of tyrannical immured under the Piombi or in the Bastille. They lacked aptitude, moreover, or perhaps opportunity, to weave their stories into thrilling narratives, such as have been preserved from the pens of more scholarly prisoners. Hence the chronicle of Newgate is somewhat bald and uninteresting as regards escapes. It rings the changes upon conventional stratagems and schemes. All more or less bear testimony to the cunning and adroitness of the prisoners, but all equally prove the keepers' carelessness or cupidity. An escape from prison argues always a want of precaution. This may come of mere neglectfulness, or it may be bought at a price. Against bribery there can be no protection, but long experience has established the watchful supervision, which to-day avails more than bolts and bars and blocks of stone. A prisoner can sooner win through a massive wall than elude a keen-eyed warder's care. Hence in all modern prison construction the old idea of mere solidity has been abandoned, and reliance is placed rather upon the upright intelligence of that which we may term the prison police. The minute inspection of cells and other parts occupied by prisoners, the examination of the prisoners themselves at uncertain times; above all, the intimate acquaintance which those in authority should have of the movements and doings of their charges at all seasons—these are the best safeguards against escapes.

In early days attempts to break prison were generally rude and imperfect. Now and again a rescue was accomplished by force, at risk, however, of a levée of the citizens in vindication of the law. This was the case in 1439, when Phillip Malpas and Robert Marshall, the sheriffs of London, recovered a prisoner who had been snatched from their officers' hands.[131] Sometimes the escape followed a riotous upheaval of the inmates of

Newgate, as when two of the Percies and Lord Egremond were committed to Newgate for an affray in the North Country between them and Lord Salisbury's sons. Soon after their committal these turbulent aristocrats "broke out of prison and went to the king; the other prisoners took to the leads of the gate, and defended it a long while against the sheriffs and all their officers," till eventually the aid of the citizens had to be called in. In 1520 a prisoner who was so weak and ill that he had to be let down out of Newgate in a basket broke through the people in the Sessions Hall, and took sanctuary in Grey Friars Church. The rest of the story, as told by Holinshed, states that after staying six or seven days in the church, before the sheriffs could speak with him, "because he would not abjure (the country) and ask a crowner, with violence they took him hence, and cast him again into prison, but the law served not to hang him."

In the 'Calendar of State Papers,' under date 1593, there is a reference to a more ingenious method of compassing the enlargement of a prisoner. The scheme was to convey a living body out of Newgate in a coffin, instead of the dead one for which it had been prepared. The prisoner was a member of a congregation or secret conventicle, and the coffin had been made by subscription of the whole society, at a cost of four-and-eightpence. The State Papers give the examination of one Christopher Bowman, a goldsmith, on the subject, but unfortunately gives few details as to the meditated escape. The idea was to write a wrong name on the coffin-lid, and no doubt to trust to a corrupt officer within the prison for the substitution of the bodies. I find another curious but brief reference to escapes in the State Papers about this date. It is the endorsement of "the examination of Robert Bellamy, of the manner of his escape from Newgate, from thence to Scotland, and then over to Hamburgh. His arrest in the Palsgrave's country, and his conveyance to Duke Casimir."

As time passed the records become fuller, and there is more variety in the operations of the prisoners in their efforts towards freedom. In 1663 a man escaped by his wife changing clothes with him, and got into a hole between two walls in Thomas Court; "but though he had a rug and food, yet the night being wet he wanted beer, and peeping out, he was taken, is brought back prisoner, and will, it is thought, be hanged." Sometimes the prisoners rose against their keepers, and tried to set the prison on fire, hoping to get out during the confusion. This was repeatedly tried. In 1615, for instance, and again in 1692, when the prison was actually alight; but the fire was discovered just as certain of the prisoners were in the act of breaking open the prison gates. Sometimes no violence was used, but the prisoner walked off with the connivance of his keeper. This was what occurred with Sir Nicholas Poyntz, who escaped between Newgate and the King's Bench, on the road to the latter prison, to which he was being transferred. The references to this case throw some light upon the interior of Newgate at the time (1623). Poyntz had been arrested for killing a man in a street brawl. He had been committed first to the King's Bench, whence on pretence of his having excited a mutiny in that prison, he was transferred to Newgate, and lodged in a dungeon without bed or light, and compelled to lie in a coffin. All this he sets forth in a petition to the high and mighty prince, George Duke of Buckingham, for whose use he paid the sum of £500 to Sir Edward Villiers, and prays that he may have leave to sue out his Habeas Corpus, or have back his money. No notice having been taken of this appeal, he made shift for himself in the manner described. He was soon afterwards retaken, as appears from other petitions from the under-sheriffs, against whom actions had been commenced for allowing the escape.

Another somewhat similar case is reported in 1635, where the deputy-keeper of Newgate, Edward James by name, was attached and committed to the Fleet for allowing Edward Lunsford, a prisoner in his custody, to go at large. Lunsford was concerned with Lewis and others in a foul attempt to kill Sir Thomas Pelham on a Sunday going to church, and committed under an order of the Star Chamber to Newgate, where he lay for a year. His imprisonment was from time to time relaxed by James: first that he might prosecute his suit to a gentlewoman worth £10,000; and afterwards on account of the prosecutions against him in the Star Chamber; ultimately on account of his lameness and sickness James gave him liberty for the recovery of his health, and he was allowed to lodge out of prison, his father being his surety, and promising that he should be produced when required. But he abused this kindness, and instead of showing himself at regular periods to the keeper, made off altogether. All this is stated in a petition from James, who prays for enlargement on bail that he may pursue and recapture Lunsford. "Lunsford is so lame that he can only go in a coach, and though it is reported that he has been at Gravelines and Cologne, yet he has been seen in town within ten days." This petition, which is in the State Papers, is underwritten that the Attorney-General be directed to prosecute the petitioner in the Star Chamber, and upon it are Secretary Windebank's notes; to the effect that James had received a bribe of £14 to allow Lunsford and his companions to go abroad without a warrant, and one of them to escape. Various sentences were proposed. Lord Cottington suggested that James should pay a fine of £1000 to the king, imprisonment during pleasure, to be bound to good behaviour when he comes out, and acknowledgments. Secretary Windebank added that he should be put from his place; the Earl Marshall suggested standing with a paper in Westminster Hall, and prosecution of the principal keeper; Archbishop Laud concluded with whipping, and that the chief keeper should be sent for to the Council Board.

The ordinary methods of attempting escape were common enough in Newgate. Quarrying into the walls, breaking up floors, sawing through bars, and picking locks were frequent devices to gain release. In 1679 several prisoners picked out the stones of the prison walls, and seven who had been committed to Newgate for burglary escaped. No part of the prison was safe from attack, provided only the prisoners had leisure and were unobserved, both of which were almost a matter of course. Now it is a hole through the back of a chimney in a room occupied by the prisoner, now a hole through a wall into a house adjoining the prison. Extraordinary perseverance is displayed in dealing with uncompromising material. The meanest and seemingly most insufficient weapons served. Bars are sawn through like butter;[132] prisoners rid themselves of their irons as though they were old rags; one man takes a bar out of the chapel window and gets away over the house-tops; a gang working in association saw through eight bars, "each as thick as a man's wrist, leaving enough iron to keep the bars together, and fitting up the notches with dirt and iron-rust to prevent discovery;" but they are detected in time, and for proper security are all chained to the floor. Another lot are discovered "working with large iron crows," meaning to get through the floor. On this occasion "a great lot of saws, files, pins, and other tools" were found among the prisoners, plainly revealing the almost inconceivable license and carelessness prevailing. Again, two men under sentence of death found means to break out of Newgate "through walls six feet in thickness." They were brothers, and one of them being ill, he was out of humanity removed from his cell to an upper room, where the other was suffered to attend him. As they were both bricklayers by trade, they easily worked through the wall in a night and so escaped. They were, however, retaken and hanged. The ease with which irons are slipped is shown repeatedly. One man having attempted to escape was as usual chained to the floor, yet he managed to get himself loose from an iron collar in which his neck was fastened and his hands extended. This man, when he got himself disengaged from the floor, had the resolution to wring the collar from his neck by fixing it between two of the bars of the gaol window, and thus by main strength he broke it in two. Others cut through their handcuffs and shackles two or three times running with the ease of the Davenport brothers freeing themselves from bonds.

Jack Sheppard's escapes from Newgate are historical, although much embellished by the novelist's art. Sheppard's success was really marvellous, but it may be explained to some extent by his indomitable pluck, his ingenuity, and his personal activity. As he was still quite a lad when he was hanged, he could have been barely twenty-two at the time of his escapes.[133] He is described as of a lithe, spare figure and of great strength. From his early apprenticeship to a carpenter he had much skill and knowledge in the handling of tools. He first became celebrated as a prison-breaker by his escapes from the St. Giles' Round House and from the New Prison. His first escape, from the condemned hold of Newgate, where he lay under sentence of death, was more a proof of ingenuity than of prowess. The usual neglect of proper precautions allowed two female visitors to have access to him and to supply him with tools, probably a file and saw. With these he partly divided a spike on the top of the hatch which led from the condemned hold. Upon a second visit from his fair friends he broke off the spike, squeezed his head and shoulders through the opening, the women then pulling him through. How he got past the lodge where the turnkeys were carousing is not recorded, but it was probably in female disguise. His second escape following his recapture, and a second sentence of death, was much more remarkable. It was, however, only rendered possible by the negligence of his keepers. They visited him at dinner-time, and after a careful examination of his irons, having satisfied themselves that he was quite secure, left him for the day. Released thus from all surveillance, time was all that Sheppard needed to effect his escape.

He had been chained to the floor by heavy irons, which were rivetted into a staple fixed in the ground. Various fancy sketches exist of the means of restraint employed, but none can be relied upon as accurate or authentic. Some irons still in existence at Newgate may be akin to those by which Sheppard was secured, but they are hardly the identical fetters. Sheppard was also handcuffed. These he is said to have rid himself of by holding the connecting chain firmly between his teeth, squeezing his fingers as small as possible, and drawing the manacles off. "He next twisted the gyves,[134] the heavy gyves, round and round, and partly by main strength, partly by a dexterous, well-applied jerk, snapped asunder the central link by which they were attached to the padlock." He was now free to move about, but the basils still confined his ancles, and he dragged at every step the long connecting chain. He drew up the basils on his calf, and removing his stockings used them to tie up the chains to his legs. He first attempted to climb up the chimney, but his upward progress was impeded by an iron bar that crossed the aperture. He descended, therefore, and from the outside with a piece of his broken chain set to work to pick out the stones and bricks so as to release the bar. This he accomplished and thus obtained an implement about an inch square and nearly a yard long, which was of the utmost service to him in his further operations. The room in which he had been confined was a part of the so-called "castle"; above it was the "Red-room," and into this he effected an entrance by climbing the chimney and making a fresh hole on the level of the floor above. In the "Red-room" he found a rusty nail, with which he tried to pick the lock, but failing in this, he wrenched off the plate that covered the bolt and forced the bolt back with his fingers. This red-room door opened on to a dark passage leading to the chapel. There was a door in it which he opened by making a hole in the wall and pushing the bolt back, and so reached the chapel. Thence he got into an entry between the chapel and the lower leads. "The door of this entry was very strong,[135] and fastened with a great lock. What was worse, the night had now overtaken him, and he was forced to work in the dark. However, in half an hour, by the help of the great nail, the chapel spike, and the iron bar, he forced off the box of the lock and opened the door, which led him to another yet more difficult, for it was not only locked, but barred and bolted. When he had tried in vain to make this lock and box give way he wrenched the fillet from the main post of the door and the box and staples came off with it.... There was yet another door betwixt him and the lower leads; but it being bolted within side he opened it easily, and mounting to the top of it he got over the wall and so to the upper leads." All that remained for him to do was to descend. There was a house adjoining, that of Mr. Bird, a turner, on to which he might drop, but he deemed the leap too dangerous, and coolly resolved to retrace his steps to the prison chamber, from whence he had so laboriously issued, and secure his blanket. Having accomplished this risky service, he returned to the leads, made fast his blanket, slid down it, entered the turner's house by a garret window, and eventually, after some delay and no little danger of detection, got away down into the street.

Mr. Austin, the Newgate turnkey, who was specially in charge of Sheppard, and who, on unbolting the castle strong room next morning found that his prisoner was gone, was amazed beyond measure. The whole of the prison warders ran up, and at sight of the cartloads of rubbish and débris "stood like men deprived of their senses." After their first surprise they got their keys to open the neighbouring strong rooms, hoping that he might not have got clean and entirely away. It was not difficult to follow his track. Six great doors, one of which it was said had not been opened for seven years, had been forced, and their massive locks, screws, and bolts lay broken in pieces and scattered about the gaol. Last of all they came to the blanket hanging pendant from the leads, and it was plain that Sheppard was already far beyond pursuit.

It may be interesting to mention here that he was recaptured, mainly through his own negligence and drunkenness, within a fortnight of his escape. In the interval, after ridding himself of his irons, he had committed several fresh robberies, the most successful being a burglary at a pawnbroker's, where he furnished himself with the fine suit, sword, and snuff-box he possessed at the time of his arrest. "When he was brought back to the jail," says a contemporary account, "he was very drunk, carry'd himself insolently, defy'd the keepers to hold him with all their irons, art, and skill." He was by this time quite a notorious personage. "Nothing contributes so much to the entertainment of the town at present," says another journal of the time, "as the adventures of the house-breaker and gaol-breaker, John Sheppard. 'Tis thought the keepers of Newgate have got above £200 already by the crowds who daily flock to see him." "On Wednesday several noblemen visited him." He sat for his portrait to Sir James Thornhill, the eminent painter,[136] and the likeness was reproduced in a mezzotint which had a large circulation. Seven different histories or narratives of his adventures were published and illustrated with numerous engravings. His importance was further increased by the special instructions issued to the Attorney-General to bring him to immediate trial. A letter from the Duke of Newcastle, then Secretary of State, is preserved in the Hardwicke MSS., wherein that great official condescends to convey the king's commands to Sir Philip Yorke that Sheppard, having made two very extraordinary escapes, and being a very dangerous person, should be forthwith brought to trial, "to the end that execution may without delay be awarded against him." This letter is dated the 6th November; he was arraigned on the 10th, found guilty, and sentenced the same day. His execution took place on the 16th November, just one month after his escape. He exhibited great coolness and effrontery during his trial. He told the Court that if they would let his handcuffs be put on he by his art would take them off before their faces. The most numerous crowds ever seen in London paid testimony to his notoriety as he passed through the streets; and Westminster Hall had not been so densely thronged in the memory of man as at the time of his trial. No pains were spared to ensure his safe custody in Newgate. He was chained to the floor in the condemned hold, and constantly watched night and day by two guards. But up to the last Sheppard entertained schemes for eluding justice. He had obtained a pen-knife by some means or other, and he had intended to cut his cords while actually in the cart going to Tyburn, throw himself in amongst the crowd at a place called Little Turnstile, and run for his life through the narrow passage along which the mounted officers could not follow him. But this plan was nullified by the discovery of the knife on his person just before he left Newgate. It is said that he had also hopes of resuscitation, and that friends had agreed to cut him down promptly, and to apply the usual restoratives. This scheme, if it had ever existed, was probably rendered abortive by the proceedings of the mob after the execution.[137]

Sheppard had many imitators, but few equals. Possibly the ease with which he broke prison led to an increase in precautions, and I can find no other cases of evasion in Jack Sheppard's manner. There are several instances of attempted escapes by the reverse process, not over the walls, but through them or along the sewers. Burnworth, while in Newgate in 1726,[138] projected a plan of escape. He got an iron crow, and assisted by certain prisoners, pulled stones out of the walls, while others sung psalms to put the turnkeys off their guard. Next day the officers came to remove five convicts awaiting execution, but found the room so full of stones and rubbish that some hours elapsed before the prisoners could be got out. Burnworth made another but equally ineffective attempt next day. Joshua Dean, capitally convicted in 1731 for counterfeiting stamps, formed a design with seven other prisoners awaiting transportations to the plantations to break gaol. They found means to get down into the common sewer no doubt by taking up the floor. Thence four of them reached a vault under a house in Fleet Lane, and so into the shop through which three got off, but the fourth was secured and carried back to Newgate. The fate of two at least of the remaining three was not known till long afterwards. In 1736, a certain Daniel Malden, who had already escaped once, again got out of Newgate by sawing his chains near the staple, by which they were fastened to the wall of the condemned hold, and getting through the brickwork, dropped into the common sewer. "Several persons were employed to search after him, but to no purpose, though the chains about him weighed nearly a hundred pounds." Malden was not discovered, but the searchers came upon "the bodies of two persons who had been smothered in trying to escape." These were no doubt two of those mentioned above. This method of evasion continued to be practised till long afterwards. In 1785 two convicts cut a hole in the floor of their cell, and got into the common sewer to make their escape. "But wading till they were almost suffocated, they at length reached the gully-hole, and calling for help, were taken out alive, but too weak to walk, and carried to their former quarters."

Daniel Malden, who twice, in 1735 and 1736, escaped from the condemned hold in Newgate in a manner little less surprising, although less notorious than Jack Sheppard, had been a man-of-war's-man, and served in several of her Majesty's ships. After his discharge he took to burglary and street-robberies, for which he was presently arrested and sentenced to suffer death. While lying in the condemned hold, on the very morning of his execution he effected his escape. A previous occupant of the same cell in the condemned hold had told him that a certain plank was loose in the floor, which he found to be true. Accordingly, between ten and eleven on the night of October 21st, 1736, before execution, he began to work, and raised up the plank with the foot of a stool that was in the cell. He soon made a hole through the arch under the floor big enough for his body to pass through, and so dropped into a cell below from which another convict had previously escaped. The window-bar of this cell remained cut just as it had been left after this last escape, and Malden easily climbed through with all his irons still on him into the press-yard. When there he waited a bit, till, seeing "all things quiet," he pulled off his shoes and went softly up into the chapel, where he observed a small breach in the wall. He enlarged it and so got into the penthouse. Making his way through the penthouse he passed on to the roof. At last, using his own words, "I got upon the top of the cells by the ordinary's house, having made my way from the top of the chapel upon the roofs of the houses, and all round the chimneys of the cells over the ordinary's house"; from this he climbed along the roofs to that of an empty house, and finding one of the garret windows open, entered it and passed down three pairs of stairs into the kitchen, where he put on his shoes again, "which I had made shift to carry in my hand all the way I came, and with rags and pieces of my jacket wrapped my irons close to my legs as if I had been gouty or lame; then I got out at the kitchen window, up one pair of stairs into Phœnix Court, and from thence through the streets to my home in Nightingale Lane."

Here he lay till six a.m., then sent for a smith who knocked off his irons, "and took them away with him for his pains." Then he sent for his wife, who came to him; but while they were at breakfast, hearing a noise in the yard he made off, and took refuge at Mrs. Newman's, "the sign of the Blackboy, Millbank; there I was kept private and locked up four days alone and no soul by myself." Venturing out on the fifth day he heard they were in pursuit of him, and again took refuge, this time in the house of a Mrs. Franklin. From thence he despatched a shoemaker with a message to his wife, and letters to two gentlemen in the city. But the messenger betrayed him to the Newgate officers, and in about an hour "the house was beset. I hid myself," says Malden,[139] "behind the shutters in the yard, and my wife was drinking tea in the house. The keepers seeing her, cried, 'Your humble servant, madam; where is your spouse?' I heard them, and knowing I was not safe, endeavoured to get over a wall, when some of them espyed me, crying, 'Here he is!' upon which they immediately laid hold of me, carried me back to Newgate, put me into the old condemned hold as the strongest place, and stapled me down to the floor."

Nothing daunted by this first failure he resolved to attempt a second escape. A fellow-prisoner conveyed a knife to him, and on the night of June 6th, 1737, he began to saw the staple to which he was fastened in two. His own story is worth quoting.

"I worked through it with much difficulty, and with one of my irons wrenched it open and got it loose. Then I took down, with the assistance of my knife, a stone in front of the seat in the corner of the condemned hold: when I had got the stone down, I found there was a row of strong iron bars under the seat through which I could not get, so I was obliged to work under these bars and open a passage below them. To do this I had no tool but my old knife, and in doing the work my nails were torn off the ends of my fingers, and my hands were in a dreadful, miserable condition. At last I opened a hole just big enough for me to squeeze through, and in I went head foremost, but one of my legs, my irons being on, stuck very fast in the hole, and by this leg I hung in the inside of the vault with my head downward for half an hour or more. I thought I should be stifled in this sad position, and was just going to call out for help when, turning myself up, I happened to reach the bars. I took fast hold of them by one hand, and with the other disengaged my leg to get it out of the hole."

When clear he had still a drop of some thirty feet, and to break his fall he fastened a piece of blanket he had about him to one of the bars, hoping to lower himself down; but it broke, and he fell with much violence into a hole under the vault, "my fetters causing me to fall very heavy, and here I stuck for a considerable time." This hole proved to be a funnel, "very narrow and straight; I had torn my flesh in a terrible manner by the fall, but was forced to tear myself much worse in squeezing through." He stuck fast and could not stir either backward or forward for more than half an hour. "But at last, what with squeezing my body, tearing my flesh off my bones, and the weight of my irons, which helped me a little here, I worked myself through."

The funnel communicated with the main sewer, in which, as well as he could, he cleaned himself. "My shirt and breeches were torn in pieces, but I washed them in the muddy water, and walked through the sewer as far as I could, my irons being very heavy on me and incommoding me much." Now a new danger overtook him: his escape had been discovered and its direction. Several of the Newgate runners had therefore been let into the sewer to look for him. "And here," he says, "I had been taken again had I not found a hollow place in the side of the brick-work into which I crowded myself, and they passed by me twice while I stood in that nook." He remained forty-eight hours in the sewer, but eventually got out in a yard "against the pump in Town Ditch, behind Christ's Hospital." Once more he narrowly escaped detection, for a woman in the yard saw and suspected him to be after no good. However, he was suffered to go free, and got as far as Little Britain, where he came across a friend who gave him a pot of beer and procured a smith to knock off his fetters.

Malden's adventures after this were very varied. He got first to Enfield, when some friends subscribed forty-five shillings to buy him a suit of clothes at Rag Fair. Thence he passed over to Flushing, where he was nearly persuaded to take foreign service, but he refused and returned to England in search of his wife. Finding her, the two wandered about the country taking what work they could find. While at Canterbury, employed in the hop-fields, he was nearly discovered by a fellow who beat the drum in a show, and who spoke of him openly as "a man who had broken twice out of Newgate." Next he turned jockey, and while thus employed was betrayed by a man to whom he had been kind. Malden was carried before the Canterbury justices on suspicion of being the man who had escaped from Newgate, and a communication sent to the authorities of that prison. Mr. Akerman and two of his officers came in person to identify the prisoner, and, if the true Malden, to convey him back to London. But Malden once more nearly gave his gaolers the slip. He obtained somehow an old saw, "a spike such as is used for splicing ropes, a piece of an old sword jagged and notched, and an old knife." These he concealed rather imprudently upon his person, where they were seen and taken from him, otherwise Mr. Akerman, as Malden told him, "would have been like to have come upon a Canterbury story" instead of the missing prisoner. However, the Newgate officers secured Malden effectually, and brought him to London on the 26th September, 1736, which he reached "guarded by about thirty or forty horsemen, the roads all the way being lined with spectators." "Thus was I got to London," he says in his last dying confession, "handcuffed, and my legs chained under the horse's belly; I got to Newgate that Sunday evening about five o'clock, and rid quite up into the lodge, where I was taken off my horse, then was conveyed up to the old condemned hole, handcuffed and chained to the floor."

On Friday the 15th October, the last day of sessions, Malden was called into Court and informed that his former judgment of death must be executed upon him, and he was accordingly hanged upon the 2nd November following.

Stratagem and disguise in some shape or other were, however, the most favourite and generally the most successful forms of escape. Extraordinary and quite culpable facilities for changing clothes were given by the lax discipline of the prison. The substitution of persons, devoted wife or friend, taking the place of the accused, as in the story of Sydney Carton, as told by Dickens, or the well-known exchange between Lord and Lady Nithsdale, occurred too at Newgate. George Flint, an imprisoned journalist, who continued to edit his objectionable periodical from the prison, got away in the costume of a footman. His wife was suffered to live with him, and helped him to the disguise. She concealed the escape for two or three days, pretending that her husband was dangerously ill in bed, "and not fit to be disturbed;" for which fidelity to her husband, who was now beyond the seas, having made the most of the time thus gained, Mrs. Flint was cast into the condemned hold, and "used after a most barbarous manner to extort a confession." Another very similar and unsuccessful case was that of Alexander Scott, a highwayman suspected of robbing the Worcester and Portsmouth mails. Scott attempted to get out in the "habit" of an oyster-woman, whom his wife had persuaded to favour their design. The change was made, and the lodge bell rung to give egress to Scott. Unfortunately for the prisoner the gate-keeper was dilatory. Meanwhile, an assistant turnkey, missing Scott, conjectured that he had escaped, and seeing the oyster-woman standing at the gate began to question her, and insisted upon looking at her face. Scott being at once detected, he struck the turnkey a blow in the face, hoping to knock him down. A scuffle ensued, the turnkey proved the strongest, and Scott was secured.

Female disguise was one of the many methods employed to compass escape by the imprisoned Jacobites after the '15, but not always successfully. Mr. Barlow of Burton Hall tried it among others. In the first instance a crazy woman, Elizabeth Powell, well known in Westminster Market, came to Mr. Barlow with a whole suit of female apparel, but "he, fearing it might be a trick, or that he might fail in the attempt, discovered her." A week or two later, as if inspired by the proposal, Mr. Barlow did make the attempt. Close shaved and neatly dressed in female clothes, he came to the gate with a crowd of ladies who had been visiting their Jacobite friends, hoping to pass out unobserved with the others. But the turnkey—escapes had been very frequent, and all officials were on the alert—caught hold of him, turned him about, and in the struggle threw him down. The rest of the women cried out in a lamentable tone, "Don't hurt the poor lady; she is with child;" and some of them cried, "Oh, my dear mother!" whereupon the turnkey, convinced he had to do with a lady, let him go. Mr. Barlow, says the account, acted the part to the life. He was padded, his face was painted red and white, and he would certainly have made his escape had not Mr. Carleton Smith, one of the special commissioners appointed to ensure the safe custody of the rebels, strictly examined the would-be fugitive and detected his disguise. Mr. Barlow offered Smith ten guineas to let him go, but instead of accepting the bribe, Mr. Smith carried his prisoner just as he was, in female disguise, before the Court then sitting at the Old Bailey. Mr. Barlow declared that the clothes had been brought him by his wife. "The Court," goes on the account, "was very well pleased to see him thus metamorphosed, but ordered him to be put in heavy irons, and the clothes to be kept as a testimony against him."

The circumstances under which Mr. Pitt the governor of Newgate was superseded in his functions have been described in a previous chapter. Mr. Pitt was so strongly suspected of Jacobite leanings that he was tried for his life. No doubt escapes were scandalously frequent during his *régime*, and it is just possible that they were due to the governor's complicity, although Mr. Pitt was actually acquitted of the charge. More probably they owed their success to the ingenuity of desperate men easily triumphing over the prevailing carelessness of their keepers. The first escape which made a considerable noise was that of Mr. Forster, commonly known as General Forster, who headed the Northumbrian rising in 1715, and lost the battle of Preston Pans. Mr. Forster was allowed considerable liberty, and lodged in apartments in the keeper's house. One afternoon, when Forster and another were drinking French wine with Mr. Pitt, Mr. Forster sent his servant to fetch a bottle of wine from his own stock to "make up the treat." The servant on pretence of going to the vault left the room. Being long away, Mr. Forster pretended to be very angry, and followed him out of the room. Meanwhile the servant had sent the governor's black man, a species of hybrid turnkey, down to the cellar for the wine, and had locked him up there. The black thus disposed of, Forster's servant returned and waited for his master just outside Mr. Pitt's parlour door. Being an adept at the locksmith's art as well as a smart intelligent fellow, the servant had previously obtained an impression in clay of Mr. Pitt's front door key, and had manufactured a counterfeit key. Directly Mr. Forster appeared, the front door was unlocked, master and servant passed through and went off together, first taking care to lock the door on the outside and leave the key in the lock to prevent their being readily pursued. Mr. Forster got to Prittlewell in Essex by four o'clock next morning with two more horsemen that had been waiting to attend them. From Prittlewell they hastened on to Leigh, where a vessel was provided, in which they made a safe voyage to France. "By this it appears," says the chronicler, evidently a stout Whig, "that Mr. Forster was much better skilled in contriving an escape than leading an army, which shows the weakness of the Pretender and his council, who put so great a trust in the hands of a person who was altogether unfit for it, and never made other campaign than to hunt a fox and drink down his companions."

The next attempt was on a larger scale. It was planned by Brigadier Macintosh, with whom were Mr. Wogan, two of the Delmehoys, Mr. James Talbot, and the brigadier's son, with several others, to the number of fifteen in all. The prime mover was the brigadier, who, having "made a shift to get off his irons, and coming down with them in his hand under his gown, caused a servant to knock at the gaol door outside, himself sitting close by it." As soon as the door was opened he pushed out with great violence, knocking down the turnkey and two or three of the sentinels. One of the soldiers made a thrust at him with his bayonet; but the brigadier parried the charge, seized the piece, unscrewed the bayonet, and "menaced it at the breast of the soldier, who thereupon gave way and suffered him and fourteen more to get into the street." Eight of the fugitives were almost immediately recaptured, but the other gentlemen got clean off. One of them was Mr. James Talbot, who, unhappily, fell again into the hands of the authorities. He was discovered by the chance gossip of a garrulous maid-servant, who, chattering at an ale-house in Windmill Street, near the Haymarket, said her master had a cousin come to see him who had the whitest hands she ever saw in her life. This caused suspicion, and suspicion brought discovery. A reward of £500 had been offered by proclamation for the arrest of any fugitives, except the brigadier, who was valued at £1000, and Talbot was given up.

The escapes did not end here. The next to get away was Mr. George Budden, an upholsterer, who had a shop near Fleet Bridge, a Jacobite, but not in the rebellion of '15. He effected his escape at the time when Mr. Pitt was himself a prisoner, suspected of collusion in the previous evasions. Mr. Budden's plan was simple. He was possessed of money, and had friends who could help to convey him away could he but get out of Newgate. One night as he sat drinking with the head turnkey, Mr. Budden purposely insulted the officer grossly, and even went so far as to strike him. The turnkey was furious, and carried off his prisoner to the lodge, there to be heavily ironed, Mr. Budden trusting that either on the way there or back he might contrive to escape. On reaching the lodge Mr. Budden apologised and "made atonement to the good-natured keeper, who was a little mellower than ordinary," and was led back to his former apartment; on the way he turned up the keeper's heels and made off through the gate. Once outside, Budden ran into Newgate Market, and thence by many windings and turnings out of London, riding post haste seventy miles to the coast, and so across to France.

There were other attempts, such as that of Mr. Robertson, who tried to make off in a clergyman's habit, but was discovered and stopped before he had passed one of the doors; and of Mr. Ramsay, who escaped with the crowd that came to hear the condemned sermon. Now and then there was the concerted action of a number, as when the prisoners thronged about the gates in order to make their escape; "and to promote the design the High Church cobbler fought with one of the servants, which occasioned a great disturbance and confusion." Trouble, again, was only prevented by timely warning that there was a design to convey large iron crows to the rebels, by which they might beat open the gaol and escape. The most important and about the last of the rebel escapes was that of Mr. Ratcliffe, brother of the unfortunate Lord Derwentwater. This was effected so easily, indeed, with so much cool impudence, that connivance must assuredly have been bought. Mr. Ratcliffe seized his opportunity one day when he was paying a visit to Captain Dalziel and others on the master's side. At the gate he met by previous agreement a "cane-jobber," or person who sold walking-sticks, and who had once been an inmate of Newgate himself. Mr. Ratcliffe paused for a time and bargained for a cane, after which he passed under the iron chain at the gate, and upon the cane-seller's saying that he was no prisoner, the turnkey and guard suffered Ratcliffe to get off. The author of the 'History of the Press-Yard' says that Mr. Ratcliffe bribed the officer, "which," as another writer adds, "must be owned to be the readiest way to turn both lock and key."

Mr. Ratcliffe, thirty years later, paid the penalty to the law which he had escaped on this occasion. A warm adherent of the Pretender, he embarked from France for Scotland to take part in the Jacobite rising in 1745. The French ship was captured, and Ratcliffe sent as a prisoner to the Tower. He was presently arraigned at the Bar of the King's Bench for having escaped from Newgate in 1716, when under sentence of death for high treason. Ratcliffe at first refused to plead, declaring that he was a subject of the French king, and that the court had no jurisdiction over him. Then he denied that he was the person named in the record produced in court, whereupon witnesses were called to prove that he was Charles Ratcliffe. Two Northumbrian men identified him as the leader of five hundred of the Earl of Derwentwater's men, remembering him by the scar on his face. They had been to see him in the Tower, and could swear to him; but could not swear that he was the same Charles Ratcliffe who had escaped from Newgate prison. A barber who had been appointed "close shaver" to Newgate in 1715, and who attended the prison daily to shave all the rebel prisoners, remembered Charles Ratcliffe, Esq., perfectly as the chum or companion of Basil Hamilton, a reputed nephew of the Duke of Hamilton; but this barber, when closely pressed, could not swear that the prisoner at the bar was the very same Charles Ratcliffe whom he had shaved, and who had afterwards escaped out of Newgate. No evidence indeed was forthcoming to positively fix Mr. Ratcliffe's identity; but "a gentleman" was called who deposed that the prisoner had in the Tower declared himself to be the same Charles Ratcliffe who was condemned in the year 1716, and had likewise told him, the witness, that he had made his escape out of Newgate in mourning, with a brown tye wig, when under sentence of death in that gaol. Upon this evidence the judge summed up against the prisoner, the jury found a verdict of guilty, and Ratcliffe was eventually beheaded on Tower Hill.

THE GAOL CALENDAR

Newgate Calendars—Their editors and publishers—All based on Sessions' papers—Demand for this literature fostered by prevalence of crime—Brief summary of state of crime in the first half of the 18th century—State of the Metropolis—Street robberies—Burglaries—Henry Fielding on the increase of robbers—The Thieves' Company—The Revolution Club—Firearms in the Law Courts—Causes of the increase of crime—Drunkenness—The Gin Act—Gaming universal—Faro's daughters—Lotteries—Repression of crime limited to hanging—No police—The Charlies or watchmen—Civil power lethargic—Efforts made by private societies for reformation of manners—Character of crimes—Murders, duels, and affrays—Richard Savage, the poet, in Newgate for murder—Major Oneby for murder, commits suicide—Marquis de Paleoti for murdering his man-servant—Colonel Charteris for rape, sentenced to death, but pardoned—Crime in high place—The Earl of Macclesfield, Lord Chancellor, convicted of venal practices—Embezzlement by public officials—Crimes more commonplace, but more atrocious—Murder committed by Catherine Hayes and her accomplices—She is burnt alive for petty treason—Sarah Malcolm the Temple murderess—Other prominent and typical murders—Jack Ketch hanged for murder—Wife murderers, Houssart, Vincent Davis, George Price, Edward Joines, John Williamson—Theodore Gardelle, the murderer of Mrs. King—Two female murderers—Mrs. Meteyard—Her cruelty to a parish apprentice—Elizabeth Brownrigg beats Mary Clifford to death.

PRISON calendars obviously reflect the criminal features of the age in which they appear. Those of Newgate since the beginning of the eighteenth century are numerous and voluminous enough to form a literature of their own. To the diligence of lawyers and publishers we owe a more or less complete collection of the most remarkable cases as they occurred. These volumes have been published under various titles. The 'Newgate Calendar,' compiled by Messrs. Knapp and Baldwin, attorneys-at-law, is one of the best known. This work, according to its title-page, professes to contain "interesting memoirs of notorious characters who have been convicted of outrages on the law of England; with essays on crimes and punishments and the last exclamations of sufferers." There are many editions of it. The first I think was published by Nuttall, Fisher, and Dixon, of Liverpool; a later edition issues from the Albion Press, Ivy Lane, London, under the auspices of J. Robins and Co. But another book of similar character had as its compiler "George Theodore Wilkinson, Esq.," barrister-at-law. It was published by Cornish and Co. in 1814, and the work was continued by "William Jackson, Esq.," another barrister, with Alexander Hogg, of Paternoster Row, and by Offor and Sons of Tower Hill as publishers. Early and perfect editions of these works are somewhat rare and curious, fondly sought out and carefully treasured by the bibliophile. But all of them were anticipated by the editors of the 'Tyburn Calendar,' or 'Malefactor's Bloody Register,' which issued soon after 1700 from the printing office of G. Swindells, at the appropriate address of Hanging Bridge, Manchester. The compilers of these volumes claimed a high mission. They desired "to fully display the regular progress from Virtue to Vice, interspersed with striking reflections on the conduct of those unhappy wretches who have fallen a sacrifice to the injured laws of their country. The whole tending to guard young minds from allurements of vice and the paths that lead to destruction." Another early work is the 'Chronicle of Tyburn, or Villainy displayed in all its branches,' which gave the authentic lives of notorious malefactors, and was published at the Shakespeare's Head in 1720. Yet another dated 1776, and printed for J. Wenman of 144, Fleet Street, bears the title of 'The Annals of Newgate,' and claims upon the title-page, that by giving the circumstantial accounts of the lives, transactions, and trial of the most notorious malefactors it is "calculated to expose the deformity of vice, the infamy, and punishments naturally attending those who deviate from the paths of virtue; and is intended as a beacon to warn the rising generation against the temptations, the allurements, and the dangers of bad company."

All Newgate calendars have seemingly a common origin. They are all based primarily upon the Sessions' Papers, the official publications which record the proceedings at the Old Bailey. There is a complete early series of these session papers in the Library of the British Museum, and another in the Home Office from the year 1730, including the December sessions of 1729. The publisher, who is stated on the title-page to be "T. Payne, at the corner of Ivy Lane, near Paternoster Row," refers in his preface to an earlier series, dating probably from the beginning of the century, and a manuscript note in the margin of the first volume of the second series also speaks of a preceding folio volume. These sessions papers did not issue from one publisher. As the years pass the publication changes hands. Now it is "J. Wilford, behind the Chapter House, St. Pauls"; now "I. Roberts at the

Oxford Arms in Warwick Lane." Ere long "T. Applebee in Bolt Court, near the Leg Tavern," turns his attention to this interesting class of periodical literature. He also published another set of semi-official documents, several numbers of which are bound up with the sessions' papers already mentioned, and like them supplying important data for the compilation of calendars. These were the accounts given by the ordinary of Newgate of the behaviour, confessions, and dying words of the malefactors "executed at Tyburn," a report rendered by command of the Mayor and corporation, but a private financial venture of the chaplains. As the ordinary had free access to condemned convicts at all times, and from his peculiar duties generally established the most confidential relations with them, he was in a position to obtain much curious and often authentic information from the lips of the doomed offenders. Hence the ordinary's account contained many criminal autobiographies, and probably was much patronized by the public. Its sale was a part of the Reverend gentleman's perquisites; and that the chaplains looked closely after the returns may be gathered from the already mentioned application made by the Rev. Mr. Loraine, chaplain in 1804, who petitioned Parliament to exempt his "execution brochure" from the paper tax.[140]

In the advertisement sheets of these sessions' papers are notices of other criminal publications proving how great was the demand for this kind of literature. Thus in 1731 is announced 'The History of Executions: being a complete account of the thirteen malefactors executed at Tyburn for robberies, price 4d.,' and this publication is continued from year to year. In 1732 "T. Applebee and others" published at 3s. 6d. the 'Lives of the most Remarkable Criminals,' a volume containing as a frontispiece the escape of Jack Sheppard from Newgate. In the description of this book the public is assured that the volume contains a first and faithful narration of each, "without any additions of feigned or romantic adventures, calculated merely to entertain the curiosity of the Reader." Jack Sheppard had many biographers. Seven accurate and authentic histories were published, all purporting to give the true story of his surprising adventures, and bequeathing a valuable legacy to the then unborn historical novelist, Mr. Harrison Ainsworth. Again, Rich, the Manager of the Lincoln's Inn Theatre, brought out 'Harlequin Jack Sheppard' in the year of that desperado's execution, an operatic pantomime founded upon his exploits. A little before this another dramatic performance, the 'Beggars Opera,' having a criminal for its hero, had taken the town by storm; and many strongly and with reason condemned the degradation of national taste which could popularize the loves of 'Polly Peachum' and 'Captain Macheath.' Besides these books and plays there was a constant publication of broad-sheets and chap-books of a still lower type, intended to pander to the same unwholesome taste, while a great novelist like Fielding did not hesitate to draw upon his personal acquaintance with crime, obtained as a police magistrate, and write the life of Jonathan Wild.

The demand was no doubt fostered by the extraordinary prevalence of crime. Criminal records would probably be read with avidity at times when ruffianism was in the ascendant, and offences of the most heinous description were of daily occurrence. New crimes cropped up daily. The whole country was a prey to lawlessness and disorder. Outrages of all kinds, riots, robberies, murders, took place continually. None of the high-roads or bye-roads were safe by night or day. Horsemen in the open country, footpads in or near towns, laid wayfarers under contribution. Armed parties ranged the rural districts attacking country houses in force, driving off cattle and deer, and striking terror everywhere. The general turbulence often broke out into open disturbance. The Riot Act, which was a product of these times, was not passed before it was needed. Riots were frequent in town and country. The mob was easily roused, as when it broke open the house of the Provost Marshal Tooley in Holborn, "to whom they owed a grudge for impressing men to sell as recruits to Flanders."[141] "They burnt his furniture in the street; many persons were killed and wounded in the affray."[142] Now political parties, inflamed with rancorous spirit, created uproars in the "mug houses"; now mutinous soldiers violently protested against the coarse linen of their "Hanover" shirts; again the idle flunkies at a London theatre rose in revolt against new rules introduced by the management and produced a serious riot.[143] In the country gangs of ruffians disguised in female attire, the forerunners of Rebecca and her daughter, ran a muck against turnpike gates, demolishing all they found. There were smuggling riots, when armed crowds overpowered the custom's officers and broke into warehouses sealed by the Crown; corn riots at periods of scarcity, when private granaries were forced and pillaged. A still worse crime prevailed—that of arson. I find in 'Hardwicke's Life' reference to a proclamation offering a reward for the detection of those who sent threatening letters "to diverse persons in the citys of London, Westminster, Bristol, and Exeter, requiring them to deposit certain sums of money in particular places, and threatening to sett fire to their houses, and to burn and destroy them and their families in case of refusal, some of which threats have accordingly been carried into execution."[144] Other threats were to murder unless a good sum were at once paid down. Thus Jepthah Big was tried in 1729 for writing two letters, demanding in one eighty-five guineas, in the other one hundred guineas from Nathaniel Newnham, "a fearful old man," and threatening to murder both him and his wife unless he got the money. Jepthah Big was found guilty and sentenced to death.

 The state of the metropolis was something frightful in the

early decades of the eighteenth century. Such was the reckless daring of evil-doers that there was but little security for life and property. Wright, in his 'Caricature History of the Georges,' says of this period, "robbery was carried on to an extraordinary extent in the streets of London even by daylight. Housebreaking was of frequent occurrence by night, and every road leading to the metropolis was beset by bands of reckless highwaymen, who carried their depredations into the very heart of the town. Respectable women could not venture in the streets alone after nightfall, even in the city, without risk of being grossly outraged." In 1720 ladies going to Court were escorted by servants armed with blunderbusses "to shoot at the rogues." Wright gives a detailed account of five-and-twenty robberies perpetrated within three weeks in January and February of the year above mentioned. A few of the most daring cases may be quoted. Three highwaymen stopped a gentleman of the Prince's household in Poland Street, and made the watchman throw away his lantern and stand quietly by while they robbed and ill-used their victim. Other highwaymen the same night fired at Colonel Montague's carriage as it passed along Frith Street Soho, because the coachman refused to stand; and the Duchess of Montrose, coming from Court in her chair, was stopped by highwaymen near Bond Street. The mails going out and coming into London were seized and rifled. Post-boys, stage-coaches, every-body and everything that travelled were attacked. A great peer, the Duke of Chandos, was twice stopped during the period above mentioned, but he and his servants were too strong for the villains, some of whom they captured. People were robbed in Chelsea, in Cheapside, in White Conduit Fields, in Denmark Street, St. Giles. Wade, in his 'British Chronology', under the head of public calamities in 1729, classes with a sickly season, perpetual storms, and incessant rains, the dangerous condition of the cities of London and Westminster and their neighbourhoods, which "proceeded from the number of footpads and street-robbers, insomuch that there was no stirring out after dark for fear of mischief. These ruffians knocked people down and wounded them before they demanded their money." Large rewards were offered for the apprehension of these offenders. Thief-catchers and informers were continually active, and the law did not hesitate to strike all upon whom it could lay its hands. Yet crime still nourished and increased year after year.

The Englishman's house, and proverbially his castle, was no more secure then than now from burglarious inroads. Housebreakers abounded, working in gangs with consummate skill and patience, hand and glove with servants past and present, associated with receivers, and especially with the drivers of night coaches. Half the hackney coachmen about this time were in league with thieves, being bribed by nocturnal depredators to wait about when a robbery was imminent, and until it was completed. Then, seizing the chance of watchmen being off their beat, these useful accomplices drove at once to the receiver with the "swag."

Towards the middle of the century, Henry Fielding, the great novelist, and at that time acting magistrate for Westminster, wrote:[145] "I make no doubt but that the streets of this town and the roads leading to it will shortly be impassable without the utmost hazard; nor are we threatened with seeing less dangerous groups of rogues amongst us than those which the Italians call banditti...." Again, "If I am to be assaulted and pillaged and plundered, if I can neither sleep in my own house, nor walk the streets, nor travel in safety, is not my condition almost equally bad whether a licensed or an unlicensed rogue, a dragoon or a robber be the person who assaults and plunders me?" Those who set the law at defiance organized themselves into gangs, and co-operated in crime. Fielding tells us in the same work that nearly a hundred rogues were incorporated in one body, "have officers and a treasury, and have reduced theft and robbery into a regular system." Among them were men who appeared in all disguises and mixed in all companies. The members of the society were not only versed in every art of cheating and thieving, but they were armed to evade the law, and if a prisoner could not be rescued, a prosecutor could be bribed, or some "rotten member of the law" forged a defence supported by false witnesses. This must have been perpetuated, for I find another reference later to the Thieves or Housebreaker's Company which had regular books, kept clerks, opened accounts with members, and duly divided the profits. According to the confession of two of the gang who were executed on Kensington Common, they declared that their profits amounted on an average to £500 a year, and that one of them had put by £2000 in the stocks, which before his trial he made over to a friend to preserve it for his family. Another desperate gang, Wade says, were so audacious that they went to the houses of the peace officers, and made them beg pardon for endeavouring to do their duty, and promise not to molest them. They went further, and even attacked and wounded a "head borough" in St. John's Street in about forty places, so that many of the threatened officers had to "lie in Bridewell for safety."

In Harris's 'Life of Lord Hardwicke' is a letter from the solicitor to the Treasury to Sir Philip Yorke, referring to "the gang of ruffians who are so notorious for their robberies, and have lately murdered Thomas Bull in Southwark, and wounded others. Their numbers daily increase, and now become so formidable that constables are intimidated by their threats and desperate behaviour from any endeavour to apprehend them." One of these ruffians was described in the proclamation offering rewards for their apprehension as "above six feet high, black eyebrows, his teeth broke before;" another had a large scar under his chin.

Still worse was the "Resolution Club," a numerous gang, regularly organized under stringent rules. It was one of their articles, that whoever resisted or attempted to fly when stopped should be instantly cut down and crippled. Any person who prosecuted, or appeared as evidence against a member of the club, should be marked down for vengeance. The members took an "infernal oath" to obey the rules, and if taken and sentenced to "die mute." Another instance of the lawlessness of the times is to be seen in the desperate attack made by some forty ruffians on a watch-house in Moorfields, where an accomplice was kept a prisoner. They were armed with pistols, cutlasses, and other offensive weapons. The watchman was wounded, the prisoner rescued. After this the assailants demolished the watch-house, robbed the constables, "committed several unparalleled outrages, and went off in triumph." The gang was too numerous to be quickly subdued, but most of the rioters were eventually apprehended, and it is satisfactory to learn that they were sentenced to imprisonment in Newgate for three, five, or seven years, according to the part they had played.

The contempt of the majesty of the law was not limited to the lower and dangerous classes. A gentleman's maid-servant, having resisted the parish officers who had a distress warrant upon the gentleman's house for unpaid rates, was committed by the magistrates to Newgate. "The gentleman," by name William Frankland, on learning what had happened, armed himself with a brace of pistols, and went to the office where the justices were then sitting, and asked which of them had dared to commit his servant to prison? "Mr. Miller," so runs the account, "smilingly replied, 'I did,' on which the gentleman fired one of his pistols and shot Mr. Miller in the side, but it is thought did not wound him mortally. He was instantly secured and committed to Newgate." At the following Old Bailey sessions, he was tried under the Black Act, when he pleaded insanity. This did not avail him, and although the jury in convicting him strongly recommended him to mercy he was sentenced to death. Another case of still more flagrant contempt of court may fitly be introduced here. At the trial of a woman named Housden for coining at the Old Bailey in 1712, a man named Johnson, an ex-butcher and highwayman by profession, came into court and desired to speak to her. Mr. Spurling, the principal turnkey of Newgate, told him no person could be permitted to speak to the prisoner, whereupon Johnson drew out a pistol and shot Mr. Spurling dead upon the spot, the woman Housden loudly applauding his act. The court did not easily recover from its consternation, but presently the recorder suspended the trial of the woman for coining, and as soon as an indictment could be prepared, Johnson was arraigned for the murder, convicted, and then and there sentenced to death, the woman Housden being also sentenced at the same time as an accessory before and after the fact.

Various causes are given for this great prevalence of crime. The long and impoverishing wars of the early years of the century, which saddled us with the national debt, no doubt produced much distress, and drove thousands who could not or would not find honest work, into evil ways. Manners among the highest and the lowest were generally profligate. Innumerable places of public diversion, ridottos, balls, masquerades, tea-gardens, and wells, offered crowds a ready means for self-indulgence. Classes aped the habits of the classes above their own, and the love of luxurious gratification "reached to the dregs of the people," says Fielding, "who, not being able by the fruits of honest labour to support the state which they affect, they disdain the wages to which their industry would entitle them, and abandoning themselves to idleness, the more simple and poor-spirited betake themselves to a state of starving and beggary, while those of more art and courage become thieves, sharpers, and robbers."

Drunkenness was another terrible vice, even then more rampant and wildly excessive than in later years. While the aristocracy drank deep of Burgundy and port, and every roaring blade disdained all heel-taps, the masses fuddled and besotted themselves with gin. This last-named pernicious fluid was as cheap as dirt. A gin-shop actually had on its sign the notice, "Drunk for 1*d*.; dead drunk for 2*d*.; clean straw for nothing," which Hogarth introduced into his caricature of Gin Lane. No pencil could paint, no pen describe the scenes of hideous debauchery hourly enacted in the dens and purlieus of the town. Legislation was powerless to restrain the popular craving. The Gin Act, passed in 1736 amidst the execrations of the mob, which sought to vent its rage upon Sir Joseph Jekyll, the chief promoter of the Bill, was generally evaded. The much-loved poisonous spirit was still retailed under fictitious names, such as Sangree, Tow Row, the Makeshift, and King Theodore of Corsica. It was prescribed as a medicine for cholic to be taken two or three times a day. Numberless tumults arose out of the prohibition to retail spirituous liquors, and so openly was the law defied, that twelve thousand persons were convicted within two years of having sold them illegally in London. Informers were promptly bought off or intimidated, magistrates "through fear or corruption" would not convict, and the Act was repealed in the hope that more moderate duty and stricter enforcement of the law would benefit the revenue and yet lessen consumption. The first was undoubtedly affected, but hardly the latter. Fielding, writing nearly ten years after the repeal of the Act, says that he has reason to believe that "gin is the principal sustenance (if it may be so called) of more than a hundred thousand people in the metropolis," and he attributed to it most of the crimes committed by the wretches with whom he had to deal. "The intoxicating draught itself disqualifies them from any honest means to acquire it, at the same time that it removes sense of fear and shame, and emboldens them to commit every wicked and desperate enterprise."

The passion for gaming, again, "the school in which most highwaymen of great eminence have been bred,"[146] was a fruitful source of immoral degeneracy. Every one gambled. In the 'Gentleman's Magazine' for 1731 there is the following entry: "At night their majesties played for the benefit of the groom porter, and the king (George II.) and queen each won several hundreds, and the Duke of Grafton several thousands of pounds." His Majesty's lieges followed his illustrious example, and all manner of games of chance with cards or dice, such as hazard, Pharoah, basset, roly-poly, were the universal diversion in clubs, public places, and private gatherings. The law had thundered, but to no purpose, against "this destructive vice," inflicting fines on those who indulged in it, declaring securities won at play void, with other penalties, yet gaming throve and flourished. It was fostered and encouraged by innumerable hells, which the law in vain strove to put down. Nightly raids were made upon them. In the same number of the 'Gentleman's Magazine' as that just quoted it is recorded that "the High Constable of Holborn searched a notorious gaming-house behind Gray's Inn Road; but the gamesters were fled, only the keeper was arrested and bound over for £200." Again, I find in Wade's 'Chronology' that "Justice Fielding, having received information of a rendezvous of gamesters in the Strand, procured a strong party of the Guards, who seized forty-five of the tables, which they broke to pieces, and carried the gamesters before the justice.... Under each of the broken tables were observed two iron rollers and two private springs, which those who were in the secret could touch and stop the turning whenever they had flats to deal with." No wonder these establishments throve. They were systematically organized, and administered by duly appointed officers. There was the commissioner who checked the week's accounts and pocketed the takings; a director to superintend the room; an operator to deal the cards, and four to five *croupiers*, who watched the cards and gathered in the money of the Bank. Besides these there were "puffs," who had money given them to decoy people to play; a clerk and a *squib*, who were spies upon the straight dealings of the puffs; a flasher to swear how often the bank was stripped; a dunner to recover sums lost; a waiter to snuff candles and fill in the wine; and an attorney or "Newgate solicitor." A flash captain was kept to fight gentlemen who were peevish about losing their money at the door was a porter, "generally a soldier of the foot guards,"[147] who admitted visitors after satisfying himself that they were of the right sort. The porter had aides-de-camp and assistants—an "orderly man," who patrolled the street and gave notice of the approaching constables; a "runner," who watched for the meetings of the justices and brought intelligence of the constables being out; and a host of linkboys, coachmen, chairmen, drawers to assist, with common-bail affidavit men, ruffians, bravos, and assassins for any odd job that might turn up requiring physical strength.

As the years passed the vice grew in magnitude. Large fortunes were made by the proprietors of gaming-houses, thanks to the methodized employment of capital, embarked regularly as in any other trading establishment, the invention of E. O. tables, and the introduction of the "foreign games of roulet and rouge et noir. Little short of a million must have been amassed in this way,"[148] individuals having acquired from £10,000 to £100,000 a-piece. The number of establishments daily multiplied. They were mounted regardless of expense. Open house was kept, and luxurious dinners laid for all comers. Merchants and bankers' clerks entrusted with large sums were especially encouraged to attend. The cost of entertainment in one house alone was £8000 for eight months, while the total expenditure on all as much as £150,000 a year. The gambling-house keepers, often prize-fighters originally, or partners admitted for their skill in card-sharping or cogging dice, possessed such ample funds that they laughed at legal prosecutions. Witnesses were suborned, officers of justice bribed, informers intimidated. Armed ruffians and bludgeon men were employed to barricade the houses and resist the civil power. Private competed with public hells. Great ladies of fashion, holding their heads high in the social world, made their drawing-rooms into gambling places, into which young men of means were enticed and despoiled. This was called "pidgeoning," and probably originated the expression. The most noted female gamesters were Lady Buckinghamshire, Lady Archer, Lady Mount Edgecombe, a trio who had earned for themselves the soubriquet of "Faro's Daughters." Their conduct came under severe reprehension of Lord Kenyon, who, in summing up a gambling case, warned them that if they came before him in connection with gambling transactions, "though they should be the first ladies of the land," they should certainly exhibit themselves in the pillory. This well-merited threat was reproduced in various caricatures of the day, under such heads as, "Ladies of Elevated Rank"; "Faro's Daughters, Beware!" "Discipline *à la* Kenyon."

The Government itself was in a measure responsible for the diffusion of the passion for gambling. The pernicious custom of public lotteries practically legalized this baneful vice. State lotteries began in the reign of Elizabeth, and existed down to 1826. They brought in a considerable revenue, but they did infinite mischief by developing the rage for speculation, which extended to the whole community. The rich could purchase whole tickets, or "great goes"; for the more impecunious the tickets were subdivided into "little goes." Those who had no tickets at all could still gamble at the lottery insurance offices by backing any particular number to win. The demorailzition was widespread. It reached a climax in the South Sea bubble, when thousands and thousands were first decoyed, then cruelly deceived and beggared. But lotteries lingered on till the Government at length awoke to the degradation of obtaining an income from such a source.

While crime thus stalked rampant through the land, the law was nearly powerless to grapple and check it. It had practically but one method of repression—the wholesale removal of convicted offenders to another world. Of prevention as we understand it our forefathers had but little idea. The metropolis, with its ill-paved, dimly-lighted streets, was without police protection beyond that afforded by a few feeble watchmen, the sorely-tried and often nearly useless "Charlies." The administration of justice was defective; the justices had not sufficient powers; they were frequently "as regardless of the law as ignorant of it,"[149] or else were defied by pettifoggers and people with money in their pockets. "A mob of chairmen or servants, or a gang of thieves, are almost too big for the civil authority to repress;"[150] and the civil power generally, according to Fielding, was in a lethargic state. Yet private enterprise had sought for some time past to second the efforts of the State, and various societies for the reformation of manners laboured hard, but scarcely with marked success, to reduce crime. The first of these societies originated in the previous century by six private gentlemen, whose hearts were moved by the dismal and desperate state of the country "to engage in the difficult and dangerous enterprise;" and it was soon strengthened by the addition of "persons of eminency in the law, members of Parliament, justices of the peace, and considerable citizens of London of known abilities and great integrity." There was a second society of about fifty persons, tradesmen, and others; and a third society of constables, who met to consider how they might best discharge their oaths; a fourth to give information; while other bodies of householders and officers assisted in the great work. These in one year, that of 1724, had prosecuted 2723 persons, and in the thirty-three years preceding 89,393; while in the same period they had given away 400,000 good books. However well meant and well directed were these efforts, it is to be feared that they were of little avail in stemming the torrent of crime which long continued to deluge the country, and which has far from abated even now.

The character of offences perpetrated will best be understood by passing from the general to the particular, and briefly indicating the salient points of a certain number of typical cases, all of which were in some way or other connected with Newgate. Crime was confined to no one class; while the lowest robbed with brutal violence, members of the highest stabbed and murdered each other on flimsy pretences, or found funds for debauchery in systematic and cleverly contrived frauds. Life was held very cheap in those days. Every one with any pretensions carried a sword, and appealed to it on the slightest excuse or provocation. Murderous duels and affrays were of constant occurrence. So-called affairs of honour could only be washed out in blood. Sometimes it was a causeless quarrel in a club or coffee-house ending in a fatal encounter. Richard Savage the poet was tried for his life for a murder of this kind. In company with two friends, all three of them being the worse for drink, he forced his way into a private room in Robinson's coffee-house, near Charing Cross, occupied by another party carousing. One of Savage's friends kicked down the table without provocation. "What do you mean by that?" cried one side. "What do *you* mean?" cried the other. Swords were drawn, and a fight ensued. Savage, who found himself in front of one Sinclair, made several thrusts at his opponent, and ran him through the body. Lights were put out, and Savage tried to escape, but was captured in a back court. He and his associates were committed first to the gatehouse and thence to Newgate. Three weeks later they were arraigned at the Old Bailey, found guilty of murder, and cast for death.[151] The king's pardon was, however, obtained for Savage through the intercession of influential friends, but contrary, it is said, to the expressed wish of his mother. Savage was the illegitimate child of the Countess of Macclesfield, the fruit of a guilty intrigue with Captain Richard Savage, afterwards Earl Rivers. Lady Macclesfield was divorced, and subsequently married Lord Rivers; but she conceived a violent hatred for the child, and only consented to settle an annuity of £50 upon him when grown to man's estate, under threat of exposure in the first publication of Savage's poems. Savage, after his release from Newgate, retired into Wales, but he continued in very distressed circumstances, and being arrested for debt, lingered out the remainder of his days in Bristol Gaol.

The case of Major Oneby is still more typical of the times. He was a military officer who had served in Marlbro's wars, and not without distinction, although enjoying an evil reputation as a duellist. When the army lay in winter quarters at Bruges, he had been "out," and had killed his man; again in Jamaica he had wounded an adversary who presently died. After the peace of Utrecht Major Oneby was placed on half pay, and to eke out his narrow means he became a professional gambler, being seldom without cards and dice in his pocket. He was soon known as a swaggerer and a bully, with whom it was wisest not to quarrel. One night, however, he was at play in the Castle Tavern in Drury Lane, when a Mr. Gower and he fell out about a bet. Oneby threw a decanter at Gower, and Gower returned the fire with a glass. Swords were drawn, but at the interposition of others put up again. Gower was for making peace, but Oneby sullenly swore he would have the other's blood. When the party broke up he called Gower into another room and shut the door. A clashing of swords was heard within, the waiter broke open the door, and the company rushed in to find Oneby holding up Gower with his left hand, having his sword in his right. Blood was seen streaming through Gower's waistcoat, and his sword lay upon the floor. Some one said to Oneby, "You have killed him;" but the Major replied, "No, I might have done it if I would, but I have only frightened him," adding, that if he had killed him in the heat of passion the law would have been on his side. But his unfortunate adversary did actually die of his wound the following day, whereupon Major Oneby was apprehended and locked up in Newgate. He was tried the following month at the Old Bailey, but the jury could not decide as to the exact measure of the Major's guilt, except that it was clear he had given the first provocation, while it was not denied he had killed the deceased.

A special verdict was agreed to, and the case with its various points referred to the twelve judges. The prisoner, who had hoped to escape with a conviction for manslaughter, was remanded to Newgate, and remained there in the State side without judgment for the space of two years. Becoming impatient, he prayed the Court of King's Bench that counsel might be heard in his case, and he was accordingly brought into Court before the Lord Chief Justice Raymond, when his counsel and those for the Crown were fully heard. The Judge reserved his judgment till he had consulted his eleven brethren; but the Major, elated at the ingenious arguments of his lawyer, fully counted upon speedy release. On his way back to gaol he entertained his friends at a handsome dinner given at the Crown and Anchor Tavern.[152] He continued to carouse and live high in Newgate for several months more, little doubting the result of the Judges' conference. They met after considerable delay in Sergeant's Inn Hall, counsel was heard on both sides, and the pleadings lasted a whole day. A friend called in the evening, and told him when he was making merry over a bowl of punch that eleven of the Judges had decided against him. This greatly alarmed him; next day the keeper of Newgate (Mr. Akerman) came to put irons on him, unless he was prepared to pay for a special keeper to occupy the same room. Oneby was indignant, but helpless. He felt the ground slipping from under his feet, and he was almost prepared for the judgment delivered in open court that he had been guilty of murder, his threat that he would have Gower's blood having had great weight in his disfavour.

Oneby spent the days before execution in fruitless efforts to get relations and friends to use their influence in obtaining him a pardon. But to the first he was so overbearing that they would not visit him in Newgate, and the latter, if he had any, would not stir a finger to help him. His last moments seem to have been spent between laughing at the broad jokes of his personal gaoler, who now never left him, one John Hooper, afterwards public executioner,[153] and fits of rage against those who had deserted him in his extremity. He was further exasperated by a letter from an undertaker in Drury Lane, who, having heard that the Major was to die on the following Monday, promised to perform the funeral "as cheap and in as decent a manner as any man alive." Another cause of annoyance was the publication of a broad sheet, entitled 'The Weight of Blood, or the Case of Major John Oneby,' the writer of which had visited the prisoner, ostensibly to offer to suppress the publication, but really as an "interviewer" to obtain some additional facts for his catch-penny pamphlet. The Major was so indignant that he laid a trap for the author by inviting him to revisit Newgate, promising himself the pleasure of thrashing him when he appeared, but the man declined to be caught. On the Saturday night before execution Oneby, learning that a petition had been presented and rejected, prepared to die. He slept soundly till four in the morning, then calling for a glass of brandy and writing materials, he wrote his will. It was brief, and to the following effect:

"Cousin Turvill, give Mr. Akerman, for the turnkey below stairs, half a guinea, and Jack Hooper who waits in my room five shillings. The poor devils have had a great deal of trouble with me since I have been here." After this he begged to be left to sleep; but a friend called about seven, the Major cried feebly to his servant, "Philip, who is that?" and it was found that he was bleeding to death from a deep gash in his wrist. He was dead before a surgeon could be called in.

In these disastrous affrays both antagonists were armed. But reckless roysterers and swaggering bobadils were easily provoked, and they did not hesitate, in a moment of mad passion, to use their swords upon defenceless men. Bailiffs and the lesser officers of justice were especially obnoxious to these high-tempered bloods. I read in 'Luttrell,' under date Feb. 1698, "Captain Dancy of the Guards killed a bailiff in Exeter Street, and is committed to Newgate." Again in 1705, "Captain Carlton, formerly a Justice of the Peace for Middlesex, is committed to Newgate for running a Marshal's man through the body who endeavoured to arrest him on the parade by the Horse Guards in St. James' Park, of which wound it is thought the man will die." I can find no mention of the fate which overtook these murderers; but the 'Calendars' contain a detailed account of another murder of much the same kind, that perpetrated by the Marquis de Paleoti upon his servant, John Niccolo, otherwise John the Italian, in 1718. The Marquis had come to England to visit his sister, who had married the Duke of Shrewsbury in Rome, and had launched out into a career of wild extravagance. The Duchess had paid his debts several times, but at length declined to assist him further. He was arrested and imprisoned, but his sister privately procured his discharge. After his enlargement, being without funds, the Marquis sent Niccolo to borrow what he could. But "the servant, having met with frequent denials, declined going, at which the Marquis drew his sword and killed him on the spot."[154] The Marquis seems to have hoped to have found sanctuary at the Bishop of Salisbury's, to whose house he repaired as soon as Niccolo's body was found. But he was arrested there after having behaved so rudely, that his sword, all bloody with gore, had to be taken from him, and he was conveyed to Newgate. His defence was weak, his guilt clear, and much to his surprise, he was sentenced to be hanged. He declared that it was disgraceful "to put a nobleman to death like a common malefactor for killing a servant;" but his plea availed little, and he suffered at Tyburn five weeks after the murder. Forty years later an English nobleman, Earl Ferrers, paid the same extreme penalty for murdering his steward. His lordship was tried by his peers, and after sentence until his execution was lodged in the Tower, and not in Newgate. His case is sufficiently well known, and has already been briefly referred to.

Another aristocratic miscreant, whose crimes only fell short of murder, was Colonel Francis Charteris. Well born, well educated, well introduced into life, he joined the army under Marlborough in the Low Countries as a cornet of horse, and soon became noted as a bold and dexterous gambler. His greed and rapacity were unbounded; he lent money at usurious rates to those whom he had already despoiled of large sums by foul play, and having thus ruined many of his brother officers, he was brought to trial, found guilty of disgraceful conduct, and sentenced by Court Martial to be cashiered. On his way back to Scotland, by falsely swearing he had been robbed at an inn, he swindled the landlord out of a large sum of money as an indemnity, and does not seem to have been called to account for his fraud. In spite of his antecedents, Charteris obtained a new commission through powerful friends, and was soon advanced to the grade of Colonel. Moving in the best society, he extended his gambling operations, and nearly robbed the Duchess of Queensbury of £3000 by placing her near a mirror, so that he could see all her cards. Escaping punishment for this he continued his depredations till he acquired a considerable fortune and several landed estates. Fate overtook him at last, and he became the victim of his own profligacy. Long notorious as an unprincipled and systematic seducer, by means of stratagems and bribes he effected the ruin of numbers, but was at length arrested on a charge of criminal assault. He lay in Newgate on the State side, lightly ironed, and enjoying the best of the prison until the trial at the Old Bailey in Feb. 1730. He was convicted and sentenced to die, but through the strenuous exertions of his son-in-law, the Earl of Wemyss, obtained the king's pardon. He died two years later, miserably, in Edinburgh, whither he had retired after his release. He was long remembered with obloquy. Dr. Arbuthnot, who wrote his epitaph, has best depicted his detestable character, as a villain, "who with an inflexible constancy and inimitable impunity of life persisted, in spite of age and infirmity, in the practice of every human vice except prodigality and hypocrisy, his insatiable avarice exempting him from the first, and his matchless impudence from the latter, … and who, having done every day of his life something worthy of a gibbet, was once condemned to one for what he had not done." Dr. Arbuthnot appears from this to have dissented from the verdict of the jury by which Charteris was tried.

In times of such general corruption it was not strange that a deplorable laxity of morals should prevail as regards trusts, whether public or private. Even a Lord Chancellor was found guilty of venal practices—the sale of offices, and the misappropriation of funds lodged in the Chancery Court. This was the twelfth Earl of Macclesfield,[155] who sought thus dishonestly to mend his fortunes, impaired, it was said, by the South Sea Bubble speculations. He was tried before his peers, found guilty, and declared for ever incapable of sitting in Parliament, or of holding any office under the Crown; and further sentenced to a fine of £30,000 with imprisonment in the Tower until it was paid. Lord Macclesfield promptly paid his fine, which was but a small part of the money he had amassed by his speculations, and was discharged. "To the disgrace of the times in which he lived," says the biographer of Lord Hardwicke,[156] "the infamy with which he had been thus covered debarred him neither from the favour of the great nor even from that of his sovereign."

Various cases of embezzlement by public officials previous to this are mentioned by Luttrell. Frauds upon the Exchequer, and upon persons holding Government annuities, were not infrequent. The first entry in Luttrell is dated 1697, May, and is to the effect that "Mr. Marriott, an underteller in the Exchequer, arrested for altering an Exchequer bill for £10 to £100, pleaded innocency, but is sent to Newgate"; others were implicated, and a proclamation was issued offering a reward for the apprehension of Domingo Autumes, a Portuguese, Robert Marriott, and another for counterfeiting Exchequer bills. A little later another teller, Mr. Darby, is sent to Newgate on a similar charge, and in that prison Mr. Marriott "accuses John Knight, Esq., M.P., treasurer of customs, who is displaced." Marriott's confession follows: "He met Mr. Burton and Mr. Knight at Somerset House, where they arranged to get twenty per cent, by making Exchequer bills specie bills; they offered Marriott £500 a year to take all upon himself if discovered. It is thought greater people are in it to destroy the credit of the nation." Following this confession, bills were brought into the House of Commons charging Burton, Knight, and Duncombe with embezzlement, but "blanks are left for the House to insert the punishment, which is to be either fine, imprisonment, or loss of estates." Knight was found guilty of endorsing Exchequer bills falsely, but not of getting money thereby. Burton was found guilty; Duncombe's name is not mentioned, and Marriott was discharged. But this does not end the business. In the May following "Mr. Ellers, master of an annuity office in the Exchequer, was committed to Newgate for forging people's hands to their orders, and receiving a considerable sum of money thereon." Again in October, "Bellingham, an old offender, was convicted of felony in forging Exchequer bills; and a Mrs. Butler, also for forging a bond of £20,000, payable by the executors of Sir Robert Clayton six years after his death." Later on (1708) I find an entry in Luttrell that Justice Dyot, who was a commissioner of the Stamp-office, was committed to Newgate for counterfeiting stamps, which others whom he informed against distributed. Of the same character as the foregoing was the offence of Mr. Lemon, a clerk in the Pell office of the Exchequer, who received £300 in the name of a gentlewoman deceased, and kept it, for which he was turned out of his place. Other unfaithful public servants were to be found in other departments. Robert Lowther, Esq., was taken into custody on the 25th October, 1721, by order of the Privy Council, for his tyrannical and corrupt administration when Governor of the Island of Barbadoes. Twenty years later the House of Commons fly at still higher game, and commit the Solicitor of the Treasury to Newgate for refusing to answer questions put to him by the Secret Committee which sat to inquire into Sir Robert Walpole's administration. This official had been often charged with the Prime Minister's secret disbursements, and he was accused of being recklessly profuse.

Returning to meaner and more commonplace offenders, I find in the records full details of all manner of crimes. Murders the most atrocious and bloodthirsty, robberies executed with great ingenuity and boldness by both sexes, remarkable instances of swindling and successful frauds, early cases of forgery, coining carried out with extensive ramifications, piracies upon the high seas, long practised with strange immunity from reprisals. Perhaps the most revolting murder ever perpetrated, not excepting those of later date, was that in which Catherine Hayes assisted. The victim was her husband, an unoffending, industrious man, whose life she made miserable, boasting once indeed that she would think it no more sin to murder him than to kill a dog. After a violent quarrel between them she persuaded a man who lodged with them, named Billings, and who was either her lover or her illegitimate son, to join her in an attempt upon Hayes. A new lodger, Wood, arriving, it was necessary to make him a party to the plot, but he long resisted Mrs. Hayes' specious arguments, till she clenched them by declaring that Hayes was an atheist and a murderer, whom it could be no crime to kill, moreover that at his death she would become possessed of £1500, which she would hand over to Wood. Wood at last yielded, and after some discussion it was decided to do the dreadful deed while Hayes was in his cups. After a long drinking bout, in which Hayes drank wine, probably drugged, and the rest beer, the victim dragged himself to bed and fell on it in a stupor. Billings now went in, and with a hatchet struck Hayes a violent blow on the head and fractured his skull; then Wood gave the poor wretch, as he was not quite dead, two other more blows and finished him. The next job was to dispose of the murdered man's remains. To evade identification Catherine Hayes suggested that the head should be cut off, which Wood effected with his pocket-knife. She then proposed to boil it, but this was over-ruled, and the head was disposed of by the men, who threw it into the Thames from a wharf near the Horseferry[157] at Westminster. They hoped that the damning evidence would be carried off by the next tide, but it remained floating near shore, and was picked up next day by a watchman, and handed over to the parish officers, by whom, when washed and the hair combed, it was placed on the top of a pole in the churchyard of St. Margaret's, Westminster. Having got rid of the head, the murderers next dealt with the body, which they dismembered, and packed the parts into a box. This was conveyed to Marylebone, where the pieces were taken out, wrapped in an old blanket, and sunk in a pond.

Meanwhile the exposed head had been viewed by curious crowds, and at last a Mr. Bennet, an organ-builder, saw a resemblance to the face of Hayes, with whom he had been acquainted; another person, a journeyman tailor, also recognized it, and inquiries were made of Catherine as to her husband. At first she threw people off the scent by confessing that Hayes had killed a man and absconded, but being questioned by several she told a different story to each, and presently suspicion fell upon her. As it had come out that Billings and Wood had been drinking with Hayes the last time he was seen, they were included in the warrant, which was now issued for the apprehension of the murderers. The woman was arrested by Mr. Justice Lambert in person, who had "procured the assistance of two officers of the Life Guards," and Billings with her. One was committed to the Bridewell, Tothill Fields, the other to the Gatehouse. Catherine's conduct when brought into the presence of her murdered husband's head almost passes belief. Taking the glass in which it had been preserved into her arms, she cried, "It is my dear husband's head," and shed tears as she embraced it. The surgeon having taken the head out of the case, she kissed it rapturously, and begged to be indulged with a lock of his hair. Next day the trunk and remains of the corpse were discovered at Marylebone without the head, and the justices, nearly satisfied as to the guilt of Catherine Hayes, committed her to Newgate. Wood was soon after captured, and on hearing that the body had been found, confessed the whole crime. Billings shortly did the same; but Mrs. Hayes obstinately refused to admit her guilt. This atrocious creature was for the moment the centre of interest: numbers visited her in Newgate, and sought to learn her reasons for committing so dreadful a crime; but she gave different and evasive answers to all.

At her trial she pleaded hard to be exempted from the penalty of petty treason,[158] which was at that time burning, alleging that she was not guilty of striking the fatal blow. She was told the law must take its course. Billings and Wood hoped they might not be hung in chains, but received no answer. Wood actually died in prison before execution; Billings suffered at Tyburn, and was hung in chains near the pond in Marylebone. Mrs. Hayes tried to destroy herself, but failed, and was literally burnt alive.[159] The fire reaching the hands of the hangman, he let go the rope by which she was to have been strangled, and the flames slowly consumed her, as she pushed the blazing faggots from her, and rent the air with her agonized cries. Hers, which took place on 9th May, 1726, was not the last execution of its kind. In November, 1750, Amy Hutchinson was burnt at Ely, after a conviction of petty treason, having poisoned a husband newly married, whom she had taken to spite a truant lover. In 1767, again, Ann Sowerly underwent the same awful sentence at York. She also had poisoned her husband. Last of all, on the 10th March, 1788, a woman was burnt before the debtors' door of Newgate. Having been tied to a stake and seated on a stool, the stool was withdrawn and she was strangled. After that she was burnt. Her offence was coining. In the following year an Act was passed (30 Geo. III., cap. 48) which abolished this cruel custom of burning women for petty treason.

Sarah Malcolm was another female monster, a wholesale murderess, whose case stands out as one of peculiar atrocity even in those bloodthirsty times. She was employed as a laundress in the Temple, where she waited on several gentlemen, and had also access in her capacity of charwoman to the chambers occupied by an aged lady named Mrs. Duncombe.[160] Sarah's cupidity was excited by the chance sight of her mistress's hoarded wealth, both in silver plate and broad coins, and she resolved to become possessed of it, hoping when enriched to gain a young man of her acquaintance named Alexander as her husband. Mrs. Duncombe had two other servants, Elizabeth Harrison, also aged, and a young maid named Ann Price, who resided with her in the Temple. One day (Feb. 2, 1733) a friend coming to call upon Mrs. Duncombe was unable to gain admittance. After some delay the rooms were broken into, and their three occupants were found barbarously murdered, the girl Price in the first room, with her throat cut from ear to ear, her hair loose, hanging over her eyes, and her hands clenched; in the next lay Elizabeth Harrison on a press bed, strangled; and last of all, old Mrs. Duncombe, also lying across her bed, quite dead. The strong box had been broken open and rifled.

That same night one of the barristers, returning to his chambers late, found Sarah Malcolm there kindling a fire, and after remarking upon her appearance at that strange hour, bade her begone, saying, that no person acquainted with Mrs. Duncombe should be in his chambers till the murderer was discovered. Before leaving she confessed to having stolen two of his waistcoats, whereupon he called the watch and gave her into custody. After her departure, assisted by a friend, the barrister made a thorough search of his rooms, and in a cupboard came upon a lot of linen stained with blood, also a silver tankard with blood upon the handle. The watchmen had suffered Sarah to go at large, but she was forthwith rearrested; on searching her, a green silk purse containing twenty-one counters was found upon her, and she was committed to Newgate. There, on arrival, she sought to hire the best accommodation, offering two or three guineas for a room upon the Master Debtors' side. Roger Johnston, a turnkey, upon this searched her, and discovered "concealed under her hair," no doubt in a species of a chignon, "a bag containing twenty moidores, eighteen guineas, and a number of other broad pieces." This money she confessed had come from Mrs. Duncombe; but she stoutly denied all complicity with the murder, or that she had done more than contrive the robbery. She charged two brothers, named Alexander, one of whom she desired to marry, and a woman, Mary Tracy, with the greater crime. Upon her information they were arrested and confronted with her. She persisted in this line of defence at her trial, but the circumstantial evidence against her was so strong that the jury at once found her guilty. She herself had but little hope of escape, and had been heard to cry out on her first commitment, "I am a dead woman." She was duly executed at Tyburn. The Alexanders and Tracy were discharged.

I have specially instanced these foul murders as exhibiting circumstances of atrocity rarely equalled in the records of crime. Catherine Hayes and Sarah Malcolm were unsexed desperadoes, whose misdeeds throw into the shade those of the Mannings and Kate Websters of later times. But women had no monopoly of assassination, in those days when life was held so cheap. Male murderers were still more numerous, and also more pitiless and bloodthirsty. The calendars are replete with homicides, and to refer to them in anything like detail would both weary and disgust the reader. I shall do no more therefore than briefly indicate a certain number of the more prominent cases remarkable either from the position of the criminals, the ties by which they were bound to their victims, or the horrible character of the crime.

The hangman figures among the murderers of this epoch. John Price, who filled the office in 1718, and who rejoiced in the usual official soubriquet of "Jack Ketch," was a scoundrel rendered still more callous and cruel by his dreadful calling. He had begun life well, as an apprentice, but he absconded, and entering the navy, "served with credit on board different king's ships for eighteen years." On his discharge, seeking employment, he obtained the situation of public executioner. He might have lived decently on the hangman's wages and perquisites, but he was a spendthrift, who soon became acquainted with the interiors of the debtors' prisons for Middlesex. Once he was arrested on his way back from Tyburn after a good day's work, having in his possession, besides fees, the complete suits of three men who had just been executed. He gave up all this to liquidate the debt, but the value being insufficient, he was lodged in the Marshalsea. When released, in due course he returned to his old employment, but was soon arrested again, and on a serious charge—that of a murderous assault upon a poor woman who sold gingerbread through the streets. He had attempted to outrage her, and maddened by her resistance, had ill-used her shamefully. "He beat her so cruelly," the account says, "that streams of blood issued from her eyes and mouth; he broke one of her arms, knocked out some of her teeth, bruised her head in a most shameful manner, and forced one of her eyes from the socket."[161] One account says that he was taken red-handed close to the scene of his guilt; another, the more probable, that he was arrested on his way to Tyburn with a convict for the gallows. In any case his unfortunate victim had just life left in her to bear testimony against him. Price was committed to Newgate, and tried for his life. His defence was, that in crossing Moorfields he found something lying in his way, which he kicked and found to be the body of a woman. He lifted her up, but she could not stand on her legs. The evidence of others was too clear, and the jury did not hesitate to convict. After sentence he abandoned himself to drink, and obstinately refused to confess. But on the day before his execution he acknowledged that he had committed the crime while in a state of intoxication. He was hanged in Bunhill Fields, and his body afterwards exhibited in chains in Holloway near the scene of the murder.

Wife-murder was of common occurrence in these reckless

times. The disgraceful state of the marriage laws, and the facility with which the matrimonial knot could be tied, often tempted unscrupulous people to commit bigamy.[162] Louis Houssart was of French extraction, settled in England, who married Ann Rondeau at the French church in Spitalfields. After about three years "he left his wife with disgust," and going into the city, passed himself off as a single man. Becoming acquainted with a Mrs. Hern, he presently married her. He had not been long married before his new wife taxed him with having another wife. He swore it was false, and offered to take the sacrament upon it. She appeared satisfied, and begged him to clear his reputation. "Do not be uneasy," he said; "in a little time I will make you sensible I have no other wife." He now resolved to make away with the first Mrs. Louis Houssart, otherwise Ann Rondeau, and reopened communications with her. Finding her in ill-health, one day he brought her "a medicine which had the appearance of conserve of roses, which threw her into such severe convulsive fits that her life was despaired of for some hours; but at length she recovered." This attempt having failed, he tried a simpler plan. Dressed in a white coat, with sword and cane, he went one evening to the end of Swan Alley, where his wife lived with her mother, and finding a boy, gave him a penny to go and tell Mrs. Rondeau that a gentleman wanted to speak to her in a neighbouring public-house. When she left the house Houssart went in, found his wife alone, and cut her throat with a razor.

"Thus murdered she was found by her mother on her return, after inquiring in vain for the gentleman who was said to be waiting for her." Suspicion fell on Houssart, who was arrested and tried, but for want of the boy's evidence acquitted of the murder. But he was detained in Newgate to take his trial for bigamy. While waiting sentence the boy, a lad of thirteen, who knew of the murder and arrest, and who thought he would be hanged if he confessed that he had carried the message to Mrs. Rondeau, came forward to give evidence. He was taken to Newgate into a room, and identified Houssart at once among seven or eight others. The brother of the deceased, Solomon Rondeau, as heir, now lodged an appeal, in the name of John Doe and Richard Roe, against Houssart, who was eventually again brought to trial. Various pleas were put forward by the defence in bar of further proceedings, among others that there was no such persons as John Doe and Richard Roe, but this plea, with the rest, was overruled, the fact being sworn to that there was a John Doe in Middlesex, a weaver, also a Richard Roe, who was a soldier, and the trial went on. The boy's evidence was very plain. He remembered Houssart distinctly, had seen him by the light of a lantern at a butcher's shop; he wore a whitish coat. The boy also recognized Mrs. Rondeau as the woman to whom he gave the message. Others swore to the white coat which Houssart had on; but the most damning evidence was that of a friend whom he had summoned to see him in Newgate, and whom he asked to swear that they had been drinking together in Newgate Street at the time the murder was committed. The prisoner, however, owned that he did give the boy a penny to call the old woman out, and that he then went in and gave his wife "a touch with the razor, but did not think of killing her." Houssart offered this witness a new shirt, a new suit of clothes, and twenty guineas to swear for him. The prisoner was found guilty and hanged at the end of Swan yard in Shoreditch, on Dec. 7, 1724.

Vincent Davis was another miscreant who murdered his wife, under much the same conditions. He had long barbarously ill-used her; he kept a small walking-cane on purpose to beat her with, and at last so frightened her by his threats to kill her that she ran away from him. She returned one night, but finding that he had put an open knife by the bedside, she placed herself under the protection of the landlady, who advised her to swear the peace against him and get him imprisoned. Next day the brutal husband drove her out of the house, declaring she had no right to be in his company, as he was married to "Little Jenny." But she implored him to be friends, and having followed him to an ale-house seeking reconciliation, he so slashed her fingers with a knife that she came back with bleeding hands. That same night, when his wife met him on his return home, he ordered her to light him to his room, then drawing his knife, stabbed her in the breast. The poor woman bled to death in half-an-hour. Davis after the deed was done was seized with contrition, and when arrested and on his way to Newgate, he told the peace officer that he had killed the best wife in the world. "I know I shall be hanged," he added; "but for God's sake don't let me be anatomized." This man is said to have assumed an air of bravado while he lay under sentence of death, but his courage deserted him as the time for execution approached. He had such a dread of falling into the hands of the surgeons that he wrote to several friends begging them to rescue his body if any attempt should be made at the gallows to remove it. He was hanged at Tyburn on the 30th April, 1825; but the calendar does not state what happened to his corpse.

George Price, who murdered his wife in 1738, had an analogous motive: he wished to release himself from one tie in order to enter into another. He was in service in Kent, his wife lived in lodgings in Highgate, and their family increased far more rapidly than he liked. Having for some time paid his addresses to a widow in Kent, he at length resolved to remove the only obstacle to a second and more profitable marriage. With this infernal object in view he went to Highgate, and told his wife that he had secured a place for her at Putney, to which he would himself drive her in a chaise. She was warned by some of his fellow-servants against trusting herself alone with him, but "she said she had no fear of him, as he had treated her with unusual kindness." They drove off towards Hounslow. On the way she begged him to stop while she bought some snuff, but he refused, laughingly declaring she would never want to use snuff again. When they reached Hounslow Heath it was nearly ten o'clock at night. The time and place being suitable, he suddenly threw his whip-lash round his wife's throat and drew it tight. As the cord was not quite in the right place he coolly altered it, and disregarding her entreaties, he again tightened the rope; then finding she was not quite dead, pulled it with such violence that it broke, but not till the murder was accomplished. Having stripped the body, he disfigured it, as he hoped, beyond recognition, then left it under a gibbet on which some malefactors were hanging in chains, and returned to London with his wife's clothes, part of which he dropped about the street, and part he gave back to her landlady, to whom they belonged. Being seen about, so many inquiries were made for his wife that he feared detection, and fled to Portsmouth.

Next day he heard the murder cried through the streets by the bellman, and found that it was his own case, with an exact description of his appearance. He at once jumped out of the window—the inn was by the waterside—and swam to another part of the shore. Thence he made his way into the country and got chance jobs as a farm-labourer. At Oxford he found that he was advertised in the local paper, and he again decamped, travelling on and on till he reached his own home in Wales. His father gave him refuge for a couple of days, but a report of his being in the house got about, and he had to fly to Gloucester, where he became an ostler at an inn. In Gloucester he was again recognized as the man who had killed his wife on Hounslow Heath by a gentleman who promised not to betray him, but warned him that he would be taken into custody if he remained in the town. "Agitated by the momentary fear of detection, Price knew not how to act," and he resolved at length to go back to

London and give himself up to justice. He called first on his former master, was apprehended, and committed to Newgate. He took his trial in due course, and was, on "the strongest circumstantial evidence ever adduced against an offender," cast for death, but fell a victim to the gaol-fever in October, 1738.

I will mention a couple more cases of wife-murder, and leave this section of criminals. The second marriage of Edward Joines, contracted at the Fleet, was not a happy one. His wife had a violent temper, and they continually disagreed. A daughter of hers lived with them, and the two women contrived to aggravate and annoy Joines to desperation. He retaliated by brutal treatment. On one occasion he pushed his wife into the grate and scorched her arm; frequently he drove her out of doors in scanty clothing at late hours and in inclement weather. One day his anger was roused by seeing a pot of ale going into his house for his wife, who was laid up with a fractured arm. He rushed in, and after striking the tankard out of her hand, seized her by the bad arm, twisted it till the bone again separated. The fracture was reset, but mortification rapidly supervened, and she died within ten days. The coroner's jury in consequence brought in a verdict of wilful murder against Joines. He was in due course convicted of murder, although it was difficult to persuade him that he had had a fair trial, seeing that his wife did not succumb immediately to the cruel injury she had received at his hands. He was executed in December, 1739.

The second wife of John Williamson received still more terribly inhuman treatment at his hands. This ruffian within three weeks after his marriage drenched his wife with cold water, and having otherwise ill-used her, inflicted the following diabolical torture. Having fastened her hands behind with handcuffs, he lifted her off the ground, with her toes barely touching it, by a rope run through a staple. She was locked up in a closet, and close by was placed a small piece of bread and butter, which she could just touch with her lips. She was allowed a small portion of water daily. Sometimes a girl who was in the house gave the poor creature a stool to rest her feet on, but Williamson discovered it, and was so furious that he nearly beat the girl to death. The wretched woman was kept in this awful plight for more than a month at a time, and at length succumbed. She died raving mad. Williamson when arrested made a frivolous defence, declaring his wife provoked him by treading on a kitten and killing it. He was found guilty and executed in 1760.

The victim of Theodore Gardelle was a woman although not his wife. This murder much exercised the public mind at the time. The perpetrator was a foreigner, a hitherto inoffensive miniature painter, who was goaded into such a frenzy by the intolerable irritation of a woman's tongue, that he first struck and then despatched her. He lodged with a Mrs. King in Leicester Fields, whose miniature he had painted, but not very successfully. She had desired to have the portrait particularly good, and in her disappointment gave the unfortunate painter no peace. One morning she came into the parlour which he used, and which was *en suite* with her bed-room, and immediately attacked him about the miniature. Provoked by her insults, Gardelle told her she was a very impertinent woman; at which she struck him a violent blow on the chest. He pushed her from him, "rather in contempt than anger," as he afterwards declared, "and with no desire to hurt her;" her foot caught in the floor-cloth, she fell backward, and her head came with great force against a sharp corner of the bedstead, for Gardelle apparently had followed her into her bed-room. The blood immediately gushed from her mouth, and he at once ran up to assist her and express his concern; but she pushed him away, threatening him with the consequences of his act. He was greatly terrified at the thought of being charged with a criminal assault; but the more he strove to pacify the more she reviled and threatened, till at last he seized a sharp-pointed ivory comb which lay upon her toilette-table and drove it into her throat. The blood poured out in still greater volume, and her voice gradually grew fainter and fainter, and she presently expired. Gardelle said afterwards he drew the bed-clothes over her, then, horrified and overcome, fell by her side in a swoon. When he came to himself he examined the body to see if Mrs. King were quite dead, and in his confusion staggered against the wainscot and hit his head so as to raise a great bump over his eye.

Gardelle now seems to have considered with himself how best he might conceal his crime. There was only one other resident in the house, a maid-servant, who was out on a message for him at the time of his fatal quarrel with Mrs. King. When she returned she found the bed-room locked, and Gardelle told her her mistress had gone into the country for the day. Later on he paid her wages on behalf of Mrs. King and discharged her, with the, explanation that her mistress intended to bring home a new maid with her. Having now the house to himself, he entered the chamber of death, and stripped the body, which he laid in the bed. He next disposed of the blood-stained bed-clothes by putting them to soak in a wash-tub in the back wash-house. A servant of an absent fellow-lodger came in late and asked for Mrs. King, but Gardelle said she had not returned, and that he meant to sit up for her and let her into the house. Next morning he explained Mrs. King's absence by saying she had come late and gone off again for the day.

This went on from Wednesday to Saturday; but no suspicion of anything wrong had as yet been conceived, and the body still lay in the same place in the back-room. On Sunday Gardelle began to put into execution a project for destroying the body in parts, which he disposed of by throwing them down the sinks, or spreading in the cock-loft. On Monday and Tuesday inquiries began to be made for Mrs. King, and Gardelle continued to say that he expected her daily, but on Thursday the stained bedclothes were found in the wash-tub. Gardelle was seen coming from the wash-house, and heard to ask what had become of the linen. This roused suspicion for the first time. The discharged maid-servant was hunted up, and as she declared she knew nothing of the wash-tub or its contents, and as Mrs. King was still missing, the neighbours began to move in the matter. Mr. Barron, an apothecary, came and questioned Gardelle, who was so much confused in his answers that a warrant was obtained for his arrest. Then Mrs. King's bed-room was examined, and that of Gardelle, now a prisoner. In both were found conclusive evidence of foul play. By-and-by in the cock-loft and elsewhere portions of the missing woman were discovered, and some jewellery known to be hers was traced to Gardelle, who did not long deny his guilt. When he was in the new prison at Clerkenwell he tried to commit suicide by taking forty drops of opium; but it failed even to procure him sleep. After this he swallowed halfpence to the number of twelve, hoping that the verdigrese would kill him, but he survived after suffering great tortures. He was removed then to Newgate for greater security, and was closely watched till the end. After a fair trial he was convicted and cast for death. His execution took place in the Haymarket near Panton Street, to which he was led past Mrs. King's house, and at which he cast one glance as he passed. His body was hanged in chains on Hounslow Heath.

Women were as capable of fiendish cruelty as men, and displayed greater and more diabolical ingenuity in devising torments for their victims. Two murders typical of this class of crime may be quoted here. One was that committed by the Meteyards, mother and daughter, upon an apprentice girl; the other that of Elizabeth Brownrigg, also on an apprentice. The Meteyards kept a millinery shop in Bruton Street, Berkeley Square, and had five parish apprentices bound to them. One was a sickly girl, Anne Taylor by name. Being unable to do as much work as her employers desired, they continually vented their spite upon her. After enduring great cruelty Anne Taylor absconded; she was caught, brought back to Bruton Street, and imprisoned in a garret on bread and water; she again escaped, and was again recaptured and cruelly beaten with a broom-handle. Then they tied her with a rope to the door of a room so that she could neither sit nor lie down, and she was so kept for three successive days, but suffered to go to bed at night time. On the third night she was so weak she could hardly creep up-stairs. On the fourth day her fellow apprentices were brought to witness her torments as an incentive to exertion, but were forbidden to afford her any kind of relief. On this the last day of her torture she faltered in speech and presently expired. The Meteyards now tried to bring their victim to with hartshorn, but finding life was extinct, they carried the body up to the garret and locked it in. Then four days later they enclosed it in a box, left the garret door ajar, and spread a report through their house that "Nanny" had once more absconded. The deceased had a sister, a fellow apprentice, who declared she was persuaded "Nanny" was dead; whereupon the Meteyards also murdered the sister and secreted the body. Anne's body remained in the garret for a couple of months, when the stench of decomposition was so great that the murderesses feared detection, and after chopping the corpse in pieces, they burnt parts and disposed of others in drains and gully holes. Four years elapsed without suspicion having been aroused, but there had been constant and violent quarrels between mother and daughter, the former frequently beating and ill-using the latter, who in return reviled her mother as a murderess. During this time the daughter left her home to live with a Mr. Rooker as servant at Ealing. Her mother followed her, and still behaved so outrageously that the daughter, in Mr. Rooker's presence, upbraided her with what they had done. He became uneasy, and cross-questioned them till they confessed the crime. Both women were arrested and tried at the Old Bailey, where they were convicted and sentenced to death. The mother on the morning of her execution was taken with a fit from which she never recovered, and she was in a state of insensibility when hanged.

Elizabeth Brownrigg was the wife of a plumber who carried on business in Flower de Luce Court, Fleet St. She practised midwifery, and received parish apprentices, whom she took to save the expense of keeping servants. Two girls, victims of her cruel ill-usage, ran away, but a third, Mary Clifford, bound to her by the parish of Whitefriars, remained to endure still worse. Her inhuman mistress repeatedly beat her, now with a hearth-broom, now with a horse-whip or a cane. The girl was forced to lie at nights in a coal-hole, with no bed but a sack and some straw. She was often nearly perished with cold. Once after a long diet of bread and water, when nearly starved to death, she rashly broke into a cupboard in search of food and was caught in the act. Mrs. Brownrigg, to punish her, made her strip, and while she was naked repeatedly beat her with the butt end of a whip. Then fastening a jack-chain around her neck she drew it as tight as possible without strangling, and sent her back to the coal-hole with her hands tied behind her back. Mrs. Brownrigg's son vied with his mother in ill-treating the apprentices, and when the mistress was tired of horsewhipping the lad continued the savage punishment. When Mary Clifford complained to a French lodger of the barbarity she experienced, Mrs. Brownrigg flew at her and cut her tongue in two places with a pair of scissors. Other apprentices were equally ill-used, and they were all covered with wounds and bruises from the cruel flagellations they received.

At length one of the neighbours, alarmed by the constant moaning and groanings which issued from Brownrigg's house, began to suspect that "the apprentices were treated with unwarrantable severity." It was impossible to gain admission, but a maid looked through a skylight into a covered yard, and saw one of the apprentices, in a shocking state of filth and wretchedness, kept there with a pig. One of the overseers now went and demanded Mary Clifford. Mrs. Brownrigg produced another, Mary Mitchell, who was taken to the workhouse, but in such a pitiable state that in removing her clothes her boddice stuck to her wounds. Mary Mitchell having been promised that she should not be sent back to Brownrigg's, gave a full account of the horrid treatment she and Mary Clifford had received. A further search was made in the Brownrigg's house, but without effect. At length, under threat of removal to prison, Mrs. Brownrigg produced Clifford "from a cupboard under a beaufet in the dining-room." "It is impossible," says the account, "to describe the miserable appearance of this poor girl; nearly her whole body was ulcerated." Her life was evidently in imminent danger. Having been removed to St. Bartholomew's Hospital, she died there within a few days. The man Brownrigg was arrested, but the woman and son made their escape. Shifting their abode from place to place, buying new disguises from time to time at rag-fairs, eventually they took refuge in lodgings at Wandsworth, where they were recognized by their landlord as answering the description of the murderers of Mary Clifford, and arrested. Mrs. Brownrigg was tried and executed; the men, acquitted of the graver charge, were only sentenced to six months' imprisonment. The story goes that Hogarth, who prided himself on his skill as a physiognomist, wished to see Mrs. Brownrigg in Newgate. The governor, Mr. Akerman, admitted him, but at the instance of a mutual friend played a trick upon the painter by bringing Mrs. Brownrigg before him casually, as some other woman. Hogarth on looking at her took Akerman aside and said, "You must have two great female miscreants in your custody, for this woman as well as Mrs. Brownrigg is from her features capable of any cruelty and any crime."

THE GAOL CALENDAR (CONTINUED)

Less atrocious murders—Consequences of ungovernable passion—Mr. Plunkett—Mr. Bird—A sensitive Guardsman—The Reverend James Hackman, in passionate despair, murders Miss Reay—Governor Wall—His severe and unaccommodating temper—Trial of Sergeant Armstrong—punished by drumhead court-martial and flogged to death—Wall's arrest and escape to the Continent—Persons of note charged with murder—Quin the actor kills Williams in self-defence—Charles Macklin kills Hallam, a fellow actor at Drury Lane—Joseph Baretti, author of the 'Italian Dictionary,' mobbed in the Haymarket, defends himself with a pocket-knife, and stabs one of his assailants—Chronic dangers and riots in the London streets—Trade terrorism—Turbulent serving-men—Footmen's riot at Drury Lane—Footmen frequently turned highwaymen—Hawkins attempts an alibi—Other alibis—James Maclane, a notorious knight of the road, once a butler and respectable grocer, has a lodging in St. James' Street—Stops Horace Walpole—His capture and fame in Newgate before execution—William Page, another footman, turned highway robber—His clever stratagems and disguises—A *confederate betrays him—Arrested in London—Hanged at Maidstone —John Rann, alias Sixteen-String Jack—His extravagant costumes— Short career ends in the gallows—- Well-born but dissolute reprobates to the road—A Baronet and a Lieutenant convicted—William Parsons, a baronet's son, related to a Duchess and a naval officer, becomes an ensign in the 34th—His extravagance—Sells out of the army—Turns swindler, and is transported to Virginia—Returns and takes to the road—Is caught and hanged—Paul Lewis, another highwayman, who had been a King's officer—Captured by a police officer —William Norton, who sometimes took a thief, captures William Belchier—Jonathan Wild, the sham thief-taker and notorious criminal—His conviction and his career summarized—Once anxious to become a freeman of the city of London—Pirates and sea-robbers— Captain Kidd—English Peers accused of complicity—Kidd's arrest, trial, and sentence—John Gow and his career in the 'Revenge'—His death at Execution Dock—Captain Massey, an involuntary pirate, through whom others are captured, is himself hung.*

I PASS now to murders of less atrocity, the result of temporary and more or less ungovernable passion, rather than of malice deliberate and aforethought. In this class must be included the case of Mr. Plunkett, a young gentleman of Irish extraction, who murdered a peruke-maker, who asked him an exorbitant price for a wig. Brown had made it to order for Mr. Plunkett, and wanted seven pounds for it. After haggling he reduced it to six. Plunkett offered four, and on this being refused, seized a razor lying handy and cut Brown's throat.

A somewhat similar case was that of Mr. Edward Bird, a wellborn youth, who had been educated at Eton, and after making the grand tour had received a commission in a regiment of horse. Unfortunately he led a wild, dissolute life, associating with low characters. One morning, after spending the night in a place of public resort, he ordered a bath. One waiter deputed the job to another, the latter went to Bird to apologize for the delay.

Bird, growing furious, drew his sword and made several passes at the waiter, who avoided them by holding the door in his hand, and then escaped down-stairs. Bird pursued, threw the man down, breaking his ribs. On this the master of the house and another waiter, by name Loxton, tried to appease Bird, but the latter, frantic at not having the bath when ordered, fell upon Loxton and ran him through with his sword. Loxton dropped and died almost instantaneously. Bird was arrested, committed to Newgate, and eventually tried for his life. He was convicted and received sentence of death, but great interest was made to get it commuted to transportation. His powerful friends might have obtained it but for the protests of Loxton's representatives, and Bird was ordered for execution. The night before he first tried poison, then stabbed himself in several places, but survived to be taken the following morning to Tyburn in a mourning coach, attended by his mother and the ordinary of Newgate. At the gallows he asked for a glass of wine and a pinch of snuff, which "he took with apparent unconcern, wishing health to those who stood near him. He then repeated the Apostle's Creed and was launched into eternity."

The military were not over-popular at times, when party disputes ran high, and the soldiery were often exposed to contumely in the streets. It must be admitted too that they were ready enough to accept any quarrel fastened upon them. Thus William Hawksworth, a guardsman, while marching through the park with a party to relieve guard at St. James, left the ranks to strike a woman who he thought had insulted his cloth. It was not she, however, but her companion who had cried, "What a stir there is about King George's soldiers!" This companion, by name Ransom, resented the blow, and called Hawksworth a puppy, whereupon the soldier clubbed his musket and knocked the civilian down. Hawksworth marched on with his guard; Ransom was removed to the hospital with a fractured skull, and died in a few hours. But a bystander, having learnt the name of the offender, obtained a warrant against Hawksworth, who was committed to Newgate. He was ably defended at his trial, and his commanding officer gave him an excellent character. But the facts were so clearly proved that conviction was imperative. For some time he was buoyed up with the hope of reprieve, but this failed him at the last, and he went to Tyburn solemnly declaring that Ransom hit him first, that he had no malice against the deceased, and he hardly remembered leaving the ranks to strike him.

Two cases may well be inserted here, although belonging to a somewhat later date. Both were murders committed under the influence of strong excitement: one was the fierce outburst of passionate despair at unrequited love, the other the rash action of a quick-tempered man who vested for the moment with absolute power. The first was the murder of Miss Reay by the Rev. James Hackman, the second the flogging to death of the Sergeant Armstrong by order of Colonel Wall, Lieutenant-Governor of Goree.

Mr. Hackman had held a commission in the 68th Foot, and while employed on the recruiting service at Huntingdon, had been hospitably received at Hinchingbroke, the seat of Lord Sandwich. At that time a Miss Reay resided there under the protection of his lordship, by whom she had had nine children. Hackman fell desperately in love with Miss Reay, and the lady did not altogether reject his attentions. A correspondence between them, which bears every appearance of authenticity, was published after the murder under the title of 'Love and Madness,' and the letters on both sides are full of ardent protestations. Hackman continued to serve for some time, but the exile from the sight of his beloved became so intolerable that he sold out, took orders, and entered the Church, obtaining eventually the living of Wiverton in Norfolk. He had determined to marry

Miss Reay if she would accept him, and one of the last letters of the correspondence above quoted proves that the marriage arrangements were all but completed. On the 1st March, 1779, he writes,—"In a month or six weeks at farthest from this time I might certainly call you mine. Only remember that my character now I have taken orders renders expedition necessary. By tonight's past I shall write into Norfolk about the alterations at *our* parsonage." But within a few weeks a cloud overshadowed his life. It is only vaguely indicated in a letter to a friend, dated the 20th March, in which he hints at a rupture between Miss Reay and himself. "What I shall do I know not—without her I do not think I can exist." A few days later he wrote to the same friend: "Despair goads me on—death only can relieve me.... What then have I to do, who only lived when she loved me, but cease to live now she ceases to love?"

At this period it is evident that the idea of suicide only occupied his over-wrought brain. He wrote on the 7th April,—"When this reaches you I shall be no more.... You know where my affections were placed; my having by some means or other lost hers (an idea which I could not support) has driven me to madness." So far he does not appear to have contemplated any violence against Miss Reay, for in his letter he commends her to the kind offices of his friend. He spent that day in self-communing and in reading a volume of Dr. Blair's sermons. In the evening he went from his lodgings in Duke's Court, St. Martin's Lane, toward the Admiralty, and saw Miss Reay drive by to the Covent Garden Theatre. He followed her into the theatre and gazed at her for the last time. Then, unable to retrain the violence of his passion, he returned to his lodgings, and having loaded two pistols, returned to Covent Garden, where he waited in the piazza till the play was over. When Miss Reay came out he stepped up with a pistol in each hand. One he fired at her, and killed her on the spot, the other he discharged at himself, but without fatal effect.

He was at once arrested, and when his wound had been dressed, was committed by Sir John Fielding to Tothill Fields, and afterwards to Newgate. He wrote from prison to the same friend as follows:

"I am alive—— and she is dead. I shot her, shot her, and not myself. Some of her blood and brains is still upon my clothes. I don't ask you to speak to me, I don't ask you to look at me, only come hither and bring me a little poison, such as is strong enough. Upon my knees I beg, if your friendship for me ever was sincere, do, *do* bring me some poison."

Next day he was more composed, and declared that nothing should tempt him to escape justice by suicide. "My death," he writes, "is all the recompense I can make to the laws of my country." He was tried before Mr. Justice Blackstone (of the Commentaries), and convicted on the clearest evidence. A plea of insanity was set up in his defence, but could not be maintained. His dignified address to the jury had nothing of madness in it, and it is probable that he had no real desire to escape the just punishment for his crime. This is shown by his answer to Lord Sandwich, who wrote:—

17th April, 1779.

"To Mr. Hackman in Newgate.

"If the murderer of Miss —— *wishes to live, the man he has most injured will use all his interest to procure his life."*

To this Hackman replied from

"*The Condemned Cell in Newgate,
17th April, 1779.*

"THE MURDERER *of her whom he preferred, far preferred to life, respects the hand from which he has just received such an offer as he neither desires nor deserves. His wishes are for death, not life. One wish he has. Could he be pardoned in this world by the man he has most injured—oh, my lord, when I meet her in another world enable me to tell her (if departed spirits are not ignorant of earthly things) that you forgive us both, that you will be a father to her dear infants!*

"J. H."

THE CONDEMNED MAN continued to fill many sheets with his reflections in the shape of letters to his friend. But they are all rhapsodical to the last degree. The 19th April was the day fixed for his execution, and on that morning he rose at 5 a.m., dressed himself, and spent some time in private meditation. About 7 a.m. he was visited by Mr. Boswell and some other friends, with whom he went to the chaplain and partook of the sacrament. During the procession to Tyburn he seemed much affected, and said but little. After having hung the usual time his body was carried to Surgeon's Hall. He appears to have written a few last words in pencil at Tyburn, while actually waiting to be turned off.

"My dear Charlie," he wrote, "*farewell for ever in this world. I die a sincere Christian and penitent, and everything I hope you can wish me. Would it prevent my example's having any bad effect if the world should know how I abhor my former ideas of suicide, my crime?*——

will be the best judge. Of her fame I charge you to be careful. My poorly will....

"Your dying H."[163]

MISS REAY WAS BURIED at Elstree, Herts., where her grave is still pointed out.

Twenty years elapsed between the commission of the murder with which Governor Wall was charged and his trial and atonement. The date of his execution was 1802, a date which would bring the story within the scope of a later rather than the present chapter. But while postponing the particulars of the execution, I propose to deal here with the offence, as it falls naturally into this branch of my subject. Colonel Wall was governor and commandant of Goree, a small island off the coast of Africa close to Cape Verd, and now in the possession of the French. It was mainly dependent upon England for its supplies, and when these ran short, as was often the case, the troops received a money compensation in lieu of rations. A sum was due to them in this way on one occasion when both the Governor and paymaster were on the point of leaving the island for England, and a number of men, anxious for an adjustment of their claims, set off in a body to interview the paymaster at his quarters. They were encountered *en route* by the Governor, who reprimanded them, and ordered them to return to their barracks. An hour or two later a second party started for the paymaster, at the head of which was a certain Sergeant Armstrong. The Governor met them as before, and addressing himself to Sergeant Armstrong, again ordered the men back to their quarters.

Upon the nature of this demonstration the whole of the

subsequent proceedings hinged. Governor Wall and his witnesses declared it was a tumultuous gathering, seventy or eighty strong; other testimony limited the number to about a dozen. Governor Wall alleged that the men with Armstrong were armed and menacing; others that they comported themselves in a quiet, orderly manner. It was sworn that Armstrong when spoken to by the Governor came up to him submissively, hat in hand, addressed him as "Your Excellency," used no disrespectful language, and withdrew, with his comrades, without noise or disturbance. This view was supported by the evidence of several officers, who swore that they saw no appearance of a mutiny on the island that day; on the other hand, the Governor urged that the men had declared they would break open the stores and help themselves if they were not settled with at once; that they prevented him from going to the shore, fearing he meant to leave the island in a hurry; and that they forced the main guard and released a prisoner. It is difficult to reconcile statements so widely divergent; but the fact that Governor Wall left the island next day, and took with him three officers out of the seven in the garrison; that he made no special report of the alleged mutiny to the military authorities in London, and did not even refer to it in minute returns prepared and forwarded at the time, must be deemed very detrimental to Governor Wall's case, and no doubt weighed with the jury which tried him. The only conclusion was that no mutiny existed, but one was assumed merely to screen the infliction of an unauthorized punishment.

To return to the events on the island. It is pretty certain that Governor Wall's mind must have been thrown off its balance after he had dismissed the party headed by Armstrong. He was either actually apprehensive for the safety of his command, or was momentarily blinded by passion at the seeming defiance of discipline, and he felt that he must make an example if his authority was to be maintained. Although many old comrades of high rank bore witness at his trial to his great humanity and good temper, there is reason to fear that to those under his command he was so severe and unaccommodating as to be generally unpopular, and this no doubt told against him at his trial. He was not a strong, self-reliant commander. It is nearly certain that he gave trifles exaggerated importance, and was only too ready to put in practice the severest methods of repression he had at hand. In this instance, however, he did not act without deliberation. It was not until six in the evening that he had resolved to punish Armstrong as the ringleader of the mutiny. By that time he had fully laid his plans. The "long roll" was beat upon the drums, the troops were assembled hurriedly as in the case of alarm, and a gun-carriage was dragged into the centre of the parade. The Governor then constituted a drum-head court-martial, which proceeded to try Armstrong for mutiny, convict, and sentence him without calling upon him to plead to any charge, or hearing him in his defence; so that he was practically punished without a trial. He was ordered eight hundred lashes, which were forthwith inflicted, not as in ordinary cases by the regimental drummers, whom the Governor thought were tinged with insubordination, but by the black interpreter and his assistants; nor was the regulation cat-of-nine-tails used, as the Governor declared they had all been destroyed by the mutineers, but with a thick rope's end, which, according to the surgeon's testimony, did more mischief than the cat. Armstrong's punishment was exemplary. It was proved that the Governor stood by, threatening to flog the blacks themselves unless they "laid on" with a will, and crying again and again, "Cut him to the heart! cut him to the liver!" Armstrong begged for mercy, but he received the whole eight hundred lashes, twenty-five at a time; and when he was cast loose, he said that the sick season was coming on, which with the punishment would certainly do for him. A surgeon was present at the infliction, but was not called upon to certify as to Armstrong's fitness or otherwise for corporal punishment, nor did he enter any protest. Armstrong was taken at once to hospital, and his back was found "as black as a new hat." From the moment of his reception the doctors had no hope of his recovery: he gradually grew worse and worse, and presently died.

The day after the punishment Governor Wall left Goree and came to England, where he arrived in August, 1782. The news of Armstrong's death followed him, and various reports as to the Governor's conduct, which were inquired into and dismissed. But in 1784 a more detailed and circumstantial account came to hand, and two messengers were despatched to Bath by Lord Sidney, then Secretary of State, to arrest Wall. They apprehended him and brought him as far as Reading in a chaise and four, where they alighted at an inn. While the officers were at supper he gave them the slip and got over to France, whence he wrote promising to surrender in the course of a few months. His excuse for absconding was that many of those who would be the principal witnesses were his personal enemies. He continued abroad, however, for some years, residing sometimes in Italy, more constantly in France, "where he lived respectably and was admitted into good company." He affected the society of countrymen serving in the French army, and was well-known to the Scotch and Irish Colleges in Paris. In 1797 he returned to England and remained in hiding, occupying lodgings in Lambeth Court, where his wife, who was a lady of good family, regularly visited him. He is described as being unsettled in mind at this time, and even then contemplating surrender. His means of subsistence were rather precarious, but he lived at the time of delivering himself up in Upper Thornhaugh St., Bedford Square. In October, 1801, he wrote twice to Lord Pelham, stating that he had returned to England for the purpose of meeting the charge against him. It was generally supposed that, had he not thus come forward voluntarily, the matter had nearly passed out of people's memory, and he would hardly have been molested. He was, however, arrested on his own letter, committed to Newgate, and tried at the Old Bailey for the murder of Benjamin Armstrong at Goree in 1782. He was found guilty and sentenced to death. After several respites and strenuous exertions to save his life, he was executed in front of Newgate on the 28th January, 1802. The whole of one day was occupied by the judges and law officers in reviewing his case, but their opinion was against him. For an account of the prisoner's demeanour after sentence and execution the reader is referred to the chapter on Executions in vol. ii.

Three persons of note and superior station found themselves in Newgate about this time upon a charge of murder. The first was James Quin, the celebrated actor, the popular diner-out and *bon vivant*, who went to the west coast of England to eat John Dory in perfection, and who preferred eating turtle in Bristol to London. He made his first hit as Falstaff in the 'Merry Wives of Windsor.' He had understudied the part, but Rich, manager of the Theatre Royal, Lincoln's Inn Fields, substituted him for it on an emergency with great reluctance. His next hit was as Cato, in which, with many other parts, he succeeded Booth. Quin was modest enough on his first appearance as Cato to announce that the part would be "attempted by Mr. Quin." The audience were, however, fully satisfied with his performance, and after one critical passage was applauded with shouts of "Booth outdone!" It was through this his great part of Cato that he was led into the quarrel which laid him open to the charge of murder. One night an inferior actor named Williams, taking the part of messenger, said, "Cæsar sends health to Cato," but pronounced Cato "Keeto." Quin, much annoyed, replied instantly with a "gag"—"Would that he had sent a better messenger."[164]

Williams was now greatly incensed, and in the Green Room later in the evening complained bitterly to Quin that he had been made ridiculous, that his professional prospects were blighted, and that he insisted upon satisfaction or an apology. Quin only laughed at his rage. Williams, goaded to madness, went out into the piazza at Covent Garden to watch for Quin. When the latter left the theatre Williams attacked him with his sword. Quin drew in his defence, and after a few passes ran Williams through the body. The ill-fated actor died on the spot. Quin surrendered himself, was committed, tried, found guilty of manslaughter, and sentenced to be burnt in the hand.

Another well-known actor, Charles Macklin, was no less unfortunate in incurring the stain of blood. He was a hot-headed, intemperate Irishman, who, when he had an engagement at Drury Lane Theatre, quarrelled with another actor over a wig. Going down between the pieces into the scene-room, "where the players warm themselves," he saw a Mr. Hallam, who was to appear as Sancho in the 'Fop's Fortune,' wearing a "stock wig" which he (Macklin) had on the night before. He swore at him for a rogue, and cried, "What business have you with my wig?" The other answered that he had as much right to it as Macklin, but presently went away and changed it for another. Macklin still would not leave the man alone, and taking the wig, began to comb it out, making grumbling and abusive remarks, calling Hallam a blackguard and a scrub rascal. Hallam replied that he was no more a rascal than Macklin was; upon which the latter "started from his chair, and having a stick in his hand, made a full lunge at the deceased, and thrust the stick into his left eye;" pulling it back again he looked pale, turned on his heel, and in a passion threw the stick on the fire. Hallam clapped his hand to his eye and said the stick had gone through his head. Young Mr. Cibber, the manager's son, came in, and a doctor was sent for; the injured man was removed to a bed, where he expired the following day. Macklin was very contrite and concerned at his rash act, for which he was arrested, and in due course tried at the Old Bailey. Many of the most renowned actors of the day, Rich, Fleetwood, Quin, Ryan, and others, bore testimony to his good character and his quiet, peaceable disposition. He also was found guilty of manslaughter only, and sentenced to be burnt in the hand.

The third case of killing by misadventure was that of Joseph Baretti, the author of the well-known Italian and English dictionary. Baretti had resided in England for some years, engaged upon this work; he was a middle-aged, respectable man, of studious habits, the friend and associate of the most noted literary men and artists of the day. He was a member of the club of the Royal Academicians at that time (1769), lodged in Soho, and went there one afternoon after a long morning's work over his proofs. Finding no one at the club, he went on to the Orange coffee-house, and returning by the Haymarket to the club, was madly assaulted by a woman at the corner of Panton Street. Very unwisely he resented her attack by giving her a blow with his hand, when the woman, finding by his accent he was a foreigner, cried for help against the cursed Frenchman, when there was at once a gathering of bullies, who jostled and beat Baretti, making him "apprehensive that he must expect no favour nor protection, but all outrage and blows." There was, generally, a great puddle at the corner of Panton Street, even when the weather was fine, and on this particular day it had rained incessantly, and the pavement was very slippery. Baretti's assailants tried hard to push him into the puddle, and at last in self-defence he drew his pocket-knife, a knife he kept, as he afterwards declared, to carve fruit and sweetmeats, and not to kill his fellow-creatures with. [165] Being hard pushed, "in great horror, having such bad eyes," lest he should run against some, and his pursuers constantly at him, jostling and beating him, Baretti "made a quick blow" at one who had knocked off his hat with his fist; the mob cried "Murder, he has a knife out," and gave way. Baretti ran up Oxenden Street, then faced about and ran into a shop for protection, being quite spent with fatigue. Three men followed him; one was a constable, who called upon Baretti to surrender. Morgan, the man whom he had stabbed, three times, as it appeared, "the third wound having hurt him more than the two former," was fast bleeding to death. Baretti was carried before Sir John Fielding; his friends came from the club and testified to his character, among others Sir Joshua Reynolds himself, but he was committed to prison. It was urged in Baretti's defence that he had been very severely handled; he had a swollen cheek, and was covered with bruises. Independent witnesses came forward, and swore that they had been subjected to personal outrage in the neighbourhood of the Haymarket. A number of personal friends, including Sir Joshua Reynolds, Dr. Johnson, Mr. Fitz-Herbert, and Mr. Edmund Burke, spoke in the highest terms of Mr. Baretti as "a man of benevolence, sobriety, modesty, and learning." In the end he was acquitted of murder or manslaughter, and the jury gave a verdict of self-defence.

Inoffensive persons were constantly in danger, day and night, of being waylaid and maltreated in the streets. Disturbance was chronic in certain localities, and a trifling quarrel might at any moment blaze into a murderous riot. On execution days the mob was always rampant; at times too, when political passion was at fever-heat, crowds of roughs were ever ready to espouse the popular cause. Thus when the court party, headed by Lord Bute, vainly strove to crush the demagogue John Wilkes, and certain prisoners were being tried at the Old Bailey for riot and wounding, a crowd collected outside the Mansion House carrying a gibbet on which hung a boot and a petticoat.[166] The Mayor interfered and a fray began. Weapons were used, some of the Lord Mayor's servants were wounded, and one of the prisoners was rescued by the mob. Sometimes the disturbance had its origin in trade jealousies. A clerk to a weaver's club was arraigned with others for tying two weavers back to back, setting them on horseback, and in a riotous manner driving them through the streets; their offence being that they had worked under price. Again, a number of men riotously assembled and destroyed a saw-mill, for which they were sentenced to seven years' imprisonment in Newgate. At the execution of two weavers on Bethnal Green for destroying work on the looms the mob behaved outrageously as the convicts were being conveyed from Newgate to Bethnal Green—insulted the sheriffs, pulled up the gallows, broke the windows, destroyed the furniture, and committed other outrages in the house of a manufacturer in Spitalfields. The sheriffs harangued them without effect, and it was not till they were threatened with calling out the military that they dispersed.

An especially turbulent class were the footmen, chairmen, and body-servants of the aristocracy. They quarrelled and wrangled and rioted in the open streets, often in the precincts of the royal residence, as when a number of them created a disturbance outside Leicester House during a drawing-room held by the Princess of Wales. The Footmen's Riot at Drury Lane Theatre, which occurred in 1737, was a still more serious affair. It had long been the custom to admit "the parti-coloured tribe," as the licensed lacqueys are called in contemporary accounts, to the upper gallery of that Theatre gratis, out of compliment to their masters on whom they were in attendance. Thus established among the gods, they comported themselves with extraordinary license; they impudently insulted the rest of the audience, who, unlike themselves, had paid for admission, and "assuming the prerogative of critics, hissed or applauded with the most offensive clamour." Finding the privilege of free entrance thus scandalously abused, Mr. Fleetwood, the manager, suspended the free list. This gave great offence to the footmen, who proceeded to take the law into their own hands. "They conceived," as it was stated in 'Fog's Weekly Journal,' "that they had an indefeasible hereditary right to the said gallery, and that this expulsion was a high infringement of their liberties." Accordingly, one Saturday night a great number of them—quite three hundred, it was said—assembled at Drury Lane doors, armed with staves and truncheons, and "well fortified with three-threads and twopenny."[167] The night selected was one when the performance was patronized by royalty, and the Prince and Princess of Wales, with other members of the royal family, were in the theatre. The rioters attacked the stage door and forced it open, "bearing down all the box-keepers, candle-snuffers, supernumeraries, and pippin women that stood in the way." In this onslaught some five-and-twenty respectable people were desperately wounded. Fortunately Colonel de Veil, an active Westminster justice, happened to be in the house, and at once interposed. He ordered the Riot Act to be read, but "so great was the confusion," says the account, "that they might as well have read Cæsar's 'Commentaries'." Colonel de Veil then got the assistance of some of the guards, and with them seized several of the principal rioters, whom he committed to Newgate. These prisoners were looked upon as martyrs to the great cause, and while in gaol were liberally supplied with all luxuries by the subscription of their brethren. They were, however, brought to trial, convicted of riot, and sentenced to imprisonment.

This did not quite end the disturbance. Anonymous letters poured into the theatre, threatening Fleetwood and vowing vengeance. The following is a specimen:—

"Sir,

"*We are willing to admonish you before we attempt our design; and provide you use us civil, and admit us into your gallery, which is our property according to formalities, and if you think proper to come to a composition this way you'll hear no further; and if not, our intention is to combine in a body, incognito, and reduce the playhouse to the ground. Valueing no detection, we are*

"Indemnified."

THE MANAGER CARRIED these letters to the Lord Chamberlain and appealed to him for protection. A detachment of the guards, fifty strong, was ordered to do duty at the theatre nightly, and "thus deterred the saucy knaves from carrying their threats into execution. From this time," says the 'Newgate Calendar,' "the gallery has been purged of such vermin."

The footmen and male servants generally of this age were an idle, dissolute race. From among them the ranks of the highwaymen were commonly recruited, and it was very usual for the gentleman's gentleman, who had long flaunted in his master's apparel, and imitated his master's vices, to turn gentleman on the road to obtain funds for the faro-table and riotous living. A large proportion of the most famous highwaymen of the eighteenth century had been in service at some time or other. Hawkins, James Maclane, John Rann, William Page, had all worn the livery coat. John Hawkins had been butler in a gentleman's family, but lost his place when the plate chest was robbed, and suspicion fell upon him because he was flush of money. Hawkins, without a character, was unable to get a fresh place, and he took at once to the road. His operations, which were directed chiefly against persons of quality, were conducted in and about London. He stopped and robbed the Earl of Burlington, Lord Bruce, and the Earl of Westmoreland, the latter in Lincoln's Inn Fields. When he got valuable jewels he carried them over to Holland and disposed of them for cash, which he squandered at once in a "hell," for he was a rash and inveterate gambler. Working with two associates, he made his head-quarters at a public-house in the London Wall, the master of which kept a livery stable, and shared in the booty. From this point they rode out at all hours and stopped the stages as they came into town laden with passengers. One of the gang was, however, captured in the act of robbing the mail and executed at Aylesbury. After this, by way of revenge, they all determined to turn mail-robbers. They first designed to stop the Harwich mail, but changed their mind as its arrival was uncertain, being dependent on the passage of the packet-boat, and determined to rob the Bristol mail instead. They overtook the boy carrying the bags near Slough, and made him go down a lane where they tied him to a tree in a wet ditch, ransacked the Bath and Bristol bags, and hurried off by a circuitous route to London, where they divided the spoil, sharing the bank-notes and throwing the letters into the fire. Soon after this, the Post-office having learnt that the public-house in the London Wall was the resort of highwaymen, it was closely watched. One of Hawkins' gang became alarmed, and was on the point of bolting to Newcastle when he was arrested. He was hesitating whether or not he should confess, when he found that he had been forestalled by an associate, who had already given information to the Post-office, and he also made a clean breast of it all. The rest of the gang were taken at their lodgings in the Old Bailey, but not without a fight, and committed to Newgate. Hawkins tried to set up an alibi, and an innkeeper swore that he lodged with him at Bedfordbury on the night of the robbery; but the jury found him guilty, and he was hanged at Tyburn, his body being afterwards hung in chains on Hounslow Heath.

The defence of an alibi was very frequently pleaded by highwaymen, and the tradition of its utility may explain why that veteran and astute coachman, Mr. Weller, suggested it in the case of 'Bardell *v.* Pickwick.' In one genuine case, however, it nearly failed, and two innocent men were all but sacrificed to mistaken identity. They had been arrested for having robbed, on the Uxbridge road, a learned sergeant-at-law, Sir Thomas Davenport, who swore positively to both. His evidence was corroborated by that of Lady Davenport, and by the coachman and footman. Also the horses ridden by the supposed highwaymen, one a brown and the other a grey, were produced in the Old Bailey courtyard, and sworn to. Yet it was satisfactorily proved that both the prisoners were respectable residents of Kentish Town; that one, at the exact time of the robbery, was seated at table dining at some club anniversary dinner, and never left the club-room; that the other was employed continuously in the bar of a public-house kept by his mother. It was proved too that the prisoners owned a brown and a grey horse respectively. The Judge summed up in the prisoner's favour, and they were acquitted. But both suffered severe mental trouble from the unjust accusation. A few years later the actual robbers were convicted of another offence, and in the cells of Newgate confessed that it was they who had stopped Sir Thomas Davenport.

A very notorious highwayman, who had also been in service at one time of his varied career, was James Maclane. He was the son of a dissenting minister in Monaghan, and had a brother a minister at the Hague. Maclane inherited a small fortune, which he speedily dissipated, after which he became a gentleman's butler, lost his situation through dishonesty, determined to enlist in the Horse Guards, abandoned the idea, and turned fortune-hunter. He was a vain man, of handsome exterior, which he decked out in smart clothes on borrowed money. He succeeded at length in winning the daughter of a respectable London horse-dealer, and with her dowry of £500 set up in business as a grocer. His wife dying early, he at once turned his stock-in-trade into cash, and again looked to win an heiress, "by the gracefulness of his person and the elegance of his appearance." He was at last reduced to his last shilling, and being quite despondent, an Irish apothecary, who was a daring robber, persuaded him to take to the highway. One of his earliest exploits was to stop Horace Walpole when the latter was passing through Hyde Park. A pistol went off accidentally in this encounter, and the bullet not only grazed Walpole's cheek-bone, but went through the roof of the carriage. At this time Maclane had a lodging in St. James' Street, for which he paid two guineas a week; his accomplice Plunkett lived in Jermyn Street. "Their faces," says Horace Walpole, "are as well known about St. James as any gentleman's who lives in that quarter, and who perhaps goes upon the road too."[168] Maclane accounted for his style of living by putting out that he had Irish property worth £700 a year. Once when he had narrowly escaped capture he went over to his brother in Holland for safety, but when the danger was passed he returned and recommenced his depredations. He made so good a show that he was often received into respectable houses, and was once near marrying a young lady of good position; but he was recognized and exposed by a gentleman who knew him. Maclane continued to rob with greater boldness till the 26th June, 1750. On this day he and Plunkett robbed the Earl of Eglinton on Hounslow Heath. Later in the day they stopped and rifled the Salisbury stage, and among the booty carried off two portmanteaus, which were conveyed to Maclane's lodgings in St. James. Information of this robbery was quickly circulated, with a description of the stolen goods. Maclane had stripped the lace off a waistcoat, the property of one of the robbed, and recklessly offered it for sale to the very laceman from whom it had been purchased. He also sent for another salesman, who immediately recognized the clothes offered for those which had been stolen, and pretending to go home for more money, he fetched a constable and apprehended Maclane. He made an elaborate defence when brought to trial, but it availed him little, and he was sentenced to death. While under condemnation he became quite a popular hero. "The first Sunday after his trial," says Horace Walpole, "three thousand people went to see him. He fainted away twice with the heat of his cell. You can't conceive the ridiculous rage there is for going to Newgate; and the prints that are published of the malefactors, and the memoirs of their lives, set forth with as much parade as Marshal Turennes'." Maclane suffered at Tyburn amidst a great concourse.

William Page did a better business as a highwayman than Maclane. Page was apprenticed to a haberdasher, but he was a consummate coxcomb, who neglected his shop to dress in the fashion and frequent public places. His relations turned him adrift, and when in the last stage of distress he accepted a footman's place. It was while in livery that he first heard of what highwaymen could do, and conceived the idea of adopting the road as a profession. His first exploits were on the Kentish road, when he stopped the Canterbury stage; his next near Hampton Court. When he had collected some £200 he took lodgings in Lincoln's Inn Fields and passed as a student of law. He learnt to dance, frequented assemblies, and was on the point of marrying well, when he was recognized as a discharged footman, and turned out of doors. He continued his depredations all this time, assisted by a curious map which he had himself drawn, giving the roads round London for twenty miles. His plan was to drive out in a phaeton and pair. When at a distance from town he would turn into some unfrequented place and disguise himself with a grizzle or black wig and put on other clothes. Then saddling one of his phaeton horses, he went on to the main road and committed a robbery. This effected, he galloped back to his carriage, resumed his former dress, and drove to London. He was often cautioned against himself; but laughingly said that he had already lost his money once and could now only lose his coat and shirt. He was nearly detected on one occasion, when some haymakers discovered his empty phaeton and drove it off with his best clothes. He had just stopped some people, who pursued the haymakers with the carriage and accused them of being accomplices in the robbery. Page heard of this, and throwing the disguise into a well, went back to town nearly naked, where he claimed the carriage, saying the men had stripped him and thrown him into a ditch. The coach-builder swore that he had sold him the carriage, and they were committed for trial, but Page did not appear to prosecute. Page after this extended his operations, and in company with one Darwell, an old school-fellow, committed more than three hundred robberies in three years. He frequented Bath, Tunbridge, Newmarket, and Scarbro', playing deep everywhere and passing for a man of fortune. Darwell and he next "worked" the roads around London, but while the former was near Sevenoaks he was captured by Justice Fielding. He turned evidence against Page, who was arrested in consequence at the Golden Lion near Hyde Park, with a wig to disguise him in one pocket and his map of the London roads in another. He was remanded to Newgate and tried for a robbery, of which he was acquitted; then removed to Maidstone and convicted of another, for which he was hanged at that place.

John Rann was first a helper, then postboy, then coachman to several gentlemen of position. While in this capacity he dressed in a peculiar fashion, wearing breeches with eight strings at each knee, and was hence nick-named Sixteen-string Jack. Having lost his character he turned pickpocket, and then took to the road. He was soon afterwards arrested for robbing a gentleman of a watch and some money on the Hounslow road. The watch was traced to a woman with whom Rann kept company, who owned that she had had it from him. Rann denied all knowledge of the transaction, which could not be brought home to him. He appeared in court on this occasion in an extravagant costume. His irons were tied up with blue ribbons, and he carried in his breast a bouquet of flowers "as big as a broom." He was fond of fine feathers. Soon afterwards he appeared at a public-house in Bagnigge Wells, dressed in a scarlet coat, tambour waistcoat, white silk stockings, and laced hat. He gave himself out quite openly as a highwayman, and getting drunk and troublesome, he was put out of the house through a window into the road. Later on he appeared at Barnet races in elegant sporting style, his waistcoat being blue satin trimmed with silver. On this occasion he was followed by hundreds who knew him, and wished to stare at a man who had made himself so notorious. At last he stopped Dr. Bell, Chaplain to the Princess Amelia, in the Uxbridge Road, and robbed him of eighteenpence and a common watch in a tortoiseshell case; the latter was traced to the same woman already mentioned, and Rann was arrested coming into her house. Dr. Bell swore to him, and his servant declared that he had seen Rann riding up Acton Hill twenty minutes before the robbery. Rann was convicted on this evidence and suffered at Tyburn, after a short career of four years. It was not the first time he had seen the gallows. A short time previously he had attended a public execution, and forcing his way into the ring kept by the constables, begged that he might be allowed to stand there, as he might some day be an actor in the scene instead of a spectator.

The road was usually the last resource of the criminally inclined, the last fatal step in the downward career which ended abruptly at the gallows. Dissolute and depraved youths of all classes, often enough gentlemen, undoubtedly well-born, adopted this dangerous profession when at their wit's ends for funds. William Butler, who did his work accompanied by his servant Jack, was the son of a military officer. Kent and Essex was his favourite line of country, but London was his head-quarters, where they lived in the "genteelest lodgings, Jack wearing a livery, and the squire dressed in the most elegant manner."

A baronet, Sir Simon Clarke, was convicted of highway robbery at Winchester assizes, with an associate, Lieutenant Robert Arnott; although the former, by the strenuous exertions of his country friends, escaped the death penalty to which he had been sentenced. A very notorious highwayman executed in 1750 was William Parsons, the son of a baronet, who had been at Eton, and bore a commission in the Royal Navy. He had hopes of an inheritance from the Duchess of Northumberland, who was a near relative, but her Grace altered her will in favour of his sister. He left the navy in a hurry, and abandoned by his friends, became quite destitute, when his father got him an appointment in the Royal African Company's service. But he soon quarrelled with the governor of James Fort on the Gambia, and returned to England again so destitute that he lived on three halfpence for four days and drank water from the street pumps. His father now told him to enlist in the Life Guards, but the necessary purchase-money, seventy guineas, was not forthcoming. He then, by personating a brother, obtained an advance on a legacy which an aunt had left the brother, and with these funds made so good a show that he managed to marry a young lady of independent fortune, whose father was dead and had bequeathed her a handsome estate. His friends were so delighted that they obtained him a commission as ensign in a marching regiment, the 34th. He immediately launched out into extravagant expenditure, took a house in Poland Street, kept three saddle-horses, a chaise and pair, and a retinue of servants. He also fell into the hands of a noted gambler and sharper, who induced him to play high, and fleeced him. Parsons was compelled to sell his commission to meet his liabilities, and still had to evade his creditors by hiding under a false name.

From this time he became an irreclaimable vagabond, put to all sorts of shifts, and adroit in all kinds of swindles, to raise means. Having served for some time he shipped as captain of marines on board a galley-privateer. He returned and lived by forgery and fraud. One counterfeit draft he drew was on the Duke of Cumberland for £500; another on Sir Joseph Hankey & Co. He defrauded tailors out of new uniforms, and a hatter of 160 hats, which he pretended he had contracted to supply to his regiment. He also robbed, by a pretended marriage, a jeweller of a wedding and several valuable diamond rings. In the '45 he borrowed a horse from an officer intending to join the rebels, but he only rode as far as Smithfield, where he sold the nag, and let the officer be arrested as a supposed traitor. He was arrested for obtaining money on a false draft at Ranelagh, tried at Maidstone, sentenced to transportation, and despatched to Virginia. There, "after working as a common slave about seven weeks," a certain Lord F. rescued him and took him as a guest into his house. Parsons robbed Lord F. of a horse and took the highway. With the proceeds of his first robbery he got a passage back to England. On arriving at Whitehaven, he represented himself as having come into a large estate, and a banker advanced him seventy pounds. With this he came on to London, took lodgings in the West End, near Hyde Park corner, and rapidly got through his cash. Then he hired a horse and rode out on to Hounslow Heath to stop the first person he met.

This became his favourite hunting-ground, although he did business also about Kensington and Turnham Green. Once having learnt that a footman was to join his master at Windsor with a portmanteau full of notes and money, he rode out to rob him, but was recognized by an old victim. The latter let him enter the town of Hounslow, then ordered him to surrender. He might still have escaped, but the landlord of the inn where he lodged thought he answered the description of a highwayman who had long infested the neighbourhood. Parsons was accordingly detained and removed to Newgate. He was easily identified, and his condemnation for returning from transportation followed as a matter of course. His father and his wife used all their interest to gain him a pardon, but he was deemed too old an offender to be a fit object for mercy.

Paul Lewis was another reprobate, who began life as a king's officer. He was the son of a country clergyman, who got him a commission in the train of artillery; but Lewis ran into debt, deserted from his corps, and took to the sea. He entered the royal navy, and rose to be first midshipman, then lieutenant. Although courageous in action, he was "wicked and base;" and while on board the fleet he collected three guineas apiece from his messmates to lay in stores for the West Indian voyages, and bolted with the money. He at once took to the road. His first affair was near Newington Butts, when he robbed a gentleman in a chaise. He was apprehended for this offence, but escaped conviction through an alibi; after this he committed a variety of robberies. He was captured by a police officer on a night that he had stopped first a lady and gentleman in a chaise, and then tried to rob a Mr. Brown, at whom he fired. Mr. Brown's horse took fright and threw him; but when he got to his feet he found his assailant pinned to the ground by Mr. Pope, the police officer, who was kneeling on his breast. It seemed the lady and gentleman, Lewis's first victims, had warned Pope that a highwayman was about, and the police officer had ridden forward quickly and seized Lewis at the critical moment. Lewis was conveyed to Newgate, and in due course sentenced to death. "Such was the baseness and unfeeling profligacy of this wretch," says the Newgate Calendar, "that when his almost heart-broken father visited him for the last time in Newgate, and put twelve guineas into his hand to repay his expenses, he slipped one of the pieces of gold into the cuff of his sleeve by a dexterous sleight, and then opening his hand, showed the venerable and reverend old man that there were but eleven; upon which his father took another from his pocket and gave it him to make the number intended. Having then taken a last farewell of his parent, Lewis turned round to his fellow prisoners, and exultingly exclaimed, 'I have flung the old fellow out of another guinea.'"

Pope's capture of the highwayman Lewis was outdone by that of William Belchier, a few years previously, by William Norton, a person who, according to his own account of himself, kept a shop in Wych Street, and who "sometimes took a thief." Norton at the trial told his story as follows. "The chaise to Devizes having been robbed two or three times, as I was informed, I was desired to go into it, to see if I could take the thief, which I did on the third of June, about half an hour after one in the morning. I got into the post-chaise; the post-boy told me the place where he had been stopped was near the half-way house between Knightsbridge and Kensington. As we came near the house the prisoner (Belchier) came to us on foot and said, 'Driver, stop.' He held a pistol and tinder box to the chaise, and said: 'Your money directly, you must not stop; this minute, your money.' I said, 'Don't frighten us, I have but a trifle—you shall have it.' Then I said to the gentlemen,—there were three in the chaise,—'Give your money.' I took out a pistol from my coat pocket, and from my breeches' pocket a five-shilling piece and a dollar. I held the pistol concealed in one hand and the money in the other. I held the money pretty hard. He said, 'Put it in my hat.' I let him take the five-shilling piece out of my hand. As soon as he had taken it I snapped my pistol at him. It did not go off. He staggered back and held up his hands, and said, 'Oh Lord! oh Lord.' I jumped out of the chaise; he ran away, and I after him about six or seven hundred yards, and then took him. I hit him a blow on his back; he begged for mercy on his knees. I took his neckcloth off and tied his hands with it, and brought him back to the chaise. Then I told the gentlemen in the chaise that was the errand I came upon, and wished them a good journey, and brought the prisoner to London."

No account of the thief-taking or of the criminality of the eighteenth century would be complete without some reference to Jonathan Wild. What this astute villain really was may be best gathered from the various sworn informations on which he was indicted. It was set forth that he had been for years the confederate of highwaymen, pickpockets, burglars, shoplifters, and other thieves; that he had formed a kind of corporation of thieves of which he was head, or director, and that, despite his pretended efforts at detection, he procured none to be hanged but those who concealed their booty or refused him his share. It was said that he had divided the town and country into districts, and had appointed distinct gangs to each, who accounted to him for their robberies; that he employed another set to rob in churches during divine service, and other "moving detachments to attend at court on birthdays and balls, and at the houses of Parliament." His chosen agents were returned transports, who lay quite at his mercy. They could not be evidence against him, and if they displeased him he could at any time have them hanged. These felons he generally lodged in a house of his own, where he fed and clothed them, and used them in clipping guineas or counterfeiting coin.[169] He himself had been a confederate in numerous robberies; in all cases he was a receiver of the goods stolen; he had under his care several warehouses for concealing the same, and owned a vessel for carrying off jewels, watches, and other valuables to Holland, where he had a superannuated thief for a factor. He also kept in his pay several artists to make alterations and transform watches, seals, snuff-boxes, rings, so that they might not be recognized, which he used to present to people who could be of service to him. It was alleged that he generally claimed as much as half the value of all articles which he pretended to recover, and that he never gave up bank-notes or paper unless the loser could exactly specify them. "In order to carry out these vile practices, and to gain some credit with the ignorant multitude, he usually carried a short silver staff as a badge of authority from the government, which he used to produce when he himself was concerned in robbing." Last of all he was charged with "selling human blood;" in other words, of procuring false evidence to convict innocent persons; "sometimes to prevent them from being evidence against himself, and at other times for the sake of the great reward offered by the government." Wild's career was brought to an abrupt conclusion by the revelations made by two of his creatures. He absconded, but was pursued, captured, and committed to Newgate. He was tried on several indictments, but convicted on that of having maintained a secret correspondence with felons, receiving money for restoring stolen goods, and dividing it with the thieves whom he did not prosecute. While under sentence of death he made desperate attempts to obtain a pardon, but in vain, and at last tried to evade the gallows by taking a large dose of laudanum. This also failed, and he was conveyed to Tyburn amidst the execrations of a countless mob of people, who pelted him with stones and dirt all the way. Among other curious facts concerning this arch-villain, it is recorded that when at the acme of his prosperity, Jonathan Wild was ambitious of becoming a freeman of the city of London. His petition to this effect is contained among the records of the Town Clerk's office, and sets forth that the petitioner "has been at great trouble and charge in apprehending and convicting divers felons for returning from transportation from Oct. 1720 ... that your petitioner has never received any reward or gratuity for such his service, that he is very desirous of becoming a freeman of this honorable city...." The names follow, and include Moll King, John Jones, &c., "who were notorious street robbers." The petition is endorsed as read Jan. 2nd, 1724, but the result is not stated.

Before I close this chapter I must refer briefly to another class of highway robbers—the pirates and rovers who ranged the high seas in the first half of the eighteenth century.[170] In those days there was no efficient ocean police, no perpetual patrolling by war-ships of all nations to prevent and put down piracy as a crime noxious to the whole world. Later, on the ascendancy of the British navy, this duty was more or less its peculiar province; but till then every sea was infested with pirates sailing under various flags. The growth of piracy has been attributed, no doubt with reason, to the narrow policy of Spain with regard to her transatlantic colonies. To baffle this colonial system the European powers long tolerated, even encouraged these reckless filibusters, who did not confine their ravages to the Spanish-American coast, but turned their hands, like nautical Ishmaels, against all the world. The mischief thus done was incalculable. One notorious rover, Captain Roberts, took four hundred sail. They were as clever in obtaining information as to the movements of rich prizes on the seas as were highwaymen concerning the traffic along the highroads. They were particularly cunning in avoiding war-ships, and knew exactly where to run for supplies. As Captain Johnson tells us, speaking of the West Indies in the opening pages of his 'History of Pirates,' "they have been so formidable and numerous that they have interrupted the trade of Europe in those parts; and our English merchants in particular have suffered more by their depredations than by the united force of France and Spain in the late war."

Pirates were the curse of the North American waters when Lord Bellamont went as Governor of New England in 1695, and no one was supposed to be more in their secrets at that time, or more conversant with their haunts and hiding-place, than a certain Captain John Kidd of New York, who owned a small vessel, and traded with the West Indies. Lord Bellamont's instructions were to put down piracy if he could, and Kidd was recommended to him as a fitting person to employ. For some reason or other Kidd was denied official status; but it was pointed out to Lord Bellamont that, as the affair would not well admit delay, "it was worthy of being undertaken by some private persons of rank and distinction, and carried into execution at their own expense, notwithstanding public encouragement was denied to it." Eventually the Lord Chancellor, Lord Somers, the Duke of Shrewsbury, the Earl of Romney, the Earl of Orford, with some others, subscribed a sum of £6000 to fit out an expedition from England, of which Kidd was to have the command; and he was granted a commission by letters patent under the great seal to take and seize pirates, and bring them to justice. The profits of the adventure, less a fifth, which went to Kidd and another, were to be pocketed by the promoters of the enterprise, and this led subsequently to a charge of complicity with the pirates, which proved very awkward, especially for Lords Orford and Somers.

Kidd sailed for New York in the Adventure galley, and soon hoisted the black flag. From New York he steered for Madeira, thence to the Cape of Good Hope, and on to Madagascar. He captured all that came in his way. French ships, Portuguese, "Moorish," even English ships engaged in legitimate and peaceful trade. Kidd shifted his flag to one of his prizes, and in her returned to the Spanish main for supplies. Thence he sailed for various ports of the West Indies, and having disposed of much of his booty, steered for Boston. He had been preceded there by a merchant who knew of his piratical proceedings, and gave information to Lord Bellamont. Kidd was accordingly arrested on his arrival in New England. A full report was sent home, and a man-of-war, the Rochester, despatched to bring Kidd to England for trial. As the Rochester became disabled, and Kidd's arrival was delayed, much great public clamour arose, caused and fed by political prejudices against Lord Bellamont and the other great lords, who were accused of an attempt to shield Kidd. It was moved in the House of Commons that the "letters patent granted to the Earl of Bellamont and others respecting the goods taken from pirates were dishonourable to the king, against the law of nations, contrary to the laws and statutes of the realm, an invasion of property, and destructive to commerce." The motion was opposed, but the political opponents of Lord Somers and Lord Orford continued to accuse them of giving countenance to pirates, while Lord Bellamont was deemed no less culpable. The East India Company, which had suffered greatly by Kidd's depredations, and which had been refused[171] letters of marque to suppress piracy in the Indian Ocean, joined in the clamour, and petitioned that Captain Kidd "might be brought to speedy trial, and that the effects taken unjustly from the subjects of the Great Mogul may be returned to them as a satisfaction for their losses."

It was ruled at last that Kidd should be examined at the bar of the House of Commons, with the idea of "fixing part of his guilt on the parties who had been concerned in sending him on his expedition." Kidd was accordingly brought to England and lodged first in the Marshalsea, the prison of the Admiralty Court, and afterwards committed to Newgate. It was rumoured that Lord Halifax, who shared the political odium of Lords Somers and Orford, had sent privately for Kidd from Newgate to tamper with him, but "the keeper of the gaol on being sent for averred that it was false."[172] It is more probable that the other side endeavoured to get Kidd to bear witness against Lord Somers and the rest; but at the bar of the House, where he made a very contemptible appearance, being in some degree intoxicated, Kidd fully exonerated them. "Kidd discovered little or nothing," says Luttrell. In their subsequent impeachment they were, notwithstanding, charged with having been Kidd's accomplices, but the accusation broke down. Kidd in the mean time had been left to his fate. He was tried with his crew on several indictments for murder and piracy at the Admiralty sessions of the Old Bailey, convicted and hung.[173] He must have prospered greatly in his short and infamous career. According to Luttrell, his effects were valued at £200,000, and one witness alone, Cogi Baba, a Persian merchant, charged him with robbing him in the Persian Gulf of £60,000. No case was made out against the above-mentioned peers. Lord Orford set up in his defence that in Kidd's affair "he had acted legally, and with a good intention towards the public, though to his own loss;"[174] and Lord Somers denied that he had ever seen or knew anything of Kidd. Hume sums up the matter by declaring that "the Commons in the whole course of the transaction had certainly acted from motives of faction and revenge."

John Gow, who took the piratical name of Captain Smith, was second mate of the George galley, which he conspired with half the crew to seize when on the voyage to Santa Cruz. On a given signal, the utterance of a password, "Who fires first?" an attack was made on the first mate, surgeon, and supercargo, whose throats were cut. The captain hearing a noise came on deck, when one mutineer cut his throat, and a second fired a couple of balls into his body. The ship's company consisted of twenty: four were now disposed of, eight were conspirators, and of the remaining eight, some of whom had concealed themselves below decks and some in the shrouds, four had joined the pirates. The other four were closely watched, and although allowed to range the ship at pleasure, were often cruelly beaten. The ship was rechristened 'The Revenge'; she mounted several guns, and the pirates steered her for the coast of Spain, where several prizes were taken—the first a ship laden with salted cod from Newfoundland, the second a Scotch ship bound to Italy with a cargo of pickled herrings, the third a French ship laden with oil, wine, and fruit. The pirates also made a descent upon the Portuguese coast and laid the people under contributions.

Dissensions now arose in the company. Gow had a certain amount of sense and courage, but his lieutenant was a brutal ruffian, often blinded by passion, and continually fermenting discord. At last he attempted to shoot Gow, but his pistol missed fire, and he was wounded himself by two of the pirates. He sprang down to the powder-room and threatened to blow up the ship, but he was secured, and put on board a vessel which had been ransacked and set free, the commander of it being desired to hand the pirate over to the first king's ship he met, "to be dealt with according to his crimes." After this the pirates steered north for the Orkneys, of which Gow was a native, and after a safe passage anchored in a bay in one of the islands. While lying there one of his crew, who had been forced into joining them, escaped to Kirkwall, where he gave information to a magistrate, and the sheriff issued a precept to the constables and others to seize 'The Revenge.' Soon afterwards ten more of the crew, also unwilling members of it, laid hands on the long boat, and reaching the mainland of Scotland, coasted along it as far as Leith, whence they made their way to Edinburgh, and were imprisoned as pirates. Gow meanwhile, careless of danger, lingered in the Orkneys, plundering and ransacking the dwelling-houses to provide himself with provisions, and carrying off plate, linen, and all valuables on which they could lay hands.

Arriving at an island named Calf Sound, Gow planned the robbery of an old schoolmate, a Mr. Fea, whom he sought to entrap. But Mr. Fea turned the tables upon him. Inviting Gow and several of the crew to an entertainment on shore, while they were carousing Mr. Fea made his servants seize the pirates' boat, and then entering by different doors, fell upon the pirates themselves, and made all prisoners. The rest, twenty-eight in number, who were still afloat, were also captured by various artifices, and the whole, under orders of the Lord Chief Justice, were despatched to the Thames in H.M.S. Greyhound, for trial at the Admiralty Court. They were committed to the Marshalsea, and thence to Newgate, and arraigned at the Old Bailey, where Gow refused to plead, and was sentenced to be pressed to death. He pretended that he wished to save an estate for a relation; but when all preparations for carrying out the sentence were completed, he begged to be allowed to plead, and "the judge being informed, humanely granted his request." Gow and six others were eventually hanged at Execution Dock.

Pirates who fell in with ships usually sought to gain recruits among the captured crews. The alternative was to walk the plank or to be set adrift in an open boat, or landed on an uninhabited island. The latter was the fate of as many in a shipload of convicts taken at sea by pirates as refused to sign articles. For those who thus agreed under compulsion a still harder fate was often in store. Captain Massey was an unfortunate instance of this. While serving in the Royal African Company he was for some time engaged in the construction of a fort upon the coast with a detachment of men. They ran short of food, and suffered frightfully from flux. When at the point of death a passing ship noticed their signals of distress, and sent a boat on shore to bring them on board. The ship proved to be a pirate. Captain Massey did not actually join them, but he remained on board while several prizes were taken. However, he gave information at Jamaica, the pirate captain and others were arrested and hanged, and Captain Massey received the thanks of the Governor, who offered him an appointment on the island. But Massey was anxious to return to England, whither he proceeded armed with strong letters of recommendation to the lords of the Admiralty. To his intense surprise, "instead of being caressed he was taken into custody," tried, and eventually executed. His case evoked great sympathy. "His joining the pirates was evidently an act of necessity, not choice," and he took the earliest opportunity of giving up his involuntary associates to justice—a conduct by which he surely merited the thanks of his country, and not the vengeance of the law.

THE GAOL FEVER

Why chapter so styled—The gaol fever the visible exponent of foul state of gaols—Their evils briefly described—Neither sufficient light nor air—Often underground—Scantiest supply of water—No bed, no exercise—Meagre rations—Water soup—Allowance to criminals denied to debtors who had to beg alms—Prison buildings wretched—Often private property of local magnates, who farmed them out, and pocketed the gains—How the Bishop of Ely kept his prisoners—All prisoners loaded with irons—Legal opinions on the practice—Description of irons used—Women also fettered—John Wilkes when sheriff protests against ironing the untried—Avarice primary cause of ill-treatment of prisoners—Drunkenness encouraged—Gaol fees—Overcrowding the parent of gaol fever—Rarity of gaol deliveries—The gaol fever explained—Its causes—Its ravages—Extends from prisons to court-houses—To villages—Into the army and the fleet—Earliest mention of gaol distemper—The Black Assize—The sickness of the House at the King's Bench prison—The gaol fever in the 17th century—Its outbreaks in the 18th—The Taunton Assize—Originated in

Newgate in 1750—Extends to Old Bailey with deadly results—The Corporation alarmed—Seek to provide a remedy—Enquiry into the sanitary condition of Newgate—A new ventilator recommended by the Rev. Dr. Hales and Dr. Pringle, F.R.S.—The ventilator described—Hopes expressed that it will check the disease, but the air of Newgate continues pestiferous—Fatal effects of working at the ventilator—Men employed show all symptoms of gaol fever—The fever constantly present in Newgate—Mr. Akerman's evidence—Statistics of deaths—The fever taken into the country gaols by prisoners removed from Newgate—Also to Southwark—Renewed dread in the Courts, which are protected by the fumes of vinegar—All this time no regular doctor at Newgate—Howard condemns construction of new Newgate as likely to produce gaol fever—Lord George Gordon dies of it in 1793—Dr. Smith reports and condemns the new prison at Newgate—Too crowded and faulty site—Mr. Akerman defends it as superior to the old, but admits that prisoners die in it, broken-hearted—Mr. Akerman a humane man—A friend of Boswell's, who panegyrizes him—Mr. Akerman's brave and judicious conduct at a fire in prison—Calms the prisoners, and remains in the midst of danger—Life at Newgate—The sexes intermixed—Debauchery—Gaming—Drunkenness—Moral contamination—Criminals willingly took military service to escape confinement in Newgate.

I HAVE given this title to the present chapter because the gaol fever while it raged was the visible exponent of the foul condition of all gaols, including Newgate, or, as Dr. Guy puts it, "the physical expression of manifold prison neglect and mismanagement." The loathsome corruption that festered unchecked or unalleviated within the prison houses was never revealed until John Howard began his self-sacrificing visitations, and it is to the pages of his 'State of Prisons' that we must refer for full details. Some would be incredible were they not vouched for on the unimpeachable testimony of the great philanthropist. All through the eighteenth century the case of all prisoners was desperate, their sufferings heart-rending, their treatment a disgrace to that or any age. They were either entirely deprived of, or at best but scantily provided with, the commonest and most indispensable necessaries of life. They were often denied both light and air, which are assuredly the free heritage of all God's creatures. Rapacity and extortion, of which more directly, were too prevalent in prison administration to allow of many windows when all such openings were heavily taxed. What windows there were looked generally down dark entries or noisome passages, and gave no light. In Newgate until the building of the new (and last) gaol, the felons' side and the common debtors' side were so dark that it was necessary to use links and burners all day long; indeed, artificial light was generally necessary all over the prison, except in the press-yard.

The place of durance was sometimes underground, a dungeon, or subterranean cellar, into which the prisoners were lowered, to fight with rats for the meagre pittance of food thrown to them through a trap-door. These terrible *oubliettes* were too often damp and noisome, half a foot deep in water, or with an open sewer running through the centre of the floor. They had no chimneys, no fireplace, no barrack beds; the wretched inmates huddled together for warmth upon heaps of filthy rags or bundles of rotten straw reeking with foul exhalations, and fetid with all manner of indescribable nastiness. There was not the slightest attempt at ventilation, as we understand the word. The windows, when they existed, were seldom if ever opened, nor the doors, for the spaces within the prison walls were generally too limited to allow of daily exercise, and the prisoners were thus kept continuously under lock and key. Water, another necessary of life, was doled out in the scantiest quantities, too small for proper ablutions or cleansing purposes, and hardly sufficient to assuage thirst. Howard tells us of one prison where the daily allowance of water was only three pints per head, and even this was dependent upon the good will of the keepers, who brought it or not, as they felt disposed. At another, water could only be had on payment, the price being a half-penny for three gallons.

The rations of food were equally meagre. In some prisons indeed nothing was given; in others, the prisoners subsisted on water-soup—"bread boiled in mere water." The poor debtors were the worst off. For the felon, thief, murderer, or highwayman there was a grant either in money or in kind—a pennyworth of bread per diem, or a shilling's worth per week, or a certain weight of bread. But the debtors, who formed three-fourths of the permanent prison population, and whose liabilities on an average did not exceed ten or fifteen pounds a piece, were almost starved to death. The bequests of charitable people, especially intended for their support, were devoted to other uses; creditors seldom if ever paid the "groat," or fourpence per diem for subsistence required by the Act. Any alms collected within the prison by direct mendicancy were commonly intercepted by the ruffians who ruled the roost. When gaolers applied to the magistrates for food for the debtors the answer was, "Let them work or starve"; yet the former was forbidden, lest the tools they used might fall into the hands of criminal prisoners, and furnish means of escape. At Exeter the prisoners were marched about the city soliciting charity in the streets. One Christmas-tide, so Howard says, the person who conducted them broke open the box and absconded with the contents. The debtors' ward in this gaol was called the "shew," because the debtors begged by letting down a *shoe* from the window.

Prison buildings were mostly inconvenient, ill-planned, and but little adapted for the purposes of incarceration. Many of them were ancient strongholds—the gate of some fortified city, the keep or castle or embattled residence of a great personage. Some lords, spiritual and temporal, with peculiar powers in their own districts, once had their prisons, so to speak, under their own roof. The prisons lingered long after the power lapsed, and in Howard's time many of the worst prisons were the private property of individuals,[175] who protected the keepers, their lessees, and pocketed the gains wrung from the wretched lodgers. The Duke of Portland was the proprietor of Chesterfield gaol, which consisted of one room with a cellar under it. For this accommodation, and the privilege it conferred upon him of demanding gaol fees, the keeper paid the Duke an annual rent of eighteen guineas. "The cellar," Howard says, "had not been cleaned for months, nor the prison door opened for several weeks." Another disgraceful prison was that owned by the Bishop of Ely. One bishop had been compelled to rebuild it in part fourteen years before Howard's visit, but it was still bad. It had been so insecure that the keeper resorted to a most cruel contrivance in order to ensure safe custody. Prisoners were "chained down upon their backs upon a floor, across which were several iron bars, with an iron collar with spikes about their necks, and a heavy iron bar over their legs." This barbarous treatment formed the subject of a special petition to the king, supported by a drawing, "with which His Majesty was much affected, and gave immediate orders for a proper inquiry and redress."

Loading prisoners with irons was very generally practised, although its legality was questioned even then. Lord Coke gave his opinion against the oppression. Bracton affirmed that a sentence condemning a man to be confined in irons was illegal, and in 'Blackstone Commentaries'[176] is this passage: "The law will not justify jailers in fettering a prisoner unless when he is unruly, or has attempted an escape. In 1728 the judges reprimanded the warders of the Fleet prison, and declared that a jailer could not answer the ironing of a man before he was found guilty of a crime." When a keeper pleaded necessity for safe custody to Lord Chief Justice King, the judge bade him "build higher his prison walls." As Buxton observes, the neglect of this legal precaution was no excuse for the infliction of an illegal punishment. Prisoners should not suffer because authorities neglect their duty. "Very rarely is a man ironed for his own misdeeds, but frequently for those of others; additional irons on his person are cheaper than additional elevation to the walls. Thus we cover our own negligence by increased severity to our captives."[177]

The irons were so heavy that "walking, even lying down to sleep, was difficult and painful." In some county gaols women did not escape this severity, Howard tells us, but London was more humane. But in the London prisons the custom of ironing even the untried males was long and firmly established. An interesting letter is extant from John Wilkes, dated 1771, the year of his shrievalty to the keeper of Newgate, Mr. Akerman. This letter expresses satisfaction with his general conduct, and admits his humanity to the unhappy persons under his care. But Wilkes takes strong exceptions to the practise of keeping the prisoners in irons at the time of arraignment and trial, which he conceives to he alike repugnant to the laws of England and humanity.

"Every person at so critical a moment ought to be without any bodily pain or restraint, that the mind may be perfectly free to deliberate on its most interesting and awful concerns, in so alarming a situation. It is cruelty to aggravate the feelings of the unhappy in such a state of distraction, and injustice to deprive them of any means for the defence of supposed innocence by calling off the attention by bodily torture at the great moment when the full exertion of every faculty is most wanting. No man in England ought to be obliged to plead while in chains; we therefore are determined to abolish the present illegal and inhuman practice, and we direct you to take off the irons before any prisoner is sent to the bar, either for arraignment or trial."[178]

Avarice was no doubt a primary cause of the ill-treatment of prisoners, and, as I have described elsewhere,[179] heavy fees were exacted to obtain "easement" or "choice" of irons. This idea of turning gaols to profit underlay the whole system of prison management. The gaolers bought or rented their places, and they had to recoup themselves as best they could. A pernicious vested interest was thus established, which even the legislature acknowledged. The sale of strong drink within the prison, and the existence of a prison tap or bar, were recognized and regulated by law. Drunkenness in consequence prevailed in all prisons, fostered by the evil practice of claiming garnish, which did not disappear, as I shall presently show, till well on into the present century. Another universal method of grinding money out of all who came within the grip of the law was the extortion of gaol fees. It was the enormity of demanding such payment from innocent men, acquitted after a fair trial, who in default were hauled back to prison, that first moved Howard to inquire into the custom at various prisons. As early as 1732 the Corporation of London had promulgated an order that all prisoners acquitted at the Old Bailey should be released without fees. But when Howard visited Newgate forty years later, Mr. Akerman the keeper showed him a table of fees "which was given him for his direction when he commenced keeper." The sums demanded varied from 8s. 10d. for a debtor's discharge, to 18s. 10d. for a felon's, and £3 6s. 8d. for a bailable warrant. The exactions for fees, whether for innocent or guilty, tried or untried, was pretty general throughout the kingdom, although Howard found a few prisons where there were none. Even he in his suggestions for the improvement of gaols, although recommending the abolition of fees and the substitution of a regular salary to the gaoler, was evidently doubtful of securing so great a reform, for he expresses a hope that if fees were not altogether abolished they may at least be reduced. However, the philanthropist found a welcome support from Mr. Popham, M.P. for Taunton, who in 1773 brought in a bill "abolishing gaolers' fees, and substituting for them fixed salaries payable out of the county rates," which bill passed into law the following year in an amended form. This Act provided that acquitted prisoners "shall be immediately set at large in open court." Yet the law was openly evaded by the clerks of assize and clerks of the place, who declared that their fees were not cancelled by the Act, and who endeavoured to indemnify themselves by demanding a fee from the gaoler for a certificate of acquittal. In one case at Durham, Judge Gould at the assizes in 1775 fined the keeper £50 for detaining acquitted prisoners under this demand of the clerk of assize, but the fine was remitted on explanation. Still another pretence often put forward for detaining acquitted prisoners until after the judge had left the town was, that other indictments might be laid against them; or yet again, prisoners were taken back to prison to have their irons knocked off, irons with which, as free, unconvicted men, they were manacled illegally and unjustly.

Perhaps the most hideous and terrible of all evils, and the immediate parent of gaol fever, was the disgraceful and almost indiscriminate overcrowding of the gaols. The rarity of gaol deliveries was a proximate cause of this. The expense of entertaining the judges was alleged as an excuse for not holding assizes more than once a year; but at some places—Hull, for instance—there had been only one gaol delivery in seven years, although, according to Howard, it had latterly been reduced to three. Often in the lapse of time principal witnesses died, and there was an acquittal with a failure of justice. Nor was it only the accused and unconvicted who lingered out their lives in gaol, but numbers of perfectly innocent folk helped to crowd the narrow limits of the prison-house. Either the mistaken leniency, or more probably the absolutely callous indifference of gaol-rulers, suffered debtors to surround themselves with their families, pure women and tender children brought thus into continuous intercourse with felons and murderers, and doomed to lose their moral sense in the demoralizing atmosphere. The prison population was daily increased by a host of visitors, improper characters, friends and associates of thieves, who had free access to all parts of the gaol. In every filthy, unventilated cell-chamber the number of occupants was constantly excessive. The air space for each was often less than 150 cubic feet, and this air was never changed. Of one room, with its beds in tiers, its windows looking only into a dark entry, its fireplace used for the cooking of food for forty persons, it was said that the man who planned it could not well have contrived "a place of the same dimensions more effectually calculated to destroy his fellow-creatures."

The gaol fever or distemper, of which I shall now give some account, was the natural product of these insanitary conditions. This fell epidemic exercised strange terrors by the mystery which once surrounded it; but this has now been dispelled by the strong light of modern medical science. All authorities are agreed that it was nothing but that typhus fever, which inevitably goes hand in hand with the herding and packing together of human beings, whether in prisons, workhouses, hospitals, or densely-populated quarters of a town. The disease is likely to crop up, as Dr. Guy remarks, "wherever men and women live together in places small in proportion to their numbers, with neglect of cleanliness and ventilation, surrounded by offensive effluvia, without proper exercise, and scantily supplied with food."[180] It is easy to understand that the poison would be generated in gaol establishments such as I have described; still more, that prisoners should be saturated with it so as to infect even healthy persons whom they approached. This is precisely what happened, and it is through the ravages committed by the disorder beyond the prison walls that we mostly hear of it. The decimation it caused within the gaol might have passed unnoticed, but the many authentic cases of the terrible mortality it occasioned elsewhere forced it upon the attention of the chronicler. It made the administration of the law a service of danger, while its fatal effects can be traced far from beyond the limits of the court-house. Prisoners carried home the contagion to the bosoms of their families, whence the disease spread into town or village. They carried it on board ship, and imported it into our fleets. "The first English fleet sent to America lost by it above 2000 men; ... the of infection were carried from the guardships into our squadrons; and the mortality thence occasioned was greater than by all other diseases or means of death put together."[181] It was the same with the army: regiments and garrisons were infected by comrades who brought the fever from the gaol; sometimes the escorts returning with deserters temporarily lodged in prison also sickened and died.

The earliest mention of a gaol distemper is that quoted by Howard from Stowe, under date 1414, when "the gaolers of Newgate and Ludgate died, and prisoners in Newgate to the number of sixty-four." In 'Wood's History of Oxford' there is a record of a contagious fever which broke out at the assize of Cambridge in 1521. The justices, gentlemen, bailiffs, and others "resorting thither took such an infection that many of them died, and almost all that were present fell desperately sick, and narrowly escaped with their lives." After this comes the Black Assize at Oxford in 1577, when, Holinshed says, "there arose amidst the people such a dampe that almost all were smouldered, very few escaping.... the jurors presently dying, and shortly after Sir Robert Bell, Lord Chief Baron." To this account we may add that in 'Baker's Chronicle,' which states that all present died within forty hours, the Lord Chief Baron, the sheriff, and three hundred more. The contagion spread into the city of Oxford, and thence into the neighbourhood, where there were many more deaths. Stowe has another reference to the fever about this date, and tells us that in the King's Bench Prison, in the six years preceding the year 1579, a hundred died of a certain contagion called "the sickness of the house." Another outbreak occurred at Exeter, 1586, on the occasion of holding the city assizes, when "a sudden and strange sickness," which had appeared first among the prisoners in the gaol, was dispersed at their trial through the audience in court, "whereof more died than escaped," and of those that succumbed, some were constables, some reeves, some tithing men or jurors. No wonder that Lord Bacon, in writing on the subject, should characterize "the smell of the jail the most pernicious infection, next to the plague. When prisoners have been long and close and nastily kept, whereof we have had in our time experience twice or thrice, both judges that sat upon the trial, and numbers of those that attended the business or were present, sickened upon it and died."

The gaol distemper is but sparingly mentioned throughout the seventeenth century, but as the conditions were precisely the same, it is pretty certain that the disease existed then, as before and after. But in the first half of the eighteenth century we have detailed accounts of three serious and fatal outbreaks. The first was at the Lent Assizes held in Taunton in 1730, "when," Howard says, "some prisoners who were brought thither from the Ilchester gaol infected the court; and Lord Chief Baron Pengelly, Sir James Shepherd, sergeant, John Pigott, Esq., sheriff, and some hundreds besides died of the gaol distemper." The second case occurred also in the west country, at Launceston, where "a fever which took its rise in the prisons was disseminated far and near by the county assizes, occasioned the death of numbers, and foiled frequently the best advice." It is described as a contagious, putrid, and very pestilential fever, attended with tremblings, twitchings, restlessness, delirium, with, in some instances, early phrenzy and lethargy; while the victims broke out often into livid pustules and purple spots. The third case of gaol fever was in London in 1750, and it undoubtedly had its origin in Newgate. At the May Sessions at the Old Bailey there was a more than usually heavy calendar, and the court was excessively crowded. The prisoners awaiting trial numbered a hundred, and these were mostly lodged in two rooms, fourteen feet by seven, and only seven feet in height; but some, and no doubt all in turn, were put into the bail dock; many had long lain close confined in the pestiferous wards of Newgate. The court itself was of limited dimensions, being barely thirty feet square, and in direct communication with the bail dock and rooms beyond, whence an open window, "at the furthest end of the room," carried a draught poisoned with infection towards the judges' bench. Of these four, viz. Sir Samuel Pennant, the Lord Mayor, Sir Thomas Abney and Baron Clark, the judges, and Sir Daniel Lambert, alderman, were seized with the distemper, and speedily died; others, to the number of forty, were also attacked and succumbed. Among them were some of the under-sheriffs, several members of the bar and of the jury; while in others of lesser note the disease showed itself more tardily, but they also eventually succumbed. Indeed, with the exception of two or three, none of those attacked escaped.[182] The symptoms were the same as these already described, including the delirium and the spots on the skin.

The Corporation of London, moved thereto by a letter from the Lord Chief Justice, and not unnaturally alarmed themselves at the ravages of a pestilence which spared neither Lord Mayor nor aldermen, set about inquiring into its origin. A committee was appointed for this purpose in October, 1750, five months after the last outbreak, and their instructions were to ascertain "the best means for procuring in Newgate such a purity of air as might prevent the rise of those infectious distempers." ... The committee consulted the Rev. Dr. Hales and Dr. Pringle, F.R.S., [183] the latter of whom subsequently published a paper in the 'Transactions of the Philosophical Society,' containing much curious information concerning the disease. The remedy suggested by Dr. Hales, and eventually approved of by the committee, was to try further the ventilator which some time previously had been placed upon the top of Newgate. Nothing less than the reconstruction on an extended plan of the prison, which was acknowledged to be too small for its average population, would have really sufficed, but this, although mooted, had not yet taken practical shape. The existing ventilator was in the nature of a main trunk or shaft, into which other air-pipes led from various parts of the prison. But these were neither numerous nor effective, while there was no process of extraction or of obtaining an up-draught. To effect this a machine was erected upon the leads of Newgate with large arms like those of a windmill. The plan was fully approved of by the Court of Aldermen, but its execution was delayed. At length, in July, 1752, [184] Dr. Pringle heard that a portion of the machine was completed and in working order, and went to inspect it, accompanied by other medical men. "Having visited several of the wards," he says, "we were all of us very sensible that such as were provided with ventilating tubes were much less offensive than the rest that wanted them." The air of the whole gaol they thought was distinctly improved. Some of the wards indeed were so free from the smell peculiar to such places that Dr. Pringle felt persuaded that if the design was completed, and persons appointed to regulate the sliders of the tubes, and keep the machine in order, the usual evil effects of overcrowding in gaols might be in a great measure if not wholly prevented in Newgate.

Nevertheless, throughout the execution of the work and afterwards the air of Newgate continued pestiferous and fatal to all who breathed it. The workmen employed in fixing the tubes ran great risks, and in several cases were seized with unmistakable gaol fever. One man had found himself indisposed for some days and left off work; then returning to Newgate, he had been employed in opening one of the tubes of the old ventilator which had stood for three or four years. Such an offensive smell had issued from the tube that he was seized with sickness and nausea. He went home, and that night fell ill of the fever, being afflicted with violent headache, retching, trembling of the hands, and last of all delirium. He was admitted into St. Thomas' Hospital, and said to be suffering from continued fever, attended with stupor and a sunk pulse. Another victim was a fellow workman, who from, having been active and full of health, fell ill after working at Newgate, and shewed the same symptoms. Three more of his companions were also attacked, all of whom had the headaches, tremblings, stupor, and "petechial" spots. One of these was a lad of fifteen, who had been forced by his fellows to go down the great trunk of the ventilator in order to bring up a wig which some one had thrown into it; on coming up again he was immediately attacked by a violent headache, a great disorder in his stomach, and nausea, none of which had left him when seen weeks later. A peculiarity in his case was, that he had been twice let down into the ventilator when the machine on the leads had been standing still, and he had suffered no ill effects; but the last time it was in motion, and the heavily-laden up-draught had well nigh poisoned him and two others who had dragged him out of the shaft. These cases did not complete the mischief done. The infection was carried home and spread in the families of those attacked in Newgate. Wives, children, friends, and nurses all fell sick in turn. Besides those who received the contagion at second-hand, there were seven originally infected in the gaol, and this out of a total of eleven workmen employed.

It is probable that the great windmill and ventilator[185] did some good, for there is no further mention of epidemic seizure in court. But the sanitary condition of the inmates of Newgate cannot have been permanently or very appreciably improved. I find in the Home Office papers, under date July, 1769, a letter from Fras Ingram to Lord —— in favour of one William Wiseman, condemned for petty larceny, and awaiting transportation. The prisoner was in chains in Newgate, and when Mr. Ingram's servant went to inquire for him he was forbidden to approach the bars of the room in which Wiseman was detained. The prison was so foul and loathsome in this hot season that there was a fear lest Mr. Ingram's servant should run the risk of taking and carrying away the infection of the gaol distemper.

The gaol fever or its germs must indeed have been constantly present in Newgate. The more crowded the prison the more sickly it was. The worst seasons were the middle of winter or the middle of summer, or when the weather was damp and wet. The place was seldom without some illness or other; but in one year, according to Mr. Akerman, about sixteen died in one month from the gaol distemper. Mr. Akerman declared that the fever was all over the gaol, and that in ten years he had buried eight or ten of his servants. He also gave a return to the Commons' committee, which showed that eighty-three prisoners had died between 1758 and 1765, besides several wives who had come to visit their husbands, and a number of children born in the gaol. This statement was supported by the evidence of the coroner for Middlesex, Mr. Beach, who went even further, and made out that one hundred and thirty-two had died between 1755 and 1765, or forty-nine more in the two additional years. In 1763 the deaths had been twenty-eight, all of them of contagion, according to Mr. Beach, who was also of opinion that a large percentage of the whole one hundred and thirty-two had died of the gaol fever.

Twenty years later, when Howard was visiting prisons, he heard it constantly affirmed by county gaolers that the gaol distemper was brought into their prisons by prisoners removed under Habeas Corpus from Newgate. In May, 1763, I find an inquisition was held in the new gaol, Southwark, upon the body of Henry Vincent, one of five prisoners removed there from Newgate. It then appeared that the Southwark prisoners had been healthy till those from Newgate arrived, all five being infected. About this date too, according to the coroner for Middlesex, there were several deaths in the new gaol, of prisoners brought from Newgate who had caught the fever in that prison. This same coroner had taken eleven "inquisitions" at Newgate in a couple of days, all of whom he thought had died of the gaol distemper. He was also made ill himself by going to Newgate. Again in 1772 there was a new alarm of epidemic. In the sessions of the preceding year there had been an outbreak of malignant distemper, of which several had died. An attempt was made to tinker up the ventilator, and other precautions taken. Among the latter was a plan to convey the fumes of vinegar through pipes into the Sessions House while the courts were sitting. At this date there was no regular medical officer in attendance on the Newgate prisoners, although an apothecary was paid something for visiting occasionally. Howard expresses his opinion strongly on the want. "To this capital prison," he says, "the magistrates would, in my humble opinion, do well to appoint a physician, a surgeon, and an apothecary." The new prison, that built by Dance, and still standing (1883), was just then in process of erection,[186] and was intended to embody all requirements in prison construction. But Howard was dissatisfied with it. Although it would avoid "many inconveniences of the old gaol," yet it had some manifest errors. "It is too late," he goes on, "to point out particulars. All I say is, that without more than ordinary care, the prisoners in it will be in great danger of gaol fever."[187]

William Smith, M.D., who, from a charitable desire to afford medical assistance to the sick, inspected and reported in 1776 upon the sanitary conditions of all the London prisons, had not a better opinion of the new Newgate than had Howard. The gaol had now a regular medical attendant, but "it was filled with nasty ragged inhabitants, swarming with vermin, though Mr. Akerman the keeper is extremely humane in keeping the place as wholesome as possible." The new prison, goes on Dr. Smith, is built upon the old principle of a great number being crowded together into one ward, with a yard for them to assemble in in the day, and a tap where they may get drink when they please and have the money to pay. He had no fault to find with the wards, which were large, airy, high, and "as clean as can well be supposed where such a motley crew are lodged." But he condemns the prison, on which so much had been already spent, and which still required an immense sum to finish it. Its site was, he thought, altogether faulty. "The situation of a gaol should be high and dry in an open field, and at a distance from the town, the building spacious, to obviate the bad effects of a putrid accumulation of infectious air, and extended in breadth rather than height. The wards should have many divisions to keep the prisoners from associating." Dr. Smith found that the numbers who sickened and died of breathing the impure and corrupted air were much greater than was imagined. Hence, he says, the absolute necessity for a sufficiency of fresh air, "the earth was made for us all, why should so small a portion of it be denied to those unhappy creatures, while so many large parts lay waste and uncultivated?"

Another person, well entitled to speak from his own knowledge and practical experience, declared that the new gaol contrasted very favourably with the old. This was Mr. Akerman the keeper, who was the friend of Johnson and Boswell, and whom Dr. Smith and others call extremely humane. But Mr. Akerman, in giving evidence before a committee of the House of Commons in 1779, while urging that few were unhealthy in the new prison, admitted that he had often observed a dejection of spirits among the prisoners in Newgate which had the effect of disease, and that "many had died broken-hearted." Mr. Akerman clearly did his best to alleviate the sufferings of those in his charge. For the poor convicted prisoner, unable to add by private means or the gifts of friends to the meagre allowance of the penny loaf per diem, which was often also fraudulently under weight, the keeper provided soup out of his own pocket, made of the coarse meat commonly called clods and stickings.

Mr. Akerman had many good friends. He was an intimate acquaintance of Mr. James Boswell, their friendship no doubt having originated in some civility shown to Dr. Johnson's biographer at one of the executions which it was Boswell's craze to attend. Boswell cannot speak too highly of Mr. Akerman. After describing the Lord George London Riots,[188] he says, "I should think myself very much to blame did I here neglect to do justice to my esteemed friend Mr. Akerman, the keeper of Newgate, who long discharged a very important trust with an uniform intrepid firmness, and at the same time a tenderness and a liberal charity, which entitles him to be recorded with distinguished honour." He goes on to describe in detail an incident which certainly proves Mr. Akerman's presence of mind and capacity as a gaol governor. The story has been often quoted, but it is so closely connected with the chronicles of Newgate that I cannot forbear giving it again to the public. "Many years ago a fire broke out in the brick part, which was built as an addition to the old gaol of Newgate. The prisoners were in consternation and tumult, calling out, 'We shall be burnt! we shall be burnt! down with the gate! down with the gate!' Mr. Akerman hastened to them, showed himself at the gate, and having after some confused vociferations of 'Hear him! hear him!' obtained a silent attention, he then calmly told them that the gate must not go down; that they were under his care, and that they should not be permitted to escape; but that he could assure them they need not be afraid of being burnt, for that the fire was not in the prison properly so called, which was strongly built with stone; and that if they would engage to be quiet he himself would come to them and conduct them to the further end of the building, and would not go out till they gave him leave. To this proposal they agreed; upon which Mr. Akerman, having first made them fall back from the gate, went in, and with a determined resolution ordered the outer turnkey upon no account to open the gate, even though the prisoners (though he trusted they would not) should break their word and by force bring himself to order it. 'Never mind me,' he said, 'should that happen.' The prisoners peaceably followed him while he conducted them through passages of which he had the keys to the extremity of the gaol which was most distant from the fire. Having by this very judicious conduct fully satisfied them that there was no immediate risk, if any at all, he then addressed them thus: 'Gentlemen, you are now convinced that I told you true. I have no doubt that the engines will soon extinguish the fire; if they should not, a sufficient guard will come, and you shall be all taken out and lodged in the compters. I assure you, upon my word and honour, that I have not a farthing insured. I have left my house that I might take care of you. I will keep my promise and stay with you if you insist upon it; but if you will allow me to go out and look after my family and property I shall be obliged to you.' Struck with his behaviour, they called out, 'Master Akerman, you have done bravely; it was very kind in you; by all means go and take care of your own concerns.' He did so accordingly, while they remained and were all preserved." Akerman received still higher praise for this, which was generally admitted to be courageous conduct. Dr. Johnson, according to Boswell, had been heard to relate the substance of the foregoing story "with high praise, in which he was joined by Mr. Edmund Burke." Johnson also touched upon Akerman's kindness to his prisoners, and "pronounced this eulogy upon his character. He who has long had constantly in his view the worst of mankind, and is yet eminent for the humanity of his disposition, must have had it originally in a great degree, and continued to cultivate it very carefully."

Another tribute to Akerman's worth comes from a less distinguished but probably not less genuine source. In the letters of the wretched Hackman already referred to,[189] he speaks in terms of warm eulogy of this humane gaoler. "Let me pay a small tribute of praise," he says. "How often have you and I complained of familiarity's blunting the edge of every sense on which she lays her hand?... what then is the praise of that gaoler who, in the midst of misery, crimes, and death, sets familiarity at defiance and still preserves the feelings of a man? The author of the 'Life of Savage' gives celebrity to the Bristol gaoler, by whose humanity the latter part of that strange man's life was rendered more comfortable. Shall no one give celebrity to the present keeper of Newgate? Mr. Akerman marks every day of his existence by more than one such deed as this. Know, ye rich and powerful, ye who might save hundreds of your fellow creatures from starving by the sweepings of your tables, know that among the various feelings of almost every wretch who quits Newgate for Tyburn, a concern neither last nor least is that which he feels upon leaving the gaol of which this man is the keeper."[190]

Life in Newgate, with its debauchery and foul discomfort, the nastiness and squalor of its surroundings, the ever-present infectious sickness due to constant overcrowding, and the utter absence of all cleanliness, or efforts at sanitation, must have been terrible. Evil practices went on without let or hindrance inside its walls. There is clear evidence to show that the sexes were intermixed during the daytime. The occupants of the various wards had free intercourse with each other: they had a reciprocal conversation, exchanged visits, and "assisted each other with such accommodation as the extension of their present circumstances permitted." Dinner was at two in the afternoon, and when prisoners possessed any variety or novelty in food, they were ready to trade or barter with it among themselves. After dinner the rest of the day and night was spent at "cards, draughts, fox and geese," or, as gambling was not interdicted, at games of chance, which led to numerous frauds and quarrels. Rapid moral deterioration was inevitable in this criminal sty. The prison was still and long continued a school of depravity, to which came tyros, some already viciously inclined, some still innocent, to be quickly taught all manner of iniquity, and to graduate and take honours in crime. It is on record that daring robberies were concocted in Newgate between felons incarcerated and others at large, who came and went as they pleased. The gaol was the receptacle for smuggled or stolen goods; false money was coined in the dark recesses of its gloomy wards and passed out into circulation. Such work was the natural employment of otherwise unoccupied brains and idle hands. Thefts inside the gaol were of common occurrence. The prisoners picked the pockets of visitors whenever they had the chance, or robbed one another.[191]

It was not strange that the inmates of Newgate should hold this miserable life of theirs pretty cheap, and be ready to risk it in any way to compass enlargement from gaol. Newgate was always constantly drawn upon by those who wanted men for any desperate enterprise. In the early days of inoculation, soon after it had been introduced by Lady Mary Wortly Montague from the East, and when it was still styled engrafting, "the process was first tried upon seven condemned prisoners, with a certain success." Again, a reprieve was granted to another convict under sentence of death, on condition that he permitted an experiment to be performed on his ear. The process, which was the invention of a Mr. Chas. Elden, was intended to cure deafness by cutting the tympanum. Sometimes a convicted criminal was allowed to choose between a year's imprisonment in Newgate or taking service under the Crown. There are also many entries in the State Papers of prisoners pardoned to join His Majesty's forces. Not that these very questionable recruits were willingly accepted. I find on 13th May, 1767, in reply to a letter forwarding a list of convicts so pardoned, a protest from the Secretary of War, who says that commanding officers are very much averse from accepting the services of these gaol-birds, and have often solicited him not to send them out to their regiments. The practice was the more objectionable as at that time the term of service for free volunteers was for life, while the exconvicts only joined the colours for a limited period. The point was not pressed therefore in its entirety, but the concession made, that these convicts should be enlarged for special service on the west coast of Africa. It was argued that "considering the unhealthiness of the climate, His Majesty is desirous that the troops stationed there should be recruited rather with such men as must look upon that duty as a mitigation of their sentences than with deserving volunteers." But to this again objections were raised by the agent to the troops at Senegal, who pointed out the extreme danger to life and property of sending "nineteen sturdy cut-throats armed and accoutred" to reside within the walls of a feeble place, having a total garrison of sixty men, adding that, "should this embarkation of thieves take place he would be glad to insure his property at seventy-five per cent."

THE NEW GAOL

Corporation anxious to check gaol fever— Appoints committee to report as to building a new prison—York Castle proposed for imitation—Plans obtained, and given to city architect, Mr. Dance—Nothing is done, and in 1757 neighbours petition Corporation that they are afraid of infection from Newgate—A new committee appointed, which furnishes designs, but Government will not give grant in aid, and project again falls through—Revived again and again to no effect—In 1762 Press-yard destroyed by fire—Two prisoners burnt to death—It is at last decided to rebuild—7 Geo. III. empowers Corporation to raise funds—Specification of expenditure—£50,000 total amount proposed—Found insufficient, and an additional £40,000 authorized—Lord Mayor Beckford lays first stone in 1770—The new gaol is gutted in the Lord George Gordon riots—Origin of these riots—Lord George presents, at head of procession, petition to House of Commons—Riotous demonstrations—Mob attracted to Newgate—The gaoler, Mr. Akerman, summoned to surrender, and release his prisoners—He refuses, and seeks help from Sheriff's—Rioters storm Newgate—Sack Governor's house—His *furniture is burnt against the gates, which finally give way—Rioters, headed by Dennis the hangman, rush in and set inmates free— Extraordinary effects of the fire—Other gaols attacked and burnt— The military called out, and much blood shed before calm is restored —Many released prisoners return to Newgate of their own accord— Some try to rekindle the fire—Lord George arrested, lodged in the Tower, and tried for high treason, but acquitted—Six years later, he takes up the case of some Newgate prisoners in a pamphlet, called libellous, for which he is prosecuted—Arrested in Jewish garb in Birmingham—He undertakes his own defence—He protests against the criminal law, and declares himself the victim of persecution—Prosecuted for second libel against Queen of France and the French Ambassador—Lord George is found guilty on both counts—Sentenced to fines and imprisonment in Newgate—Dies in Newgate of gaol fever, 1793—Recovery of Newgate keys, stolen during riots—Cost of repairing gaol after the fire.*

I HAVE described in the preceding chapter how the gaol fever spread from Newgate to the Old Bailey in 1750, and the havoc it occasioned. An account has also been given of the steps taken by the Corporation to minimize the chances of a fresh outbreak. The erection of a ventilator and windmill might do something towards rendering Newgate less foul, but much more was needed to make it a suitable receptacle for the numbers it was often called upon to hold. The total acreage covered by its ill-contrived, ruinous buildings was under three quarters of an acre, and upon this space as many as three hundred persons were sometimes crowded together;[192] while a part of this limited area was otherwise occupied by the Old Bailey Sessions' House, gardens, and yards. The existing prison was obviously inadequate. One of the sheriffs in the year of the great mortality stigmatizes it as an abominable sink of beastliness and corruption. The Lord Mayor, judges, and the whole of the Court of Aldermen were so thoroughly persuaded, we are told, that notwithstanding all precautions, no effectual remedy could be applied to check the gaol infection but that of reconstruction, that a committee of the Common Council was appointed to consider the best method of building a new prison. It was for this reason, says a letter from one of the sheriffs who had been in office in 1750, that the old ruinous buildings between the Old Bailey Sessions' House and Newgate belonging to the city were allowed to fall in, and that a plan for a new gaol became the general topic, as well as the general desire. Many people sought to have a finger in the pie. The committee to which the subject had been referred was lectured and advised in numerous letters, some authenticated, and many anonymous. It was suggested that they should imitate the example of the county of York, which had not long before rebuilt the gaol on an excellent plan, with sufficient internal area, water in great plenty, and all other conveniences, so that the inmates, averaging from a hundred to a hundred and twenty at most, are almost certain of being preserved in a healthy state at all times. Application was actually made to the Yorkshire county authorities, who forwarded four plans of their prison—"the noble prison in a spacious area," of which Howard speaks in 1772. These plans came into the hands of Mr. Dance, the city surveyor, who seems to have been guided by them in the design he furnished the Newgate committee in 1755 for a new prison.

This committee was not ambitious, and was satisfied with endeavouring to improve and extend rather than reconstruct. "The business of enlarging the gaol engaged its attention," we are told. It was to be effected according to their idea by making an "airy" or walking place for prisoners. For this purpose all the houses between Newgate and the Sessions' House Gate were to be taken down, and an enclosure made on the space, surrounded by a strong wall. This recommendation when brought forward by the committee scarcely went far enough for the Common Council, who were at first strongly of opinion that it would be more proper to rebuild the gaol. But although they were convinced of the propriety, they speedily let the matter drop, and nothing was done as regards Newgate for another couple of years.

In 1757, however, the residents in the immediate neighbourhood of Newgate raised their protest against the gaol, and petitioned the Corporation, "setting forth their apprehensions from their vicinity to Newgate, and from the stenches proceeding therefrom, of being subject to an infectious disease called the gaol distemper." Upon receipt of this petition, the Common Council appointed a fresh committee, and the various allegations were gone into seriatim. They next surveyed the gaol itself and the surrounding premises, examined the site with a view to rebuilding, and had plans prepared with estimates and specifications as to cost of ground and construction. The projected design embraced a series of quadrangles, one for the debtors and another for the felons, with an area to each. The probable expense for a work which the committee were of opinion was greatly needed would amount to about £40,000, for which sum "they did resolve to petition Parliament for a grant." This petition was, however, never presented. Mr. Alderman Dickens, having spoken privately to the Chancellor of the Exchequer on the subject, was informed that no public money would be forthcoming, and the project again fell through.

It did not entirely drop notwithstanding. To the credit of the Corporation it must be stated, that many attempts were made to grapple with the difficulties of ways and means. Application was made to Parliament more than once for powers to raise money for the work by some proportionable tax on the city and county, but always without avail. Parties differed as to the manner in which funds should be obtained, yet all were agreed upon the "immediate necessity for converting this seat of misery and disease, this dangerous source of contagion, into a secure and wholesome place of confinement." The matter became more urgent, the occasion more opportune, when that part of the prison styled the press-yard was destroyed by fire in 1762.

Some account of this fire may be inserted here. It broke out in the middle of the night at the back of the staircase in the press-yard, and in a few hours consumed all the apartments in that place, and greatly damaged the chapel. Other adjoining premises, particularly that of a stocking-trimmer in Phœnix Court, were greatly injured by the fire. Worst of all, two prisoners perished in the flames. One was Captain Ogle, who had been tried for murdering the cook of the Vine Tavern, near Dover St., Piccadilly, but had been found insane on arraignment, and had accordingly been detained in prison "during His Majesty's pleasure." There was no Broadmoor asylum in those days for criminal lunatics, and Newgate was a poor substitute for the palatial establishment now standing among the Berkshire pine woods. The fire was supposed to have originated in Captain Ogle's room. Beneath it was one occupied by Thomas Smith, a horse-dealer, committed to prison on suspicion of stealing corn from Alderman Masters. Smith's wife the night before the conflagration had carried him the whole of his effects, amounting to some five or six hundred pounds in notes and bank bills. When the fire was raging Smith was heard to cry out for help. He was seen also to put his arm through the iron grating, which, however, was so excessively hot that it set his shirt on fire. About this time it is supposed that he threw out his pocket-book containing the notes; it was caught and the valuables saved. A few minutes later the floor fell in, and both Captain Ogle and Smith were buried in the ruins. The fire had burnt so fiercely and so fast that no one could go to the assistance of either of these unfortunates. By six a.m., there being an abundance of water handy, the flames had greatly abated, but the fire continued to burn till two in the afternoon, and ended by the fall of a party wall, which happily did no great damage. About four a.m. the Lord Mayor and sheriffs arrived upon the scene, and took an active part in the steps taken to check the fire and provide for the safety of the prisoners.

This was no doubt the fire at which Mr. Akerman behaved with such intrepidity, and which has already been described. [193]

After the fire it was admitted that the proper time was arrived for "putting in execution the plan of rebuilding this inconvenient goal, which was thought of some time ago." Once more a committee of the Common Council was appointed, and once more the question of site was considered, with the result that the locality of the existing prison was decided upon as the most suitable and convenient. Upon the receipt of this report, 1763, it was resolved to petition Parliament again for assistance, and this time the petition was actually presented. But the zeal of the Corporation for prison reform must have waxed cold, for I find it recorded in 1765 (5th March) that the project for rebuilding Newgate was laid aside. But the House of Commons, however, had not ignored the city's petition. They had referred the whole subject to a committee, which took the evidence of all persons closely concerned. It was clearly proved that a new gaol was indispensable. Mr. Dance, the city surveyor, was quite against extension or reappropriation by adding on the Sessions' House, and there was nothing to be done but to build a new prison. An Act was accordingly passed in 1766 (the 7 Geo. III.), authorizing the Corporation to raise for various works a certain sum at 3½ per cent. per annum, to be paid off by a tax at the rate of 6*d*. per ton on coal or culm imported into the city, of which £50,000 were to be applied to the purpose of erecting the new Newgate.

The following is a short summary of the various items of

proposed expenditure, extracted from a pamphlet published by the Corporation under date 1767.

Leasehold interests to be purchased in the Old Bailey from the Mason's Yard to Newgate, and some houses opposite thereto

£6000 N.B.—The old materials will pay for taking down and clearing away the rubbish to the surface of the streets.

The new prison, to answer the present Sessions' House and to contain distinct wards for the men and women debtors, the men and women felons, transports, and convicts, a chapel, a keeper's house, tap-houses, sutlery, yards, area, ponds of water, will require 160 square yards of new building, which, on account of the requisite strength per square, will cost £250 per square

£40,000 Salaries and gratuities to the surveyor, the committee clerk, the chamberlain's clerks, &c.

2,750 Incidental Expenses

1,250

£50,000

The sum of £50,000 already referred to, and raised under the powers granted by the 7 Geo. III., was not found sufficient to complete the gaol, after the manner of building estimates, which too often mislead all those who are beguiled into expenditure upon bricks and mortar. The foundations cost £19,000. It was necessary to sink them a depth of forty feet, as the site was that of the ditch of the old London Wall, besides which the neighbouring houses had to be shored. Ten years later, when the building was still incomplete, another Act of Parliament became necessary to increase the funds at the disposal of the Corporation. This Act, the 18 Geo. III. cap. 48, authorized the city to raise £40,000 for Newgate buildings upon the credit of the surpluses of a fund known as the Orphans' Fund. It set forth that the Corporation had "proceeded in the erection of a new, spacious, and commodious gaol, and for that purpose have given up to the public the freehold of a very large and extensive tract of ground;" moreover, that they had already laid out £50,000 on this new gaol, as well as £15,000 on a new Sessions' House, and £6,250 to buy several houses in the Old Bailey, "in order to make the new gaol more healthy and the avenues thereto more convenient." The Act then goes on to say, that as the new prison still lacks an infirmary, which if built would "greatly contribute to the health of the prisoners, and thereby be of great public utility," that the Corporation are in possession of a piece of ground quite handy and suitable for the purpose, and that as a sum of £20,000 would build it, while another £20,000 would complete the gaol, the Corporation are empowered to raise the money in the manner already mentioned, by the issue of bonds at 4½ per cent. interest.

The first stone of the new gaol was laid on the 31st May, 1770, by the Lord Mayor, William Beckford, Esquire, the founder of that family.

Within a year or two of its completion, the new Newgate had to pass through an ordeal which nearly threatened its existence. Its boasted strength as a place of durance was boldly set at naught, and almost for the first and last time in this country this gaol, with others in the metropolis, was sacked and its imprisoned inmates set free. The occasion grew out of the so-called Lord George Gordon Riots in 1780. These well-known disturbances had their origin in the relaxation of the penal laws against the Roman Catholics. Such concessions raised fanatical passion to fever pitch. Ignorance and intolerance went hand in hand, and the malcontents, belonging mainly to the lowest strata of society, found a champion in a weak-minded and misguided cadet of the ducal house of Gordon. Lord George Gordon,[194] who was a member of the House of Commons, showed signs of eccentricity soon after he took his seat, but it was at first more ridiculous than mischievous. Lord George became more dangerously meddlesome when the anti-Catholic agitation began. It was to him that the Protestant association looked for countenance and support, and when Lord North at his instance refused to present a petition from that society to Parliament, Lord George Gordon promised to do so in person, provided it was backed by a multitude not less than 20,000 strong.

This led to the great gathering in St. George's Fields on the 2nd June, 1780, when thousands organized themselves into three columns, and proceeded to the House of Commons across the three bridges, Westminster, Blackfriars, and London Bridge. Lord George headed the Westminster procession, and all three concentrated at St. Stephens between two and three in the afternoon. There the mob filled every avenue and approach; crowds overflowed the lobbies, and would have pushed into the body of the House. Lord George went ahead with the monster petition, which bore some 120,000 signatures or "marks," and which the Commons by a negative vote of 192 to 6 refused to receive. After this the rioters, at the instigation of their leader, hastened *en masse* to destroy the chapels of the foreign ambassadors. This was followed by other outrages. While some of their number attacked and rifled the dwellings of persons especially obnoxious to them, others set fire to public buildings, and ransacked the taverns. The military had been called out early in the day, and had made many arrests. As the prisoners were taken to Newgate, the fury of the populace was attracted to this gaol, and a large force, computed at quite two-thirds of the rioters, proceeded thither, determined to force open its gates. This mob was composed of the lowest scum of the town, roughs brutal and utterly reckless, having a natural loathing for prisons, their keepers, and all the machinery of the law. Many already knew, and but too well, the inside of Newgate, many dreaded to return there, either as lodgers or travellers bound on the fatal road to Tyburn. One wild fierce desire was uppermost with all, one thought possessed their minds to the exclusion of all others—to destroy the hateful prison-house and raze it to the ground.

On arriving at the Old Bailey in front of the stone façade, as grim and solid as that of any fortress, the mob halted and demanded the gaoler, Mr. Akerman, who appeared at a window, some say on the roof, of his house, which forms the centre of the line of buildings facing Newgate street. When he appeared the mob called on him to release their confederates and surrender the place unconditionally. Mr. Akerman distinctly and without hesitation refused, and then, dreading what was coming, he made the best of his way to the sheriffs, "in order to know their pleasure." As the front of the prison was beset by the densely-packed riotous assemblage, Mr. Akerman probably made use of the side wicket and passage which leads direct from Newgate into the Sessions' House. The magistrates seemed to have been in doubt how to act; and for some time did nothing. "Their timidity and negligence," says Boswell, helped the almost incredible exertions of the mob. And he is of opinion, that had proper aid been given to Mr. Akerman, the sacking of Newgate would certainly have been prevented. While the magistrates hesitated the mob were furiously active; excited to frenzy, they tried to beat down the gate with sledge-hammers, and vainly sought to make some impression on the massive walls. A portion of the assailants forced their way into the governor's house, and laying hands upon his furniture, with all other combustibles, dragged them out and made a great pile in front of the obdurate door, which still resisted force. The heap of wood, having been anointed with rosin and turpentine, was kindled, and soon fanned into a mighty blaze. The door, heavily barred and bolted, and strongly bound with iron, did not ignite quite readily, but presently it took fire and burnt steadily, though slowly. Meanwhile the rioters fed the flames with fresh fuel, and snatching burning brands from the fire, cast them on to the roof and over the external wall into the wards and yards within. The prisoners inside, who had heard without fully understanding the din, and saw the flames without knowing whether they promised deliverance or foreboded a dreadful death, suffered the keenest mental torture, and added their agonized shouts to the general uproar.

Charles Dickens has drawn an awful picture of the scene, based upon contemporary and authentic accounts. He has described in glowing language the yielding of the door.

"A shout! Another! another yet, though few knew why, or what it meant. But those around the gate had seen it slowly yield and drop from its topmost hinge. It hung on that side by but one, but it was upright still because of the bar, and of its having sunk of its own weight into the heap of ashes at its foot. There was now a gap at the top of the doorway, through which could be descried a gloomy passage, cavernous and dark. Pile up the fire!

"It burnt fiercely. The door was red hot and the gap wider. They vainly tried to shield their faces with their hands, and standing as if in readiness for a spring, watched the place. Dark figures, some crawling on their hands and knees, some carried in the arms of others, were seen to pass along the roof. It was plain the gaol could hold out no longer. The keeper and his officers and their wives and children were escaping. Pile up the fire!

"The door sank down again; it settled deeper in the cinders —tottered—yielded—was down!"

Dickens gives a prominent place among the rioters to John Dennis the hangman, who himself was, as the records state, sentenced to be hanged for his complicity in these dark doings. Dennis was likely to be familiar with the interior of the gaol. There were no doubt many others who had threaded its gloomy passages before. With such experienced guides the way must have been easy to find. The outer barriers down, the mob surged like a tidal wave into and through the whole gaol. I will again draw from fiction, which is the more powerful in this case that it is founded upon fact, and will quote from 'Barnaby Rudge.'

"Now they came rushing through the gaol, calling to each other in the vaulted passages; clashing the iron gates dividing yard from yard; beating at the doors of cells and wards; wrenching off bolts and locks and bars; tearing down the doorposts to let men out; endeavouring to drag them by main force through gaps and windows where a child could scarcely pass; whooping and yelling without a moment's rest, and running through the heat and flames as if they were cased in metal. By their legs, their arms, the hair upon their heads, they dragged the prisoners out. Some threw themselves upon their captives as they got towards the door, and tried to file away their irons; some danced about them with a frenzied joy, and rent their clothes, and were ready as it seemed to tear them limb from limb. Now a party of a dozen men came dashing through the yard, ... dragging a prisoner along the ground, whose dress they had nearly torn from his body in their mad eagerness to set him free, and who was bleeding and senseless in their hands. Now a score of prisoners ran to and fro who had lost themselves in the intricacies of the prison, and were so bewildered with the noise and the glare that they knew not where to turn or what to do, and still cried out for help as loudly as before. Anon some famished wretch, whose theft had been a loaf of bread or a scrap of butcher's meat, came skulking past barefooted, going slowly away because that gaol, his house, was burning; not because he had another, or had friends to meet, or old haunts to revisit, or any liberty to gain, but liberty to starve and die. And then a knot of highwaymen went trooping by, conducted by the friends they had amongst the crowd, who muffled their fetters as they went along with handkerchiefs and bands of hay, and wrapped them in coats and cloaks, and gave them drink from bottles, and held it to their lips because of their handcuffs, which there was no time to remove. All this, and Heaven knows how much, was done amidst a noise, a hurry and distraction like nothing that we know of even in our dreams; which seemed for ever on the rise, and never to decrease for the space of a single instant."

Through all this tumult and destruction the law was paralyzed. After much delay the sheriff sent a party of constables to the gaolers' assistance. But they came too late, and easily fell into a trap. The rioters suffered them to pass on till they were entirely encircled, then attacked them with great fury, disarmed them, took their staves, and quickly converted them at the fire into blazing brands, which they threw about to extend the flames. "It is scarcely to be credited," says a narrator, "with what celerity a gaol which to a common observer appeared to be built with nothing that would burn, was destroyed by the flames. So efficient were the means employed, that the work of destruction was very rapid. Stones two or three tons in weight, to which the doors of the cells were fastened, were raised by that resistless species of crow known to housebreakers by the name of the pig's foot. Such was the violence of the fire, that the great iron bars and windows were eaten through and the adjacent stones vitrified.[195] Nor is it less astonishing that from a prison thus in flames a miserable crew of felons in irons and a company of confined debtors, to the number in the whole of more than three hundred, could all be liberated as it were by magic, amidst flames and firebrands, without the loss of a single life.... But it is not at all to be wondered that by a body of execrable villains thus let loose upon the public, the house of that worthy and active magistrate Sir John Fielding should be the first marked for vengeance." In the same way, even before the destruction of Newgate, the house of Justice Hyde, whose activity the rioters resented, had also been stripped of its furniture, which was burnt in front of the door.

Crabbe's account written at the time to a friend is graphic, and contains several new details—"How Akerman, the governor, escaped," he says, "or where he is gone, I know not; but just at the time I speak of they set fire to his house, broke in, and threw every piece of furniture they could find into the street, firing them also in an instant. The engines came, but they were only suffered to preserve the private houses near the prison. As I was standing near the spot, there approached another body of men —I suppose five hundred—and Lord George Gordon, in a coach drawn by the mob, towards Alderman Bull's, bowing as he passed along. He is a lively-looking young man in appearance and nothing more, though just now the popular hero. By eight o'clock Akerman's house was in flames. I went close to it, and never saw anything so dreadful. The prison was, as I have said, a remarkably strong building; but, determined to force it, they broke the gates with crows and other instruments, and climbed up outside of the cell part, which joins the two great wings of the building where the felons were confined; and I stood where I plainly saw their operations; they broke the roof, tore away the rafters, and having got ladders, they descended. Not Orpheus himself had more courage or better luck. Flames all around them, and a body of soldiers expected, yet they laughed at all opposition. The prisoners escaped. I stood and saw about twelve women and eight men ascend from their confinement to the open air, and they were conducted through the streets in their chains. Three of these were to be hanged on Friday (two days later).

"You have no conception of the frenzy of the multitude. This now being done, and Akerman's house now a mere shell of brick-work, they kept a store of flame for other purposes. It became red-hot, and the doors and windows appeared like the entrance to so many volcanoes. With some difficulty they then fired the debtors' prison, broke the doors, and they too all made their escape. Tired of the scene, I went home, and returned again at eleven o'clock at night. I met large bodies of horse and foot soldiers coming to guard the Bank and some houses of Roman Catholics near it. Newgate was at this time open to all; any one might get in, and what was never the case before, any one might get out. I did both, for the people were now chiefly lookers-on. The mischief was done, and the doers of it gone to another part of the town.... But I must not omit what struck me most: about ten or twelve of the mob getting to the top of the debtors' prison whilst it was burning, to halloo, they appeared rolled in black smoke mixed with sudden bursts of fire—like Milton's infernals, who were as familiar with flames as with each other."

It should be added here that the excesses of the rioters did not end with the burning of Newgate; they did other mischief. Five other prisons, the new prison, Clerkenwell, the Fleet, the King's Bench, the Borough Clink in Tooley Street, and the new Bridewell, were attacked, their inmates released, and the buildings set on fire. At one time the town was convulsed with terror at a report that the rioters intended to open the gates of Bedlam, and let loose gangs of raving lunatics to range recklessly about. They made an attempt upon the Bank of England, but were repulsed with loss by John Wilkes and the soldiers on guard. At one time during the night as many as thirty-six incendiary fires were ablaze. The troops had been called upon to support the civil power, and had acted with vigour. There was fighting in nearly all the streets, constant firing. At times the soldiers charged with the bayonet. The streets ran with blood. In all, before tranquillity was restored, nearly five hundred persons had been killed and wounded, and to this long bill of mortality must be added the fifty-nine capitally convicted under the special commission appointed to try the rioters.

It was in many cases cruel kindness to set the prisoners free. Numbers of the debtors of the King's Bench were loth to leave their place of confinement, for they had no friends and nowhere else to go. Of the three hundred released so unexpectedly from Newgate, some returned on their own accord a few days later and gave themselves up. It is said that many others were drawn back by an irresistible attraction, and were actually found loitering about the open wards of the prison. Fifty were thus retaken within the walls the day after the fire, and others kept dropping by twos and threes to examine their old haunts and see for themselves what was going on. Some, Dickens says, were found trying to rekindle the fire; some merely prowled about the place, "being often found asleep in the ruins, or sitting talking there, or even eating and drinking, as in a choice retreat."[196]

The ringleader and prime mover, Lord George Gordon, was arrested on the evening of the 9th, and conveyed to the Tower. His trial did not come on till the following February at the King's Bench, where he was indicted for high treason. He was charged with levying war against the majesty of the king; "not having the fear of God before his eyes, but being moved and seduced by the instigation of the devil; ... that he unlawfully, maliciously, and traitorously did compass, imagine, and intend to raise and levy war, insurrection, and rebellion," and assembled with some five hundred more, "armed and arrayed in a warlike manner, with colours flying, and with swords, clubs, bludgeons, staves, and other weapons," in the liberty of Westminster. It was proved in evidence that Lord George directed the Associated Protestants to meet him at Westminster in their best clothes, and with blue cockades in their hats, and said he should wear one himself. He was also heard to declare that the king had broken his coronation oath, and to exhort the mob to continue steadfast in so good and glorious a cause. For the defence it was urged that Lord George Gordon had desired nothing but to compass by all legal means the repeal of the Act of Toleration; that he had no other view than the Protestant interest, and had always demeaned himself in the most loyal manner. He had hoped that the great gathering would be all peaceable; that the mob "should not so much as take sticks in their hands," should abstain from all violence, surrender at once any one riotously disposed; in a word, should exhibit the true Protestant spirit, and if struck should turn the other cheek. Mr. Erskine, Lord George's counsel, after pointing out that his client had suffered already a long and rigorous imprisonment, his great youth, his illustrious lineage and zeal in parliament for the constitution of his country, urged that the evidence and the whole tenor of the prisoner's conduct repelled the belief of traitorous purpose.

Lord Mansfield, who had been a chief victim to the riots, and whose house had been gutted and burnt,[197] summed up the case fairly and impartially. He laid it down that insurrection, or any forcible attempt to alter laws or gain any end, amounted to levying war against the majesty of the realm. The point was not whether the Toleration Act was a good or a bad one; "whether grievances be real or pretended, whether a law be good or bad, it is equally high treason, by the strong hand of a multitude to force the repeal or redress." It was for the jury to decide, first, whether the multitude did assemble with intent to terrify the legislature into the repeal of the obnoxious act, and secondly, whether the prisoner at the bar incited, encouraged, and promoted the insurrection. If there was any doubt, however, and the jury were not fully satisfied of Lord George Gordon's guilt, they must acquit him. The jury retired for half an hour, and then brought in a verdict of not guilty.

Lord George, unhappily, could not keep out of trouble, although naturally of mild disposition. He was an excitable, rather weak-minded man, easily carried away by his enthusiasm on particular points. Six years later he espoused, with customary warmth and want of judgment, the case of other prisoners in Newgate, and published a pamphlet purporting to be a petition from them presented to himself, praying him to "interfere and secure their liberties by preventing their being sent to Botany Bay." Prisoners labouring under severe sentences cried out from their dungeons for redress. "Some were about to suffer execution without righteousness, others to be sent off to a barbarous country." "The records of justice have been falsified," the pamphlet went on to say, "and the laws profanely altered by men like ourselves. The bloody laws against us have been enforced, under a normal administration, by mere whitened walls, men who possess only the show of justice, and who condemned us to death contrary to law."

That this silly production should be made the subject of a criminal information for libel, rather justifies the belief that an exaggerated importance was given to Lord George's vagaries, both by the Government and his own relations and friends. No doubt he was a thorn in the side of his family, but the ministry could well have afforded to treat him and his utterances with contempt. He was, however, indicted at the King's Bench for publishing the petition, which he had actually himself written, with a view to raise a tumult among the prisoners within Newgate, or cause a disturbance by exciting the compassion of those without. The pamphlet included the law and judges in indiscriminate abuse. "The laws," said the Attorney-General, "might not be absolutely perfect, but those who condemned them should not reside under their jurisdiction. The criminal law was nowhere attended to with more, or enforced with so much lenity."[198] Lord George when "wanted" on these charges was not to be found. At first it was thought he had escaped to Holland, but he was at length arrested in Birmingham, dressed in Jewish garb, and wearing a long beard. Some time before this he had espoused Judaism, even submitting, it was alleged, to circumcision, a change of religious belief for which he was excommunicated at Marylebone church. When put upon his trial he conducted his own defence, and made a long and desultory harangue, which included a history of the English criminal law from the days of Athelstan.

He had been induced, he said, to look into the laws against felony because of a petty fraud in his family, which he had found constituted a capital offence, although the sum stolen was only eighteenpence. He went on to protest against the code as much too sanguinary, an opinion which proves that there was some method in Lord George Gordon's madness, and that he only lived a little before his time as regards the reform of our criminal law. His pamphlet, every word of which he contended was actually to be found in the Bible, he urged was but the enlargement of this idea, which he had already communicated to Lord Mansfield and other judges, who admitted the propriety of his views, and recommended him to put them on paper. In the course of his address, Lord George complained bitterly of the vexatious prosecutions instituted against him, thus giving colour to the presumption that he was the victim of persecution. He quoted Blackstone to show that *ex officio* informations, such as those filed against him, "are only proper for such enormous misdemeanours as peculiarly tend to disturb or endanger the king's government, and in the punishment or execution of which a moment's delay would be fatal." Yet in his case the informations against him had been pending six and ten months. He complained also that spies had been set over him by the Treasury for several months, and concluded by solemnly declaring that his object had been reformation, not tumult.

The case against him was very clearly made out. It was proved by a Newgate turnkey that Lord George frequently came to the lodge of the prison and asked to see various prisoners, particularly those under sentence of death, "which request was often denied;" presumably, therefore, he was sometimes admitted. When he had published his pamphlet he had been at great pains to distribute it, especially among the prisoners and prison officials. A man and woman were employed in handing them about at the door of the prison. Copies were also sent to Mr. Akerman, the governor, Mr. Villette, the chaplain, and the turnkeys. One of the latter waited on him at his house in Welbeck Street, and said there was sad work about the distribution of the pamphlet. Lord George replied, "No matter; let them come on as soon as they please; I am ready for them." There were numbers of the pamphlet about, one of which, at Lord George's request, the turnkey took to Mr. Akerman. Upon all this, and notwithstanding his lordship's defence, the jury without hesitation returned a verdict of guilty against him for having written and published the libel as alleged.

Before sentence the court passed on to the consideration of a second libel, published by Lord George Gordon in the 'Public Advertizer.' This was an account of his visit to the French embassy accompanied by the notorious Count Cagliostro, whose cause, like that of the Newgate prisoners, Lord George had warmly espoused. The article enlarged upon the merits and sufferings of the count, and reflected severely upon Marie Antoinette, at that time Queen of France, the French ambassador, and the secretary of the embassy. The defence of the diplomatic body, no less than of that of a royal personage, was undertaken by the Government. Lord George attempted to justify all that he had written. Count Cagliostro, he averred, had been persecuted by a faction in Paris, of which the queen was the head; and although acquitted by the Parliament of Paris, Count d'Adhemar, the French ambassador, had continued to vilify him by inserting infamous paragraphs about him in the 'Courrier de l'Europe,' a French paper published in London. "Count d'Adhemar," said Lord George, "was a low man of no family; but being plausible and clever, had pushed himself forward to the notice of men in authority; in short, what Jenkinson was in Britain, d'Adhemar was in France." This allusion to Lord Hawkesbury[199] caused a great laugh in the court. Lord George went on to indulge in very scurrilous abuse of Marie Antoinette. He said he was charged with libelling the Queen of France, whereas that was impossible, as her character was well known in every street in Paris. He could only compare her to Catherine of Russia. "He was proceeding in this strain," says the report of the trial, "when the court was compelled to interfere, and the Attorney-General told him he was a disgrace to the name of Briton."

Although Lord George contended that what he had published was no libel, as it contained nothing but truth of Count Cagliostro, who had as much right as Count d'Adhemar, or any other foreigner, to the protection of the laws, the jury promptly returned a verdict of guilty on this count. The court then passed sentence, and addressed his lordship in scathing terms. The judge told him that his "petition" was calculated to excite insurrection, discontent, and sedition, and that he might make a better use of Bible phraseology than employ it for the wicked purpose of undermining the laws of his country. "One is sorry," remarked Mr. Justice Ashurst, "that you, descended of an illustrious line of ancestors, should have so much dishonoured your family ... that you should prefer the mean ambition of being popular among thieves and pickpockets, and to stand as the champion of mischief, anarchy, and confusion." As to the second libel, the judge charged the prisoner with endeavouring to rekindle animosities between the two nations, France and England, now once more at peace, by personal abuse of the sovereign of one of them. He (Lord George) had insulted her most Christian Majesty, and it was highly necessary to repress an offence of so dangerous a nature. As his crime consisted of two parts, Lord George Gordon must be subjected to two different sentences. For the first, the publication of the "prisoners' petition," the judge awarded him three years' imprisonment in Newgate. For the second offence, being "trespasses, contempts, and misdemeanours against the royal consort of his most Christian Majesty," the sentence was a fine of £500, with a farther imprisonment in Newgate at the termination of the other three; and in addition he was required to give security for fourteen years for his good behaviour, himself in £10,000, and two sureties of £2500 each.

Lord George Gordon remained in Newgate till his death, from gaol-fever, in 1793. He made two or three ineffectual attempts to put in his bail, but they were objected to as insufficient. It was thought to the last that the government and his friends sought pretences to keep him in confinement and out of mischief. His somewhat premature death must have been a relief to them. But it can hardly be denied that hard measure was meted out to him, and if he escaped too easily at his first trial, he was too heavily punished at the second. It is impossible to absolve him from responsibility for the outrages committed by the rioters in 1780, although he was doubtless shocked at their excesses. Lord George could not have foreseen the terrible consequences which would follow his rash agitation, and little knew how dangerous were the elements of disturbance he unchained. But it can hardly be denied that he meant well. Had he lived a century later, he would probably have found a more legitimate outlet for his peculiar tendencies, and would have figured as an ardent philanthropist and platform orator, instead of as a criminal in the dock.

Two more facts must be mentioned concerning these riots and the successful attacks on Newgate. The first is with regard to the prison keys. I find it recorded in Southey's Commonplace Book (Book iv. p. 371), that on draining the basin in St. James's Square for the purpose of erecting a statue of King William IV. there, the keys of Newgate were found at the bottom. These keys had been stolen at the fire in 1780, and thrown in here. A quantity of iron chains and fetters were recovered at the same time. The second fact is the probable extent of the damage done, as shown by the amount required for repairs. This must have been about £20,000. I see by the report of a Committee of the House of Commons, dated May 16, 1782, that a sum of £10,000 had been voted to meet the repairs of Newgate, and again in February 1783, at a Court of Common Council, a motion was made to petition Parliament for the grant of a further sum of £10,000 to complete these repairs.

END OF VOL. I.

FOOTNOTES TO VOLUME 1

[1] This chapter originally appeared in the 'Fortnightly Review,' June 1882.

[2] See post, chap. iv.

[3] See vol. ii. cap. ii.

[4] See vol. ii. cap. iii.

[5] See vol. ii. cap. v.

[6] Something of the same ambition filled the breasts of the projectors of Seville Cathedral.

[7] An entry in a letter book at Guildhall speaks of the "heynouse gaol of Newgate," and its fetid and corrupt atmosphere. Loftie, 'Hist. of London,' vol. i. 437.

[8] Noorthouck, 'Hist. of London,' p. 60.

[9] The term "roarer," and "roaring boy," signifying a riotous person, was in use in Shakespeare's day, and still survives in slang (Riley).

[10] The word is so given in the text, although this text is in Latin, fol. cxxxii. 6 (Riley).

[11] The indictment charged John Brid for having sought to

falsely and maliciously obtain his own private advantage "by skilfully and artfully causing a certain hole to be made upon a table of his, called a *moldingborde*, pertaining to his bakehouse after the manner of a mouse-trap in which mice are caught, there being a certain wicket, warily provided for closing and opening such a hole." When neighbours brought dough to make into bread and bake at his oven, John Brid got them to put it on his *moldingborde* table, having "one of his household ready provided for the same sitting in secret beneath such table; which servant of his, so seated beneath the hole, and carefully opening it, piecemeal and bit by bit craftily withdrew some of the dough aforesaid, frequently collecting great quantities from such dough, falsely, wickedly, and maliciously." It was proved that the hole was made of aforethought, that large quantities of dough were drawn through the table and found beneath, and that the neighbours suffered grievous loss. Numerous other cases of similar fraud were brought forward at the same time, and all were equally proved, after "due inquisition as to the truth of the matter had been made." Whereupon at a full court of aldermen, and in the presidency of Richard de Botoigne, Mayor, it was ordered that all male offenders against whom the charge was proved should be out upon the pillory with a certain quantity of the dough round their necks, in the cases where dough had been found; where it had not, the sentence was one of simple exposure. Two female bakers sought to escape by laying the crime upon their husbands, but "it was agreed and ordained that they should be sent back to the prison of Newgate, there to remain until as to them it should be otherwise ordained," and there, according to the same document, they should linger *sine die*. To wipe out the disgrace, it was further ordered that all the *moldingborde* tables "should be thrown down and utterly destroyed," and that any baker in future guilty of such an offence "should stand upon the pillory for a whole day, and afterwards abjure the city, so as at no time to return thereto."

[12] A prison for night-walkers and other suspicious persons, and called the Tun because the same was built somewhat in fashion of a Tun standing on the one end. It was built in 1282 by Henry Walers, Mayor.

[13] "Our ancestors, with a strong love for practical jokes and an equally strong aversion to falsehood and boasting, checked an indulgence in such vices when they became offensive by very plain satire. A confirmed liar was presented with a *whetstone* to jocularly infer that his invention, if he continued to use it so freely, would require sharpening."—Chambers' 'Book of Days,' ii. 45.

[14] Pressing to death. See post, chap. vi.

[15] Skinner or furrier.

[16] Noorthouck calls him John Gate. See 'Hist. of London,' p. 49.

[17] Sir Edward Coke derives the title of the court from the fact that justice was done in them as speedily as dust can fall from the foot.

[18] A toll had been levied thirty years earlier (1373) for the cleansing of Smithfield, which may be referred to here. It is interesting as showing the status at this period of the keeper of Newgate. He, Adam Fernham by name, was one of those selected to levy the toll, and with two others was sworn faithfully to collect and receive the pennies, and cleanse the field, for a term of three years. Fernham must have been a man of credit and good repute to have been thus chosen.

[19] For full account see Riley's 'Liber Albus,' p. 41.

[20] Sheriff Hoare (1740-1) tells us how the names of the prisoners in each gaol were read over to him and his colleagues; the keepers acknowledged them one by one to be in their custody, and then tendered the keys, which were delivered back to them

again, and after executing the indentures, the sheriffs partook of sack and walnuts, provided by the keepers of the prison, at a tavern adjoining Guildhall. Formerly the sheriffs attended the Lord Mayor on Easter Eve through the streets to collect charity for the prisoners in the city prison. Sheriffs were permitted to keep prisoners in their own houses, hence the Sponging Houses. The "Sheriffs' Fund" was started in 1807 by Sir Richard Phillips, who, in his letter to the Livery of London, states that he found, on visiting Newgate, so many claims on his charity that he could not meet a tenth part of them. A suggestion to establish a sheriffs' fund was thereupon made public and found general support. In 1867 the fund amounted to £13,000.

[21] 'Liber Albus,' Riley, p. 108.

[22] 'Harleian Miscell.,' vol. vi.

[23] The exemption of St. Martin's from both ecclesiastical and civil jurisdiction until the time of James I., and by affording easy sanctuary to malefactors of the city, was a great nuisance. Loftie, i. 118.

[24] Or "Porti-foug," a breviary which could be carried about.

[25] Riley's 'Memorials of London,' p. 466.

[26] State Papers.

[27] See chap. iv.

[28] This abjuring the king's land was an act of self-banishment, akin in its effects to the old Roman penalty of *aquæ et ignis interdictio*. Any criminal who took sanctuary might escape the law, provided that within forty days he clothed himself in sackcloth, confessed his crime before the coroner, and after solemnly abjuring the land, proceeded, cross in hand, to some appointed port, where he embarked and left the country. If apprehended within forty days he was again suffered to depart.—Note in Thom's 'Stow,' p. 157.

[29] It was based on a passage in the commentaries of Jerome Cardan. Cardan, in a calculation of the horoscope of Edward VI.,

amidst much astrological rubbish relates, on hearsay, his authority being the Bishop of Lisieux, that seventy-two thousand criminals had perished by the executioner in the reign of Henry VIII.—Froude, iii. 227.

[30] Froude.

[31] Stowe's 'Survey,' p. 72.

[32] Fabian's 'Chronicle.'

[33] 'Maitland,' i. 226.

[34] Cromwell's house was in the city in Throgmorton Street, close to the site of the monastic house of the Austin Friars.

[35] This Benedict Spinola must have been an Italian with some influence. His personal relations with Burghley are manifest from a letter of congratulation sent by him to Burghley on the safe arrival of the Earl of Oxford at Milan. Other more or less confidential matters are mentioned in connection with Pasqual and Jacob Spinola, Benedict's brothers.

[36] Vol. iv. pp. 6, 7.

[37] Of these ten friars of the Charterhouse sent to Newgate, Froude says "nine died of prison fever and filth, the tenth survivor was executed." Secretary Bedyll, writing to Cromwell concerning them, says, "It shall please your lordship to understand that the monks of the Charterhouse here in London, which were committed to Newgate for their traitorous behaviour long time continued against the king's Grace, be almost despatched by the hand of God, as may appear, to you by the bill enclosed."

[38] 'Foxe,' v. 180.

[39] 'Foxe,' v. 451.

[40] 'Foxe,' vi. 612.

[41] 'Foxe,' vii. 684.

[42] 'Harleian Miscell.'

[43] Friday continued the day of horse-market until the closing of Smithfield as a market for live cattle.

[44] The bell which was rung at mass on the elevation of the host.

[45] Clink prison.

[46] State Papers.

[47] Stowe, who adds: "note that gaolers buying their offices will deal hardly with pitiful prisoners."

[48] Before Dios? See p. 90.

[49] The priests were subject to espionage even beyond the limits of the realm. A deposition is given in the State Papers made by one Arthur Saul, a prisoner in Newgate, to the effect that he had been employed by Secretary Winwood and the Archbishop of Canterbury to report what English were at Douay College, particulars of priests who have returned to England, of their meeting-places and conveyance of letters. "One of them," it is added, "helped four recusants to escape from Newgate."

[50] Chief of the Jesuits in England, afterwards executed (1608).

[51] "On the Queen's day ten were taken at mass in Newgate."—State Papers, 1602.

[52] This is beyond explanation.

[53] Without paying gaoler's fees.

[54] There was a keeper and a deputy: the latter was resident, and did most of the work.

[55] Calendar, "The prisoners of Newgate's condemnation," declaring every verdict of the whole Bench at the Sessions House in the Old Bailey. April 22, 1642.

[56] The Jack Ketch of the period.

[57] See *ante*, p. 113.

[58] A homily against play-acting and masquerades.

[59] Printed by F. Coles and G. Lindsey, 1642.

[60] The rebellion in Ireland.

[61] As Colonel Gerard had been rescued by Mr. Anthuser, and next day the Portuguese, to the number of fifty, fell upon a

Colonel Mayo, mistaking him for Anthuser, wounded him dangerously, and killed another person, Mr. Greenaway. The murderers were arrested in spite of the protection afforded them by the Portuguese ambassador and committed to Newgate. Whitelocke's 'Memorials,' p. 569.

[62] Their first victim, Colonel Gerard, survived only to be executed on Tower Hill the same year for conspiring to murder the Lord Protector. 'State Trials,' v. 518.

[63] See *ante*, chap. i. p. 58.

[64] The disgusting brutality with which this operation was carried out will be realized from the following extract from the life of J. Ellwood, who found himself in Newgate in the beginning of Charles II.'s reign:—

"When we first came into Newgate," says Mr. Ellwood, "there lay (in a little by-place like a closet, near the room where we were lodged) the quartered bodies of three men, who had been executed some days before, for a real or pretended plot; ... and the reason why their quarters lay there so long, was, the relatives were all that while petitioning to have leave to bury them; which, at length, with much ado, was obtained for the quarters, but not for the heads, which were ordered to be set up in some part of the City. I saw the heads when they were brought up to be boiled; the hangman fetched them in a dirty dust basket, out of some by-place; and setting them down among the felons, he and they made sport with them. They took them by the hair, flouting, jeering, and laughing at them; and then, giving them some ill names, boxed them on the ears and cheeks. Which done, the Hangman put them into his kettle, and parboiled them with Bay-Salt and Cummin-seed,—that to keep them from putrefaction, and this to keep off the fowls from seizing on them. The whole sight (as well that of the bloody quarters first, and this of the heads afterwards) was both frightful and loathsome, and begat an abhorrence in my nature."

[65] "Bilboes" were bars of iron with fetters attached. The name comes from the Spanish town Bilbao, where they were first made.

[66] Cf. chap. 6, vol. ii. Executions.

[67] Who were responsible for the keeper and the prison generally.

[68] Luttrell.

[69] Luttrell.

[70] Luttrell.

[71] Macaulay, i. 380.

[72] Still the seat of the Thynnes; and the property of the head of the family—the present Marquis of Bath.

[73] Reresby's Memoirs, p. 256.

[74] Reresby.

[75] Luttrell.

[76] Reresby's Memoirs.

[77] Reresby.

[78] Luttrell.

[79] Luttrell.

[80] See chap. vi.

[81] 'Celebrated Trials,' ii. 322.

[82] 'Celebrated Trials,' ii. 326.

[83] Dr. Oates in the next reign was to some extent indemnified for his sufferings. When quite an old man he married a young city heiress with a fortune of £2000; and a writer who handled this "Salamanca wedding," as it was called, was arrested. Oates was in the receipt of a pension of £300 from the Government when he died in 1705.

[84] The practice of fining jurors for finding a verdict contrary to the direction of the judge had already been declared arbitrary, unconstitutional, and illegal.

[85] 'History of the Press-yard.'

[86] *Ibid.*

[87] See chap. x.

[88] This cobbler of Highgate was a zealous Jacobite, who turned out in his best suit of clothes on King James's birthday. For this he was prosecuted, and sentenced to be whipped up and down Highgate Hill, with a year's imprisonment in Newgate. He lived on the fat of the land during his incarceration, had quarters in the press-yard, and "lay in lodgings at ten or twelve shilling a week."

[89] This was Bernardi. See post, p. 226.

[90] Bernardi.

[91] Mr. Marvell was either principal hangman or the assistant.

[92] 'History of the Press-yard.'

[93] 'Secret History of the Rebels in Newgate: giving an account of their daily behaviour from their commitment to their gaol delivery.' Taken from the diary of a gentleman in the same prison—who was evidently no particular admirer of theirs.

[94] 'History of the Press-yard.'

[95] It will be remembered that Mr. Forster's want of generalship lost the battle of Prestonpans.

[96] See chap. vii. for this and other escapes.

[97] For this Dalton was convicted and fined fifty marks, with imprisonment for one year, also to find security for three more years.

[98] Parson Paul was the Rev. William Paul, M.A., vicar of Orton-on-the-Hill, in Leicestershire. He met the rebels at Preston, and performed service there, praying for the Pretender as King James the Third. When the royal troops invested Preston, Mr. Paul escaped "in coloured clothes, a long wig, a laced hat, and a sword by his side." He came to London, and was recognized in St. James's Park by a Leicestershire magistrate, who apprehended him, and he was committed to Newgate.

[99] One of the Halls of Otterburn, Northumberland, and a

magistrate for the county. He joined the Pretender early, and was one of his most active and staunch supporters.

[100] No doubt a form of the gaol fever.

[101] 'Secret History.'

[102] See *ante*, p. 203.

[103] According to the deposition of Harris the informer, Bernardi came with Rookwood to London on purpose to meet Barclay the chief conspirator.

[104] Pike, 'Hist, of Crime,' ii. 83.

[105] Camden's 'Annals of the Year 1581.'

[106] Dr. Bastwick's daughter, Mrs. Poe, after his ears were cut off, called for them, put them in a clean handkerchief, and carried them away with her.

[107] No. 45 of the 'North Briton' charged the king with falsehood, and was the basis of the prosecutions; 45 became in consequence a popular number with the patriots. Tradesmen called their goods "forty-five"; and snuff so styled was still sold in Fleet Street only a few years ago. Horne Tooke declares that the Prince of Wales aggravated his august father, when the latter was flogging him, by shouting "Wilkes and 45 for ever!"

[108] Lords of Leet were obliged to keep up a pillory or tumbrel, on pain of forfeiture of the leet; and villages might also be compelled to provide them.

[109] The last stocks in London were those of St. Clement's Dane's in Portugal Street, which were removed in 1826, to make way for local improvements.—Wade, 'British Chronology.'

[110] 'Punishments in the Olden Time,' by William Andrews, F.R.H.S., to which I am indebted for many of my facts.

[111] This was not an uncommon offence. One Mary Hamilton was married fourteen times to members of her own sex. A more inveterate, but a more natural, bigamist was a man named Miller, who was pilloried, in 1790, for having married thirty different women on purpose to plunder them.

[112] The 'Reliquary,' edited by Llewellyn Jewitt, F.S.A.

[113] On the first introduction of the treadwheel in the early decades of the present century, its use was not restricted to males, and women were often made to suffer this punishment.

[114] Whipping females was not abolished till 1817.

[115] 'Ancient Law.'

[116] Bernardo Visconti, Duke of Milan, in the 14th century, made a capital punishment, or more exactly the act of killing, last for forty days.

[117] Pike, 'Hist. of Crime,' i. 210.

[118] By "Halifax law" any thief who within the precincts of the liberty stole thirteen pence could on conviction before four burghers be sentenced to death. The same law obtained at Hull, hence the particular prayer in the thieves' Litany, which ran as follows: "From Hull, Hell, and Halifax, good Lord, deliver us."

[119] Loftie, 'Hist. of London,' 1883, vol. ii. 215.

[120] Waller, the Tyebourne and Westbourne paper read before the London and Middlesex Archæological Society.

[121] 'History of Paddington.'

[122] See account of Courvoisier's trial in cap. vii., vol. ii.

[123] See *ante*, p. 186.

[124] 'Memorials of George Selwyn,' I. 11.

[125] The season was the summer, and on the Sunday following the execution, London was like a deserted city; hundreds of thousands went out to see him hanging in chains.

[126] The negligence and perfunctory performance of duty of the ordinary, Mr. Ford, is strongly animadverted upon in the 'Report of Commons' Committee in 1814.' See vol. ii. cap. 2.

[127] The Rev. Paul Lorraine.

[128] The Scotch Dalziels bear sable, a hanged man with his arms extended. A Spanish hidalgo has in his coat armour, a ladder with gibbet; and various implements of torture have been borne by German families of distinction.

[129] Many of the immediate successors of Brandon above-mentioned were called Gregory.

[130] 'Natural History of Oxfordshire,' cap. 8.

[131] See *ante*, chap. i.

[132] The most ingenious and painstaking attempt of this kind was that made by some Thugs awaiting sentence in India, who sawed through the bars of their prison with packthread smeared with oil and coated with fine stone-dust.

[133] In the proclamation for his apprehension after his second escape, he is described as about twenty-two years of age, five feet four inches in height, very slender, of a pale complexion, having an impediment or hesitation in his speech, and wearing a butcher's blue frock with a great-coat over it; a carpenter or house-joiner by trade. Twenty guineas reward was offered to any who might discover or apprehend him.

[134] I have followed the text of Ainsworth's novel, which gives a clear and picturesque account. It is also accurate, and based on the best accounts extant.

[135] I am quoting now from the 'Tyburn Calendar,' the wording of which is preserved in all other accounts.

[136] The following stanzas were written at the time, and appeared in the 'British Journal' of Nov. 28, 1724:—

"Thornhill, 'tis thine to gild with fame

The obscure and raise the humble name;

To make the form elude the grave,

And Sheppard from oblivion save.

Tho' life in vain the wretch implores,

An exile on the farthest shores,

Thy pencil brings a kind reprieve,

And bids the dying robber live.

. . . .

Apelles Alexander drew,

Cæsar is to Aurelius due,

Cromwell in Lilly's works doth shine,
And Sheppard, Thornhill, lives in thine."

[137] See *ante*, p. 268.

[138] See *ante*, p. 254.

[139] Ordinary's account of executions, Nov. 1736.

[140] See *ante*, p. 273.

[141] Luttrell, iii. 1695.

[142] *Ibid.*

[143] I have described this in detail in the next chapter.

[144] 'Life of Lord Hardwicke,' i. 215.

[145] 'An inquiry into the causes of the late increase of robbers,' &c. London: 1751.

[146] Fielding, 'Robbers,' p. 35.

[147] Soldiers in the Guards, after long and faithful service, were granted leave of absence from military duty in order to take civil situations which did not monopolize all their time. By this means they eked out their scanty pay.

[148] 'A Treatise on the Police of the Metropolis,' by P. Colquhoun, LL.D. London, 1800.

[149] Fielding, p. xxviii.

[150] *Ibid.*, p. xxix.

[151] Savage was tried before Sir Francis Page, commonly known as "the hanging judge," and whose severity was most notorious. He afterwards admitted that he had been most anxious to hang Savage. In his old age when his health was inquired after, he is reported to have replied, "I keep hanging on, hanging on."

[152] 'Celebrated Trials,' iii. 457. 'Newgate Calendar,' i. 39. Thornbury, in his 'Old Stories Retold,' calls it the King's Arms, on what authority he does not say.

[153] "What do you bring this fellow here for?" Oneby had

cried to the keeper of Newgate when he appeared with Hooper. "Whenever I look at him I shall think of being hanged." Hooper had a forbidding countenance, but he was an inimitable mimic, and he soon made himself an agreeable companion to the condemned man.

[154] 'Calendar,' i. 146.

[155] The husband of the Lady Macclesfield, who was mother to Richard Savage. See *ante*, p. 340.

[156] 'Life of Lord Chancellor Hardwicke,' by George Harris, i. 176.

[157] Where Lambeth Suspension Bridge now stands.

[158] The crime of petty treason was established when any person out of malice took away the life of another to whom he or she owed special obedience—as when a servant killed his master, a wife her husband, or an ecclesiastic his superior. The wife's accomplices in the murder of a husband were not deemed guilty of petty treason.

[159] The infamous Judge Jeffries in 1685 sentenced Elizabeth Gaunt to be burnt alive at Tyburn, for sheltering persons concerned in Monmouth's rebellion.

[160] As barristers often preferred to do business at their own homes, chambers in the Temple were rather at a discount just then, and their landlords, "preferring tenants of no legal skill to no tenants at all, let them out to any that offered, ..." consequently many private people creep about the Inns of Court. —'Newgate Calendar,' i. 470.

[161] 'Newgate Calendar,' i. 189.

[162] "Beau" Fielding, who was tried at the Old Bailey in 1706 for committing bigamy with the Duchess of Cleveland, is one of the most remarkable instances of this. See 'Celebrated Trials,' iii. 534. Also see the trial of the Duchess of Kingston, 'Remarkable Trials,' 203. She was tried by the House of Lords, found guilty, but pleaded her peerage and was discharged.

[163] Hackham was present at Dr. Dodd's execution a short time previously. His remarks on the subject will be found in vol. ii. chap. i.

[164] Quin could not resist the chance of making a sharp speech. When desired by the manager of Covent Garden to go to the front to apologize for Madame Rollau, a celebrated dancer, who could not appear, he said, "Ladies and Gentlemen, Madame Rollau cannot dance to-night, having dislocated her ancle—I wish it had been her neck."

[165] At this date abroad, Mr. Baretti pointed out, it was not the custom to put knives on the dinner-table, so that even ladies carried them in their pockets for general use.

[166] The boot was the usual punning allusion to Lord Bute in the caricatures of the day; and the petticoat no doubt referred to his undue influence over the Princess of Wales, mother of the reigning sovereign, George III. See *ante*, p. 238.

[167] Cant names of the period for drinks.

[168] Walpole's Letters to Sir Horace Mann.

[169] Wild at last had the audacity to occupy a house in the Old Bailey, opposite the present Sessions House.

[170] There were sometimes as many as sixty or seventy pirates awaiting trial at a time in Newgate, about this period.

[171] By Lord Orford and the Board of Admiralty.

[172] Luttrell.

[173] See *ante*, chap. vi. p. 279.

[174] Hume, xi. 418.

[175] The following are some of the great people who owned prisons in those days: "The Dukes of Portland, Devonshire, Norfolk, and Leeds, the Marquis of Carnarvon, Lords Salisbury, Exeter, Arundel, and Derby, the Bishops of Salisbury, Ely, and Durham, the Dean and Chapter of Westminster."

[176] Book iv. c. 22.

[177] 'Buxton on Prison Discipline,' p. 11.

[178] As late as 1818 the most capricious rules prevailed as to ironing in various prisons in the country. Thus at Newgate all felons were ironed; it was the same at Chelmsford; but at Bury and Norwich all felons were without irons. Again at Coldbath Fields, only the untried and those sent for re-examination were ironed; at other places the untried were not ironed, and so on. Dr. Dodd, in his 'Thoughts in Prison,' refers to the horror he experienced in Newgate from the constant rattling of chains. It seems the most hardened prisoners often clanked their irons for an amusement.

[179] See *ante*, chap. v. p. 211.

[180] 'Dr. Guy on Public Health,' 183.

[181] Lind, 'Health of our Seamen.'

[182] According to Lord Campbell, Lord Chief Justice Lee was attacked with the gaol fever in this year, but recovered. It was through Lee's remonstrances that certain precautions were adopted, such as plunging a hot iron into a bucket full of vinegar and sweet smelling herbs. 'Lives of the Lord Chief Justices.'

[183] Dr. (afterwards Sir John) Pringle had already published (1750) a pamphlet on hospital and 'jayl' fevers, in which he traced the distemper to jails being too small for their numbers, and too insecure to forego the use of dungeons. The only resource, he said, until these two evils were removed, was in ventilators.

[184] In this year 1752 another Lord Mayor, Winterbottom, died of the gaol fever. Lord Campbell's 'Lives of Lord Chief Justices.'

[185] A full account of the ventilator from the pen of Dr. Hales is published in the 'Gentleman's Magazine,' vol. xxii. p. 180 (1752), where also is the plan of the windmill which worked it, which plan I have introduced into this chapter. The various letters on the plan refer to the detailed description in the original.

[186] For full account of this see next chapter.

[187] Lord George Gordon died of it in the new Newgate in 1793.

[188] See next chapter.

[189] See page 379.

[190] Dr. Dodd in his 'Prison Thoughts' animadverts strongly upon the evils of Newgate, but completely exonerates Mr. Akerman. "No man could do more," says Dr. Dodd. "His attention is great, and his kindness and humanity to those in sickness or affliction peculiarly pleasing."

[191] There is a brief account of Newgate about this period in the 'Memoirs of Casanova,' who saw the interior of the prison while awaiting bail for an assault. Casanova was committed in ball dress, and received with hisses, which increased to furious abuse when they found he did not answer their questions, being ignorant of English. He felt as if he was in one of the most horrible circles of Dante's hell. He saw, "Des figures fauves, des regards de vipères, des sinistres sourires tous les caractères de l'envie de la rage, du désespoir; c'était un spectacle épouvantable."—'Mémoires,' vi. 48.

[192] Some notion of the density of the prison population in Newgate in those times will be obtained by comparing it with modern ideas on this subject. The following figures give the acreage and average population of three comparatively new prisons.

Prison Acreage Average prison population. Warwick 9A. 3R. 2P. 300 St. Albans 4 2 1 100 Lincoln 16 0 15 180 [193] See last chapter.

[194] Lord George Gordon was the son of Cosmo, Duke of Gordon, and was born in 1750. He entered the navy as a midshipman, but left the service in consequence of a dispute with Lord Sandwich. He sat in Parliament for Ludgershall, and was a bitter opponent of the ministry.

[195] Pennant's 'London.'

[196] 'Barnaby Rudge.'

[197] Lord Mansfield's impartiality at the trial was the subject of general admiration. "He never shewed the slightest tinge of resentment or bias." Yet with his house were destroyed not only much valuable property, but a mass of private journals and letters, which he had been collecting to form the basis of memoirs of his own times, and the loss of which was quite irreparable.

[198] This position may well be questioned. *Vide* vol. ii. cap. i.

[199] The Right Honourable Charles Jenkinson was created Lord Hawkesbury in 1787, and made Chancellor of the Duchy of Lancaster, as well as President of the Board of Trade. He was an authority in all mercantile and commercial affairs.

VOLUME 2

CRIMES AND CRIMINALS

State of crime on opening new gaol—Newgate full—Executions very numerous—Ruthless penal code—Forgery punished with death—Its frequency—How fostered—Some notable forgers—The first forgery of Bank of England notes—Gibson—Bolland—The two Perreaus—Dr. Dodd—Charles Price, alias Old Patch—Clipping still largely practised—John Clarke hanged for it—Also William Guest, a clerk in Bank of England—His elaborate apparatus for filing guineas—Coining—Forty or fifty private mints for making counterfeits—Always at work—Town and country orders regularly executed—650 prosecutions for coining in seven years—Offences against life and property—Streets unsafe—High roads infested by robbers—No regular police—Inefficiency of watchmen—Assaults on the weaker sex—Renwick Williams "the monster"—Daring Robberies at lévees—The Duke of Beaufort robbed by gentleman Harry—George Barrington, the gentleman thief, frequents Ranelagh, the Palace, the Opera House—His depredations—He aids authorities to suppress a mutiny, turns police officer and becomes chief constable of New South Wales before he dies—Gentlemen of the road *ubiquitous and always busy—Highwaymen put down by the horse patrol—Horse patrol described—Executions still numerous, but transportation now adopted as a secondary punishment for lesser offenders—Some of these described—"Long firm" swindlers—Alexander Day, alias Marmaduke Davenport, Esq.—Female Sharpers—Elizabeth Grieve pretends to sell places under the Crown—So does David James Dignam—Traffic in places flourished in this corrupt age—Mrs. Clarke and the Duke of York—Other forms of swindling—Jacques defrauds Warden of the Fleet—Juvenile depravity—Increased by committing the young to Newgate—Various youthful crimes—A girl for sale—Prize-fighting—Writers in gaol—The North Briton—Wilkes—The Press oppressed—Mr. Walter of the 'Times' in Newgate—Sir Francis Burdett and Mr. John Gale Jones—William Cobbett in Newgate—Also the Marquis of Sligo.*

IN the years immediately following the erection of the new gaol, crime was once more greatly in the ascendant. After the peace which gave independence to the United States, the country was overrun with discharged soldiers and sailors. They were mostly in dire poverty, and took to depredation almost as a matter of course. The calendars were particularly heavy. At the September Sessions of the Old Bailey in 1783, fifty-eight were convicted for capital offences. The Deputy Recorder, in passing sentence, remarked that it gave him inexpressible pain, and that it was truly alarming "to behold a bar so crowded with persons whose wickedness and imprudence had induced them to commit such enormous crimes as the laws of their country justly and necessarily punish with death. Those laws," he added, being thoroughly imbued with the ferocious spirit of the times, "while they are founded in equity, and executed with lenity, (!) impartiality, and rectitude, are written in blood." The exemplary punishment of so many failed to have a very deterrent effect. In the December Sessions following the number of trials was greater, although there were not so many capital convictions. Twenty-four received sentence of death, and ninety were convicted of single felonies. "Two such sessions," says a contemporary writer, "were never known before in London." The same depravity, dealt with in the same ruthless manner, prevailed throughout England. In the Lent Assizes of 1785 the judges on every circuit dealt out death with a liberal hand. At Kingston there were twenty-one capital sentences, and nine executions. At Lincoln twelve of the former, and at Gloucester sixteen, with, in both cases, nine executions; seven executions at Warwick, six at Exeter, Winchester, and Salisbury, five at Shrewsbury, and so on. The total number of capital sentences in England alone was two hundred and forty-two, of whom one hundred and three suffered, and only at Stafford, Oakham, and Ludlow was there a "maiden assize," or no capital conviction. At this date there were forty-nine persons lying in Newgate under sentence of death, one hundred and eighty under sentence of transportation, and prisoners of other categories, making the total prison population up to nearly six hundred souls.

Speaking of those times, Mr. Townshend, a veteran Bow Street runner, in his evidence before a Parliamentary Committee in 1816,[1] declared that in the years 1781-7 as many as twelve, sixteen, or twenty were hanged at one execution; twice he saw forty hanged at one time. In 1783 there were twenty at two consecutive executions. He had known, he said, as many as two hundred and twenty tried at one sessions. He had himself obtained convictions of from thirteen to twenty-five for returning from transportation. Upon the same authority we are told that in 1783 the Secretary of State advised the King to punish with all severity. The enormity of the offences was so great, says Mr. Townshend, and "plunder had got to such an alarming pitch," that a letter was circulated among judges and recorders then sitting, to the effect that His Majesty would dispense with the recorders' reports, and that the worst criminals should be picked out and at once ordered for execution.

The penal code was at this period still ruthlessly severe. There were some two hundred capital felonies upon the statute book. Almost any member of parliament eager to do his share in legislation could "create a capital felony." A story is told of Edmund Burke, that he was leaving his house one day in a hurry, when a messenger called him back on a matter which would not detain him a minute: "Only a felony without benefit of clergy." Burke also told Sir James Mackintosh, that although scarcely entitled to ask a favour of the ministry, he thought he had influence enough to create a capital felony.[2] It is true that of the two hundred, not more than five-and-twenty sorts of felonies actually entailed execution. It is true too that some of the most outrageous and ridiculous reasons for its infliction had disappeared. It was no longer death to take a falcon's egg from the nest, nor was it a hanging matter to be thrice guilty of exporting live sheep. But a man's life was still appraised at five shillings. Stealing from the person, or in a dwelling, or in a shop, or on a navigable river, to that amount, was punished with death. "I think it not right nor justice," wrote Sir Thomas More in 1516, "that the loss of money should cause the loss of man's life; for mine opinion is that all the goods in the world are not able to countervail man's life." Three hundred years was still to pass before the strenuous efforts of Sir Samuel Romilly bore fruit in the amelioration of the penal code. In 1810 he carried a bill through the House of Commons, which was, however, rejected by the Lords, to abolish capital punishment for stealing to the amount of five shillings in a shop. His most bitter opponents were the great lawyers of the times, Lords Ellenborough, Eldon, and others, Lords Chancellors and Lords Chief Justice, who opposed dangerous innovations, and viewed with dismay any attempt "to alter laws which a century had proved to be necessary." Lord Eldon on this occasion said that he was firmly convinced of the wisdom of the principles and practice of our criminal code. Romilly did not live to see the triumph of his philanthropic endeavours. He failed to procure the repeal of the cruel laws against which he raised his voice, but he stopped the hateful legislation which multiplied capital felonies year by year, and his illustrious example found many imitators. Within a few years milder and more humane ideas very generally prevailed. In 1837 the number of offences to which the extreme penalty could be applied was only seven, and in that year only eight persons were executed, all of them for murders of an atrocious character.[3]

Forgery, at the period of which I am now treating, was an offence especially repugnant to the law. No one guilty of it could hope to escape the gallows. The punishment was so certain, that as milder principles gained ground, many benevolent persons gladly withdrew from prosecution where they could. Instances were known in which bankers and other opulent people compromised with the delinquent rather than be responsible for taking away a fellow-creature's life.[4] The prosecutor would sometimes pretend his pockets had been picked of the forged instrument, or he destroyed it, or refused to produce it. An important witness sometimes kept out of the way. Persons have gone so far as to meet forged bills of exchange, and to a large amount. In one case it was pretty certain they would not have advanced the money had the punishment been short of death, because the culprit had already behaved disgracefully, and they had no desire he should escape a lesser retribution. Prosecutors have forfeited their recognizances sooner than appear, and have even, when duly sworn, withheld a portion of their testimony.

But at the time of which I am now writing the law generally took its course. In the years between 1805 and 1818 there had been two hundred and seven executions for forgery; more than for either murder, burglary, or robbery from the person. It may be remarked here that the Bank of England was by far the most bitter and implacable as regards prosecutions for forgery. Of the above-mentioned two hundred and seven executions for this crime, no less than seventy-two were the victims of proceedings instituted by the Bank. Forgeries upon this great monetary corporation had been much more frequent since the stoppage of specie payments, which had been decreed by Parliament in 1797 to save the Bank from collapse. Alarms of invasion had produced such a run upon it, that on one particular day little more than a million in cash or bullion remained in the cellars, which had already been drained of specie for foreign subsidies and subventions. Following the cessation of cash payments to redeem its paper in circulation, the Bank had commenced the issue of notes to the value of less than five pounds, and it was soon found that these, especially the one-pound notes, were repeatedly forged. In the eight years preceding 1797 but few prosecutions had been instituted by the Bank; but in the eight immediately following there were one hundred and forty-six convictions for the offence. At last, about 1818, a strong and general feeling of dissatisfaction grew rife against these prosecutions. The crime had continued steadily to increase, in spite of the awful penalties conviction entailed. It was proved, moreover, that note forgery was easily accomplished. Detection, too, was most difficult. The public were unable to distinguish between the good and bad notes. Bank officials were themselves often deceived, and cases were known where the clerks had refused payment of the genuine article. Juries began to decline to convict on the evidence of inspectors and clerks, unless substantiated by the revelation of the private mark, a highly inconvenient practice, which the Bank itself naturally discountenanced. Efforts were made to improve the quality of the note, so as to defy imitation; but this could not well be done at the price, and, as the only effective remedy, specie payments were resumed, and the one-pound note withdrawn from circulation.[5] But execution for forgery continued to be the law for many more years. Fauntleroy suffered for it in 1824;[6] Joseph Hunton, the Quaker linen-draper, in 1828; and Maynard, the last, in the following year.

I am, however, anticipating somewhat, and must retrace my steps, and indicate briefly one or two of the early forgers who passed through Newgate and suffered for the crime. The first case I find recorded is that of Richard Vaughan, a linen-draper of Stafford, who was committed to Newgate in March, 1758, for counterfeiting Bank of England notes. He employed several artists to engrave the notes in various parts, one of whom informed against him. The value of the note he himself added. Twenty which he had thus filled up he had deposited in the hands of a young lady to whom he was paying his addresses, as a guarantee of his wealth. Vaughan no doubt suffered, although I see no record of the fact in the Newgate Calendar.

Mr. Gibson's was a curious case. He was a prisoner in Newgate for eighteen months between conviction and execution, the jury having found a special verdict, subject to the determination of the twelve judges. As Gibson remained so long in gaol, it was the general opinion that no further notice would be taken of the case. The prisoner himself must have been buoyed up with this hope, as he petitioned repeatedly for judgment. He had been sentenced in Sept. 1766, and in 1768, at Hilary Term, the judges decided that his crime came within the meaning of the law. Gibson had been a solicitor's clerk, who gave so much satisfaction that he was taken into partnership. The firm was doing a large business, and among other large affairs was intrusted with a Chancery case, respecting an estate for which an *ad interim* receiver had been appointed. Gibson's way of life was immoral and extravagant. He had urgent need of funds, and in an evil hour he forged the signature of the Accountant-

General to the Court of Chancery, and so obtained possession of some of the rents of the above-mentioned estate. The fraud was presently discovered; Gibson was arrested, and eventually, as already stated, condemned. "After sentence," says the Calendar, "his behaviour was in every way becoming his awful situation; ... he appeared rational, serious, and devout. His behaviour was so pious, so resigned, and in all respects so admirably adapted to his unhappy situation, that the tears of the commiserating multitude accompanied his last ejaculation. He was carried to execution in a mourning coach," an especial honour reserved for malefactors of aristocratic antecedents and gentle birth.

James Bolland, who was executed in 1772, deserved and certainly obtained less sympathy. Bolland long filled the post of a sheriff's officer, and as such became the lessee of a spunging-house, where he practised boundless extortion. He was a man of profligate life, whose means never equalled his extravagant self-indulgence, and he was put to all manner of shifts to get money. More than once he arrested debtors, was paid all claims in full, and appropriated the money to his own use, yet escaped due retribution for his fraud. He employed bullies, spies, and indigent attorneys to second his efforts, some of whom were arrested and convicted of other crimes with the clothes Bolland provided them still on their backs. His character was so infamous, that when he purchased the situation of upper city marshal for £2400, the court of aldermen would not approve of the appointment. He tried also to succeed to a vacancy as Sergeant-at-mace, and met with the same objection. The deposit-money paid over in both these affairs was attached by his sureties, and he was driven to great necessities for funds. When called upon to redeem a note of hand he had given, he pleaded that he was short of cash, and offered another man's bill, which, however, was refused unless endorsed. Bolland then proceeded to endorse it with his own name, but it was declared unnegotiable, owing to the villanous character it bore. Whereupon Bolland erased all the letters after the capital, and substituted the letters "anks," the name of Banks being that of a respectable victualler of Rathbone Place, in a large way of trade. When the bill became due, Banks repudiated his signature, and Bolland, who sought too late to meet it and hush up the affair, was arrested for the forgery. He was tried and executed in due course.

The case of the twin brothers Perreau in 1776 was long the talk of the town. It evoked much public sympathy, as they were deemed to be the dupes of a certain Mrs. Rudd, who lived with Daniel Perreau, and passed as his wife. Daniel was a man of reputed good means, with a house in Harley Street, which he kept up well. His brother, Robert Perreau, was a surgeon enjoying a large practice, and residing in Golden Square. The forged deed was a bond for £7500, purporting to be signed by William Adair, a well-known agent. Daniel Perreau handed this to Robert Drummond Perreau, who carried it to the Bank, where its validity was questioned, and the brothers, with Mrs. Rudd, were arrested on suspicion of forgery. Daniel on his trial solemnly declared that he had received the instrument from Mrs. Rudd; Robert's defence was that he had no notion the document was forged. Both were, however, convicted of knowingly uttering the counterfeit bond. It was, however, found impossible to prove Mrs. Rudd's complicity in the transaction, and she was acquitted. The general feeling was, however, so strong that she was the guilty person, that the unfortunate Perreaus became a centre of interest. Strenuous efforts were made to obtain a reprieve for them. Robert Perreau's wife went in deep mourning, accompanied by her three children, to sue for pardon on their knees from the Queen. Seventy-two leading bankers and merchants signed a petition in his favour, which was presented to the King two days before the execution. But all to no purpose. Both brothers suffered the extreme penalty at

Tyburn on the 17th January, 1776, before an enormous multitude estimated at 30,000. They asserted their innocence to the last.

In the following year a clergyman, who had at one time achieved some eminence, also fell a victim to the vindictive laws regarding forgery. Dr. Dodd was the son of a clergyman. He had been a wrangler at Cambridge, and was early known as a littérateur of some repute. While still on his promotion, and leading a gay life in London, he made a foolish marriage, and united himself to the daughter of one of Sir John Dolben's servants, a young lady largely endowed with personal attractions, but certainly deficient in birth and fortune. This sobered him, and he took orders in the year that his 'Beauties of Shakespeare' was published. He became a zealous curate at West Ham; thence he went to St. James', Garlick Hill, and took an active part in London church and charitable work. He was one of the promoters of the Magdalen Hospital, also of the Humane Society, and in 1763, twelve years after ordination, he was appointed chaplain in ordinary to the King. About the same time he was presented to a prebend's stall in Brecon Cathedral, and was recommended to Lord Chesterfield as tutor to his son. He hoped to succeed to the rectory of West Ham, but being disappointed he now came to London, and launched out into extravagance. He had a town house, and a country house at Ealing, and he exchanged his chariot for a coach. Having won a prize of £1000 in a lottery, he became interested in two proprietary chapels, but could not make them pay. But just then he was presented with a living, that of Hockliffe, in Bedfordshire, which he held with the vicarage of Chalgrove, and his means were still ample. They were not sufficient, however, for his expenditure, and in an evil moment he attempted to obtain the valuable cure of St. George's, Hanover Square, by back-stair influence. The living was in the gift of the Crown, and Dodd was so ill advised as to write to a great lady at Court, offering her £3000 if he were presented. The letter was forthwith passed on to the Lord Chancellor, and the King, George III., hearing what had happened, ordered Dr. Dodd's name to be struck off the list of his chaplains. The story was made public, and Dodd was satirized in the press and on the stage.

Dodd was now greatly encumbered by debts, from which the presentation to a third living, that of Winge, in Buckinghamshire, could not relieve him. He was in such straits that, according to his biographer, "he descended so low as to become the editor of a newspaper," and he tried to obtain relief in bankruptcy, but failed. At length, so sorely pressed was he by creditors that he resolved to do a dishonest deed. He forged the name of his old pupil, now Lord Chesterfield, who had since become his patron, to a bond for £4200. He applied to certain usurers, in the name of a young nobleman who was seeking an advance. The business was refused by many, because Dr. Dodd declared that they could not be present at the execution of the bond. A Mr. Robertson proved more obliging, and to him Dr. Dodd, in due course, handed a bond for £4200 executed by Lord Chesterfield, and witnessed by himself. A second witness being necessary, Mr. Robertson signed his name beneath Dr. Dodd's. The bond was no sooner presented for payment, and referred to Lord Chesterfield, than it was repudiated. Robertson was forthwith arrested, and soon afterwards Dr. Dodd. The latter at once, in the hope of saving himself, returned £3000; he gave a cheque upon his bankers for £700, a bill of sale on his furniture worth £400 more, and the whole sum was made up by another hundred from the brokers. Nevertheless Dr. Dodd was taken before the Lord Mayor and charged with the forgery. Lord Chesterfield would not stir a finger to help his old tutor, although the poor wretch had made full restitution. Dr. Dodd, when arraigned, declared that he had no intention to defraud, that he had only executed the bond as a temporary resource to meet some pressing claims. The jury after consulting only five minutes found him guilty, and he was regularly sentenced to death. Still greater exertions were made to obtain a reprieve for Dr. Dodd than in the case of the Perreaus. The newspapers were filled with letters pleading for him. All classes of people strove to help him; the parish officers went in mourning from house to house, asking subscriptions to get up a petition to the King, and this petition, when eventually drafted, filled twenty-three skins of parchment. Petitions from Dodd and his wife, both drawn up by Dr. Johnson, were laid before the King and Queen. Even the Lord Mayor and Common Council went in a body to St. James's Palace to beg mercy from the King. As, however, clemency had been denied to the Perreaus, it was deemed unadvisable to extend it to Dr. Dodd.[7] The concourse at his execution, which took place at Tyburn, was immense. It has been stated erroneously that Dr. Dodd preached his own funeral sermon. He only delivered an address to his fellow-prisoners in the prison chapel by the permission of Mr. Villette, the ordinary. The text he chose was Psalm li. 3, "I acknowledge my faults; and my sin is ever before me." It was delivered some three weeks before the Doctor's execution, and subsequently printed. It is a curious fact that among other published works of Dr. Dodd, is a sermon on the injustice of capital punishments. He was, however, himself the chief witness against a highwayman, who was hanged for stopping him. Among other spectators at the execution of Dr. Dodd was the Rev. James Hackman, who afterwards murdered Miss Reay.[8]

It is said that a scheme was devised to procure Dodd's escape from Newgate. He was treated with much consideration by Mr. Akerman, allowed to have books, papers, and a reading-desk. Food and other necessaries were brought him from outside by a female servant daily. This woman was found to bear a striking resemblance to the Doctor, which was the more marked when she was dressed up in a wig and gown. She was asked if she would co-operate in a scheme for taking the Doctor's place in gaol, and consented. It was arranged that on a certain day, Dr. Dodd's irons having been previously filed, he was to change clothes with the woman. She was to seat herself at the reading-desk while Dr. Dodd, carrying a bundle under his arm, coolly walked out of the prison. The plan would probably have succeeded, but Dodd would not be a party to it. He was so buoyed up with the hope of reprieve that he would not risk the misconstruction which would have been placed upon the attempt to escape had it failed. In his own profession Dr. Dodd was not very highly esteemed. Dr. Newton, Bishop of Bristol, is said to have observed that Dodd deserved pity, because he was hanged for the least crime he had committed.

One of the most notorious depredators in this line, whose operations long eluded detection, was Charles Price, commonly called Old Patch. He forged bank-notes wholesale. His plans were laid with the utmost astuteness, and he took extraordinary precautions to avoid discovery. He did everything for himself; made his own paper, with the proper water-mark, engraved his own plates, and manufactured his own ink. His method of negotiating the forged notes was most artful. He had three homes; at one he was Price, properly married, at a second he lived under another name with a woman who helped him in his schemes, at a third he did the actual business of passing his notes. This business was always effected in disguise; none of his agents or instruments saw him except in disguise, and when his work was over he put it off to return home. One favourite personation of his was that of an infirm old man, wearing a long black camlet cloak, with a broad cape fastened up close to his chin. With this he wore a big, broad-brimmed slouch hat, and often green spectacles or a green shade. Sometimes his mouth was covered up with red flannel, or his corpulent legs and gouty feet were swathed in flannel. His natural appearance as Price was a compact middle-aged man, inclined to stoutness, erect, active, and not bad-looking, with a beaky nose, keen grey eyes, and a nutcracker chin. His schemes were very ingenious. On one occasion he pretended, in one disguise, to expose a swindler (himself in another disguise), whom a respectable city merchant inveigled into his house in order to give him up to the police. The swindler proposed to buy himself off for £500; the offer was accepted, the money paid by a thousand-pound note, for which the swindler got change. The note, of course, was forged. He victimized numbers of tradesmen. Disguised as an old man, he passed six forged fifty-pound notes on a grocer, and then as Price backed up his victim in an action brought against the bank which refused payment of the counterfeits. But his cleverest coup was that organized against the lottery offices. Having in one of his disguises engaged a boy to serve him, he sent the lad, dressed in livery, round the town to buy lottery tickets, paying for them in large (forged) notes, for which change was always required. By these means hundreds and hundreds of pounds were obtained upon the counterfeits. The boy was presently arrested, and a clever plot was laid to nab the old man his master, but Price by his vigilance outwitted the police. Another dodge was to hire boys to take forged notes to the Bank, receive the tickets from the teller, and carry them back to him (Price). He forthwith altered the figures, passed them on by the same messenger to the Bank cashier, and obtained payment for the larger amount.

These wholesale forgeries produced something like consternation at the Bank. It was supposed that they were executed by a large gang, well organized and with numerous ramifications, although Price, as I have said, really worked single-handed. The notes poured in day after day, and still no clue was obtained as to the culprits. The Bow Street officials were hopelessly at fault.

"Old Patch" was advertised for, described in his various garbs. It was now discovered that he had a female accomplice. This was a Mrs. Poultney, alias Hickeringill, his wife's aunt, a tall, rather genteel woman of thirty, with a downcast look, thin face and person, light hair, and pitted with the small-pox. Fate at last unexpectedly overtook Old Patch. One of many endorsements upon a forged note was traced to a pawnbroker, who remembered to have had the note from one Powel. The runners suspected that Powel was Price, and that he was a member of Old Patch's gang. A watch was set at the pawnbroker's, and the next time Powel called he was arrested, identified as Price, searched, and found to have upon his person a large number of notes, with a quantity of white tissue-paper, which he declared he had bought to make into air-balloons for his children. Price was committed to prison, and a close inquiry made into his antecedents. He was found to be the man who had decoyed Foote the actor into a partnership in a brewery, and decamped with the profits, leaving Foote to pay liabilities to the extent of £500. Then, he had started an illicit still, and had been arrested and sent to Newgate till he had paid a fine of £1600. He was released through the intercession of Lord Littleton and Foote, and forgiven the fine. He next set up as a fraudulent lottery office keeper, and bolted with a big prize. After this he elaborated his system of forgery, which ended in the way I have said. Price was alert and cunning to the last. One of his first acts was to pass out a clandestine letter to Mrs. Poultney, briefly telling her to "destroy everything." This she effected by burning the whole of his disguises in the kitchen fire, on the pretence that the clothes were infected by the plague. The engraving press was disposed of; the copper plates heated red hot, then smashed into pieces and thrown with the water-mark wires on to a neighbouring dust-heap, where they were subsequently discovered. Price attempted to deny his identity, but to no purpose, and when he saw the grip of the law tightening upon him, he committed suicide to avoid the extreme penalty. He was found hanging behind the door of his cell, suspended from two hat-screws, strengthened by gimlets. Price's depredations, it was said, amounted to £200,000; but how he disposed of his ill-gotten gains, seeing that he always lived obscurely, and neither gambled nor drank, remained an inscrutable secret to the last.

Two deliberate cases of forging Bank of England notes about this time may be mentioned, although neither of the criminals passed through Newgate. One was James Elliot, who suffered at Maidstone in 1777, the other Joshua Crompton, who was executed at Gangley Green, near Guildford, in 1778.

The circulation of counterfeit paper was not the only kind of monetary fraud in vogue. The coinage of the realm still suffered. Clipping could not be quite put down by act of Parliament. The punishment was still capital, and generally inflicted without hope of reprieve. It was a crime affected more particularly by workers in the precious metals. Thus John Clarke, in 1767, was a London watch-case maker of good repute, who was in the habit of working alone in a private closet. His apprentice, jealously suspecting him to be engaged in some secret branch of his trade, bored a hole through the wainscot, and caught his master filing guineas. The apprentice immediately informed; Clarke was arrested, convicted, and soon afterwards hanged.

Persons in a higher station, however, succumbed to special temptations. William Guest was the son of a clergyman living at Worcester, who had sufficient interest to get him a clerkship in the Bank of England. The constant handling of piles of gold was too much for Guest's integrity, and he presently resolved to turn his opportunities to account. Taking a house in Broad Street Buildings, he devoted the upper part of it to his nefarious trade. He abstracted guineas from his drawer in the Bank, carried them home, filed them, then remilled them in a machine he had designed for the purpose, and returned them—now light weight—to the Bank. The filings he converted into ingots and disposed of to the trade. No suspicion of his malpractices transpiring, he was in due course advanced to the post of teller. But a fellow-teller having observed him one day picking out new guineas from a bag, watched him, and found that he did this constantly. On another occasion he was seen to pay away guineas some of which, on examination, proved to have been recently filed. They were weighed, and found short weight. To test Mr. Guest still further, his money-bags were opened one night after hours, and the contents counted and examined. The number was short, and several guineas found which appeared to have been recently filed, and which on weighing proved to be light.

A descent was forthwith made upon Guest's house, and in the upper rooms the whole apparatus for filing was laid bare. In a nest of drawers were found vice, files, the milling machine, two bags of gold filings, and a hundred guineas. A flap in front of the nest of drawers could be let down, and inside was a skin fastened to the back of the flap, with a hole in it to button on to the waistcoat, and equip the workman after the method of jewellers. More evidence was soon forthcoming against Guest. His fellow-teller had seen him in possession of a substantial bar of gold; jewellers and others swore to having bought ingots from him, and an assayer at Guest's trial deposed to their being of the same standard as the guinea coinage. His guilt was clearly made out to the jury, and he was sentenced to death. A petition signed by a number of influential persons was forwarded to the Crown, praying for mercy, but it was decided that the law ought to take its course. As his crime amounted to high treason, he went to Tyburn on a sledge, but he suffered no other penalty than hanging.

The flagitious trade of coining was in a most flourishing condition during the last decades of the eighteenth and the early part of the nineteenth centuries. The condition of the national coinage was at this time far from creditable to the Mint. A great part of both the silver and copper money in circulation was much worn and defaced. Imitation thus became much easier than with coins comparatively fresh and new. Hence the nefarious practice multiplied exceedingly. There were as many as forty or fifty private mints constantly at work, either in London or in the principal country towns. The process was rapid, not too laborious, and extremely profitable. A couple of hands could turn out in a week base silver coins worth nominally two or three hundred pounds. The wages of a good workman were as much as a couple of guineas a day. Much capital was invested by large dealers in the trade, who must have made enormous sums. One admitted that his transactions in seven years amounted to the production of £200,000 in counterfeit half-crowns and other silver coins. So systematic was the traffic, that orders for town and country were regularly executed by the various manufacturers. Boxes and parcels of base coin were despatched every morning by coach and waggon to all parts of the kingdom, like any other goods. The trade extended to foreign countries.[9] The law, until it was rectified by the 37 Geo. III. cap. 126, did not punish the counterfeiting of foreign money, and French louis-d'or, Spanish dollars, German florins, and Turkish sequins were shipped abroad in great quantities. Our Indian possessions even did not escape, and a manufactory of spurious gold or silver pagodas was at one time most active in London, whence they were exported to the East. The number of persons employed in London as capitalists and agents for distribution alone amounted to one hundred and twenty at one time; and besides there was a strong force of skilful handicraftsmen, backed up by a whole army of "utterers" or "smashers," constantly busy in passing the base money into the currency. The latter comprised hawkers, peddlers, market-women, hackney-coach drivers, all of whom attended the markets held by the dealers in the manufactured article, and bought wholesale to distribute retail by various devices, more particularly in giving change. They obtained the goods at an advantage of about one hundred per cent. When the base money lost its veneer, the dealers were ready to repurchase it in gross, and after a repetition of the treatment, issue it afresh at the old rates.

Gold coins were not so much counterfeited as silver and copper, but there were bad guineas in circulation. The most dexterous method of coining them was by mixing a certain amount of alloy with the pure metal. They were the proper weight, and had some semblance of the true ring, but their intrinsic value was not more than thirteen or fourteen shillings, perhaps only eight or nine. The fabrication was, however, limited by the expense and the nicety required in the process. To counterfeit silver was a simpler operation. Of base silver money there were five kinds; viz. flats, plated goods, plain goods, castings, and fig things. The *flats* were cut out of prepared flattened plates composed of silver and blanched copper. When cut out the coins were turned in a lathe, stamped in a press with the proper die, and subjected to rubbing with various materials, including aquafortis to bring the silver to the surface, sandpaper, cork, cream of tartar, and last of all blacking to give the appearance of age. *Plated goods* were prepared from copper; the coins cut the proper size and plated, the stamping being done afterwards. As these coins were most like silver, they generally evaded detection. *Plain goods* consisted of copper blanks the size of a shilling, turned out from a lathe, then given the colour and lustre of metal buttons, after which they were rubbed with cream of tartar and blacking. *Castings*, as the word implies, were coins made of blanched copper, cast in moulds of the proper die; they were then silvered and treated like the rest. It was very common to give this class of base money a crooked appearance, by which means they seemed genuine, and got into circulation without suspicion. The *figs*, or *fig things*, were the lowest and meanest class, and was confined chiefly to sixpences. Copper counterfeit money was principally of two kinds, stamped and plain, made out of base metal; the profit on them being about a hundred per cent. They were mostly halfpennies; but farthings were also largely manufactured, the material being real copper, but the fraud was in their being of light weight, and very thin.

The prosecutions for coining were very numerous. The register of the solicitor to the Mint recorded as many as 650 in a period of seven years. The offence of making or uttering, till a very recent date, constituted petty treason, and met with the usual penalties. These, in the case of female offenders, included hanging and burning at a stake. The last woman who suffered in this way was burnt before the debtors' door, in front of Newgate, in 1788, having been previously strangled. In the following year, as I have already said, the 30 Geo. III. cap. 48 was passed, which abolished the practice of burning women convicted of petty treason.[10] Persons guilty of only selling or dealing in base money were more leniently dealt with. The offence was long only a misdemeanour, carrying with it a sentence of imprisonment for a year and a day, which the culprit passed not unpleasantly in Newgate, while his friends or relations kept the business going outside, and supplied him regularly with ample funds.

There was as yet little security for life and property in town or country. The streets of London were still unsafe; high roads and bye roads leading to it were still infested by highway robbers. The protection afforded to the public by the police continued very inefficient. It was still limited to parochial effort; the watchmen were appointed by the vestries, and received a bare pittance,—twelve and sixpence a week in summer, seventeen and sixpence in winter,—which they often eked out by taking bribes from the women of the town, or by a share in a burglar's "swag," to whose doings they were conveniently blind. These watchmen were generally middle-aged, often old and feeble men, who were appointed either from charitable motives, to give them employment, or save them from being inmates of the workhouse and a burthen to the parish. Their hours of duty were long, from night-fall to sunrise, during which, when so disposed, they patrolled the streets, calling the hour, the only check on their vigilance being the occasional rounds of the parish beadle, who visited the watchmen on their various beats. In spite of this the watchmen were often invisible; not to be found when most wanted, and even when present, powerless to arrest or make head against disorderly or evilly-disposed persons.

Besides the watchmen there were the parish constables, nominated by the court of burgesses, or court leet. The obligation of serving in the office of constable might fall upon any householder in turn, but he was at liberty to escape it by buying a substitute or purchasing a "Tyburn ticket," of which more directly. The parish constables were concerned with pursuit rather than prevention, with crime after rather than before the fact. In this duty they were assisted by the police constables, although there was no love lost between the two classes of officer. The police constables are most familiar to us under the name of "Bow Street runners," but they were attached to all the police offices, and not to Bow Street alone. They were nominated from Whitehall by the Secretary of State, the minister now best known as the Home Secretary. The duties of the "runners" were mainly those of detection and pursuit, in which they were engaged in London and in the country, at home and abroad. Individuals or public bodies applied to Bow Street, or some other office, for the services of a runner. These officers took charge of poaching cases, of murders, burglaries, or highway robberies. Some were constantly on duty at the Court, as depredations were frequently committed in the royal palaces, or the royal family were "teased by lunatics." The runners were remunerated by a regular salary of a guinea a week; but special services might be recognized by a share in the private reward offered, or, in case of conviction, by a portion of the public parliamentary reward of £40, which might be granted by the bench.[11]

The policy of making these grants was considered questionable. It tended to tempt officers of justice "to forswear themselves for the lucre of the reward," and the thirst for "blood-money," as it was called, was aggravated till it led many to sell the lives of their fellow-creatures for gain. There were numerous cases of this. Jonathan Wild was one of the most notorious of the dishonest thief-takers. In 1755 several scoundrels of the same kidney were convicted of having obtained the conviction of innocent people, simply to pocket the reward. Their offence did not give under penal statute, so they were merely exposed in the pillory, where, however, the mob pelted one to death and nearly killed another. Again, in 1816, a police officer named Vaughan was guilty of inciting to crime, in order to betray his victims and receive the blood-money. On the other hand, when conviction was doubtful the offender enjoyed long immunity from arrest. Officers would not arrest him until he "weighed his weight," as the saying was, or until they were certain of securing the £40 reward. Another form of remuneration was the bestowal on conviction of a "Tyburn ticket"; in other words, of an exemption from service in parish offices. This the officer sold for what it would fetch, the price varying in different parishes from £12 or £14 to £30 or £40.

It was not to be wondered at that a weak and inadequate police force, backed up by such uncertain and injudicious incentives to activity, should generally come off second-best in its struggles with the hydra-headed criminality of the day.

Robberies and burglaries were committed almost under the eyes of the police. It was calculated that the value of the property stolen in the city in one month (*circa* 1808) amounted to £15,000, and none of the parties were even known or apprehended, although sought after night and day.[12] Such cases as the following were of frequent occurrence. "Seven ruffians, about eight o'clock at night, knocked at the door of Mrs. Abercrombie in Charlotte Street, Rathbone Place, calling out 'Post!' and on its being opened, rushed in and took from Mrs. A. her jewels and fifty or sixty guineas in money, with all the clothes and linen they could get. The neighbourhood was alarmed, and a great crowd assembled, but the robbers sallied forth, and with swords drawn and pistols presented, threatened destruction to any who opposed them. The mob tamely suffered them to escape with their booty without making any resistance." The officers of justice were openly defied. There were streets, such as Duck Lane, Gravel Lane, or Cock Lane, in which it was unsafe for any one to venture without an escort of five or six of his fellows. "They (the ruffians) would have cut him to pieces if he was alone."

Still more dastardly were the wanton outrages perpetrated upon unprotected females, often in broad daylight, and in the public streets. These at one time increased to an alarming extent. Ladies were attacked and wounded without warning, and apparently without cause. The injuries were often most serious. On one occasion a young lady was stabbed in the face by means of an instrument concealed in a bouquet of flowers which a ruffian had begged her to smell. When consternation was greatest, however, it was reported that the cowardly assailant was in custody. He proved to be one Renwick Williams, now generally remembered as "the monster." The assault for which he was arrested was made in St. James's Street, about midnight, upon a young lady, Miss Porter, who was returning from a ball to her father's house. Renwick struck at her with a knife, and wounded her badly through her clothes, accompanying the blow with the grossest language. The villain at the time escaped, but Miss Porter recognized him six months later in St. James's Park. He was followed by a Mr. Coleman to his quarters at No. 52, Jermyn Street, and brought to Miss Porter's house. The young lady, crying "That is the wretch!" fainted away at the sight of him. The prisoner indignantly repudiated that he was "the monster" who was advertised for, but he was indicted at the Old Bailey, and the jury found him guilty without hesitation. His sentence was two years' imprisonment in Newgate, and he was bound over in £400 to be of good behaviour.

Gentlemen, some of the highest station, going or returning from court, were often the victims of the depredations committed in the royal precincts. In 1792 a gang of thieves dressed in court suits smuggled themselves into a drawing-room of St. James's Palace, and tried to hustle and rob the Prince of Wales. The Duke of Beaufort, returning from a levee, had his "George," pendant to his ribbon of the Garter, stolen from him in the yard of St. James's Palace. The order was set with brilliants, worth a very large sum of money. The duke called out to his servants, who came up and seized a gentlemanly man dressed in black standing near. The "George" was found in this gentleman's pocket. He proved to be one Henry Sterne, commonly called Gentleman Harry,[13] who, being of good address and genteel appearance, easily got admission to the best company, upon whom he levied his contributions.

George Barrington, the notorious pickpocket, also found it to his advantage to attend levees and drawing-rooms. Barrington, or Waldron, which was his real name, began crime early. When one of a strolling company in Ireland, he recruited the empty theatrical treasury and supplemented meagre receipts by stealing watches and purses, the proceeds being divided among the rest of the actors. He found thieving so much more profitable than acting that he abandoned the latter in favour of the former profession, and set up as a gentleman pickpocket. Having worked Dublin well, his native land became too hot to hold him, and came to London. At Ranelagh one night he relieved both the Duke of Leinster and Sir William Draper of considerable sums. He visited also the principal watering places, including Bath, but London was his favourite hunting-ground. Disguised as a clergyman, he went to court on drawing-room days, and picked pockets or removed stars and decorations from the breasts of their wearers. At Covent Garden Theatre one night he stole a gold snuff-box set with brilliants, and worth £30,000, belonging to Prince Orloff, of which there had been much talk, and which, with other celebrated jewels, Barrington had long coveted. The Russian prince felt the thief's hand in his pocket, and immediately seized Barrington by the throat, on which the latter slipped back the snuff-box. But Barrington was arrested and committed for trial, escaping this time because Prince Orloff would not prosecute. He was, however, again arrested for picking a pocket in Drury Lane Theatre, and sentenced to three years' hard labour on board the hulks in the Thames.

From this he was released prematurely through the good offices of a gentleman who pitied him, only to be reimprisoned, but in Newgate, not the hulks, for fresh robberies at the Opera House, Pantheon, and other places of public resort. Once more released, he betook himself to his old evil courses, and having narrowly escaped capture in London, wandered through the northern counties in various disguises, till he was at length taken at Newcastle-on-Tyne. Another narrow escape followed, through the absence of a material witness; but he was finally arrested for picking a pocket on Epsom Downs, and sentenced to seven years' transportation. He made an affecting speech at his trial, urging, in extenuation of his offence, that he had never had a fair chance of earning an honest livelihood. He may have been sincere, and he certainly took the first opportunity of trying to do well. On the voyage out to New South Wales there was a mutiny on board the convict ship, which would have been successful but for Barrington's aid on the side of authority. He kept the passage to the quarter-deck single-handed, and the mob of convicts at bay with a marline-spike, till the captain and crew were able to get arms and make head against the revolt. As a reward for his conduct, Barrington was appointed to a position of trust, in charge of other prisoners at Paramatta. Within a year or two he was advanced to the more onerous and responsible post of chief constable, and was complimented by the governor of the colony for his faithful performance of the duty. He fell away in health, however, and retiring eventually upon a small pension, died before he was fifty years of age.

The gentlemen of the highway continued to harass and rob all travellers. All the roads were infested. Two or three would be heard of every morning; some on Hounslow Heath, some on Finchley Common, some on Wimbledon Common, some on the Romford Road. Townshend, the Bow Street runner, declared that on arriving at the office of a morning people came in one after the other to give information of such robberies. "Messrs. Mellish, Bosanquet, and Pole, merchants of the city," says a contemporary chronicle, "were stopped by three highwaymen on Hounslow Heath. After robbing them, without resistance, of their money and their watches, one of the robbers wantonly fired into the chaise and mortally wounded Mr. Mellish." The first successful effort made to put down this levying of blackmail upon the king's highway was the establishment of the police horse patrol in 1805. It was organized by the direction of the chief magistrate at Bow Street, then Sir Nathaniel Conant, and under the immediate orders of a conductor, Mr. Day. This force consisted of mounted constables, who every night regularly patrolled all the roads leading into the metropolis. They worked singly between two stations, each starting at a fixed time from each end, halting midway to communicate, then returning. The patrol acted on any information received *en route*, making themselves known as they rode along to all persons riding horses or in carriages, by calling out in a loud tone "Bow Street Patrol." They arrested all known offenders whom they met with, and were fully armed for their own and the public protection. The members of this excellent force were paid eight-and-twenty shillings a week, with turnpike tolls and forage for their horses, which, however, they were obliged to groom and take care of. Marked and immediate results obtained from the establishment of this patrol. Highway robbery ceased almost entirely, and in the rare cases which occurred before it quite died out, the guilty parties were invariably apprehended.

There was as yet no very marked diminution in the number of executions, but other forms of punishment were growing into favour. Already transportation beyond the seas had grown into a system. Since the settlement of New South Wales as a penal colony in 1780, convicts were sent out regularly, and in increasingly large batches. The period between conviction and embarkation was spent in Newgate, thus adding largely to its criminal population, with disastrous consequences to the health and convenience of the place. Besides these, the most heinous criminals, there were other lesser offenders, for whom various terms of imprisonment was deemed a proper and sufficient penalty. Hence gaols were growing much more crowded, Newgate more especially, as I shall presently show. For the present I propose to give the reader some of the types of persons who became lodgers in Newgate, not temporarily, as in the case of all who passed quickly from the condemned cells to the gallows, but who remained there for longer periods, whether awaiting removal as transports, or working out a sentence of imprisonment in the course of law.

As London, increased in size and life, became more complex, chances multiplied for rogues and sharpers, who tried with chicane and stratagem to prey upon society. Swindling was carried out more systematically and upon a wider scale than in the days of Jenny Diver or the sham German Princess.[14] A woman named Robinson was arrested in 1801, who, under the pretence of being a rich heiress, had obtained goods fraudulently from tradesmen to the value of £20,000. Again, some years later, a gang resembling somewhat the "long firms" of modern days carried on a fictitious trade, and obtained goods from city merchants worth £50,000. There were many varieties of the professional swindler in those days. Some did business under the guise of licensed and outwardly respectable pawnbrokers, who *sub rosâ* were traffickers in stolen goods. Others roamed the country as hawkers, general dealers, and peddlers, distributing exciseable articles which had been smuggled into the country, carrying on fraudulent raffles, purchasing stolen horses in one county and disposing of them in another. The "duffer" went from door to door in the town, offering for sale smuggled tobacco, muslins, or other stuffs, and, if occasion served, passing forged notes or bad money as small change.

Where the swindler possessed such qualifications as a pleasing manner and a gentlemanly address, with a small capital to start with, he flew at higher game. Alexander Day, alias Marmaduke Davenport, Esq., was one of the first of a long line of impostors who made a great show, in a fine house in a fashionable neighbourhood, with sham footmen in smart liveries, and a grand carriage and pair. The latter he got in on approval, taking care while he used them to be driven to the Duke of Montague's and other aristocratic mansions. In the carriage too he called on numbers of tradesmen and gave large orders for goods: yards of Spanish point-lace, a gold "equipage" or dinner-service, silks in long pieces, table and other linen enough to furnish several houses. By clever excuses he postponed payment, or made off with the property by a second door. Among other things ordered was a gold chain for his squirrel, which already wore a silver one. The goldsmith recognized the silver chain as one he had recently sold to a lady, and his suspicions were aroused. On reference to her she denounced Day as a swindler, who had cheated her out of a large sum of money. Day was forthwith arrested and sent to Newgate. At his trial he declared that he meant to pay for everything he had ordered, that he owned an estate in Durham worth £1200 a year, but that it was heavily mortgaged. The case occupied some time, but in the end Day was sentenced to two years' imprisonment in Newgate, to stand twice in the pillory, find security for his good behaviour, and pay a fine of £200.

The cleverest swindles were often effected by the softer sex. Female sharpers infested all places of public resort. They dressed in the best clothes, and personating ladies of the highest fashion, attended entertainments and masquerades; they even succeeded in gaining admission to St. James's Palace, where they got into the general circle and pilfered right and left. One woman, the wife of a notorious Chevalier d'Industrie, was known to have been at court at the King's birthday (George III.). Her costume was in irreproachable good taste; her husband attended her in the garb of a dignitary of the Church. Between them they managed to levy contributions to the extent of £1700, and made off before these thefts were discovered or suspected. A notable female sharper was Elizabeth Harriet Grieve, whose line of business was to pretend that she possessed great influence at court, and promise preferment. She gave out that she was highly connected: Lord North was her first cousin, the Duke of Grafton her second; she was nearly related to Lady Fitz-Roy, and most intimate with Lord Guildford and other peers. In those days places were shamelessly bought and sold, and tradesmen retiring from business, or others who had amassed a little property, invested their savings in a situation under the Crown. When the law at length laid hands on the Hon. Elizabeth Harriet, as she styled herself, a great number of cases were brought against her. A coach-carver, whose trade was declining, had paid her £36 to obtain him a place as clerk in the Victualling Office. Another man gave her £30 down, with a conditional bond for £250, to get the place of a "coast" or "tide"-waiter. Both were defrauded. There were many more proved against her, and she was eventually sentenced to transportation.

She was only one of many who followed the same trade. David James Dignum was convicted in 1777 of pretending to sell places under Government, and sentenced to hard labour on the Thames. Dignum's was a barefaced kind of imposition. He went the length of handing his victims, in exchange for the fees, which were never less than a hundred guineas, a stamped parchment duly signed by the head of the public department, with seals properly attached. In one case he got £1000 for pretending to secure a person the office of "writer of the 'London Gazette.' " Of course the signatures to these instruments were forged, and the seals had been removed from some legal warrant. When the time came for Dignum's departure for the hulks, he resolved to go to Woolwich in state, and travelled down in a post-chaise, accompanied by his negro servant. But on reaching the ballast lighter on which Dignum was to work, his valet was refused admittance, and the convict was at once "put to the duty of the wheelbarrow." He made a desperate effort to get off by forging a cheque on Drummonds, which he got others to cash. They were arrested, but their innocence was clearly shown. Dignum had hoped to be brought up to London for examination. He had thought to change his lot, to exchange the hulks for Newgate, even at the risk of winding up at Tyburn. But in this he was foiled, as the authorities thought it best to institute no prosecution, but leave him to work out his time at the hulks.

That the dishonest and evilly-disposed should thus try to turn the malversation of public patronage to their own advantage was not strange. The traffic in places long flourished unchecked in a corrupt age, and almost under the very eyes of careless, not to say culpable, administrators. The evil practice culminated in the now nearly forgotten case of Mrs. Mary Ann Clarke, who undoubtedly profited liberally by her pernicious influence over the Duke of York when commander-in-chief of the army. The scandal was brought prominently before the public by Colonel Wardle, M.P., who charged her with carrying on a traffic in military commissions, not only with the knowledge, but the participation, of the Duke of York. A long inquiry followed, at which extraordinary disclosures were made. Mrs. Clarke was proved to have disposed of both military and ecclesiastical patronage. She gave her own footman a pair of colours, and procured for an Irish clergyman the honour of preaching before the King. Her brokership extended to any department of state, and her lists of applicants included numbers of persons in the best classes of society. The Duke of York was exonerated from the charge of deriving any pecuniary benefit from this disgraceful traffic; but it was clear that he was cognizant of Mrs. Clarke's proceedings, and that he knowingly permitted her to barter his patronage for filthy lucre. Mrs. Clarke was examined in person at the bar of the house. In the end a vote acquitted the duke of personal corruption, and the matter was allowed to drop. But a little later Colonel Wardle was sued by an upholsterer for furniture supplied at his order to Mrs. Clarke, and the disinterestedness of the colonel's exposure began to be questioned. In 1814 Mrs. Clarke was sentenced to nine months' imprisonment for a libel on the Irish Chancellor of the Exchequer.

A clever scheme of deception which went very near success was that perpetrated by Robert Jaques. Jaques filled the post of "clerk of the papers" to the warden of the Fleet, a place which he had himself solicited, on the plea that he was a man of experience, able to guard the warden against the tricks incident to his trust. Jaques admitted that his own antecedents were none of the best, that he had been frequently in gaol, but he pleaded that "men like himself, who had been guilty of the worst offences, had afterwards become the best officers." No sooner was Jaques appointed than he began to mature a plot against his employer. The warden of the Fleet by his office became responsible for the debt of any prisoner in his custody who might escape. Jaques at once cast about for some one whom he might through a third party cause to be arrested, brought to the Fleet on a sham action, and whom he would assist to escape. The third party's business would then be to sue the warden for the amount of the evaded debt. Jaques applied to a friend, Mr. Tronson, who had been a servant, an apothecary, a perfumer, and a quack doctor. Tronson found him one Shanley, a needy Irishman, short of stature and of fair complexion, altogether a person who might well be disguised as a woman. Jaques next arranged that a friend should get a warrant against Shanley for £450. Upon this, Shanley, who was easily found, being a "dressy young gentleman, fond of blue and gold," was arrested and carried to a spunging-house. While there a second writ was served upon Shanley for £850, at the suit of another friend of Jaques. Shanley was next transferred to the Fleet on a Habeas, applied for by a fictitious attorney. The very next Sunday, Jaques gave a dinner-party, at which his wife, a brother, Mr. John Jaques, and his wife, with some of the parties to the suits, and of course Shanley, were present. Later in the day Shanley exchanged clothes with Mrs. John Jaques, and, personating her, walked out of the prison. It was at a time when an under turnkey was on duty at the gate, and he let the disguised prisoner pass without question. By-and-by Mrs. Jaques got back her clothes, and also left. Shanley had meanwhile proceeded post haste to Dover, and so reached the continent.

As soon as the escape was discovered, suspicion fell on Jaques's friends, who were openly taxed with connivance. The matter looked worse for them when they laid claim to the money considered forfeited by the disappearance of the debtor, and the law stepped in to prosecute inquiry. The head turnkey, tracking Shanley to Calais, went in pursuit. At the same time a correspondence which was in progress between the conspirators on either side of the Channel was intercepted by order of the Secretary of State, and the letters handed over to the warden's solicitors. From these the whole plot was discovered, and the guilt of the parties rendered the more sure by the confession of Shanley. Jaques was arrested, tried, and convicted at the Old Bailey, receiving the sentence of three years' imprisonment, with one public exposure on the pillory at the Royal Exchange. A curious accident, however, helped to obtain the premature release of Jaques from Newgate. A Sir James Saunderson having been robbed of a large sum in cash and notes, portion of the stolen property was brought into Newgate by some of the thieves, who were arrested on another charge. The notes were intrusted to Jaques, who pretended he could raise money on them. Instead of this, he gave immediate notice to their rightful owner that he had them in his possession. Jaques afterwards petitioned Sir James Saunderson to interest himself in his behalf, and through this gentleman's good offices he escaped the exposure upon the pillory, and was eventually pardoned.

A peculiar feature in the criminal records of the early part of the present century was the general increase in juvenile depravity. This was remarked and commented upon by all concerned in the administration of justice: magistrates of all categories, police officers, gaolers, and philanthropists. It was borne out, moreover, by the statistics of the times. There were in the various London prisons, in the year 1816, three thousand inmates under twenty years of age. Nearly half of this number were under seventeen, and a thousand of these alone were convicted of felony. Many of those sent to prison were indeed of tender years. Some were barely nine or ten. Children began to steal when they could scarcely crawl. Cases were known of infants of barely six charged in the courts with crimes. This deplorable depravity was attributable to various causes: to the profligacy prevailing in the parish schools; the cruel and culpable neglect of parents who deserted their offspring, leaving them in a state of utter destitution, or were guilty of the no less disgraceful wickedness of using them as instruments for their nefarious designs; the artfulness of astute villains—prototypes of old Fagin—who trained the youthful idea in their own devious ways. The last-named was a fruitful source of juvenile crime. Children were long permitted to commit small thefts with impunity. The offence would have been death to those who used them as catspaws; for them capital punishment was humanely nearly impossible; moreover, the police officers ignored them till they "weighed their weight," or had been guilty of a forty-pound crime.[15] The education in iniquity continued steadily. They went from bad to worse, and ere long became regular inmates of "flash houses," where both sexes mixed freely with vicious companions of their own age, and the most daring enjoyed the hero-worship of their fellows. When thus assembled, they formed themselves into distinct parties or gangs, each choosing one of their number as captain, and dividing themselves into reliefs to work certain districts, one by day and by night. When they had "collared their swag," they returned to divide their plunder, having gained sometimes as much as three or four hundred pounds. A list of these horrible dens prepared about this date showed that there were two hundred of them, frequented by six thousand boys and girls, who lived solely by this way, or were the associates of thieves. These haunts were situated in St. Giles, Drury Lane, Chick Lane, Saffron Hill, the Borough, and Ratcliffe Highway. Others that were out of luck crowded the booths of Covent Garden, where all slept promiscuously amongst the rotting garbage of the stalls. During the daytime all were either actively engaged in thieving, or were revelling in low amusements. Gambling was a passion with them, indulged in without let or hindrance in the open streets; and from tossing buttons there they passed on to playing in the low publics at such games as "put," or "the rocks of Scylla," "bumble puppy," "tumble tumble," or "nine holes."

Still more demoralizing than the foregoing was the pernicious habit, commonly, but happily not invariably followed, of committing these young thieves to Newgate. Here these tyros were at once associated with the veterans and great leaders in crime. Old house-breakers expatiated upon their own deeds, and found eager and willing pupils among their youthful listeners. The elder and more evilly experienced boys soon debased and corrupted their juniors. One with twenty previous convictions against him, who had been in Newgate as often, would have alongside him an infant of seven or eight, sent to gaol for the first time for stealing a hearth-broom. It was as bad or worse for the females. Girls of twelve or thirteen were mixed up with the full-grown felons; one of the latter, as in a known case, who was what we should style in these days an habitual criminal, and who had been committed thirty times to Newgate, residing there generally nine months out of every twelve, was the wardswoman or prisoner-officer, with nearly unlimited power.

The crying evils of the system had moved private philanthropy to do something in remedy. Charitable schools, the forerunners of our modern reformatories, or the germ and nucleus of time-honoured institutions still flourishing, and worthy all praise, were started. I shall refer to these more particularly in a later chapter.[16] Other well-meaning people, each with their own pet scheme, began to theorize and propose the construction of juvenile penitentiaries, economical imitations mostly of the great penitentiary which was nearly completed at Millbank. But juvenile crime still grew and flourished, the offences were as numerous as ever, and their character was mostly the same. The most favourite pastime was that of picking pockets. Boys then as now were especially skilful at this in a crowd; short, active little chaps, they slipped through quickly with their booty, and passed it on to the master who was directing the operations. Shop-lifting, again, was much practised, the dodge being to creep along on hands and feet to the shop fronts of haberdashers and linen-drapers, and snatch what they could. Again, there were clever young thieves who could "starr" a pane in a window, and so get their hands through the glass. But there were boys convicted of highway robbery, like Joseph Wood and Thomas Underwood, one fourteen and the other twelve, both of whom were hanged. Another boy, barely sixteen, was executed for setting his master's house on fire. The young incendiary was pot-boy at a public-house, and having been reprimanded for neglect, vowed revenge. Another boy was condemned for forming one of a gang of boys and girls in a street robbery, who fell upon a man in liquor. The girls attacked him, and the boys stripped him of all he had.

Perhaps the most astounding precocity in crime was that displayed by a boy named Leary, who was tried and sentenced to death at thirteen years of age for stealing a watch and chain from some chambers in the Temple. He began at the early age of eight, and progressed regularly from stealing apples to burglary and household robbery. He learnt the trade first from a companion at school. After exacting toll from the tart-shops, he took to stealing bakers' loaves, then money from shop counters and tills, or breaking shop windows and drawing their contents through. He often appeared at school with several pounds in his pocket, the proceeds of his depredations. He soon became captain of a gang known as Leary's gang, who drove about, armed with pistols, in a cart, watching for carriages with the trunks fastened outside, which they could cut away. In these excursions the gang was often out for a week or more, Leary's share of the profits amounting sometimes to £100. Once, the result of several robberies in and about London, he amassed some £350, but the money was partly stolen from him by older thieves, or he squandered it in gambling, or in the flash houses. After committing innumerable depredations, he was captured in a gentleman's dining-room in the act of abstracting a quantity of plate. He was found guilty, but out of compassion committed to the Philanthropic School. He was recaptured, however, and eventually sentenced to transportation for life.

The prevailing tastes of the populace were in these times low and depraved. Their amusements were brutal, their manners and customs disreputable, their morality at the lowest ebb. It is actually on record that little more than a hundred years ago a man and his wife were convicted of offering their niece, "a fine young girl, apparently fourteen years of age," for sale at the Royal Exchange. Mr. and Mrs. Crouch were residents of Bodmin, Cornwall, to which remote spot came a report that "maidens were very scarce in London, and that they sold there for a good price." They accordingly travelled up to town by road, two hundred and thirty-two miles, and on arrival hawked the poor girl about the streets. At length they "accosted an honest captain of a ship, who instantly made known the base proposal they had made to him." The Crouches were arrested and tried; the man was sentenced to six months' imprisonment in Newgate, but his wife, as having acted under his influence, was acquitted.

Traffic in dead bodies was more actively prosecuted. The wretches who gained the name of Resurrection men despoiled graveyards to purvey subjects for the dissecting knife. There were dealers who traded openly in these terrible goods, and, as has been seen in the chapter on executions, their agents haggled for corpses at the foot of the gallows. Sometimes the culprits were themselves the guardians of the sacred precincts. I find that the grave-digger of St. George's, Bloomsbury, was convicted, with a female accomplice, of stealing a dead body, and sentenced to imprisonment. They were also "whipped twice on their bare backs from the end of King's Gate Street, Holborn, to Dyot Street, St. Giles, being half a mile." To this crime, and its development in the persons of Burke and Hare, I shall recur on a later page.

Disorderly gatherings for the prosecution of the popular sports were of constant occurrence. The vice of gambling was openly practised in the streets. It was also greatly fostered by the metropolitan fairs, of which there were eighty annually, lasting from Easter to September, when Bartholomew Fair was held. These fairs were the resort of the idle and the profligate, and most of the desperate characters in London were included in the crowd. Another favourite amusement was bull-baiting or bullock-hunting. Sunday morning was generally chosen for this pastime. A subscription was made to pay the hire of an animal from some drover or butcher, which was forthwith driven through the most populous parts of the town; often across church-yards when divine service was in progress, pursued by a yelling mob, who goaded the poor brute to madness with sharp pointed sticks, or thrust peas into its ears. When nearly dead the poor beast rejoined its herd, and was driven on to Smithfield market. A system of bull-baits was introduced at Westminster by two notorious characters known as Caleb Baldwin and Hubbersfield, otherwise Slender Billy, which attracted great crowds, and led to drunkenness and scenes of great disorder.

Towards the close of the eighteenth century a still lower and more debasing amusement sprang suddenly into widespread popularity. The patronage of pugilism or prize-fighting was no doubt supposed by many to be the glorification of the national virtues of courage and endurance. It was also greatly due to the gradual disuse of the practice of carrying side-arms, when it was thought that quarrels would be fought out with fists instead of swords. Hence the "noble art of self-defence," as it was styled magniloquently, found supporters in every class of society. Prize-fights first became fashionable about 1788, following a great encounter between two noted pugilists, named Richard Humphreys and Daniel Mendoza, a Jew. Sporting papers were filled with accounts of the various fights, which peer and pickpocket attended side by side, and which even a Royal Prince did not disdain to honour. These professional bruisers owned many noble patrons. Besides, the Prince of Wales, the Dukes of Clarence and York, the Duke of Hamilton, Lords Barrymore and others, attended prize-fights and sparring matches at theatres and public places. A well-known pugilist, who was summoned for an assault at Covent Garden Theatre, brought forward in his defence the terms of intimacy he was on with noted people; the very day on which he was charged, that he had dined at the Piazza Coffee House with General Gwynne, Colonel McDouel, Captains Barkley and Hanbury, after which they had all gone to the theatre. These aristocratic friends were, moreover, ready to be useful at a pinch, and would bail out a pugilist in trouble, or give him their countenance and support. At the trial of one William Ward, who had killed a man in a fight, the pugilist was attended by his patrons in court. The case was a bad one. Ward, on his way to see a fight in the country, had been challenged by a drunken blacksmith, and proved to him after a few rounds that he was no match for the trained bruiser. The blacksmith did not like his "punishment," and tried to escape into the bar, when his antagonist followed him, and actually beat him to death. At the trial Ward was found guilty of manslaughter, fined one shilling, and only sentenced to be imprisoned three months in Newgate. Yet the judge who inflicted this light punishment condemned boxing as an inhuman and disgraceful practice, a disgrace to any civilized nation.

To the foregoing categories of undoubted criminals must be added another pretty numerous class of offenders, who were at least so deemed by contemporary codes, and who now frequently found themselves relegated to Newgate. These were days when the press had far from achieved its present independence; when writers, chafing under restraints and reckless of consequence, were tempted into licence from sheer bravado and opposition; when others far more innocent were brought under the same ban of the law, and suffered imprisonment and fine for a hardly unwarrantable freedom of speech. It is to be feared that the frequent prosecutions instituted had often their origin in political antipathy. While ministerial prints might libel and revile the opponents of the governments, journals which did not spare the party in power were humiliated and brow-beaten, difficulties were thrown in the way of their obtaining intelligence, and if they dared to express their opinions freely, "an information *ex officio*," as it was styled, was issued by the Attorney-General. Prosecution followed, protracted to the bitter end. Even what seems to us the harmless practice of parliamentary reporting was deemed a breach of privilege; it was tolerated, but never expressly permitted. Offending journalists were often reprimanded at the bar of the House, and any member who felt aggrieved at the language attributed to him was at liberty to claim the protection of the House. When legislators and executive were so sensitive, it was hardly likely that the great ones, the supposed salt of the earth, should be less thin-skinned. Any kind of criticism upon princes of the blood was looked upon as rank blasphemy; the morals of a not blameless or too reputable aristocracy were guaranteed immunity from attack, while the ecclesiastical hierarchy was apparently not strong enough to vindicate its tenets or position without having recourse to the secular arm.

As time passed, the early martyrs to freedom of speech, such men as Prynne Bastwick and Daniel Defoe, were followed by many victims to similar oppression. One of the first to suffer after Defoe was the nonjuring clergyman Lawrence Howell, who died in Newgate. He was prosecuted about 1720 for writing a pamphlet in which he denounced George I. as a usurper. He was tried at the Old Bailey, convicted, and sentenced to pay a fine of £500 to the king, to find sureties for an additional sum, to be imprisoned in Newgate for three years, and during that term to be twice whipped. He was also to be degraded and stripped of his gown by the common executioner. Howell asked indignantly of his judges, "Who will whip a clergyman?" "We pay no deference to your cloth," replied the court, "because you are a disgrace to it, and have no right to wear it." The validity of his ordination was also denied by the court, and as Howell continued to protest, the hangman was ordered to tear off his gown as he stood there at the bar. The public whipping was not inflicted, but Howell died soon afterwards in Newgate.

Next came Nathaniel Mist, who was sentenced in 1721 to stand in the pillory, to pay a fine, and suffer imprisonment for reflecting upon the action of George I. as regards the Protestants in the Palatinate. His paper, the 'Weekly Journal' or 'Saturday's Post,' was notoriously Jacobite in its views. Soon afterwards he came under the displeasure of the House of Commons for instituting comparisons between the times of the '15 rebellion and those which followed, and was committed to Newgate for uttering a "false, malicious, and scandalous libel." This interference by the House with Mist's publications in a matter which did not concern its privileges is characterized by Hallam as an extraordinary assumption of parliamentary power. Tom Paine, whose rationalist writings gained him much obloquy later on, was one of the next in point of time to feel the arm of the law. In 1724 he was convicted of three libels on the Government, fined £100, and imprisoned for a year. A clergyman, William Rowland, was put in the pillory in 1729 for commenting too freely in print on two magistrates who had failed to convict and punish prisoners charged with unnatural crimes. Mr. Rowland was pilloried in his canonical habit, and preached all the time to the multitude, complaining of the injustice of his sentence, "whereupon the people, and amongst them were several women, made a collection for him."

About 1730, newspapers were especially established for purposes of political party warfare, and each side libelled or prosecuted the other in turn. The 'Craftsman' about this date sprang into the first rank for wit and invective. Its editors were constantly in trouble; the statesmen who supported it had to defend their bantling with their swords. In 1738 the printer, Henry Haines, was sentenced to two years' imprisonment for producing the paper. In 1759 Dr. Shebbeare was fined, put in the pillory, and imprisoned for three years, his offence being the publication of what was deemed a scandalous libel in his 'Sixth Letter to the English People.' Four years later, John Wilkes, M.P., started the 'North Briton,' a Liberal print, in opposition to Smollet's 'Briton,' a Tory paper, which was subsidized and supported by Lord Bute, then in power. John Wilkes was no doubt assisted by Lord Temple and John Churchill the satirist. The 'North Briton' had been intended to assail Lord Bute's government, but it was not until its forty-fifth number that the dash and boldness of its contributors attracted general attention. In this number a writer rashly accused the king of falsehood.[17] The matter was at once taken up; proceedings were instituted against printer and publisher, who were arrested, as was also Wilkes. These arrests subsequently formed the subject of lengthy lawsuits; they were in the end declared illegal, and all three got heavy damages. Wilkes was, however, expelled from the House, by whose order the offending numbers of the 'North Briton' were burnt by the common hangman. But these measures did not extinguish the 'North Briton,' which was continued as far as the two hundred and seventeenth number, when Mr. William Bingley, a bookseller, who at that time owned it, was committed to Newgate, and kept there a couple of years for refusing to reply to interrogatories connected with an earlier number of the paper. Wilkes, who had fled to France to escape imprisonment, next fell under the displeasure of the House of Lords. The 'London Evening Post,' a paper which had already come into collision with the Commons for presuming to publish reports of debates, committed the seemingly venial offence of inserting a letter from Wilkes, in which he commented rather freely upon a peer of the realm at that time British Ambassador in Paris. The House of Lords could not touch Wilkes, but they took proceedings against the printer for breach of privilege in presuming to mention the name of one of its members,[18] and fined him £100. The precedent soon became popular, and in succeeding sessions printers were constantly fined whenever they mentioned, even by accident, the name of a peer.

Journalism was in these days an ill-used profession. The reign of George III. must always be remembered as a time when newspapers and those who wrote them were at the mercy of the people in power. Grant[19] declares that the despotic and tyrannical treatment of the press during the several administrations under George III. had no parallel in English history. The executive was capriciously sensitive to criticism, and readily roused to extreme measures. No newspaper indeed was safe; the editors of Liberal prints, or their contributors, who touched on political subjects were at the mercy of the Attorney-General. Any morning's issue might be made the subject of a prosecution, and every independent writer on the wrong side went in daily dread of fine, the pillory, or committal to Newgate.[20] Among the early records of the great organ which custom has long honoured with the title of the "leading journal," are several instances of the dangers journalists ran. The 'Daily Universal Register,' started by the first Mr. John Walter in 1785, became the 'Times' in 1788. On the 11th July, 1789, the publisher—at that time Mr. Walter himself—of the paper was tried and convicted of alleged libels on three royal dukes, York, Gloucester, and Cumberland, whose joy at the recovery of the king the 'Times' dared to characterize as "insincere." The sentence decreed and inflicted was a fine of £50, imprisonment in Newgate for one year, and exposure on the pillory at Charing Cross. A second prosecution followed, intended to protect, and if possible rehabilitate, the Prince of Wales, and Mr. Walter, having been brought from Newgate for the trial, was sentenced to a further fine of £100, and a like sum for a libel on the Duke of Clarence. Mr. Walter remained in Newgate for eighteen months, and was released in March 1791, having been pardoned at the instance of the Prince of Wales.

Nor was the law invoked in favour of our own princes alone. A few years later a foreign monarch obtained equal protection, and the editor, printer, and publisher of the 'Courier' were fined and imprisoned for stigmatizing the Czar of Russia as a tyrant among his own subjects, and ridiculous to the rest of Europe. The House of Peers, including the Bench of Bishops, continued very sensitive. In 1799 the printer of the 'Cambridge Intelligence' was brought to the bar of the House, charged for reflecting on the speech of the Bishop of Llandaff concerning the union with

Ireland. Lord Grenville moved that the printer should be fined £100 and committed to Newgate; Lord Holland protested, but it was justified by Lord Kenyon, and the motion was carried. Lord Kenyon did not spare the unfortunates arraigned before him for libel. One Thomas Spence, who published a pamphlet called 'Spence's Restorer of Society,' in which the abolition of private ownership of land was advocated, and its investment in parishes for the good of the public at large, was brought before Lord Kenyon, and sentenced by him to twelve months' imprisonment and a fine of £50. Another peer, Lord Ellenborough, who prosecuted Messrs. White and Hart for a libel in 1808, obtained a conviction against them, and a sentence of three years' imprisonment.

In 1810 the House of Commons distinguished itself by a prosecution which led to rather serious consequences. At a debate on the Walcheren expedition, a member, Mr. Yorke, had insisted from day to day upon the exclusion of strangers, and another, Mr. Windham, had inveighed violently against press reporting. Upon this a question was discussed at a debating society known as the "British Forum," as to whether Mr. Yorke's or Mr. Windham's conduct was the greater outrage on the public feeling. The decision was given against Mr. Yorke, and the result announced in a placard outside. This placard was constituted a breach of privilege, "comment upon the proceedings of the House being deemed a contravention of the Bill of Rights." A Mr. John Gale Jones confessing himself the author of the placard, he was forthwith committed to Newgate. Sir Francis Burdett took Jones' part, and published his protest, signed, in Cobbett's 'Weekly Register.' The House on this ordered the Sergeant-at-arms to arrest Sir Francis and take him to the Tower. Sir Francis resisted, and was carried off by force.[21] A riot occurred *en route*, the crowd attacked the escort, and the troops fired, with fatal consequences, upon the crowd. Sir Francis appealed to the law courts, which in the end refused to take cognizance of the questions at issue, and he was released, returning home in triumph. Mr. John Gale Jones claimed to be tried, and refused to leave Newgate without it; but he was got out by a stratagem, loudly complaining that he had been illegally imprisoned, and illegally thrust out. Jones was sentenced in the autumn of the same year to twelve months' imprisonment in Coldbath Fields Gaol. Another and a better known writer found himself in Newgate about this time. In 1810 William Cobbett was tried for animadverting too openly upon the indignity of subjecting English soldiers to corporal punishment, for which he was sentenced to two years' imprisonment in Newgate, and a fine of £1000. This was not his first prosecution, but it was by far the most serious. Shorter sentences of imprisonment were imposed on his printers and publishers, Messrs. Hansard, Budd, and Bagshaw.

Some other notable criminals found themselves in Newgate about this date. In 1809 it became the place of punishment for two Government officials who were convicted of embezzlement on a large scale. The first, Mr. Alexander Davison, was employed to purchase barrack-stores for the Government on commission. He was intrusted with this duty by the barrack-master general, as a person of extensive mercantile experience, to avoid the uncertainty of trusting to contractors. Mr. Davison was to receive a commission of 2½ per cent. Instead of buying in the best and cheapest markets, he himself became the seller, thus making a profit on the goods and receiving the commission as well; or, in the words of Mr. Justice Grose, Davison, when "receiving a stipend to check the frauds of others, and insure the best commodities at the cheapest rate, became the tradesman and seller of the article, and had thereby an interest to increase his own profit, and to commit that fraud it was his duty to prevent." Davison disgorged some £18,000 of his ill-won profits, and this was taken into consideration in his sentence, which was limited to imprisonment in Newgate for twenty-one months. The other delinquent was Mr. Valentine Jones, who had been appointed commissary-general and superintendent of forage and provisions in the West Indies in 1795. A large British force was at that time stationed in the West Indian Islands, which entailed vast disbursements from the public exchequer. The whole of this money passed through the hands of Mr. Jones. His career of fraud began directly he took over his duties. Mr. Higgins, a local merchant, came to him proposing to renew contracts for the supply of the troops, but Mr. Jones would only consent to their renewal on condition that he shared Mr. Higgins' profits. Higgins protested, but at length yielded. Within three years the enormous sum of £87,000 sterling was paid over to Jones as his share in this nefarious transaction. Mr. Jones was tried at the King's Bench and sentenced to three years' imprisonment in Newgate.

Soon afterwards a person of very high rank was committed to Newgate. This was the Marquis of Sligo, who was convicted of enticing British men-of-war's men to desert, and sentenced to imprisonment, with a fine of £5000. Lord Sligo went to Malta soon after leaving College, and there hired a brig, the 'Pylades,' intending to make a yachting tour in the Grecian Archipelago. The admiral at Malta and other naval officers helped Lord Sligo to fit out the 'Pylades,' and he was welcomed on board the various king's ships. From one of these several trusty seamen were shortly afterwards missing. Their captain trusted to Lord Sligo's honour that he had not decoyed these men, and that he would not receive them; but at that moment the deserters were actually on board the 'Pylades,' having been enticed from the service by Lord Sligo's servants. The 'Pylades' then went on her cruise along the Mediterranean. Suspicion seems to have still rested on Lord Sligo, and after leaving Palermo the 'Pylades' was chased and brought to by H.M.S. 'Active.' A boat boarded the

'Pylades,' her crew was mustered and examined, but the deserters had been securely hidden in the after hold, and were not discovered. A little later Lord Sligo sailed for Patmos, where some of the crew landed and were left behind; among them were the men-of-war's-men, through whom the whole affair was brought to light. Lord Sligo was arrested on his return to England, and tried at the Old Bailey. The evidence was conclusive. In the course of the trial a letter was put in from Lord Sligo, to the effect that if the business was brought into court he should do his best to defend himself; if he did not succeed, he had an ample fortune, and could pay the fines. No money, however, could save him from incarceration, and in accordance with the sentence of Sir William Scott, who was supported on the bench by Lord Ellenborough and Mr. Baron Thompson, the Marquis of Sligo was sent to Newgate for four months.

NEWGATE DOWN TO 1818

Newgate still overcrowded—Some statistics—Description of interior—The various "sides" and wards—Their dimensions and uses—Debtors in Middlesex, generally paltry debts and colossal costs—Various debtors' prisons in London described—The King's Bench—The Fleet—The Marshalsea—The Compters, Ludgate, Giltspur Street, and Borough—Debtors in Newgate—Fees extorted—Garnish—Scanty food—Little bedding—Squalor and wretchedness prevail throughout—Constant quarrels and fighting—Discipline maintained only by prisoner wardsmen—Their tyranny and extortion—A new debtors' prison indispensable—Building of Whitecross Street—The criminal side—Indiscriminate association of all classes—The middle yard greatly crowded with transports awaiting deportation, and with whom mere children were constantly mixed—Deterioration rapid—Mock courts for trials of new-comers who would not adopt the ways of the gaol—Case of a decent man completely ruined—Greater ease in the master felons' side—Fees—The best accommodation was in the state side, and open to all who could pay—High fees charged—Cobbett in state side, and the

Marquis of Sligo—The press yard—Recklessness of the condemned—Cashman—The condemned cells—Summary of glaring defects in Newgate—Scanty diet—Irons—Visitors admitted in crowds, including low females—Crimes constantly being hatched in Newgate—The Corporation roused to reform Newgate—Appoint committee to examine other gaols—Its report, and many useful recommendations—Few are carried out.

UNDER the conditions referred to in the previous chapter, with criminals and misdemeanants of all shades crowding perpetually into its narrow limits, the latter state of Newgate was worse than the first. The new gaol fell as far short of the demands made on it as did the old. The prison population fluctuated a great deal, but it was almost always in excess of the accommodation available, and there were times when the place was full to overflowing. Neild[22] gives some figures which well illustrate this. On the 14th June, 1800, there were 199 debtors and 289 felons in the prison. On the 27th April, in the following year, these numbers had risen to 275 and 375 respectively, or 650 in all. For two more years these high figures were steadily maintained, and in 1803 the total rose to 710. After that they fell as steadily, till, 1808, the lowest point was touched of 197 debtors and 182 felons, or 379 in all. The numbers soon increased, however, and by 1811 had again risen to 629; and Mr. Neild was told that there had been at one time 300 debtors and 900 criminals in Newgate, or 1200 prisoners in all. Previous to that date there had been 700 or 800 frequently, and once, in Mr. Akerman's time, 1000. Trustworthy evidence is forthcoming to the effect that these high figures were constantly maintained for many months at a time. The inadequacy of the gaol was noticed and reported upon again and again by the grand juries of the city of London, who seldom let a session go by without visiting Newgate. In 1813 the grand jury made a special presentment to the Court of Common Council, pointing out that on the debtors' side, which was intended for only 100, no less than 340 were crowded, to the great inconvenience and danger of the inmates. On the female side matters were much worse; "the apartments set apart for them, being built to accommodate 60 persons, now contain about 120." Returns laid before the House of Commons showed that 6439 persons had been committed to Newgate in the three years between 1813 and 1816, and this number did not include the debtors, a numerous class, who were still committed to Newgate pending the completion of the White Cross Street prison.

In order to realize the evils entailed by incarceration in Newgate in these days, it is necessary to give some account of its interior as it was occupied and appropriated in 1810. Full details of the arrangements are to be found in Mr. Neild's 'State of Prisons in England, Scotland, and Wales,' published in 1812. The gaol at that date was divided into eight separate and more or less distinct departments, each of which had its own wards and yard. These were—

i. The male debtors' side. ii. The female debtors' side. iii. The chapel yard. iv. The middle yard. v. The master felons' side. vi. The female felons' side. vii. The state side. viii. The press yard. i. The male debtors' side consisted of a yard forty-nine feet by thirty-one, leading to thirteen wards on various floors, and a day room. Of these wards, three were appropriated to the "cabin side," so called because they each contained four small rooms or "cabins" seven feet square, intended to accommodate a couple of prisoners apiece, but often much more crowded.[23] Two other wards were appropriated to the master's side debtors; they were each twenty-three feet by fourteen and a half, and supposed to accommodate twenty persons. The eight remaining wards were for the common side debtors, long narrow rooms—one thirty-six feet, six twenty-three feet, and the eighth eighteen, the whole about fifteen feet wide. The various wards were all about eleven feet in height, and were occupied as a rule by ten to fifteen people when the prison was not crowded, but double the number was occasionally placed in them. The day room was fitted with benches and settles after the manner of the tap in a public-house.

ii. The female debtors' side consisted of a court-yard forty-nine by sixteen feet, leading to two wards, one of which was thirty-six feet by fifteen, and the other eighteen by fifteen; and they nominally held twenty-two persons. A high wall fifteen feet in height divided the females' court-yard from the men's.

iii. The chapel yard was about forty-three feet by twenty-five. It had been for some time devoted principally to felons of the worst types, those who were the oldest offenders, sentenced to transportation, and who had narrowly escaped the penalty of death. This arrangement was, however, modified after 1811, and the chapel yard was allotted to misdemeanants and prisoners awaiting trial. The wards in this part were five in number, all in dimensions twenty feet by fifteen, with a sixth ward fifteen feet square. These wards were all fitted with barrack-beds, but no bedding was supplied. The chapel yard led to the chapel, and on the staircase were two rooms frequently set apart for the king's witnesses, those who had turned king's evidence, whose safety might have been imperilled had they been lodged with the men against whom they had informed. But these king's witnesses were also put at times into the press yard among the capital convicts, seemingly a very dangerous proceeding, or they lodged with the gatesmen, the prisoner officers who had charge of the inner gates.

iv. The middle yard was at first given up to the least heinous offenders. After 1812 it changed functions with the chapel yard. It was fifty feet by twenty-five, and had five wards each thirty-eight by fifteen. At one end of the yard was an arcade, directly under the chapel, in which there were three cells, used either for the confinement of disorderly and refractory prisoners, or female convicts ordered for execution.

v. The master felons' side consisted of a yard the same size as the preceding, appropriated nominally to the most decent and better-behaved prisoners, but really kept for the few who had funds sufficient to gain them admission to these more comfortable quarters. Here were also lodged the gatesmen, the prisoners who had charge of the inner gates, and who were intrusted with the duty of escorting visitors from the gates to the various wards their friends occupied.

vi. The state side was the part stolen from the female felons' side. It was large and comparatively commodious, being maintained on a better footing than any other part of the prison. The inmates were privileged, either by antecedents or the fortunate possession of sufficient funds to pay the charges of the place. Neild takes it for granted that the former rather than the latter prevailed in the selection, and tells us that in the state side "such prisoners were safely associated whose manners and conduct evince a more liberal style of education, and who are therefore lodged apart from all other districts of the gaol." The state side contained twelve good-sized rooms, from twenty-one by eighteen feet to fifteen feet square, which were furnished with bedsteads and bedding.

vii. The press yard was that part set aside for the condemned. Its name and its situation were the same as those of the old place of carrying out the terrible sentence inflicted on accused persons who stood mute.[24] The long narrow yard still remained as we saw it in Jacobite times, and beyond it was now a day room for the capital convicts or those awaiting execution. Beyond the press yard were three stories, condemned cells, fifteen in all, with vaulted ceilings nine feet high to the crown of the arch. The ground floor cells were nine feet by six; those on the first floor were rather larger on account of a set-off in the wall; and the uppermost were the largest, for the same reason. Security was provided for in these condemned cells by lining the substantial stone walls with planks studded with broad-headed nails; they were lighted by a double-grated window two feet nine inches by fourteen inches; and in the doors, which were four inches thick, a circular aperture had been let in to give ventilation and secure a free current of air. In each cell there was a barrack bedstead on the floor without bedding.

viii. The female felons were deprived of part of the space which the architect had intended for them. More than half their quadrangle had been partitioned off for another purpose, and what remained was divided into a master's and a common side for female felons. The two yards were adjoining, that for the common side much the largest. There were nine wards in all on the female side, one of them in the attic, with four casements and two fireplaces, being allotted for a female infirmary, and the rest being provided with barrack beds, and in dimensions varying from thirty feet by fifteen to fifteen feet by ten.

The eight courts above enumerated were well supplied with water; they had dust-bins, sewers, and so forth, "properly disposed,"[25] and the city scavenger paid periodical visits to the prison. The prisoners had few comforts, beyond the occasional use of a bath at some distance, situated in the press yard, to which access was granted rarely and as a great favour. But they were allowed the luxury of drink—if they could pay for it. A recent reform had closed the tap kept by the gaoler within the precincts, but there was still a "convenient room" which served, and "near it a grating through which the debtors receive their beer from the neighbouring public-houses. The felons' side has a similar accommodation, and this mode of introducing the beverage is adopted because no publican as such can be permitted to enter the interior of this prison."[26] The tap-room and bar were just behind the felons' entrance lodge, and beyond it was a room called the "wine room," because formerly used for the sale of wine, but in which latterly a copper had been fixed for the cooking of provisions sent in by charitable persons. "On the top of the gaol," continues Neild, "are a watch-house and a sentry-box, where two or more guards, with dogs and firearms, watch all night. Adjoining the felons' side lodge is the keeper's office, where the prison books are kept, and his clerk, called the clerk of the papers, attends daily."[27]

Having thus briefly described the plan and appropriation of the prison, I propose to deal now with the general condition of the inmates, and the manner of their life. Of these the debtors, male and female, formed a large proportion. The frequency and extent of processes against debtors seventy or eighty years ago will appear almost incredible in an age when insolvent acts and bankruptcy courts do so much to relieve the impecunious, and imprisonment for debt has almost entirely disappeared.[28] But at the time of which I am writing the laws were relentless against all who failed to meet their engagements. The number of processes against debtors annually was extraordinary. Neild gives, on the authority of Mr. Burchell, the under sheriff of Middlesex, a table showing the figures for the year ending Michaelmas 1802. In that period upwards of 200,000 writs had been issued for the arrests of debtors in the kingdom, for sums varying from fourpence to £500 and upwards. Fifteen thousand of these were issued in Middlesex alone, which at that time was reckoned as only a fifteenth of Great Britain. The number of arrests actually made was 114,300 for the kingdom, and 7020 for Middlesex. Barely half of these gave bail bonds on arrests, and the remainder went to prison. Quite half of the foregoing writs and arrests applied to sums under £30. Neild also says that in 1793, 5719 writs and executions for debts between £10 and £20 were issued in Middlesex, and the aggregate amount of debts sued for was £81,791. He also makes the curious calculation that the costs of these actions if undefended would have amounted to £68,728, and if defended, £285,950; in other words, that to recover eighty odd thousand pounds, three times the amount would be expended.

An elaborate machinery planned for the protection of the trader, and altogether on his side, had long existed for the recovery of debts. Alfred the Great established the Court Baron, the Hundred Court, and the County Court, which among other matters entertained pleas for debt. The County Court was the sheriff's, who sat there surrounded by the bishop and the magnates of the county; but as time passed, difficulties and delays in obtaining judgment led to the removal of causes to the great Court of King's Bench, and the disuse of the inferior courts. So much inconvenience ensued, that in 1518 the Corporation obtained from Parliament an act empowering two aldermen and four common councilmen to hold Courts of Requests, or Courts of Conscience, to hear and determine all causes of debt under 40s. arising within the city. These courts were extended two centuries later to several large provincial towns, and all were in full activity when Neild wrote, and indeed supplied the bulk of the poor debtors committed to prison. These courts were open to many and grave objections. The commissioners who presided were "little otherwise than self-elected,[29] and when once appointed continued to serve *sine die*;"[30] they were generally near in rank to the parties whose causes they decided. Often a commissioner had to leave the bench because he was himself a party to the suit that was *sub judice*. The activity as well as the futility of these courts may be estimated from the statement given by Neild, that 1312 debtors were committed by them to Newgate between 1797 and 1808, and that no more than 197 creditors recovered debts and costs. The latter indeed hung like millstones round the neck of the unhappy insolvent wretches who found themselves in limbo. Costs were the gallons of sack to the pennyworth of debt. Neild found at his visit to Newgate in 1810, fourteen men and women who had lain there ten, eleven, and thirteen years for debts of a few shillings, weighted by treble the amount of costs. Thus, amongst others, Thomas Blackburn had been committed on October 15th for a debt of 1s. 5d., for which the costs were 6s. 10d. Thomas Dobson, on 22nd August, 1799, for 1s., with costs of 8s. 10d.; and Susannah Evans, in October the same year, for 2s., with costs of 6s. 8d. Other cases are recorded elsewhere, as at the Giltspur Street Compter, where in 1805 Mr. Neild found a man named William Grant detained for 1s. 9d., with costs of 5s., and John Lancaster for 1s. 8d., with costs of 7s. 6d. "These surely, I thought," says Mr. Neild, "were bad enough! But it was not so." He recites another most outrageous and extraordinary case, in which one John Bird, a market porter, was arrested and committed at the suit of a publican for the paltry sum of 4d., with costs of 7s. 6d. Bird was, however, discharged within three days by a subscription raised among his fellow-prisoners.

Mr. Buxton, in his 'Inquiry into the System of Prison Discipline,' quotes a case which came within his own knowledge of a boy sent to prison for non-payment of one penny. The lad in question was found in Coldbath Fields prison, to which he had been sent for a month in default of paying a fine of forty shillings. He had been in the employ of a corn-chandler at Islington, and went into London with his master's cart and horse. There was in the City Road a temporary bar, with a collector of tolls who was sometimes on the spot and sometimes not. The boy declared he saw no one, and accordingly passed through without paying the toll of a penny. For this he was summoned before a magistrate, and sentenced as already stated. The lad was proved to be of good character and the son of respectable parents. Mr. Buxton's friends at once paid the forty shillings, and the boy was released.

The costs in heavier debts always doubled the sum; if the arrest was made in the country it trebled it. Neild gives a list of the various items charged upon a debt of £10, which included instructions to sue, affidavit of debt, drawing præcipe (£1 5s.), capias, fee to officer on arrest, affidavit of service, and many more, amounting in all to twenty-seven, and costing £11 15s. 8d., within ten days.[31]

Before dealing with the debtors in Newgate, I may refer incidentally to those in other London prisons, for Newgate was not the only place of durance for these unfortunate people. There were also the King's Bench, the Fleet, and the Marshalsea prisons especially devoted to them, whilst Ludgate, the Giltspur Street, and Borough Compters also received them—the latter two being also a prison for felons and vagrants arrested within certain limits.

The King's Bench was a national prison, in which were confined all debtors arrested for debt or for contempt of the court of the King's Bench. The population generally amounted to from five hundred to seven hundred, the accommodation being calculated for two hundred. Every new-comer was entitled to a "chummage" ticket, but did not always get it, being often obliged to pay a high rent for a bed at the coffee-house or in some room which was vacated by its regular occupant. No fixed rates or rules governed the hiring out of rooms or parts of a room, and all sorts of imposition was practised. The best, or at least the most influential prisoners, got lodging in the State House, which contained "eight large handsome rooms." Besides those actually resident within the walls, another two hundred more or less took advantage of "the rules," and lived outside within a circumference of two miles and a half. In these cases security was given for the amount of the debt, and a heavy fee at the rate of £8 per £100, with £4 for every additional hundred. Besides these, a number had the privilege of a "run on the key," which allowed a prisoner to go into the rules for the day. The foregoing rentals and payments for privileges, together with fees exacted on commitment and discharge, went to the marshal or keeper of the prison, whose net annual income thus entirely derived from the impecunious amounted to between three and four thousand pounds. The office of marshal had been hereditary, but in the 27th Geo. II. the right of presentation was bought by the Crown for £10,500. The marshal was supposed to be resident either within the prison or the rules. He seems to have felt no responsibility as to the welfare or comfort of those in charge, and out of whom he made all his money. The prison was always in "the most filthy state imaginable."[32] The half or wholly starved prisoners fished for alms or food at the gratings. When they were sick no more notice was taken of them than of a dog. A man dying of liver complaint lay on the cold stones without a bed or food to eat. Dissolute habits prevailed on all sides; drunkenness was universal, gambling perpetual. The yards were taken up with rackets and five courts, and here and there were "bumble puppy grounds," a game in which the players rolled iron balls into holes marked with numbers. How to make most profit out of the wretched denizens of the gaol was the marshal's only care. He got a rent for the coffee-house and the bake-house; the keeper of the large tap-room called the Brace, because it was once kept by two brothers named Partridge, also paid him toll. The sale of spirits was forbidden, but gin could always be had at the whistling shops, where it was known as Moonshine, Sky Blue, Mexico, and was consumed at the rate of a hogshead per week.

The Fleet, which stood in Farringdon Street, was a prison for debtors and persons committed for contempt by the courts of Chancery, Exchequer, and Common Pleas. It was so used for the date of the abolition of the Star Chamber in the 16th Charles I. The shameful malpractices of Bambridge, the warden of the

Fleet at the commencement of the eighteenth century, are too well known to need more than a passing reference. A committee of the House of Commons investigated the charges against Bambridge, who was proved to have connived at the escape of some debtors, and to have been guilty of extortion to others. One Sir William Rich, Bart., he had loaded with heavy irons. In consequence of these disclosures, both Bambridge and Huggin, his predecessor in the office, were committed to Newgate, and many reforms instituted. But the condition of the prison and its inmates remained unsatisfactory to the last. It contained generally from six to seven hundred inmates,[33] while another hundred more or less resided in the rules outside. The principle of "chummage" prevailed as in the King's Bench, but a number of rooms, fifteen more or less, were reserved for poor debtors under the name of Bartholomew Fair. The rentals of rooms and fees went to the warden, whose income was £2372. The same evils of overcrowding, uncleanliness, want of medical attendance, absence or neglect of divine service, were present as in the King's Bench, but in an exaggerated form. The Committee on Gaols[34] reported that "although the house of the warden looked into the court, and the turnkeys slept in the prison, yet scenes of riot, drunkenness, and disorder were most prevalent." The state of morals was disgraceful. Any woman obtained admission if sober, and if she got drunk she was not turned out. There was no distinct place for the female debtors, who lived in the same galleries as the men. Disturbances were frequent, owing to the riotous conduct of intoxicated women. Twice a week there was a wine and beer club held at night, which lasted till two or three in the morning. In the yard behind the prison were places set apart for skittles, fives, and tennis, which strangers frequented as any other place of public amusement.

Matters were rather better at the Marshalsea. This very ancient prison, which stood in the High Street, Southwark, was used for debtors arrested for the lowest sums within twelve miles of the palace of Whitehall; also for prisoners committed by the Admiralty Court. At one time the Marshalsea was the receptacle of pirates, but none were committed to it after 1789. The court of the Marshalsea was instituted by Charles I. in the sixth year of his reign, to be held before the steward of the royal household, the knight marshal, and the steward of the court, with jurisdiction to hold pleas in all actions within the prescribed limits. The court was chiefly used for the recovery of small debts under £10, but its business was much reduced by the extension of the Courts of Conscience. The prison was a nest of abuses, like its neighbour the King's Bench, and came under the strong animadversion of the Gaol Committee of 1729. As the business of the Marshalsea Court declined, the numbers in its prison diminished. The population, as reported by the committee in 1814, averaged about sixty, and the prison, although wives and children resided within the walls, was not overcrowded. Their conduct too was orderly on the whole. Drunkenness was not common, chiefly because liquor was not to be had freely, although the tapster paid a rent of two guineas a week for permission to sell it. The inmates, who euphemistically styled themselves "collegians," were governed by rules which they themselves had framed, and under which subscriptions were levied and fines imposed for conduct disapproved of by the "college." A court of the collegians was held every Monday to manage its affairs, at which all prisoners were required to attend. A committee of collegians was elected to act as the executive, also a secretary or accountant to receive monies and keep books, and a master of the ale-room, who kept this the scene of their revels clean, and saw that boiling water was provided for grog. Bad language, quarrelling, throwing water over one another was forbidden on pain of fine and being sent to Coventry; but the prevailing moral tone may be guessed from the penalty inflicted upon persons singing obscene songs *before* nine p.m. Yet the public opinion of the whole body seems to have checked dissipation. The poorer prisoners were not in abject want, as in other prisons, owing to many charitable gifts and bequests, which included annual donations from the Archbishop of Canterbury, the Lord Steward of the Household, the steward and officers of the Marshalsea Court, and others. Legacies had also been left to free a certain number of debtors, notably that of £100 per annum left by a Mr. Henry Allnutt, who was long a prisoner in the Marshalsea, and came into a fortune while there. His bequest, which was charged upon his manor at Goring, Oxon, and hence called the Oxford Charity, was applied only to the release of poor debtors whom £4 each could free. The supreme control of the Marshalsea was vested in the marshal of the royal household; but although he drew a salary of £500 a year, he did nothing beyond visiting the prison occasionally, and left the administration to the deputy marshal. The latter's salary, with fees, the rent of the tap and of the chandler's shop, amounted to about £600 a year.

The compters of Ludgate, Giltspur Street, and the Borough were discontinued as debtors' prisons (as was Newgate also) on the opening of Whitecross prison for debtors in 1815. Ludgate to the last was the debtors' prison for freemen of the city of London, clergymen, proctors, attorneys, and persons specially selected by the Corporation. At one time the Ludgate debtors, accompanied by the keeper, went outside and beyond the prison to call on their creditors, and try to arrange their debts, but this practice was discontinued. There were fifteen rooms of various sizes, and as the numbers imprisoned rarely exceeded five-and-twenty, the place was never overcrowded, while the funds of several bequests and charities were applied in adding to the material comfort of the prisoners. The Giltspur Street Compter received sheriffs' debtors, also felons, vagrants, and night charges. It was generally crowded, as debtors who would have gone to the Poultry Compter were sent to Giltspur Street when the former was condemned as unfit to receive prisoners.[35] The demands for fees were excessive in Giltspur Street. Those who could not pay were thrown into the wards with the night charges, and denied admission to the "charity wards," which partook of all the benefits of bequests and donations to poor debtors. The Borough Compter was in a disgraceful state to the last. The men's ward had an earth, or rather a mud, floor, and was so unfit to sleep on that it had not been used for many years, so that the men and women associated together indiscriminately. The rooms had no fireplaces, so it mattered little that no coals were allowed. There were no beds or bedding, no straw even. In one room Mr. Neild found a woman ill of a flux shut up with three men; the latter raised eighteenpence among them to pay for a truss of straw for the poor woman to lie on. Neild found the prisoners in the Borough Compter ragged, starving, and dirty.

I come now to the debtors in Newgate. The quarters they occupied were divided, as I have said,[36] into three principal divisions—the master's side, the cabin side, and the common side. Payment of a fee of 3s. gained the debtor admission to the two first named; those who could pay nothing went, as a matter of course, to the common side; a further fee was, however, demanded from the new-comer before he was made free of either the master's or the cabin side. This was the reprehensible claim for "garnish," which had already been abolished in all well-conducted prisons, but which still was demanded in Newgate. Garnish on the cabin side was a guinea at entrance for coals, candles, brooms, &c., and a gallon of beer on discharge; on the master's side it was thirteen and fourpence, and a gallon of beer on entrance, although Mr. Newman, in his evidence in 1814, said it was more, and gave the garnish for the common side at that sum, which is five shillings more than Mr. Neild says was extorted on the common side. Numerous tyrannies were practised on all who would not and could not pay the garnish. They were made to wash and swab the ward, or they were shut out from the ward fireplace, and forbidden to pass a chalked line drawn on the floor, and so were unable either to warm themselves or to cook their food. Besides these fees, legitimate and illegitimate, there were others which must be paid before release. The sheriff demanded 4s. 6d. for his liberate, the gaoler 6s. 10d. more, and the turnkey 2s.; and thus when the debtor's debt had been actually paid, or when he had abandoned his property to the creditors, and, almost destitute, looked forward to his liberty, he was still delayed until he had paid a new debt arising "only out of a satisfaction of all his former debts." The fees were not always extorted, it is true; nor was non-payment made a pretext for further imprisonment, thanks to the humanity of the gaoler, or the funds provided by various charities.

There was this much honest forbearance in Newgate in these days, that debtors who could afford the cabin and master's side were not permitted to share in the prison charities. These were lumped together into a general fund, and a calculation made as to the amount that might be expended per week from the whole sum, so that the latter might last out the year. It generally ran to about six pounds per week. The money, which at one time had been distributed quarterly, and all went in drink, was after 1807, through the exertions of the keeper[37] of the gaol, spent in the purchase of necessaries. But this weekly pittance did not go far when the debtors' side was crowded, as it often was; notably as when numbers filled Newgate in anticipation of Lord Redesdale's bill for insolvent debtors, and there were as many as three hundred and fifty prisoners in at one time. The city also allowed the poor debtors fourteen ounces of bread daily, and their share of eight stone of meat, an allowance which never varied, issued once a week, and divided as far as it would go—a very precarious and uncertain ration. The bread was issued every alternate day; and while some prisoners often ate their whole allowance at once, others who arrived just after the time of distribution were often forty-eight hours without food. The latter might also be six days without meat. Share in the weekly allowance of meat might also be denied to debtors who had not paid "garnish," as well as in the weekly grant from the charitable fund. Hence starvation stared many in the face,[38] unless friends from outside came to their assistance, or the keeper made them a special grant of 6*d.* per diem out of the common stock; or the sixpenny allowance was claimed for the creditors, which seldom happened, owing to the expense the process entailed. The poor debtors were not supplied with beds. Those who could pay the price might hire them from each other, or from persons who made a trade of it, or they might bring their beds with them into the prison. Failing any of these methods, seeing that straw was forbidden for fear of fire, they had to be satisfied with a couple of the rugs provided by the city, the supply of which was, however, limited, and there were not always enough to give bedding to all. The stock was diminished by theft; female visitors carried them out of the prisons, or the debtors destroyed them when the weather was warm, and they were not in great demand, in order to convert them into mop-heads or cleaning-rags. Sometimes rugs were urgently required and not forthcoming; a severe winter set in, the new stock had not been supplied by the contractors, and the poor debtors perished of cold. Again, there was no regular allowance of fuel. Coals were purchased out of the garnish money and the charitable fund; so were candles, salt, pepper, mops and brooms. But the latter could have been of little service. Dirt prevailed everywhere; indeed the place, with its oak floors caulked with pitch, and smoked ceilings, could not be made even to look clean while there was no obligation of personal cleanliness on individuals, who often came into the prison in filthy rags. Only now and again, in extreme cases, an unusually nasty companion was stripped, haled to the pump, and left under it in a state of nature until he was washed clean.

The squalor and uncleanness of the debtors' side was intensified by constant overcrowding. Prisoners were committed to it quite without reference to its capacity. No remonstrance was attended to, no steps taken to reduce the number of committals, and the governor was obliged to utilize the chapel as a day and night room. Besides this, although the families of debtors were no longer permitted to live with them inside the gaol, hundreds of women and children came in every morning to spend the day there, and there was no limitation whatever to the numbers of visitors admitted to the debtors' side. Friends arrived about nine a.m., and went out at nine p.m., when as many as two hundred visitors have been observed leaving the debtors' yards at one time. The day passed in revelry and drunkenness. Although spirituous liquors were forbidden, wine and beer might be had in any quantity, the only limitation being that not more than one bottle of wine or one quart of beer could be issued at one time. No account was taken of the amount of liquors admitted in one day, and debtors might practically have as much as they liked, if they could only pay for it. No attempt was made to check drunkenness, beyond the penalty of shutting out friends from any ward in which a prisoner exceeded. Quarrelling among the debtors was not unfrequent. Blows were struck, and fights often ensued. For this and other acts of misconduct there was the discipline of the refractory ward, or "strong room" on the debtors' side. Bad cases were removed to a cell on the felons' side, and here they were locked in solitary confinement for three days at a time.

Order throughout the debtors' side was preserved and discipline maintained by a system open to grave abuses, and which had the prescription of long usage, and which was never wholly rooted out for many years to come. This was the pernicious plan of governing by prisoners, or of setting a favoured few in authority over the many. The head of the debtors' prison was a prisoner called the steward, who was chosen by the whole body from six whom the keeper nominated. This steward was practically supreme. All the allowances of food passed through his hands; he had the control of the poor-box for chance charities, he collected the garnish money, and distributed the weekly grant from the prison charitable fund. In the latter duties he was, however, supervised by three auditors, freely chosen by the prisoners among themselves. The auditors were paid a shilling each for their services each time the poor-box was opened. The steward was also remunerated for his trouble. He had a double allowance of bread, deducted, of course, from the already too limited portion of the rest, and no doubt made the meat also pay toll. Under the steward there were captains of wards, chosen in the same way, and performing analogous duties. These subordinate chiefs were also rewarded out of the scanty prison rations. The same system was extended to the criminal side, and cases were on record of the place of wardsman being sold for considerable sums. So valuable were they deemed, that as much as fifty guineas was offered to the keeper for the post.

Enough has been said, probably, to prove that there was room for improvement in the condition and treatment of debtors in the prisons of the city of London. This gradually was forced upon the consciousness of the Corporation, and about 1812 application was made to Parliament for funds to build a new debtors' prison. Authority was given to raise money on the Orphans' Fund to the extent of £90,000. A site was purchased between Red Lion and White Cross streets, and a new prison planned, which would accommodate the inmates of Newgate and of the three compters, Ludgate, Giltspur Street, and the Poultry, or about four hundred and seventy-six in all. The evils of association for these debtors were perpetuated, although the plan provided for the separation of the various contingents committed to it. There was no lack of air and light for the new gaol, and several exercising yards. The completion of this very necessary building was, however, much delayed for want of funds, and it was not ready to relieve Newgate till late in 1815. The reforms which were to be attempted in that prison, more particularly as regarded the classification of prisoners, and which were dependent on the space to be gained by the removal of the debtors, could not be carried out till then. It is to be feared that long after the opening of White Cross Street prison, Newgate continued to be a reproach to those responsible for its management.

I pass now to the criminal side of Newgate, which consisted of the six quarters or yards already enumerated and described. [39] The inmates of this part, as distinguished from the debtors, were comprised in four classes:—(1) those awaiting trial; (2) persons under sentence of imprisonment for a fixed period, or until they shall have paid certain fines; (3) transports awaiting removal to the colonies, and (4) capital convicts, condemned to death and awaiting execution. At one time the whole of these different categories were thrown together pell-mell, young and old, the untried with the convicted. An imperfect attempt at classification was, however, made in 1812, and a yard was as far as possible set apart for the untried, or class (1), with whom, under the imperious demand for accommodation, were also associated the misdemeanants, or class (2). This was the chapel yard, with its five wards, which were calculated to hold seventy prisoners, but often held many more. A further sub-classification was attempted by separating at night those charged with misdemeanours from those charged with felony, but all mingled freely during the day in the yard. The sleeping accommodation in the chapel-yard wards, and indeed throughout the prison, consisted of a barrack bed, which was a wooden flooring on a slightly inclined plane, with a beam running across the top to serve as a pillow. No beds were issued, only two rugs per prisoner. When each sleeper had the full lateral space allotted to him, it amounted to one foot and a half on the barrack bed; but when the ward was obliged to accommodate double the ordinary number, as was frequently the case, the sleepers covered the entire floor, with the exception of a passage in the middle. All the misdemeanants, whatever their offence, were lodged in this chapel ward. As many various and, according to our ideas, heinous crimes came under this head, in the then existing state of the law, the man guilty of a common assault found himself side by side with the fraudulent, or others who had attempted abominable crimes. In this heterogeneous society were also thrown the unfortunate journalists to whom I have already referred,[40] and on whom imprisonment in Newgate was frequently adjudged for so-called libels, or too out-spoken comments in print. It was particularly recommended by the Committee on Gaols in 1814 that some other and less mixed prison should be used for the confinement of persons convicted of libels. But this suggestion was ignored. Indeed the partial classification attempted seems to have been abandoned within a year or two. The Hon. H. G. Bennet, who visited Newgate in 1817, saw in one yard, in a total of seventy-two prisoners, thirty-five tried and thirty-seven untried. Of the former, three were transports for life, four for fourteen years, and three of them persons sentenced to fines or short imprisonment—one for little more than a month. Two of the untried were for murder, and several for house-breaking and highway robbery. Nor were the misdemeanants and bail prisoners any longer separated from those whose crimes were of a more serious character. Mr. Bennet refers to a gentleman confined for want of bail, who occupied a room with five others—two committed by the Bankruptcy Commissioner, one for perjury, and two transports. Persons convicted of publishing libels were still immured in the same rooms with transports and felons.

The middle yard, as far as its limits would permit, was appropriated to felons and transports. The wards here were generally very crowded. Each ward was calculated to hold twenty-four, allowing each individual one foot and a half; "a common-sized man," says the keeper, Mr. Newman, "can turn in nineteen inches."[41] These twenty-four could just sleep on the barrack bed; when the number was higher, and it often rose to forty, the surplus had to sleep on the floor. The crowding was in consequence of the delay in removing transports. These often remained in Newgate for six months, sometimes a year, in some cases longer; in one, for seven years—that of a man sentenced to death, for whom great interest had been made, but whom it was not thought right to pardon. Occasionally the transports made themselves so useful in the gaol that they were passed over. Mr. Newman admitted that he had petitioned that certain "trusty men" might be left in the gaol. Constantly associated with these convicted felons were numbers of juveniles, infants of tender years. There were frequently in the middle yard seven or eight children, the youngest barely nine, the oldest only twelve or thirteen, exposed to all the contaminating influences of the place. Mr. Bennet mentions also the case of young men of better stamp, clerks in city offices, and youths of good parentage, "in this dreadful situation," who had been rescued from the hulks through the kindness and attention of the Secretary of State. "Yet they had been long enough," he goes on to say, "in the prison associated with the lowest and vilest criminals, with convicts of all ages and characters, to render it next to impossible but that, with the obliteration of all sense of self-respect, the inevitable consequence of such a situation, their morals must have been destroyed; and though distress or the seduction of others might have led to the commission of this their first offence, yet the society they were driven to live in, the language they daily heard, and the lessons they were taught in this academy, must have had a tendency to turn them into the world hardened and accomplished in the ways of vice and crime."

Mr. Buxton, in the work already quoted, instances another grievous case of the horrors of indiscriminate association in Newgate. It was that of a person "who practised in the law, and who was connected by marriage with some very respectable families. Having been committed to Clerkenwell, he was sent on to Newgate in a coach, handcuffed to a noted house-breaker, who was afterwards cast for death. The first night in Newgate, and for the subsequent fortnight, he slept in the same bed with a highwayman on one side, and a man charged with murder on the other. Spirits were freely introduced, and although he at first abstained, he found he must adopt the manners of his companions, or that his life would be in danger. They viewed him with some suspicion, as one of whom they knew nothing. He was in consequence put out of the protection of their internal law." Their code was a subject of some curiosity. When any prisoner committed an offence against the community or against an individual, he was tried by a court in the gaol. A prisoner, generally the oldest and most dexterous thief, was appointed judge, and a towel tied in knots was hung on each side in imitation of a wig. The judge sat in proper form; he was punctiliously styled "my lord." A jury having been selected and duly sworn, the culprit was then arraigned. Justice, however, was not administered with absolute integrity. A bribe to the judge was certain to secure acquittal, and the neglect of the formality was as certainly followed by condemnation. Various punishments were inflicted, the heaviest of which was standing in the pillory. This was carried out by putting the criminal's head through the legs of a chair, and stretching out his arms and tying them to the legs. The culprit was then compelled to carry the chair about with him. But all punishments might readily be commuted into a fine to be spent in gin for judge and jury.

The prisoner mentioned above was continually persecuted by trials of this kind. The most trifling acts were magnified into offences. He was charged with moving something which should not be touched, with leaving a door open, or coughing maliciously to the disturbance of his companions. The evidence was invariably sufficient to convict, and the judge never hesitated to inflict the heaviest penalties. The unfortunate man was compelled at length to adopt the habits of his associates; "by insensible degrees he began to lose his repugnance to their society, caught their flash terms and sung their songs, was admitted to their revels, and acquired, in place of habits of perfect sobriety, a taste for spirits." His wife visited him in Newgate, and wrote a pitiable account of the state in which she found her husband. He was an inmate of the same ward with others of the most dreadful sort, "whose language and manners, whose female associates of the most abandoned description, and the scenes consequent with such lost wretches, prevented me from going inside but seldom, and I used to communicate with him through the bars from the passage." One day he was too ill to come down and meet her. She went up to the ward and found him lying down, "pale as death, very ill, and in a dreadfully dirty state, the wretches making game of him, and enjoying my distress; and I learned he had been up with the others the whole night. Though they could not force him to gamble, he was compelled to drink, and I was obliged afterwards to let him have five shillings to pay his share, otherwise he would have been stripped of his clothes."

Felons who could pay the price were permitted, irrespective of their character or offences, to purchase the greater ease and comfort of the master's side. The entrance fee was at least 13s. 6d. a head, with half-a-crown a week more for bed and bedding, the wards being furnished with barrack bedsteads, upon which each prisoner had the regulation allowance of sleeping room, or about a foot and a half laterally. These fees were in reality a substantial contribution towards the expenses of the gaol; without them the keeper declared that he could not pay the salaries of turnkeys and servants, nor keep the prison going at all. Besides the gaol fees, there was garnish of half-a-guinea, collected by the steward, and spent in providing coals, candles, plates, knives, and forks; while all the occupants of this part of the prison supported themselves; they had the ration of prison bread only, but they had no share in the prison meat or other charities, and they or their friends found them in food. All who could scrape together the cash seem to have gladly availed themselves of the privilege of entering the master's side. It was the only way to escape the horrors, the distress, penury, and rags of the common yards. Idleness was not so universally the rule in this part of the gaol. Artizans and others were at liberty to work at their trades, provided they were not dangerous. Tailoring and shoemaking was permitted, but it was deemed unsafe to allow a carpenter or blacksmith to have his tools. All the money earned by prisoners was at their own disposal, and was spent almost habitually in drink, chambering, and wantonness.

The best accommodation the gaol could offer was reserved for the prisoners on the state side, from whom still higher fees were exacted, with the same discreditable idea of swelling the revenues of the prison. To constitute this the aristocratic quarter, unwarrantable demands were made upon the space properly allotted to the female felons,[42] and no lodger was rejected, whatever his status, who offered himself and could bring grist to the mill. The luxury of the state side was for a long time open to all who could pay—the convicted felon, the transport awaiting removal, the lunatic whose case was still undecided,[43] the misdemeanant tried or untried, the debtor who wished to avoid the discomfort of the crowded debtors' side, the outspoken newspaper editor, or the daring reporter of parliamentary debates. The better class of inmate complained bitterly of this enforced companionship with the vile, association at one time forbidden by custom, but which greed and rapacity long made the rule. The fee for admission to the state side, as fixed by the table of fees, was three guineas, but Mr. Newman declared that he never took more than two. Ten and sixpence a week more was charged as rent for a single bed; where two or more slept in a bed the rent was seven shillings a week each. Prisoners who could afford it sometimes paid for four beds, at the rate of twenty-eight shillings, and so secured the luxury of a private room. A Mr. Lundy, charged with forgery, was thus accommodated on the state side for upwards of five years. But the keeper protested that no single prisoner could thus monopolize space if the state side was crowded. The keeper went still further in his efforts to make money. He continued the ancient practice of letting out a portion of his own house, and by a poetical fiction treated it as an annexe of the state side. Mr. Davison, sent to Newgate for embezzlement, and whose case is given in the preceding chapter, was accommodated with a room in Mr. Newman's house at the extravagant rental of thirty guineas per week; Mr. Cobbett was also a lodger of Mr. Newman's; and so were any members of the aristocracy, if they happened to be in funds—among whom was the Marquis of Sligo in 1811.

The female felons' wards I shall describe at length in the next chapter, which will deal with Mrs. Fry's philanthropic exertions at this period in this particular part of the prison. These wards were always full to overflowing; sometimes double the number the rooms could accommodate were crowded into them. There was a master's side for females who could pay the usual fees, but they associated with the rest in the one narrow yard common to all. The tried and the untried, young and old, were herded together; sometimes girls of thirteen, twelve, even ten or nine years of age, were exposed to "all the contagion and profligacy which prevailed in this part of the prison." There was no separation even for the women under sentence of death, who lived in a common and perpetually crowded ward. Only when the order of execution came down were those about to suffer placed apart in one of the rooms in the arcade of the middle ward.

I have kept till the last that part of the prison which was usually the last resting-place of so many. The old press yard has been fully described in a previous chapter.[44] The name still survived in the new press yard, which was the receptacle of the male condemned prisoners. It was generally crowded, like the rest of the prison. Except in murder cases, where the execution was generally very promptly performed, strange and inconceivable delay occurred in carrying out the extreme sentence. Hence there was a terrible accumulation of prisoners in the condemned cells. Once, during the long illness of George III., as many as one hundred were there waiting the "Report," as it was called. At another time there were fifty, one of whom had been under sentence a couple of years. Mr. Bennet speaks of thirty-eight capital convicts he found in the press yard in February 1817, five of whom had been condemned the previous July, four in September, and twenty-nine in October. This procrastination bred certain callousness. Few realizing that the dreadful fate would overtake them, dismissed the prospect of death, and until the day was actually fixed, spent the time in roystering, swearing, gambling, or playing at ball. Visitors were permitted access to them without stint; unlimited drink was not denied them provided it was obtained in regulated quantities at one time. These capital convicts, says Mr. Bennet, "lessened the ennui and despair of their situation by unbecoming merriment, or sought relief in the constant application of intoxicating stimulants. I saw Cashman[45] a few hours before his execution, smoking and drinking with the utmost unconcern and indifference." Those who were thus reckless reacted upon the penitent who knew their days were numbered, and their gibes and jollity counteracted the ordinary's counsels or the independent preacher's earnest prayers. For while Roman Catholics and Dissenters were encouraged to see ministers of their own persuasion, a number of amateurs were ever ready to give their gratuitous ministrations to the condemned.

The prisoners in the press yard had free access during the day to the yard and large day room; at night they were placed in the fifteen cells, two, three, or more together, according to the total number to be accommodated. They were never left quite alone for fear of suicide, and for the same reason they were searched for weapons or poisons. But they nevertheless frequently managed to secrete the means of making away with themselves, and accomplished their purpose. Convicted murderers were kept continuously in the cells on bread and water, in couples, from the time of sentence to that of execution, which was about three or four days generally, from Friday to Monday, so as to include one Sunday, on which day there was a special service for the condemned in the prison chapel. This latter was an ordeal which all dreaded, and many avoided by denying their faith. The condemned occupied an open pew in the centre of the chapel, hung with black; in front of them, upon a table, was a black coffin in full view. The chapel was filled with a curious but callous congregation, who came to stare at the miserable people thus publicly exposed. Well might Mr. Bennet write that the condition of the condemned side was the most prominent of the manifold evils in the present system of Newgate, "so discreditable to the metropolis."

Yet it must have been abundantly plain to the reader that the other evils existing were great and glaring. A brief summary of them will best prove this. The gaol was neither suitable nor sufficiently large. It was not even kept weather-tight. The roof of the female prison, says the grand jury in their presentment in 1813, let in the rain. Supplies of common necessaries, such as have now been part of the furniture of every British gaol for many years, were meagre or altogether absent. The rations of food were notoriously inadequate, and so carelessly distributed, that many were left to starve. So unjust and unequal was the system, that the allowance to convicted criminals was better than that of the innocent debtor, and the general insufficiency was such that it multiplied beyond all reason the number of visitors, many of whom came merely as the purveyors of food to their friends.

The prison allowances were eked out by the broken victuals generously given by several eating-house keepers in the city, such as Messrs. Birch of Cornhill and Messrs. Leach and Dollimore of Ludgate Hill. These were fetched away in a large tub on a truck by a turnkey. Amongst the heap was often the meat that had made turtle soup, which, when heated and stirred together in a saucepan, was said to be very good eating. The bedding was scanty; fuel and light had to be purchased out of prisoners' private means; clothing was issued but rarely, even to prisoners almost in nakedness, and as a special charitable gift. Extortion was practised right and left. Garnish continued to be demanded long after it had disappeared in other and better-regulated prisons. The fees on reception and discharge must be deemed exorbitant, when it is remembered the impoverished class who usually crowded the gaol; and they were exacted to relieve a rich corporation from paying for the maintenance of their own prison. This imposition of fees left prisoners destitute on their discharge, without funds to support them in their first struggle to recommence life, with ruined character, bad habits, and often bad health contracted in the gaol. A further and a more iniquitous method of extorting money was still practised, that of loading newly-arrived prisoners until they paid certain fees. Ironing was still the rule, not only for the convicted, but for those charged with felonies; only the misdemeanants escaped. At the commencement of every sessions, such of the untried as had purchased "easement" of irons were called up and re-fettered, preparatory to their appearance in the Old Bailey. Irons were seldom removed from the convicted until discharge; sometimes the wearer was declared medically unfit, or he obtained release by long good conduct, or the faithful discharge of some petty office, such as gatesman or captain of a ward. The irons weighed from three to four pounds, but heavier irons, seven or eight pounds' weight, were imposed in case of misconduct; and when there had been an attempt at escape, the culprit was chained down to the floor by running a chain through his irons which prevented him from climbing to the window of his cell. Among other excuses offered for thus manacling all almost without exception, was that it was the best and safest method of distinguishing a prisoner from a stranger and temporary visitor. Clothes or prison uniform would not have served the purpose, for a disguise can be rapidly and secretly put on, whereas irons cannot well be exchanged without loss of time and attracting much attention.[46]

The unchecked admission of crowds of visitors to the felons' as well as the debtors' side was another unmixed evil. By this means spirits, otherwise unattainable and strictly prohibited, were smuggled into the gaol. Searches[47] were made certainly, but they were too often superficial, or they might be evaded by a trifling bribe. Hence the frequent cases of drunkenness, of which no notice was taken, unless people grew riotous in their cups, and attracted attention by their disorderly behaviour. Another frightful consequence of this indiscriminate admission was the influx of numbers of abandoned women, only a few of whom had the commendable prudery to pass themselves off as the wives of prisoners. Any reputed, and indeed any real, wife might spend the night in Newgate if she would pay the shilling fee, commonly known as the "bad money," a base payment which might have done something towards increasing the prison receipts, had it not been appropriated by the turnkey who winked at this evasion of the rules. Among the daily visitors were members of the criminal classes still at large, the thieves and burglars who carried on the active business of their profession, from which their confederates were temporarily debarred. One notorious character, while a prisoner awaiting transfer to the hulks, kept open house, so to speak, and entertained daily within the walls a select party of the most noted thieves in London. This delectable society enticed into their set a clerk who had been imprisoned for fraud, and offered him half the booty if he would give full information as to the transactions and correspondence of his late employers. Owing to the facility of intercourse between inside and outside, many crimes were doubtless hatched in Newgate. Some of the worst and most extensive burglaries were planned there. Forged notes had been fabricated, false money coined, and both passed out in quantities to be circulated through the country. "I believe," says Mr. Bennet in the letter already largely quoted, "that there is no place in the metropolis where more crimes are projected or where stolen property is more secreted than in Newgate."

These malpractices were fostered by the absence of all supervision and the generally unbroken idleness. Although attempted partially at Bridewell, and more systematically at the new Millbank penitentiary, but just open (1816), the regular employment of prisoners had never yet been accepted as a principle in the metropolitan prisons. Insuperable difficulties were still supposed to stand in the way of any general employment of prisoners at their trades. There was fear as to the unrestricted use of tools, limits of space, the interference of the ill-disposed, who would neither work nor let others do so, and the danger of losing material, raw or manufactured. Many years were to elapse before these objections should be fairly met and universally overcome. It was not strange, therefore, that the inmates of Newgate should turn their unoccupied brains and idle hands to all manner of mischief; that when they were not carousing, plotting, or scheming, they should gamble with dice or cards, and play at bumble puppy or some other disreputable game of chance.

The report of the Committee of the House of Commons painted so black a picture of Newgate as then conducted, that the Corporation were roused in very shame to undertake some kind of reform. The above-mentioned report was ordered to be printed upon the 9th May. Upon the 29th July the same year, the court of aldermen appointed a committee of its own body, assisted by the town clerk, Mr. Dance, city surveyor, son to the architect of Newgate, and Mr. Addison, keeper of Newgate, to make a visitation of the gaols supposed to be the best managed, including those of Petworth and Gloucester.[48] This committee was to compare allowances, examine rules, and certify as to the condition of prisoners; also to make such proposals as might appear salutary, and calculated to improve Newgate and the rest of the city gaols.

This committee made its report in September the following year, and an excellent report it is, so far as its recommendations are concerned. The committee seems to have fully realized, even at this early date (1815), many of the indispensable conditions of a model prison according to modern ideas. It admitted the paramount necessity for giving every prisoner a sleeping cell to himself, an amount of enlightenment which is hardly general among European nations at this the latter end of the nineteenth century,[49] several of which still fall far short of our English ideal, that all prisoners should always be in separate cells by night, and those of short sentences by day. It recommended day cells or rooms for regular labour, which should be compulsory upon all transports and prisoners sentenced to hard labour, the work being constant and suitable, with certain hours of relaxation and for food and exercise. The personal cleanliness of all prisoners was to be insisted upon; they should be made to wash at least once a day, with the penalty of forfeiting the day's allowance of food, an increase of which the committee had recommended. The provision of more baths was also suggested, and the daily sweeping out of the prison. The clothes of prisoners arriving dirty, or in rags, should be fumigated before worn in the gaol, but as yet no suggestion was made to provide prison uniform. A laundry should be established, and a matron appointed on the female side, where all the prisoners' washing could be performed. Proper hours for locking and unlocking prisoners should be insisted upon; a bell should give notice thereof, and of meal-hours, working-hours, or of escapes.

The committee took upon itself to lay down stringent rules for the discipline of the prison. The gaoler should be required to visit every part and see every prisoner daily; the chaplain should perform service, visit the sick, instruct the prisoners, "give spiritual advice and administer religious consolation" to all who might need them;[50] the surgeon should see all prisoners, whether ill or well, once a week, and take general charge of the infirmaries. All three, governor, chaplain, and surgeon, should keep journals, which should be inspected periodically by the visiting magistrates. It should be peremptorily forbidden to the keeper or any officer to make a pecuniary profit out of the supplies of food, fuel, or other necessaries. No prisoner should be allowed to obtain superior accommodation on the payment of any fees. Fees indeed should be generally abolished, garnish also. No prisoners should in future be ironed, except in cases of misconduct, provided only that their security was not jeopardized, and dependent upon the enforcement of another new rule, which recommended restrictions upon the number of visitors admitted. No wine or beer should be in future admitted into or sold in the gaol, except for the use of the debtors, or as medical comforts for the infirmary. Drunkenness, if it ever occurred, should be visited with severe punishment; gaming of all sorts should be peremptorily forbidden under heavy pains and penalties. The feelings of the condemned prisoners should no longer be outraged by their exposure in the chapel, and the chapel should be rearranged, so that the various classes might be seated separately, and so as not to see each other.

It will hardly be denied that these proposals went to the root of the matter. Had they been accepted in their entirety, little fault could in future have been found with the managers of Newgate. In common justice to them, it must be admitted that immediate effect was given to all that could be easily carried out. The state side ceased to exist, and the female prisoners thus regained the space of which their quadrangle had been robbed. The privileges of the master's side also disappeared; fees were nominally abolished, and garnish was scotched, although not yet killed outright. A certain number of bedsteads were provided, and there was a slight increase in the ration of bread. But here the recommendations touched at once upon the delicate subject of expense, and it is clear that the committee hesitated on this score. It made this too the excuse for begging the most important issue of the whole question. The committee did not deny the superior advantages offered by such prisons as Gloucester and Petworth, but it at once deprecated the idea that the city could follow the laudable example thus set in the provinces. "Were a metropolitan prison erected on the same lines, with all the space not only for air and exercise, but for day rooms and sleeping cells," it would cover some thirty acres, and cost a great deal more than the city, with the example of Whitecross Street prison before it, could possibly afford. The committee does not seem to have yet understood that Newgate could be only and properly replaced by a new gaol built on the outskirts, as Holloway eventually was,[51] and permitted itself to be altogether countered and checked in its efforts towards reform by the prohibitory costliness of the land about Newgate. With the seeming impossibility of extending the limits of the prison as it then stood, all chances of classification and separation vanished, and the greatest evils remained untouched. All the committee could do in this respect was to throw the responsibility on others. It pointed out that the Government was to blame for the overcrowding, and might diminish it if it chose. It was very desirable that there should be a more speedy removal of transports from Newgate to the ships. Again, there was the new Millbank penitentiary now ready for occupation. Why not relieve Newgate by drawing more largely upon the superior accommodation which Millbank offered?

PHILANTHROPY IN NEWGATE

Absence of religious and moral instruction in Newgate a hundred years ago—Chaplains not always zealous—Unprofessional amateur enthusiasts minister to the prisoners—Christian Knowledge Society—Silas Told, his life and work—Wesley leads him to prison visitation—Goes to Newgate regularly—Chaplain opposes his visits—Attends the condemned to the gallows—Attends Mary Edmondson—The gentlemen Highwaymen—Mrs. Brownrigg—Alexander Cruden of the 'Concordance' also visits Newgate—More precise account of a neglectful Chaplain—Dr. Forde—His hatred of amateur preachers—In his element in the chair of a 'free-and-easy'—Private philanthropy active—Various societies formed—Prison schools—The female side the most disgraceful part of the prison—Mrs. Fry's first visit—Her second visit—Awful description of interior of gaol—Ill-treatment of female prisoners—Their irons—Where Mrs. Fry commenced—The School—The Matron—Work obtained—Rules framed—Rapid improvement of Newgate—Female prison reformed—Publicity follows—Newgate becomes a show.

AMONG the many drawbacks from which the inmates of Newgate suffered through the eighteenth and the early part of the nineteenth century, was the absence of proper religious and moral instruction. The value of the ministrations of the ordinary, who was the official ghostly adviser, entirely depended upon his personal qualities. Now and again he was an earnest and devoted man, to whom the prisoners might fully open their hearts. More often he was careless and indifferent, satisfied to earn his salary by the slightest and most perfunctory discharge of his sacred duties. There were ordinaries whose fame rested rather upon their powers of digestion than in polemics or pulpit oratory. The Newgate chaplain had to say grace at city banquets, and was sometimes called upon to eat three consecutive dinners without rising from the table. One in particular was noted for his skill in compounding a salad, another for his jovial companionship. But the ordinary took life easy, and beyond conducting the services, did little work. Only when executions were imminent was he especially busy. It behoved then to collect matter for his account of the previous life and the misdeeds of the condemned, with their demeanour at Tyburn, and this, according to contemporary records, led him to get all the information he could from the malefactors who passed through his hands. In the history of the press yard there is an account of the proceedings of the chaplain, Mr. Smith, which may be somewhat over-coloured, but which has the appearance of truth. It was the ordinary's custom to give interviews in his private closet to those condemned to death, and cross-examine them closely. One day a young fellow was brought before him, to whom he said at once, "Well, boy, now is the time to unbosom thyself to me. Thou hast been a great sabbath-breaker in thy time I warrant thee? The neglect of going to church regularly has brought thee under these unhappy circumstances." "Not I, good sir," was the reply; "I never neglected going to some church, if I was in health, morning and evening every Lord's day." The lad told truth, for his business took him to such places of resort for the better carrying on his trade, which was that of a pickpocket. Mr. Smith was not to be done out of his confession. "No sabbath-breaker? then thou hast been an abominable drunkard?" This the criminal denied, declaring that he had always had a mortal aversion to strong drinks. The chaplain continued to press the criminal, but could find that he had been guilty of nothing more than thieving, and as this was a topic he could not enlarge upon in his pamphlet, he dismissed the lad, to be entered in his account as an obstinate, case-hardened rogue.

But while the official lacked zeal or religious fervour, there were not wanting others more earnest and enthusiastic to add their unprofessional but devoted efforts to the half-hearted ministrations of the ordinary of Newgate. Towards the end of the seventeenth century, when the Society for the Promotion of Christian Knowledge was first formed, Dr. Bray and other members visited Newgate, and made its inmates their especial care for a time. A prominent figure in the philanthropic annals of Newgate a little later is that of Silas Told, who devoted many years of his life to the spiritual needs of the prisoners. Told's career is full of peculiar interest. He was a pious child; both father and mother were religious folk, and brought him up carefully. According to his own memoirs, when quite an infant he and his sister Dulcibella were wont to wander into the woods and fields to converse about "God and happiness." Told passed through many trials and vicissitudes in his early years. At thirteen he went to sea as an apprentice, and suffered much ill-usage. He made many voyages to the West Indies and to the Guinea coast, being a horrified and unwilling witness of some of the worst phases of the slave trade. He fell into the hands of piratical Spaniards, was cast away on a reef, saved almost by a miracle, last of all was pressed on board a man-of-war. Here, on board H.M.S. 'Phœnix,' his religious tendencies were strengthened by a pious captain, and presently he married and left the sea for ever. After this he became a schoolmaster in Essex, then a clerk and book-keeper in London. Here he came under the influence of John Wesley, and although predisposed against the Methodists, he was profoundly impressed by their leader's preaching. While listening to a sermon by John Wesley on the suddenness of conversion, Told heard another voice say to him, "This is the truth," and from that time forth he became a zealous Methodist.

It was Wesley who led him to prison visitation. He was at that time schoolmaster of the Foundry school, and his call to his long and devoted labours in Newgate were brought about in this wise. "In the year 1744," to quote his own words, "I attended the children one morning at the five o'clock preaching, when Mr. Wesley took his text out of the twenty-fifth chapter of St. Matthew. When he read 'I was sick and in prison, and ye visited me not,' I was sensible of my negligence in never visiting the prisoners during the course of my life, and was filled with horror of mind beyond expression. This threw me well-nigh into a state of despondency, as I was totally unacquainted with the measures requisite to be pursued for that purpose. However, the gracious God, two or three days after, sent a messenger to me in the school, who informed me of the malefactors that were under sentence of death, and would be glad of any of our friends who could go and pray with them. The messenger, whose name was Sarah Peters, gave me to understand that they were all much awakened, and that one of them, John Lancaster, was converted, and full of the grace of God. In consequence of this reviving information, I committed my school without an hour's delay to my trusty usher, and went with Sarah Peters to Newgate, where we had admittance to the cell wherein they were confined."

Silas Told found Lancaster in a state of religious exaltation, thanking God that he had been sent to Newgate, and praying while they knocked his irons off, till even the attendant sheriff shed tears.

Silas accompanied the condemned men to Tyburn, and saw the gallows for the first time. He tells us that he went not without much shame and fear, because he clearly perceived the greater part of the spectators considered him as one of the sufferers. Lancaster, on arriving at the fatal tree, lifted up his eyes thereto, and said, "Blessed be God," then prayed extemporary in a very excellent manner, and the others behaved with great discretion. Lancaster was friendless, and no one came forward to give the body interment; so the "surgeon's mob" secured it, and carried it over to Paddington for dissection. Scarcely had it disappeared before a party of sailors came on the scene and demanded what had become of it. They followed the "surgeon's mob," recovered the body, and carried it in state through Islington and Hounsditch till they were tired. Then they dropped it upon the first doorstep. The story ends most dramatically, and Told declares that an old woman, disturbed by the uproar, came down and recognized in John Lancaster's corpse the body of her own son.

After this first visit Told went regularly to Newgate. He describes the place, twenty-one years later, but still remembered vividly, as "such an emblem of the infernal pit as he never saw before." However, he struggled bravely on, having a constant pressure upon his mind "to stand up for God in the midst of them," and praying much "for wisdom and fortitude." He preached as often as he was permitted to both felons and debtors. But for the first few years, when attending the malefactors, he met with so many repulses from the keeper and ordinary, as well as from the prisoners themselves, that he was often greatly discouraged. "But notwithstanding I more vehemently pressed through all," becoming the more resolute and "taking no denial." His most bitter opponent, as was not unnatural, was the ordinary, Mr. Taylor, who would constantly station himself on Sunday mornings a few doors from Newgate, and wait there patiently for a couple of hours or more to obstruct his entrance, at the same time forbidding the turnkeys to give him admittance. Told's persistence generally got him through, so that most Sunday mornings he had an opportunity of preaching on the debtors' side to a congregation of forty or more. His influence among the debtors was so great that they readily formed themselves, at his request, into a society or organization, bound by rules and regulations to strict religious observances. In this he was ably seconded by the "circumspection" of two or three prisoners who highly approved of his proposals, and exercised a close watch on the others, whom they would not "suffer to live in any outward sin." For a considerable time the debtors paid regular attention to his preachings and the meetings of the society. After some time, however, the ordinary "raised a great tumult," and managed ever after to shut Silas Told out from that side of the prison.

Told was not to be repressed entirely. In spite of all opposition, he still visited the felons, among whom there was a blessed work, especially among the condemned malefactors. He frequently preached during the space which intervened between sentence and execution; he constantly visited the sick in all parts of the prison, which he tells us he had "reason to believe was made a blessing to many of their souls." His zeal was so great that he spared no pains to do all the good in his power, "embracing every opportunity, both in hearing and speaking, so that in process of time he preached in every prison, as well as in every workhouse, in and about London, and frequently travelled to almost every town within twelve miles of the metropolis."

Silas Told has left us several of his personal experiences in attending upon the condemned. One of the most interesting cases is that of Mary Edmonson, who was convicted of murdering her aunt, on slight evidence, and whose guilt seems doubtful. When the time of her departure for Tyburn approached, Silas begged the sheriff to let him visit her as soon as possible. The sheriff asked him if he was a clergyman. "No, sir," replied Told. "Are you a Dissenting minister?" "I answered him 'No.'" "What are you then?" he went on. Silas replied that he was one who preached the gospel, and who wished to be the means of bringing the prisoner to confession. The sheriff then bade Told seize hold of his bridle-rein, and go by his side to the place of execution; although he cautioned him against the attempt, there being a riotous mob all along the streets, who were fiercely incensed against the poor condemned woman. "As we were proceeding on the road,"—let Silas tell his own story, —"the sheriff's horse being close to the cart, I looked at her from under the horse's bridle, and said, 'My dear, look to Jesus.' This salutary advice quickened her spirit, insomuch that although she did not look about her before, yet she turned herself round to me and joyfully answered, 'Sir, I bless God I can look to Jesus for my comfort!' This produced a pleasant smile on her countenance, which when the sons of violence perceived, they d—d her in a shameful manner; this was accompanied with a vengeful shout, 'See how bold she is! See how the ---- laughs!'

"At length we came to the gallows, where many officers were stationed on horseback, besides numbers more on foot, furnished with constables' staves. When the cart was backed under the gallows, a very corpulent man trod on my foot with such weight that I really thought he had taken it quite off; however, the sheriff soon cleared the way, and formed an arrangement of constables round the cart, then directed some of them to put me into it, in order that I might be of all the service to the malefactor which lay in my power; the sheriff himself standing behind the cart, the better to avail himself of my discourses with her. When she was tied up I began to address her nearly in the same words I did at the Peacock, pressing upon her an acknowledgment of the murder in the most solemn manner, but she declared her innocence in the presence of the sheriff. I then interrogated her. 'Did you not commit the fact? Had you no concern therein? Were you not interested in the murder?' She answered, 'I am as clear of the whole affair as I was the day my mother brought me into the world.' The sheriff on hearing these words shed plenty of tears, and said, 'Good God! it is a second Coleman's case!' This circumstance likewise brought tears from many persons who heard her. When I was getting out of the cart the executioner put the handkerchief over her eyes, but she quickly moved it away, and, addressing herself to the multitude, begged them to pray that God would bring to light, when she was departed, the cause of the assassination, saying she had no doubt but the prayers of such persons would be heard; but repeated her innocence, solemnly declaring that she was as ignorant of the crime for which she was going to suffer as at the day of her birth; and added also, 'I do not lay anything to the charge of my Maker, He has an undoubted right to take me out of this world as seemeth Him good; and although I am clear of this murder, yet I have sinned against Him in many various instances; but I bless God He hath forgiven me all my sins.' Her kinsman then came up into the cart, and would fain have saluted her; but she mildly turned her face aside, strongly suspecting him to be the assassin.

"After her kinsman had gone out of the cart, the executioner a second time was putting the handkerchief over her face, when she again turned it aside, looking at the sheriff, and saying, 'I think it cruel that none is suffered to pray by me.' The sheriff then desired me, for God's sake, to go a second time into the cart and render my prayers with her, which when finished, she began to pray extempore, and in a most excellent manner. When she had concluded her prayer, the executioner performed his part, and being turned off, her body dropped against my right shoulder, nor did she once struggle or move, but was as still as if she had hung for three hours."

One other case I will extract from Silas Told, as it possesses some peculiar features. It is that of the amateur highwaymen who took to the road as a fitting frolic to end a day's pleasure. Messrs. Morgan, Whalley, Brett, and Dupree, and two more, had dined freely at Chelmsford to celebrate an election. Having "glutted themselves with immoderate eating and drinking," they went out on the highway to rob the first person they came across. This happened to be an Essex farmer, whom they stripped of all he had. The farmer got help, followed them into Chelmsford, where they were captured, sent to London, tried at the Old Bailey, and cast for death. They were all of good station —Brett the son of a clergyman in Dublin, Whalley a man of fortune, Dupree a gentleman, and Morgan an officer on board one of His Majesty's ships of war. The last was engaged to Lady E—— Howard, a daughter of the Duke of Norfolk, who frequently visited Mr. Morgan in Newgate, Told being generally present at their interviews. Lady E—— went daily to the king, as did many other persons of great influence, to beg Mr. Morgan's life; but His Majesty steadfastly rejected all petitions, stating that to do so would be to show partiality and a want of justice. But the devoted woman would not forego all hope, and, the morning before the execution, again appeared, and fell upon her knees at the king's feet. "My lady," said His Majesty, "there is no end to your importunity. I will spare his life upon condition that he is not acquainted therewith till he arrives at the place of execution." This was accordingly carried. Brett, Whalley, and Dupree were actually tied up to the gallows. Morgan and two others followed in a second cart, when the sheriff rode up with the respite for Morgan.

"It is hard to express"—I again quote from Told—"the sudden alarm this made among the multitude; and when I turned round and saw one of the prisoners out of the cart, falling to the ground, he having fainted away at the sudden news, I was seized with terror, as I thought it was a rescue rather than a reprieve; but when I beheld Morgan put into a coach, and perceived that Lady E. H. was seated therein, my fear was at an end.

"As soon as Morgan was gone, a venerable gentleman, addressing himself to Dupree, begged him to look steadfastly to God, in whose presence he would shortly appear, and hoped the mercy his companion had received would have no bad effect upon him. Dupree, with all calmness and composure of mind, said, 'Sir, I thank God that him they reprieved; it doesn't by any means affect me.' This gave the gentleman much satisfaction. When prayers were ended, I addressed each of them in the most solemn words I was capable of, which I hope was not in vain, as they all appeared entirely resigned to their fate. Brett earnestly craved the prayers of the multitude, and conjured them all to take warning by the untimely end of the three objects of their present attention. When they were turned off, and the mob nearly dispersed, I hastened back to Newgate, and there seriously conversed with Morgan, who, in consequence of the unexpected reprieve, was scarcely recovered."

Silas Told continued his labours for many years. In 1767 he visited the notorious Mrs. Brownrigg, who was sentenced to be hanged for whipping her servant-maid to death, and whom he accompanied to the gallows. His death occurred in 1779. He lived to hear of Howard's philanthropic exertions, and to see the introduction of some small measure of prison reform.

While Silas Told was thus engaged, another but a more erratic and eccentric philanthropist paid constant visits to Newgate. This was Alexander Cruden, the well-known, painstaking compiler of the 'Concordance.' For a long time he came daily to the gaol, to preach and instruct the prisoners in the gospel, rewarding the most diligent and attentive with money, till he found that the cash thus disbursed was often spent in drink the moment his back was turned. He did more good than this. Through Mr. Cruden's solicitations a sentence of death upon a forger, Richard Potter, was commuted to one of transportation.

More precise details of the manner in which a Newgate ordinary interpreted his trust will be found in the evidence of the Rev. Brownlow Forde, LL.D., before the committee of 1814. Dr. Forde took life pretty easy. Had a prisoner sent for him, he told the committee, he might have gone, but as no one did send, except they were sick and thought themselves at death's door, he confined his ministrations to the condemned, whom he visited twice a week in the day room of the press yard, or daily after the order for execution had arrived. He repudiated the notion that he had anything to do with the state of morals of the gaol. He felt no obligation to instruct youthful prisoners, or attend to the spiritual needs of the mere children so often thrown into Newgate. He never went to the infirmary unless sent for, and did not consider it his duty to visit the sick, and often knew nothing of a prisoner's illness unless he was warned to attend the funeral. Among other reasons, he said that as the turnkeys were always busy, there was no one to attend him. While the chaplain was thus careless and apathetic, the services he conducted were little likely to be edifying or decorous. The most disgraceful scenes were common in the prison chapel. As the prisoners trooped into the galleries they shouted and hallooed to their friends in the body of the church. Friends interchanged greetings, and "How d'ye do, Sall?" was answered by "Gallows well, Conkey Beau," as the men recognized their female acquaintances, and were recognized in turn. The congregation might be pretty quiet after the chaplain had made his appearance, but more often it was disorderly from first to last. Any disposed to behave well were teased and laughed at by others. Unrestricted conversation went on, accompanied by such loud yawning, laughing, or coughing as almost impeded the service. No one in authority attempted to preserve order; the gatesmen, themselves prisoners, might expostulate, but the turnkeys who were present ignored any disturbance until reminded of their duty by the chaplain. The keeper never attended service. It was suggested to him that he might have a pew in the chapel with a private entrance to it from his own house, but nothing came of the proposal. It was not incumbent upon the prisoners, except those condemned to death, to attend chapel. Sometimes it was crowded, sometimes there was hardly a soul. In severe weather the place, in which there was no fire, was nearly empty. It was very lofty, very cold, and the prisoners, ill clad, did not care to shiver through the service. On "curiosity days," those of the condemned sermon, more came, including debtors and visitors from outside, who thronged to see the demeanour of the wretched convicts under the painful circumstances already described. The service must have been conducted in a very slovenly and irreverent manner. Dr. Forde had no clerk, unless it chanced that some one in the condemned pew knew how to read. If not, there were sometimes no responses, and the "whole service was apt to be thrown into confusion."[52]

A man who did so little himself could hardly be expected to view with much favour the undisciplined efforts of amateurs and outsiders. In his opinion the prisoners were only harassed and worried by the Dissenting ministers and others who "haunted the gaol." Dr. Forde said they (the prisoners) did not like it. "It was not to be expected of them, with their habits, that they should be crammed with preaching and prayers." They bore with the visitation, however, hoping to get from the preacher a loaf, or money, or bread and cheese; although the tables were occasionally turned on them, and the visitor, according to Dr. Forde, "would eat up the mutton chop and drink the beer of some well-to-do prisoner, then go to prayers, and depart." These ministers he styled Methodist preachers, or "clergymen who affect to be methodistical preachers," although one, according to him, was a "raggedly-dressed Thames lighterman," who presumed to come in and expound the Scriptures. Dr. Forde makes no mention of Mr. Baker, who must have been a constant visitor in his day—a "white-headed old man" who was in frequent attendance upon the prisoners when Mrs. Fry began her labours, and who had for years "devoted much time and attention to unostentatious but invaluable visits in Newgate."[53]

Dr. Forde seems to have been more in his element when taking the chair at a public-house 'free-and-easy.' In the 'Book for a Rainy Day,' already quoted, Mr. Smith gives us an account of a visit paid to Dr. Forde at a public-house in Hatton Garden. "Upon entering the club-room, we found the Doctor most pompously seated in a superb masonic chair, under a stately crimson canopy placed between the windows. The room was clouded with smoke, whiffed to the ceiling, which gave me a better idea of what I had heard of the 'Black Hole of Calcutta' than any place I had seen. There were present at least a hundred associates of every denomination."

It is consoling to find that while officials slumbered, private philanthropy was active, and had been in some cases for years. Various societies and institutions had been set on foot to assist and often replace public justice in dealing with criminals. The Marine Society grew out of a subscription started by Justices Fielding and Welch, in 1756, for the purpose of clothing vagrant and friendless lads and sending them on board the fleet. The Philanthropic Society had been established in 1789 by certain benevolent persons, to supply a home for destitute boys and girls, and this admirable institution steadily grew and prospered. In 1794 it moved to larger premises, and in 1817 it had an income of £6000 a year, partly from subscriptions and legacies, partly from the profit on labour executed by its inmates.[54] In 1816 another body of well-meaning people, moved by the "alarming increase of juvenile delinquency in the metropolis," formed a society to investigate its causes, inquire into the individual cases of boys actually under sentence, and afford such relief upon release as might appear deserved or likely to prevent a relapse into crime. The members of this society drew up a list containing seven hundred names of the friends and associates of boys in Newgate, all of whom they visited and sought to reform. They went further, and seriously discussed the propriety of establishing a special penitentiary for juveniles, a scheme which was never completely carried out. Another institution was the Refuge for the Destitute, which took in boys and girls on their discharge from prison, to teach them trades and give them a fair start in life. There were also the Magdalen Hospital and the Female Penitentiary, both of which did good work amongst depraved women.

Matters had improved somewhat in Newgate after the report of the committee in 1814, at least as regards the juveniles. A school had been established, over which the new ordinary, Mr. Cotton, who about this time succeeded Dr. Forde, presided, and in which he took a great interest. The chaplain was in communication with the Philanthropic and other institutions, and promising cases were removed to them. The boys were kept as far as possible apart from the men, but not at first from one another. Hence in the one long room they occupied and used for all purposes, eating, drinking, and sleeping, the elder and more vitiated boys were still able to exercise a baneful influence over the young and innocent. More space became available by the removal of the debtors to Whitecross Street, and then the boys were lodged according to categories in four different rooms. Mr. Cotton believed that the boys benefited morally from the instruction and care they received. This juvenile school was one bright spot in the prevailing darkness of Newgate at that particular time. Another and a still more remarkable amelioration in the condition of the prisoners was soon to attract universal attention. The great and good work accomplished by that noble woman Mrs. Fry on the female side of Newgate forms an epoch in prison history, and merits a particular description.

Bad as were the other various courts and so called "sides" in Newgate prison, the quadrangle appropriated to the females was far worse. Its foul and degraded condition had attracted the sympathies of Elizabeth Fry as early as 1813. The winter had been unusually severe, and Mrs. Fry had been induced by several Friends, particularly by William Forster, to visit Newgate and endeavour to alleviate the sufferings of the female prisoners. The space allotted to the women was at that time still curtailed by the portion given over to the state side.[55] They were limited to two wards and two cells, an area of about one hundred and ninety-two superficial yards in all, into which, at the time of Mrs. Fry's visit, some three hundred women with their children were crowded, all classes together, felon and misdemeanant, tried and untried; the whole under the superintendence of an old man and his son. They slept on the floor, without so much as a mat for bedding. Many were very nearly naked, others were in rags; some desperate from want of food, some savage from drink, foul in language, still more recklessly depraved in their habits and behaviour. Everything was filthy beyond description. The smell of the place was quite disgusting. The keeper himself, Mr. Newman, was reluctant to go amongst them. He strove hard to dissuade Mrs. Fry from entering the wards, and failing in that, begged her at least to leave her watch in his office, assuring her that not even his presence would prevent its being torn from her. Mrs. Fry's own account fully endorses all this. "All I tell thee is a faint picture of the reality; the filth, the closeness of the rooms, the ferocious manners and expressions of the women towards each other, and the abandoned wickedness which everything bespoke, are quite indescribable." "One act, the account of which I received from another quarter, marks the degree of wretchedness to which they were reduced at that time. Two women were seen in the act of stripping a dead child for the purpose of clothing a living one."[56]

Mrs. Fry must have gone again, for she wrote under date Feb. 16th, 1813—"Yesterday we were some hours in Newgate with the poor female felons, attending to their outward necessities; we had been twice previously. Before we went away dear Anna Buxton uttered a few words in supplication, and very unexpectedly to myself I did also. I heard weeping, and I thought they appeared much tendered. A very solemn quiet was observed; it was a striking scene, with the poor people around in their deplorable condition." Mrs. Fry's charity extended to the gift of clothing, for it is recorded in her memoirs that many members of her domestic circle had long a vivid recollection of the "green baize garments," and their pleasure in assisting to prepare them.

Nearly four years elapsed before Elizabeth Fry resumed her visits. Newgate and what she had seen there had no doubt made a deep impression on her mind, but a long illness and family afflictions had prevented her from giving her philanthropic yearnings full play. She appears to have recommenced her visits about Christmas 1816, and on Feb. 16th, 1817, there is an entry in her journal to the effect that she had been "lately much occupied in forming a school in Newgate for the children of the poor prisoners, as well as the young criminals." It was in this way that she struck at the hearts of these poor degraded wretches, who were only too eager to save their children from a life of crime.

"The proposal was received," Mrs. Fry says, "even by the most abandoned with tears of joy." The three intervening years between 1813 and 1816 had brought no improvement in the female side. Its inmates—the very scum of the town—were filthy in their habits and disgusting in their persons. Mrs. Fry tells us she found the railings in the inner yard crowded with half-naked women, struggling together for the front situations with the most boisterous violence, and begging with the utmost vociferation. As double gratings had now been fixed at some distance apart to prevent close communication between prisoners and their visitors, the women had fastened wooden spoons to the end of long sticks, which they thrust across the space as they clamoured for alms. Mrs. Fry tells us that she felt as if she were going into a den of wild beasts, and that she well recollects quite shuddering when the door closed upon her, and she was locked in with such a herd of novel and desperate companions. The women, according to another eye-witness, sat about the yard on the stones, squalid in attire, ferocious in aspect. On this occasion a woman rushed out from the ward "yelling like a wild beast;" she made the circuit of the yard, brandishing her arms and tearing the caps or coverings from the heads of the other women. In spite of these terrible scenes, the ladies, several Friends having joined with Mrs. Fry, continued to give their attention to the school. "It was in our visits to the school," she afterwards observed, when giving evidence before the Parliamentary committee of 1818, "where some of us attended every day, that we were witnesses of the dreadful proceedings that went forward on the female side of the prison; the begging, swearing, gaming, fighting, singing, dancing, dressing up in men's clothes; the scenes are too bad to be described, so that we did not think it suitable to admit young persons with us." This awful place had long been aptly entitled "Hell above ground."

It was not strange that these miserable women should be absolutely unsexed. They were often subjected to brutal ill-treatment even before their arrival at Newgate. Many were brought to the prison almost without clothes. If coming from a distance, as in the case of transports lodged in Newgate until embarkation, they were almost invariably ironed, and often cruelly so. One lady saw the female prisoners from Lancaster Castle arrive, not merely handcuffed, but with heavy irons on their legs, which had caused swelling and inflammation. Others wore iron-hoops round their legs and arms, and were chained to each other. On the journey these poor souls could not get up or down from the coach without the whole of them being dragged together. A woman travelled from Cardigan with an iron hoop round her ankle, and fainted when it was removed. This woman's story was, that during a long imprisonment she had worn an iron hoop round her waist, a second round her leg above the knee, a third at the ankle, and all these connected by chains. In the waist hoop were two bolts or fastenings, in which her hands were confined at night when she went to bed. Her bed was only of straw. These wretched and ill-used creatures might be forgiven if they at times broke out into rebellion. For a long time it was the practice with the female transports to riot previous to their departure from Newgate, breaking windows, furniture, or whatever came in their reach. Their outrageous conduct continued all the way from the gaol to the water-side, whither they were conveyed in open waggons, noisy and disorderly to the last, amidst the jeers and shouts of the assembled crowds.

Mrs. Fry, as I have said, endeavoured first to form a school. For this purpose an unoccupied room was set apart by the authorities. Although looking upon her experiment as hopeless, she received cordial support from the sheriffs, the governor, Mr. Newman, and the ordinary of Newgate, Mr. Cotton. The prisoners selected from among themselves a schoolmistress, Mary

Connor by name, who had been committed for stealing a watch, and "who proved eminently qualified for her task." The school, which was for children only and young persons under twenty-five, prospered, and by degrees the heroic band of ladies were encouraged to greater efforts. The conduct of the prisoners, their entreaties not to be excluded from the benefits of the school, inspired Mrs. Fry with confidence, and she resolved to attempt the introduction of order, industry, and religious feeling into Newgate. In April 1817 eleven members of the Society of Friends and another lady, the wife of a clergyman, formed themselves into "an association for the improvement of the female prisoners in Newgate."[57] These devoted persons gave themselves up entirely to their self-imposed task. With no interval of relaxation, and with but few intermissions from the call of other and more imperious duties, they lived among the prisoners.[58] They arrived, in fact, at the hour of unlocking, and spent the whole day in the prison.

The more crying needs of the Newgate female prison at that date are indicated in a memorandum found among Mrs. Fry's papers. It was greatly in need of room, she said. The women should be under the control and supervision of female, and not, as heretofore, of male officers. The number of visitors should be greatly curtailed, and all communications between prisoners and their friends should take place at stated times, under special rules. The prisoners should not be dependent on their friends for food or clothing, but should have a sufficiency of both from the authorities. Employment should be a part of their punishment, and be provided for them by Government. They might work together in company, but should be separated at night according to classes, under a monitor. Religious instruction should be more closely considered. It was to supply these needs that the committee devoted its efforts, the ladies boldly promising that if a matron could be found who would engage never to leave the prison day or night, they would find employment for the prisoners and the necessary funds until the city could be induced to meet the expense.

The matron was found, and the first prison matron appointed, an elderly respectable woman, who proved competent, and discharged her duties with fidelity. Mrs. Fry next sought the countenance and support of the governor and chaplain, both of whom met her at her husband's house to listen to her views and proposals. Mr. Cotton, the ordinary, was not encouraging; he frankly told her that "this, like many other useful and benevolent designs for the improvement of Newgate, would inevitably fail." Mr. Newman, however, bade her not despair; "but he has since confessed that when he came to reflect on the subject, and especially upon the character of the prisoners, he could not see even the possibility of success. Both, however, promised their warmest co-operation." Mrs. Fry next saw one of the sheriffs, asking him to obtain a salary for the matron, and a room in the prison for the Ladies' Committee. This sheriff, Mr. Bridges, was willing to help her if his colleagues and the Corporation agreed, "but told her that his concurrence or that of the city would avail her but little—the concurrence of the women themselves was indispensable; and that it was in vain to expect such untamed and turbulent spirits would submit to the regulations of a woman armed with no legal authority, and unable to inflict any punishment." Nevertheless, the two sheriffs met Mrs. Fry at Newgate one Sunday afternoon. The women, seventy in number, were assembled, and asked whether they were prepared to submit to the new rules. All "fully and unanimously" agreed to abide by them, to the surprise of the sheriffs, who doubted their submitting to such restraints. Upon this the sheriffs addressed the prisoners, telling them that the scheme had official support; then turning to Mrs. Fry, one of the two magistrates said, "Well, ladies, you see your materials."

The next business was to obtain work. It had occurred to Mrs. Fry that the manufacture of clothing for Botany Bay would be a suitable sort of employment, and she accordingly called upon the city firm, Messrs. Richard Dixon and Co., of Fenchurch Street, who had hitherto supplied these articles. She told them plainly that she was seeking to deprive them of a part of their trade, whereupon they magnanimously altogether relinquished it, feeling loth "to obstruct her laudable designs." The work obtained, the work-room was next prepared. The sheriffs sent in carpenters, and the old prison laundry was speedily cleaned, whitewashed, and got ready; after which Mrs. Fry assembled all the convicted prisoners, told them her views and hopes, read them her proposed rules, which, as she did not come among them with "any absolute or authoritative pretensions," should be put to the vote. The women present voluntarily subscribed to all, although they were stringent, and aimed at the reform of evil and probably long-cherished habits. These rules need not be inserted here at length. It will suffice to say that they laid down the principle of constant employment at knitting, needlework, or so forth; that begging, swearing, gambling, quarrelling, and immoral conversation were forbidden; that the women should submit themselves to their monitors, elected by themselves, to the yard-keeper, similarly elected, and to the matron; that personal cleanliness, a quiet, orderly demeanour, and silence at the work-tables should be incumbent on all.

These rules were not only adopted readily, but strictly observed. In one month a complete transformation had taken place in the women. At first Mrs. Fry had wished to keep this gratifying result a secret, but it was thought expedient to report progress to the Corporation, so that the new system might be approved and established by the authority of the city. On a day fixed the Lord Mayor, accompanied by the sheriffs and several aldermen, attended at Newgate, and saw with their own eyes the remarkable change effected in so short a time. The daily routine went on before them exactly as usual. The prisoners assembled; one of the ladies read a chapter in the Bible, then the women proceeded quietly to their work. "Their attention during the time of reading, their orderly and sober deportment, their decent dress, the absence of anything like tumult, noise, or contention, the obedience and respect showed by them, and the cheerfulness exhibited in their countenance and manners, conspired to excite the astonishment and admiration of their visitors. Many of these knew Newgate, had visited it a few months before, and had not forgotten the painful impressions made by a scene exhibiting perhaps the very utmost limits of misery and guilt."[59] The city magistrates at once accepted the results achieved. Mrs. Fry's rules were adopted into the prison system, power was conferred on the ladies to punish the refractory, and the salary of the matron was incorporated with the regular expenses of the prison.

The evidence of a gentleman who visited Newgate within a fortnight of the adoption of the new rules may fitly be added here. He went one day to call on Mrs. Fry at the prison, and was conducted to the women's side. "On my approach," he says, "no loud or dissonant sounds or angry voices indicated that I was about to enter a place which I was credibly assured had long had for one of its titles that of 'Hell above ground.' The court-yard into which I was admitted, instead of being peopled with beings scarcely human, blaspheming, fighting, tearing each other's hair, or gaming with a filthy pack of cards for the very clothes they wore, which often did not suffice even for decency, presented a scene where stillness and propriety reigned. I was conducted by a decently-dressed person, the newly-appointed yards-woman, to the door of a ward where at the head of a long table sat a lady belonging to the Society of Friends. She was reading aloud to about sixteen women prisoners, who were engaged in needlework around it. Each wore a clean-looking blue apron and bib, with a ticket having a number on it suspended from her neck by a red tape. They all rose on my entrance, curtsied respectfully, and then at a signal given resumed their seats and employments. Instead of a scowl, leer, or ill-suppressed laugh, I observed upon their countenances an air of self-respect and gravity, a sort of consciousness of their improved character, and the altered position in which they were placed. I afterwards visited the other wards, which were the counterparts of the first."

The efforts of the ladies, which had been at first concentrated upon the convicted, were soon directed also upon the untried. These still continued in a deplorable state, quarrelling and disorderly, bolder and more reckless because they were in doubt as to their future fate. Unhappily the same measure of success did not wait upon the attempt on this side. Many of these women counted upon an early release, and would not take heartily to work, although when they did they were "really and essentially improved." Nor could it be expected that the new régime could be established without occasional insubordination and some backsliding. The rules were sometimes broken. Spirits had been introduced more than once; six or seven cases of drunkenness had occurred. But the women were careful not to break out before the ladies; if they swore, it was out of hearing, and although they still played cards, it was when the ladies' backs were turned. Mrs. Fry told the Parliamentary committee how she expostulated with the women when she found they still gambled, and how she impressed upon them, "if it were true that there were cards in the prison," that she should consider it a proof of their regard if they would have the candour and kindness to bring her their packs. By and by a gentle tap came at her door as she sat alone with the matron, and a trembling woman entered to surrender her forbidden cards; another and another followed, till Mrs. Fry had soon five packs of cards in her possession. The culprits fully expected reproof, but Mrs. Fry assured them that their fault was fully condoned, and, much to their surprise, rewarded them for their spontaneous good feeling. This seems to have been in the ascendant on the whole, and at the end of the first year it was satisfactorily proved to competent judges, the past and present Lord Mayor, the sheriffs, gaolers, and various grand juries, the ordinary, and others, that an extraordinary change for the better had shown itself in the conduct of the females.

The work done in Newgate soon obtained much publicity, to the undoubted and manifest distaste of those who had accomplished it. It was first noticed in the newspapers by the well-known Robert Owen, who adduced it as a proof of the effects of kindness and regular habits. Prison discipline was at this time attracting attention, and Mrs. Fry's labours were very remarkable in this line. Very soon the female side at Newgate became quite a show. Every one of any status in society, every distinguished traveller, all people with high aims or deep feelings, were constrained to visit the prison. Royalty for the first time took an interest in the gaol. The Duke of Gloucester was among the visitors, and was escorted round by Mrs. Fry in person. Another day she was engaged with the Chancellor of the Exchequer; on a third with the Home Secretary and the Speaker of the House of Commons. Still higher and more public honour was done to this noble woman by the Marquis of Lansdowne in the House of Lords, who in 1818, in moving an address on the state of the English prisons, spoke in terms of the highest eulogy of what had been effected "by Mrs. Fry and other benevolent persons in Newgate." After this, admission to view the interior of Newgate was eagerly sought by numbers of persons whose applications could not well be refused, in spite of the inconvenience occasioned by thus turning a place of durance into a sentimental lounge. A more desirable and useful result of these ministrations was the eagerness they bred in others to imitate this noble example. Numbers of persons wrote to Mrs. Fry from all parts of the country, seeking advice and encouragement as to the formation of similar societies. Even magistrates appealed to her regarding the management of their prisons. In consequence of the numerous communications received by the Newgate Association, a "corresponding committee" was formed to give information and send replies. Letters came from various capitals of Europe, including St. Petersburgh, Turin, and Amsterdam, which announced the formation of Ladies' Societies for prison visiting.

During many years following its inauguration, the "Ladies' Association" continued their benevolent exertions with marked and well-deserved success. They did not confine their labours to Newgate, but were equally active in the other metropolitan prisons. They also made the female transports their peculiar charge, and obtained many reforms and ameliorations in the arrangement of the convict ships, and the provision for the women on landing at the Antipodes. That the first brilliant successes should be long and continuously maintained could hardly be expected. As time passed and improvements were introduced, there was not the same room for active intervention, and it was difficult to keep alive the early fire. The energy of the Ladies' Committee might not exactly flag, but it came later on to be occasionally misapplied. And it will be found in a later chapter, that the inspectors of prisons were not altogether satisfied with the ground taken up by the association.

THE BEGINNINGS OF PRISON REFORM

P*rison reform generally taken up—Mr. Neild's visitation—Howard's great work repeated—Neglect of prisons not the fault of the legislature—Numerous gaol Acts passed, but not carried out by local authorities—Prison Discipline Society formed in 1817—Its distinguished members—Mr. Buxton a leading spirit—His views and arguments for insisting on prison reform—Idea of classification first given in gaol Act of 1784, but never carried out—The society animadverts upon condition of various prisons—The Borough compter—Guildford—Irons—Their weight—Overcrowding—Underground dungeons—"The pit"—A few brilliant exceptions—Bury St. Edmunds—Ilchester—Newgate compared badly with last-named, but diet improved, and irons removed from untried—Complete reform still indispensable for real improvement—Prisoners committed to Newgate taken through the streets in gangs, chained—Opponents of reform—Sydney Smith laughs at efforts of Prison Discipline Society—It continues to work undeterred—Gives attention to tread-wheels—Also to plans for prison construction—Faulty prison architecture—Society rewarded by new legislation, and devotes itself* *to seeing that new Acts are observed—Borough prisons the worst—Acts did not apply to them—Great diversity of practice and discipline prevail—Various hours of labour—Borough gaols continue bad because municipalities beyond reach of the law—Description of worst borough gaols—Newgate continues a bye-word—Its shortcomings—Further legislation—Report of Lords' Committee in 1835—Reform of Municipal Corporations brings about reform in borough prisons.*

WHILE Mrs. Fry was diligently engaged upon her self-imposed task in Newgate, other earnest people, inspired doubtless by her noble example, were stirred up to activity in the same great work. It began to be understood that prison reform could only be compassed by continuous and combined effort. The pleadings, however eloquent, of a single individual were unable to more than partially remedy the widespread and colossal evils of British prisons. Howard's energy and devotion were rewarded by lively sympathy, but the desire to improve which followed his exposures was but short-lived. It was so powerless against the persistent neglect of those intrusted with prison management, that, five-and-twenty years later, Mr. Neild, a second Howard, as indefatigable and self-sacrificing, found by personal visitation that the condition of gaols throughout the kingdom was, with a few bright exceptions, still deplorable and disgraceful. Mr. Neild was compelled to admit in 1812 that "the great reformation produced by Howard was in several places merely temporary: some prisons that had been ameliorated under the persuasive influence of his kind advice were relapsing into their former horrid state of privation, filthiness, severity, or neglect; many new dungeons had aggravated the evils against which his sagacity could not but remonstrate; the motives for a transient amendment were becoming paralyzed, and the effect had ceased with the cause."

I have shown in a previous chapter what Newgate was at this period, despite a vast expenditure and boasted efforts to introduce reforms. Some of the county gaols, and one or two borough gaols, had been rebuilt, generally through the personal activity of influential and benevolent local magnates, but the true principles of prison construction were as yet but imperfectly understood, and such portions of the "improved" gaols of that period as were still extant a few years back, contrast ludicrously with the prison architecture based upon a century's experience of our own age.

The neglect of prison reform in those days was not to be visited upon the legislature. The executive, although harassed by internal commotion and foreign war, was not entirely callous to the crying need for amelioration in gaols. Measures remedial, although at best partial and incomplete, were introduced from time to time. Thus in 1813 the exaction of gaol fees had been forbidden by law, and two other acts more peremptory and precise followed on the same subject in succeeding years. In 1814 a bill was brought in to insist upon the appointment of chaplains in gaols, and when this had passed into law, it was subsequently amplified, and the rates of salaries fixed. Various acts were also passed to consolidate and amend previous gaol acts. The erection of new prison buildings was made imperative under certain conditions and following certain rules; the principle of classification was freshly enunciated; prison regulations were framed for general observance. But the effect of this legislation was rather weakened by the remoteness of the pressure exercised. The onus of improvement lay upon the magistracy, the local authorities administering local funds, and they were not threatened with any particular penalties if they evaded or ignored the new acts. Moreover, the laws applied more particularly to county jurisdictions. The borough gaols, those in fact under corporate management, were not included in the new measures; it was hoped that their rulers would hire accommodation in the county prisons, and that the inferior establishments would in course of time disappear. Yet the borough gaols were destined to survive many years, and to exhibit for a long time to come all the worst features of gaol mismanagement.

It was in 1817 that a small band of philanthropists resolved to form themselves into an association for the improvement of prison discipline. They were hopeless of any general reform by the action of the executive alone. They felt that private enterprise might with advantage step in, and by the collection and diffusion of information, and the reiteration of sound advice, greatly assist the good work. The association was organized under the most promising auspices. A king's son, the Duke of Gloucester, was the patron; among the vice-presidents were many great peers of the realm, several bishops, and a number of members of the House of Commons, including Mr. Manners Sutton, Mr. Sturges Bourne, Sir James Mackintosh, Sir James Scarlett, and William Wilberforce. An active committee was appointed, comprising many names already well known, some of them destined to become famous in the annals of philanthropy. One of the moving spirits was the Honourable H. G. Bennet, M.P., whose vigorous protests against the lamentable condition of Newgate have already been recorded. Mrs. Fry's brother, Mr. Samuel Hoare, Junior, was chairman of the committee, on which also served many noted members of the Society of Friends—Mr. Gurney, Mr. Fry, Messrs. Forster, and Mr. T. F. Buxton, the coadjutor of Wilberforce in the great anti-slavery struggle. Mr. Buxton had already been associated with Mrs. Fry in the Newgate visitation, and his attention had thus been drawn to the neglected state of English prisons. When in Belgium he had examined with great satisfaction the admirable management of the great "Maison de Force" at Ghent,[60] which Howard had eulogized some forty years before. Mr. Buxton communicated what he had seen at Ghent to the Prison Discipline Society, and was induced to make the account public. In order to give greater value to the pamphlet, he personally visited several English gaols, and pointed his observations by drawing forcible contrasts between the good and bad.

Mr. Buxton's small work on prison discipline[61] gave a new aspect to the question he had so much at heart. For the first time the doctrine was enunciated that prisoners had rights of their own. The untried, and in the eyes of the law still innocent, could claim pure air, wholesome and sufficient food, and opportunities for exercise. They had a right, Mr. Buxton affirmed, to be employed in their own crafts, provided it could be safely followed in prison. "You have no right," he says, addressing the authorities, "to subject a prisoner to suffering from cold, by want of bed-clothing by night or firing by day; and the reason is plain: you have taken him from his home, and have deprived him of the means of providing himself with the necessaries or comforts of life, and therefore you are bound to furnish him with moderate indeed but suitable accommodation." "You have for the same reason," he goes on, "no right to ruin his habits by compelling him to be idle, his morals by compelling him to mix with a promiscuous assemblage of hardened and convicted criminals, or his health by forcing him at night into a damp, unventilated cell, with such crowds of companions as very speedily render the air foul and putrid; or to make him sleep in close contact with the victims of contagious and loathsome disease, or amidst the noxious effluvia of dirt and corruption. In short, attention to his feelings, mental and bodily, a supply of every necessary, abstraction from evil society, the conservation of his health and industrious habits, are the clear, evident, undeniable rights of an unconvicted prisoner." Nor even when found guilty and his liberty forfeited did his privileges cease. The law appointed a suitable punishment for the offence; it was for those charged with the administration of the law to guard carefully against any aggravation of that punishment, to see that "no circumstances of severity are found in his treatment which are not found in his sentence." No judge ever condemned a man to be half-perished with cold by day, or half-suffocated with heat by night. "Who ever heard of a criminal being sentenced to catch the rheumatism or the typhus fever?" "Disease, cold, famine, nakedness, and contagious and polluted air are not lawful punishments in the hands of the civil magistrates; nor has he a right to poison or starve his fellow-creatures."[62] "The convicted delinquent has his rights," said Mr. Buxton authoritatively. "All measures and practices in prison which may injure him in any way are illegal, because they are not specified in his sentence; he is therefore entitled to a wholesome atmosphere, decent clothing and bedding, and a diet sufficient to support him."

These somewhat novel but undoubtedly indisputable propositions were backed up, not by sound arguments only, but by the letter of the law. As Mr. Buxton pointed out, many old acts of parliament designed to protect the prisoner were still in full force. Some might be in abeyance, but they had never been repealed, and some were quite freshly imported upon the Statute Book. As far back as the reign of Charles II., a law was passed[63] declaring that sufficient provision should be made for the relief and setting on work of "poor and needy prisoners committed to the common jail for felony and other misdemeanours, who many times perish before their trial; and the poor there living idle and unemployed become debauched, and come forth instructed in the practice of thievery and lewdness." As a remedy, justices of the peace were empowered to provide materials for the setting of poor prisoners to work, and to pay overseers or instructors out of the county rates. Again, the 22 Charles II. c 20 ordered the gaoler to keep felons and debtors "separate and apart from one another, in distinct rooms, on pain of forfeiting his office and treble damages to the party aggrieved." A much later act, the 14 Geo. III. c. 59 (1774), which was contemporaneous with Howard's first journeys, laid down precise rules as regards cleanliness, and the proper supply of space and air. This act set forth that "whereas the malignant fever commonly called the jail distemper is found to be owing to want of cleanliness and fresh air in the several jails, the fatal consequences whereof might be prevented if the justices of the peace were duly authorized to provide such accommodations in jails as may be necessary to answer this salutary purpose, it is enacted that the justices shall order the walls of every room to be scraped and white-washed once every year." Ventilators, hand and others, were to be supplied. An infirmary, consisting of two distinct rooms, one for males and one for females, should be provided for the separate accommodation of the sick. Warm and cold baths, or "commodious bathing tubs," were to be kept in every gaol, and the prisoners directed to wash in them before release. These provisions were almost a dead letter. Yet another act passed in 1791, if properly observed, should have insured proper attention to them. By the 31 Geo. III. c. 46, s. 5, two or more justices were appointed visitors of prisons, and directed to visit and inspect three times every quarter. They were to report in writing to quarter sessions as to the state of the gaol, and as to all abuses which they might observe therein.

The most important gaol act of that early period, however, was the 24 Geo. III. c. 54, s. 4 (1784), which was the first legislative attempt to compel the classification of prisoners, or their separation into classes according to their categories or crimes. It was made incumbent upon the justices to provide distinct places of confinement for five classes of prisoners, viz.—

1. Prisoners convicted of felony.
2. Prisoners committed on a charge or suspicion of felony.
3. Prisoners guilty of misdemeanours.
4. Prisoners charged with misdemeanours.

5. Debtors.

It was further ordered that male prisoners should be kept perfectly distinct from the females. King's evidences were also to be lodged apart. Infirmaries separating the sexes were also to be provided, a chapel too, and warm and cold baths. "Care also was to be taken that the prisoners shall not be kept in any apartment underground."

In an early report of the Prison Discipline Improvement Society, published some six-and-thirty years after the promulgation of this act, the flagrant and persistent violations of it and others, which had continued through that long period, are forcibly pointed out. In 1818, out of five hundred and eighteen prisons in the United Kingdom, to which a total of upwards of one hundred thousand prisoners had been committed in the year, only twenty-three prisons were divided according to law; fifty-nine had no division whatever to separate males and females; one hundred and thirty-six had only one division for the purpose; sixty-eight had only two divisions, and so on. In four hundred and forty-five prisons no work of any description had been introduced for the employment of prisoners; in the balance some work was done, but with the most meagre results. The want of room was still a crying evil. In one hundred gaols, capable of accommodating only eight thousand five hundred and forty-five persons, as many as thirteen thousand and fifty-seven were crowded. Many of the gaols were in the most deplorable condition: incommodious, as has been stated, insecure, unhealthy, and unprovided with the printed or written regulations required by law. To specify more particularly one or two of the worst, it may be mentioned that in the Borough Compter the old evils of indiscriminate association still continued unchecked. All prisoners passed their time in absolute idleness, or killed it by gambling and loose conversation. The debtors were crowded almost inconceivably. In a space twenty feet long by six wide, twenty men slept on eight straw beds, with sixteen rugs amongst them, and a piece of timber for a bolster. Mr. Buxton, who found this, declared that it seemed physically impossible, but he was assured that it was true, and that it was accomplished by "sleeping edgeways." One poor wretch, who had slept next the wall, said he had been literally unable to move for the pressure. "In the morning the stench and heat were so oppressive that he and every one else on waking rushed unclothed into the yard;" and the turnkey told Mr. Buxton that the "smell on first opening the door was enough to knock down a horse." The hospital was filled with infectious cases, and in one room, seven feet by nine, with closed windows, where a lad lay ill with fever, three other prisoners, at first perfectly healthy, were lodged. Of course they were seized with the fever; so that the culprit, in addition to his sentence, had to endure by "the regulations of the city a disease very dangerous in its nature," and ran the risk of a lingering and painful death.[64]

At Guildford prison, which Mr. Buxton also visited in 1818, there was no infirmary, no chapel, no work, no classification. The irons, which nearly every one wore, were remarkably heavy; those double ironed could not take off their small clothes.[65] No prison dress was allowed, and half the inmates were without shirts or shoes or stockings. The diet was limited to dry bread, which was of the best certainly, and a pound and a half in weight. Matters were on much the same footing at St. Albans. They were far worse at Bristol, although at Mr. Buxton's visit a new gaol was in process of erection, the first step towards reform since Howard's visitation in 1774. In 1818 the old gaol was so densely packed that it was nearly impossible to pass through the yards for the throng. One hundred and fifty were lodged in a prison just capable of holding fifty-two. In the crowd, all of them persons who had "no other avocation or mode of livelihood but thieving," Mr. Buxton counted eleven children—children hardly old enough to be released from the nursery. All charged with felony were in heavy irons, without distinction of age. All were in ill health; almost all were in rags; almost all were filthy in the extreme. The state of the prison, the desperation of the prisoners, broadly hinted in their conversation and plainly expressed in their conduct, the uproar of oaths, complaints, and obscenity, "the indescribable stench," presented together a concentration of the utmost misery and the utmost guilt. It was "a scene of infernal passions and distresses," says Buxton, "which few have imagination sufficient to picture, and of which fewer still would believe that the original is to be found in this enlightened and happy country."

There was still worse to come. Having explored the yards and adjacent day rooms, and sleeping cells, a door was unlocked, the visitors were furnished with candles, and they descended eighteen long steps into a vault. At the bottom was a circular space, through which ran a narrow passage, and the sides of which were fitted with barrack bedsteads. The floor was on the level of the river, and very damp. The smell at one o'clock of the day "was something more than can be expressed by the term disgusting." On the dirty bedstead lay a wretched being in the throes of severe illness. The only ventilation of this pit, this "dark, cheerless, damp, unwholesome cavern—a dungeon in its worst sense"—was by a kind of chimney, which the prisoners kept hermetically sealed, and which had never been opened in the memory of the turnkey. Untried persons were often lodged in this nauseous underground den, and sometimes slept in "the pit," loaded with heavy irons for a whole year, waiting the gaol delivery. Confinement for twelve months in the Bristol gaol was counted a punishment equivalent to seven years' transportation.

In this prison there was no female infirmary. Sick women and their children remained in the ordinary wards, and propagated disease. No prison dress was allowed; no reception-room was provided, no soap, towels, or baths. The bedclothes consisted only of a single "very slight" rug. The allowance of food daily to felons was a fourpenny loaf, a price which in those days fluctuated enormously—as much as a hundred per cent. in a couple of years; but as no similar variation occurred in the prisoner's appetite, his ration was somewhat precarious. As for the debtors, they had no allowance whatever, and were often in imminent danger of starvation. With all this, the inmates were crowded together at night to such a degree as to excite surprise that they should escape suffocation. There reigned through the whole edifice a chilly, damp, unwholesome atmosphere, and the effluvia from the prisoners was so nauseous that the chaplain found it necessary to take his place before they entered chapel, as he could not otherwise have faced the smell.

It is consoling to know that there were a few brilliant exceptions to this cruel, callous neglect. Already, as early as 1818, a prison existed at Bury St. Edmunds which was a model for imitation to others at that time, and which even fulfilled many of the exacting requirements of modern days. The great principles of classification, cleanliness, and employment were closely observed. There were eighty-four separate sleeping-cells, and unless the gaol was overcrowded, every inmate passed the night alone, and in comparative comfort, with a bed and proper bedding. The prison stood on a dry, airy situation outside the town. Prisoners on reception were treated as they are now-a-days—bathed, dressed in prison clothes, and inspected by the surgeon. No irons were worn except as a punishment. Personal cleanliness was insisted upon, and all parts of the prison were kept scrupulously clean. There was an infirmary, properly found and duly looked after. No idleness was permitted among the inmates. Trades were taught, or prisoners were allowed to follow their own if suitable. There was, besides, a mill for grinding corn, somewhat similar to a turn-spit, which prisoners turned by walking in rows. This made exertion compulsory, and imposed hard labour as a proper punishment. Another gaol, that of Ilchester, was also worthy of all commendation. It exhibited all the good points of that at Bury. At Ilchester the rule of employment had been carried further. A system not adopted generally till nearly half a century later had already prevailed at Ilchester. The new gaol had been in a great measure constructed by the prisoners themselves. Masons, bricklayers, carpenters, painters had been employed upon the buildings, and the work was pronounced excellent by competent judges. Industrial labour had also been introduced with satisfactory results. Blanket weaving and cloth spinning was carried on prosperously, and all the material for prisoners' apparel was manufactured in the gaol. There were work-rooms for wool-washing, dyeing, carding, and spinning. The looms were constantly busy. Tailors were always at work, and every article of clothing and bedding was made up within the walls. There was a prison laundry too, where all the prisoners' linen was regularly washed. The moral welfare of the inmates was as closely looked after as the physical. There was an attentive chaplain, a schoolmaster, and regular religious and other instruction.

Compared with those highly meritorious institutions Newgate still showed but badly. Its evils were inherent and irremediable, but some ameliorating measures had been introduced, mainly through the exertions of a new governor, Mr. Brown, who succeeded Mr. Newman at Newgate in 1817.[66] The most noticeable of the improvements introduced was a better regulation of dietaries within the prison. The old haphazard system, by which meat was issued in bulk, a week's allowance at a time, was abolished, and there was a regular scale of daily rations adopted. The diet was now ample. It consisted of a pound and a half of bread per diem; for breakfast a pint of gruel;

for dinner half a pound of boiled meat, or a quart of soup with vegetables, on alternate days. The food was properly prepared in the prison kitchen. Meat was no longer issued raw, to be imperfectly cooked before a ward fire and bolted gluttonously, the whole two pounds at one sitting. Mr. Brown confidently asserted that no gaol in England now fed its inmates so well as did Newgate. So plentiful was this dietary, that although the old permission remained in force of allowing the friends of prisoners to bring them supplies from outside, the practice was falling into abeyance, and the prisoners seldom required private assistance to eke out their meals.[67] It was also claimed for the more ample and more orderly distribution of victuals, that the general health of the prisoners had greatly improved. Mr. Brown also, much to his own credit, brought about the abandonment of the practice of ironing all prisoners as a matter of course.

In 1818 prisoners awaiting trial in Newgate, were at length relieved from this illegal infliction. Convicts were not even compelled to wear irons, providing they behaved well. It was found that shackles might be safely dispensed with, even in the case of the most desperate characters. This was effected by stopping the nearly indiscriminate admission of visitors, which had hitherto prevailed all over the gaol. Ironing it will be remembered,[68] was a distinguishing badge, so that when the gaol was cleared the free might be readily known from the captive, and escapes prevented. Under the new rule visitors were not allowed to pass into the interior of the prison, but were detained between the grating. This change led to some discontent, until it was found that the much greater boon of relief from irons accompanied it, and the reform was quietly accepted. Indeed the best consequences followed from the removal of irons. The prisoners were much better disposed; there were no riots, and fewer disturbances.

But nothing short of radical reform and complete reconstruction could touch the deep-seated evils of association, overcrowding, and idleness. The first still produced deplorable results—results to be observable for many years to come. Mr. Buxton mentions the case of a boy whose apparent innocence and artlessness had attracted his attention. He had been committed for an offence for which he was acquitted. He left Newgate utterly corrupted, and after lapsing into crime, soon returned with a very different character. Other cases of moral deterioration have already been recorded. Some attempt was made to reduce the overcrowding, on the recommendation of the House of Commons Committee of 1818, but this applied only a partial remedy. The bulk of the prisoners were still left in idleness. A few fortunate criminals, many of them kept back from transportation on purpose, who were skilled in trades, were employed at them. Painters, plasterers, and carpenters were allowed to follow their handicrafts, with the reward of sixpence per diem and a double allowance of food. They used their own tools, and this without any dangerous consequences as regards facilitating the escape of others, thus disposing of the objection so long raised against the industrial employment of prisoners in Newgate. But this boon of toil was denied to all but a very limited number. As the Prison Discipline Society pertinently observed in a report dated 1820, "It is obvious that reformation must be materially impeded, and in some cases utterly defeated, when the prisoners are defectively classed, remain without constant inspection or employment, and are consequently condemned to habits of idleness and dissipation."

Newgate prisoners were the victims to another most objectionable practice which obtained all over London. Persons committed to a metropolitan gaol at that time were taken in gangs, men and women handcuffed together, or linked on to a long chain, unless they could afford to pay for a vehicle out of their own funds. Even then they were not certain of the favour, for I find a reference to a decent and respectable woman sent to Newgate, who handed a shilling to the escort warder to provide her with a hackney coach; but this functionary pocketed the cash, and obliged the woman to walk, chained to the rest. As the miserable crew filed through the public streets, exposed to the scornful gaze of every passenger, they were followed by a crowd of reckless boys, who jeered at and insulted them. Many thus led in procession were in a shocking condition of dirt and misery, frequently nearly naked, and often bearing upon them the germs, more or less developed, of contagious disease. "Caravans," the forerunners of the prison vans, were first made use of about 1827. That the need for prison reform was imperative may be gathered from the few out of many instances I have adduced, yet there were those who, wedded to ancient ideas, were intolerant of change; they would not admit the existence of any evils. One smug alderman, a member of the House of Commons, sneered at the ultra philanthropy of the champions of prison improvement. Speaking on a debate on prison matters, he declared that "our prisoners have all that prisoners ought to have, without gentlemen think they ought to be indulged with Turkey carpets." The Society for the Improvement of Prison Discipline was taxed with a desire to introduce a system tending to divest punishment of its just and salutary terrors; an imputation which the Society indignantly and very justly repudiated, the statement being, as they said, "refuted by abundant evidence, and having no foundation whatever in truth."

Among those whom the Society found arrayed against it was Sydney Smith, who, in a caustic article contributed to the 'Edinburgh Review,' protested against the pampering of criminals. While fully admitting the good intentions of the Society, he condemned their ultra humanitarianism as misplaced. He took exception to various of the proposals of the Society. He thought they leant too much to a system of indulgence and education in gaols. He objected to the instruction of prisoners in reading and writing. "A poor man who is lucky enough," he said, "to have his son committed for a felony educates him under such a system for nothing, while the virtuous simpleton who is on the other side of the wall is paying by the quarter for these attainments." He was altogether against too liberal a diet; he disapproved of industrial occupations in gaols, as not calculated to render prisons terrible. "There should be no tea and sugar, no assemblage of female felons around the washing-tub, nothing but beating hemp and pulling oakum and pounding bricks—no work but what was tedious, unusual."... "In prisons, which are really meant to keep the multitude in order, and to be a terror to evil-doers, there must be no sharings of profits, no visiting of friends, no education but religious education, no freedom of diet, no weavers' looms or carpenters' benches. There must be a great deal of solitude, coarse food, a dress of shame, hard, incessant, irksome, eternal labour, a planned and regulated and unrelenting exclusion of happiness and comfort."[69]

Undeterred by these sarcasms and misrepresentations, the Society pursued its laudable undertaking with remarkable energy and great singleness of purpose. The objects it had in view were set forth in one of its earliest meetings. It sought to obtain and diffuse useful information, to suggest beneficial regulations, and circulate tracts demonstrating the advantages of classification, constant inspection, regular employment, and humane treatment generally, with religious and moral instruction. It earnestly advocated the appointment of female officers to take exclusive charge of female prisoners, a much-needed and, according to our ideas, indispensable reform, already initiated by the Ladies' Committee at Newgate.[70] It made the subject of the newly-invented tread-wheels, or stepping-wheels, as they were at first called, its peculiar affair, and obtained full details, from places where they had been adopted, of the nature of these new machines,[71] the method by which they were worked, and the dietaries of the prisoners employed upon them. Nor did it confine itself to mere verbal recommendations. The good it tried to do took active shape in the establishment of temporary refuges—at Hoxton for males, and in the Hackney Road for females—for the reception of deserving cases discharged from prison. The governor of Newgate and other metropolitan prisons had orders of admission to this refuge, which he could bestow on prisoners on release, and so save the better-disposed or the completely destitute from lapsing at once into crime. The refuge, which had for its object the training of its inmates in habits of industry, and in moral and religious duty, and which after a time sought to provide them with suitable situations, was supported entirely out of the funds of the Society. At the time of its greatest prosperity, its annual income from donations and subscriptions was about £1600.

Another point to which the Society devoted infinite pains was the preparation of plans for the guidance of architects in the construction of prisons. A very valuable volume published by the Society traced the progress of prison architecture from the days when the gaol was the mere annexe of the baronial or episcopal castle, or a dungeon above or below the gate of a town, to the first attempts at systematic reconstruction carried out under the advice and supervision of Howard.[72] It is interesting to observe that the plan of "radiation," by which the prison blocks radiated from a central hall, like spokes in a wheel, was introduced as early as 1790 by Mr. Blackburn, an architect of eminence who was very largely employed in the erection of prison buildings at the close of the last century. With some important modifications this principle of radiation is still the rule. The Society did not limit its remarks to the description of what had already been done, but it offered suggestions for future buildings, with numerous carefully-executed drawings and designs of the model it recommended for imitation. Experience has since shown that in some respects these plans are defective, especially in the placing of the governor's residence in the centre of the prison. It was thought that this would guarantee constant supervision and inspection, but it did nothing of the kind, and only the presence of warders on duty is found now-a-days to be really efficacious. The main recommendations, however, are based upon common sense, and none are more commendable than that which deprecates the excessive ornamentation of the external parts of the edifice. "The new gaols," as Howard says, "having pompous fronts, appear like palaces to the lower class of people, and many persons are against them on this account." The Prison Society reproves the misdirected efforts of ambitious architects, who by a lavish and improvident expenditure of public money sought to "rank the prisons they built among the most splendid buildings of the city or town." Absence of embellishment is in perfect unison with the character of the establishment. These are principles fully recognized now-a-days, and it may fairly be conceded that the Prison Discipline Society's ideal differed little from that kept in view in the construction of the latest and best modern gaols.

After a few years of active exertion the Society was rewarded by fresh legislation. To its efforts, and their effect upon Parliament and the public mind, we must attribute the new Gaol Acts of 4 Geo. IV. cap. 64, and 5 Geo. IV. cap. 85, which having gone through several sessions, at last became law in 1823-4. By the preamble of the first-named act it was declared "expedient to introduce such measures and arrangements as shall not only provide for the safe custody, but shall also tend more effectually to preserve the health and improve the morals of the prisoners, and shall insure the proper measure of punishment to convicted offenders." Accordingly due provision was made for the enforcement of hard labour on all prisoners sentenced to it, and for the employment of all others. As a rider to this enactment, it was laid down that any prisoner who could work and would not had no claim to be supported in gaol, "unless such ability (to work) should cease by reason of sickness, infirmity, the want of sufficient work, or from any other cause." It was distinctly laid down that male and female prisoners should be confined in separate buildings or parts of the prison, "so as to prevent them from seeing, conversing, or holding any intercourse with each other." Classification was insisted upon, in the manner laid down by the 24 Geo. III. cap. 54,[73] with such further separation as the justices should deem conducive to good order and discipline. Female prisoners were in all cases to be under the charge of female officers. Every prison containing female prisoners was to have a matron who was to reside constantly in the prison. The religious and moral welfare of the prisoners were to be attended to, the first by daily services, the latter by the appointment of schoolmasters and instruction in reading and writing. Last, but not least, the use of irons was strictly forbidden, "except in cases of urgent and absolute necessity," and every prisoner was to be provided with a hammock or cot to himself, suitable bedding, and, if possible, a separate cell. The second act, passed in the following year, enlarged and amended the first, and at the same time gave powers to the House to call for information as to the observance of its provisions.

The promulgation of these two Gaol Acts strengthened the hands of the Prison Discipline Society enormously. It had now a legal and authoritative standard of efficiency to apply, and could expose all the local authorities that still lagged behind, or neglected to comply with the provisions of the new laws. The Society did not shrink from its self-imposed duty, but continued year after year, with unflagging energy and unflinching spirit, to watch closely and report at length upon the condition of the prisons of the country. For this purpose it kept up an extensive correspondence with all parts of the kingdom, and circulated queries to be answered in detail, whence it deduced the practice and condition of every prison that replied. Upon these and the private visitations made by various members the Society obtained the facts, often highly damnatory, which were embodied in its annual reports. The progress of improvement was certainly extremely slow. It was long before the many jurisdictions imitated the few. Gaols, of which the old prison at Reading was a specimen, were still left intact. In that prison, with its cells and yards arranged within the shell of an ancient abbey chapel, the prisoners, without firing, bedding, or sufficient food, spent their days "in surveying their grotesque prison, or contriving some means of escape by climbing the fluted columns which supported the Gothic arches of the aisles, and so passing by the roof down into the garden and on to freedom." In a county prison adjoining the metropolis, the separation between the male and female quarters was supposed to be accomplished by the erection of an iron railing; in this same prison capital convicts were chained to the floor until execution. In another gaol not far off male and female felons still occupied the same room—underground, and reached by a ladder of ten steps. In others the separation between the sexes consisted in a hanging curtain, or an imaginary boundary line, and nothing prevented parties from passing to either side but an empty regulation which all so disposed could defy. Numbers of the gaols were still unprovided with chaplains, and the prisoners never heard Divine service. In many others there were no infirmaries, no places set apart for the confinement of prisoners afflicted with dangerous and infectious disorders. No attempt was made to maintain discipline. Half the gaols had no code of rules properly prepared and sanctioned by the judges, according to law.

By degrees, however, the changes necessary to bring the prisons into conformity with the recent acts were attempted, if not actually introduced into the county prisons, to which, with a few of the more important city or borough prisons, these acts more especially applied.[74] Most of the local authorities embarked into considerable expenditure, determined to rebuild their gaols *de novo* on the most approved pattern, or to reappropriate, reconstruct, and patch up the existing prisons till they were more in accordance with the growing requirements of the times. Religious worship became more generally the rule; chaplains were appointed, and chapels provided for them; surgeons and hospitals also. Workshops were built at many prisons, various kinds of manufactures and trades were set on foot, including weaving, matting, shoe-making, and tailoring. The interior of one prison was illuminated throughout with gas,— still a novelty, which had been generally adopted in London only four years previously,—"a measure which must greatly tend to discourage attempts to escape." There were tread-wheels at most of the prisons, and regular employment thereon or at some other kind of hard labour. In many places too where the prisoners earned money by their work, they were granted a portion of it for their own use after proper deduction for maintenance. Only a few glaring evils still demanded a remedy. The provision of separate sleeping cells was still quite inadequate. For instance, in twenty-two county gaols there were 1063 sleeping cells in all (in 1823), and the average daily number committed that year amounted to 3985. The want of sleeping cells long continued a crying need. Four years later the Prison Society reported that in four prisons, which at one time of the year contained 1308 prisoners, there were only sixty-eight sleeping rooms or cells, making an average of nineteen persons occupying each room. At the New Prison, Clerkenwell, which had become the principal reception gaol of Middlesex, and so took all the untried, the sleeping space per head was only sixteen inches, and often as many as 293 men[75] had to be accommodated on barrack beds occupying barely 390 feet lineal. The "scenes of tumult and obscenity" in these night rooms are said to have been beyond description; a prisoner in one nocturnal riot lost an eye. Yet to Clerkenwell were now committed the juveniles, and all who were inexperienced in crime.

Great want of uniformity in treatment in the various prisons was still noticeable, and was indeed destined to continue for another half century, in other words, until the introduction of the Prison Act of 1877.[76] At the time of which I am writing there was great diversity of practice as regards the hours of labour. In some prisons the prisoners worked seven hours a day, in others ten and ten and a half. The nature of the employment varied greatly in severity, especially the tread-wheel labour. In some county gaols, as I have already said, female prisoners were placed upon the tread-wheel; in others women were very properly exempted from it, and also from all severe labour. Earnings were very differently appropriated. Here the prisoners were given the whole amount, there a half or a third. Sometimes this money might be expended in the purchase of extra articles of food.[77] The rations varied considerably everywhere. It was still limited to bread in some places, the allowance of which varied from one to three pounds; in others meat, soup, gruel, beer were given. Here and there food was not issued in kind, but a money allowance which the prisoner might expend himself. Bedding and clothing was still denied, but only in a few gaols; in others both were supplied in ample quantities, the cost varying per prisoner from twenty shillings to five pounds. It was plain that although the law had defined general principles of prison government, too much discretion was still left to the magistracy to fill in the details. The legislature only recommended, it did not peremptorily insist. Too often the letter of the law was observed, but not its spirit.

One great impediment to wide amelioration was that a vast number of small gaols lay out of reach of the law. When the new acts were introduced, numerous prisons under local jurisdiction were exempted from the operation of the law. They were so radically bad that reform seemed hopeless, and it was thought wiser not to bring them under provisions which clearly could not be enforced. Mr. Peel, who as Home Secretary had charge of the bill, which became the 4 Geo. IV. cap. 64, said that he had abstained from legislating for these small jurisdictions "on mature deliberation." "It is not," he said, "that I am insensible of the lamentable and disgraceful situation in which many of them are, but I indulge a hope that many of them will contract with the counties, that many of them will build new gaols, and that when in a year or two we come to examine their situation, we shall find but few which have not in one or other of these ways removed the grievance of which such just complaint is made. When that time arrives I shall not hesitate to ask Parliament for powers to compel them to make the necessary alterations, for it is not to be endured that these local jurisdictions should remain in the deplorable situation in which many of them now are."

At this time there were in England one hundred and seventy boroughs, cities, towns, and liberties which possessed the right of trying criminals for various offences. Nearly every one of these jurisdictions had its own prison, and there were one hundred and sixty such gaols in all. Many of them consisted of one or two rooms at most. The total number of prisoners they received during the year varied from two persons to many hundreds. It was in these gaols, withdrawn from the pressure of authority, that the new rules were invariably ignored. The right and privilege of the borough to maintain its own place of confinement was so "ancient and indisputable," that for long no idea of interfering with them was entertained. All that was urged was that the borough magistracy had no right to govern their gaols so as to corrupt those committed, "to the injury of the peace and morals of the public." As time passed, however, these magistrates made no effort at reform. They neither built new gaols nor contracted with the counties, as had been expected, for the transfer of their prisoners. As the Society put it in 1827, "the friends to the improvement of prison discipline will regret to learn that the gaols attached to corporate jurisdictions continue to be the fruitful sources of vice and misery, debasing all who are confined within their walls, and disseminating through their respective communities the knowledge and practice of every species of criminality." The Society proceeded to support this indictment by facts. It is much the old story. The prisoners were lodged in rooms whence they could converse with passengers in the streets, and freely obtain spirits and other prohibited articles. All descriptions of offenders congregated together in the felons' wards. The keeper and his officers resided at a distance from the gaol, and left its inmates to their own devices. There was no decency whatever in the internal arrangements; still no separation of the sexes, no means of ablution or other necessary services. One borough prison consisted of nothing more than a couple of cells, about ten yards square, and absolutely nothing more. In another borough, with a population of ten thousand, the prison was of the same dimensions. One cell was a dungeon, and the other an "improper and unhealthy abode for any human being," with a watercourse running through it.

Most of these small gaols were still in existence and in much the same state eight years later, as is shown by the report of the Commissioners to inquire into the state of the municipal corporations in 1835. An examination of this report shows how even the most insignificant township had its gaol. Thus Dinas Mwddy, in Merionethshire, had, "besides the pinfold and the stocks or crib, a little prison." Clun, in Shropshire, had a lock-up under the town hall. At Eye, in Suffolk, the gaol was part of the poor-house; so it was at Richmond, in Yorkshire, where the master of the workhouse was also keeper of the gaol. At Godmanchester there was no gaol, but a cage to secure prisoners till they could be taken before a magistrate. Kidderminster had a prison, one damp chill room, "the only aperture through which air could be admitted being an iron grating level with the street, through the bars of which quills or reeds were inserted, and drink conveyed to the prisoners." At Walsall, in Staffordshire, the gaol consisted of six cells, frequently so damp that the moisture trickled down the walls; there was not space for air or exercise, and the prison allowance was still limited to bread and water.

Newgate through all these years continued a bye-word with the Society. Some reforms had certainly been introduced, such as the abolition of irons, already referred to, and the establishment of male and female infirmaries. The regular daily visitation of the chaplain was also insisted upon. But it was pointed out in 1823 that defective construction must always bar the way to any radical improvement in Newgate. Without enlargement no material change in discipline or interior economy could possibly be introduced. The chapel still continued incommodious and insufficient; female prisoners were still exposed to the full view of the males, the netting in front of the gallery being perfectly useless as a screen. In 1824 Newgate had no glass in its windows, except in the infirmary and one ward of the chapel yard; and the panes were filled in with oiled paper, an insufficient protection against the weather; and as the window-frames would not shut tight, the prisoners complained much of the cold, especially at night. There was a diminution in the numbers in custody, due to the adoption of the practice of not committing at once to Newgate every offender for trial at the Old Bailey, but nothing had been done to improve the prison buildings. In 1827 the Society was compelled to report that "no material change had taken place in Newgate since the passing of the prison laws,[78] and that consequently the observance of their most important provisions was habitually neglected." It was enacted that the court of aldermen should make rules for the government of the prison, and that these should be posted publicly within the walls. As yet no rules or regulations had been printed or prepared. By another clause of the Gaol Act, two justices were to be appointed to visit the prison at least thrice in every quarter, and "oftener if occasion required." These justices were to inspect every part of the prison, and examine into the state and condition of prisoners. The city justices had not fulfilled this obligation. Idleness was still the general rule for all prisoners in Newgate, in defiance of the law. There was no instruction of adult prisoners, in accordance with the law. The sleeping accommodation was still altogether contrary to the latest ideas. The visits of friends was once more unreservedly allowed, and these incomers freely brought in extra provisions and beer. Last, and worst of all, the arrangements for keeping the condemned prisoners between sentence and execution were more than unsatisfactory. They were not confined apart from each other, but were crowded thirty or forty together in the press yard, so that "corrupt conversation obliterated from the mind of him who is doomed to suffer every serious feeling and valuable impression."[79] I shall have more to say on this subject, and upon the state of Newgate generally, in the following chapter.

The Prison Society did not relax its efforts as time passed, but its leading members had other and more pressing claims upon their energies. Mr. Buxton had succeeded to the great work which William Wilberforce had commenced, and led the repeated attacks upon slavery in British colonies till the whole body of the slaves were manumitted in 1833. In the year immediately preceding this, Parliament was too busy with the great question of its own reform to spare much time for domestic legislation. Nevertheless a committee of the House of Commons was appointed in 1831 to report upon the whole system of secondary punishments, which dealt with gaols of all classes, as well as transportation. This committee animadverted strongly upon the system in force at the metropolitan gaols, and more especially upon the condition of Newgate, where "prisoners before and after trial are under no efficient superintendence," and where "there was no restraint, or attempt at restraint." Mr. Samuel Hoare was examined by this committee, and stated that in his opinion Newgate, as the common gaol of Middlesex, was wholly inadequate to the proper confinement of its prisoners. From the moment of a person's committal he was certain to be plunged deeper and deeper in guilt. The prisoners were crowded together in the gaol, contrary to the requirements of the 4 Geo. IV. Again in 1835 prisons and their inmates became once more the care of the senate, and the subject was taken up this time by the House of Lords. A committee was appointed, under the presidency of the Duke of Richmond, "to inquire into and report upon the several gaols and houses of correction in the counties, cities, and corporate towns within England and Wales; upon the rules and discipline therein established with regard to the treatment of unconvicted as well as convicted persons." The committee was also to report upon the manner in which sentences were carried out, and to recommend any alterations necessary in the rules in order to insure uniformity of discipline. It met on the 31st March, 1835, and continued its sittings well into July, during which time a host of witnesses were examined, and the committee presented three separate reports, embodying recommendations which may be said to have formed the basis of modern prison management.

It was laid down as a first and indispensable principle that uniformity of discipline should prevail everywhere, a theory which did not become a practical fact for forty more years. As a means of securing this uniformity, it was suggested that the rules framed for prison government should be subjected to the Secretary of State for approval, and not, as heretofore, to the judges of assize; that, both to check abuses and watch the progress of improvement, inspectors of prisons should be appointed, who should visit all the prisons from time to time and report to the Secretary of State. It was recommended that the dietaries should be submitted and approved like the rules; that convicted prisoners should not receive any food but the gaol allowance; that food and fuel should be issued in kind, and never provided by the prisoners themselves out of monies granted them. The use of tobacco, hitherto pretty generally indulged in both by men and women, should be strictly prohibited, "as a stimulating luxury inconsistent with any notion of strict discipline and the due pressure of just punishment." Prison officers should not have any share in prisoners' earnings, which should be paid into general prison funds, and no part of them handed over to the prisoners themselves. As a means of increasing the severity of imprisonment, letters and visits from outside should not be permitted during the first six months of an imprisonment. Various other recommendations were made as regards the appointment of chaplain and schoolmasters; the limitation of the powers of wardsmen, or prisoners employed in positions of trust, who should not be permitted to traffic with their fellow-prisoners in any way. The committee most of all insisted upon the entire individual separation of prisoners, except during the hours of labour, religious worship, and instruction, as "absolutely necessary for preventing contamination, and for securing a proper system of prison discipline." This was the first enunciation of the system of separate confinement, which was eventually to replace the attempted arrangement of prisoners by classes according to antecedents and crimes, an incomplete and fallacious method of preventing contamination. The Lords'

Committee fully recognized the painful fact that the greatest mischief followed from the intercourse which was still permitted in so many prisons; to use its words, "the comparatively innocent are seduced, the unwary are entrapped, and the tendency to crime in offenders not entirely hardened is confirmed by the language, the suggestions, and the example of more depraved and systematic criminals."

This committee, as well as the one preceding it, also reported in terms of strong reprobation on the small prisons and gaols still under the borough corporations. The Commons' Committee gave it as their opinion that they were in a deplorable state. The same language was used by the commissioners appointed to inquire into the municipal corporations in 1835, when speaking more particularly of the borough gaols. In these the commissioners found "additional proof of the evils of continuing the present constitution of the local tribunals. Instances rarely occur in which the borough gaols admit of any proper classification of the prisoners. In some large towns, as at Berwick on Tweed, Southampton, and Southwark, they (the prisons) are in a very discreditable condition. In many of the smaller boroughs they are totally unfit for the confinement of human beings. In these places the prisoners are often without a proper supply of air and light; frequently the gaols are mere dungeons under the town hall.... It was frequently stated in evidence that the gaol of the borough was in so unfit a state for the reception of prisoners, that plaintiffs were unwilling to consign the defendants against whom they had obtained execution to confinement within its walls." The Lords' Committee on Gaols were of the same opinion, and considered the prisons under corporate or peculiar jurisdiction in a very unsatisfactory condition. They therefore recommended that the prisoners should be removed to the county gaols from such prisons as were past improvement, and that the borough funds should be charged for the accommodation. The whole question was again dealt with in Lord John Russell's bill for the reform of the municipal corporations, and with a more liberal election of town councillors, and the establishment of municipal institutions upon a proper footing, the borough gaols were brought more into accordance with the growing demand for a more humane system of prison management.

THE FIRST REPORT OF THE INSPECTORS OF PRISONS

Appointment of inspectors of prisons—Their names and antecedents—Mr. Crawford and Mr. Whitworth Russell at once visit Newgate, and make a searching inquiry—Find old evils still present—Overcrowding no longer excusable—Want of classification—The governor, Mr. Cope, blamed for this—Prisoners' treatment—No beds, uncleanly, and in rags—Baleful despotism of prisoner wardsmen, who have more power than the officers—Again proofs of Mr. Cope's neglect—Scenes of horror in Newgate—Gambling, drinking, debauchery—Flash books allowed—Libel of Stockdale v. Hansard grows out of this—Serious affrays in the wards—Prisoners badly wounded by one another—Extra and luxurious food admitted—Also visitors of both sexes indiscriminately—Same evils to a lesser degree on female side—Ladies' Association—No real separation of the sexes—Mr. Cope an offender in this respect—The press-yard or condemned convicts' yard the worst of all—Culpable and indiscriminate association—Brutal behaviour of many of those sentenced to death—The ordinary checked in his zeal—Criminal lunatics allowed to remain in Newgate—House of Commons' *prisoners monopolize hospital and best accommodation in the gaol— Abuses of State Side revived in their case—Evils rampant briefly recapitulated by inspectors—Their report raises a storm in the city— Protest of the Corporation—Some attempt at reform—Many of the charges reiterated in later reports—No radical reform possible without complete reconstruction.*

IN the preceding chapter I have been tempted by the importance of the general question to give it prominence and precedence over the particular branch of which I am treating. Newgate has remained rather in the background while the whole of the gaols as a body were under discussion. But this digression was necessary in order to present a more complete picture of the state of gaols in the early part of the present century, just before the public mind was first awakened to the need for thorough reform. I shall now return to the great gaol of the city of London, and give a more detailed account of its condition and inner life as the inspectors of prisons found them in 1835-6. These gentlemen were appointed in October 1835, owing to the strong representations of the Lords' Committee,[80] backed up by the evidence of several influential witnesses. Mr. Samuel Hoare, when examined, considered it indispensably necessary, to carry out whatever system might be established, that inspectors should watch over the observance of the law. He saw no objection on the score of their probable interference with the local jurisdiction, but he would not arm them with any authority lest their co-operation might be offensive. Sir Frederick Roe was of the same opinion as regards the appointment, but he would give the inspectors the power of acting as well as reporting. They should be persons, he thought, selected from the highest class; the duty was most important, one which required discretion, judgment, and knowledge of law, with sufficient insight and experience to discover defects in prison discipline. These considerations no doubt had weight with those who made the selection of the first inspectors, and the two gentlemen appointed were probably the most fitted in England to be so employed. One was Mr. William Crawford, the other the Rev. Whitworth Russell.

The first named had long been an active philanthropist, devoting himself more particularly to the reformation of juvenile criminals.[81] William Crawford had been one of the promoters and managers of the Philanthropic Society's farm school. Later on he had devoted himself to the personal investigation of the prisons of the United States. At that time the mild and intelligent prison discipline in force in Pennsylvania, the legacy of the old Quaker immigrants, had made such prisons as Auburn a model for imitation. Several European states had despatched emissaries to examine and report upon them. France had sent MM. Beaumont and De Tocqueville, who subsequently published several interesting works on the subject. England was represented by Mr. Crawford, and the result of his inquiry was given to the public as an appendix to the House of Commons' 'Report on Secondary Punishments.' It is an able and exhaustive state paper, testifying to the keenness of the writer's perception, and his unremitting labour in pursuing his researches. Mr. Crawford was thoroughly versed in the still imperfectly understood science of prison management, and fully qualified for his new duties.

The second inspector, the Rev. Whitworth Russell, was the chaplain of Millbank penitentiary, the great architectural experiment which grew out of the strong representations of Jeremy Bentham and others, and was the first national recognition of the principle that punishment must be reformatory as well as deterrent.

Messrs. Crawford and Russell proceeded to carry out their new functions with commendable energy, and without a moment's loss of time. The ink was barely dry upon their letters of appointment before they appeared at Newgate, and commenced a searching investigation. They attended early and late; they mustered the prisoners, examined into their condition, took voluminous evidence from all classes of individuals, from the governor down to the convict in the condemned cells. They visited the wards after locking-up time, and saw with their own eyes what went on. Having started with the proposition that the metropolitan prisons must monopolize their attention, as constituting, to use their own words, "a subject of magnitude and importance sufficient to exclude other gaols," they soon narrowed their inquiry still further, and limited it to Newgate alone. Newgate indeed became the sole theme of their first report. The fact was that the years as they passed, nearly twenty in all, had worked but little permanent improvement in this detestable prison. Changes introduced under pressure had been only skin deep. Relapse was rapid and inevitable, so that the latter state of the prison was worse than the first. The disgraceful overcrowding had been partially ended, but the same evils of indiscriminate association were still present; there was the old neglect of decency, the same callous indifference to the moral well-being of the prisoners, the same want of employment and of all disciplinary control.

All these evils were set forth at length in the inspectors' first report. There was no longer the faintest possible excuse for overcrowding. The numbers now committed to Newgate had sensibly diminished. The prison had become more or less a place of detention only, harbouring mainly those awaiting trial. To these were still added an average of about fifty expecting the last penalty of the law; a certain number of transports awaiting removal to the colonies; an occasional prisoner or two committed by the Houses of Parliament, the Courts of King's Bench, Common Pleas, and Exchequer, the Commissioners of bankruptcy and of taxes; smugglers, and a larger number sentenced for very short terms, and for offences of the most varying description, by the Central Criminal Court. The sum total thus produced was inconsiderable compared with the hundreds that had formerly filled the gaol, and the whole by proper management might have been so accommodated as to prevent overcrowding. But incredible as it may appear, the authorities of Newgate declined to avail themselves of the advantages offered them, and when the population fell they shut up one half the gaol and crowded up the other. Some rooms remained quite empty and unoccupied, while others were full to overflowing. Not only were the wards thus needlessly crammed, and for no reason but the niggardliness of the corporation which refused a proper supply of bedding, but the occupants of each were huddled together indiscriminately. The inspectors found in the same wards in the chapel yard the convicted and the untried, the felon and the misdemeanant, the sane and the insane, the old and young offender. The classification prescribed by the Gaol Act, which laid down that certain prisoners should not intermix, was openly neglected, and "the greatest contempt shown for the law." In another part there were men charged with and convicted of unnatural offences shut up with lads of tender years; minor offenders charged with small thefts or non-payment of small sums were cheek by jowl with convicts sentenced to long terms of transportation. In the master's side yard, which had only one washing place, as many as seventy-eight prisoners, frequently more, were associated together, "of every variety of age, habit, and delinquency, without employment, oversight, or control." In the middle yard it was still worse. "Here," say the inspectors, "are herded together the very worst class of prisoners; certainly a more wretched combination of human beings can hardly be imagined. We have reason to fear that poverty, ragged clothes, and an inability to pay the ward dues, elsewhere exacted for better accommodation, consign many of the more petty and unpractised offenders to this place, where they inevitably meet with further contamination from the society of the most abandoned and incorrigible inmates of the gaol."

No doubt the governor for the time being, Mr. Cope, was in a great measure to blame for all this, and for the want of proper classification. I shall have occasion to speak again, and more at length, of Mr. Cope's careless and perfunctory discharge of his many manifest duties, but I shall here confine myself to animadverting on his neglect as regards the appropriation of his prison. He was unable to give any reason whatever for not utilizing the whole of the wards. He saw certain rooms fill up, and yet took no steps to open others that were locked up and empty. He blamed the construction of Newgate for the neglect of classification, and was yet compelled to confess that he had made no attempt whatever to carry it out. The fact was, he did not keep the classification of prisoners on first arrival in his own hands, nor even in that of his officers. A new prisoner's fate, as to location, rested really with a powerful fellow-prisoner. The inspectors found that prisoners had their places assigned to them by the inner gatesman, himself a convicted prisoner, and a "wardsman" or responsible head of a room. The wardsman still exacted dues, of which more directly, and this particular official took excellent care to select as residents for his own ward those most suitable from his own point of view. "So great is the authority exercised by him, and so numerous were his opportunities of showing favouritism, that all the prisoners may be said to be in his power. If a man is poor and ragged, however inexperienced in crime, or however trifling may be the offence for which he has been committed, his place is assigned among the most depraved, the most experienced, and the most incorrigible offenders in the middle yard." It must be admitted that so far but little effort had been made to counteract the evils of indiscriminate association.

It was not likely that a system which left innocent men—for the great bulk of new arrivals were still untried—to be pitchforked by chance anywhere, into any sort of company, within this the greatest nursery of crime in London, should exercise even the commonest care for the personal decency or comfort of the prisoners. Their treatment was also a matter of chance. They still slept on rope mats on the floor, herded together in companies of four or more to keep one another warm, and under the scanty covering of a couple of dirty stable-rugs apiece. So closely did they lie together, that the inspectors at their night visits found it difficult in stepping across the room to avoid treading on them. Sometimes two mats were allotted to three sleepers. Sometimes four slept under the same bedding, and left their mats unoccupied. The rugs used were never washed; an order existed that the bedding should be taken into the yards to be aired, but it was not very punctually obeyed. The only convenience for personal ablutions were the pumps in the yards, and the far-off baths in the condemned or press-yard. Water might not be taken into the ward for washing purposes. There was some provision of clothing, but it was quite insufficient, and nothing at all was given if prisoners had enough of their own to cover their nakedness. The inspectors paraded the prisoners, and found them generally ragged and ill-clad, squalid and filthy in the extreme; many without stockings, and with hardly shoes to their feet; some, who had the semblance of covering on the upper part of their feet, had no soles to the shoes, and their bare feet were on the ground. This, too, was in the depth of the winter, and during a most inclement season. The allowance of food was not illiberal, but its issue was precarious, and dependent on the good will of the wardsmen, who measured out the portions to each according to his eye, and not with weights and measures, no turnkey being present. Too much was left to the wardsman. It was he who could issue small luxuries; he sold tea, coffee, sugar, tobacco, although prohibited, and extra beer. He charged a weekly sum as ward dues for the use of knives, forks, and plates—a perpetuation under another form of the old detestable custom of garnish. He had power where his exactions were resisted of making the ward most uncomfortable for the defaulter. He could trump up a false complaint against his fellow-prisoner, and so get him punished; he might keep him from the fire, or give him his soup or gruel in a pail instead of a basin.

The authority of these wardsmen so improperly exalted, and so entirely unchecked, degenerated into a baneful despotism. They bought their offices from one another, and were thus considered to have a vested interest in them. Their original capital had been a few shillings, and for this they purchased the right to tax their fellows to the extent of pounds per week. The wardsman had a monopoly in supplying provisions, gave dinner and breakfast at his own price, and was such complete master of the ward that none of its inmates were suffered to make tea or coffee for themselves lest it should interfere with his sales. He made collections when it suited him for ward purposes, to be spent as he chose, in candles and so forth. When the wardsman was a man of some education, with some knowledge of legal chicanery gained by personal experience, he might add considerably to his emoluments by drawing briefs and petitions for his fellows. There was a recognized charge of 5*s*. per brief, for a petition of from 1*s*. 6*d*. to 8*s*., according to its length, and by these payments a wardsman had been known to amass as much as £40. The man intrusted with this privilege was often the inner gatesman, the prisoner official already mentioned, who held the fate of new arrivals as regards location in his hands. It was not strange that he should sometimes misuse his power, and when prisoners were not to be cajoled into securing his legal services, had been known to employ threats, declaring that he was often consulted by the governor as to a prisoner's character, in view of speaking to it at the trial, and he could easily do them a good turn—or a very bad one. The brief-drawing gatesman and wardsman at the time of the inspectors' first visit must have been a particularly powerful personage. He was on the most intimate and improperly familiar terms with the turnkeys, had a key of both the master's side and middle side yards, was the only person present at the distribution of beer, and was trusted to examine, and, if he chose, pass in, all provisions, money, clothes, and letters brought for prisoners by their friends.

All the wardsmen alike were more or less irresponsible. The turnkeys complained bitterly that these old prisoners had more power than they themselves. The governor himself admitted that a prisoner of weak intellect who had been severely beaten and much injured by a wardsman did not dare complain, the victim of this cruel ill-usage having "more fear of the power of the wardsman to injure him, than confidence in the governor's power to protect him." These wardsmen, besides thus ruling the roast, had numerous special privileges, if such they can be called. They were not obliged to attend chapel, and seldom if ever went; "prisoners," said one of them under examination, "did not like the trouble of going to chapel." They had a standing bedstead to sleep on, and a good flock mattress; double allowance of provisions, filched from the common stock. Nobody interfered with them or regulated their conduct. They might get drunk when so disposed, and did so frequently, alone or in company. Evidence was given before the inspectors of eight or ten prisoners seen "giddy drunk, not able to sit upon forms." The female wards-women were also given to intemperance. The matron deposed to having seen the gates-woman "exceedingly drunk," and having been insulted by her. There was no penalty attached to drunkenness. A wardsman did not necessarily lose his situation for it. Nor was drink the only creature comfort he might enjoy. He could indulge in snuff if a snuff-taker, and might always smoke his pipe undisturbed; for although the use of tobacco had been prohibited since the report of the Lords Committee, it was still freely introduced into the prison.

Probably authority would not have been so recklessly usurped by the wardsmen had not the proper officials too readily surrendered it. The turnkeys left the prisoners very much to themselves, never entering the wards after locking-up time, at dusk, till unlocking next morning, and then only went round to count the number. Many of them were otherwise and improperly occupied for hours every day in menial services for the governor, cleaning his windows or grooming his horse. One turnkey had been so employed several hours daily for nearly eleven years. It was not strange that subordinates should neglect their duty when superiors set the example. Nothing was more prominently brought out by the inspectors than the inefficiency of the governor at that time, Mr. Cope. He may have erred in some points through ignorance, but in others he was clearly guilty of culpable neglect. We have seen that he took no pains to classify and separate prisoners on reception. This was only one of many grave omissions on his part. He did not feel it incumbent on himself to visit his prison often or see his prisoners. The act prescribed that he should do both every twenty-four hours, but days passed without his entering the wards. The prisoners declared that they did not see him oftener than twice a week; one man who had been in the condemned ward for two months, said the governor only came there four times. Again, a turnkey deposed that his chief did not enter the wards more than once a fortnight.

But it is only fair to Mr. Cope to state that he himself said he went whenever he could find time, and that he was constantly engaged attending sessions and going with drafts to the hulks. But when he did visit, his inspections were of the most superficial character; sometimes he looked at his bolts and bars, but he never examined the cupboards, coal-boxes, or other possible hiding-places for cards, dice, dangerous implements, or other prohibited articles. He only attended chapel once on Sunday, never on the week-day, and generally devoted the time service was in progress to taking the descriptions of newly-arrived prisoners. He really did not know what passed in his gaol, and was surprised when the inspectors proved to him that practices of which he was ignorant, and which he admitted that he reprehended, went on without hindrance. He was satisfied to let matters run on as in the old times, he said in his own justification; with him what was, was right, and evils that should have been speedily rooted out remained because they had the prescription of long usage. He kept no daily journal of occurrences, and nothing, however important, was recorded at the time. The aldermen never called upon him to report, and left him nearly unsupervised and uncontrolled. In his administration of discipline he was quite uncertain; the punishments he inflicted were unequal, and it was not the least part of the blame imputed to him that he made special favourites of particular prisoners, retaining of his own accord in Newgate, and for years, felons who should have been sent beyond the seas. But, indeed, his whole rule was far too mild, and under this mistaken leniency the interior of the gaol was more like a bear-garden or the noisy purlieus of a public-house than a prison.

It was the same old story—evil constantly in the ascendant, the least criminal at the mercy of the most depraved. Under the reckless contempt for regulations, the apathy of the authorities, and the undue ascendancy of those who, as convicted felons, should have been most sternly repressed, the most hardened and the oldest in vice had the best of it, while the inexperienced beginner went to the wall. Edward Gibbon Wakefield,[82] who spent three years in Newgate a little before the time of the inspectors' first report, said with justice that "incredible scenes of horror occur in Newgate." It was, moreover, in his opinion undoubtedly the greatest nursery of crime in London. The days were passed in idleness, debauchery, riotous quarrelling, immoral conversation, gambling, indirect contravention of parliamentary rules, instruction in all nefarious processes, lively discourse upon past criminal exploits, elaborate discussion of others to be perpetrated after release. No provision whatever was made for the employment of prisoners, no materials were purchased, no trade instructors appointed. There was no school for adults; only the boys were taught anything, and their instructor, with his assistant, were convicted prisoners. Idle hands and unoccupied brains found in mischief the only means of whiling away the long hours of incarceration. Gaming of all kinds, although forbidden by the Gaol Acts, was habitually practised. This was admitted in evidence by the turnkeys, and was proved by the appearance of the prison tables, which bore the marks of gaming-boards deeply cut into them. Prisoners confessed that it was a favourite occupation, the chief games being "shoving halfpence" on the table, pitch in the hole, cribbage, dominoes, and common tossing, at which as much as four or five shillings would change hands in an hour.

But this was not the only amusement. Most of the wards took in the daily papers, the most popular being the 'Times,' 'Morning Herald,' and 'Morning Chronicle'; on Sunday the 'Weekly Dispatch,' 'Bell's Life,' and the 'Weekly Messenger.' The newsman had free access to the prison; he passed in unsearched and unexamined, and, unaccompanied by an officer, went at once to his customers, who bought their paper and paid for it themselves. The news-vendor was also a tobacconist, and he had thus ample means of introducing to the prisoners the prohibited but always much-coveted and generally procurable weed. In the same way the wardsman laid in his stock to be retailed. Other light literature besides the daily journals were in circulation: novels, flash songs, play-books, such as 'Jane Shore,' 'Grimm's German Tales,' with Cruikshank's illustrations, and publications which in these days would have been made the subject of a criminal prosecution. One of these, published by Stockdale, the inspectors styled "a book of the most disgusting nature."[83] There was also a good supply of Bibles and prayers, the donation of a philanthropic gentleman, Captain Brown, but these, particularly the Bibles, bore little appearance of having been used. Drink, in more or less unlimited quantities, was still to be had. Spirits certainly were now excluded; but a potman, with full permission of the sheriffs, brought in beer for sale from a neighbouring public-house, and visited all the wards with no other escort than the prisoner gatesman. The quantity to be issued per head was limited by the prison regulations to one pint, but no steps were taken to prevent any prisoner from obtaining more if he could pay for it. The beer-man brought in as much as he pleased; he sold it without the controlling presence of an officer. Not only did prisoners come again and again for a "pint," but large quantities were carried off to the wards to be drunk later in the day.

There were more varied, and at times, especially when beer had circulated freely, more uproarious diversions. Wrestling, in which legs were occasionally broken, was freely indulged in; also such low games as "cobham," leap-frog, puss in the corner, and "fly the garter," for which purpose the rugs were spread out to prevent feet slipping on the floor. Feasting alternated with fighting. The weekly introduction of food, to which I shall presently refer, formed the basis of luxurious banquets, washed down by liquor and enlivened by flash songs and thrilling long-winded descriptions of robberies and other "plants." There was much swearing and bad language, the very worst that could be used, from the first thing in the morning to the last thing at night.[84] New arrivals, especially the innocent and still guileless debutant, were tormented with rude horse-play, and assailed by the most insulting "chaff." If any man presumed to turn in too early he was "toed," that is to say, a string was fastened to his big toe while he was asleep, and he was dragged from off his mat, or his bedclothes were drawn away across the room. The ragged part of the prisoners were very anxious to destroy the clothes of the better dressed, and often lighted small pieces of cloth, which they dropped smouldering into their fellow-prisoners' pockets. Often the victim, goaded to madness, attacked his tormentors; a fight was then certain to follow. These fights sometimes took place in the daytime, when a ring was regularly formed, and two or three stood by the door to watch for the officer's approach. More often they occurred at night, and were continued to the bitter end. The prisoners in this way administered serious punishment on one another. Black eyes and broken noses were always to be seen.

More cruel injuries were common enough, which did not result from honest hand-to-hand fights. The surgeon's journal produced to the inspectors contained numerous entries of terrible wounds inflicted in a cowardly way. "A serious accident: one of the prisoners had a hot poker run into his eye." "A lad named Matthew White has had a wound in his eye by a bone thrown at him, which very nearly destroyed vision." "There was a disturbance in the transport yard yesterday evening, and the police were called in. During the tumult a prisoner, ... who was one of the worst of the rioters, was bruised about the head and body." "Watkins' knee-joint is very severely injured." "A prisoner Baxter is in the infirmary in consequence of a severe injury to his wrist-joint." Watkins' case, referred to above, is made the subject of another and a special report from the surgeon. He was in the transport side, when one of his fellows, in endeavouring to strike another prisoner with a large poker, missed his aim, and struck Watkins' knee.... Violent inflammation and extensive suppuration ensued, and for a considerable time amputation seemed inevitable. After severe suffering prolonged for many months, the inflammation was subdued, but the cartilage of the knee-joint was destroyed, and he was crippled for life. On another occasion a young man, who was being violently teased, seized a knife and stabbed his tormentor in the back. The prisoner who used the knife was secured, but it was the wardsman, and not the officers, to whom the report was made, and no official inquiry or punishment followed.

Matters were at times still worse, and the rioting went on to such dangerous lengths as to endanger the safety of the building. On one occasion a disturbance was raised which was not quelled until windows had been broken and forms and tables burnt. The officers were obliged to go in among the prisoners to restore order with drawn cutlasses, but the presence and authority of the governor himself became indispensable. The worst fights occurred on Sunday afternoons; but nearly every night the act of locking up became, from the consequent removal of all supervision, the signal for the commencement of obscene talk, revelry, and violence.

Other regulations laid down by the Gaol Acts were still defied. One of these was that prisoners should be restricted to the gaol allowance of food; but all could still obtain as much extra, and of a luxurious kind, as their friends chose to bring them in. Visitors were still permitted to come with supplies on given days of the week, about the only limitation being that the food should be cooked, and cold; hot meat, poultry, and fish were also forbidden. But the inspectors found in the ward cupboards mince-pies and other pasties, cold joints, hams, and so forth. Many other articles were introduced by visitors, including money, tobacco, pipes, and snuff. From the same source came the two or three strong files which the inspectors found in one ward, together with four bradawls, several large iron spikes, screws, nails, and knives; "all of them instruments calculated to facilitate attempts at breaking out of prison, and capable of becoming most dangerous weapons in the hands of desperate and determined men." The nearly indiscriminate admission of visitors, although restricted to certain days, continued to be an unmixed evil. The untried might see their friends three times a week, the convicted only once. On these occasions precautions were supposed to be taken to exclude bad characters, yet many persons of notoriously loose life continually obtained egress. Women saw men if they merely pretended to be wives; even boys were visited by their sweethearts. Decency was, however, insured by a line of demarcation, and visitors were kept upon each side of a separated double iron railing. But no search was made to intercept prohibited articles at the gate, and there was no permanent gate-keeper, which would have greatly helped to keep out bad characters. Some idea of the difficulty and inconvenience of these lax regulations as regards visiting, may be gathered from the statement that as many as three hundred were often admitted on the same day—enough to altogether upset what small show of decorum and discipline was still preserved in the prison. Perhaps the worst feature of the visiting system was the permission accorded to male prisoners "under the name of husbands, brothers, and sons" to have access to the female side on Sundays and Wednesdays, in order to visit their supposed relations there.

On this female side, where the Ladies' Association still reigned supreme, more system and a greater semblance of decorum was maintained. But there were evils akin to those on the male side, prominent amongst which was the undue influence accorded to prisoners. A female prisoner kept the registers. Wards-women were allowed much the same authority, with the same temptations to excess, and intoxication was not unknown among them and others. The clothing was still meagre and ragged: the washing places insufficient, and wanting in decency; in some yards the pump was the only provision, and this in a place within sight of visitors, of the windows of the male turnkeys, and unprotected from the weather. There was the same crowding in the sleeping arrangements as on the male side; the same scarcity of bedding. It was a special evil of this part of the prison, that the devotional exercises, originally so profitable, had grown into a kind of edifying spectacle, which numbers of well-meaning but inquisitive people were anxious to witness. Thus, when the inspectors visited there were twenty-three strangers, and only twenty-eight prisoners. The presence of so many strangers, many of them gentlemen, distracted the prisoners' attention, and could not be productive of much good.

The separation of the sexes was not indeed rigidly carried out in Newgate as yet. We have seen that male prisoners visited their female relations and friends on the female side. Besides this, the gatesman who prepared the briefs had interviews with female prisoners alone while taking their instructions; a female came alone and unaccompanied by a matron to clean the governor's office in the male prison; male prisoners carried coal into the female prison, when they saw and could speak or pass letters to the female prisoners; and the men could also at any time go for tea, coffee, and sugar to Mrs. Brown's shop, which was inside the female gate. In the bail-dock, where most improper general association was permitted, the female prisoners were often altogether in the charge of male turnkeys. The governor was also personally responsible for gross contravention of this rule of separation, and was in the habit of drawing frequently upon the female prison for prisoners to act as domestic servants in his own private dwelling. Some member of the Ladies' Association observed and commented upon the fact that a "young rosy-cheeked girl" had been kept by the governor from transportation, while older women in infirm health were sent across the seas. His excuse was that he had given the girl his promise that she should not go, an assumption of prerogative which by no means rested with him; but he afterwards admitted that the girl had been recommended to him by the principal turnkey, who knew something of her friends. This woman was really his servant, employed to help in cleaning, and taken on whenever there was extra work to be done. The governor had a great dislike, he said, to seeing strangers in his house. This girl had been first engaged on account of the extra work entailed by certain prisoners committed by the House of Commons, who had been lodged in the governor's own house. The house at this time was full of men and visitors; waiters came in from the taverns with meals. Some of the prisoners had their valets, and all these were constantly in and out of the kitchen where this female prisoner was employed. There was revelling and roystering, as usual, with "high life below-stairs." The governor sent down wine on festive occasions, of which no doubt the prisoner housemaid had her share. It can hardly be denied that the governor, in his treatment of this woman, was acting in flagrant contravention of all rules.

Eighteen years had elapsed since the formation of the "Ladies' Association," and Mrs. Fry with her colleagues still laboured assiduously in Newgate, devoting themselves mainly to the female prison, although their ministrations were occasionally extended to the male side. The inspectors paid tribute to the excellence of the motives of these philanthropic ladies, and recognized the good they did. They had introduced "much order and cleanliness," had provided work for those who had hitherto passed their time in total idleness, and had made the treatment of female transports on the way to New South Wales their especial care. They had tried, moreover, by their presence and their pious, disinterested efforts, to restrain the dissolute manners and vicious language of the unhappy and depraved inmates. But it was already plain that they constituted an independent authority within the gaols; they were frequently in conflict with the chaplain, who not strangely resented the orders issued by the aldermen, that women should be frequently kept from chapel in order that they might attend the ladies' lectures and exhortations. The admission of a crowd of visitors to assist in these lay services has already been remarked upon; as the inspectors pointed out, it had the bad effect of distracting attention, it tended to "dissipate reflection, diminish the gloom of the prison, and mitigate the punishment which the law has sentenced the prisoner to undergo."

It is to be feared too that although the surface was thus whitewashed and decorous, much that was vicious still festered and rankled beneath, and that when the restraining influences of the ladies were absent, the female prisoners relapsed into immoral and uncleanly discourse. Even in the daytime, when supervision was withdrawn, "the language used to be dreadful," says one of the women when under examination; "swearing and talking of what crimes they had committed, and how they had done it." Another witness declared she had heard the most shocking language in the yard; she said "she had never witnessed such scenes before, and hopes she never shall again—it was dreadful!" After locking-up time, which varied, as on the male side, according to the daylight, the scenes were often riotous and disgraceful. The poor, who could afford no luxuries, went to bed early, but were kept awake by the revelries of the rich, who supped royally on the supplies provided from outside, and kept it up till ten or eleven o'clock. There were frequent quarrels and fights; shoes and other missiles were freely bandied about; and with all this "the most dreadful oaths, the worst language, too bad to be repeated," were made use of every night.

Bad as were the various parts of the gaol already dealt with, there still remained one where the general callous indifference and mismanagement culminated in cruel culpable neglect. The condition of the capitally-convicted prisoners after sentence was still very disgraceful. The side they occupied, still known as the press-yard, consisted of two dozen rooms and fifteen cells. In these various chambers, until just before the inspectors made their report, all classes of the condemned, those certain to suffer, and the larger number who were nearly certain of a reprieve, were jumbled up together, higgledy-piggledy, the old and the young, the murderer and the child who had broken into a dwelling.[85] All privacy was impossible under the circumstances. At times the numbers congregated together were very great; as many as fifty and sixty, even more, were crowded indiscriminately into the press-yard. The better-disposed complained bitterly of what they had to endure; one man declared that the language of the condemned rooms was disgusting, that he was dying a death every day in being compelled to associate with such characters. In the midst of the noisy and blasphemous talk no one could pursue his meditations; any who tried to pray became the sport and ridicule of his brutal fellows.

Owing to the repeated entreaties of the criminals who could hardly hope to escape the gallows, some show of classification was carried out, and when the inspectors visited Newgate they found the three certain to die in a day-room by themselves; in a second room were fourteen more who had every hope of a reprieve. The whole of these seventeen had, however, a common airing-yard, and took their exercise there at the same time, so that men in the most awful situation, daily expecting to be hanged, were associated continually with a number of those who could look with certainty on a mitigation of punishment. The latter, light-hearted and reckless, conducted themselves in the most unseemly fashion, and "with as much indifference as the inmates of the other parts of the prison." They amused themselves after their own fashion; played all day long at blind-man's-buff and leap-frog, or beat each other with a knotted handkerchief, laughing and uproarious, utterly unmindful of the companionship of men upon whom lay the shadow of an impending shameful death. "Men whose cases were dangerous, and those most seriously inclined, complained of these annoyances," so subversive of meditation, so disturbing to the thoughts; they suffered sickening anxiety, and wished to be locked up alone. This indiscriminate association lasted for months, during the whole of which time the unhappy convicts who had but little hope of commutation were exposed to the mockery of their reckless associates.

The brutal callousness of the bulk of the inmates of the press-yard may be gathered from the prison punishment-book, which frequently recorded such entries as the following: "Benjamin Vines and Daniel Ward put in irons for two days for breaking the windows of the day room in the condemned cells." "Joseph Coleman put in irons for three days for striking one of the prisoners," in the same place. There were disputes and quarrels constantly among these doomed men; it was a word and blow, an argument clenched always with a fight. The more peaceably disposed found some occupation in making Newgate tokens, leaden hearts,[86] and "grinding the impressions off penny-pieces, then pricking figures or words on them to give to their friends as memorials." Turnkeys occasionally visited the press-yard, but its occupants were under little or no control. The chaplain, who might have been expected to make these men his peculiar care, and who at one time had visited them frequently, often several times a week, had relaxed his efforts, because, according to his own account, he was so frequently stopped in the performance of his duties. In his evidence before the inspectors he declared that "for years he gave his whole time to his duties, from an early hour in the morning till late in the afternoon. He left off because he was so much interfered with and laughed at, and from seeing that no success attended his efforts, owing to the evils arising from association." Latterly his ministrations to the condemned had been restricted to a visit on Sunday afternoons, and occasionally about once a fortnight on a week-day.

It is only fair to Mr. Cotton to add that, according to his own journal, he was unremitting in his attentions to convicts who were actually cast for death, and the day of whose execution was fixed. He had no doubt a difficult mission to discharge; on the one hand, the Ladies' Association, supported and encouraged by public approval, trenched upon his peculiar province; on the other, the governor of the gaol sneered at his zeal, stigmatized his often most just strictures on abuses as "a bundle of nonsense," and the aldermen, when he appealed to them for protection and countenance, generally sided with his opponents. Nevertheless the inspectors summed up against him. While admitting that he had had many difficulties to contend with, and that he had again and again protested against the obstacles thrown in his way, the inspectors "cannot forbear expressing their opinion that he might have shown greater perseverance, in the face of impediments confessedly discouraging," as regards the private teaching of prisoners; and they went on to say that "a resolved adherence, in spite of discouragements the most disheartening, to that line of conduct which his duty imposed on him, would, it is probable, have eventually overcome the reluctance of some of the prisoners at least, and would have possessed so much moral dignity as effectually to rebuke and abash the profane spirit of the more insolent and daring of the criminals."

The lax discipline maintained in Newgate was still further deteriorated by the presence of two other classes of prisoners who ought never to have been inmates of such a gaol. One of these were the criminal lunatics, who were at this time and for long previous continuously imprisoned there. As the law stood since the passing of the 9th Geo. IV. c. 40, any two justices might remove a prisoner found to be insane, either on commitment or arraignment, to an asylum, and the Secretary of State had the same power as regards any who became insane while undergoing sentence. These powers were not invariably put in force, and there were in consequence many unhappy lunatics in Newgate and other gaols, whose proper place was the asylum. At the time the Lords' Committee sat there were eight thus retained in Newgate, and a return in the appendix of the Lords' report gives a total of thirty-nine lunatics confined in various gaols, many of them guilty of murder and other serious crimes. The inspectors in the following year, on examining the facts, found that some of these poor creatures had been in confinement for long periods: at Newgate and York Castle as long as five years; "at Ilchester and Morpeth for seven years; at Warwick for eight years, at Buckingham and Hereford for eleven years, at Appleby for thirteen years, at Anglesea for fifteen years, at Exeter for sixteen years, and at Pembroke for not less a period than twenty-four years."

It was manifestly wrong that such persons, "visited by the most awful of calamities," should be detained in a common prison. Not only did their presence tend greatly to interfere with the discipline of the prison, but their condition was deplorable in the extreme. The lunatic became the sport of the idle and the depraved. His cure was out of the question; he was placed in a situation "beyond all others calculated to confirm his malady and prolong his sufferings." The matter was still further complicated at Newgate by the presence within the walls of sham lunatics. Some of those included in the category had actually been returned as sane from the asylum to which they had been sent, and there was always some uncertainty as to who was mad and who not. Prisoners indeed were known to boast that they had saved their necks by feigning insanity. It was high time that the unsatisfactory state of the law as regards the treatment of criminal lunatics should be remedied, and not the least of the good services rendered by the new inspectors was their inquiry into the status of these unfortunate people, and their recommendation to improve it.

The other inmates of the prison of an exceptional character, and exempted from the regular discipline, such as it was, were the ten persons committed to Newgate by the House of Commons in 1835. These were the gentlemen concerned in the bribery case at Ipswich in 1835, when a petition was presented against the return of Messrs. Adam Dundas and Fitzroy Kelly. Various witnesses, including Messrs. J. B. Dasent, Pilgrim, Bond, and Clamp, had refused to give evidence before the House of Commons' Committee; a Speaker's warrant was issued for their arrest when they absconded. Mr. J. E. Sparrow and Mr. Clipperton, the parliamentary agents of the members whose election was impugned, were implicated in aiding and abetting the others to abscond, and a Mr. O'Mally, counsel for the two M.P.'s, was also concerned. Pilgrim and Dasent were caught and given into the custody of the sergeant-at-arms, and the rest were either arrested or they surrendered. A resolution at once passed the House without division to commit the whole to Newgate, where they remained for various terms. Dasent and Pilgrim were released in ten days, on making due submission. O'Mally sent in a medical certificate, declaring that the imprisonment was endangering his life, and after some question he was also released. The rest were detained for more than a month, it being considered that they were the most guilty, as being either professional agents, who advised the others to abscond, or witnesses who did not voluntarily come forward when the chance was given them.

Many of the old customs once prevalent in the State Side, so properly condemned and abolished, were revived for the convenience of these gentlemen, whose incarceration was thus rendered as little like imprisonment as possible. A certain number, who could afford the high rate of a guinea per diem, fixed by the under sheriff, were lodged in the governor's house, slept there, and had their meals provided for them from the Sessions House or London Coffee-House. A few others, who could not afford a payment of more than half a guinea, were permitted to monopolize a part of the prison infirmary, where the upper ward was exclusively appropriated to their use. They also had their meals sent in, and, with the food, wine almost *ad libitum*. A prisoner, one of the wardsmen, waited on those in the infirmary; the occupants of the governor's house had their own servants, or the governor's. As a rule, visitors, many of them persons of good position, came and went all day long, and as late as nine at night; some to the infirmary, many more to the governor's house. There were no restraints, cards and backgammon were played, and the time passed in feasting and revelry. Even Mr. Cope admitted that the committal of this class of prisoners to Newgate was most inconvenient, and the inspectors expressed themselves still more strongly in reprehension of the practice. The infirmary at this particular period epitomized the condition of the gaol at large. It was diverted from its proper uses, and, as the "place of the greatest comfort," was allotted to persons who should not have been sent to Newgate at all. All the evils of indiscriminate association were strongly accentuated by the crowd collected within its narrow limits. "It may easily be imagined," say the inspectors, in speaking of the prison generally, "what must be the state of discipline in a place filled with characters so various as were assembled there, where the tried and the untried, the sick and the healthy, the sane and the insane, the young and the old, the trivial offender and the man about to suffer the extreme penalty of the law, are all huddled together without discrimination, oversight, or control."

Enough has probably been extracted from this most damnatory report to give a complete picture of the disgraceful state in which Newgate still remained in 1835. The inspectors, however, honestly admitted that although the site of the prison was convenient, its construction was as bad as bad could be. Valuable space was cumbered with many long and winding passages, numerous staircases, and unnecessarily thick and cumbrous inner walls. The wards were in some cases spacious, but they were entirely unsuited for separation or the inspection of prisoners. The yards were narrow and confined, mainly because the ground plan was radically vicious. These were evils inseparable from the place. But there were others remediable under a better system of management. More attention to ventilation, which was altogether neglected and inadequate, would have secured a better atmosphere for the unhappy inmates, who constantly breathed an air heavy, and, when the wards were first opened in the morning, particularly offensive.

Again, the discipline commonly deemed inseparable from every place of durance was entirely wanting. The primary object of committing a prisoner to gaol, as the inspectors pointed out, was to deter not only the criminal himself, but others from crime, and "to dispose him, by meditation and seclusion, to return to an honest life." But at Newgate the convicted prisoner, instead of privation and hard fare, "is permitted to purchase whatever his own means or the means of his friends in or out of prison can afford, and he can almost invariably procure the luxuries of his class of life, beer and tobacco, in abundance. Instead of seclusion and meditation, his time is passed in the midst of a body of criminals of every class and degree, in riot, debauchery, and gaming, vaunting his own adventures, or listening to those of others; communicating his own skill and aptitude in crime, or acquiring the lessons of greater adepts. He has access to newspapers, and of course prefers that description which are expressly prepared for his own class, and which abound in vulgar adventure in criminal enterprise, and in the histories of the police, the gaol, and the scaffold. He is allowed intercourse with prostitutes who, in nine cases out of ten, have originally conduced to his ruin; and his connection with them is confirmed by that devotion and generosity towards their paramours in adversity for which these otherwise degraded women are remarkable. Having thus passed his time, he returns a greater adept in crime, with a wider acquaintance among criminals, and, what perhaps is even more injurious to him, is generally known to all the worst men in the country; not only without the inclination, but almost without the ability of returning to an honest life."

These pungent and well-grounded strictures applied with still greater force to the unconvicted prisoner, the man who came to the prison innocent, and still uncontaminated, to be subjected to the same baneful influences, and to suffer the same moral deterioration, whether ultimately convicted or set free. The whole system, or more correctly the want of system, was baneful and pernicious to the last degree. The evils of such association were aggravated by the unbroken idleness; one "evil inflamed the other;" reformation or any kind of moral improvement was impossible; the prisoner's career was inevitably downward, till he struck the lowest depths. "Forced and constant intercourse with the most depraved individuals of his own class; the employment of those means and agents by which the lowest passions and the most vulgar propensities of man are perpetually kept in the highest state of excitement—drink, gaming, obscene and blasphemous language; utter idleness, the almost unrestricted admission of money and luxuries; uncontrolled conversation with visitors of the very worst description—prostitutes, thieves, receivers of stolen goods; all the tumultuous and diversified passions and emotions which circumstances like these must necessarily generate, forbid the faintest shadow of a hope that in a soil so unfavourable for moral culture, any awakening truth, salutary exhortation, or imperfect resolutions of amendment can take root or grow."

Strong as were the foregoing remarks, the inspectors wound up their report in still more trenchant language, framing a terrible indictment against those responsible for the condition of Newgate. Their words deserve to be quoted in full.

"We cannot close these remarks," say the inspectors, "without an expression of the painful feelings with which we submit to your Lordship[87] this picture of the existing state of Newgate. That in this vast metropolis, the centre of wealth, civilization, and information; distinguished as the seat of religion, worth, and philanthropy, where is to be found in operation every expedient by which Ignorance may be superseded by Knowledge, Idleness by Industry, and Suffering by Benevolence; that in the metropolis of this highly-favoured country, to which the eyes of other lands turn for example, a system of prison discipline such as that enforced in Newgate should be for a number of years in undisturbed operation, not only in contempt of religion and humanity, but in opposition to the recorded denunciations of authority, and in defiance of the express enactments of the law, is indeed a subject which cannot but impress every considerate mind with humiliation and sorrow. We trust, however, that the day is at hand when this stain will be removed from the character of the city of London, and when the first municipal authority of our land will be no longer subjected to the reproach of fostering an institution which outrages the rights and feelings of humanity, defeats the ends of justice, and disgraces the profession of a Christian country."

The publication of this report raised a storm in the city, and the corporation was roused to make an immediate protest. A committee of aldermen was forthwith appointed to report upon the inspectors' report, and the result was another lengthy blue book, printed in the parliamentary papers, 1836, traversing where it was possible the statements of the inspectors, and offering explanation and palliation of such evils as could not be denied. The inspectors retorted without loss of time, reiterating their charges, and pointing out that the committee of aldermen by its own admission justified the original allegations. It was impossible to deny the indiscriminate association; the gambling, drinking, smoking, quarrelling in the gaol; the undue authority given to prisoners, the levying of garnish under another name, the neglect of the condemned convicts, the filthy condition of the wards, the insufficiency of bedding and clothing, the misemployment of officers and prisoners by the governor. The corporation evidently had the worst of it, and began to feel the necessity for undertaking the great work of reform. Next year we find the inspectors expressing their satisfaction that "the full and faithful exposure which we felt it our duty to make of Newgate has been productive of at least some advantage, inasmuch as it has aroused the attention of those upon whom parliamentary reports and grand jury presentments had hitherto failed to make the slightest impression."

The measures of improvement introduced were mainly as follows: the fixing of "inspection holes" in the doors and walls, so as to insure more supervision; of windows opening into the well-holes, to give better light and ventilation; the construction of bed-places, three tiers high alongside the walls for males, two tiers for females; the provision of dining-rooms and dining-tables. The infirmary was enlarged, the admission of visitors limited, and the passing of articles prevented by a wire screen. The windows were to be glazed and painted to prevent prisoners from looking out; baths, fumigating places for clothing, wash-house, and the removal of dust-bins, completed the new arrangements in the main prison. In the press-yard, the press-room and ward above it were parcelled out into nine separate sleeping cells; each was provided with an iron bedstead, and a small desk at which the condemned man might read or write. But the one great and most crying evil remained unremedied. "The mischief of gaol associations," say the inspectors, "which has been demonstrably proved to be the fruitful source of all the abuses and irregularities which have so long disgraced Newgate, is not only permitted still to exist in the prison, but is rendered more powerful than before."... In endeavouring to arrest contamination, prisoners were more closely confined, and associated in smaller numbers; but this had the effect of throwing them into closer contact, and of making them more intimately acquainted with, more directly influential upon, one another.

In the inspectors' fourth report, dated 1839, they return to the charge, and again call the corporation to task for their mismanagement of Newgate. Abuses and irregularities, which had been partially remedied by the reform introduced in 1837, were once more in the ascendant. "In our late visits," they say, "we have seen manifest indications of a retrograde movement in this respect, and a tendency to return to much of that laxity and remissness which formerly marked the management of this prison." Again the following year the inspectors repeat their charge. "The prominent evils of this prison (Newgate)—evils which the alterations made within the last four years have failed to remove—are the association of prisoners, and the unusual contamination to which such association gives rise. For nearly twenty-two hours out of the twenty-four the prisoners are locked up, during which time no officer is stationed in the ward with them." They go on to say—"Newgate is only less extensively injurious than formerly because it is less crowded. The effects of the imprisonment are to vitiate its inmates, to extend their acquaintanceship with each other, to corrupt the prisoner charged with an offence of which he may be innocent, and to confirm in guilt the young and inexperienced offender."

The reports as the years flow on reiterate the same complaints. Much bitterness of feeling is evidently engendered, and the corporation grows more and more angry with the inspectors. The prison officials appear to be on the side of the inspectors, to the great dissatisfaction of the corporation, who claimed the full allegiance and support of its servants. In a resolution passed by the Court of Aldermen on 18th March, 1842, I find it ordered "that the ordinary of Newgate be restricted from making any communications to the Home Office or the Inspectors of Prisons, and that he be required wholly to confine himself to the performance of his duty as prescribed by Act of Parliament." The inspectors were not to be deterred, however, by any opposition from the earnest discharge of their functions, and continued to report against Newgate. In their tenth report they state that they are compelled by an imperative sense of duty to advert in terms of decided condemnation to the lamentable condition of the prisons of the city of London,—Newgate, Giltspur St. Compter, and the City Bridewell,—in which the master evil of gaol association and consequent contamination still continues to operate directly to the encouragement of crime. "The plan adopted for ventilating the dining-room on the 'master's side' and that of the middle yard is very inefficient; it consists of several circular perforations, about two inches in diameter, slanting downwards from the top of the walls to the outside adjoining the slaughter-houses of Newgate market; and occasionally, in hot weather, instead of ventilating the apartments, they only serve to convey the offensive effluvia arising from the decaying animal matter into the dining-rooms. Sometimes the stench in hot weather is said to be very bad. Many rats also come through these so-called ventilators, as they open close to the ground at the back of the prison." At the same time the inspectors animadvert strongly upon the misconduct of prisoners and the frequency of prison punishments, both offences and punishments affording a sufficient index to the practices going forward; and they wind up by declaring that a strict compliance with their duties gave them no choice "but to report matters as we found them, and again and again to protest against Newgate as it at present exists."

No complete and permanent improvement was indeed possible while Newgate remained unchanged. It was not till the erection of the new prison at Holloway in 1850, and the entire internal reconstruction of Newgate according to new ideas, that the evils so justly complained of and detailed in this chapter were entirely removed. But these are matters which will occupy a later page in my narrative.

EXECUTIONS (CONTINUED).

Executions not always in front of Newgate after discontinuance of Tyburn—Old Bailey by degrees monopolizes the business—Description of the new gallows—Same system had already been used in Dublin—"The fall of the leaf"—Last case of burning before Newgate—Phœbe Harris, in 1788—Crowds as great as ever at the Old Bailey, and as brutal as of old—Pieman, ballad-monger, and "rope"-seller did a roaring trade—Governor Wall—His demeanour and dress—Enormous crowd at Wall's execution—Also at that of Holloway and Haggerty—Frightful catastrophe and terrible loss of life in the crowd—The same anticipated at execution of Bellingham, but avoided by extreme precautions taken—Crowds to see Fauntleroy and Courvoisier suffer—Description of an execution in 1851—The demeanour, generally, of the condemned—Long protracted uncertainty as to their fate—Awful levity displayed—Reasons for delay—The Recorder's report—Its arrival—Communicated to convicts by chaplain—Tenderness really shown to those certain to die—Chaplain improves the occasion in preaching the condemned sermon—The chapel service on day it was preached described—Demeanour of the condemned

EXECUTIONS (continued).

described in detail—Abstract of a condemned sermon—Service and returning thanks by the respited the day after the execution—Callousness of those present—Crowded congregation to hear Courvoisier's condemned sermon, and dense throng to see him hanged—Amelioration of the criminal code—Executions more rare—Capital punishment gradually restricted to murderers—Dissection of the bodies abolished—Some details of dissection—Public exhibition of bodies also discontinued—The body of Williams, who murdered the Marrs, so shown—Hanging in chains given up—Failures at executions—Culprits fight for life—Case of Charles White, of Luigi Buranelli, of William Bousfield—Calcraft and his method of hanging—Other hangmen—Story of the cost of a hangman.

I PROPOSE to return now to the subject of Newgate executions, which we left at the time of the discontinuance of the long-practised procession to Tyburn. The reasons for this change were fully set forth in a previous chapter.[88] The terrible spectacle was as demoralizing to the public, for whose admonition it was intended, as the exposure was brutal and cruel towards the principal actors. The decision to remove the scene of action to the immediate front of the gaol itself was in the right direction, as making the performance shorter and diminishing the area of display. But the Old Bailey was not exclusively used; at first, and for some few years after 1784, executions took place occasionally at a distance from Newgate. This was partly due to the survival of the old notion that the scene of the crime ought also to witness the retribution; partly perhaps because residents in and about the Old Bailey raised a loud protest against the constant erection of the scaffold in their neighbourhood. As regards the first, I find that in 1786 John Hogan, the murderer of a Mr. Odell, an attorney who resided in Charlotte Street, Rathbone Place, was executed on a gibbet in front of his victim's house. Lawrence Jones, a burglar, was in 1793 ordered for execution in Hatton Garden, near the house he had robbed; and when he evaded the sentence by suicide, his body was exhibited in the same neighbourhood, "extended upon a plank on the top of an open cart, in his clothes, and fettered." Again, as late as 1809 and 1812, Execution Dock, on the banks of the Thames, was still retained. Here John Sutherland, commander of the British armed transport 'The Friends,' suffered on the 29th June, 1809, for the murder of his cabin-boy, whom he stabbed after much ill-usage on board the ship as it lay in the Tagus. On the 18th December, 1812, two sailors, Charles Palm and Sam Tilling, were hanged at the same place for the murder of their captain, James Keith, of the trading vessel 'Adventure,' upon the high seas. They were taken in a cart to the place of execution, amidst a vast concourse of people. "Palm, as soon as he was seated in the cart, put a quid of tobacco into his mouth, and offered another to his companion, who refused it with indignation.... Some indications of pity were offered for the fate of Tilling; Palm, execration alone."[89]

But the Old Bailey gradually, and in spite of all objections urged, monopolized the dread business of execution. The first affair of the kind on this spot was on the 3rd December, 1783, when, in pursuance of an order issued by the Recorder to the sheriffs of Middlesex and the keeper of His Majesty's gaol, Newgate, a scaffold was erected in front of that prison for the execution of several convicts named by the Recorder. "Ten were executed; the scaffold hung with black; and the inhabitants of the neighbourhood, having petitioned the sheriffs to remove the scene of execution to the old place, were told that the plan had been well considered, and would be persevered in." The following 23rd April, it is stated that the malefactors ordered for execution on the 18th inst. were brought out of Newgate about eight in the morning, and suspended on a gallows of a new construction. "After hanging the usual time they were taken down, and the machine cleared away in half-an-hour. By practice the art is much improved, and there is no part of the world in which villains are hanged in so neat a manner, and with so little ceremony."

A full description of this new gallows, which was erected in front of the debtors' door, is to be found in contemporary records. "The criminals are not exposed to view till they mount the fatal stage. The last part of the stage, or that next to the gaol, is enclosed by a temporary roof, under which are placed two seats for the reception of the sheriffs, one on each side of the stairs leading to the scaffold. Round the north, west, and south sides are erected galleries for the reception of officers, attendants, &c., and at the distance of five feet from the same is fixed a strong railing all round the scaffold to enclose a place for the constables. In the middle of this machinery is placed a movable platform, in form of a trap-door, ten feet long by eight wide, on the middle of which is placed the gibbet, extending from the gaol across the Old Bailey. This movable platform is raised six inches higher than the rest of the scaffold, and on it the convicts stand; it is supported by two beams, which are held in their place by bolts. The movement of the lever withdraws the bolts, the platform falls in;" and this, being much more sudden and regular than that of a cart being drawn away, has the effect of immediate death. A broadsheet dated April 24th, 1787,[90] describing an execution on the newly-invented scaffold before the debtors' door, Newgate, says, "The scaffold on which these miserable people suffered is a temporary machine which was drawn out of the yard of the sessions house by horses; ... it is supported by strong posts fixed into grooves made in the street; ... the whole is temporary, being all calculated to take to pieces, which are preserved within the prison."

This contrivance appears to have been copied with improvements from that which had been used in Dublin at a still earlier date, for that city claims the priority in establishing the custom of hanging criminals at the gaol itself. The Dublin "engine of death," as the gallows are styled in the account from which the following description is taken, consisted of an iron bar parallel to the prison wall, and about four feet from it, but strongly affixed thereto with iron scroll clamps. "From this bar hang several iron loops, in which the halters are tied. Under this bar at a proper distance is a piece of flooring or platform, projecting somewhat beyond the range of the iron bar, and swinging upon hinges affixed to the wall. The entrance upon this floor or leaf is from the middle window over the gate of the prison; and this floor is supported below, while the criminals stand upon it, by two pieces of timber, which are made to slide in and out of the prison wall through apertures made for that purpose. When the criminals are tied up and prepared for their fate, this floor suddenly falls down, upon withdrawing the supporters inwards. They are both drawn at once by a windlass, and the unhappy culprits remain suspended." This mode of execution, it is alleged, gave rise to the old vulgar "chaff," "Take care, or you'll die at the fall of the leaf." The machinery in use in Dublin is much the same as that employed at many gaols now-a-days. But the fall apart and inwards of two leaves is considered superior. The latter is the method still followed at Newgate.

The sentences inflicted in front of Newgate were not limited to hanging. In the few years which elapsed between the establishment of the gallows at Newgate and the abolition of the practice of burning females for petty treason, more than one woman suffered this penalty at the Old Bailey. One case is preserved by Catnach, that of Phœbe Harris, who in 1788 was "barbariously" (*sic* in the broadsheet) executed and burnt before Newgate for coining. She is described as a well-made little woman, something more than thirty years of age, of a pale complexion and not disagreeable features. "When she came out of prison she appeared languid and terrified, and trembled greatly as she advanced to the stake, where the apparatus for the punishment she was about to experience seemed to strike her mind with horror and consternation, to the exclusion of all power of recollectedness in preparation for the approaching awful moment." She walked from the debtors' door to a stake fixed in the ground about half-way between the scaffold and Newgate Street. She was immediately tied by the neck to an iron bolt fixed near the top of the stake, and after praying fervently for a few minutes, the steps on which she stood were drawn away, and she was left suspended. A chain fastened by nails to the stake was then put round her body by the executioner with his assistants. Two cart-loads of faggots were piled about her, and after she had hung for half-an-hour the fire was kindled. The flames presently burned the halter, the body fell a few inches, and hung then by the iron chain. The fire had not quite burnt out at twelve, in nearly four hours, that is to say. "A great concourse of people attended on this melancholy occasion."

The change from Tyburn to the Old Bailey had worked no improvement as regards the gathering together of the crowd or its demeanour. As many spectators as ever thronged to see the dreadful show, and they were packed into a more limited space, disporting themselves as heretofore by brutal horse-play, coarse jests, and frantic yells. It was still the custom to offer warm encouragement or bitter disapproval, according to the character and antecedents of the sufferer. The highwayman, whose exploits many in the crowd admired or emulated, was cheered and bidden to die game; the man of better birth could hope for no sympathy, whatever his crime. At the execution of Governor Wall, in 1802, the furious hatred of the mob was plainly apparent in their appalling cries. His appearance on the scaffold was the signal for three prolonged shouts from an innumerable populace, "the brutal effusion of one common sentiment." It was said that so large a crowd had never collected since the execution of

Mrs. Brownrigg, nor had the public indignation risen so high. Pieman and ballad-monger did their usual roaring trade amidst the dense throng. No sooner was the "job" finished than half-a-dozen competitors appeared, each offering the identical rope for sale at a shilling an inch. One was the "yeoman of the halter," a Newgate official, the executioner's assistant, whom Mr. J. T. Smith,[91] who was present at the execution, describes as "a most diabolical-looking little wretch—Jack Ketch's head man." The yeoman was, however, under-sold by his wife, "Rosy Emma," exuberant in talk and hissing hot from Pie Corner, where she had taken her morning dose of gin-and-bitters.[92] A little further off, says Mr. Smith, was "a lath of a fellow past three-score years and ten, who had just arrived from the purlieus of Black Boy Alley, woebegone as Romeo's apothecary, exclaiming, 'Here's the identical rope at sixpence an inch.' "

Mr. Smith's account of the condemned convict, whose cell he was permitted to enter, may be inserted here. He was introduced by the ordinary, Dr. Forde, a name familiar to the reader,[93] who met him at the felons' door "in his canonicals, and with his head as stiffly erect as a sheriff's coachman." The ordinary "gravely uttered, 'Come this way, Mr. Smith.' As we crossed the press yard a cock crew, and the solitary clanking of a restless chain was dreadfully horrible. The prisoners had not risen." They entered a "stone cold room," and were presently joined by the prisoner. "He was death's counterfeit, tall, shrivelled, and pale; and his soul shot out so piercingly through the port-holes of his head, that the first glance of him nearly petrified me.... His hands were clasped, and he was truly penitent. After the yeoman had requested him to stand up, 'he pinioned him,' as the Newgate phrase is, and tied the cord with so little feeling that the governor (Wall), who had not given the wretch his accustomed fee, observed, 'You have tied me very tight,' upon which Dr. Forde ordered him to slacken the cord, which he did, but not without muttering. 'Thank you, sir,' said the governor to the doctor, 'it is of little moment.' He then made some observations to the attendant about the fire, and turning to the doctor, questioned him. 'Do tell me, sir; I am informed I shall go down with great force; is it so?' After the construction and action of the machine had been explained, the doctor asked the governor what kind of men he had commanded at Goree, where the murder for which he was condemned had been committed. 'Sir,' he answered, 'they sent me the very riff-raff.' The poor soul then joined the doctor in prayer, and never did I witness more contrition at any condemned sermon than he then evinced. The sheriff arrived, attended by his officers, to receive the prisoner from the keeper. A new hat was partly flattened on his head, for, owing to its being too small in the crown, it stood many inches too high behind. As we were crossing the press yard, the dreadful execrations of some of the felons so shook his frame that he observed 'the clock had struck;' and quickening his pace, he soon arrived at the room where the sheriff was to give a receipt for his body, according to the usual custom. Before the colonel[94] had been pinioned he had pulled out two white handkerchiefs, one of which he bound over his temples so as nearly to conceal his eyes, the other he kept between his hands. Over the handkerchief around his brows he placed a white cap, the new hat being on top of all. He was dressed in a mixed-coloured loose coat with a black collar, swandown waistcoat, blue pantaloons, and white silk stockings. Thus apparelled he ascended the stairs at the debtors' door, and stepped out on to the platform, to be received, as has been said, by prolonged yells. These evidently deprived him of the small portion of fortitude he had summoned up. He bowed his head under extreme pressure of ignominy, and at his request the ordinary drew the cap further down over his face, when in an instant, without waiting for any signal, the platform dropped, and he was launched into eternity."

Whenever the public attention had been specially called to a particular crime, either on account of its atrocity, the doubtfulness of the issue, or the superior position of the perpetrator, the attendance at the execution was certain to be tumultuous, and the conduct of the mob disorderly. This was notably the case at the execution of Holloway and Haggerty in 1807, an event long remembered from the fatal and disastrous consequences which followed it. They were accused by a confederate, who, goaded by conscience, had turned approver, of the murder of a Mr. Steele, who kept a lavender warehouse in the city, and who had gardens at Feltham, whither he often went to distil the lavender, returning to London the same evening. One night he was missing, and after a long interval his dead body was discovered, shockingly disfigured, in a ditch. This was in 1802. Four years passed without the detection of the murderers, but in the beginning of 1807 one of them, at that time just sentenced to transportation, made a full confession, and implicated Holloway and Haggerty. They were accordingly apprehended and brought to trial, the informer, Hanfield by name, being accepted as king's evidence. Conviction followed mainly on his testimony; but the two men, especially Holloway, stoutly maintained their innocence to the last. Very great excitement prevailed in the town throughout the trial, and this greatly increased when the verdict was known.

An enormous crowd assembled to witness the execution, amounting, it was said, to the hitherto unparalleled number of 40,000. By eight o'clock not an inch of ground in front of the platform was unoccupied. The pressure soon became so frightful that many would have willingly escaped from the crowd; but their attempts only increased the general confusion. Very soon women began to scream with terror; some, especially of low stature, found it difficult to remain standing, and several, although held up for some time by the men nearest them, presently fell, and were at once trampled to death. Cries of Murder! murder! were now raised, and added greatly to the horrors of the scene. Panic became general. More women, children, and many men were borne down, to perish beneath the feet of the rest. The most affecting and distressing scene was at Green Arbour Lane, just opposite the debtors' door of the prison. Here a couple of piemen had been selling their wares; the basket of one of them, which was raised upon a four-legged stool, was upset. The pieman stooped down to pick up his scattered stock, and some of the mob, not seeing what had happened, stumbled over him. No one who fell ever rose again. Among the rest was a woman with an infant at the breast. She was killed, but in the act of falling she forced her child into the arms of a man near her, and implored him in God's name to save it; the man, needing all his care for his own life, threw the child from him, and it passed along the heads of the crowd, to be caught at last by a person who struggled with it to a cart and deposited it there in safety. In another part seven persons met their death by suffocation.

In this convulsive struggle for bare existence people fought fiercely with one another, and the weakest, of course the women, went under. One cart-load of spectators having broken down, some of its occupants fell off the vehicle, and were instantly trampled to death. This went on for more than an hour, and until the malefactors were cut down and the gallows removed; then the mob began to thin, and the streets were cleared by the city marshals and a number of constables. The catastrophe exceeded the worst anticipations. Nearly one hundred dead and dying lay about; and after all had been removed, the bodies for identification, the wounded to hospitals, a cart-load of shoes, hats, petticoats, and fragments of wearing apparel were picked up. St. Bartholomew's Hospital was converted into an impromptu *Morgue*, and all persons who had relatives missing were admitted to identify them. Among the dead was a sailor lad whom no one knew; he had his pockets filled with bread and cheese, and it was generally supposed that he had come a long distance to see the fatal show.

A tremendous crowd assembled when Bellingham was executed in 1812 for the murder of Spencer Percival, at that time prime minister; but there were no serious accidents, beyond those caused by the goring of a maddened, over-driven ox which forced its way through the crowd. Precautions had been taken by the erection of barriers, and the posting of placards at all the avenues to the Old Bailey, on which was printed, "Beware of entering the crowd! Remember thirty poor persons were pressed to death by the crowd when Haggerty and Holloway were executed!" The concourse was very great, notwithstanding these warnings. It was still greater at Fauntleroy's execution in 1824, when no less than 100,000 persons assembled, it was said. Every window and roof which could command a view of the horrible performance was occupied. All the avenues and approaches, places even whence nothing whatever could be seen of the scaffold, were blocked by persons who had overflowed from the area in front of the gaol. At Courvoisier's execution in 1840 it was the same, or worse. As early as six a.m. the number assembled already exceeded that seen on ordinary occasions; by seven a.m. the whole space was so thronged that it was impossible to move one way or the other. Some persons were kept for more than five hours standing against the barriers, and many nearly fainted from exhaustion. Every window had its party of occupants; the adjoining roofs were equally crowded. High prices were asked and paid for front seats or good standing room. As much as £5 was given for the attic story of the Lamb's Coffee House; £2 was a common price for a window. At the George public-house to the south of the drop, Sir W. Watkin Wynn, Bart., hired a room for the night and morning, which he and a large party of friends occupied before and during the execution; in an adjoining house, that of an undertaker, was Lord Alfred Paget, also with several friends. Those who had hired apartments spent the night in them, keeping up their courage with liquids and cigars. Numbers of ladies were present, although the public feeling was much against their attendance. One well-dressed woman fell out of a first-floor window on to the shoulders of the crowd below, but neither she nor any one else was greatly hurt. The city authorities had endeavoured to take all precautions against panic and excitement among the crowd, and caused a number of stout additional barriers to be erected in front of the scaffold, and although one of these gave way owing to the extraordinary pressure, no serious accident occurred.

Some years later an eye-witness published a graphic account of one of these scenes.[95] Soon after midnight on the Sunday night, for by this time the present practice of executing on Monday morning had been pretty generally introduced, the crowd began to congregate in and about the Old Bailey. Gin-shops and coffee-houses were the first to open doors, and touts began to bid for tenants for the various rooms upstairs. Cries of "Comfortable room!" "Excellent situation!" "Beautiful prospect!" "Splendid view!" resounded on every side. By this time the workmen might be heard busily erecting the gallows; the sounds of hammer and saw intermingled with the broad jeers and coarse jests of the rapidly increasing mob. One by one the huge uprights of black timber were fitted together, until presently the huge stage loomed dark above the crowd which was now ranged round the barriers; a throng of people whom neither rain, snow, storm, nor darkness ever hindered from attending the show. They were mainly members of the criminal classes; their conversation was of companions and associates of former years, long ago imprisoned, transported, hanged, while they, hoary-headed and hardened in guilt, were still at large. They talked of the days when the convicts were hung up a dozen or more in a row; of those who had shown the white, and those who had died game. The approaching ceremony had evidently no terrors for these "idolaters of the gallows." With them were younger men and women: the former already vowed to the same criminal career, and looking up to their elders with the respect due to successful practitioners; the latter unsexed and brutalized by dissipation, slipshod and slovenly, in crushed bonnet and dirty shawl, the gown fastened by a single hook, their harsh and half-cracked voices full of maudlin, besotted sympathy for those about to die. "Above the murmur and tumult of that noisy assembly, the lowing and bleating of cattle as they were driven into the stalls and pens of Smithfield fell with a strange unnatural sound upon the ear.... Hush! the unceasing murmur of the mob now breaks into a loud deep roar, a sound as if the ocean had suddenly broken through some ancient boundary, against which its ever restless billows had for ages battered; the wide dark sea of heads is all at once in motion; each wave seems trying to overleap the other as they are drawn onwards towards this outlet. Every link in that great human chain is shaken, along the whole lengthened line has the motion jarred, and each in turn sees, coiled up on the floor of the scaffold like a serpent, the hangman's rope! The human hand that placed it there was only seen for a moment, as it lay, white and ghastly, upon the black boards, and then again was as suddenly withdrawn, as if ashamed of the deed it had done. The loud shout of the multitude once more subsided, or only fell upon the abstracted ear like the dreamy murmur of an ocean shell. Then followed sounds more distinct and audible, in which ginger-beer, pies, fried fish, sandwiches, and fruit were vended under the names of notorious murderers, highwaymen, and criminals, famous in the annals of Newgate for the hardihood they had displayed in the hour of execution, when they terminated their career of crime at the gallows. Threading his way among these itinerant vendors was seen the meek-faced deliverer of tracts, the man of good intentions, now bonneted, now laughed at, the skirt of his seedy black coat torn across; yet, though pulled right and left, or sent headlong into the crowd by the swing of some brutal and muscular arm, never once from that pale face passed away its benign and patient expression, but ever the same form moved along in the fulfilment of his mission, in spite of all persecution. Another fight followed the score which had already taken place; this time two women were the combatants. Blinded with their long hair, they tore at each other like two furies; their bonnets and caps were trodden underfoot in the kennel, and lay disregarded beside the body of the poor dog which, while searching for its master in the crowd, was an hour before kicked to death by the savage and brutal mob.

"Another deep roar, louder than any which had preceded it, broke from the multitude. Then came the cry of 'Hats off!' and 'Down in front!' as at a theatre. It was followed by the deep and solemn booming of the death-bell from the church of St. Sepulchre—the iron knell that rang upon the beating heart of the living man who was about to die; and with blanched cheek, and sinking, we turned away from the scene."

In thus describing the saturnalia before the gallows I have been drawn on somewhat beyond the period with which I am at present dealing. Let me retrace my steps, and speak more in detail of the treatment of the condemned in those bloodthirsty and brutally indifferent days, and of their demeanour after sentence until the last penalty was paid. One of the worst evils was the terrible and long-protracted uncertainty as to the result. In the case of convicted murderers only was prompt punishment inflicted, and with them indeed this despatch amounted to undue precipitancy. Forty-eight hours was the limit of time allowed to the unhappy man to make his peace, and during that time he was still kept on a bare allowance of bread and water. But the murderers formed only a small proportion of the total number sentenced to death, and for the rest there was a long period of anxious suspense, although in the long run mercy generally prevailed, and very few capitally convicted for crimes less than murder actually suffered. Thus in the years between May 1st, 1827, and 30th April, 1831, no less than four hundred and fifty-one sentences of death for capital crimes were passed at the Old Bailey; but of these three hundred and ninety-six were reversed by the king in council, and only fifty-two were really executed. Already the severity of our criminal code, and the number of capital felonies upon the statute book, had brought a reaction; and while the courts adhered to the letter of the law, appeals were constantly made to the royal prerogative of mercy. This was more particularly the practice in London. Judges on assize were satisfied with simply recording a sentence of death against offenders whom they did not think deserved the extreme penalty. At the Old Bailey almost every one capitally convicted by a jury was sentenced to be hanged. The result in the latter case was left in the first place to the king in council, but there was a further appeal then, as now, to the king himself, or practically to the Home Secretary. Neither in town or country were cases entirely taken on their own merits. Convicted offenders might have good or bad luck; they might be arraigned when their particular crime was uncommon, and were then nearly certain to escape; or theirs might be one of many, and it might be considered necessary to "make an example." In this latter it might fairly be said that a man was put to death less for his own sins than for the crimes of others.

The absurdity of the system, its irregularity and cruelty, were fully touched upon by the inspectors of prisons in their first report. They found at Newgate, under disgraceful conditions as already described,[96] seventeen capital convicts, upon all of whom the sentence of death had been passed. Eventually two only of the whole number suffered; two others were sentenced to three months' imprisonment, and the balance to varying terms. Nothing could be more strongly marked than the contrast between the ultimate destiny of different individuals all abiding the same awful doom: on the one hand the gallows, on the other a short imprisonment. The inspectors very properly desired to call attention to the inevitable tendency in this mode of dealing with "the most awful sanctions of the law," to make those sanctions an object of contemptuous mockery. The consequences were plainly proved to the inspectors. Capitally convicted prisoners did, as a matter of fact, "treat with habitual and inexpressible levity the sentence of death." Of this I have treated at length in the last chapter.

The time thus spent varied considerably, but it was seldom less than six weeks. It all depended upon the sovereign's disposition to do business. Sometimes the Privy Council did not meet for months, and during all that time the convicts languished with hope nearly indefinitely deferred. When the council had decided, the news was conveyed to Newgate by the Recorder, who made his "report," as it was called. The time of the arrival of this report was generally known at Newgate, and its contents were anxiously awaited by both convicts in the press-yard and their friends collected in a crowd outside the gates. Sometimes the report was delayed. On one occasion, Mr. Wakefield tells us, the Recorder, who had attended the council at Windsor, did not deliver the report till the following day. "The prisoners and their friends, therefore, were kept in a state of the most violent suspense for many hours, during which they counted the moments—the prisoners in their cells as usual, and their friends in the street in front of Newgate, where they passed the night. I have heard the protracted agony of both classes described by those who witnessed it in terms so strong, that I am unwilling to repeat them."...[97] "The crowd of men and women who passed the night in front of Newgate, began, as soon as the hour was passed when they had expected the report, to utter imprecations against the Recorder, the Secretary of State, the Council, and the King; they never ceased cursing until the passion of anger so excited was exchanged for joy in some and grief in others. I myself heard more than one of those whose lives were spared by that decision of the council, afterwards express a wish to murder the Recorder for having kept them so long in suspense."

The Recorder's report generally reached Newgate late at night. Its receipt was immediately followed by the promulgation of its contents to the persons most closely concerned, which was done with a sort of ceremony intended to be impressive. The whole of the convicts were assembled together in one ward, and made to kneel down. To them entered the chaplain or ordinary of Newgate in full canonicals, who in solemn tones communicated to each in turn the fate in store for him. The form of imparting the intelligence was generally the same. "So-and-so, I am sorry to tell you that it is all against you;" or, "A. B., your case has been taken into consideration by the king in council, and His Majesty has been mercifully pleased to spare your life." The fatal news was not always received in the same way. The men who were doomed often fell down in convulsions upon the floor. Sometimes any who had had a narrow escape fainted, but the bulk of those respited looked on with unfeeling indifference. The concluding part of the ceremony was, for those who had been pardoned, to recite a thanksgiving to God and the king.

It is satisfactory to be able to record that some consideration was shown the capital convict actually awaiting execution. Even so severe a critic as Mr. Wakefield states that "a stranger to the scene would be astonished to observe the peculiar tenderness, I was going to add respect, which persons under sentence of death obtain from all the officers of the prison. Before sentence a prisoner has only to observe the regulations of the gaol in order to remain neglected and unnoticed. Once ordered to the cells, friends of all classes suddenly rise up; his fellow-prisoners, the turnkeys, the chaplain, the keepers, and the sheriffs all seem interested in his fate, and he can make no reasonable request that is not at once granted by whomsoever he may address. This rule has some, but very few, exceptions; such as where a hardened offender behaves with great levity and brutality, as if he cared nought for his life, and thought every one anxious to promote his death." Mr. Wakefield goes on to remark that persons convicted of forgery "excited an extraordinary degree of interest in all who approached them." This was noticeable with Fauntleroy, who, on account of his birth and antecedents, was allowed to occupy a turnkey's room, and kept altogether separate from the other prisoners until the day of his death. It cannot be denied, however, that the ordinary's treatment was somewhat unfeeling, and in proof thereof I will quote an extract from the reverend gentleman's own journal. He seems to have improved the occasion when preaching the condemned sermon before Fauntleroy, by pointing a moral from that unhappy man's own case. For this the chaplain was a few days later summoned before the gaol committee of aldermen, and informed that the public would not in future be admitted to hear the condemned sermon. "I was also informed," writes Mr. Cotton, "that this resolution was in consequence of their (the aldermen's) disapproving of the last discourse delivered by me, previous to the execution of Henry Fauntleroy for uttering a forged security, in which it was said I had enlarged upon the heinous nature of his crime, and warned the public to avoid such conduct. I was informed that this unnecessarily harassed his feelings, and that the object of such sermons was solely to console the prisoner, and that from the time of his conviction nothing but what is consolatory should be addressed to a criminal. One of the aldermen, moreover, informed me that the whole court of aldermen were unanimous in their opinion on this subject. As to the exclusion of strangers on these occasions, the experience I have had convinces me that one, and perhaps the only, good of an execution, *i. e.* the solemn admonition to the public, will thereby be lost."

Probably the reader will side with the aldermen against the ordinary. This episode throws some doubt upon the tenderness and proper feeling exhibited by the chaplain towards the most deserving members of his criminal flock; and the idea will be strengthened by the following account of the Sunday service in the prison chapel on the occasion when the condemned sermon was preached. The extract is from Mr. E. Gibbon Wakefield's brochure, the date 1828, just three years after Fauntleroy's death. Strangers were now excluded, but the sheriffs attended in state, wearing their gold chains, while behind their pew stood a couple of tall footmen in state liveries. The sheriffs were in one gallery; in the other opposite were the convicts capitally convicted who had been respited. Down below between the galleries was the mass of the prison population; the schoolmaster and the juvenile prisoners being seated round the communion-table, opposite the pulpit. In the centre of the chapel was the condemned pew, a large dock-like erection painted black. Those who sat in it were visible to the whole congregation, and still more to the ordinary, whose desk and pulpit were just in front of the condemned pew, and within a couple of yards of it. The occupants of this terrible black pew were the last always to enter the chapel. Upon the occasion which I am describing they were four in number; and here I will continue the narrative in Mr. Wakefield's own words:—

"First is a youth of eighteen, condemned for stealing in a dwelling-house goods valued above five pounds. His features have no felonious cast; ... he steps boldly with head upright, looks to the women's gallery, and smiles. His intention is to pass for a brave fellow, but the attempt fails; he trembles, his knees knock together, and his head droops as he enters the condemned pew. The next convict is clearly and unmistakably a villain. He is a hardened offender, previously cast for life, reprieved, transported to Australia, and since returned without pardon. For this offence the punishment is death. He has, however, doubly earned his sentence, and is actually condemned for burglary committed since his arrival in England. His look at the sheriffs and the ordinary is full of scorn and defiance. The third convict is a sheep-stealer, a poor ignorant fellow in whose crime are mitigating circumstances, but who is left to die on the supposition that this is not his first conviction, and still more because a good many sheep have of late been stolen by other people. He is quite content to die; indeed the chaplain and others have brought him firmly to believe that his situation is enviable, and that the gates of heaven are open to receive him." The last of the four is said to have been a clergyman of the Church of England,[98] condemned for forgery, "a miserable old man in a tattered suit of black. Already he is half dead. Great efforts have been made to save his life. Friends, even utter strangers, have interceded for him, and to the last he has buoyed himself up by hope of reprieve. Now his doom is sealed irrevocably, and he has given himself up to despair. He staggers towards the pew, reels into it, stumbles forward, flings himself on the ground, and, by a curious twist of the spine, buries his head under his body. The sheriffs shudder, their inquisitive friends crane forward, the keeper frowns on the excited congregation, the lately smirking footmen close their eyes and forget their liveries, the ordinary clasps his hands, the turnkeys cry 'Hush!' and the old clerk lifts up his cracked voice, saying, 'Let us sing to the praise and glory of God.'

"The morning hymn is sung first, as if to remind the condemned that next morning at eight a.m. they are to die. The service proceeds. At last the burial service is reached. The youth alone is able to read, but from long want of practice he is at a loss to find the place in his prayer-book. The ordinary observes him, looks to the sheriffs, and says aloud, 'The service for the dead!' The youth's hands tremble as they hold the book upside down. The burglar is heard to mutter an angry oath. The sheep-stealer smiles, and, extending his arms upwards, looks with a glad expression to the roof of the chapel. The forger has never moved.

"Let us pass on. All have sung 'the Lamentation of a Sinner,' and have seemed to pray 'especially for those now awaiting the awful execution of the law.' We come to the sermon.

"The ordinary of Newgate is an orthodox, unaffected, Church of England divine, who preaches plain, homely discourses, as fit as any religious discourse can be fit for the irritated audience. The sermon of this day, whether eloquent or plain, useful or useless, must produce a striking effect at the moment of its delivery. The text, without another word, is enough to raise the wildest passions of the audience.... For a while the preacher addresses himself to the congregation at large, who listen attentively—except the clergyman and the burglar, the former of whom is still rolled up at the bottom of the condemned pew, while the eyes of the latter are wandering round the chapel, and one of them is occasionally winked impudently at some acquaintance amongst the prisoners for trial. At length the ordinary pauses, and then, in a deep tone, which, though hardly above a whisper, is audible to all, says, 'Now for you, my poor fellow mortals, who are about to suffer the last penalty of the law.' But why should I repeat the whole? It is enough to say that in the same solemn tone he talks about the minutest of crimes, punishments, bonds, shame, ignominy, sorrow, sufferings, wretchedness, pangs, childless parents, widows and helpless orphans, broken and contrite hearts, and death to-morrow morning for the benefit of society. What happens? The dying men are dreadfully agitated. The young stealer in a dwelling-house no longer has the least pretence to bravery. He grasps the back of the pew, his legs give way, he utters a faint groan, and sinks on the floor. Why does no one stir to help him? Where would be the use? The hardened burglar moves not, nor does he speak; but his face is of an ashy paleness; and if you look carefully you may see the blood trickling from his lip, which he has bitten unconsciously, or from rage, or to rouse his fainting courage. The poor sheep-stealer is in a frenzy. He throws his hands far from him, and shouts aloud, 'Mercy, good Lord! mercy is all I ask. The Lord in His mercy come! There! there! I see the Lamb of God! Oh! how happy! Oh! this is happy!' Meanwhile the clergyman, still bent into the form of a sleeping dog, struggles violently; his feet, legs, hands, and arms, even the muscles of his back, move with a quick, jerking motion, not naturally, but, as it were, like the affected parts of a galvanized corpse. Suddenly he utters a short sharp scream, and all is still.

"The silence is short. As the ordinary proceeds 'to conclude,' the women set up a yell, which is mixed with a rustling noise, occasioned by the removal of those whose hysterics have ended in fainting. The sheriffs cover their faces, and one of their inquisitive friends blows his nose with his glove. The keeper tries to appear unmoved, but his eye wanders anxiously over the combustible assembly. The children round the communion-table stare and gape with childish wonder. The two masses of prisoners for trial undulate and slightly murmur, while the capital convicts who were lately in that black pew appear faint with emotion.

"This exhibition lasts for some minutes, and then the

congregation disperses, the condemned returning to the cells: the forger carried by turnkeys; the youth sobbing aloud convulsively, as a passionate child; the burglar muttering curses and savage expressions of defiance; whilst the poor sheep-stealer shakes hands with the turnkeys, whistles merrily, and points upwards with madness in his look."

Mr. Wakefield winds up his graphic but somewhat sensational account by describing another religious service, which may appropriately be inserted here. He says, "On the day of execution there is no service in the chapel of Newgate. On the following day the capital convicts, whose companions have been hanged, are required to return thanks for their narrow escape. The firmest disbeliever in religion, if he had not lately been irritated by taking part in such a scene as the condemned service in Newgate, could hardly witness this ceremony without being affected. The men, who were so lately snatched from the jaws of death, kneel, whilst the rest of the congregation sit, and the ordinary, in a tone of peculiar solemnity, says, 'Almighty God, Father of all mercies, we thine unworthy servants do give thee most humble and hearty thanks for all thy goodness and loving-kindness to us, and to all men; *particularly to those who desire now to offer up their praises and thanksgivings for thy late mercies vouchsafed unto them.*' Could any one, knowing the late situation of the kneeling men, looking as they do at the empty pew, occupied when they saw it last, but a few hours ago, by their comrades who are now dead; could any one, not disgusted with the religious ceremonials of Newgate, witness this scene without emotion? Hardly any one. But what are the feelings of those who take part in it? I have been present at the scene not less than twenty times, and have invariably observed that many of the kneeling men or boys laughed while they knelt, pinched each other, and, when they could do so without fear of being seen by any officer of the prison, winked at other prisoners in derision of what was taking place; and I have frequently heard men and lads who had been of the kneeling party boast to their companions after the service that they had wiped their eyes during the thanksgiving, to make the ordinary believe they had been crying."

Although this misapplication of religious services still went on, the outside public continued to be excluded from the Newgate chapel on the day the condemned sermon was preached. This very proper rule was, however, set aside on the Sunday preceding Courvoisier's execution. So many applications for admission were made to the sheriffs, that they reluctantly agreed to open the gallery which had formerly been occupied by strangers on these occasions. Cards were issued, and to such an extent, that although the service was not to commence till half-past ten, by nine a.m. all the avenues to the prison gates were blocked by ticket-holders. In spite of the throng, owing to the excellent arrangements made by the sheriffs, no inconvenience was suffered by the congregation, among whom were Lord Adolphus Fitz Clarence, Lord Coventry, Lord Paget, Lord Bruce, several members of the House of Commons, and a few ladies. Contemporary accounts give a minute description of the demeanour of the convict upon this solemn occasion. He sat on a bench before the pulpit,—the hideous condemned pew had been swept away,—and never once raised his eyes during the service. "In fact his looks denoted extreme sorrow and contrition, and he seemed to suffer great inward agitation when the ordinary particularly alluded to the crime for the perpetration of which he stood condemned." Mr. Carver, the ordinary, appears to have addressed himself directly to Courvoisier, and to have dwelt with more emphasis than good taste upon the nature of the crime, and the necessity for repentance. But the chaplain admitted that the solitude of the convict's cell was more appropriate for serious reflection and profitable ministration than "this exciting occasion before a large and public assembly." So far as I can find, Courvoisier was the last condemned criminal who was thus exhibited to a crowd of morbidly curious spectators.

The atrocity of the murder no doubt attracted extraordinary attention to it. The crowd outside Newgate on the day of execution has already been described; but there was also a select gathering of distinguished visitors within the gaol. First came the sheriffs, the under-sheriffs, and several aldermen and city officials, then Lord Powerscourt and several other peers of the realm. Mr. Charles Kean the tragedian was also present, drawn to this terrible exhibition by the example of his father, the more celebrated Edmund Kean, who had witnessed the execution of Thistlewood "with a view," as he himself said, "to his professional studies."

But there is little doubt that as executions became more rare they made more impression on the public mind. Already a strong dislike to the reckless and almost indiscriminate application of the extreme penalty was apparent in all classes, and the mitigation of the criminal code, for which Romilly had so strenuously laboured, was daily more and more of an accomplished fact. In 1832 capital punishment was abolished for forgery, except in cases of forging or altering wills or powers of attorney to transfer stock. Nevertheless, after that date no person whatever was executed for this offence. In the same year capital punishment was further restricted, and ceased to be the legal sentence for coining, sheep or horse stealing, and stealing in a dwelling-house. House-breaking, as distinguished from burglary, was similarly exempted in the following year; next, the offences of returning from transportation, stealing post-office letters, and sacrilege were no longer punishable with death. In 1837 Lord John Russell's acts swept away a number of capital offences, including cutting and maiming, rick-burning, robbery, burglary, and arson. Within a couple of years the number of persons sentenced to death in England had fallen from four hundred and thirty-eight in 1837 to fifty-six in 1839. Gradually the application of capital punishment became more and more restricted, and was soon the penalty for murder alone. While in London, for instance, in 1829, twenty-four persons had been executed for crimes other than murder, from 1832 to 1844 not a single person had been executed in the metropolis except for this the gravest crime. In 1837 the death penalty was practically limited to murder or attempts to murder, and in 1841 this was accepted as the almost universally established rule. Seven other crimes, however, were still capital by law, and so continued till the passing of the Criminal Consolidation Acts of 1861.

With the amelioration of the criminal code, other cruel concomitants of execution also disappeared. In 1832 the dissection of bodies cut down from the gallows, which had been decreed centuries previously,[99] was abolished; the most recent enactment in force was the 9th Geo. IV. cap. 31, which directed the dissection of all bodies of executed murderers, the idea being to intensify the dread of capital punishment. That such dread was not universal or deep-seated may be gathered from the fact that authentic cases were known previous to the first cited act of criminals selling their own bodies to surgeons for dissection. This dissection was carried out for Newgate prisoners in Surgeons' Hall, adjoining Newgate, the site of the present Sessions House of the Old Bailey, and the operation was witnessed by students and a number of curious spectators. Lord Ferrers' body was brought to Surgeons' Hall after execution in his own carriage and six; after the post mortem had been carried out, the corpse was exposed to view in a first-floor room. Pennant speaks of Surgeons' Hall as a handsome building, ornamented with Ionic pilasters, and with a double flight of steps to the first floor. Beneath is a door for the admission of the bodies of murderers and other felons. There were other public dissecting rooms for criminals. One was attached to Hicks' Hall, the Clerkenwell Sessions House, built out of monies provided by Sir Baptist Hicks, a wealthy alderman of the reign of James I.[100] Persons were still living in 1855 who had witnessed dissections at Hicks' Hall, and "whom the horrid scene, with the additional effect of some noted criminals hanging on the walls, drove out again sick and faint, as we have heard some relate, and with pale and terrified features, to get a breath of air."[101] The dissection of executed criminals was abolished soon after the discovery of the crime of burking, with the idea that ignominy would no longer attach to an operation which ceased to be compulsory for the most degraded beings; and that executors or persons having lawful possession of the bodies of people who had died friendless, would voluntarily surrender them for the advancement of medical science.

Another brutal practice had nearly disappeared about the time of the abolition of dissection. This was the public exhibition of the body, as was done in the case of Mrs. Phipoe, the murderess, who was executed in front of Newgate in 1798, and "her body publicly exhibited in a place built for the purpose in the Old Bailey." About this time I find that the bodies of two murderers, Clench and Mackay, "were publicly exposed in a stable in Little Bridge Street, near Apothecaries' Hall, Surgeons' Hall being let to the lieutenancy of the county for the accommodation of the militia." In 1811 Williams, who murdered the Marrs in Ratcliffe Highway,[102] having committed suicide in gaol to escape hanging, it was determined that a public exhibition should be made of the body through the neighbourhood which had been the scene of the monster's crimes. A long procession was formed, headed by constables, who cleared the way with their staves. Then came the newly-formed horse patrol, with drawn cutlasses, parish officers, peace officers, the high constable of the county of Middlesex on horseback, and then the body of Williams, "extended at full length on an inclined platform erected on the cart, about four feet high at the head, and gradually sloping towards the horse, giving a full view of the body, which was dressed in blue trousers and a blue-and-white striped waistcoat, but without a coat, as when found in the cell. On the left side of the head the fatal mall, and on the right the ripping chisel, with which the murders had been committed, were exposed to view. The countenance of Williams was ghastly in the extreme, and the whole had an appearance too horrible for description." The procession traversed Ratcliffe twice, halting for a quarter of an hour in front of the victims' dwelling, and was accompanied throughout by "an immense concourse of persons, eager to get a sight of the murderer's remains.... All the shops in the neighbourhood were shut, and the windows and tops of the houses were crowded with spectators."

Hanging in chains upon the gibbet which had served for the execution, or on another specially erected on some commanding spot, had fallen into disuse by 1832. But there was an attempt to revive it at that date, when the act for dispensing with the dissection of criminals was passed. A clause was inserted to the effect that "the bodies of all prisoners convicted of murder should either be hung in chains, or buried under the gallows on which they had been executed, ... according to the discretion of the court before whom the prisoners might be tried." The revival of this barbarous practice caused much indignation in certain quarters, but it was actually tried in two provincial towns, Leicester and Durham. At the first-named the exhibition nearly created a tumult, and the body was taken down and buried, but not before the greatest scandal had been caused by the unseemly proceedings of the crowd that flocked to see the sight. A sort of fair was held, gaming-tables were set up, cards were played under the gibbet, to the disturbance of the public peace and the annoyance of all decent people.[103] At Jarrow Stake, where the Durham murderer's body was exposed, there were similar scenes, mingled with compassion for the culprit's family, and a subscription was set on foot for them then and there at the foot of the gibbet. Later on, after dark, some friends of the deceased stole the body and buried it in the sand, and this was the end of hanging in chains. After this a law was passed which prescribed that the bodies of all executed murderers should be buried within the walls of the gaol.

Although these objectionable practices had disappeared, there were still many shocking incidents at executions, owing to the bungling and unskilful way in which the operation was performed. The rope still broke sometimes, although it was not often that the horrid scene seen at Jersey at the beginning of the century was repeated. There the hangman added his weight to that of the suspended culprit, and having first pulled him sideways, then got upon his shoulders, so that the rope broke. "To the great surprise of all who witnessed this dreadful scene, the poor criminal rose straight upon his feet, with the hangman on his shoulders, and immediately loosened the rope with his fingers." After this the sheriffs sent for another rope, but the spectators interfered, and the man was carried back to gaol. The whole case was referred to the king, and the poor wretch, whose crime had been a military one, was eventually pardoned. A somewhat similar event happened at Chester not long afterwards; the ropes by which two offenders were turned off broke a few inches from their necks. They were taken back to gaol, and were again brought out in the afternoon, by which time fresh and stronger ropes had been procured, and the sentence was properly and completely carried out. Other cases might be quoted, especially that of William Snow, *alias* Sketch, who slipped from the gallows at Exeter and fell to the ground. He soon rose to his feet, and hearing the sorrowful exclamations of the populace, coolly said, "Good people, do not be hurried; I am not, I can wait."

Similar cases were not wanting as regards the executions before Newgate. Others were not less horrible, although there was no failure of apparatus. Sometimes the condemned man made a hard fight for life. When Charles White was executed in 1823 for arson, he arranged a handkerchief in such a way that the executioner found a difficulty in pinioning his hands. White managed to keep his wrists asunder, and continued to struggle with the officials for some time. Eventually he was pinioned with a cord in the usual manner. On the scaffold he made a violent attempt to loosen his bonds, and succeeded in getting his hands free. Then with a strong effort he pushed off the white cap, and tried to liberate his neck from the halter, which by this time had been adjusted. The hangman summoned assistance, and with help tied the cap over White's face with a handkerchief. The miserable wretch during the whole of this time was struggling with the most determined violence, to the great horror of the spectators. Still he resisted, and having got from the falling drop to the firm part of the platform, he nearly succeeded in tearing the handkerchief from his eyes. However, the ceremony went forward, and when the signal was given the drop sank. The wretched man did not fall with it, but jumped on to the platform, and seizing the rope with his hands, tried to avoid strangulation. The spectacle was horrible; the convict was half on the platform, half hanging, and the convulsions of his body were appalling. The crowd vociferously yelled their disapproval, and at length the executioner forced the struggling criminal from the platform, so that the rope sustained his whole weight. His face was visible to the whole crowd, and was fearful to behold. Even now his sufferings were not at an end, and his death was not compassed until the executioner terminated his sufferings by hanging on to his legs.

When Luigi Buranelli was executed in 1855, through the improper adjustment of the rope his sufferings were prolonged for five minutes; "his chest heaved, and it was evident that his struggle was a fearful one."[104] A worse case still was that of William Bousfield, who, when awaiting execution for murder, about the same date, had attempted to throw himself upon the fire in his condemned cell. He was in consequence so weak when brought out for execution, that he had to be carried by four men, two supporting his body and two his legs. His wretched, abject condition, seated in a chair under the drop, was such as almost to unnerve the executioner Calcraft, who bad been further upset by a letter threatening to shoot him when he appeared to perform his task. Calcraft, the moment he had adjusted the cap and rope, ran down the steps, drew the bolt, and disappeared. "For a second or two the body hung motionless, then, with a strength that astonished the attendant officials, Bousfield slowly drew himself up, and rested with his feet on the right side of the drop. One of the turnkeys rushed forward and pushed him off. Again the wretched creature succeeded in obtaining foothold, but this time on the left side of the drop." Calcraft was forced to return, and he once more pushed Bousfield off, who for the fourth time regained his foothold. Again he was repelled, this time Calcraft adding his weight to the body, and the strangulation was completed.

It was stated in evidence before the Commission on Capital Punishment in 1864, that Calcraft's method of hanging was very rough, much the same as if he had been hanging a dog. There has never been much science in the system of carrying out the extreme penalty in this country; the "finisher of the law" has come more by chance than fitness or special education to exercise his loathsome office. Calcraft, of whom mention has just been made, was by trade a lady's shoemaker, and before he took to hanging he was employed as a watchman at Reid's brewery in

Liquorpond Street. He was at first engaged as assistant to the executioner Tom Cheshire, but in due course rose to be chief. He was always known as a mild-mannered man of simple tastes, much given to angling in the New River, and a devoted rabbit fancier. He was well known in the neighbourhood where he resided, and the street *gamins* cried "Jack Ketch" as he went along the street. While Calcraft was in office other aspirants to fame appeared in the field. One was Askern, who had been a convicted prisoner at York, but who consented to act as hangman when Calcraft was engaged, and no other functionary could be obtained. It was not always easy to hire a hangman. There is still extant a curious petition presented to the Treasury by Ralph Griffith, Esq., high sheriff of Flintshire, which sets forth that the petitioner had been at great expense by sending clerks and agents to Liverpool and Shrewsbury to hire an executioner. The man to be hanged belonged to Wales, and no Welshman would do the job. Travelling expenses of these agents cost £15, and another £10 were spent in the hire of a Shropshire man, who deserted, and was pursued, but without success. Another man was hired, himself a convict, whose fees for self and wife were twelve guineas. Then came the cost of the gallows, £4 12s.; and finally the funeral, cart, coffin, and other petty expenses, amounting to £7 10s., making the whole outlay close on £50.

NEWGATE NOTORIETIES

Diminution in certain kinds of crime—Fewer street robberies because people carried less cash about them—Corresponding increase in cases of fraud, forgeries, jewel and bullion robberies—Great commercial frauds—Offences against the person confined to murder and manslaughter, the character of which remained much the same—Another crime, that of attempt upon the sovereign—Other forms of treason—The Cato Street conspiracy—Thistlewood's history—Discovery of the plot—The conspirators' plan—How defeated—Their trial at the Old Bailey—The informer Edwards—Their sentence and execution—Attacks on the sovereign—Oxford fires at Queen Victoria—His attempt due to a craze for notoriety—"Young England"—Francis—Bean—Mr. Pate—Celebrated frauds and forgeries—Fauntleroy—The last execution for forgery—Captain Montgomery—Joseph Hunton the Quaker—Richard Gifford—Maynard—Sir Robert Peel's bill to amend forgery laws—The Forgery Act—Latest cases of abduction—E. Gibbon Wakefield and Miss Turner—Big "jobs," burglaries and other robberies, still perpetrated—Howard robs Mr. Mullay—Strange *assault upon Mr. Gee—Thieves prosper through connivance of fences and receivers—Ikey Solomons—His escape from custody—He leaves the country, but returns, and is eventually sentenced to transportation—Large robbery of the Custom House—While still undiscovered, robbery of diamonds at the Custom House Quay—Leads to detection of both—The gold-dust robbery in 1839—How discovered—Done by Jews, who cheat each other all round—A few of the most remarkable murders of this epoch—Thurtell, Hunt, and Probert kill Mr. Weare—Burke and Hall—Their imitators, Bishop and Williams, in London, murder an Italian boy and sell the body—Greenacre and Mrs. Gale murder Hannah Brown—Horrible means of disposing of the corpse—Detection, trial, and sentence.*

IN chapter two of the present volume I brought down the record of crime to the second decade of the present century. I propose now to continue the subject, and to devote a couple of chapters to criminal occurrences of a more recent date, only premising that as accounts become more voluminous I shall be compelled to deal with fewer cases, taking in preference those which are typical and invested with peculiar interest. It is somewhat remarkable that a marked change soon comes over the Calendar. Certain crimes, those against the person especially, diminished gradually. They became less easy or remunerative. Police protection was better and more effective; the streets of London were well lighted, the suburbs were more populous and regularly patrolled. People, too, were getting into the habit of carrying but little cash about them, and no valuables but their watches or personal jewellery. Street robberies offered fewer inducements to depredators, and evil-doers were compelled to adopt other methods of preying upon their fellows. This led to a rapid and marked increase in all kinds of fraud; and prominent in the criminal annals of Newgate in these later years will be found numerous remarkable instances of this class of offence—forgeries committed systematically, and for long periods, as in the case of Fauntleroy, to cover enormous defalcations; the fabrication of deeds, wills, and false securities for the purpose of misappropriating funds or feloniously obtaining cash; thefts of bullion, bank-notes, specie, and gold-dust, planned with consummate ingenuity, eluding the keenest vigilance, and carried out with reckless daring; jewel-boxes cleverly stolen under the very noses of owners or care-takers. As time passed, the extraordinary extension of all commercial operations led to many entirely novel and often gigantic financial frauds. The credulity of investors, the unscrupulous dishonesty of bankers, the slackness of supervision over wholly irresponsible agents, produced many terrible monetary catastrophes, and lodged men like Cole, Robson, and Redpath in Newgate.

While the varying conditions of social life thus brought about many changes in the character of offences against property, those against the person became more and more limited to the most heinous, or those which menaced or destroyed life. There was no increase in murder or manslaughter; the number of such crimes remained pretty constant proportionately to population. Nor did the methods by which they were perpetrated greatly vary from those in times past. The causes also continued much the same. Passion, revenge, cupidity, sudden ebullitions of homicidal rage, the cold-blooded, calculating atrocity born of self-interest, were still the irresistible incentives to kill. The brutal ferocity of the wild beast once aroused, the same means, the same weapons were employed to do the dreadful deed, the same and happily often futile precautions taken to conceal the crime. Pegsworth, and Greenacre, and Daniel Good merely reproduced types that had gone before, and that have since reappeared. Esther Hibner was as inhuman in her ill-usage of the parish apprentice she killed as Martha Brownrigg had been. Thurtell and Hunt followed in the footsteps of Billings, Wood, and Catherine Hayes. Courvoisier might have lived a century earlier. Hocker was found upon the scene of his crime, irresistibly attracted thither, as was Theodore Gardelle. Now and again there seemed to be a recurrence of a murder epidemic, as there had been before; as in the year 1849, a year memorable for the Rush murders at Norwich, the Gleeson Wilson murder at Liverpool, that of the Mannings in London, and of many more. Men like Mobbs, the miscreant known as "General Haynau" on account of his blood-thirstiness, still murdered their wives; or like Cannon the chimney-sweeper, who savagely killed the policeman.

A not altogether new crime, however, akin to murder, although happily never passing beyond dastardly attempts, cropped up in these times, and was often frequently repeated within a short interval. The present Queen very soon after her accession became the victim of the most cowardly and unmanly outrages, and the attempted murder of the sovereign by Oxford in 1840 was followed in the very next year by those of Francis and of Bean in two consecutive months, while in 1850 Her Majesty was the victim of another outrage at the hands of one Pate. These crimes had their origin too often in the disordered brains of lunatics at large, like Captain Goode. Their perpetrators were charged with high treason, but met with merciful clemency as irresponsible beings. But at various dates treason more distinct and tangible came to the front: attempts to levy war against the State. The well-known Cato Street conspiracy, which grew out of disturbed social conditions after the last French war, amidst general distress, and when the people were beginning to agitate for a larger share of political power, was among the earliest, and to some extent the most desperate, of these. Its ringleaders, Thistlewood and the rest, were after capture honoured by committal as State prisoners to the Tower, but they came one and all to Newgate for trial at the Old Bailey, and remained there after conviction till they were hanged. Later on, the Chartists agitated persistently for the concession embraced in the so-called People's Charter, many of which are by this time actually, and by more legitimate efforts, engrafted upon our Constitution. But the Chartists sought their ends by riot and rebellion, and gained only imprisonment for their pains. Some five hundred in all were arrested, but as only three of these were lodged in Newgate, I shall not recur to them in my narrative.

The Cato Street conspiracy would have been simply ridiculous but for the recklessness of the desperadoes who planned it. That some thirty or more needy men should hope to revolutionize England is a sufficient proof of the absurdity of their attempt. But they proceeded in all seriousness, and would have shrunk from no outrage or atrocity in furtherance of their foolhardy enterprise. The massacre of the whole of the Cabinet Ministers at one stroke was to be followed by an attack upon "the old man and the old woman," as they styled the Mansion House and the Bank of England. At the former the "Provisional Government" was to be established, which under Thistlewood as dictator was to rule the nation, by first handing over its capital to fire and pillage. This Thistlewood had seen many vicissitudes throughout his strange, adventurous career. The son of a respectable Lincolnshire farmer, he became a militia officer, and married a woman with £10,000, in which, however, she had only a life interest. She died early, and Thistlewood, left to his own resources, followed the profession of arms, first in the British service, and then in that of the French revolutionary Government. It was during this period that he was said to have imbibed his revolutionary ideas. Returning to England, he found himself rich in a small landed property, which he presently sold to a man who became bankrupt before he had paid over the purchase money. After this he tried farming, but failed. He married again and came to London, where he soon became notorious as a reckless gambler and a politician holding the most extreme views. In this way he formed the acquaintance of Watson and others, with whom he was arraigned for treasonable practices, and imprisoned. On his release he sent a challenge to Lord Sidmouth, the Home Secretary, and was again arrested and imprisoned. On his second release, goaded by his fancied wrongs, he began to plot a dark and dreadful revenge, and thus the conspiracy in which he was the prime mover took shape, and came to a head.

The Government obtained early and full information of the nefarious scheme. One of the conspirators, by name Edwards, made a voluntary confession to Sir Herbert Taylor one morning at Windsor; after which Thistlewood and his accomplices were closely watched, and measures taken to arrest them when their plans were so far developed that no doubt could remain as to their guilt. The day appointed for the murder and rising actually arrived before the authorities interfered. It was the day on which Lord Harrowby was to entertain his colleagues at dinner in Grosvenor Square. The occasion was considered excellent by the conspirators for disposal of the whole Cabinet at one blow, and it was arranged that one of their number should knock at Lord Harrowby's door on the pretence of leaving a parcel, and that when it was opened the whole band should rush in. While a few secured the servants, the rest were to fall upon Lord Harrowby and his guests. Hand-grenades were to be thrown into the dining-room, and during the noise and confusion the assassination of the ministers was to be completed, the heads of Lord Castlereagh and Lord Sidmouth being carried away in a bag. Lord Harrowby's dinner-party was postponed, but the conspirators knew nothing of it, and those who watched his house were further encouraged in their mistake by the arrival of many carriages, bound, as it happened, to the Archbishop of York's. Meanwhile the main body remained at their headquarters, a ruined stable in Cato Street, Edgeware Road, completing their dispositions for assuming supreme power after the blow had been struck. Here they were surprised by the police, headed by a magistrate, and supported by a strong detachment of Her Majesty's Guards. The police were the first to arrive on the spot, the Guards having entered the street at the wrong end. The conspirators were in a loft, approached by a ladder and a trap-door, access through which could only be obtained one by one. The first constable who entered Thistlewood ran through the body with a sword, but others quickly followed, the lights were extinguished, and a desperate conflict ensued. The Guards, headed by Lord Adolphus Fitz Clarence, now reinforced the police, and the conspirators gave way. Nine of the latter were captured, with all the war material, cutlasses, pistols, hand-grenades, and ammunition. Thistlewood and fourteen more succeeded for the moment in making their escape, but most of them were subsequently taken. Thistlewood was discovered next morning in a mean house in White Street, Moorfields. He was in bed with his breeches on (in the pockets of which were found a number of cartridges), the black belt he had worn at Cato Street, and a military sash.

The trial of the conspirators came on some six weeks later, at the Old Bailey. Thistlewood made a long and rambling defence, the chief features of which were abuse of Lord Sidmouth, and the vilification of the informer Edwards. Several of the other prisoners took the same line as regards Edwards, and there seems to have been good reason for supposing that he was a greater villain than any of those arraigned. He had been in a state of abject misery, and when he first joined "the reformers," as the Cato Street conspirators called themselves, he had neither a bed to lie upon nor a coat to his back. His sudden access to means unlimited was no doubt due to the profitable *rôle* he soon adopted of Government informer and spy, and it is pretty certain that for some time he served both sides; on the one inveigling silly enthusiasts to join in the plot, and denouncing them on the other. The employment of Edwards, and the manner in which the conspirators were allowed to commit themselves further and further before the law was set in motion against them, were not altogether creditable to the Government. It was asserted, not without foundation, at these trials, that Edwards repeatedly incited the associates he was betraying to commit outrage, to set fire to houses, throw hand-grenades into the carriages of ministers; that he was, to use Thistlewood's words, "a contriver, instigator, and entrapper." The Government were probably not proud of their agent, for Edwards, after the conviction had been assured, went abroad to enjoy, it was said, an ample pension, so long as he did not return to England.

Five of the conspirators, Thistlewood, Ings, Brunt, Davidson, and Tidd, were sentenced to death, and suffered in the usual way in front of Newgate, with the additional penalty of decapitation, as traitors, after they had been hanged. A crowd as great as any known collected in the Old Bailey to see the ceremony, about which there were some peculiar features worth recording. The reckless demeanour of all the convicts except Davidson was most marked. Thistlewood and Ings sucked oranges on the scaffold; they with Brunt and Tidd scorned the ordinary's ministrations, but Ings said he hoped God would be more merciful to him than men had been. Ings was especially defiant. He sought to cheer Davidson, who seemed affected, crying out, "Come, old cock-of-wax, it will soon be over." As the executioner fastened the noose, he nodded to a friend he saw in the crowd; and catching sight of the coffins ranged around the gallows, he smiled at the show with contemptuous indifference. He roared out snatches of a song about Death or Liberty, and just before he was turned off, yelled out three cheers to the populace whom he faced. He told the executioner to "do it tidy," to pull it tight, and was in a state of hysterical exaltation up to the very last. Davidson, who was the only one who seemed to realize his awful situation, listened patiently and with thankfulness to the chaplain, and died in a manner strongly contrasting with that of his fellows. After the five bodies had hung for half-an-hour, a man in a mask came forward to complete the sentence. Contemporary reports state that from the skilful manner in which he performed the decapitation, he was generally supposed to be a surgeon. Be this as it may, the weapon used was only an ordinary axe, which rather indicates that force, not skill, was employed. This axe is still in existence, and is preserved at Newgate with various other unpleasant curiosities, but is only an ordinary commonplace tool. These were the last executions for high treason, but not the last prisoners by many who passed through Newgate charged with sedition.

Attacks upon the sovereign, as I have said, became more common after the accession of the young Queen Victoria in 1838. It was a form of high treason not unknown in earlier reigns. In 1786 a mad woman, Margaret Nicholson, tried to stab George III. as he was alighting from his carriage at the gate of St. James's Palace. She was seized before she could do any mischief, and eventually lodged in Bethlehem Hospital, where she died after forty years' detention, at the advanced age of one hundred. Again, a soldier, by name Hatfield, who had been wounded in the head, and discharged from the army for unsoundness of mind, fired a pistol at George III. from the pit of Drury Lane theatre in 1800. William IV. was also the victim of a murderous outrage on Ascot race-course in 1832, when John Collins, "a person in the garb of a sailor, of wretched appearance, and having a wooden leg," threw a stone at the king, which hit him on the forehead, but did no serious injury. Collins, when charged, pleaded that he had lost his leg in action, that he had petitioned without success for a pension, and that, as he was starving, he had resolved on this desperate deed, feeling, as he said, that he might as well be shot or hanged as remain in such a state. He was eventually sentenced to death, but the plea of lunacy was allowed, and he was confined for life.

None of the foregoing attempts were, however, so dastardly or determined as that made by Oxford upon our present gracious Queen two years after she ascended the throne. The cowardly crime was probably encouraged by the fearless and confiding manner in which the Queen, secure as it seemed in the affections of her loyal people, freely appeared in public. Oxford, who was only nineteen at the time his offence was committed, had been born at Birmingham, but he came as a lad to London, and took service as a pot-boy to a publican. From this he was promoted to barman, and as such had charge of the business in various public-houses. He left his last situation in April 1840, and established himself in lodgings in Lambeth, after which he devoted himself to pistol practice in shooting-galleries, sometimes in Leicester Square, sometimes in the Strand, or the West End. His acquaintances often asked his object in this, but he kept his own counsel till the 10th June. On that day Oxford was on the watch at Buckingham Palace. He saw Prince Albert return there from a visit to Woolwich, and then passed on to Constitution Hill, where he waited till four p.m., the time at which the Queen and Prince Consort usually took an afternoon drive. About six p.m. the royal carriage, a low open vehicle drawn by four horses, ridden by postilions, left the palace. Oxford, who had been pacing backwards and forwards with his hands under the lapels of his coat, saw the carriage approach. He was on the right or north side of the road. Prince Albert occupied the same side of the carriage, the Queen the left. As the carriage came up to him Oxford turned, put his hand into his breast, drew a pistol, and fired at the Queen.

The shot missed, and as the carriage passed on, Oxford drew

a second pistol and fired again. The Queen saw this second movement, and stooped to avoid the shot; the Prince too rose to shield her with his person. Again, providentially, the bullet went wide of the mark, and the royal party drove back to Clarence House, the Queen being anxious to give the first news of the outrage and of her safety to her mother, the Duchess of Kent. Meanwhile the pistol-shots had attracted the attention of the bystanders, of whom there was a fair collection, as usual, waiting to see the Queen pass. Oxford was seized by a person named Lowe, who was at first mistaken for the assailant. But Oxford at once assumed the responsibility for his crime, saying, "It was I. I did it. I'll give myself up. There is no occasion to use violence. I will go with you." He was taken into custody, and removed first to a police cell, thence committed to Newgate, after he had been examined before the Privy Council. Oxford expressed little anxiety or concern. He asked more than once whether the Queen was hurt, and acknowledged that the pistols were loaded with ball.

A craze for notoriety, to be achieved at any cost, was the one absorbing idea in young Oxford's disordered brain. After his arrest he thought only of the excitement his attempt had raised, nothing of its atrocity, or of the fatal consequences which might have ensued. When brought to trial he hardly realized his position, but gazed with complacency around the crowded court, and eagerly inquired what persons of distinction were present. He smiled continually, and when the indictment was read, burst into loud and discordant fits of laughter. These antics may have been assumed to bear out the plea of insanity set up in his defence, but that there was madness in his family, and that he himself was of unsound mind, could not be well denied. His father, it was proved in evidence, had been at times quite mad; and Oxford's mental state might be inferred from his own proceedings. Among his papers was found a curious document, purporting to be the rules of an association called "Young England," which Oxford had evolved out of his own inflated self-conceit, and which had never any real corporeal existence. "Young England" was a secret society, with no aim or object. Its sworn members, known only to Oxford, and all of them mere shadows, were bound to provide themselves with sword, rifle, dagger, and a pair of pistols; to wear a black crape mask, to obey punctually the orders of their commander-in-chief, and to assume any disguise, if required to go into the country on the business of the association.

The officers of the society were to be known only by "factitious (sic) names." Thus, among the presidents were those of Gowrie, Justinian, Aloman, Colsman, Kenneth, and Godfrey; Hannibal and Ethelred were on the council; Anthony, Augustus, and Frederic were among the generals; Louis and Amadeus among the captains; and Hercules, Neptune, and Mars among the lieutenants of the association. The various grades were distinguished by cockades and bows of different colours. The society was supposed to meet regularly, and its proceedings, together with the speeches made, were duly recorded. With Oxford's other papers were found letters from the secretary, written as it seemed by Oxford to himself, after the manner of Mr. Toots, all of which declared their approval of the commander-in-chief. One expressed pleasure that Oxford improved so much in speaking, and declared that his (Oxford's) speech the last time "was beautiful." This letter went on to say that a new member had been introduced by Lieut. Mars, "a fine, tall, gentlemanly young man, and it is said that he is a military officer, but his name has not yet transpired. Soon after he was introduced we were alarmed by a violent knocking at the door; in an instant our faces were covered, we cocked our pistols, and with drawn swords stood waiting to receive the enemy. While one stood over the fire with the papers, another stood with lighted torch to fire the house. We then sent the old woman to open the door, and it proved to be some little boys who had knocked and ran away." Another letter directed Oxford to attend an extraordinary meeting of "Young England" in consequence of having received some information of an important nature from Hanover. "You must attend; and if your master will not give you leave, you must come in defiance of him."

No serious importance could be attached to these, the manifest inventions of a disordered intellect. The whole of the evidence pointed so strongly towards insanity, that the jury brought in a verdict of acquittal on that ground, and Oxford was ordered to be detained during Her Majesty's pleasure. He went from Newgate first to Bethlehem, from which he was removed to Broadmoor on the opening of the great criminal lunatic asylum at that place. He was released from Broadmoor in 1878, and went abroad.

Within a couple of years a second attempt to assassinate the Queen was perpetrated in nearly the same spot, by a man named John Francis, who was arrested in the very act, just as he had fired one shot. His motives for thus imitating the dastardly crime of Oxford are shrouded in obscurity. He could not plead insanity like his predecessor, and no attempt was made at his trial to prove him of unsound mind. Here again probably it was partly the love of notoriety which was the incentive, backed possibly with the hope that, as in a much more recent case,[105] he would be in some way provided for, he having been for some time previously in abject circumstances. The deed was long premeditated, and would have been executed a day earlier had not his courage failed him at the last moment. A youth named Pearson had seen him present a pistol at the Queen's carriage, but draw it back again, exclaiming presently, "I wish I had done it." Pearson weakly allowed Francis to go off without securing his apprehension, but later he gave full information. The Queen was apprised of the danger, and begged not to go abroad; but she declared she would not remain a prisoner in her own palace, and next day drove out as usual in an open barouche. Nothing happened till Her Majesty returned to Buckingham Palace about six p.m., when, on descending Constitution Hill, with an equerry riding close on each side of her carriage, a man who had been leaning against the palace garden wall suddenly advanced, levelled a pistol at the Queen, and fired. He was so close to the carriage that the smoke of his pistol enveloped the face of Colonel Wylde, one of the equerries. The Queen was untouched, and at first, it is said, hardly realized the danger she had escaped. Francis had already been seized by a policeman named Trounce, who saw his movement with the pistol, but too late to prevent its discharge. The prisoner was conveyed without delay to the Home Office, and there examined by the Privy Council, which had been hastily summoned for the purpose. On searching him the pistol was found in his pocket, the barrel still warm; also some loose powder and a bullet. There was some doubt as to whether the pistol when fired was actually loaded with ball, but the jury brought in a verdict of guilty of the criminal intent to kill. Francis was sentenced to be hanged, decapitated, and quartered, the old traitor's doom, but was spared, and subsequently transported for life. The enthusiasm of the people at the Queen's escape was uproarious, and her drive next day was one long triumphal progress. At the Italian Opera in the evening the audience, on the Queen's appearance, greeted her with loud cheers, and called for the national anthem. This was in May 1842.

Undeterred by the well-merited punishment which had overtaken Francis, a third miscreant made a similar but far less serious attempt in the month of July following. As the Queen was driving from Buckingham Palace to the Chapel Royal, a deformed lad among the crowd was seen to present a pistol at

Her Majesty's carriage, in the Mall, about half-way between Buckingham and St. James's Palaces. Only one person saw the movement, a lad named Dasset, who at once collared the cripple, and taking him up to two policemen, charged him with the offence. The policemen treated the matter as a hoax, and allowed the culprit to make off. Later on, however, Dasset was himself seized and interrogated, and on his information handbills were circulated, giving the exact description of the deformed youth, who had "a hump-back, and a long, sickly, pale face, with light hair;" his nose was marked with a scar or black patch, and he was altogether of a dirty appearance. It happened that a lad named Bean had absconded from his father's home some weeks before, whose description, as given by his father to the police, exactly tallied with that of the deformed person "wanted" for the assault on the Queen. A visit to the father's residence was followed by the arrest of the son, who had by this time returned. This son, John William Bean, was fully identified by Dasset, and presently examined by the Privy Council. He was eventually charged with a misdemeanour, the capital charge having been abandoned, and committed for trial. Much the same motives of seeking notoriety seem to have impelled Bean, who was perfectly sane, to his rash act; but it was proved that the pistol was not loaded with ball, and he was only convicted of an attempt "to harass, vex, and grieve the sovereign." Lord Abinger sentenced him to eighteen months' imprisonment in Newgate, but the place of durance was changed, to meet the existing law, to Millbank Penitentiary.

I shall mention briefly one more case, in which, however, there was no murderous intent, before I pass on to other crimes. On June 1850 the Queen was once more subjected to cowardly outrage, the offender being a Mr. Pate, a gentleman by birth, who had borne the Queen's commission, first as cornet, and then lieutenant, in the 10th Hussars. Pate was said to be an eccentric person, given to strange acts and antics, such as mixing whiskey and camphor with his morning bath-water, and walking for choice through prickly gorse bushes. He always kept the blinds down at his chambers in Jermyn Street; and as the St. James's clock chimed quarter-past three, invariably went out in a cab, for which he always paid the same fare, nine shillings, all in shillings, and no other coin. But this was not sufficient to constitute lunacy, nor was his plea of "momentary uncontrollable impulse" deemed valid as any palliation of his offence. That offence was a brutal assault upon Her Majesty, whom he struck in the face with a small stick just as she was leaving Cambridge House. The blow crushed the bonnet and bruised the forehead of the Queen, who was happily not otherwise injured. Pate was found guilty, and sentenced to seven years' transportation, the judge, Baron Alderson, abstaining from inflicting the penalty of whipping, which was authorized by a recent act, on account of Mr. Pate's family and position in life.

I have already remarked that as violence was more and more eliminated from crimes against the person, frauds indicating great boldness, extensive design, and ingenuity became more prevalent. The increase of bank forgeries, and its cause, I referred to in a previous chapter.[106] At one session of the Old Bailey, in 1821, no less than thirty-five true bills were found for passing forged notes. But there were other notorious cases of forgery. That of Fauntleroy the banker, in 1824, caused much excitement at the time on account of the magnitude of the fraud, and the seeming probity of the culprit. Mr. Fauntleroy was a member of a banking firm, which his father had established in conjunction with a gentleman of the name of Marsh, and others. He had entered the house as clerk in 1800; in 1807, and when only twenty-two, he succeeded to his father's share in the business. According to Fauntleroy's own case, he found at once that the firm was heavily involved, through advances made to various builders, and that it could only maintain its credit by wholesale discounting. Its embarrassments were greatly increased by the bankruptcy of two of its clients in the building trade, and the bank became liable for a sum of £170,000. New liabilities were incurred to the extent of £100,000 by more failures, and in 1819, by the death of one of the partners, a large sum in cash had to be withdrawn from the bank to pay his heirs. "During these numerous and trying difficulties"—it is Mr. Fauntleroy who speaks—"the house was nearly without resources, and the whole burthen of management falling on me, ... I sought resources where I could;" in other words, he forged powers of attorney, and proceeded to realize securities lodged in his bank under various names. Among the prisoner's private papers, one was found giving full details of the stock he had feloniously sold out, the sum total amounting to some £170,000, with a declaration in his own handwriting to the following effect. "In order to keep up the credit of our house, I have forged powers of attorney for the above sums and parties, and sold out to the amount here stated, and without the knowledge of my partners. I kept up the payments of the dividends, but made no entries of such payments in my books. The bank began first to refuse our acceptances, and to destroy the credit of our house; the bank shall smart for it."

Many stories were in circulation at the time of Fauntleroy's trial with regard to his forgeries. It was said that he had by means of them sold out so large an amount of stock, that he paid £16,000 a year in dividends to escape detection. Once he ran a narrow risk of being found out. A lady in the country, who had £13,000 in the stocks, desired her London agent to sell them out. He went to the bank, and found that no stocks stood in her name. He called at once upon Fauntleroy, his client's bankers, for an explanation, and was told by Mr. Fauntleroy that the lady had desired *him* to sell out, "which I have done," added the fraudulent banker, "and here are the proceeds," whereupon he produced exchequer bills to the amount. Nothing more was heard of the affair, although the lady declared that she had never instructed Fauntleroy to sell. On another occasion the banker forged a gentleman's name while the latter was sitting with him in his private room, and took the instrument out to a clerk with the ink not dry. It must be added that the Bank of England, on discovering the forgeries, replaced the stock in the names of the original holders, who might otherwise have been completely ruined. A newspaper report of the time describes Fauntleroy as "a well-made man of middle stature. His hair, though gray, was thick, and lay smooth over his forehead. His countenance had an expression of most subdued resignation. The impression which his appearance altogether was calculated to make was that of the profoundest commiseration."

The crime, long carried on without detection, was first discovered in 1820, when it was found that a sum of £10,000, standing in the name of three trustees, of whom Fauntleroy was one, had been sold out under a forged power of attorney. Further investigations brought other similar frauds to light, and fixed the whole sum misappropriated at £170,000, the first forgery dating back to 1814. A run upon the bank immediately followed, which was only met by a suspension of payment and the closing of its doors. Meanwhile public gossip was busy with Fauntleroy's name, and it was openly stated in the press and in conversation that the proceeds of these frauds had been squandered in chambering, gambling, and debauchery. Fauntleroy was scouted as a licentious libertine, a deep and determined gamester, a spendthrift whose extravagance knew no bounds. [107] The veil was lifted from his private life, and he was accused of persistent immorality. In his defence he sought to rebut these charges, which indeed were never clearly made out, and it is pretty certain that his own account of the causes which led him into dishonesty was substantially true. He called many witnesses, seventeen in all, to speak of him as they had found him; and these, all respectable city merchants and business men, declared that they had hitherto formed a high opinion of his honour, integrity, and goodness of disposition, deeming him the last person capable of a dishonourable action.

These arguments availed little with the jury, who after a short deliberation found Fauntleroy guilty, and he was sentenced to death. Every endeavour was used, however, to obtain a commutation of sentence. His case was twice argued before the judges on points of law, but the result in both cases was unfavourable. Appeals were made to the Home Secretary, and all possible political interest brought to bear, but without success. Fauntleroy meanwhile lay in Newgate, not herded with other condemned prisoners, as the custom was,[108] but in a separate chamber, that belonging to one of the warders of the gaol. I find in the chaplain's journal, under date 1824, various entries relative to this prisoner. "Visited Mr. Fauntleroy. My application for books for him not having been attended, I had no prayer-book to give him." "Visited Mr. Fauntleroy. The sheriffs have very kindly permitted him to remain in the turnkey's room where he was originally placed; nor can I omit expressing a hope that this may prove the beginning of a better system of confinement, and that every description of persons who may be unfortunately under sentence of death will no longer be herded indiscriminately together."[109] The kindliness of the city authorities to Fauntleroy was not limited to the assignment of a separate place of durance.

As I have already said, they took the chaplain seriously to task for the bad taste shown in the condemned sermon preached before Fauntleroy. This was on the text, "Wherefore let him that thinketh he standeth take heed lest he fall," and was full of the most pointed allusions to the culprit. Fauntleroy constantly groaned aloud while the sermon proceeded, and contemporary reports declared that "he appeared to feel deeply the force of the reverend gentleman's observations," especially when the chaplain spoke "of the great magnitude of our erring brother's offence, one of the most dangerous description in a trading community." The sermon ended with an appeal to the dying man, exhorting him to penitence. This "personality," and it can be called by no other name, is carefully excluded from prison pulpit utterances on the eve of an execution.

A very curious and, in its way, amusing circumstance in connection with this case was the offer of a certain Italian, Edmund Angelini, to take Fauntleroy's place. Angelini wrote to the Lord Mayor to this effect, urging that Fauntleroy was a father, a citizen: "his life is useful, mine a burthen, to the State." He was summoned to the Mansion House, where he repeated his request, crying, "Accordez moi cette grâce," with much urgency. There were doubts of his sanity. He wrote afterwards to the effect that the moment he had offered himself, an unknown assassin came to aim a blow at him. "Let this monster give his name; I am ready to fight him. I am still determined to put myself in the place of Mr. Fauntleroy. If the law of this country can receive such a sacrifice, my death will render to heaven an innocent man, and to earth a repentant sinner."

Fauntleroy was not entirely dependent upon the ordinary for ghostly counsel in his extremity. He was also attended by the Rev. Mr. Springett and the indefatigable Mr. Baker, whose name has already been mentioned.[110] When led out on the morning of his execution, these two last-named gentlemen each took hold of one of his arms, and so accompanied him to the scaffold. The concourse in front of Newgate was enormous, but much sympathy was evinced for this unfortunate victim to human weakness and ruthless laws. A report was, moreover, widely circulated, and the impression long prevailed, that he actually escaped death. It was said that strangulation had been prevented by the insertion of a silver tube in his wind-pipe, and that after hanging for the regulated time he was taken down and easily restored to consciousness. Afterwards, according to the common rumour, he went abroad and lived there for many years; but the story is not only wholly unsubstantiated, but there is good evidence to show that the body after execution was handed over to his friends and interred privately.

Some years were still to elapse before capital punishment ceased to be the penalty for forgery, and in the interval several persons were sentenced to or suffered death for this crime. There were two notable capital convictions for forgery in 1828. One was that of Captain Montgomery, who assumed the aliases of Colonel Wallace and Colonel Morgan. His offence was uttering forged notes, and there was strong suspicion that he had long subsisted entirely by this fraud. The act for which he was taken into custody was the payment of a forged ten-pound note for half-a-dozen silver spoons. Montgomery was an adept at forgery. He had gone wrong early. Although born of respectable parents, and gazetted to a commission in the army, he soon left the service and betook himself to dishonest ways. His first forgery was the marvellous imitation of the signature of the Hon. Mr. Neville, M.P., who wrote an extremely cramped and curious hand. He was not prosecuted for this fraud on account of the respectability of his family, and soon after this escape he came to London, where he practised as a professional swindler and cheat. For a long time justice did not overtake him for any criminal offence, but he was frequently in Newgate and in the King's Bench for debt. After three years' confinement in the latter prison he passed himself off as his brother, Colonel Montgomery, a distinguished officer, and would have married an heiress had not the imposture been discovered in time. He then took to forging bank-notes, and was arrested as I have described above. Montgomery was duly sentenced to death, but he preferred suicide to the gallows. After sentence his demeanour was serious yet firm. The night previous to that fixed for his execution he wrote several letters, one of them being to Edward Gibbon Wakefield, a fellow-prisoner,[111] and listened attentively to the ordinary, who read him the well-known address written and delivered by Dr. Dodd previous to his own execution for forgery. But next morning he was found dead in his cell. In one corner after much search a phial was found labelled "Prussic acid," which it was asserted he had been in the habit of carrying about his person ever since he had taken to passing forged notes, as an "antidote against disgrace." This phial he had managed to retain in his possession in spite of the frequent searches to which he was subjected in Newgate.

The second conviction for forgery in 1828 was that of the Quaker Joseph Hunton, a man of previously the highest repute in the city of London. He had prospered in early life, was a slop-seller on a large scale at Bury St. Edmunds, and a sugar-baker in the metropolis. He married a lady also belonging to the Society of Friends, who brought him a large fortune, which, and his own money, he put into a city firm, that of Dickson and Co. He soon, however, became deeply involved in Stock Exchange speculations, and losing heavily, to meet the claims upon him he put out a number of forged bills of exchange or acceptances, to which the signature of one Wilkins of Abingdon was found to be forged. Hunton tried to fly the country on the detection of the fraud, but was arrested at Plymouth just as he was on the point of leaving England in the New York packet. He had gone on board in his Quaker dress, but when captured was found in a light-green frock, a pair of light-grey pantaloons, a black stock and a foraging cap. Hunton was put upon his trial at the Old Bailey, and in due course sentenced to death. His defence was that the forged acceptances would have been met on coming to maturity, and that he had no real desire to defraud. Hunton accepted his sentence with great resignation, although he protested against the inhumanity of the laws which condemned him to death. On entering Newgate he said, "I wish after this day to have communication with nobody; let me take leave of my wife, and family, and friends. I have already suffered an execution; my heart has undergone that horrible penalty." He was, however, visited by and received his wife, and several members of the Society of Friends. Two elders of the meeting sat up with him in the press yard the whole of the night previous to execution, and a third, Mr. Sparks Moline, came to attend him to the scaffold. He met his death with unshaken firmness, only entreating that a certain blue handkerchief, to which he seemed fondly attached, should be used to bandage his eyes, which request was readily granted.

Hunton's execution no doubt aroused public attention to the cruelty and futility of the capital law against forgery. A society which had already been started against capital punishment devoted its efforts first to a mitigation of the forgery statute, but could not immediately accomplish much. In 1829 the gallows claimed two more victims for this offence. One was Richard Gifford, a well-educated youth who had been at Christ's Hospital, and afterwards in the National Debt Office. Unfortunately he took to drink, lost his appointment, and fell from bad to worse. Suddenly, after being at the lowest depths, he emerged, and was found by his friends living in comfort in the Waterloo Road. His funds, which he pretended came to him with a rich wife, were really the proceeds of frauds upon the Bank of England. He forged the names of people who held stock on the Bank books, and got the value of the stock; he also forged dividend receipts and got the dividends. He was only six-and-twenty when he was hanged. The other and the last criminal executed for forgery in this country was one Maynard, who was convicted of a fraud upon the Custom House. In conjunction with two others, one of whom was a clerk in the Custom House, and had access to the official records, he forged a warrant for £1973, and was paid the money by the comptroller general. Maynard was convicted of uttering the forged document, Jones of being an accessory; the third prisoner was acquitted. Maynard was the only one who suffered death.

This was on the last day of 1829. In the following session Sir Robert Peel brought in a bill to consolidate the acts relating to forgery. Upon the third reading of this bill Sir James Macintosh moved as an amendment that capital punishment should be abolished for all crimes of forgery, except the forgery of wills and powers of attorney. This amendment was strongly supported outside the House, and a petition in favour of its passing was presented, signed by more than a thousand members of banking firms. Macintosh's amendment was carried in the Commons, but the new law did not pass the Lords, who re-enacted the capital penalty. Still no sentence of death was carried out for the offence, and in 1832 the Attorney-General introduced a bill to abolish capital punishment entirely for forgery. It passed the Commons, but opposition was again encountered in the Lords. This time they sent back the bill, re-enacting only the two penalties for will forging and the forging of powers of attorney; in other words, they had advanced in 1832 to the point at which the Lower House had arrived in 1830. There were at the moment in Newgate six convicts sentenced to death for forging wills. The question was whether the Government would dare to take their lives at the bidding of the House of Lords, and in defiance of the vote of the assembly which more accurately represented public opinion. It was indeed announced that their fate was sealed; but Mr. Joseph Hume pressed the Government hard, and obtained an assurance that the men should not be executed. The new Forgery Act with the Lords' amendment passed into law, but the latter proved perfectly harmless, and no person ever after suffered death for any variety of this crime.

I will include in this part of the present chapter almost one of the last instances[112] of a crime which in time past had invariably been visited with the death penalty, and which was of a distinctly fraudulent nature. The abduction of Miss Turner by the brothers Wakefield bore a strong resemblance to the carrying off and forcible marrying of heiresses as already described.[113] Miss Turner was a school-girl of barely fifteen, only child of a gentleman of large property in Cheshire, of which county he was actually high sheriff at the time of his daughter's abduction. The elder brother, Edward Gibbon Wakefield, the prime mover in the abduction, was a barrister, not exactly briefless, but without a large practice. He had, it was said, a good private income, and was already a widower with two children at the time of his committing the offence for which he was subsequently tried. He had eloped with his first wife from school. While on a visit to Macclesfield he heard by chance of Miss Turner, and that she would inherit all her father's possessions. He thereupon conceived an idea of carrying her off and marrying her willy nilly at Gretna Green. The two brothers started at once for Liverpool, where Miss Turner was at school with a Mrs. Daulby. At Manchester, *en route*, a travelling carriage was purchased, which was driven up to Mrs. Daulby's door at eight in the morning, and a servant hurriedly alighted from it, bearing a letter for Miss Turner. This purported to be from the medical attendant of Mr. Turner, written at Shrigley, Mr. Turner's place of residence; and it stated that Mrs. Turner had been stricken with paralysis. She was not in immediate danger, but she wished to see her daughter, "as it was possible she might soon become incapable of recognizing any one." Miss Turner, greatly agitated, accompanied the messenger who had brought this news, a disguised servant of Wakefield's, who had plausibly explained that he had only recently been engaged at Shrigley. The road taken was *viâ* Manchester, where the servant said a Dr. Hull was to be picked up to go on with them to Shrigley.

At Manchester, however, the carriage stopped at the Albion Hotel. Miss Turner was shown into a private room, where Mr. Wakefield soon presented himself. Miss Turner, not knowing him, would have left the room, but he said he came from her father, and she remained. Wakefield, in reply to her inquiries, satisfied her that her mother was well, and that the real reason for summoning her from school was the state of her father's affairs. Mr. Turner was on the verge of bankruptcy. He was at that moment at Kendal, and wished her to join him there at once. Miss Turner consented to go on, and they travelled night and day towards the north. But at Kendal there was no Mr. Turner, and, to allay Miss Turner's growing anxiety, Wakefield found it necessary to become more explicit regarding her father's affairs. He now pretended that Mr. Turner was also on his way to the border, pursued by sheriffs' officers. The fact was, Wakefield went on to say, an uncle of his had advanced Mr. Turner £60,000, which had temporarily staved off ruin. But another bank had since failed, and nothing could save Mr. Turner but the transfer of some property to Miss Turner, and its settlement on her, so that it might become the exclusive property of her husband, "whoever he might be." Wakefield added that it had been suggested he should marry Miss Turner, but that he had laughed at the idea. Wakefield's uncle took the matter more seriously, and declared that unless the marriage came off Mr. Turner must be sold up. Miss Turner, thus pressed, consented to go on to Gretna Green. Passing through Carlisle, she was told that Mr. Turner was in the town, but could not show himself. Nothing could release him from his trouble but the arrival of the marriage certificate from Gretna Green. Filial affection rose superior to all scruples, and Miss Turner, having crossed the border, was married to Wakefield by the blacksmith in the usual way. Returning to Carlisle, she now heard that her father had been set free, and had gone home to Shrigley, whither they were to follow him. They set out, but at Leeds Wakefield found himself called suddenly to Paris; the other brother was accordingly sent on a pretended mission to Shrigley to bring Mr. Turner on to London, whither Wakefield and Miss Turner also proceeded. On arrival, Wakefield pretended that they had missed Mr. Turner, and must follow him over to France. The strangely-married couple thereupon pressed on to Dover, and crossed over to Calais.

The fact of the abduction did not transpire for some days. Then Mrs. Daulby learnt that Miss Turner had not arrived at Shrigley, but that she had gone to Manchester. Friends went in pursuit and traced her to Huddersfield and further north. The terror and dismay of her parents were soon intensified by the receipt of a letter from Wakefield, at Carlisle, announcing the marriage. Mr. Turner at once set off for London, where he sought the assistance of the police, and presently ascertained that Wakefield had gone to the Continent with his involuntary bride. An uncle of Miss Wakefield's, accompanied by his solicitor and a Bow Street runner, at once went in pursuit. Meanwhile, a second letter turned up from Wakefield at Calais, in which he assured Mrs. Turner that Miss Turner was fondly attached to him, and went on to say, "I do assure you, madam, that it shall be the anxious endeavour of my life to promote her happiness by every means in my power." The game, however, was nearly up. Miss Turner was met by her uncle on Calais pier as she was walking with Wakefield. The uncle claimed her. The husband resisted. M. le Maire was appealed to, and decided to leave it to the young lady, who at once abandoned Wakefield. As he still urged his rights over his wife, Miss Turner cried out in protest, "No, no, I am not his wife; he carried me away by fraud and stratagem, and forced me to accompany him to Gretna Green.... By the same forcible means I was compelled to quit England, and to trust myself to the protection of this person, whom I never saw until I was taken from Liverpool, and never want to see again." On this Wakefield gave in. He surrendered the bride who had never been a wife, and she returned to England with her friends, while Wakefield went on alone to Paris.

Mr. William Wakefield was arrested at Dover, conveyed to Chester, and committed to Lancaster Gaol for trial at the next assizes, when indictments were preferred against both brothers "for having carried away Ellen Turner, spinster, then a maid and heir apparent unto her father, for the sake of the lucre of her substance; and for having afterwards unlawfully and against her will married the said Ellen Turner." They were tried in March of the following year, Edward Wakefield having apparently given himself up, and found guilty, remaining in Lancaster Gaol for a couple of months, when they were brought up to the court of King's Bench for judgment. The prosecution pressed for a severe penalty. Edward Wakefield pleaded that his trial had already cost him £3000. Mr. Justice Bayley, in summing up, spoke severely of the gross deception practised upon an innocent girl, and sentenced the brothers each to three years' imprisonment, William Wakefield in Lancaster Gaol, and Edward Gibbon Wakefield in Newgate, which sentences were duly enforced. The marriage was annulled by an Act of Parliament, although Wakefield petitioned against it, and was brought from Newgate, at his own request, to oppose the second reading of the bill. He also wrote and published a pamphlet from the gaol to show that Miss Turner had been a consenting party to the marriage, and was really his wife. Neither his address nor his pamphlet availed much, for the bill for the divorce passed both Houses. That Mr.

Wakefield was a shrewd critic and close observer of all that went on in the Newgate of those days, will be admitted by those who have read his book on "the punishment of death," which was based on his gaol experiences, and of which I have availed myself in the last chapter.

After their release from Lancaster and Newgate respectively, both Wakefields went abroad. Mr. W. Wakefield served in a continental army, and rose to the rank of colonel, after which he went to New Zealand, and held an important post in that colony. Mr. E. G. Wakefield took part in the scheme for the colonization of North Australia, and for some years resided in that colony. Miss Turner subsequently married Mr. Legh of Lym Hall, Cheshire.

It must not be imagined that although highway robbery was now nearly extinct,[114] and felonious outrages in the streets were rare, that thieves or depredators were idle or entirely unsuccessful. Bigger "jobs" than ever were planned and attempted, as in the burglary at Lambeth Palace, when the thieves were fortunately disappointed, the archbishop having, before he left town, sent his plate-chests, eight in number, to the silversmith's for greater security. The jewellers were always a favourite prey of the London thieves. Shops were broken into, as when that of Grimaldi and Johnson, in the Strand, was robbed of watches to the value of £6000. Where robbery with violence was intended, the perpetrators had now to adopt various shifts and contrivances to secure their victim. No more curious instance of this ever occurred than the assault made by one Howard upon a Mr. Mullay, with intent to rob him. The latter had advertised, offering a sum of £1000 to any one who would introduce him to some mercantile employment. Howard replied, desiring Mr. Mullay to call upon him in a house in Red Lion Square. Mr. Mullay went, and a second interview was agreed upon, when a third person, Mr. Owen, through whose interest an appointment under Government was to be obtained for Mullay, would be present. Mr. Mullay called again, taking with him £500 in cash. Howard discovered this, and his manner was very suspicious; there were weapons in the room—a long knife, a heavy trap-ball bat, and a poker. Mr. Mullay became alarmed, and as Mr. Owen did not appear, withdrew; Howard, strange to say, making no attempt to detain him; probably because Mullay promised to return a few days later, and to bring more money. On this renewed visit Mr. Owen was still absent, and Mr. Mullay agreed to write him a note from a copy Howard gave him. While thus engaged, Howard thrust the poker into the fire. Mullay protested, and then Howard, under the influence of ungovernable rage, as it seemed, jumped up, locked the door, and attacked Mullay violently with the trap-ball bat and knife. Mullay defended himself, and managed to break the knife, but not before he had cut himself severely. A life and death struggle ensued. Mullay cried "Murder!" Howard swore he would finish him, but proved the weaker of the two, and Mullay got him down on the floor. By this time the neighbours were aroused, and several people came to the scene of the affray. Howard was secured, given into custody, and committed to Newgate. The defence he set up was, that Mullay had used epithets towards him while they were negotiating a business matter, and that, being an irritable temper, he had struck Mullay, after which a violent scuffle took place. It was, however, proved that Howard was in needy circumstances, and that his proposals to Mr. Mullay could only have originated in a desire to rob him. He was found guilty of an assault with intent, and sentenced to transportation for fourteen years.

A more complicated and altogether most extraordinary case of assault, with intent to extort money, occurred a few years later. It was perpetrated upon a respectable country solicitor, Mr. Gee, of Bishop Stortford, who administered the estate of a certain Mr.

Canning, deceased. This Mr. Canning had left his widow a life interest in £2000 so long as she remained unmarried. The money went after her to her children. Mr. Gee had invested £1200 of this, and was seeking how best to place the remaining £800, when he was asked to meet a Mr. Heath in London with regard to the sale of certain lands at Bishop Stortford. An appointment was made and kept by Mr. Gee, but on arrival he was met by a young sailor with a letter which begged Mr. Gee to go to Heath's house, as the latter was not well. Mr. Gee went in the coach sent for him, and alighted at 27, York Street, West, Commercial Road. The coach immediately drove off; Mr. Gee entered the house, asked for Mr. Heath, was told he would find him in the back kitchen at breakfast. He was about to descend the stairs when three persons, one of them the young sailor, fell upon him, and in spite of his resistance carried him into a sort of den partitioned off at the end of the back kitchen. There he was seated on some sort of wooden bench and securely fastened. "A chain fixed to staples at his back passed round his chest under his arms, and was padlocked on the left side;" his feet were bound with cords and made fast to rings in the floor. Thus manacled, one of the party, who pretended to be Mrs. Canning's brother, addressed him, insisting that he should forthwith sign a cheque for the £800 of the Canning inheritance still uninvested, and write an order sufficient to secure the surrender of the other £1200. Mr. Gee at first stoutly refused. Then, as they warned him that he would be kept a prisoner in total darkness in this horrible den until he agreed to their demands, he gave in, and signed the documents thus illegally extorted. One was a cheque for £800 on his bankers, the other an order to Mr. Bell of Newport, Essex, requesting the surrender of a deed.

His captors having thus succeeded in their designs, left him, no doubt to realize the money. The door of his place of durance stood open, and Mr. Gee began to consider whether he might not escape. For three hours he struggled without success with his bonds, but at length managed to wriggle out of the chain which confined his body, and soon loosened the ropes round his feet. Thus free, he eluded the vigilance of two of the party, who were at dinner in the front kitchen, and creeping out into the garden at the back, climbed the wall, and got into the street. His first act was to send a messenger to stop the cheque and the order to Mr. Bell, his next to seek the help of the police. Two Bow Street runners were despatched to the house in York Street, which had evidently been taken on purpose for the outrage. There was no furniture in the place, and the den in the kitchen had been recently and specially constructed of boards of immense strength and thickness. It was a cell five feet by three, within another, the intervening being filled with rammed earth to deaden the sound. A fixed seat, two feet, was at one end, and a foot above it was a bar with a staple, to which hung the body chain.

On the arrival of the police the house was empty. The two men on guard had gone off immediately after Mr. Gee had escaped, but they returned later in the day, and were apprehended. Inquiries set on foot also elicited the suspicion that the person who had represented Mrs. Canning's brother was a blind man named Edwards, who had taken this house in York Street, and who was known to be a frequent visitor at Mrs. Canning's. A watch was set on him at her house, where he was soon afterwards arrested. Edwards, whom Mr. Gee easily identified with the others, at once admitted that he was the prime mover of the conspiracy. He had sought by all legal means to obtain possession of the £2000, but had failed, and had had recourse to more violent means. It turned out that he was really married to Mrs. Canning, both having been recognized by the clergyman who had performed the ceremony, and the assault had been committed to secure the money which Mrs. Canning had lost by re-marriage. All three men were committed for trial, although Edwards wished to exculpate the others as having only acted under his order. At the trial the indictment charging them with felony could not be sustained, but they were found guilty of conspiracy and assault. Edwards was sentenced to two years' imprisonment in Newgate, Weedon and Lecasser to twelve and six months respectively in Coldbath Fields.

At no period could thieves in London or elsewhere have prospered had they been unable to dispose of their ill-gotten goods. The trade of fence, or receiver, therefore, is very nearly as old as the crimes which it so obviously fostered.[115] One of the most notorious, and for a time most successful practitioners in this illicit trade, passed through Newgate in 1831. The name of Ikey Solomons was long remembered by thief and thief-taker. He began as an itinerant street vendor at eight, at ten he passed bad money, at fourteen he was a pickpocket and a "duffer," or a seller of sham goods. He early saw the profits to be made out of purchasing stolen goods, but could not embark in it at first for want of capital. He was taken up when still in his teens for stealing a pocket-book, and was sentenced to transportation, but did not get beyond the hulks at Chatham. On his release an uncle, a slop-seller in Chatham, gave him a situation as "barker," or salesman, at which he realized £150 within a couple of years. With this capital he returned to London and set up as a fence. He had such great aptitude for business, and such a thorough knowledge of the real value of goods, that he was soon admitted to be one of the best judges known of all kinds of property, from a glass bottle to a five hundred guinea chronometer. But he never paid more than a fixed price for all articles of the same class, whatever their intrinsic value. Thus, a watch was paid for as a watch, whether it was of gold or silver; a piece of linen as such, whether the stuff was coarse or fine. This rule in dealing with stolen goods continues to this day, and has made the fortune of many since Ikey.

Solomons also established a system of provincial agency, by which stolen goods were passed on from London to the seaports, and so abroad. Jewels were re-set, diamonds re-faced; all marks by which other articles might be identified, the selvages of linen, the stamps on shoes, the number and names on watches, were carefully removed or obliterated after the goods passed out of his hands. On one occasion the whole of the proceeds of a robbery from a boot shop was traced to Solomons'; the owner came with the police, and was morally convinced that it was his property, but could not positively identify it, and Ikey defied them to remove a single shoe. In the end the injured bootmaker agreed to buy back his stolen stock at the price Solomons had paid for it, and it cost him about a hundred pounds to re-stock his shop with his own goods.

As a general rule Ikey Solomons confined his purchases to small articles, mostly of jewellery and plate, which he kept concealed in a hiding-place with a trap-door just under his bed. He lived in Rosemary Lane, and sometimes he had as much as £20,000 worth of goods secreted on the premises. When his trade was busiest he set up a second establishment, at the head of which, although he was married, he put another lady, with whom he was on intimate terms. The second house was in Lower Queen Street, Islington, and he used it for some time as a depot for valuables. But it was eventually discovered by Mrs. Solomons, a very jealous wife, and this, with the danger arising from an extensive robbery of watches in Cheapside, in which Ikey was implicated as a receiver, led him to think seriously of trying his fortunes in another land. He was about to emigrate to New South Wales, when he was arrested at Islington and committed to Newgate on a charge of receiving stolen goods. While thus incarcerated he managed to escape from custody, but not actually from gaol, by an ingenious contrivance which is worth mentioning. He claimed to be admitted to bail, and was taken from Newgate on a writ of *habeas* before one of the judges sitting at Westminster. He was conveyed in a coach driven by a confederate, and under the escort of a couple of turnkeys. Solomons, while waiting to appear in court, persuaded the turnkeys to take him to a public-house, where all might "refresh." While there he was joined by his wife and other friends. After a short carouse the prisoner went into Westminster, his case was heard, bail refused, and he was ordered back to Newgate. But he once more persuaded the turnkeys to pause at the public, where more liquor was consumed. When the journey was resumed, Mrs. Solomons accompanied her husband in the coach. Half-way to Newgate she was taken with a fit. One turnkey was stupidly drunk, and Ikey persuaded the other, who was not much better, to let the coach change and pass Petticoat Lane *en route* to the gaol, where the suffering woman might be handed over to her friends. On stopping at a door in this low street, Ikey jumped out, ran into the house, slamming the door behind him. He passed through and out at the back, and was soon beyond pursuit. By-and-by the turnkeys, sobered by their loss, returned to Newgate alone, and pleaded in excuse that they had been drugged.

Ikey left no traces, and the police could hear nothing of him. He had in fact gone out of the country, to Copenhagen, whence he passed on to New York. There he devoted himself to the circulation of forged notes. He was also anxious to do business in watches, and begged his wife to send him over a consignment of cheap "righteous" watches, or such as had been honestly obtained, and not "on the cross." But Mrs. Solomons could not resist the temptation to dabble in stolen goods, and she was found shipping watches of the wrong category to New York. For this she received a sentence of fourteen years' transportation, and was sent to Van Diemen's Land. Ikey joined her at Hobart Town, where they set up a general shop, and soon began to prosper. He was, however, recognized, and ere long an order came out from home for his arrest and transfer to England, which presently followed, and he again found himself an inmate of Newgate, waiting trial as a receiver and a prison-breaker. He was indicted on eight charges, two only of which were substantiated, but on each of them he received a sentence of seven years' transportation. At his own request he was reconveyed to Hobart Town, where his son had been carrying on the business. Whether Ikey was "assigned" to his own family is not recorded, but no doubt he succeeded to his own property when the term of servitude had expired.

No doubt, on the removal of Ikey Solomons from the scene, his mantle fell upon worthy successors. There was an increase rather than an abatement in jewel and bullion robberies in the years immediately following, and the thieves seem to have had no difficulty in disposing of their spoil. One of the largest robberies of its class was that effected upon the Custom House in the winter of 1834. A large amount of specie was nearly always retained here in the department of the Receiver of Fines. This was known to some clerks in the office, who began to consider how they might lay hands on a lot of cash. Being inexperienced, they decided to call in the services of a couple of professional housebreakers, Jordan and Sullivan, who at once set to work in a business-like way to obtain impressions of the keys of the strong room and chest. But before committing themselves to an attempt on the latter, it was of importance to ascertain how much it usually contained. For this purpose Jordan waited on the receiver to make a small payment, for which he tendered a fifty-pound note. The chest was opened to give change, and a heavy tray lifted out which plainly held some £4000 in cash. Some difficulty then arose as to gaining admission to the strong room, and it was arranged that a man, May, another Custom House clerk, should be introduced into the building, and secreted there during the night to accomplish the robbery. May was smuggled in through a window on the esplanade behind an opened umbrella. When the place was quite deserted he broke open the chest and stole £4700 in notes, with a quantity of gold and some silver. He went out next morning with the booty when the doors were re-opened, and attracted no attention. The spoil was fairly divided; part of the notes were disposed of to a travelling "receiver," who passed over to the Continent and there cashed them easily.

This occurred in November 1834. The Custom House officials were in a state of consternation, and the police were unable at first to get on the track of the thieves. While the excitement was still fresh, a new robbery of diamonds was committed at a bonded warehouse in the immediate neighbourhood, on Custom House Quay. The jewels had belonged to a Spanish countess recently deceased, who had sent them to England for greater security on the outbreak of the first Carlist war. At her death the diamonds were divided between her four daughters, but only half had been claimed, and at the time of the robbery there were still £6000 worth in the warehouse. These were deposited in an iron chest of great strength on the second floor. The thieves it was supposed had secreted themselves in the warehouse during business hours, and waited till night to carry out their plans. Some ham sandwiches, several cigar ends, and two empty champagne bottles were found on the premises next day, showing how they had passed their time. They had had serious work to get at the diamonds. It was necessary to force one heavy door from its hinges, and to cut through the thick panels of another. The lock and fastenings of the chest were forced by means of a "jack," an instrument known to housebreakers, which if introduced into a keyhole, and worked like a bit and brace, will soon destroy the strongest lock. The thieves were satisfied with the diamonds; they broke open other cases containing gold watches and plate, but abstracted nothing.

The police were of opinion that these robberies were both the work of the same hand. But it was not until the autumn that they traced some of the notes stolen from the Custom House to Jordan and Sullivan. About this time also suspicion fell upon Huey, one of the clerks, who was arrested soon afterwards, and made a clean breast of the whole affair. There was a hunt for the two well-known house-breakers, who were eventually heard of at a lodging in Kennington. But they at once made tracks, and took up their residence under assumed names in a tavern in Bloomsbury. The police lost all trace of them for some days, but at length Sullivan's brother was followed from the house in Kennington to the above-mentioned tavern. Both the thieves were now apprehended, but only a small portion of the lost property was recovered, notwithstanding a minute search through the room they had occupied. After their arrest, Jordan's wife and Sullivan's brother came to the inn, and begged to be allowed to visit this room; but their request, in spite of their earnest entreaties, was refused, at the instigation of the police. A few days later a frequent guest at the tavern arrived, and had this same room allotted to him. A fire was lit in it, and the maid in doing so threw a lot of rubbish, as it seemed, which had accumulated under the grate, on top of the burning coals. By-and-by the occupant of the room noticed something glittering in the centre of the fire, which, to inspect more closely, he took out with the tongs. It was a large gold brooch set in pearls, but a portion of the mounting had melted with the heat. The fire was raked out, and in the ashes were found seven large and four dozen small brilliants, also seven emeralds, one of them of considerable size. A part of the "swag" stolen from the bonded warehouse was thus recovered, but it was supposed that a number of the stolen notes had perished in the fire.

The condign punishment meted out to these Custom House robbers had no deterrent effect seemingly. Within three months, three new and most mysterious burglaries were committed at the West End, all in houses adjoining each other. One was occupied by the Portuguese ambassador, who lost a quantity of jewellery from an escritoire, and his neighbours lost plate and cash. Not the slightest clue to these large affairs was ever obtained, but it is probable that they were "put up" jobs, or managed with the complicity of servants. The next year twelve thousand sovereigns were cleverly stolen in the Mile End Road.

The gold-dust robbery of 1839, the first of its kind, was cleverly and carefully planned with the assistance of a dishonest *employé*. A young man named Caspar, clerk to a steam-ship company, learnt through the firm's correspondence that a quantity of gold-dust brought in a man-of-war from Brazil had been transhipped at Falmouth for conveyance to London. The letter informed him of the marks and sizes of the cases containing the precious metal, and he with his father arranged that a messenger should call for the stuff with forged credentials, and anticipating the rightful owner. The fraudulent messenger, by the help of young Caspar, established his claim to the boxes, paid the wharfage dues, and carried off the gold-dust. Presently the proper person arrived from the consignees, but found the gold-dust gone. The police were at once employed, and after infinite pains they discovered the person, one Moss, who had acted as the messenger. Moss was known to be intimate with the elder Caspar, father of the clerk to the steam-ship company, and these facts were deemed sufficient to justify the arrest of all three. They also ascertained that a gold-refiner, Solomons, had sold bar gold to the value of £1200 to certain bullion dealers. Solomons was not straightforward in his replies as to where he got the gold, and he was soon placed in the dock with the Caspars and Moss. Moss presently turned approver, and implicated "Money Moses," another Jew, for the whole affair had been planned and executed by members of the Hebrew persuasion. "Money Moses" had received the stolen gold-dust from Moss' father-in-law, Davis, or Isaacs, who was never arrested, and passed it on to Solomons by his daughter, a widow named Abrahams. Solomons was now also admitted as a witness, and his evidence, with that of Moss, secured the transportation of the principal actors in the theft. In the course of the trial it came out that almost every one concerned except the Caspars had endeavoured to defraud his accomplices. Moss peached because he declared he had been done out of the proper price of the gold-dust; but it was clear that he had tried to appropriate the whole of the stuff, instead of handing it or the price of it back to the Caspars. "Money Moses" and Mrs. Abrahams imposed upon Moss as to the price paid by Solomons; Mrs. Abrahams imposed upon her father by abstracting a portion of the dust and selling it on her own account; Solomons cheated the whole lot by retaining half the gold in his possession, and only giving an I. O. U. for it, which he refused to redeem on account of the row about the robbery.

Moses, it may be added, was a direct descendant of Ikey Solomons.[116] He was ostensibly a publican, and kept the Black Lion in Vinegar Yard, Drury Lane, where secretly he did business as one of the most daring and successful fencers ever known in the metropolis. His arrest and conviction cast dismay over the whole gang of receivers, and for a time seriously checked the nefarious traffic. It may be added that prison life did not agree with "Money Moses"; a striking change came over his appearance while in Newgate. Before his confinement he had been a sleek round person, addicted obviously to the pleasures of the table. He did not thrive on prison fare, now more strictly meagre, thanks to the inspectors and the more stringent discipline, and before he embarked for Australia to undergo his fourteen years, he was reported to have fallen away to a shadow.

Having brought down the records of great frauds, forgeries, and thefts from about 1825 to 1840, I will now retrace my steps and give some account of the more remarkable murders during that period. No murder has created greater sensation and horror throughout England than that of Mr. Weare by Thurtell, Hunt, and Probert. As this was accomplished beyond the limits of the metropolis, and its perpetrators arraigned at Hertford, where the principal actor suffered death, the case hardly comes within the limits of my subject. But Probert, who turned king's evidence, and materially assisted conviction, was tried at the Old Bailey the following year for horse-stealing, and hanged in front of Newgate. The murder was still fresh in the memory of the populace, and Probert was all but lynched on his way to gaol. According to his statement, when sentenced to death, he had been driven to horse-stealing by the execration which had pursued him after the murder. "Every door had been closed against him, every hope of future support blasted. Since the calamitous event," he went on, "that happened at Hertford, I have been a lost man." The event which he styles calamitous we may well characterize as one of the most deliberately atrocious murders on record. Thurtell was a gambler, and Weare had won a good deal of money from him. Weare was supposed to carry a "private bank" about with him in a pocket in his under waistcoat. To obtain possession of this, Thurtell with his two associates resolved to kill him. The victim was invited to visit Probert's cottage in the country near Elstree. Thurtell drove him down in a gig, "to be killed as he travelled," in Thurtell's own words. The others followed, and on overtaking Thurtell, found he had done the job alone in a retired part of the road known as Gill's Hill Lane. The murderer explained that he had first fired a pistol at Weare's head, but the shot glanced off his cheek. Then he attacked the other's throat with a penknife, and last of all drove the pistol barrel into his forehead. After the murder the villains divided the spoil, and went on to Probert's cottage, and supped off pork-chops brought down on purpose. During the night they sought to dispose of the body by throwing it into a pond, but two days later had to throw it into another pond. Meanwhile the discovery of pistol and knife spattered with human blood and brains raised the alarm, and suspicion fell upon the three murderers, who were arrested. The crime was brought home to Thurtell by the confession of Hunt, one of his accomplices, who took the police to the pond, where the remains of the unfortunate Mr. Weare were discovered, sunk in a sack weighted by stones. Probert was then admitted as a witness, and the case was fully proved against Thurtell, who was hanged in front of Hertford Gaol. Hunt, in consideration of the information he had given, escaped death, and was sentenced to transportation for life.

Widespread horror and indignation was evoked throughout the kingdom by the discovery of the series of atrocious murders perpetrated in Edinburgh by the miscreants Burke and Hare, the first of whom has added to the British language a synonym for illegal suppression. The crimes of these inhuman purveyors to medical science do not fall within the limits of this work. But Burke and Hare had their imitators further south, and of these Bishop and Williams, who were guilty of many peculiar atrocities, ended their murderous careers in front of the debtors' door at Newgate. Bishop, whose real name was Head, married a half-sister of Williams'. Williams was a professional resurrectionist, or body-snatcher, a trade almost openly countenanced when "subjects" for the anatomy schools were only to be got by rifling graves, or worse. Bishop was a carpenter, but having been suddenly thrown out of work, he joined his brother-in-law in his line of business. After a little Bishop got weary of the dangers and fatigues of exhumation, and proposed to Williams that instead of disinterring they should murder their subjects. Bishop confessed that he was moved to this by the example of Burke and Hare. They pursued their terrible trade for five years without scruple and without detection. Eventually the law overtook them, but almost by accident. They presented themselves about noon one day at the dissecting room of King's College Hospital, accompanied by a third man, an avowed "snatcher" and *habitué* of the Fortune of War, a public-house in Smithfield frequented openly by men of this awful profession. This man, May, asked the porter at King's College if "he wanted anything?" the euphemism for offering a body. The porter asked what he had got, and the answer was, a male subject. Reference was made to Mr. Partridge, the demonstrator in anatomy, and after some haggling they agreed on a price, and in the afternoon the snatchers brought a hamper which contained a body in a sack. The porter received it, but from its freshness became suspicious of foul play. Mr. Partridge was sent for, and he with some of the students soon decided that the corpse had not died a natural death. The snatchers were detained, the police sent for, and arrest followed as a matter of course.

An inquest was held on the body, which was identified as that of an Italian boy, Carlo Ferrari, who made a living by exhibiting white mice about the streets, and the jury returned a verdict of wilful murder against persons unknown, expressing a strong opinion that Bishop, Williams, and May had been concerned in the transaction. Meanwhile, a search had been made at Nova Scotia Gardens, Bethnal Green, where Bishop and Williams lived. At first nothing peculiar was found; but at a second search the back-garden ground was dug up, and in one corner, at some depth, a bundle of clothes were unearthed, which, with a hairy cap, were known to be what

Ferrari had worn when last seen. In another portion of the garden more clothing, partly male and partly female, was discovered, plainly pointing to the perpetration of other crimes. These facts were represented before the police magistrate who examined Bishop and his fellows, and further incriminating evidence adduced, to the effect that the prisoners had bartered for a coach to carry "a stiff 'un"; they had also been seen to leave their cottage, carrying out a sack with something heavy inside. On this they were fully committed to Newgate for trial. This trial came off in due course at the Central Criminal Court, where the prisoners were charged on two counts, one that of the murder of the Italian boy, the other that of a boy unknown. The evidence from first to last was circumstantial, but the jury, after a short deliberation, did not hesitate to bring in a verdict of guilty, and all three were condemned to death.

Shortly before the day fixed for execution, Bishop made a full confession, the bulk of which bore the impress of truth, although it included statements that were improbable and unsubstantiated. He asserted that the victim was a Lincolnshire lad, and not an Italian boy, although the latter was fully proved. According to the confession, death had been inflicted by drowning in a well, whereas the medical evidence all pointed to violence. It was, however, pretty clear that this victim, like preceding ones, had been lured to Nova Scotia Gardens, and there drugged with a large dose of laudanum. While they were in a state of insensibility the murder was committed. Bishop's confession was endorsed by Williams, and the immediate result was the respite of May. A very painful scene occurred in Newgate when the news of his escape from death was imparted to May. He fainted, and the warrant of mercy nearly proved his death-blow. The other two looked on at his agitation with an indifference amounting to apathy. The execution took place a week or two later, in the presence of such a crowd as had not been seen near Newgate for years.

I will close this chapter with a brief account of another murder, the memory of which is still fresh in the minds of Londoners, although half a century has passed since it was committed. The horror with which Greenacre's crime struck the town was unparalleled since the time when Catherine Hayes slew her husband. There were many features of resemblance in these crimes. The decapitation and dismemberment, the bestowal of the remains in various parts of the town, the preservation of the head in spirits of wine, in the hope that the features might some day be recognized, were alike in both. The murder in both cases was long a profound mystery. In this which I am now describing, a bricklayer found a human trunk near some new buildings in the Edgeware Road, one morning in the last week of 1836. The inquest on these remains, which medical examination showed to be those of a female, returned a verdict of wilful murder against some person unknown. On the 7th July, 1837, the lockman of "Ben Jonson lock," in Stepney Fields, found a human head jammed into the lock gates. Closer investigation proved that it belonged to the trunk already discovered on the 2nd February. A further discovery was made in an osier bed near Cold Harbour Lane, Camberwell, where a workman found a bundle containing two human legs, in a drain. These were the missing members of the same mutilated trunk, and there was now evidence sufficient to establish conclusively that the woman thus collected piecemeal had been barbarously done to death. But the affair still remained a profound mystery. No light was thrown upon it till, towards the end of March, a Mr. Gay of Goodge Street came to view the head, and immediately recognized it as that of a widowed sister, Hannah Brown, who had been missing since the previous Christmas Day.

The murdered individual was thus identified. The next step

was to ascertain where and with whom she had last been seen. This brought suspicion on to a certain James Greenacre, whom she was to have married, and in whose company she had left her own lodgings to visit his in Camberwell. The police wished to refer to Greenacre, but as he was not forthcoming, a warrant was issued for his apprehension, which was effected at Kennington on the 24th March. A woman named Gale, who lived with him, was arrested at the same time. The prisoners were examined at the Marylebone police court. Greenacre, a stout, middle-aged man, wrapped in a brown greatcoat, assumed an air of insolent bravado; but his despair must have been great, as was evident from his attempt to strangle himself in the station-house. Suspicion grew almost to certainty as the evidence was unfolded. Mrs. Brown was a washer-woman, supposed to be worth some money; hence Greenacre's offer of marriage. She had realized all her effects, and brought them with her furniture to Greenacre's lodgings. The two when married were to emigrate to Hudson's Bay. Whether it was greed or a quarrel that drove Greenacre to the desperate deed remains obscure. They were apparently good friends when last seen together at a neighbour's, where they seemed "perfectly happy and sociable, and eager for the wedding day." But Greenacre in his confession pretended that he and his intended had quarrelled over her property or the want of it, and that in a moment of anger he knocked her down. He thought he had killed her, and in his terror began at once to consider how he might dispose of the body and escape arrest. While she was senseless, but really still alive, he cut off her head, and dismembered the body in the manner already described. It is scarcely probable that he would have gone to this extremity if he had had no previous evil intention, and the most probable inference is that he inveigled Mrs. Brown to his lodgings with the set purpose of taking her life.

His measures for the disposal of the *corpus delicti* remind us of those taken by Mrs. Hayes and her associates, or of Gardelle's frantic efforts to conceal his crime. The most ghastly part of the story is that which deals with his getting rid of the head. This, wrapped up in a silk handkerchief, he carried under his coat-flaps through the streets, and afterwards on his cap in a crowded city omnibus. It was not until he left the 'bus, and walked up by the Regent's Canal, that he conceived the idea of throwing the head into the water. Another day elapsed before he got rid of the rest of the body, all of which, according to his own confession, made no doubt with the idea of exonerating Mrs. Gale, he accomplished without her assistance. On the other hand, it was adduced in evidence that Mrs. Gale had been at his lodgings the very day after the murder, and was seen to be busily engaged in washing down the house with bucket and mop.

Greenacre, when tried at the Old Bailey, admitted that he had been guilty of manslaughter. While conversing with Mrs. Brown, he declared the unfortunate woman was rocking herself to and fro in a chair; as she leant back he put his foot against the chair, and so tilted it over. Mrs. Brown fell with it, and Greenacre, to his horror, found that she was dead. But the medical evidence was clear that the decapitation had been effected during life, and the jury, after a short deliberation, without hesitation brought in a verdict of wilful murder. The woman Gale was also found guilty, but sentence of death was only passed on Greenacre. The execution was, as usual, attended by an immense concourse, and Greenacre died amidst the loudest execrations. Gale was sentenced to penal servitude for life.

NEWGATE NOTORIETIES (CONTINUED)

Increase in crimes of fraud—Edward Beaumont Smith—Casting away ships—The 'Dryad'—Wrecked by the Wallaces—Another clergyman-forger, Dr. Bailey—The Barber Fletcher frauds to obtain unclaimed stock in the funds—The Bank of England robbed by one of its clerks of £8000—Other daring robberies—Burglaries at Windsor Castle and Buckingham Palace—Ingenious plate robbery at Lord Fitzgerald's in Belgrave Square—Stealing plate from clubs by a member—A large parcel of rough diamonds stolen—More murders—The valet Courvoisier murders his master, Lord William Russell—His trial and sentence—His confession, attempted suicide, and demeanour at the scaffold—Daniel Good murders his wife—Strange discovery of the crime—Pursuit and arrest of the murderer—Hocker kills Mr. Delarue—Murderer cannot tear himself from the scene of his crime—Epidemic of murder in 1848-9—Rush—Gleeson Wilson—The Mannings and their victim, O'Connor—The cold-blooded scheme—How carried out, and how discovered—One of the first instances of the employment of the electric telegraph to arrest the murderers—Their trial—Violent conduct of Mrs. Manning—The *execution at Horsemonger Lane Gaol—Charles Dickens on this execution—Other murderers—Robert Marley—Cannon, the chimney-sweep, who makes a murderous assault upon and nearly killed a policeman—Mobbs, the brutal husband—Barthelemy—Series of gigantic frauds, commencing in 1850—Walter Watts, the inventor of the new crime—The two lives he led—Immense defalcations—Sentenced for stealing a bit of paper value one penny—Commits suicide—The forgeries of R. F. Pries—Those of Joseph Windle Cole—Raises funds on fictitious dock warrants—The bankers Messrs. Strahan, Paul, and Bates tried for disposing of securities they held on deposit—Systematic embezzlement by Robson, a clerk in the Crystal Palace Company—Lionel Redpath carries on still more audacious frauds—His way of life—A patron of art, and foremost in all good works—His detection and flight—Is captured, tried, and sentenced to transportation—Big prizes still to be had by daring thieves—The bullion robbery on the South-Eastern—How planned and carried out—Detected by accident—The bold and systematic forgeries of Saward, or Jem the Penman—His method—How caught—Sentenced to transportation.*

AS the century advanced crimes of fraud increased. They not only became more numerous, but they were on a wider scale. The most extensive and systematic robberies were planned and carried out so as long to escape detection. One of the earliest of the big operators in fraudulent finance was Edward Beaumont Smith, who was convicted in 1841 of uttering false exchequer bills to an almost fabulous amount. A not entirely novel kind of fraud, but one carried out on a larger scale than heretofore, came to light in this same year, 1841. This was the wilful shipwreck and casting away of a vessel which, with her supposed cargo, had been heavily insured. The 'Dryad' was a brig owned principally by two persons named Wallace, one a seaman, the other merchant. She was freighted by the firm of Zulueta and Co. for a voyage to Santa Cruz. Her owners insured her for a full sum of £2000, after which the Wallaces insured her privily with other underwriters for a second sum of £2000. After this, on the faith of forced bills of lading, the captain, Loose by name, being a party to the intended fraud, they obtained further insurances on goods never shipped. It was fully proved in evidence that when the 'Dryad' sailed she carried nothing but the cargo belonging to Zulueta and Co. Yet the Wallaces pretended to have put on board quantities of flannels, cloths, cotton prints, beef, pork, butter, and earthenwares, on all of which they effected insurances. Loose had his instructions to cast away the ship on the first possible opportunity, and from the time of his leaving Liverpool he acted in a manner which excited the suspicions of the crew. The larboard pump was suffered to remain choked up, and the long-boat was fitted with tackles and held ready for use at a moment's notice. The ship, however, met with exasperatingly fine weather, and it was not until the captain reached the West India Islands that he got a chance of accomplishing his crime. At a place called the Silver Keys he ran the ship on the reef. But another ship, concluding that he was acting in ignorance, rendered him assistance. The 'Dryad' was got off, repaired, and her voyage renewed to Santa Cruz. He crept along the coast close in shore, looking for a quiet spot to cast away the ship, and at last, when within fifteen miles of port, with wind and weather perfectly fair, he ran her on to the rocks. Even then she might have been saved, but the captain would not suffer the crew to act. Nearly the whole of the cargo was lost as well as the ship. The captain and crew, however, got safely to Jamaica, and so to England; the captain dying on the voyage home.

The crime soon became public. Mate, carpenter, and crew were eager to disavow complicity, and voluntarily gave information. The Wallaces were arrested, committed to Newgate, and tried at the Old Bailey. The case was clearly proved against them, and both were sentenced to transportation for life. While lying in Newgate, awaiting removal to the convict ship, both prisoners made full confessions. According to their own statements the loss of the 'Dryad' was only one of six intentional shipwrecks with which they had been concerned. The crime of fraudulent insurance they declared was very common, and the underwriters must have lost great sums in this way. The merchant Wallace said he had been led into the crime by the advice and example of a city friend who had gone largely into this nefarious business; this Wallace added that his friend had made several voyages with the distinct intention of superintending the predetermined shipwrecks. The other Wallace, the sailor, also traced his lapse into crime to evil counsel. He was an honest sea-captain, he said, trading from Liverpool, where once he had the misfortune to be introduced to a man of wealth, the foundations of which had been laid by buying old ships on purpose to cast them away. This person made much of Wallace, encouraged his attentions to his daughter, and tempted him to take to fraudulent insurance as a certain method of achieving fortune. Wallace's relations warned him against his Liverpool friend, but he would not take their advice, and developing his transactions, ended as we have seen.

A clergyman nearly a century later followed in the steps of Dr. Dodd, but did not under more humane laws lose his life. The Rev. W. Bailey, LL.D., was convicted at the Central Criminal Court, in February 1843, of forgery. A notorious miser, Robert Smith, had recently died in Seven Dials, where he had amassed a considerable fortune. But among the charges on the estate he left was a promissory note for £2875, produced by Dr. Bailey, and purporting to be signed by Smith. The executors to the estate disputed the validity of this document. Miss Bailey, the doctor's sister, in whose favour the note was said to have been given, then brought an action against the administrators, and at the trial Dr. Bailey swore that the note had been given him by Smith. The jury did not believe him, and the verdict was for the defendants. Subsequently Bailey was arrested on a charge of forgery, and after a long trial found guilty. His sentence was transportation for life.

A gigantic conspiracy to defraud was discovered in the following year, when a solicitor named William Henry Barber, Joshua Fletcher a surgeon, and three others were charged with forging wills for the purpose of obtaining unclaimed stock in the funds. There were two separate affairs. In the first a maiden lady, Miss Slack, who was the possessor of two separate sums in consols, neglected through strange carelessness on her own part and that of her friends to draw the dividends on more than one sum. The other, remaining unclaimed for ten years, was transferred at the end of that time to the commissioners for the reduction of the National Debt. Barber, it was said, became aware of this, and that he gained access to Miss Slack on pretence of conveying to her some funded property left her by an aunt. By this means her signature was obtained; a forged will was prepared bequeathing the unclaimed stock to Miss Slack; a note purporting to be from Miss Slack was addressed to the governor of the Bank of England, begging that the said stock might be handed over to her, and a person calling herself Miss Slack duly attended at the bank, where the money was handed over to her in proper form. A second will, also forged, was propounded at Doctors Commons as that of a Mrs. Hunt of Bristol. Mrs. Hunt had left money in the funds which remained unclaimed, and had been transferred, as in Miss Slack's case. Here again the money, with ten years' interest, was handed over to Barber and another calling himself Thomas Hunt, an executor of the will. It was shown that the will must be a forgery, as its signature was dated 1829, whereas Mrs. Hunt actually died in 1806. A third similar fraud to the amount of £2000 was also brought to light. Fletcher was the moving spirit of the whole business. It was he who had introduced Barber to Miss Slack, and held all the threads of these intricate and nefarious transactions. Barber and Fletcher were both transported for life, although Fletcher declared that Barber was innocent, and had no guilty knowledge of what was being done. Barber was subsequently pardoned, but was not replaced on the rolls as an attorney till 1855, when Lord Campbell delivered judgment on Barber's petition, to the effect that "the evidence to establish his (Barber's) connivance in the frauds was too doubtful for us to continue his exclusion any longer."

Banks and bankers continued to be victimized. In 1844 the Bank of England was defrauded of a sum of £8000 by one of its clerks, Burgess, in conjunction with an accomplice named Elder. Burgess fraudulently transferred consols to the above amount, standing in the name of Mr. Oxenford, to another party. A person, Elder of course, who personated Oxenford, attended at the bank to complete the transfer and sell the stock. Burgess, who was purposely on leave from the bank, effected the sale, which was paid for with a cheque for nearly the whole amount on Lubbock's Bank. Burgess and Elder proceeded in company to cash this, but as they wanted all gold, the cashier gave them eight Bank of England notes for £1000 each, saying that they could get so much specie nowhere else. Thither Elder went alone, provided with a number of canvas and one large carpet-bag. But when the latter was filled with gold it was too heavy to lift, and Elder had to be assisted by two bank porters, who carried it for him to a carriage waiting near the Mansion House. The thieves, for Elder was soon joined by Burgess, drove together to Ben Caunt's, the pugilist's, public-house in St. Martin's Lane, where the cash was transferred from the carpet-bag to a portmanteau. The same evening both started for Liverpool, and embarking on board the mail steamer 'Britannia,' escaped to the United States.

Burgess' continued absence was soon noticed at the bank. Suspicions were aroused when it was found that he had been employed in selling stock for Mr. Oxenford, which developed into certainty as soon as that gentleman was referred to. Mr. Oxenford having denied that he had made any transfer of stock, the matter was at once put into the hands of the police. A smart detective, Forrester, after a little inquiry, established the fact that the man who had personated Mr. Oxenford was a horse-dealer named Joseph Elder, an intimate acquaintance of Burgess'. Forrester next traced the fugitives to Liverpool, and thence to Halifax, whither he followed them, accompanied by a confidential clerk from the bank. At Halifax Forrester learnt that the men he wanted had gone on to Boston, thence to Buffalo and Canada, and back to Boston. He found them at length residing at the latter place, one as a landed proprietor, the other as a publican. Elder, the former, was soon apprehended at his house, but he evaded the law by hanging himself with his pocket-handkerchief. The inn belonging to Burgess was surrounded, but he escaped through a back door on to the river, and rowed off in a boat to a hiding-place in the woods. Next day a person betrayed him for the reward, and he was soon captured. The proceeds of the robbery were lodged in a Boston bank, but four hundred sovereigns were found on Elder, while two hundred more were found in Burgess' effects. Burgess was eventually brought back to England, tried at the Central Criminal Court, and sentenced to transportation for life.

Within a month or two the bank of Messrs. Rogers and Co., Clement's Lane, was broken into. Robberies as daring in conception as they were boldly executed were common enough. One night a quantity of plate was stolen from Windsor Castle; another time Buckingham Palace was robbed. Of this class was the ingenious yet peculiarly simple robbery effected at the house of Lord Fitzgerald in Belgrave Square. The butler, on the occasion of a death in the family, when the house was in some confusion, arranged with a burglar to come in, and with another carry off the plate-chest in broad daylight, and as a matter of business. No one interfered or asked any questions. The thief walked into the house in Belgrave Square, and openly carried off the plate-chest, deposited it in a light cart at the door, and drove away. Howse, the steward, accused the other servants, but they retorted, declaring that he had been visited by the thief the day previous, whom he had shown over the plate closet. Howse and his accomplice were arrested; the former was found guilty and sentenced to fifteen years, but the latter was acquitted.

Stealing plate was about this period the crime of a more aristocratic thief. The club spoons and other articles of plate were long a source of profitable income to a gentleman named Ashley, who belonged to five good London clubs—the Junior United Service, the Union, Reform, Colonial, and Erecthæum clubs. When one of these clubs was taken in at the Army and Navy, that establishment also suffered. Suspicion fell at length upon Ashley, who was seen to handle the forks and spoons at table in a strange manner. A watch was set on his house, in Allington Street, Pimlico, and one day a police constable tracked him to a silversmith's in Holborn Hill, where Ashley produced four silver spoons, and begged that his initials might be engraved upon them. Ashley was arrested as he left the shop; the spoons were impounded, and it was found that the club monogram had been erased from them. On a search of the prisoner's lodgings in Allington Street, a silver fork was found, a number of pawnbrokers' duplicates, and three small files. It was proved at the trial that Ashley had asked his landlady for brick-dust and leather, and it was contended that these with the files were used to alter the marks on the plate. At most of the clubs the servants had been mulcted to make good lost plate, which had no doubt been stolen by the prisoner. Several pawnbrokers were subpœnaed and obliged to surrender plate, to the extent in some cases of a couple of dozen of spoons or forks, which the various club secretaries identified as the property of their respective clubs. Ashley was the son of an army agent and banker, and many witnesses were brought to attest to his previous good character, but he was found guilty and sentenced to seven years' transportation.

A robbery of a somewhat novel kind was executed in rather a bungling fashion by Ker, a sea-captain, whose ship brought home a mixed cargo from Bahia and other ports. Part of the freight were four hundred rough diamonds valued at £4000. These packages were consigned to Messrs. Shroeder of London; and as it was known that they were to arrive in Ker's ship, one of the owners had met her at Deal, but the captain had already absconded with the packages of precious stones in his pocket. Ker came at once to London, and, by the help of the landlord of a public-house in Smithfield and others, disposed of the whole of the diamonds. A Jew named Benjamin effected the sale to certain merchants named Blogg and Martin, who declared that the rough diamond market was in such a depressed condition that they could only afford to give £1750 for stones worth £4000. The circumstances of this purchase of brilliants from a stranger at such an inadequate price was strongly commented upon at Ker's trial. The moment it was discovered that the diamonds had disappeared, the affair was taken up by the police. Forrester, the detective who had pursued and captured Burgess at Boston,[117] tracked Ker to France, and following him there, eventually captured him at Montreuil. He was arraigned at the Old Bailey, and the case fully proved. His sentence was seven years' transportation.

The gravest crimes continued at intervals to inspire the town with horror, and concentrate public attention upon the gaol of Newgate, and the murderers immured within its walls. Courvoisier's case made a great stir. There was unusual atrocity in this murder of an aged, infirm gentleman, a scion of the ducal house of Bedford, by his confidential valet and personal attendant. Lord William Russell lived alone in Norfolk Street, Park Lane. He was a widower, and seventy-three years of age. One morning in May his lordship was found dead in his bed with his throat cut. The fact of the murder was first discovered by the housemaid, who, on going down early, was surprised to find the dining-room in a state of utter confusion; the furniture turned upside down, the drawers of the escritoire open and rifled, a bundle lying on the floor, as though thieves had been interrupted in the act. The housemaid summoned the cook, and both went to call the valet, Courvoisier, who came from his room ready dressed, a suspicious circumstance, as he was always late in the morning. The housemaid suggested that they should see if his lordship was all right, and the three went to his bed-room. While Courvoisier opened the shutters, the housemaid, approaching the bed, saw that the pillow was saturated with blood.

The discovery of the murdered man immediately followed. The neighbourhood was alarmed, the police sent for, and a close inquiry forthwith commenced. That Lord William Russell had committed suicide was at once declared impossible. It was also clearly proved that no forcible entry had been made into the house; the fresh marks of violence upon the door had evidently been made inside, and not from outside; moreover, the instruments, poker and chisel, by which they had no doubt been effected, were found in the butler's pantry, used by Courvoisier. The researches of the police soon laid bare other suspicious facts. The bundle found in the dining-room contained, with clothes, various small articles of plate and jewellery which a thief would probably have put into his pocket. Upstairs in the bed-room a *rouleaux* box for sovereigns had been broken open, also the jewel-box and note-case, from the latter of which was abstracted a ten-pound note known to have been in the possession of the deceased. His lordship's watch was gone. Further suspicion was caused by the position of a book and a wax candle by the bedside. The latter was so placed that it could throw no light on the former, which was a 'Life of Sir Samuel Romilly.' The intention of the real murderer to shift the crime to burglars was evident although futile, and the police, feeling convinced that the crime had been committed by some inmate of the house, took Courvoisier into custody, and placed the two female servants under surveillance. The valet's strange demeanour had attracted attention from the first. He had hung over the body in a state of dreadful agitation, answering no questions, and taking no part in the proceedings.

Three days later a close search of the butler's pantry produced fresh circumstantial evidence. Behind the skirting board several of his lordship's rings were discovered; near it was his Waterloo medal, and the above-mentioned ten-pound note. Further investigation was rewarded by the discovery in the pantry of a split gold ring, used by Lord William to carry his keys on; next, and in the same place, a chased gold key; and at last his lordship's watch was found secreted under the leads of the sink. All this was evidence sufficient to warrant Courvoisier's committal for trial; but still he found friends, and a liberal subscription was raised among the foreign servants in London to provide funds for his defence. Courvoisier, when put on his trial, pleaded not guilty; but on the second day the discovery of fresh evidence, more particularly the recovery of some of Lord William's stolen plate, induced the prisoner to make a full confession of his crime to the lawyers who defended him. This placed them in a position of much embarrassment. To have thrown up their brief would have been to have secured Courvoisier's conviction. Mr. Phillips, who led in the case, went to the other extreme, and in an impassioned address implored the jury not to send an innocent man to the gallows. It will be remembered that the question whether Mr. Phillips had not exceeded the limits usually allowed to counsel was much debated at the time.

The jury without hesitation found Courvoisier guilty, and he was sentenced to death. The prisoner's demeanour had greatly changed during the trial. Coolness amounting almost to effrontery gave way to hopeless dejection. On his removal to Newgate after sentence, he admitted that he had been justly convicted, and expressed great anxiety that his fellow-servants should be relieved from all suspicion. Later in the day he tried to commit suicide by cramming a towel down his throat, but was prevented. Next morning he made a full confession in presence of his attorney, and the governor, Mr. Cope. In this he gave as the motives of his crime a quarrel he had with his master, who threatened to discharge him without a character. Lord William, according to the valet, was of a peevish, difficult temper; he was annoyed with his man for various small omissions and acts of forgetfulness, and on the night of the murder had taken Courvoisier to task rather sharply. Finally, on coming downstairs after bed-time, Lord William had found Courvoisier in the dining-room. "What are you doing here?" asked his lordship. "You can have no good intentions; you must quit my service to-morrow morning." This seems to have decided Courvoisier, who took a carving-knife from the sideboard in the dining-room, went upstairs to Lord William's bed-room, and drew the knife across his throat. "He appeared to die instantly," said the murderer, in conclusion. His account of his acts and movements after the deed varied so considerably in the several documents he left behind, that too much reliance cannot be placed upon his confession. His last statement contains the words, "The public now think I am a liar, and they will not believe me when I say the truth." This was no doubt the case, but this much truth his confession may be taken to contain: that Courvoisier was idle, discontented, ready to take offence, greedy of gain; that he could not resist the opportunity for robbery offered him by his situation at Lord William Russell's; that when vexed with his master he did not shrink from murder, both for revenge and to conceal his other crimes.

Courvoisier wished to commit suicide in Newgate, but was prevented by the vigilant supervision to which he was subjected while in gaol. The attempt was to have been made by opening a vein and allowing himself to bleed to death. The Sunday night before his execution he would not go to bed when ordered. The governor insisted, but Courvoisier showed great reluctance to strip. The order was, however, at length obeyed, and the whole of the prisoner's clothes were minutely searched. In the pocket of the coat Mr. Cope, the governor, found a neatly-folded cloth, and asked what it was for. Courvoisier admitted that he had intended to bind it tightly round his arm and bleed himself to death in the night. The next inquiry was how he hoped to open a vein. "With a bit of sharpened stick picked out of the ordinary firewood." "Where is it?" asked the governor. The prisoner replied that he had left it in the mattress of which he had just been deprived. The bed was searched, but no piece of sharpened wood was found. It was thought that it might have been lost in changing the mattresses. The cloth above referred to belonged to the inner seam of his trousers, which he had managed to tear out. There is nothing to show that Courvoisier really contemplated self-destruction.

A murder which reproduced many of the features of that committed by Greenacre soon followed, and excited the public mind even more than that of Courvoisier's. Daniel Good's crime might have remained long undiscovered but for his own careless stupidity. He was coachman to a gentleman at Roehampton. One day he went into a pawnbroker's at Wandsworth, and bought a pair of breeches on credit. At the same time he was seen to steal and secrete a pair of trousers. The shop-boy gave information. Good was followed to his stables by a policeman, but obstinately denied the theft. The policeman insisted on searching the premises, at which Good displayed some uneasiness. This increased when the officer, accompanied by two others, a neighbour and a bailiff, entered one of the stables. Good now offered to go to Wandsworth and satisfy the pawnbroker. Just at this moment, however, the searchers found concealed under two trusses of hay a woman's headless and dismembered trunk. At the constable's cry of alarm Good rushed from the stable and locked the door behind him. Some time elapsed before the imprisoned party could force open the doors, and by then the fugitive had escaped. Medical assistance having been summoned, it was ascertained how the dismemberment had been effected. At the same time an overpowering odour attracted them to the adjoining harness-room, where the missing remains were raked out half consumed in the ashes of a wood fire. In the same room a large axe and saw were found covered with blood.

Inquiry into the character of Good exposed him as a loose liver, who "kept company" with several women. One called his sister, but supposed to be his wife, had occupied a room in South Street, Manchester Square, with a son of Good's by a former wife. Another wife, real or fictitious, existed in Spitalfields, and evidence was given of close relation between Good and a third woman, a girl named Butcher, residing at Woolwich. The victim was the first of these three. Good had told her, much to her perturbation, that she was to move from South Street to Roehampton, and one day he fetched her. They were seen together on Barnes Common, and again in Putney Park Lane, where they were talking loud and angrily. The poor creature was never seen again alive. The actual method of the murder was never exactly ascertained. Good himself remained at large for some weeks. He had tramped as far as Tunbridge, where he obtained work as a bricklayer's labourer; he there gave satisfaction for industry, but he was taciturn, and would hold no converse with his fellows. The woman where he lodged noticed that he was very restless at night, moaning and sighing much. Detection came unexpectedly. He was recognized by an ex-policeman who had known him at Roehampton, and immediately arrested. In his effects were found the clothes he had on at the time of his escape from the stables, and under the jacket he was wearing was a piece of a woman's calico apron stained with blood, which he had used to save the pressure on his shoulder by the hod. Good was committed to Newgate, and tried at the Central Criminal Court before a crowded court. He made a rambling defence, ending by saying, "Good ladies and gentlemen all, I have a great deal more to say, but I am so bad I cannot say it." The case was clearly proved against him, and he was condemned, sentenced, and duly executed.

Hocker's murder is in its way interesting, as affording another proof of the extraordinary way in which the culprit returned to the scene of his guilt. The cries of his victim, a Mr. Delarue, brought passers-by and policemen to the spot, a lonely place near a dead wall beyond Belsize Hall, Hampstead, but too late to give substantial aid. While the body lay there still warm, battered and bleeding from the cruel blows inflicted upon him by his cowardly assailant, a man came by singing. He entered into conversation with the policemen, and learnt, as it seemed for the first time, what had happened. His remark was, "It is a nasty job;" he took hold of the dead hand, and confessed that he felt "queer" at the shocking sight. This sight was his own handiwork, yet he could not overcome the strange fascination it had for him, and remained by the side of the corpse till the stretcher came. Even then he followed it as far as Belsize Lane. It was here that the others engaged in their dismal office in removing the dead first got a good look at the stranger's face. He wanted a light for a cigar, and got it from a lantern which was lifted up and fully betrayed his features. It was noticed that he wore a mackintosh. Next day the police, in making a careful search of the scene of the murder, picked up a coat-button, which afterwards played an important part in the identification of the murderer. A letter, which afforded an additional clue, was also found in the pocket of the deceased. Still it was many weeks before any arrest was made. In the mean time the police were not idle. It came out by degrees that the person who had been seen in Belsize Lane on the night the body was found was a friend of the deceased. His name was Hocker; he was by trade a ladies' shoemaker; and it was also ascertained that after the day of the murder he was flush of money. He was soon afterwards arrested on suspicion, and a search of his lodgings brought to light several garments saturated with blood; a coat among them much torn and stained, with three buttons missing, one of which corresponded with that picked up at Hampstead. The letter found in the pocket of the deceased was sealed with a wafer marked F, and many of the same sort were found in the possession of the accused. This was enough to obtain a committal, after several remands; but the case contained elements of doubt, and the evidence at the trial was entirely circumstantial. A witness deposed to meeting Hocker, soon after the cries of murder were heard, running at a dog-trot into London, and others swore that they plainly recognized him as the man seen soon afterwards in the lane. A woman whom he called on the same evening declared he had worn a mackintosh, his coat was much torn, there was a stain of blood on his shirt-cuff, and he was in possession, the first time to her knowledge, of a watch. This was Delarue's watch, fully identified as such, which Hocker told his brother Delarue had given him the morning of the murder.

These were damnatory facts which well supported the prosecution. The prisoner made an elaborate defence, in which he sought to vilify the character of deceased as the seducer of an innocent girl to whom he (Hocker) had been fondly attached. When her ruin was discovered her brother panted for revenge. Hocker, whose skill in counterfeiting handwriting was known, was asked to fabricate a letter making an assignation with Delarue in a lonely part of Hampstead. Hocker and the brother went to the spot, where the latter left him to meet his sister's seducer alone. Soon afterwards Hocker heard cries of "murder," and proceeding to where they came from, found Delarue dead, slain by the furious brother. Hocker was so overcome, feeling himself the principal cause of the tragedy, that he rushed to a slaughter-house in Hampstead and purposely stained his clothes with blood. Such an extravagant defence did not weigh with judge or jury; the first summed up dead against the prisoner, and the latter, after retiring for ten minutes, found him guilty. Hocker's conduct in Newgate while under sentence of death was most extraordinary. He drew up several long statements, containing narratives purely fictitious, imputing crimes to his victim, and repeating his line of defence, that Delarue had suffered by the hands of imaginary outraged brothers acting as the avengers of females deeply injured by him. Hocker made several pretended confessions and revelations, all of which were proved to be absolutely false by the police on inquiry. His demeanour was a strange compound of wickedness, falsehood, and deceit. But at the fatal hour his hardihood forsook him, and he was almost insensible when taken out of his cell for execution. Restoratives were applied, but he was in a fainting condition when tied, and had to be supported by the assistant executioner while Calcraft adjusted the noose.

There was an epidemic of murder in the United Kingdom about 1848-9. In November of the first-named year occurred the wholesale slaughter of the Jermys in their house, Stanfield Hall, by the miscreant Rush. Soon afterwards, in Gloucestershire, a maidservant, Sarah Thomas, murdered her mistress, an aged woman, by beating out her brains with a stone. Next year John Gleeson Wilson, at Liverpool, murdered a woman, Ann Henrichson, also a maidservant and two children; while in Ireland a wife dashed out her husband's brains with a hammer. London did not escape the contagion, and prominent among the detestable crimes of the period stands that of the Mannings at Bermondsey. These great criminals suffered at Horsemonger Lane Gaol, but they were tried at the Central Criminal Court, and were for some time inmates of Newgate. Their victim was a man named Patrick O'Connor, a Custom-House gauger, who had been a suitor of Marie de Roux before she became Mrs. Manning. Marie de Roux up to the time of her marriage had been in service as lady's-maid to Lady Blantyre, daughter of the Duchess of Sutherland, and Manning hoped to get some small Government appointment through his wife's interest. He had failed in this as well as in the business of a publican, which he had at one time adopted. After the marriage a close intimacy was still maintained between O'Connor and the Mannings. He lived at Mile End, whence he walked often to call at 3, Minver Place, Bermondsey, the residence of his old love. O'Connor was a man of substance. He had long followed the profitable trade of a money-lender, and by dint of usurious interest on small sums advanced to needy neighbours, had amassed as much as £8000 or £10,000. His wealth was well known to "Maria," as he called Mrs. Manning, who made several ineffectual attempts to get money out of him. At last this fiendish woman made up her mind to murder O'Connor and appropriate all his possessions. Her husband, to whom she coolly confided her intention, a heavy brutish fellow, was yet aghast at his wife's resolve, and tried hard to dissuade her from her bad purpose. In his confession after sentence he declared that she plied him well with brandy at this period, and that during the whole time he was never in his right senses. Meanwhile this woman, unflinching in her cold, bloody determination, carefully laid all her plans for the consummation of the deed.

One fine afternoon in August, O'Connor was met walking in the direction of Bermondsey. He was dressed with particular care, as he was to dine at the Mannings and meet friends, one a young lady. He was seen afterwards smoking and talking with his hosts in their back parlour, and never seen again alive. It came out in the husband's confession that Mrs. Manning induced O'Connor to go down to the kitchen to wash his hands, that she followed him to the basement, that she stood behind him as he stood near the open grave she herself had dug for him, and which he mistook for a drain, and that while he was speaking to her she put the muzzle of a pistol close to the back of his head and shot him down. She ran upstairs, told her husband, made him go down to look at her handiwork, and as O'Connor was not quite dead, Manning gave the *coup de grâce* with a crowbar. After this Mrs. Manning changed her dress and went off in a cab to O'Connor's lodgings, which, having possessed herself of the murdered man's keys, she rifled from end to end. Returning to her own home, where Manning meantime had been calmly smoking and talking to the neighbours over the basement wall, the corpse lying just inside the kitchen all the while, the two set to work to strip the body and hide it under the stones of the floor. This job was not completed till the following day, as the hole had to be enlarged, and the only tool they had was a dust-shovel. A quantity of quicklime was thrown in with the body to destroy all identification. This was on a Thursday evening. For the remainder of that week and part of the next the murderers stayed in the house, and occupied the kitchen, close to the remains of their victim. On the Sunday Mrs.

Manning roasted a goose at this same kitchen fire, and ate it with relish in the afternoon. This cold-blooded indifference after the event was only outdone by the premeditation of this horrible murder. The hole must have been excavated and the quicklime purchased quite three weeks before O'Connor met his death, and during that time he must frequently have stood or sat over his own grave.

Discovery of the murder came in this wise. O'Connor, a punctual and well-conducted official, was at once missed at the London Docks. On the third day his friends began to inquire for him, and at their request two police officers were sent to Bermondsey to inquire for him at the Mannings, with whom it was well known that he was very intimate. The Mannings had seen or heard nothing of him, of course. As O'Connor still did not turn up, the police after a couple of days returned to Minver Place. The house was empty, bare and stripped of all its furniture, and its former occupants had decamped. The circumstance was suspicious, and a search was at once made of the whole premises. In the back kitchen one of the detectives remarked that the cement between certain stones looked lighter than the rest, and on trying it with a knife, he found that it was soft and new, while elsewhere it was set and hard. The stones were at once taken up; beneath them was a layer of fresh mortar, beneath that a lot of loose earth, amongst which a stocking was turned up, and presently a human toe. Six inches lower the body of O'Connor was uncovered. He was lying on his face, his legs tied up to his hips so as to allow of the body fitting into the hole. The lime had done its work so rapidly that the features would have been indistinguishable but for the prominent chin and a set of false teeth.

The corpse settled all doubts, and the next point was to lay hands upon the Mannings. It was soon ascertained that the wife had gone off in a cab with a quantity of luggage. Part of this she had deposited to be left till called for at one station, while she had gone herself to another, that at Euston Square. At the first the boxes were impounded, opened, and found to contain many of O'Connor's effects. At the second exact information was obtained of Mrs. Manning's movements. She had gone to Edinburgh. A telegraphic message, then newly adapted to the purposes of criminal detection, advised the Edinburgh police of the whole affair, and within an hour an answer was telegraphed, stating that Mrs. Manning was in custody. She had been to brokers to negotiate the sale of certain foreign railway stock, with which they had been warned from London not to deal, and they had given information to the police. Her arrest was planned, and, when the telegram arrived from London, completed. An examination of her boxes disclosed a quantity of O'Connor's property. Mrs. Manning was transferred to London and lodged in the Horsemonger Lane Gaol, where her husband soon afterwards joined her. He had fled to Jersey, where he was recognized and arrested. Each tried to throw the blame on the other; Manning declared his wife had committed the murder, Mrs. Manning indignantly denied the charge.

The prisoners were in due course transferred to Newgate, to be put upon their trial at the Central Criminal Court. A great number of distinguished people assembled as usual at the Old Bailey on the day of trial. The Mannings were arraigned together; the husband standing at one of the front corners of the dock, his wife at the other end. Manning, who was dressed in black, appeared to be a heavy, bull-necked, repulsive-looking man, with a very fair complexion and light hair. Mrs. Manning was not without personal charms; her face was comely, she had dark hair and good eyes, and was above the middle height, yet inclined to be stout. She was smartly dressed in a plaid shawl, a white lace cap; her hair was dressed in long *crêpe* bands. She had lace ruffles at her wrist, and wore primrose-coloured kid gloves.

The case rested upon the facts which have been already set forth, and was proved to the satisfaction of the jury, who brought in a verdict of guilty. Manning, when sentence of death was passed on him, said nothing; but Mrs. Manning, speaking in a foreign accent, addressed the court with great fluency and vehemence. She complained that she had no justice; there was no law for her, she had found no protection either from judges, the prosecutor, or her husband. She had not been treated like a Christian, but like a wild beast of the forest. She declared that the money found in her possession had been sent her from abroad; that O'Connor had been more to her than her husband, that she ought to have married him. It was against common sense to charge her with murdering the only friend she had in the world; the culprit was really her husband, who killed O'Connor out of jealousy and revengeful feelings. When the judge assumed the black cap Mrs. Manning became still more violent, shouting, "No, no, I will not stand it! You ought to be ashamed of yourselves!" and would have left the dock had not Mr. Cope, the governor of Newgate, restrained her. After judgment was passed she repeatedly cried out Shame! and stretching out her hand, she gathered up a quantity of the rue which, following ancient custom dating from the days of the gaol fever, was strewn in front of the dock, and sprinkled it towards the bench with a contemptuous gesture.

On being removed to Newgate from the court Mrs. Manning became perfectly furious. She uttered loud imprecations, cursing judge, jury, barristers, witnesses, and all who stood around. Her favourite and most often-repeated expression was, "D—n seize you all." They had to handcuff her by force against the most violent resistance, and still she raged and stormed, shaking her clenched and manacled hands in the officers' faces. From Newgate the Mannings were taken in separate cabs to Horsemonger Lane Gaol. On this journey her manner changed completely. She became flippant, joked with the officers, asked how they liked her "resolution" in the dock, and expressed the utmost contempt for her husband, whom she never intended to acknowledge or speak to again. Later her mood changed to abject despair. On reaching the condemned cell she threw herself upon the floor and shrieked in an hysterical agony of tears. After this, until the day of execution, she recovered her spirits, and displayed reckless effrontery, mocking at the chaplain, and turning a deaf ear to the counsels of a benevolent lady who came to visit. Now she abused the jury, now called Manning a vagabond, and through all ate heartily at every meal, slept soundly at nights, and talked with cheerfulness on almost any subject. Nevertheless, she attempted to commit suicide by driving her nails, purposely left long, into her throat. She was discovered just as she was getting black in the face. Manning's demeanour was more in harmony with his situation, and the full confession he made elucidated all dark and uncertain points in connection with the crime. The actual execution, which took place at another prison than Newgate, is rather beyond the scope of this work. But it may be mentioned that the concourse was so enormous that it drew down the well-merited and trenchant disapproval of Charles Dickens, who wrote to the 'Times,' saying that he believed "a sight so inconceivably awful as the wickedness and levity of the immense crowd collected at the execution this morning could be imagined by no man, and presented by no heathen land under the sun. The horrors of the gibbet, and of the crime which brought the wretched murderers to it, faded in my mind before the atrocious bearing, looks, and language of the assembled spectators. When I came upon the scene at midnight, the shrillness of the cries and howls that were raised from time to time, denoting that they came from a concourse of boys and girls already assembled in the best places, made my blood run cold." It will be in the memory of many that

Mrs. Manning appeared on the scaffold in a black satin dress, which was bound tightly round her waist. This preference brought the costly stuff into disrepute, and its unpopularity lasted for nearly thirty years.

I will briefly describe one or two of the more remarkable murders in the years immediately following, then pass on to another branch of crime.

Robert Marley at the time of his arrest called himself a surgical instrument maker. It was understood also that he had served in the army as a private, and had, moreover, undergone a sentence of transportation. But it was supposed that he had been once in a good position, well born, and well educated. When lying under sentence of death in Newgate, he was visited by a lady, a gentlewoman in every sense of the word, who was said to be his sister. His determined addiction to evil courses had led to his being cast off by his family, and he must have been at the end of his resources when he committed the crime for which he suffered. His offence was the murder of Richard Cope, a working jeweller, shopman to a Mr. Berry of Parliament Street. It was Cope's duty to stay in the shop till the last, close the shutters, secure the stock of watches and jewellery, then lock up the place and take on the keys to Mr. Berry's private house in Pimlico. Cope, a small man, crippled, and of weakly constitution, was alone in the shop about 9.30; the shutters were up, and he was preparing to close, when Marley entered and fell upon him with a life-preserver, meaning to kill him and rifle the shop. The noise of the struggle was heard outside in the street, and bystanders peeped in through the shutters, but no one entered or sought to interfere in what seemed only a domestic quarrel. A milliner's porter, Lerigo, was also attracted by the noise of the row, but after walking a few paces he felt dissatisfied, and returned to the spot. Pushing the shop-door open, he saw Marley finishing his murderous assault. Lerigo turned for assistance to take the man into custody. Marley, disturbed, picked up a cigar and parcel from the counter, then ran out, pursued by Lerigo only. Marley ran along the street, down into Cannon Row, then into Palace Yard, where the waterman of the cab-tank, in obedience to Lerigo's shouts, collared the fugitive. Escorted by his two captors, Marley was taken back into Parliament Street to the jeweller's shop. The policemen were now in possession; two of them supported Cope, who was still alive, although insensible, and Marley was apprehended. The evidence against him was completed by his identification by Cope in Westminster Hospital, who survived long enough to make a formal deposition before Mr. Jardine, the police magistrate, that Marley was the man who had beaten him to death.

Marley at his trial was undefended, and the sheriffs offered him counsel; but he declined. The witnesses against him all spoke the truth, he said; there was no case to make out; why waste money on lawyers for the defence? His demeanour was cool and collected throughout; he seemed while in Newgate to realize thoroughly that there was no hope for him, and was determined to face his fate bravely. After sentence, the Newgate officers who had special charge of him noticed that he slept well and ate well, enjoying all his meals. One of them went into his cell just at dinner-time; the great clock of St. Sepulchre's close by was striking the hour, and Marley, who had his elbows on the table, with his head resting on his hands, looked up and observed calmly, "Go along, clock; come along, gallows." On the dread morning he came out to execution quite gaily, and tripped up the stairs to the scaffold. His captors, it may be added (Lerigo and Allen), were warmly commended by the judge for their courage and activity. The former was given a reward of twenty and the latter of ten pounds.

A murderous assault on a police constable, which so nearly ended fatally that the culprit was sentenced to death, although not executed, was perpetrated in 1852. The case was accompanied with the most shocking brutality. Cannon, by trade a chimney-sweep, had long been characterized by the bitterest hatred of the police force, and had been repeatedly sentenced to imprisonment for most desperate and ferocious attacks upon various constables. His last victim was Dwyer, a fine young officer who had been summoned to take Cannon into custody when the latter was drunk and riotous in front of a public-house. Dwyer found Cannon bleeding profusely from a wound in the head, and persuaded him to go to a doctor's. They walked together quietly for some little distance, then Cannon, without the slightest warning, threw the constable on his back, and violently assaulted him by jumping on his chest and stomach, and by getting his hand inside Dwyer's stock, with the idea of strangling him. Dwyer managed to overpower his assailant, and got to his feet; but Cannon butted at him with his head, and again threw him to the ground, after which he kicked his prostrate foe in the most brutal and cowardly manner, and until he was almost senseless, and bruised from head to foot. Once more Dwyer got to his feet, and managed, by drawing his staff, to keep Cannon at bay until a second constable came to his aid. All this time not one of a numerous body of bystanders offered to assist the policeman in his extremity. On the contrary, many of them encouraged the brutal assailant in his savage attack. To Cannon's infinite surprise, he was indicted for attempt to murder, and not for a simple assault, and found guilty. The judge, in passing sentence of death, told him he richly deserved the punishment. As Dwyer survived, Cannon escaped the death sentence, which was commuted to penal servitude for life. A handsome sum was subscribed for the injured constable, who was disabled for life.

Only a few have vied with Cannon in fiendish cruelty and brutality. One of these was Mobbs, who lived in the Minories, generally known by the soubriquet of "General Haynau," a name execrated in England about this time. Mobbs systematically ill-used his wife for a long space of time, and at last cut her throat. For this he was executed in front of Newgate in 1833. Emmanuel Barthelemy again, the French refugee, was a murderer of the same description, who despatched his victim with a loaded cane, after which, to secure his escape, he shot an old soldier who had attempted to detain him. He was convicted and executed. He died impenitent, declaring that he had no belief, and that it was idle to ask forgiveness of God. "I want forgiveness of man; I want those doors (of the prison) opened." Barthelemy was generally supposed to have been a secret agent of the French police.

I will now pass to grave but less atrocious crimes. In 1850 occurred the first of a series of gigantic frauds, which followed each other at no long intervals, which had a strong family likeness, and originated all of them to make money easily, without capital, and at railroad speed. Walter Watts was an inventor, a creator, who struck an entirely new and original line of crime. Employed as a clerk in the Globe Assurance, he with unusual quickness of apprehension discovered and promptly turned to account an inexcusably lax system of management, which offered peculiar chances of profit to an ingenious and unscrupulous man. It was the custom in this office to make the banker's pass-book the basis of the entries in the company's ledgers. Thus, when a payment was made by the company, the amount disbursed was carried to account in the general books from its entry in the pass-book, and without reference to or comparison with the documents in which the payment was claimed. This pass-book, when not at the bank, was in the exclusive custody of Watts. The cheques drawn by the directors also passed through his hands; to him too they came back to be verified and put by, after they had been cashed by the bank. In this way Watts had complete control over the whole of the monetary transactions of the company. He could do what he liked with the pass-book, and by its adoption, as described as the basis of all entries, there was no independent check upon him if he chose to tamper with it. This he did to an enormous extent, continually altering, erasing, and adding figures to correspond with and cover the abstractions he made of various cheques as they were drawn. It seems incredible that this pass-book, which when produced in court was a mass of blots and erasures, should not have created suspicion of foul play either at the bank or at the company's board. Implicit confidence appears to have been placed in Watts, who was the son of an old and trusted *employé*, and, moreover, a young man of plausible address.

Watts led two lives. In the West End he was a man of fashion, with a town house, a house at Brighton, and a cellar full of good wine at both. He rode a priceless hack in Rotten Row, or drove down to Richmond in a mail phaeton and pair. He played high, and spent his nights at the club, or in joyous and dissolute company. When other pleasures palled he took a theatre, and posed as a munificent patron of the dramatic art. Under his auspices several "stars" appeared on the boards of the Marylebone theatre, and later he became manager of the newly rebuilt Olympic at Wych Street. No one cared too closely to inquire into the sources of wealth. Some said he was a fortunate speculator in stocks, others that he had had extraordinary luck as a gold-digger. Had his West End and little-informed associates followed him into the city, whither he was taken every morning in a smart brougham, they would have seen him alight from it in Cornhill, and walk forward on foot to enter as a humble and unpretending *employé* the doors of the Globe Assurance office. His situation exactly described was that of check clerk in the cashier's department, and his salary was £200 a year. Nevertheless, in this position, through the culpable carelessness which left him unfettered, he managed between 1844 and 1850 to embezzle and apply to his own purposes some £71,000. The detection of these frauds came while he was still prominently before the world as the lessee of the Olympic. Rumours were abroad that serious defalcations had been discovered in one of the insurance offices, but it was long before the public realized that the fraudulent clerk and the great theatrical manager were one and the same person. Watts's crime was discovered by the secretary of the Globe Company, who came suddenly upon the extensive falsification of the pass-book. An inquiry was at once set on foot, and the frauds were traced to Watts. The latter, when first taxed with his offence, protested his innocence boldly, and positively denied all knowledge of the affair; and he had so cleverly destroyed all traces that it was not easy to bring home the charge. But it was proved that Watts had appropriated one cheque for £1400, which he had paid into his own bankers, and on this he was committed to Newgate for trial. There were two counts in the indictment: one for stealing a cheque value £1400, the second for stealing a bit of paper value one penny. The jury found him guilty of the latter only, with a point of law reserved. This was fully argued before three judges, who decided that the act of stealing the bit of paper involved a much more serious offence, and told him they should punish him for what he had really done, and not for the slight offence as it appeared on the record. The sentence of the court, one of ten years' transportation, struck the prisoner with dismay. He had been led to suppose that twelve months' imprisonment was the utmost the law could inflict, and he broke down utterly under the unexpected blow. That same evening he committed suicide in Newgate.

The details of the suicide were given at the inquest. Watts had been in ill-health from the time of his first arrest. In Giltspur Street Compter, where he was first lodged, he showed symptoms of delirium tremens, and admitted that he had been addicted to the excessive use of stimulants. His health improved, but was still indifferent when he was brought up for sentence, and he was an occupant of the Newgate infirmary. He returned from court in a state of gloomy dejection, and in the middle of the night one of the fellow-prisoners who slept in the same ward noticed that he was not in his bed. This man got up to look for him, and found him hanging from the bars of a neighbouring room. He had made use of a piece of rope cut out from the sacking of his bedstead, and had tied his feet together with a silk pocket-handkerchief. The prison officers were called, but Watts was quite cold and stiff when he was cut down. Strange to say, a second suicide occurred in Newgate the same night, that of a prize-fighter named Donovan, tried the same day, and convicted of manslaughter. Sentence of death had been recorded against Donovan, who, like Watts, had seemingly been overcome with sudden despair.

In 1853 a second case of gigantic fraud alarmed and scandalized the financial world. It outshone the defalcations of Watts. Nothing to equal the excitement caused by the forgeries of Robert Ferdinand Pries had been known before in the city of London. He was a corn merchant who operated largely in grain. So enormous were his transactions, that they often affected the markets, and caused great fluctuations in prices. These had been attributed to political action; some thought that the large purchases in foreign grains, effected at losing prices, were intended by the protectionists to depress the wheat market, and secure the support of the farmers at the forthcoming election; others, that Napoleon III., but recently proclaimed Emperor of the French, wished to gain the popularity necessary to secure the people. Few realized that these mysterious operations were the "convulsive attempt" of a ruined and dishonest speculator to sustain his credit. Pries, although enjoying a high reputation in the city, had long been in a bad way. His extensive business had been carried on by fraud. His method was to obtain advances twice over on the same bills of lading or corn warrants. The duplicates were forged. In this way he obtained vast sums from several firms, and one to which he was indebted upwards of £50,000 subsequently stopped payment. Pries at length was discovered through a dishonoured cheque for £3000, paid over as an instalment of £18,000 owing for an advance on warrants. Inquiries were instituted when the cheque was protested, which led to the discovery of the forgeries. Pries was lodged in Newgate, tried at the Old Bailey, and transported for life.

Another set of frauds, which resembled those of Pries in principle, although not in practice, were soon afterwards discovered. These were the forgeries of Joseph Windle Cole. This clever but unscrupulous trader proposed to gain the capital he needed for business purposes by raising money on dock warrants for imported goods which had no real existence. When such goods arrived they were frequently left at a wharf, paying rent until it suited the importer to remove them. The dock warrant was issued by the wharfinger as certificate that he held the goods. The warrant thus represented money, and was often used as such, being endorsed and passed from hand to hand as other negotiable bills. Cole's plan was to have a wharf of his own, nominally occupied by a creature trading as Maltby and Co. Goods would be landed at this wharf; Maltby and Co. would issue warrants on them deliverable to the importer, and the goods were then passed to be stored in neighbouring warehouses. The owners of the latter would then issue a second set of warrants on these goods, in total ignorance of the fact that they were already pledged. Cole quickly raised money on both sets of warrants. He carried on this game for some time with great success, and so developed his business that in one year his transactions amounted to a couple of millions of pounds. He had several narrow escapes. Once a warrant-holder sent down a clerk to view certain goods, and the clerk found that these goods had already a "stop" upon them, or were pledged. Cole escaped by throwing the blame on a careless partner, and at once removed the "stop." Again, some of the duplicate and fictitious warrants were held by a firm which suspended payment, and there was no knowing into whose hands they might fall. Cole found out where they were, and redeemed them at a heavy outlay, thus obtaining business relations with the firm that held them, which were soon developed, much to that firm's subsequent anger and regret. Last of all, the well-known bankers Overend and Gurney, whose own affairs created much excitement some years later, wishing to verify the value of warrants they held, and sending to Maltby and Co.'s wharf, found out half the truth. These bankers, wishing for more specific information, asked Davidson and Gordon, a firm with which Cole was closely allied, whether the warrants meant goods or nothing. They could not deny that the latter was the truth, and were forthwith stigmatized by Mr. Chapman, Overend and Gurney's representative, as rogues. But Overend and Gurney took no steps to make the swindle public, and therefore, according to people of more rigid principle, became in a measure a party to the fraud.

The course of the swindlers was by no means smooth, but it was not till 1854 that suspicion arose that anything was wrong. A firm which held a lot of warrants suddenly demanded the delivery of the goods they covered. The goods having no existence, Cole of course could not deliver them. About this time Davidson and Gordon, the people above-mentioned, who had fraudulent warrants out of their own to the extent of £150,000, suspended payment and absconded. This affected Cole's credit, and ugly reports were in circulation charging him with the issue of simulated warrants. These indeed were out to the value of £367,800. Cole's difficulties increased more and more; warrant-holders came down upon him demanding to realize their goods.

Cole now suspended payment. Maltby, who had bolted, was pursued and arrested, to end his life miserably by committing suicide in a Newgate cell. Cole too was apprehended, and in due course tried at the Central Criminal Court. He was found guilty, and sentenced to the seemingly inadequate punishment of four years' transportation. Davidson and Gordon were also sentenced to imprisonment.

A more distressing case stands next on the criminal records—the failure and subsequent sentence of the bankers Messrs. Strahan, Paul, and Bates, for the fraudulent disposal of securities lodged in their hands. This firm was one of the oldest banking establishments in the kingdom, and dated back to the Commonwealth, when, under the title of Snow and Walton, it carried on business as pawnbrokers. The Strahan of the firm which came to grief was a Snow who changed his name for a fortune of £200,000; he was a man esteemed and respected in society and the world of finance, incapable as it was thought of a dishonest deed. Sir John Dean Paul had inherited a baronetcy from his father, together with an honoured name; he was himself a prominent member of the Low Church, of austere piety, active in all good works. Mr. Bates had been confidential managing clerk, and was taken into the firm not alone as a reward for long and faithful service, but that he might strengthen it by his long experience and known business capacity. The bank enjoyed an excellent reputation, it had a good connection, and was supposed to be perfectly sound. Moreover, the partners were sober, steady men, who paid unremitting attention to business. Yet even so early as the death of the first Sir John Paul, the bank was insolvent, and instead of starting on a fresh life with a new name, it should then and there have closed its doors. In December 1851 the balance sheet showed a deficiency of upwards of £70,000. The bank had been conducted on false principles; it had assumed enormous responsibilities—on one side by the ownership of the Mostyn collieries, a valueless property, and on the other by backing up an impecunious and rotten firm of contractors with vast liabilities and pledged to impossible works abroad. The engagements of the bank on these two heads amounting to nearly half a million of money, produced immediate embarrassment and financial distress.

The bank was already insolvent, and the partners had to decide between suspending payment or continuing to hold its head above water by flagitious processes. They chose, unhappily for themselves, the latter alternative. Money they must have, and money they raised to meet their urgent necessities upon the balances and securities deposited with them by their customers. This borrowing continued, and on such a scale that their paper was soon at a discount, and the various discount houses would not advance sufficient sums to relieve the necessities of the bank. Then it was that instead of merely pledging securities, the bank sold them outright, and thus passed the Rubicon of fraud. This went on for some time, and might never have been discovered had some good stroke of luck provided any of the partners with money enough to retrieve the position of the bank. But that passed from bad to worse; the firm's paper went down further and further in value; an application to the Committee of Bankers for assistance was peremptorily refused, then came a run on the bank, and it was compelled to stop payment. Its debts amounted to three-quarters of a million, and the dividend it eventually paid was three and twopence in the pound. But worse than the bankruptcy was the confession made by the partners in the court. They admitted that they had made away with many of the securities intrusted to their keeping. Following this, warrants were issued for their arrest, the specific charge being the unlawful negotiation of Danish bonds and other shares belonging to the Rev. Dr. Griffiths of Rochester, to the value of £20,000.

Bates was at once captured in Norfolk Street, Strand. Police officers went down at night to Nutfield, near Reigate, and arrested Sir John Paul, but allowed the prisoner to sleep there. Next morning they only just saved the train to town, and left Sir John behind on the platform, but he subsequently surrendered himself. Mr. Strahan was arrested at a friend's house in Bryanston Square. All three were tried at the Central Criminal Court, and sentenced to fourteen years' transportation, passing some time in Newgate *en route*. Bates, the least guilty, was pardoned in 1858.

Two cases of extensive embezzlement which were discovered almost simultaneously, those of Robson and Redpath, will long be remembered both within and without the commercial world. They both reproduced many of the features of the case of Watts, already described, but in neither did the sums misappropriated reach quite the same high figure. But neither Robson nor Redpath would have been able to pursue their fraudulent designs with success had they not, like Watts, been afforded peculiar facilities by the slackness of system and the want of methodical administration in the concerns by which they were employed. Robson was of humble origin, but he was well educated, and he had some literary abilities. His proclivities were theatrical, and he was the author of several plays, one at least of which, 'Love and Loyalty,' with Wallack in a leading part, achieved a certain success. He began life as a law-writer, earning thereby some fifteen or eighteen shillings a week; but the firm he served got him a situation as clerk in the office of the Great Northern Railway, whence he passed to a better position under the Crystal Palace Company. He now married, although his salary was only a pound a week; but he soon got on. He had a pleasant address, showed good business aptitudes, and quickly acquired the approval of his superiors. Within a year he was advanced to the post of chief clerk in the transfer department, at a salary of £150 a year. His immediate chief was a Mr. Fasson, upon whose confidence he gained so rapidly, through his activity, industry, and engaging manners, that ere long the whole management of the transfer department was intrusted to him.

Some time elapsed before Robson succumbed to temptation. He was not the first man of loose morality and expensive tastes who preferred to risk his future reputation and liberty to the present discomfort of living upon narrow means. The temptation was all the greater because the chances of successful fraud lay ready to hand. Shares in the company were represented by certificates, which often enough never left the company's, or more exactly Robson's, hands. He conceived the idea of transferring shares, bogus shares from a person who held none, to any one who would buy them in the open market. He took it for granted that the certificates representing these bogus shares, and which practically did not exist, would never be called for. This ingenious method of raising funds he adopted and carried on without detection, till the defalcations from fraudulent transfers and fraudulent issues combined amounted to £27,000. With the proceeds of these flagitious frauds Robson feasted and made merry. He kept open house at Kilburn Priory; entertained literary, artistic, and dramatic celebrities; had a smart "turn out," attended all the race-meetings, and dressed in the latest fashion. To his wife, poor soul, he made no pretence of fidelity, and she enjoyed only so much of his company as was necessarily spent in receiving guests at home, or could be spared from two rival establishments in other parts of the town. To account for his revenues he pretended to have been very lucky on the Stock Exchange, which was at one time true to a limited extent, and to have succeeded in other speculations. When his friends asked why he, a wealthy man of independent means, continued to slave on as a clerk on a pittance, he replied gaily that his regular work at the Crystal Palace office was useful as a sort of discipline, and kept him steady.

All this time his position was one of extreme insecurity. He was standing over a mine which at any moment might explode. The blow fell suddenly, and when least expected. One morning Mr. Fasson asked casually for certain certificates, whether representing real or fictitious shares does not appear; but they were certificates connected in some way with Robson's long-practised frauds, and he could not produce them. His chief asked sternly where they were. Robson said they were at Kilburn Priory. "Let us go to Kilburn for them together," said Mr. Fasson, growing suspicious. They drove there, and Robson on arrival did the honours of his house, rang for lunch to gain time, but at Mr. Fasson's pressing demands went upstairs to fetch the certificates. He came back to explain that he had mislaid them. Mr. Fasson, more and more ill at ease, would not accept this subterfuge, and declared they must be found. Robson again left him, but only to gather together hastily all the money and valuables on which he could lay his hands, with which he left the house. Mr. Fasson waited and waited for his subordinate to re-appear, and at last discovered his flight. A reward was forthwith offered for Robson's apprehension. Meanwhile the absconding clerk had coolly driven to a favourite dining-place in the West End, where a fish curry and a brace of partridges were set before him, and he discussed the latter with appetite, but begged that they would never give him curry again, as he did not like it. After dinner he went into hiding for a day or two, then, accompanied by a lady, not Mrs. Robson, he took steamer and started for Copenhagen. But the continental police had been warned to look out for him, and two Danish inspectors got upon his track, followed him over to Sweden, and arrested him at Helsingfors. Thence he was transferred to Copenhagen and surrendered in due course to a London police officer.

Little more remains to be said about Robson. He appears to have accepted his position, and to have at once resigned himself to his fate. When brought to trial he took matters very coolly, and at first pleaded "Not Guilty," but subsequently withdrew the plea. Sergeant Ballantine, who prosecuted, paid him the compliment of describing him as "a young man of great intelligence, considerable powers of mind, and possessed of an education very much beyond the rank of life to which he originally belonged." Robson was found guilty, and sentenced to two terms of transportation, one for twenty and one for fourteen years. Newgate officers who remember Robson still describe him as a fine young man, who behaved well as a prisoner, but who had all the appearance of a careless, thoughtless, happy-go-lucky fellow.

In many respects the embezzlement of which Leopold Redpath was guilty closely resembled that of Robson, but it was based upon more extended and audacious forgeries. Redpath's crime arose from his peculiar and independent position as registrar of stock of the Great Northern Railway Company. This offered him great facilities for the creation of artificial stock, its sale from a fictitious holder, and transfer to himself. All the signatures in the transfer were forged. Not only did he thus transfer and realize "bogus" stock, but he bought *bonâ fide* amounts, and increased their value by altering the figures, by inserting say 1 before 500, and thus making it £1500, which larger amount was duly carried to his credit on the register, and entered upon the certificates of transfer. By these means Redpath misappropriated vast sums during a period extending over ten years. The total amount was never exactly made out, but the false stock created and issued by him was estimated at £220,000. Even when the bubble burst Redpath, who had lived at the rate of twenty thousand a year, had assets in the shape of land, house, furniture, pictures, and *objets d'art* to the value of £50,000.

He began in a very small way. First a lawyer's clerk, he then got an appointment in the Peninsular and Oriental Company's office; afterwards he set up as an insurance broker on his own account, but presently failed. His fault was generosity, an open-handed, unthinking charity which gave freely to the poor and needy the money which belonged to his creditors. After his bankruptcy he obtained a place as clerk in the Great Northern Railway office, from which he rose to be assistant registrar, with the special duties of transferring shares. He soon proved his ability, and by unremitting attention mastered the whole work of the office. Later on he became registrar, and in this more independent position developed to a colossal extent the frauds he had already practised as a subordinate. Now he launched out into great expenditure, took a house in Chester Terrace, and became known as a Mæcenas and patron of the arts. He had a nice taste in *bric-à-brac*, and was considered a good judge of pictures. Leading social and artistic personages were to be met with at his house, and his hospitality was far famed. The choicest wines, the finest fruits, peas at ten shillings a quart, five-guinea pines, and early asparagus were to be found on his table. But his chief extravagance, his favourite folly, was the exercise of an ostentatious benevolence. The philanthropy he had displayed in a small way when less prosperous became now a passion. His name headed every subscription list; his purse was always open. Not content with giving where assistance was solicited, he himself sought out deserving cases and personally afforded relief. When the crash came there were pensioners and other recipients of his bounty who could not believe that so good a man had really been for years a swindler and a rogue. Down at Weybridge, where he had a country place, his name was long remembered with gratitude by the poor. During the days of his prosperity he was a governor of Christ's Hospital, of the St. Ann's Society, and one of the supporters and managers of the Patriotic Fund. In his person he was neat and fastidious; he patronized the best tailors, and had a fashionable *coiffeur* from Hanover Square daily to curl his hair.

There was something dramatic in Redpath's detection. Just after Robson's frauds had agitated the minds of all directors of companies, the chairman of the Great Northern (Mr. Denison) was standing at a railway station talking to a certain well-known peer of the realm. Redpath passed and lifted his hat to his chairman; the latter acknowledged the salute. But the peer rushed forward and shook Redpath warmly by the hand. "What do you know of our clerk?" asked Mr. Denison of his lordship. "Only that he is a capital fellow, who gives the best dinners and balls in town." Redpath had industriously circulated reports that he had prospered greatly in speculation; but the chairman of the Great Northern could not realize that a clerk of the company could honestly be in the possession of unlimited wealth. It was at once decided at the board to make a thorough examination of all his books. Redpath was called in and informed of the intended investigation. He tried to stave off the evil hour by declaring that everything was perfectly right; but finding he could not escape, he said he would resign his post, and leaving the board-room, disappeared.

The inquiry soon revealed the colossal character of the frauds. Warrants were issued for Redpath's arrest, but he had flown to Paris. Thither police officers followed, only to find that he had returned to London. A further search discovered him at breakfast at a small house in the New Road. He was arrested, examined before a police magistrate, and committed to Newgate. Great excitement prevailed in the city and the West End when Redpath's defalcations were made public. The Stock Market was greatly affected, and society, more especially that which frequents Exeter Hall, was convulsed. The Central Criminal Court, when the trial came on, was densely crowded, and many curious eyes were turned upon the somewhat remarkable man who occupied the dock. He is described by a contemporary account as a fresh-looking man of forty years of age, slightly bald, inclined to embonpoint, and thoroughly embodying the idea of English respectability. His manner was generally self-possessed, but his face was marked with "uneasy earnestness," and he looked about him with wayward, furtive glances. When the jury found a verdict of guilty he remained unmoved. He listened without emotion to the judge's well-merited censures, and received his sentence of transportation for life without much surprise. Redpath passed away into the outer darkness of a penal colony, where he was still living a year or two back. But his name lingers still in this country as that of the first swindler of his time, and the prototype of a class not uncommon in our later days—that of dishonest rogues who assume piety and philanthropy as a cloak for their misdeeds.

In Newgate Redpath is remembered by the prison officer as a difficult man to deal with. From the moment of his reception he gave himself great airs, as a martyr and a man heavily wronged. By-and-by, when escape seemed hopeless, and after sentence, he suddenly degenerated into the lowest stamp of criminal, and behaved so as to justify a belief that he had been a gaol-bird all his life.

It has been already remarked in these pages that with changed social conditions came a great change in the character of crimes. Highway robberies, for instance, had disappeared, if we except the spasmodic and severely repressed outbreak of "garotting," which at one time spread terror throughout London. Thieves preferred now to use ingenuity rather than brute force. It was no longer possible to stop a coach or carriage, or rob the postman who carried the mail. The improved methods of locomotion had put a stop to these depredations. People travelled in company, as a rule; only when single and unprotected were they in any danger of attack, and that but rarely. There were still big prizes, however, to tempt the daring, and none appealed more to the thievish instinct than the custom of transmitting gold by rail. The precious metal was sent from place to place carefully locked up and guarded, no doubt; but were the precautions too minute, the vigilance too close to be eluded or overcome? This was the question which presented itself to the fertile brain of one Pierce, who had been concerned in various "jobs" of a dishonest character, and who for the moment was a clerk in a betting office. He laid the suggestion before Agar, a professional thief, who was of opinion it contained elements of success. But the collusion and active assistance of *employés* of the railway carriers were indispensable, and together they sounded one Burgess, a guard on the South-Eastern Railway, a line by which large quantities of bullion were sent to the Continent. Burgess detailed the whole system of transmission. The gold, packed in an iron-bound box, was securely lodged in safes locked with patent Chubbs. Each safe had three sets of double keys, all held by confidential servants of the company. One pair was with the traffic superintendent in London, another with an official in Folkestone, a third with the captain of the Folkestone and Boulogne boat. At the other side of the Channel the French railway authorities took charge.

The safes while on the line *en route* between London and Folkestone were in the guard's van. This was an important step, and they might easily be robbed some day when Burgess was the guard, provided only that they could be opened. The next step was to get impressions and fabricate false keys. A new accomplice was now needed within the company's establishment, and Pierce looked about long before he found the right person. At last he decided to enlist one Tester, a clerk in the traffic department, whom he thought would prove a likely tool. The four waited patiently for their opportunity, which came when the safes were sent to Chubbs' to be repaired; and Chubbs sent them back, but only with one key, in such a way that Tester had possession of this key for a time. He lent it to Agar for a brief space, who promptly took an impression on wax. But the safes had a double lock; the difficulty was to get a copy of the second key. This was at length effected by Agar and Pierce. After hanging about the Folkestone office for some time, they saw at last that the key was kept in a certain cupboard. Still watching and waiting for the first chance, they seized it when the clerks left the office empty for a moment. Pierce boldly stepped in, found the cupboard unlocked; he removed the key, handed it to Agar outside, who quickly took the wax impression, handed it back to Pierce; Pierce replaced it, left the office, and the thing was done.

After this nothing remained but to wait for some occasion when the amount transmitted would be sufficient to justify the risks of robbery. It was Tester's business, who had access to the railway company's books, to watch for this. Meanwhile the others completed their preparations with the utmost care. A weight of shot was bought and stowed in carpet bags ready to replace exactly the abstracted gold. Courier bags were bought to carry the "stuff" slung over the shoulders; and last, but not least, Agar frequently travelled up and down the line to test the false keys he had manufactured with Pierce's assistance. Burgess admitted him into the guard's van, where he fitted and filed the keys till they worked easily and satisfactorily in the locks of the safe. One night Tester whispered to Agar and Pierce, "All right," as they cautiously lounged about London Bridge. The thieves took first-class tickets, handed their bags full of shot to the porters, who placed them in the guard's van. Just as the train was starting Agar slipped into the van with Burgess, and Pierce got into a first-class carriage. Agar at once got to work on the first safe, opened it, took out and broke into the bullion box, removed the gold, substituted the shot from a carpet bag, re-fastened and re-sealed the bullion box, and replaced it in the safe. At Redhill Tester met the train and relieved the thieves of a portion of the stolen gold. At the same station Pierce joined Agar in the guard's van, and there were now three to carry on the robbery. The two remaining safes were attacked and nearly entirely despoiled in the same way as the first, and the contents transferred to the courier bags. The train was now approaching Folkestone, and Agar and Pierce hid themselves in a dark part of the van. At that station the safes were given out, heavy with shot, not gold; the thieves went on to Dover, and by-and-by, with Ostend tickets previously procured, returned to London without mishap, and by degrees disposed of much of the stolen gold.

The theft was discovered at Boulogne, when the boxes were found not to weigh exactly what they ought. But no clue was obtained to the thieves, and the theft might have remained a mystery but for the subsequent bad faith of Pierce to his accomplice Agar. The latter was ere long arrested on a charge of uttering forged cheques, convicted, and sentenced to transportation for life. When he knew that he could not escape his fate, he handed over to Pierce a sum of £3000, his own, whether rightly or wrongly acquired never came out, together with the unrealized part of the bullion, amounting in all to some £15,000, and begged his accomplice to invest it as a settlement on a woman named Kay, by whom he had had a child. Pierce made Kay only a few small payments, then appropriated the rest of the money. Kay, who had been living with Agar at the time of the bullion robbery, went to the police in great fury and distress, and disclosed all she knew of the affair. Agar too, in Newgate, heard how Pierce had treated him, and at once readily turned approver. As the evidence he gave incriminated Pierce, Burgess, and Tester, all three were arrested and committed to Newgate for trial. The whole strange story, the long incubation and the elaborate accomplishment of the plot, came out at the Old Bailey, and was acknowledged to be one of the most extraordinary on record.

Scarcely had the conviction of these daring and astute thieves been assured, than another gigantic fraud was brought to light. The series of boldly-conceived and cleverly-executed forgeries in which James Townshend Saward, commonly called "Jem the Penman," was the prime mover, has probably no parallel in the annals of crime. Saward himself is a striking and in some respects an unique figure in criminal history. A man of birth and education, a member of the bar, and of acknowledged legal attainments, his proclivities were all downward. Instead of following an honourable profession, he preferred to turn his great natural talents and ready wits to the most nefarious practices. He was known to the whole criminal fraternity as a high-class receiver of stolen goods, a negotiator more especially of stolen paper, cheques and bills, of which he made a particular use. He dealt too in the precious metals, when they had been improperly acquired, and it was to him that Agar, Pierce, and the rest applied when seeking to dispose of their stolen bullion. But Saward's operations were mainly directed to the fabrication and uttering of forged cheques. His method was comprehensive and deeply laid. Burglars brought him the cheques they stole from houses, thieves what they got in pocket-books. Cheques blank and cancelled were his stock-in-trade. The former he filled up by exact imitation of the latter, signature and all. When he could get nothing but the blank cheque, he set in motion all sorts of schemes for obtaining signatures, such as commencing sham actions, and addressing formal applications, merely for the reply. One stroke of luck which he turned to great account was the return from transportation of an old "pal" and confederate, who brought with him some bills of exchange.

Saward's method of negotiating the cheques was equally well planned. Like his great predecessor Old Patch,[118] he never went to a bank himself, nor did any of his accomplices. The bearer of the cheque was always innocent and ignorant of the fraudulent nature of the document he presented. In order to obtain messengers of this sort, Saward answered advertisements of persons seeking employment, and when these presented themselves, intrusted them as a beginning with the duty of cashing cheques. A confederate followed the emissary closely, not only to insure fair play and the surrender of the proceeds if the cheque was cashed, but to give timely notice if it was not, so that Saward and the rest might make themselves scarce. As each transaction was carried out from a different address, and a different messenger always employed, the forgers always escaped detection. But fate overtook two of the gang, partly through their own carelessness, when transferring their operations to Yarmouth. One named Hardwicke assumed the name of Ralph, and, to obtain commercial credit in Yarmouth, paid in £250 to a Yarmouth bank as coming from a Mr. Whitney. He forgot to add that it was to be placed to Ralph's credit, and when he called as Ralph, he was told it was only at Mr. Whitney's disposal, and that it could be paid to no one else. Hardwicke, or "Ralph," appealed to Saward in his difficulty, and that clever schemer sent an elaborate letter of instructions how to ask for the money. But while Hardwicke was in communication with Saward, the bank was in communication with London, and the circumstances were deemed sufficiently suspicious to warrant the arrest of the gentlemen at Yarmouth on a charge of forgery and conspiracy.

Saward's letter to Hardwicke fell into the hands of the police and compromised him. While Hardwicke and Atwell were in

Newgate awaiting trial, active search was made for Saward, who was at length taken in a coffee-shop near Oxford Street, under the name of Hopkins. He resisted at first, and denied his identity, but on being searched, two blank cheques of the London and Westminster Bank were found in his pocket. He then confessed that he was the redoubtable Jem Saward, or Jem the Penman, and was conveyed to a police-court, and thence to Newgate. At his trial Atwell and Hardwicke, two of his chief allies and accomplices, turned approvers, and the whole scheme of systematic forgery was laid bare. The evidence was corroborated by that of many of the victims who had acted as messengers, and others who swore to the meetings of the conspirators and their movements. Saward was found guilty, and the judge, in passing sentence on him of transportation for life, expressed deep regret that "the ingenuity, skill, and talent, which had received so perverted and mistaken direction, had not been guided by a sense of virtue, and directed to more honourable and useful pursuits." The proceeds of these forgeries amounted, it was said, to some thousands per annum. Saward spent all his share at low gaming houses, and in all manner of debaucheries. He was in person a short, square-built man of gentlemanly address, sharp and shrewd in conversation and manner. He was fifty-eight at the time of his conviction, and had therefore enjoyed a long innings.

LATER RECORDS

L atest cases of escape—Charles Thomas White—John Williams—Henry Williams—Other attempts frustrated—Bell, Brown, and Barry escape together—Krapps the sailor—The last case on record—Suicides—Latest executions—Some account of Calcraft and Marwood—Public executions continue, but much reprehended—The crowd at the 'Flowery Land' executions—Prices paid for seats—The same at Müller's—'Times'' account of that execution—Efforts to make executions private in gaols—Royal commission—Mr. Hibbert's bill—- The Fenian Barrett's, last public execution at Newgate—First private one, that of Alexander Mackay—Private executions not popular with Newgate officials—Some account, by them, of the demeanour of murderers—Wainwright—Catherine Wilson—Kate Webster.

THE old notion always prevailed that Newgate was impregnable, so to speak, from within, and that none of its inmates could hope to escape from its secure precincts. Yet the gaol, in spite of its fortress-like aspect, was by no means really safe. Year after year prisoners determined to get free, and occasionally succeeded in their efforts. The inspectors' reports mention many cases of evasion accomplished. There were others less successful. Charles Thomas White, awaiting execution for arson, made a desperate effort to escape from Newgate in 1827. He had friends and auxiliaries inside the gaol and out. The cell he occupied was near the outer wall, and had he but been able to remove its iron bars, he might have descended into Newgate Street by means of a rope ladder. The ladder was actually made, of black sewing-thread firmly and closely interwoven. But White could not remove the bars; the instruments needed for the purpose never reached him. It was noticed that he was most anxious to receive a pair of shoes for which he had asked, and when they arrived they were closely examined. Sewn in between the upper and lower leathers several spring saws were found, which would have easily cut through any bars. White, when taxed with his attempt, admitted that the accusation was true, and spoke "with pride and satisfaction of the practicability of his scheme."

There is an attempt at escape mentioned in Mr. Wakefield's book, which might have been an intended suicide. John Williams, a young fellow only twenty-three years of age, awaited execution in 1827 for stealing in a dwelling-house. On the very morning on which he was to suffer he eluded the vigilance, such as it was, of his officers, and climbed up the pipe of a cistern in the corner of the press yard; some thought with the idea of drowning himself. He never reached the cistern, but fell back into the yard, injuring his legs severely. Although his execution was imminent, a surgeon attended to his wounds, and he was carried more dead than alive to the scaffold. A harrowing scene followed; the wounds broke open and bled profusely while the last dread penalty was being performed, to the manifest excitement and indignation of the crowd.

A more daring and skilful escape was effected in 1836 by the chimney-sweep Henry Williams, who, while detained in the press-yard as a capital convict, under sentence of death for burglary, managed to get away in the very same spot where his namesake had nine years before so miserably failed. Escape seemed absolutely hopeless, and would certainly have been impossible to any one less nimble than a chimney-sweep, trained under the old system to ascend the most intricate flues. Even after Williams had got out, persons were disposed to disbelieve that the escape had been accomplished in the manner indicated; they preferred to credit it to carelessness or collusion from officers of the gaol. Yet from the circumstantial account given by Williams after recapture, there can be little doubt that he got away as will be described. Williams as a capital convict was lodged in the press-yard or condemned ward. He had access to the airing yard, and there was for hours no kind of supervision. In one corner of the airing yard stood a cistern at some height from the ground; the wall beneath and above it was "rusticated," in other words, the granite surface had become roughened, and offered a sort of foothold. About fifty feet from the ground level, and above the cistern, a revolving chevaux-de-frise of iron was fixed, with only a short interval between it and the wall, supported by a horizontal iron railing with upright points; in the wall above the chevaux-de-frise projected a series of iron spikes sharp enough to forbid further ascent. Williams surveyed these formidable obstacles to evasion, and calmly proceeded to surmount them. His first task was to gain the top of the cistern; this he effected by keeping his back to one side of the angle, and working with his hands behind him, while he used his bare feet like claws upon the other side of the wall angle. The condition of the stone surface just mentioned assisted him in this, and he managed to get beyond the cistern to the railing below the chevaux-de-frise. The least slip now would have been fatal to him. But he could not thrust his body in through the narrow space left by the chevaux-de-frise, and was compelled to work along the railing round three-quarters of the square of the yard, and at length reached a point opposite the top of the building containing the condemned wards. This had been a perilous and painful task; the spikes of the railing penetrated his flesh and made progression slow and difficult. But the worst part of the business was to jump from this irksome foothold of the iron grating on to the top of the building just mentioned, a distance of eight or nine feet. He had here completed his ascent. His next job was to descend outside Newgate. Clambering along the roof, he passed to the top of the ordinary's residence, hoping to find an open sky-light by which he might enter and so work downstairs. If the worst came to the worst, he intended to have gone down some chimney, as he had often done before in the way of business. But he did not like the risk of entering a room by the fireplace, and the chances of detection it offered.

He traversed vainly all the roofs in Newgate Street, running a great risk of discovery as he passed by a lot of workmen at Tyler's manufactory in Warwick Square, which had formerly been the College of Physicians. As his coat was an incumbrance, he left it on the top of the third house in Newgate Street, and thus in shirt-sleeves, barefoot and bareheaded, he worked along to the roofs in Warwick Lane. Here he came upon a woman on the leads hanging out clothes to dry. Williams concealed himself behind a chimney till she had re-entered her garret, and then following her down a step ladder into the house, told his story, appealed to and won her compassion. She suffered him to pass downstairs. Below he met another woman and a girl, both of whom were terrified at his appearance, but when he explained that he was running away from the gallows they left him the road clear. To walk out into the street was an easy affair, and he was now free, with one and fourpence in his pocket and a shirt and trousers for all his clothing. Denied admission everywhere as a ragged, half-naked beggar, he tramped across

London Bridge to Wandsworth, where he refreshed himself with a pint of strong ale, the first sustenance he had taken since his escape, and continued his march to Kingston, where he slept soundly under a hedge till next morning. Entering a town, he obtained employment at once as a chimney-sweep from a widow woman, who gave him "bub and grub," or food and one-and-sixpence, for every nine days' work. Dissatisfied with this remuneration, he again took to the road, and tramped into Hampshire, where he presently committed a burglary at Lymington, was caught, and lodged in Winchester Gaol. Mr. Cope, the governor of Newgate, having been communicated with, proceeded to Winchester, where he at once identified Williams.

The success, although very short-lived, which attended him, no doubt inspired other inmates of Newgate to follow his example. It was for some time after this a constant practice to go up the chimneys in the hopes of escaping by the flue. Even then, however, irons across barred the ascent after a certain distance, and in no one case did a fugitive get clear away. A man named Lears, under sentence of transportation for an attempt at murder on board ship, got up part of the way, but had to come down again covered with soot and filth just as the officers entered the ward. Lears was rewarded by being obliged to wear cross irons on his legs, a punishment rarely inflicted in Newgate, and probably one of the few cases of a recurrence, but under proper safeguards and limitations, to the old system of chains. On another occasion Mr. Cope the governor came in and missed a man. The ward was one short of its number. What had become of the fellow? No one would answer. It was summer-time, and the grate was empty, but the governor promptly ordered a fire to be lighted. The effect was nearly instantaneous; the fugitive, uncomfortably ensconced in the flue, came down of his own accord, like Colonel Colt's racoon. After this great iron guards, just as are to be seen in lunatic asylums, were fixed over the fireplaces, and the prisoners had no longer access to the chimneys.

Among the escapes still remembered was one in 1849, accomplished by a man who had been employed working at the roof of the chapel on the female side. He was engaged in whitewashing and cleaning; the officer who had him in charge left him on the stairs leading to the gallery. Taking advantage of being unobserved, he got out through the roof on to the leads, and travelled along them towards No. 1, Newgate Street. This was a public-house. He stepped in at a garret window, coolly walked downstairs, and entered the bar. They asked him how he had cut his hand, which was bleeding, and he said he had done it while working up on the roof. No further notice was taken of him; no one seemingly suspected that he was a prisoner, and he was suffered to walk off without let or hindrance.

In 1853 three men escaped in company from one of the wards in the middle yard. They were penal servitude men, their names Bell, Brown, and Barry, and they were awaiting transfer to Leicester, which with Wakefield was utilized as a receptacle for convicts not going to Western Australia, or any of the new establishments at home, at Portland, Dartmoor, or elsewhere. These men managed to cut a hole in the ceiling of the ward near the iron cage[119] on the landing, and so got access to the roof. At that time rope mats were still used as beds. One of the three, shamming ill, remained all day in his ward, where he employed himself unravelling the rope from the sleeping-mats. By evening he manufactured a good long length, and after all was quiet the three got on to the roof through the hole, and so on to Tyler's manufactory close by, whence they let themselves down into the street by the rope. These men were all in prison dress at the time of their escape, but one of their number, Bell, sent back his clothes a few days later by parcel's delivery, with a civil note to the governor, saying he had no further use for them. All three fugitives were recaptured, Brown almost at once; then Barry, who was taken at the East End in a public-house where he had arranged to meet a pal. The Newgate officers obtained information of this, and went to the spot, where they effected the capture, but not till they had had an exciting chase down the street. The third, Bell, remained longest at large. He too was run into at a lodging in the Kingsland Road. The officers dropped on to him while he was still in bed, but as they came upstairs he jumped up and hid in a cupboard. All three after recapture passed on, as originally intended, to Leicester, where they did their "bit"[120] and were released; but only to be taken soon afterwards for a fresh offence, and again pass through Newgate with sentences of penal servitude.

A later case was still more remarkable, as it was effected after the alteration of the prison and its reconstruction on the newest lines. A sailor, Krapps by name, occupied one of the upper cells in the new block. The doors, through incomplete knowledge of prison needs, were not, as now, sheeted with iron. The prisoner had nothing to deal with but wooden panels, and by dint of cutting and chopping he got both the lower panels out. Through the aperture he crept out on to the landing at the dead of night, and so down into the central space of the building. Under superior orders all the doors and gates of this block were left open at night, to allow the night watchman to pass freely to all parts. This was considered safer than intrusting him with keys. Krapps walked at once into the yard and across to the female side, where he found some of the washing still hanging out to dry. He made a strong rope with several of the sheets; then, returning to the male yard, got hold of the step ladder used in lighting the gas, and which under our more careful supervision would have been, as now-a-days, chained up. Cutting the cord which fastened the two legs of the step ladder, he opened them out and made one long length; with this, placed against the wall near the chevaux-de-frise, he made an escalade. The top of the wall was gained without difficulty. Along this Krapps crawled, and then dropped down on to the cook-house. He now put in requisition the rope made of the sheets, and with its help lowered himself into the street. Down below were market-carts waiting for daylight, and among them Krapps found a refuge and friends. The first intimation of his escape was afforded by the police, who informed the prison authorities next day that a rope was hanging down from the cook-house roof. Nothing more was heard of Krapps. The curious thing in his case was that his offence was a trifling one; he was still untried, but would almost certainly have escaped with a minor penalty, say of three or four months' imprisonment. There is, however, no explanation of the motives which prompt prisoners to attempt escapes. Cases well authenticated have been known of men who had all but completed their sentences, and for whom the prison gates would open within a few days, who yet faced extraordinary risks to advance their enlargement by only a few hours. On the other hand, at the great convict establishments, such is the moral restraint of a systematic discipline, that numbers of men, "lifers," and others with ten, fourteen, or twenty years to do, can be trusted to work out of doors without bolts and bars at a distance from the prison.

The last escape from Newgate was only three years ago, and occurred just before the final closing of the prison. No report of it was made public, as the man was almost immediately recaptured. He was at work under the supervision of the artisan warder of the prison, who permitted him to go up on to the roof of the old wards, in order to throw water for flushing purposes down a shoot. He was out of sight while so employed, and remained so long absent that the warder, becoming uneasy, went in search of him. He had disappeared. Encouraged by the shouts and signals of some workmen employed on a building outside, the prisoner made one of the most marvellous jumps on record, from the building he was on to a distant wall, with a drop of sixty feet between. Then he ran along the coping of the wall towards its angle with Tyler's manufactory, and dropped down on to the gridiron below. This was not strong enough to carry him, and he fell through.

Suicides and executions were, however, always the most effectual methods of making exit from durance. Suicides at Newgate were numerous enough, but they seldom possessed any novel or unusual features; prison suicides seldom do, except as regards ingenuity and determination. Only great resolution indeed, persisted in to the bitter end, would make death a certainty, so limited and imperfect are the means generally available. When a bit of rope carefully secreted, braces, shoe-strings, shirt torn into strips are the only instruments, and a bar or small hook at no elevation affords the only drop, strangulation would seldom supervene but for the resolution of the miserable *felo de se*. One curious instance of a suicide carried out under the most adverse and extraordinary circumstances may be quoted. It was that of a "Long Firm" swindler, by name Johnson, who contrived to hang himself from a hammock hook only eighteen inches from the ground. The noose was one of his hammock straps, which he buckled round his throat. Having carefully spread out a blanket on the floor just below the hammock as it lay suspended, he fastened one end of the strap above mentioned to the hook, and then fell down. He might have saved himself at any moment by merely extending an arm; but he lay there patiently till death supervened. When discovered next morning, quite dead, it was found that the strap actually did not touch his throat; three fingers might have been inserted between it and the flesh; the pressure was all on the arteries behind the ears, and surgical opinion stated that the stoppage of circulation was the cause of death. Probably dissolution came as easily and almost without pain.

A laudable desire to invest executions with more and more solemnity and decorum gained ground as they became more rare. As more humane principles were introduced into prison management, greater attention was paid to the capital convicts, and the horrors of their situation while awaiting sentence were as far as possible mitigated and toned down. But there was little improvement in the ceremony itself. There were still untoward accidents occasionally at executions, and even the chief practitioner of recent times, Calcraft, was not always to be trusted to do his fell work efficiently.

Having mentioned Calcraft's name, I may be permitted to digress for a moment to give a few particulars concerning the last officially appointed hangman of the city of London. After Calcraft's resignation no successor was really appointed. Marwood, whose name is so familiar with the present generation, had no official status, and was merely an operator selected by the Corporation, and who, on the strength of it, contracted with sheriffs and conveners to work by the job. But Calcraft regularly succeeded Foxen, who followed Botting, and Dennis, the actor in the 1780 riots. Calcraft was born at Baddow, in Essex, in 1800; he was a shoemaker by trade, and settled in London after his marriage in 1825. The story goes, that about 1828 his attention was drawn early one morning to a man who leant against a lamp-post in Finsbury Square, coughing violently. Calcraft, who, in spite of the dreadful calling he subsequently followed, was always reputed a kindly man, invited the man with the cough to enter a neighbouring house and try a little peppermint for it. The other accepted, and they got into conversation. He told Calcraft that he was Foxen the executioner, and that he was that moment on his way to Newgate to hang a man, but that his cough was getting so much the master of him that he feared he would not be able to carry on his duties much longer. "I have no idea who the sheriffs will get to do the work after me," said Foxen, adding that his assistant, Tom Cheshire, was given to drink, and not to be trusted. "I think I could do that sort of job," said Calcraft, on the spur of the moment. Foxen asked him his name and address, and went away. Calcraft thought no more of what had occurred till the next sessions at the Old Bailey, when the sheriffs sent for him, and offered him the post of executioner for the city of London and Middlesex. He accepted, having at first Tom Cheshire as his assistant, then for a time, when Cheshire was dismissed for drunkenness, a man named Osborne. After that he worked alone.

I cannot find that Calcraft was sworn in when appointed, or any exact information when the old forbidding ceremony ceased to be practised. It was customary to make the executioner take the Bible in his hand, and swear solemnly that he would despatch every criminal condemned to die, without favouring father or mother or any other relation or friend. When he had taken the oath he was dismissed with the words, "Get thee hence, wretch!"

Calcraft's emoluments were a guinea per week, and an extra guinea for every execution. He got besides half-a-crown for every man he flogged, and an allowance to provide cats or birch rods. For acting as executioner of Horsemonger Lane Gaol he received a retaining fee of £5 5s., with the usual guinea for each job; he was also at liberty to engage himself in the country, where he demanded and was paid £10 on each occasion. It was not always easy to get a hangman so cheap, as I have already indicated on a previous page. The onus and responsibility of carrying out the sentence is personal to the sheriff. A good story is told illustrating this. Some wags in Scotland seized Calcraft and kept him in durance the night before the execution. Meanwhile the convener or sheriff was in despair, expecting that, failing the executioner, he would have to do the job himself. But, fortunately for him, just at the last moment Calcraft was set free.

Calcraft's salary was more than the proverbial "thirteenpence halfpenny—hangman's wages." The origin of this expression dates, it is said, from the time when the Scottish mark, a silver coin bearing the same relation to the Scottish pound that an English shilling does to an English pound, was made to pass current in England. The mark was valued at thirteenpence halfpenny, or rather more than the shilling, which from time immemorial had been the hangman's wages. That very ancient perquisite the convict's clothes was never claimed by Calcraft, and it may be doubted whether he was entitled to it. On one particular occasion, however, he got them. A gentleman whose sins brought him to the gallows at Maidstone wished to do Calcraft a good turn, and sent to his London tailor for a complete new suit, in which he appeared at his execution. He expressly bequeathed them to Calcraft, who was graciously pleased to accept them. On another occasion an importunate person begged Calcraft eagerly to claim his right to the clothes, and give them to him. Calcraft consented, got and bestowed the clothes, only to find that the person he had obliged exhibited them publicly. It may be added that of late years the clothes in which a convict has suffered are invariably burnt. Capital convicts go to the gallows in their own clothing, and not in prison dress, unless the former is quite unfit to be worn.

Calcraft shared the odium which his office, not strangely, has always inspired. But he was admitted into the gaol, which his predecessors were not, and who were paid their wages over the gate to obviate the necessity for letting them enter. To this curious etiquette was due the appointment of an official whose office has long since disappeared, "the yeoman of the halter," whose business it was to provide the rope and do the pinioning, and who was paid a fee of five shillings. They did not dislike

Calcraft, however, at Newgate. He was an illiterate, simple-minded man, who scarcely remembered what executions he had performed. He kept no record of them, and when asked questions, referred to the officers of the gaol. His nature must have been kindly. When he came to the prison for his wages his grand-children often accompanied him, affectionately clinging to his hands; and he owned a pet pony which would follow him about like a dog. In his own profession he was not unskilful, but he proceeded entirely by rule of thumb, leaving the result very much to chance and the strength of the rope. He was so much in favour of short drops that his immediate successor, Marwood, stigmatized him as a "short-drop" man; Marwood being, on the other hand, in favour of giving a man as much rope as possible. With Calcraft's method there were undoubtedly many failures, and it was a common custom for him to go below the gallows "just to steady their legs a little;" in other words, to add his weight to that of the hanging bodies. Marwood till latterly seemed to have done his work more effectually, and has been known to give as much as six feet fall. This generally produces instantaneous death, although cases where complete fracture of the spinal cord occurred are said to be rare.

Calcraft served the city of London till 1874, when he was pensioned at the rate of twenty-five shillings per week. The last execution at which he acted was that of Godwin, on the 25th May, 1874.

Marwood, who succeeded him, and who died while these sheets were in the press, was a Lincolnshire man, a native of Horncastle, who first took to the work from predilection, and the idea of being useful in his generation, as he himself assured the writer of these pages. Until the time of his death he kept a small shop close to the church in Horncastle. Over the door, in gilt letters, were the words "Crown Office"; in the window was a pile of official envelopes, ostentatiously displayed, while round about were shoe-strings, boot-laces, and lasts. Marwood, strange to say, followed the same trade as Calcraft. Marwood was proud of his calling, and when questioned as to whether his process was satisfactory, replied that he heard "no complaints." The strange competition amongst hundreds to succeed Marwood is a strange fact too recently before the public to need mention here. It may, however, be remarked that the wisdom of appointing any regular hangman is very open to question, and must be strongly deprecated on moral grounds, as tending to the utter degradation of one individual. Possibly such changes may be introduced into the method of execution that the ceremony may be made more mechanical, thus rendering the personal intervention of a skilled functionary unnecessary.

Executions long continued to be in public, in spite of remonstrance and reprobation. The old prejudices, such as that which enlisted Dr. Johnson on the side of the Tyburn procession, still lingered and prevented any change. It was thought that capital punishment would lose its deterrent effect if it ceased to be public, and the *raison d'être* of the penalty, which in principle so many opposed, would be gone. This line of argument prevailed over the manifest horrors of the spectacle. These increased as time passed. The graphic and terrible account given by Charles Dickens of the awful scene before Horsemonger Lane Gaol, at the execution of the Mannings, has already been quoted. Again, the concourse of people collected in front of Newgate to witness the execution, simultaneously, of the five pirates, part of the mutinous crew of the 'Flowery Land,' was greater than on any previous occasion. It was a callous, careless crowd of coarse-minded, semi-brutalized folk, who came to enjoy themselves. Few, if any, showed any feeling of terror, none were impressed with the solemnity, or realized the warning which the sight conveyed. The upturned faces of the eager spectators resembled those of the 'gods' at Drury Lane on Boxing Night; the crowd had come to witness a popular and gratuitous public performance—better than a prize-fight or a play. No notion that they were assisting at a vindication of the law filled the minds of those present with dread. On the contrary, the prevailing sentiment was one of satisfaction at the success of the spectacle. The remarks heard amongst the crowd were of coarse approval. "S'help me, ain't it fine?" one costermonger was heard to exclaim to his companion. "Five of them, all darkies in a row!" The reply evinced equal satisfaction, and the speaker, with a profane oath, declared that he would like to act as Jack Ketch to the whole lot.

To the disgrace of the better-educated and better-bred public, executions could still command the attendance of curious aristocrats from the West End. At Müller's execution there was great competition for front seats, and the windows of the opposite houses, which commanded a good view, as usual fetched high prices. As much as £25 was paid for a first-floor front on this occasion. Never, indeed, had an execution been more generally patronized. This is proved by contemporary accounts, especially one graphic and realistic article which appeared in the 'Times,' and which contributed in no small degree to the introduction of private executions. A great crowd was expected, and a great crowd came. They collected over night in the bright light of a November moon. "There were well-dressed and ill-dressed, old men and lads, women and girls." Rain fell heavily at intervals, but did not thin the concourse. "Till three o'clock it was one long revelry of songs and laughter, shouting, and often quarrelling, though, to do them mere justice, there was at least till then a half-drunken ribald gaiety among the crowd that made them all akin." There were preachers among the crowd, but they could not get a patient hearing. Then one struck up the hymn of the Promised Land, and the refrain was at once taken up with a mighty chorus—

"Oh, my!
Think I've got to die."

This was presently superseded by a fresh catch—
"Müller, Müller,
He's the man";

till a diversion was created by the appearance of the gallows, which was received with continuous yells. As day broke the character of the crowd was betrayed. There were but few women, except of the most degraded sort; the men were mostly young men—"sharpers, thieves, gamblers, betting men, the outsiders of the boxing ring, bricklayers' labourers, dock workmen, German artisans and sugar-bakers, ... with the rakings of cheap singing-halls and billiard-rooms, the fast young men of London. But all, whether young or old, men or women, seemed to know nothing, feel nothing, to have no object but the gallows, and to laugh, curse, or shout, as in this heaving and struggling forward they gained or lost in their strong efforts to get nearer where Müller was to die." The actual execution made some impression. The crowd was for a moment awed and stilled by the quiet rapid passage from life to death! But before "the slight slow vibrations of the body had well ended, robbery and violence, loud laughing, oaths, fighting, obscene conduct, and still more filthy language reigned round the gallows far and near. Such too the scene remained with little change or respite till the old hangman (Calcraft) slunk again along the drop, amid hisses and sneering inquiries of what he had had to drink that morning. He, after failing once to cut the rope, made a second attempt more successfully, and the body of Müller disappeared from view."[121]

It was preposterous to claim for such a scene as this that it conveyed any great moral lesson, or had any deterring influence. Numbers of humane and thoughtful persons had long been convinced of this. Already the urgent necessity for abolishing public executions had been brought before the House of Commons by Mr. Hibbert, and the question, as part of the whole subject of capital punishment, had been referred to a royal commission in January 1864. Full evidence was taken on all points, and on that regarding public executions there was a great preponderance of opinion towards their abolition, yet the witnesses were not unanimous. Some of the judges would have retained the public spectacle; the ordinary of Newgate was not certain that public executions were not the best. Another distinguished witness feared that any secrecy in the treatment of the condemned would invest them with a new and greater interest, which was much to be deprecated. Foreign witnesses, too, were in favour of publicity. On the other hand, Lords Cranworth and Wensleydale recommended private executions; so did Mr. Spencer Walpole, M.P. Sir George Grey thought there was a growing feeling in favour of executions within the prison precincts. Colonel (now Sir Edmund) Henderson was strongly in favour of them, based on his experience of them in Western Australia. He not only thought them likely to be more deterrent, but believed that a public ceremony destroyed the whole value of an execution. Other officials, great lawyers, governors of prisons, and chaplains supported this view. The only doubts expressed were as to the sufficiency of the safeguards, as to the certainty of death and its subsequent publication. But these, it was thought, might be provided by the admission of the press and the holding of a coroner's inquest.

Duly impressed with the weight of evidence in favour of abolition, the commission recommended that death sentences should be carried out within the gaol, "under such regulations as might be considered necessary to prevent abuse, and satisfy the public that the law had been complied with." But it is curious to note that there were several dissentients among the commissioners to this paragraph of the report. The judge of the Admiralty Court, the Right Hon. Stephen Lushington, the Right Hon. James Moncrieff, Lord Advocate, Mr. Charles Neate, Mr. William Ewart, and last, but not least, Mr. John Bright declared that they were not prepared to agree to the resolution respecting private executions. Nevertheless, in the very next session a bill was introduced by Mr. Hibbert, M.P., and accepted by the Government, providing for the future carrying out of executions within prisons. It was read for the first time in March 1866, but did not become law till 1868.

The last public execution in front of Newgate was that of the Fenian Michael Barrett, who was convicted of complicity in the Clerkenwell explosion, intended to effect the release of Burke and Casey from Clerkenwell prison, by which many persons lost their lives. Unusual precautions were taken upon this occasion, as some fresh outrage was apprehended. There was no interference with the crowd, which collected as usual, although not to the customary extent. But Newgate and its neighbourhood was carefully held by the police, both city and metropolitan. In the houses opposite the prison numbers of detectives mixed with the spectators; inside the gaol was Colonel Frazer, the chief commissioner of the city police, and at no great distance, although in the background, troops were held in readiness to act if required. Everything passed off quite quietly, however, and Calcraft, who had been threatened with summary retribution if he executed Barrett, carried out the sentence without mishap. The sufferer was stolid and reticent to the last.

The first private execution under the new law took place within the precincts of Maidstone Gaol. The sufferer was a porter on the London, Chatham, and Dover railway, sentenced to death for shooting the station-master at Dover. The ceremony, which was witnessed by only a few officials and representatives of the press, was performed with the utmost decency and decorum. The fact that the execution was to take place within the privacy of the gloomy walls, a fact duly advertised as completed by the hoisting of the black flag over the gaol, had undoubtedly a solemn, impressive effect upon those outside. The same was realized in the first private execution within Newgate, that of Alexander Mackay, who murdered his mistress at Norton Folgate by beating her with a rolling-pin and furnace-rake, and who expiated his crime on the 8th September, 1868. A more marked change from the old scene can hardly be conceived. Instead of the roar of the brutalized crowd, the officials spoke in whispers; there was but little moving to and fro. Almost absolute silence prevailed until the great bell began to toll its deep note, and broke the stillness with its regular and monotonous clangour, and the ordinary, in a voice trembling with emotion, read the burial service aloud. Mackay's fortitude, which had been great, broke down at the supreme moment before the horror of the stillness, the awful impressiveness of the scene in which he was the principal actor. No time was lost in carrying out the dread ceremony; but it was not completed without some of the officials turning sick, and the moment it was over, all who could were glad to escape from the last act of the ghastly drama at which they had assisted.

Private executions at their first introduction were not popular with the Newgate officials, and for intelligible reasons. The change added greatly to the responsibilities of the governor and his subordinates. Hitherto the public had seemed to assist at the ceremony; the moment too that the condemned man had passed through the debtors' door on to the scaffold the prison had done with him, and the great outside world shared in the completion of the sacrifice. This feeling was the stronger because all the ghastly paraphernalia, the gallows itself and the process of erecting and removing it, rested with the city architect, and not with the prison officials. Moreover, after the execution, under the old system, the latter had only to receive the body for burial after it had been cut down by the hangman, and placed decently in a shell by the workmen who removed the gallows. Under the new system the whole of the arrangements from first to last fell upon the officers. It was they who formed the chief part of the small select group of spectators; upon them devolved the painful duty of cutting down the body and preparing for the inquest. All that the hangman, whoever he may be, does under the new regime is to unhook the halter and remove the pinioning straps. The interment in a shell filled with quicklime in the passage-way leading to the Old Bailey is also a part of the duty of the prison officials. This strange burial-ground is one of the most ghastly of the remaining "sights" in Newgate. It was sometimes used as an exercising yard, and for the greater security of prisoners it is roofed in with iron bars which gives it, at least overhead, the aspect of a huge cage. Underfoot and upon the walls roughly cut into the stones, are single initial letters, the brief epitaphs of those who lie below. As this burial-ground leads to the adjacent Central Criminal Court, accused murderers, on going to and returning from trial, literally walked over what, in case of conviction, would be their own graves.

The older officers, with several of whom I have conversed, have thus had unusual opportunities of watching the demeanour of murderers both before trial and after sentence. All as a rule, unless poignant remorse has brought a desire to court their richly-merited retribution, are buoyed up with hope to the last. There is always the chance of a flaw in the indictment, of a missing witness, or extenuating circumstances. Even when in the condemned cell, with a shameful death within measurable distance, many cling still to life, expecting much from the intercession of friends or the humanitarianism of the age. All almost without exception sleep soundly at night, except the first after sentence, when the first shock of the verdict and the solemn notification of the impending blow keeps nearly all awake, or at least disturbs their night's rest. But the uneasiness soon wears off. The second night sleep comes readily, and is sound; many of the most abandoned murderers snore peacefully their eight hours, even on the night immediately preceding execution. All too have a fairly good appetite, and eat with relish, up to the last moment. A few go further, and are almost gluttonous. Giovanni Lanni, the Italian boy who murdered a Frenchwoman in the Haymarket, and was arrested on board ship just as he was about to leave the country, had a little spare cash, which he devoted entirely to the purchase of extra food. He ate constantly and voraciously after sentence, as though eager to cram as many meals as possible into the few hours still left him to live. Jeffrey, who murdered his own child, an infant of six, by hanging him in a cellar in Seven Dials, called for a roast duck directly he entered the condemned cell. The request was not granted, as the old custom of allowing capital convicts whatever they asked for in the way of food has not been the rule in Newgate. The diet of the condemned is the ordinary diet of the prison, but to which additions are sometimes made, chiefly of stimulants, if deemed necessary, by the medical officer of the gaol. The craving for tobacco which so dominates the habitual smoker often leads the convicted to plead hard for a last smoke. As a special favour Wainwright was allowed a cigar the night before execution, which he smoked in the prison yard, walking up and down with the governor, Mr. Sydney Smith.

Wainwright's demeanour was one of reckless effrontery steadily maintained to the last. His conversation turned always upon his influence over the weaker sex, and the extraordinary success he had achieved. No woman could resist him, he calmly assured Mr. Smith that night as they walked together, and he recounted his villanies one by one. His effrontery was only outdone by his cool contempt for the consolations of religion. The man who had made a pious life a cloak for his misdeeds, the once exemplary young man and indefatigable Sunday School teacher, went impenitent to the gallows. The only sign of feeling he showed was in asking to be allowed to choose the hymns on the Sunday the condemned sermon was preached in the prison chapel, and this was probably only that he might hear the singing of a lady with a magnificent voice who generally attended the prison services. During the singing of these hymns Wainwright fainted, but whether from real emotion or the desire to make a sensation was never exactly known. On the fatal morning he came gaily out of his cell, nodded pleasantly to the governor, who stood just opposite, and then walked briskly towards the execution shed, smiling as he went along. There was a smile on his face when it was last seen, and just as the terrible white cap was drawn over it. Wainwright's execution was within the gaol, but only nominally private. No less than sixty-seven persons were present, admitted by special permission of the sheriff. Rumour even went so far as to assert that among the spectators were several women, disguised in male habiliments; but the story was never substantiated, and we may hope that it rested only on the idle gossip of the day.

Many, like Wainwright, were calm and imperturbable throughout their trying ordeal. Catherine Wilson, the poisoner, [122] was reserved and reticent to the last, expressing no contrition, but also no fear—a tall, gaunt, repulsive-looking woman, who no more shrank from cowardly, secret crimes than from the penalty they entailed. Kate Webster, who was tried at the Central Criminal Court, and passed through Newgate, although she suffered at Wandsworth, is remembered at the former prison as a defiant, brutal creature who showed no remorse, but was subject to fits of ungovernable passion, when she broke out into language the most appalling. The man Marley[123] displayed fortitude of a less repulsive kind. He acknowledged his guilt from the first. When the sheriff offered him counsel for his defence, he declined, saying he wished to make none—"the witnesses for the prosecution spoke the truth." During the trial and after sentence he remained perfectly cool and collected. When visited one day in the condemned cell, just as St. Sepulchre's clock was striking, he looked up and said laughingly, "Go along, clock; come along, gallows." He tripped up the chapel-stairs to hear the condemned sermon, and came out with cheerful alacrity on the morning he was to die.

Some condemned convicts converse but little with the warders who have them unceasingly in charge. Others talk freely enough on various topics, but principally upon their own cases. When vanity is strongly developed there is the keen anxiety to hear what is being said about them outside. One was vexed to think that his victims had a finer funeral than he would have. The only subject another showed any interest in was the theatres and the new pieces that were being produced. A third, Christian Sattler, laughed and jested with the officers about "Jack Ketch," who, through the postponement of the execution, would lose his Christmas dinner. When they brought in the two watchers to relieve guard one night, Sattler said, "Two fresh men! May I speak to them? Yes! I must caution you," he went on to the warders, "not to go to sleep, or I shall be off through that little hole," pointing to an aperture for ventilating the cell. On the morning of execution he asked how far it was to the gallows, and was told it was quite close. "Then I shall not wear my coat," he cried; "Jack Ketch shall not have it," being under the erroneous impression that the convict's clothes were still the executioner's perquisite.

Often the convicts give way to despair. They are too closely watched to be allowed to do themselves much mischief, or suicides would probably be more frequent. But it is neither easy to obtain the instruments of self-destruction nor to elude the vigilance of their guard. The man, Bousfield, however, whose execution was so sadly bungled,[124] made a determined effort to burn himself to death by throwing himself bodily on to the fire in the condemned ward. He was promptly rescued from his perilous condition, but not before his face and hands were badly scorched. They were still much swollen when he was led out to execution. Miller, the Chelsea murderer, who packed his victim's body in a box, and tried to send it by parcels delivery, tried to kill himself, but ineffectively, by running his head against his cell wall. A few other cases of the kind have occurred, but they have been rare of late years, whether in Newgate or elsewhere.

NEWGATE NOTORIETIES

Latest records of crimes—Poisoning, revived and more terrible—Palmer's case—His trial at the Central Criminal Court, and demeanour in Newgate—His imitators—Dove—Dr. Smethurst—Catherine Wilson—Dr. Taylor's opinion that poisoning very prevalent—Piracy and murder—The 'Flowery Land'—Arrest of the mutineers—Their trial and sentence—Details of their behaviour while in Newgate—Murder of Mr. Briggs in a railway carriage—How brought home to Müller—Pursuit of murderer and his arrest in New York—Müller's conviction—His protest against justice of sentence—Confesses guilt when rope is actually round his neck—Christian Sattler murders a police Inspector—Latest frauds and robberies—The forgeries of Wagner, Bateman, and others—Principal forger, an aged man, Kerp, escapes arrest—Robbery of Bank of England bank-note paper at Tavistock—Reward offered—Arrests made, followed by expressions which lead to capture of whole gang—Buncher and Griffiths sentenced—Cummings acquitted: his delight—Cummings an adroit and inveterate coiner.

AS these records draw to a close, the crimes I chronicle

become so much more recent in date that they will be fresh in the memory of most of my readers. Nevertheless, in order to give completeness to the picture I have attempted to draw of crime in connection with Newgate, from first to last, I must make some mention, in this my penultimate chapter, of some of the most heinous offences of modern times.

The crime of poisoning has always been viewed with peculiar loathing and terror in this country. It will be remembered that as far back as the reign of Henry VIII. a new and most cruel penalty was devised for the punishment of the Bishop of Rochester's cook, who had poisoned his master and many of his dependents. Sir Thomas Overbury was undoubtedly poisoned by Lord Rochester in the reign of James I., and it is hinted that James himself nearly fell a victim to a nefarious attempt of the Duke of Buckingham. But secret poisoning on a wholesale scale such as was practised in Italy and France was happily never popularized in England. The well-known and lethal aqua Toffania, so called after its inventress, a Roman woman named Toffana, and which was so widely adopted by ladies anxious to get rid of their husbands, was never introduced into this country. Its admission was probably checked by the increased vigilance at the custom houses, the necessity for which was urged by Mr. Addison, when Secretary of State, in 1717. The cases of poisoning in the British calendars are rare, nor indeed was the guilt of the accused always clearly established. It is quite possible that Catherine Blandy, who poisoned her father at the instigation of her lover, was ignorant of the destructive character of the powders, probably arsenic, which she administered. Captain Donellan, who was convicted of poisoning his brother-in-law, Sir Theodosius Broughton, and executed for it, would probably have had the benefit in these days of the doubts raised at his trial. A third case, more especially interesting to us as having passed through Newgate, was that of Eliza Fenning, who was convicted of an attempt to poison a whole family by putting arsenic in the dumplings she had prepared for them. The charge rested entirely on circumstantial evidence, and as Fenning, although convicted and executed, protested her innocence in the most solemn manner to the last, the justice of the sentence was doubted at the time. Yet it was clearly proved that the dumplings contained arsenic, that she, and she alone, had made the dough, that arsenic was within her reach in the house, that she had had a quarrel with her mistress, and that the latter with all others who tasted the dumplings were similarly attacked, although no one died.

The crime of poisoning is essentially one which will be most prevalent in a high state of civilization, when the spread of scientific knowledge places nefarious means at the disposal of many, instead of limiting them, as in the days of the Borgias and Brinvilliers, to the specially informed and unscrupulously powerful few. The first intimation conveyed to society of the new terror which threatened it was in the arrest and arraignment of William Palmer, a medical practitioner, charged with doing to death persons who relied upon his professional skill. The case contained elements of much uncertainty, and yet it was so essential, in the interests and for the due protection of the public, that the fullest and fairest inquiry should be made, that the trial was transferred to the Central Criminal Court, under the authority of an Act passed on purpose, known as the Trial of Offences Act, and sometimes as Lord Campbell's Act. That the administration of justice should never be interfered with by local prejudice or local feeling is obviously of paramount importance, and the powers granted by this Act have been frequently put in practice since. The trial of Catherine Winsor, the baby farmer, was thus brought to the Central Criminal Court from Exeter assizes, and that of the Stauntons from Maidstone.

Palmer's trial caused the most intense excitement. The

direful suspicions which surrounded the case filled the whole country with uneasiness and misgiving, and the deepest anxiety was felt that the crime, if crime there had been, should be brought home to its perpetrator. The Central Criminal Court was crowded to suffocation. Great personages occupied seats upon the bench; the rest of the available space was allotted by ticket, to secure which the greatest influence was necessary. People came to stare at the supposed cold-blooded prisoner; with morbid curiosity to scan his features and watch his demeanour through the shifting, nicely-balanced phases of his protracted trial. Palmer, who was only thirty-one at the time of his trial, was in appearance short and stout, with a round head covered rather scantily with light sandy hair. His skin was extraordinarily fair, his cheeks fresh and ruddy; altogether his face, though commonplace, was not exactly ugly; there was certainly nothing in it which indicated cruel cunning or deliberate truculence. His features were not careworn, but rather set, and he looked older than his age. Throughout his trial he preserved an impassive countenance, but he clearly took a deep interest in all that passed. Although the strain lasted fourteen days, he showed no signs of exhaustion, either physical or mental. On returning to gaol each day he talked freely and without reserve to the warders in charge of him, chiefly on incidents in the day's proceedings. He was confident to the very last that it would be impossible to find him guilty; even after sentence, and until within a few hours of execution, he was buoyed up with the hope of reprieve. The conviction that he would escape had taken so firm a hold of him, that he steadily refused to confess his guilt, lest it should militate against his chances. In the condemned cell he frequently repeated, "I go to my death a murdered man." He made no distinct admissions even on the scaffold; but when the chaplain at the last moment exhorted him to confess, he made use of the remarkable words, "If it is necessary for my soul's sake to confess this murder,[125] I ought also to confess the others: I mean my wife and my brother's." Yet he was silent when specifically pressed to confess that he had killed his wife and his brother.

Palmer was ably defended, but the weight of evidence was clearly with the prosecution, led by Sir Alexander Cockburn, and public opinion at the termination of the trial coincided with the verdict of the jury. Originally a doctor in practice at Rugeley, in Staffordshire, he had gradually withdrawn from medicine, and devoted himself to the turf; but his sporting operations did not prosper, and he became a needy man, always driven to desperate straits for cash. To meet his liabilities, he raised large sums on forged bills of acceptance drawn upon his mother, a woman of some means, whose signature he counterfeited. In 1854 he owed a very large sum of money, but he was temporarily relieved by the death of his wife, whose life he had insured for £13,000. There is every reason to suppose that he poisoned his wife to obtain possession of this sum upon her death. His brother was supposed to have been his next victim, upon whose life he had also effected an insurance for another £13,000. The brother too died conveniently, but the life office took some exception to the manner of the death, and hesitated to disburse the funds claimed by Palmer. After this Palmer tried to get a new insurance on the life of a hanger-on, one Bates, but no office would accept it, no doubt greatly to Bates's longevity.

Meanwhile the bill discounters who held the forged acceptances, with other promissory notes, began to clamour for payment, and talk of issuing writs. Palmer, alive to the danger he ran of a prosecution for forgery, should the fraud he had committed be brought to light, sought about for a fresh victim to supply him with funds. He fixed upon a sporting friend, Mr. John Parsons Cook, who had been in luck at Shrewsbury races, both as a winner and a backer, whom he persuaded to go and stay at Rugeley in an hotel just opposite his own house. It was there that Cook was first taken ill with violent retchings and vomitings, all dating from visits of Palmer, who brought him medicines and food. Palmer's plan was to administer poison in quantities insufficient to cause death, but enough to produce illness which would account for death. For this purpose he gave, or there was the strongest presumption that he gave, antimony, which caused Cook's constant sickness. Quantities of antimony were found in the body after death. While Cook lay ill, Palmer in his name pocketed the proceeds of the Shrewsbury settling, and so got the money for which he was prepared to barter his soul. The last act now approached, and in order to avoid the detection of this last fraud, Palmer laid his plans for disposing of Cook. He decided to use strychnia, or the vegetable poison otherwise known as *nux vomica*; and one of the many links in the long chain of evidence was an entry in a book of Palmer's to the effect that "strychnia kills by causing tetanic fixing of the respiratory muscles."

The purchase by Palmer of strychnia was proved. The night he bought it, Cook, who had been taking certain pills under medical advice, not Palmer's, was seized with violent convulsions. He had swallowed his pills as usual, at least Palmer had administered them—whether the ordinary or his own pills will never be known, except as may be inferred from the results, which indicate that he had taken the latter. Cook recovered this time; it was probably Palmer's intention that he should recover, wishing to encourage the supposition that Cook was in a bad way. Next night Cook had a second and a more violent attack. That day Palmer had bought more strychnia, and had called in a fresh doctor. The second attack was fatal, and ended in Cook's death from tetanus. This tetanus, according to the prosecution, was produced by strychnia, and followed the administration of pills by Palmer prescribed nominally by the fresh doctor, for which Palmer had substituted his own. Cook's death was horrible—fearful paroxysms and cramps, ending in suffocation by the tetanic rigour which caught the muscles of the chest.

After Cook's death his stepfather, who was much attached to him, came to Rugeley. He was struck with the appearance of the corpse, which was not emaciated, as after a long disease ending in death; while the muscles of the fingers were tightly clenched, not open, as usual in a corpse. He said nothing, but began to feel uneasy when he found that Cook's betting-book was missing, and that Palmer put it forward that his friend had died greatly embarrassed, with bills to the amount of £4000 out in his name. Palmer too showed an indecent haste in preparing the body for interment, and in obtaining the usual certificate. After this the step-father insisted upon a post-mortem, which was conducted somewhat carelessly. The intestines were, however, preserved and sent for analysis, but it was proved that Palmer tried hard to get possession of the jar containing them, and even sought to upset the vehicle by which they were being conveyed a part of the way to London. The examination of the stomach betrayed the presence of antimony in large quantities, but no strychnia, and it was on the entire absence of the latter that the defence was principally based when Palmer was brought to trial. All the circumstances were so suspicious that he could not escape the criminal charge. He had already been arrested on a writ issued at the instance of the money-lenders, and an action had been commenced against Mrs. Palmer on her acceptances. It came out at once that these had been forged, and the whole affair at once took the ugliest complexion. A government prosecution was instituted, and Palmer was brought to Newgate for trial at the Central Criminal Court. There was not much reserve about him when there. He frequently declared before and during the trial that it would be impossible to find him guilty. He never actually said that he was not guilty, but he was confident he would not be convicted. He relied on the absence of the strychnia. But the chain of circumstantial evidence was strong enough to satisfy the jury, who agreed to their verdict in an hour. At the last moment Palmer tossed a bit of paper over to his counsel, on which he had written, "I think there will be a verdict of Not Guilty." Even after the death sentence had been passed upon him he clung to the hope that the Government would grant him a reprieve. To the last, therefore, he played the part of a man wrongfully convicted, and did not abandon hope even when the high sheriff had told him there was no possibility of a reprieve, and within a few hours of execution. He suffered at Stafford in front of the gaol.

Palmer speedily found imitators. Within a few weeks occurred the Leeds poisoning case, in which the murderer undoubtedly was inspired by the facts made public at Palmer's trial. Dove, a fiendish brute, found from the evidence in that case that he could kill his wife, whom he hated, with exquisite torture, and with a poison that would leave, as he thought, no trace. In the latter hope he was happily disappointed. But as this case is beyond my subject, I merely mention it as one of the group already referred to. Three years later came the case of Dr. Smethurst, presenting still greater features of resemblance with Palmer's, for both were medical men, and both raised difficult questions of medical jurisprudence. In both the jury had no doubt as to the guilt of the accused, only in Smethurst's case the then Home Secretary, Sir George Cornewall Lewis, could not divest his mind of serious doubt, and of which the murderer got the benefit. Smethurst's escape may have influenced the jury in the Poplar poisoning case, which followed close on its heels, although in that the verdict of "Not Guilty" was excusable, as the evidence was entirely circumstantial. There was no convincing proof that the accused had administered the poison, although beyond question that poison had occasioned the death.

Dr. Smethurst was long an inmate of Newgate, and was tried at the Central Criminal Court. He had all the characteristics of the poisoner—the calm deliberation, the protracted dissimulation, as with unshrinking, relentless wickedness the deadly work is carried on to the end. Smethurst's victim was a Miss Bankes, with whom he had contracted a bigamous marriage. He had met her at a boarding-house, where he lived with his own wife, a person of "shady" antecedents, and whom he left without scruple to join Miss Bankes. The latter seems to have succumbed only too willingly to his fascinations, and to have as readily agreed to marry him, in spite of the existence of the other Mrs. Smethurst. Probably the doctor had told her the story he brought forward when tried for bigamy, namely, that Mrs. Smethurst had no right to the name, but had a husband of her own, one Johnson, alive—a story subsequently disproved. Miss Bankes seems to have counted upon some species of whitewashing, no less than the repudiation of the other marriage, and told her sister as much when they last met. For some months Smethurst and Miss Bankes lived together as man and wife, first in London, and then at Richmond. She had a little fortune of her own, some £1700 or £1800, and a life-interest in £5000, a fact on which Smethurst's counsel dwelt with much weight, as indicating a motive for keeping her alive rather than killing her. But probably the lump sum was the bait, or perhaps Smethurst wished to return to his temporarily deserted first wife. Whatever the exact cause which impelled him to crime, it seems certain that he began to give her some poison, either arsenic or antimony, or both, in small quantities, with the idea of subjecting her to the irritant poison slowly but surely until the desired effect, death, was achieved. As she became worse and worse, Smethurst called in the best medical advice in Richmond, but was careful to prime them with his facts and lead them if possible to accept his diagnosis of the case. Smethurst was found guilty by the jury, and sentenced to death. But a long public discussion followed, and in consequence he was reprieved. The Home Secretary, in a letter to the Lord Chief Baron, stated that "although the facts are full of suspicion against Smethurst, there is not absolute and complete evidence of his guilt." Smethurst was therefore given a free pardon for the offence of murder, but he was subsequently again tried for bigamy, and sentenced to twelve months' imprisonment.

Catherine Wilson was a female poisoner who did business wholesale. She was tried in April 1862 on suspicion of having attempted to poison a neighbour with oil of vitriol. The circumstances were strange. Mrs. Wilson had gone to the chemist's for medicine, and on her return had administered a dose of something which burnt the mouth badly, but did not prove fatal. Wilson was acquitted on this charge, but other suspicious facts cropped up while she was in Newgate. It appeared that several persons with whom she was intimate had succumbed suddenly. In all cases the symptoms were much the same, vomiting, violent retching, purging, such as are visible in cholera, and all dated from the time when she knew a young man named Dixon, who had been in the habit of taking colchicum for rheumatism. Mrs. Wilson heard then casually from a medical man that it was a very dangerous medicine, and she profited by what she had heard. Soon afterwards Dixon died, showing all the symptoms already described. Soon afterwards a friend, Mrs. Atkinson, came to London from Westmoreland, and stayed in Mrs. Wilson's house. She was in good health on leaving home, and had with her a large sum of money. While with Mrs. Wilson she became suddenly and alarmingly ill, and died in great agony. Her husband, who came up to town, would not allow a post-mortem, and again Mrs. Wilson escaped. Mrs. Atkinson's symptoms had been the same as Dixon's. Then Mrs. Wilson went to live with a man named Taylor, who was presently attacked in the same way as the others, but, thanks to the prompt administration of remedies, he recovered. After this came the charge of administering oil of vitriol, which failed, as has been described. Last of all Mrs. Wilson poisoned her landlady, Mrs. Soames, under precisely the same conditions as the foregoing.

Here, however, the evidence was strong and sufficient. It was proved that Mrs. Wilson had given Mrs. Soames something peculiar to drink, that immediately afterwards Mrs. Soames was taken ill with vomiting and purging, and that Mrs. Wilson administered the same medicine again and again. The last time Mrs. Soames showed great reluctance to take it, but Wilson said it would certainly do her good. This mysterious medicine Wilson kept carefully locked up, and allowed no one to see it, but its nature was betrayed when this last victim also died. The first post-mortem indicated death from natural causes, but a more careful investigation attributed it beyond doubt to overdoses of colchicum. Dr. Alfred Taylor, the great authority and writer on medical jurisprudence, corroborated this, and in his evidence on the trial fairly electrified the court by declaring it his opinion that many deaths, supposed to be from cholera, were really due to poison. This fact was referred to by the judge in his summing up, who said that he feared it was only too true that secret poisoning was at that time very rife in the metropolis. Wilson was duly sentenced to death, and suffered impenitent, hardened, and without any confession of her guilt.

Although murder by insidious methods had become more common, cases where violence of the most deadly and determined kind was offered had not quite disappeared. I will mention two cases of this class, one accompanied with piracy on the high seas, the other perpetrated in a railway-carriage, and showing the promptitude with which criminals accept and utilize altered conditions of life, more particularly as regards locomotion.

The first case was that of the 'Flowery Land,' which left London for Singapore on the 28th July, 1863, with a cargo of wine and other goods. Her captain was John Smith; the first and second mates, Karswell and Taffir; there were two other Englishmen on board, and the rest of the crew were a polyglot lot, most of them, as was proved by their subsequent acts, blackguards of the deepest dye. Six were Spaniards, or rather natives of Manilla, and men of colour; one was a Greek, another a Turk; there were also a Frenchman, a Norwegian (the carpenter), three Chinamen, a "Sclavonian," and a black on board. Navigation and discipline could not be easy with such a nondescript crew. The captain was kindly but somewhat intemperate, the first mate a man of some determination, and punishment such as rope's-ending and tying to the bulwarks had to be applied to get the work properly done. The six Spaniards, the Greek, and the Turk were in the same watch, eight truculent and reckless scoundrels, who, brooding over their fancied wrongs, and burning for revenge, hatched amongst them a plot to murder their officers and seize the ship. The mutiny was organized with great secrecy, and broke out most unexpectedly in the middle of the night. A simultaneous attack was made upon the captain and the first mate. The latter had the watch on deck. One half of the mutineers fell upon him unawares with handspikes and capstan-bars. He was struck down, imploring mercy, but they beat him about the head and face till every feature was obliterated, and then, still living, flung him into the sea. Meanwhile the captain, roused from his berth, came out of the cabin, was caught near the 'companion' by the rest of the mutineers, and promptly despatched with daggers. His body was found lying in a pool of blood in a night-dress, stabbed over and over again in the left side. The captain's brother, a passenger on board the 'Flowery Land,' was also stabbed to death and his body thrown overboard.

The second mate, who had heard the hammering of the capstan-bars and the handspikes, with the first mate's and captain's agonized cries, had come out, verified the murderers, and then shut himself up in his cabin. He was soon summoned on deck, but as he would not move, the mutineers came down and stood in a circle round his berth. Leon, or Lyons, who spoke English, when asked said they would spare his life if he would navigate the ship for them to the River Plate or Buenos Ayres. Taffir, the second mate, agreed, but constantly went in fear of his life for the remainder of the voyage; and although the mutineers spared him, they ill-treated the Chinamen, and cut one badly with knives. Immediately after the murder cases of champagne, which formed part of the cargo, were brought on deck and broached; the captain's cabin ransacked, his money and clothes divided amongst the mutineers, as well as much of the merchandise on board. Leon wished to make every one on board share and share alike, so as to implicate the innocent with the guilty; but Vartos, or Watto, the Turk, would not allow any but the eight mutineers to have anything. The murders were perpetrated on the 10th September, and the ship continued her voyage for nearly three weeks, meeting and speaking one ship only. On the 2nd October they sighted land, ten miles distant; the mutineers took command of the ship, put her about till night-fall, by which time they had scuttled her, got out the boats, and all left the ship. The rest of the crew were also permitted to embark, except the Chinamen, one of whom was thrown into the water and drowned, while the other two were left to go down in the ship, and were seen clinging to the tops until the waters closed over them.

The boats reached the shore on the 4th October. Leon had prepared a plausible tale to the effect that they belonged to an American ship from Peru bound to Bordeaux, which had foundered at sea; that they had been in the boats five days and nights, but that the captain and others had been lost. The place at which they landed was not far from the entrance to the River Plate. A farmer took them in for the night, and drove them next day to Rocha, a place north of Maldonado. Taffir, the mate, finding there was a man who could speak English at another place twenty miles off, repaired there secretly, and so gave information to the Brazilian authorities. The mutineers were arrested, the case inquired into by a naval court-martial, and the prisoners eventually surrendered to the British authorities, brought to England, and lodged in Newgate. Their trial followed at the Central Criminal Court. Eight were arraigned at the same time: six Spaniards, Leon, Blanco, Durano, Santos, and Marsolino; Vartos the Turk, and Carlos the Greek. Seven were found guilty of murder on the high seas, and one, Carlos, acquitted. Two of the seven, Santos and Marsolino, were reprieved, and their sentences commuted to penal servitude for life; the remaining five were executed in one batch. They were an abject, miserable crew, cowards at heart; but some, especially Lopez, continued bloodthirsty to the last. Lopez took a violent dislike to the officer of the ward in charge of them, and often expressed a keen desire to do for him. They none of them spoke much English except Leon, commonly called Lyons. After condemnation, as the rules now kept capital convicts strictly apart, they could not be lodged in the two condemned cells, and they were each kept in an ordinary separate cell of the newly-constructed block, with the "traps," or square openings in the cell door, let down. A full view of them was thus at all times obtainable by the officers who, without intermission, day and night patrolled the ward. On the morning of execution the noise of fixing the gallows in the street outside awoke one or two of them. Lyons asked the time, and was told it was only five. "Ah!" he remarked, "they will have to wait for us then till eight." Lopez was more talkative. When the warder went in to call him he asked for his clothes. He was told he would have to wear his own. "Not give clothes? In Russia, Italy, always give chaps clothes." Then he wanted to know when the policemen would arrive, and was told none would come. "The soldiers then?" No soldiers either. "What, you not afraid let us go all by ourselves? Not so in Russia or Spain." The convicts were pinioned one by one and sent singly out to the gallows. As the first to appear would have some time to wait for his fellows, a difficult and painful ordeal, the seemingly most courageous was selected to lead the way. This was Duranno; but the sight of the heaving mass of uplifted, impassioned faces was too much for his nerves, and he so nearly fainted that he had to be seated in a chair. The execution went off without mishap.

In July 1864 occurred the murder of Mr. Briggs, a gentleman advanced in years and chief clerk in Robarts' bank. As the circumstances under which it was perpetrated were somewhat novel,[126] and as some time elapsed before the discovery and apprehension of the supposed murderer, the public mind was greatly agitated by the affair for several months. The story of the murder must be pretty familiar to most of my readers. Mr. Briggs left the bank one afternoon as usual, dined with his daughter at Peckham, then returned to the city to take the train from Fenchurch Street home, travelling by the North London Railway. He lived at Hackney, but he never reached it alive. When the train arrived at Hackney station, a passenger who was about to enter one of the carriages found the cushions soaked with blood. Inside the carriage was a hat, a walking-stick, and a small black leather bag. About the same time a body was discovered on the line near the railway-bridge by Victoria Park. It was that of an aged man, whose head had been battered in by a life-preserver. There was a deep wound just over the ear, the skull was fractured, and there were several other blows and wounds on the head. Strange to say, the unfortunate man was not yet dead, and he actually survived more than four-and-twenty hours. His identity was established by a bundle of letters in his pocket, which bore his full address: "T. Briggs, Esq., Robarts & Co., Lombard Street."

The friends of Mr. Briggs were communicated with, and it was ascertained that when he left home the morning of the murderous attack, he wore gold-rimmed eye-glasses and a gold watch and chain. The stick and bag were his, but not the hat. A desperate and deadly struggle must have taken place in the carriage, and the stain of a bloody hand marked the door. The facts of the murder and its object, robbery, were thus conclusively proved. It was also easily established that the hat found in the carriage had been bought at Walker's, a hatter's in Crawford Street, Marylebone; while within a few days Mr. Briggs' gold chain was traced to a jeweller's in Cheapside, Mr. Death, who had given another in exchange for it to a man supposed to be a foreigner. More precise clues to the murderer were not long wanting; indeed the readiness with which they were produced and followed up showed how greatly the publicity and wide dissemination of the news regarding murder facilitate the detection of crime. In little more than a week a cabman came forward and voluntarily made a statement which at once drew suspicion to a German, Franz Müller, who had been a lodger of his. Müller had given the cabman's little daughter a jeweller's cardboard box bearing the name of Mr. Death. A photograph of Müller shown the jeweller was identified as the likeness of the man who had exchanged Mr. Briggs' chain. Last of all, the cabman swore that he had bought the very hat found in the carriage for Müller at the hatter's, Walker's of Crawford Street.

This fixed the crime pretty certainly upon Müller, who had already left the country, thus increasing suspicion under which he lay. There was no mystery about his departure; he had gone to Canada, by the 'Victoria' sailing ship, starting from the

London docks, and bound to New York. Directly the foregoing facts were established, a couple of detective officers, armed with a warrant to arrest Müller, and accompanied by Mr. Death the jeweller and the cabman, went down to Liverpool and took the first steamer across the Atlantic. This was the 'City of Manchester,' which was expected to arrive some days before the 'Victoria,' and did so. The officers went on board the 'Victoria' at once, Müller was identified by Mr. Death, and the arrest was made. In searching the prisoner's box, Mr. Briggs' watch was found wrapped up in a piece of leather, and Müller at the time of his capture was actually wearing Mr. Briggs' hat, cut down and somewhat altered. The prisoner was forthwith extradited and sent back to England, which he reached with his escort on the 17th September the same year. His trial followed at the next sessions of the Central Criminal Court, and ended in his conviction. The case was one of circumstantial evidence, but, as Sir Robert Collyer the Solicitor-General pointed out, it was the strongest circumstantial evidence which had ever been brought forward in a murder case. It was really evidence of facts which could not be controverted or explained away. There was the prisoner's poverty, his inability to account for himself on the night of the murder, and his possession of the property of the murdered man. An alibi was set up for the defence, but not well substantiated, and the jury without hesitation returned a verdict of guilty.

Müller protested after sentence of death had been passed upon him that he had been convicted on a false statement of facts. He adhered to this almost to the very last. His case had been warmly espoused by the Society for the Protection of Germans in this country, and powerful influence was exerted both here and abroad to obtain a reprieve. Müller knew that any confession would ruin his chances of escape. His arguments were specious and evasive when pressed to confess. "Why should man confess to man?" he replied; "man cannot forgive man, only God can do so. Man is therefore only accountable to God." But on the gallows, when the cap was over his eyes and the rope had been adjusted round his neck, and within a second of the moment when he would be launched into eternity, he whispered in the ear of the German pastor who attended him on the scaffold, "I did it." While in the condemned cell he conversed freely with the warders in broken English or through an interpreter. He is described as not a bad-looking man, with a square German type of face, blue eyes which were generally half closed, and very fair hair. He was short in stature, his legs were light for the upper part of his body, which was powerful, almost herculean. It is generally supposed that he committed the murder under a sudden access of covetousness and greed. He saw Mr. Briggs' watch-chain, and followed him instantly into the carriage, determined to have it at all costs. His crime under this aspect of it was less premeditated, and less atrocious therefore, than that of Lefroy.

One other curious murder may be added to the two foregoing. Christian Sattler was by birth a German. He had led a wild life; had left his native land and enlisted first in the French army in Algeria, afterwards in the British German Legion raised for the Crimean War. At the disbandment of the force, as he was without resources, he turned his attention to hotel robberies, by which he lived for some years. He at length stole a carpet-bag containing valuables, and fled to Hamburgh. Thither he was pursued by a detective officer, Inspector Thain, who, being unable to obtain his extradition legally, had him inveigled on board an English steamer, where the arrest was made. Sattler was ironed for safe custody, a proceeding which he vehemently resented, and begged that they might be removed, as the handcuffs hurt his wrists. The inspector said that they could not be removed till he reached England. This reply of his contained no promise of immediate release. Sattler probably misunderstood, and he declared that the police officer had broken faith with him, having, moreover, stated that while at sea the captain of the ship was responsible for the security of the prisoner. As Sattler brooded over his wrongs, his rage got the upper hand, and he resolved to wreak it upon Thain. Although manacled, he managed to get a pistol from his chest and load it. The next time Thain entered his cabin he fired at him point-blank, and lodged three bullets in his breast. The unfortunate man survived till he landed, but died in Guy's Hospital. Sattler was tried for murder and convicted; his defence being that he had intended to commit suicide, but that, on the appearance of this officer who had wronged him, he had yielded to an irresistible impulse to kill him.

Sattler was a very excitable although not an ill-tempered man. While in Newgate awaiting trial he frequently tried to justify his murder by declaring that the police officer had broken faith with him. He would shoot any man or any policeman like a dog, or any number of them, who had treated him in that way. His demeanour immediately preceding his execution I have referred to in the last chapter.

Several cases of gigantic fraud, rivalling any already recorded, were brought to light between 1856 and 1873. I propose next to describe the leading features of the most important of these. Another case of long-continued successful forgery was brought to light two years after the convictions of Saward and his accomplices. This conspiracy was cleverly planned, but had scarcely so many ramifications as that of Saward. Its originators were a couple of men, Wagner and Bateman, who had already been convicted of systematic forgery, and sentenced to transportation, but they had been released on ticket-of-leave in 1856. As a blind for their new frauds, they set up as law-stationers in York Buildings, Adelphi, and at once commenced their nefarious traffic. Forged cheques and bills were soon uttered in great numbers, as well as base coin. The police suspecting the house in York Buildings, put a watch on the premises, which they kept up for more than a year, and thus obtained personal knowledge of all who passed in and out, but without obtaining any direct evidence. At length a man was caught in the act of passing a forged cheque at the Union Bank, and recognized as one of the frequenters of the bogus law-stationers. His arrest led to that of others. Among them was a man named Chandler, formerly a bill discounter by profession, who by degrees, to meet his extravagant expenditure, took to appropriating the bills intrusted to him, and so lost his business, after which he became a clerk to Messrs. Wagner and Bateman. Chandler while in Newgate turned informer, and betrayed the whole conspiracy. Besides his employers, a jeweller named Humphreys was in the "swim," at whose shop in Red Lion Square was discovered a quantity of base gold and silver coins, with all the latest appliances for coining, including those of electroplating; also a furniture dealer and one or two more commonplace rogues. The arch villain was never taken into custody. He, like Saward, was an artist in penmanship. He was a German named Kerp, eighty years of age, who had spent his whole life in imitating other people's signatures, and had acquired the most consummate skill in the practice. His copies were generally pronounced indistinguishable from and as good as the originals. The aged but wary Kerp, the moment the plot was discovered, vanished, and was never more heard of. Much the same plan was adopted by these forgers as by Saward to get their cheques cashed. They advertised for clerks, and employed the most likely of the applicants by sending them to the bank. It was one of these, Glendinning, who had allowed himself to be utilized for some time in this way, whose capture led to the breaking up of the gang. The principals in this conspiracy, Wagner and Bateman, were sentenced to penal servitude for life, the others to twenty and ten years. It was stated in evidence that the monies obtained by these forgeries amounted to £8000 or £10,000, and that the forged cheques which had been presented, but refused, amounted to double the sum. Wagner, after conviction, offered to reveal, for a reward of £3000, a system which had long been in practice of defrauding the Exchequer of vast sums by means of forged stamps. His offer was not, however, accepted.

A more elaborate plot in many ways, more secretly, more patiently prepared than the preceding, or indeed than any in the calendar, was the case of the forgeries upon the Bank of England discovered in 1863, but not before the forged paper had been put in circulation for more than a couple of years. In 1861 a man named Burnett came with his wife and took up his residence at Whitchurch, Hampshire, at no great distance from Laverstock, where are Messrs. Portal's mills for the manufacture of banknote paper. Burnett had only just come out of gaol after completing a sentence of penal servitude. His object in visiting Whitchurch was to undermine the honesty of some workman in the mills; and he eventually succeeded, his wife making the first overtures, in persuading a lad named Brown to steal some of the bank paper. Brown took several sheets, and then was detected by Brewer, a fellow-workman of superior grade, who threatened to betray the theft. But Brewer, either before or after this, succumbed to temptation, and stole paper on a much larger scale than Brown. All that was taken was handed over to Burnett, or a "woman in black" whom Brown met by appointment at Waterloo station. To facilitate his operations, Brewer obtained a false master key from Burnett, which gave him access to all parts of the mills, the packing-room included. In this part of the mills a large quantity of bank-note paper was kept at the period of the robbery, and in the states known as "water-leaf" and "sized," which are the penultimate processes of manufacture. One more remains, that of "glazing," without which no paper is issued for engraving. None of the stolen paper was glazed, and this was an important clue to the subsequent discovery of the crime.

Some time in 1862 a large deficiency in the stock of bank paper unglazed was discovered at the mills. Soon afterwards the inspectors of bank-notes at the Bank of England detected the presentation at the bank of spurious notes on genuine paper. The two facts taken in conjunction led to the employment of the police, and the offer of a reward of £1500 for the detection of the offenders. By this time Brown alone had stolen three or four hundred sheets, each containing two notes, many of the sheets suitable for engraving any kind of note from £1000 downwards. The amount of Brewer's abstractions (who was eventually acquitted) was never exactly estimated. Suspicion appears to have rested on Brown, who had left Laverstock, and he was soon approached by the police. Almost directly he was questioned he made a clean breast of the whole affair. The next step was to take the principals, and under such circumstances as would insure their conviction. A watch was set on Burnett, who was followed to the shop of one Buncher, a butcher in Strutton Ground. Buncher was then tracked to North Kent Terrace, New Cross, where a Mr. and Mrs. Campbell resided, with whom he did business in exchanging the false notes. The police officers now taxed Mrs. Campbell with complicity, and frightened her into collusion. With her assistance on a certain day a couple of bricks were taken out of the wall dividing her front and back parlours; the officers ensconced themselves in the latter, and waited for Buncher's expected visit. He came to complete a sale of forged notes, and he wanted a couple of hundred pounds for what he had. Mrs. Campbell offered him less, and there was an altercation, in the course of which Buncher became very violent, and at length, after using much intemperate language, he left the place in a huff. In the course of his remarks, however, he said, "I am the man that has got all the bank paper; I have £30,000 now, and the Bank of England cannot stop it." This was all the police wanted to know.

They next watched Buncher, and found that he paid frequent visits to Birmingham. They also discovered that through the intermediacy of one Robert Cummings, well known as a reputed coiner, he had been introduced to a man named Griffiths, an engraver and copper-plate printer. Griffiths was an unusually clever and skilful workman, who had devoted all his talent and all his energies for some seventeen years to the fabrication of false bank-notes. On a certain day, the 27th October, 1862, the two were arrested simultaneously; Buncher in London, and Griffiths in Birmingham. Nothing was found in Buncher's premises in Strutton Ground, which were thoroughly searched, but proofs of Griffiths' guilt were at once apparent on entering his work-room. In one corner was a printing-press actually in use, and on it were twenty-one forged Bank of England notes, without date or signature. On the bed were twenty forged ten-pound notes complete and ready for use, and twenty-five five-pound notes. "Mother plates" for engraving the body of the notes lay about, and other plates for various processes. More than this, Griffiths took the police to a field where, in a bank, a number of other plates were secreted. Griffiths afterwards admitted that he had been employed in defrauding the bank since 1846, and the prominent part he played secured for him on conviction the heaviest sentence of the law. This was penal servitude for life, Buncher's sentence being twenty-five, and Burnett's twenty years.

Cummings, who had introduced Buncher to Griffiths, was also tried for being in possession of stolen bank paper for improper purposes. But as there was no independent corroboration of the informer's evidence, according to the custom of the British law, the case was considered not proved, and he was acquitted. On his return to Newgate to be finally discharged, Cummings jumped up the stairs and fairly danced for joy. But he was not long at large; he was too active an evil-doer, and was perpetually in trouble. Commencing life as a resurrection man, when that trade failed through the change in the law, and no more bodies were to be bought, he devoted his energies to coining and forgery, and in the latter line was a friend and associate of Saward's. One narrow escape he had, however, before he abandoned his old business. A Bow Street officer saw him leaving London in the evening by Camberwell Green, accompanied by two other men. It was well known that they were resurrectionists, and a strict watch was kept at all the turnpike gates on the southern roads leading into London. An officer was placed for this purpose at New Cross, Camberwell, and Kennington gates. Presently "Old Bob" drove up to Camberwell Gate in the same cart in which he had been seen to start. The officers rushed out to detain him. "What have you got here? We must search the cart," they cry. "By all means," replies Bob, and a close investigation follows, without any detection of the corpse concealed. Bob was therefore allowed to pass on. But they had the body, all the same; it had been dressed up in decent clothes and made to stand upright in the cart. With the police officers it had passed muster as a living member of the party.

Cummings was repeatedly "run in" for the offence of coining and uttering bad money, whether coin or notes. His regular trade, followed before he took to the life of resurrectionist, was that of an engraver. He was a notorious criminal, an habitual offender in his own particular line, one who would stick at no trifles to evade detection or escape capture. It is told of "Bob" Brennan, an official specially employed for years by the Mint to watch and prosecute coiners, that he received information that coining was carried on by Cummings and others at a place in Westminster. He went there with a posse of officers and forced his way upstairs to the first floor, where the coiners, unexpectedly disturbed, fell an easy prey. But the police nearly paid the penalty of capture with their lives. Proceeding cautiously down the stairs, they found that the flooring at the bottom had been taken up. Where it had lain was a yawning gulf or trap sufficient to do for the whole body of police engaged in the capture. Cummings was caught shortly afterwards. He was a tall, slender man, with a long face and iron-gray hair. The community of coiners of which he was so notorious a member were a low lot, the lowest among criminals except, perhaps, the 'smashers,' or those who passed the counterfeit money. It was not easy to detect coiners, or bring home their guilt to them. Those who manufactured and those who passed had no direct dealings with each other. The false coin was bought by an agent from an agent, and dealings were carried on secretly at the "Clock House" in Seven Dials.

The annals of fraudulent crime probably contain nothing which in dramatic interest can compare with the conviction of William Roupell for forgery. As the case must still be well remembered by the present generation, it will be necessary to give here only the briefest summary. William Roupell was the eldest but illegitimate son of a wealthy man who subsequently married Roupell's mother, and had further legitimate issue. William was brought up as an attorney, and became in due course his father's man of business. As such he had pretty general control over his father's estates and affairs. In 1855 he instructed certain solicitors to prepare a deed of gift as from his father, conveying to him estates near Kingston. The old gentleman's signature to this deed of gift was a forgery, but upon this forged and false conveyance William Roupell, who had already embarked upon a career of wild extravagance, obtained a mortgage of £7000. In 1856 the father died. It had been supposed up to this date that he had willed his property, amounting in all to upwards of £200,000, but after the funeral William Roupell produced another and a later will, leaving everything to the widow, and constituting William sole executor. This will was a deliberate forgery.

Five or six years later, William Roupell minutely described how he had effected the fraud. The day his father died he got the keys of his private bureau, opened it, and took out the authentic will. After reading it, and finding this unfavourable to himself, he resolved to carry out his deliberate plan, namely, to suppress it and substitute another. He himself prepared it on a blank form which he had brought with him on purpose. To this fraudulent instrument he appended forged signatures, and in due course obtained probate. As he possessed nearly unbounded influence over his mother, her accession to the property meant that William could dispose of it as he pleased. He embarked forthwith in a career of the wildest extravagance, and ere long he had parted in his mother's name with most of the landed estates. One large item of his expenditure was a contested election at Lambeth, which he gained at a cost of £10,000. No fortune could stand the inroads he made into his mother's money, and in 1862 he was obliged to fly the country, hopelessly and irretrievably ruined.

His disappearance gave colour and substance to evil reports already in circulation that the will and conveyance above referred to were fictitious documents. His next brother, who should have inherited under the authentic will, forthwith brought an ejectment on the possessor of lands purchased on the authority of the forged conveyance and will. The case was tried at Guildford Assizes, and caused intense excitement, the hardship to the holders of these lands being plain, should the allegations of invalidity be made good. The effect of establishing the forgeries would be to restore to the Roupell family lands for which a price had already been paid in all good faith to another, but a criminal member of the family. At first the case was contested hotly, but, to the profound astonishment of every one inside and outside the court, William Roupell himself was brought as a principal witness to clench the case by a confession altogether against himself. He told his story with perfect coolness and self-possession, but in a grave and serious tone. "Every word he uttered was said with consideration, and sometimes with a long pause, but at the same time with an air of the most entire truthfulness and candour." He confessed himself a perjurer in having sworn to the false will, and a wholesale forger, having manufactured no less than ten false signatures to deeds involving on the whole some £350,000.

For these crimes William Roupell was tried at the Central Criminal Court on the 24th September, 1862. He declined to plead, but a plea of "Not Guilty" was recorded. The case was easily and rapidly disposed of. Roupell made a long statement more in exculpation than in his defence. He complained that he had at first been the dupe of others, and admitted that he had too readily fallen astray. But while repudiating the charges made against him of systematic extravagance and immorality, he confessed that his whole life had been a gigantic mistake, and he was ready to make what atonement he could. Mr. Justice Byles, in passing sentence, commented severely upon the commission of such crimes by a man in Roupell's position in life, and passed the heaviest sentence of the law, transportation for life. Roupell received the announcement with a cheerful countenance, and left the dock with evident satisfaction and relief at the termination of a most painful ordeal. Roupell was quiet and submissive while in Newgate, unassuming in manner, and ready to make the best of his position. He carried this character with him into penal servitude, and after enduring the full severity of his punishment for several years, was at length advanced to the comparative ease of a post much coveted by convicts, that of hospital nurse. His uniform good conduct gained him release from Portland on ticket-of-leave in 1882, just twenty years after his conviction.

A daring and cleverly-planned robbery of diamonds was that of the Tarpeys, man and wife, from an assistant of Loudon and Ryder's, the jewellers in Bond Street. The trick was an old one. The assistant called with the jewels on approbation at a house specially hired for the purpose in the West End, and was rendered insensible by chloroform, after which he was bound and the precious stones stolen. Mrs. Tarpey was almost immediately captured and put on her trial, but she was acquitted on the plea that she had acted under the coercion of her husband. Tarpey was caught through his wife, who was followed, disguised, and with her hair dyed black, to a house in the Marylebone Road, where she met her husband. On Tarpey's defence it was stated that the idea of the theft had been suggested to him by a novel, at a time he had lost largely on the turf. The first plot was against Mr. Harry Emmanuel, but he escaped, and the attempt was made upon Loudon and Ryder.

The last great case of fraud upon the Bank of England will fitly close this branch of the criminal records of Newgate. This was the well and astutely devised plot of the brothers Bidwell, assisted by Macdonell and Noyes, all of them citizens of the United States, by which the bank lost upwards of £100,000. The commercial experience of these clever rogues was cosmopolitan. Their operations were no less world-wide. In 1871 they crossed the Atlantic, and by means of forged letters of credit and introduction from London, obtained large sums from continental banks, in Berlin, Dresden, Bordeaux, Marseilles, and Lyons. With this as capital they came back to England *viâ* Buenos Ayres, and Austin Bidwell opened a *bonâ fide* credit in the Burlington or West End branch of the Bank of England, to which he was introduced by a well-known tailor in Saville Row.

After this the other conspirators travelled to obtain genuine bills and master the system of the leading houses at home and abroad. When all was ready, Bidwell first "refreshed his credit" at the Bank of England, as well as disarmed suspicion, by paying in a genuine bill of Messrs. Rothschilds' for £4500, which was duly discounted. Then he explained to the bank manager that his transactions at Birmingham would shortly be very large, owing to the development of his business there in the alleged manufacture of Pullman cars. The ground thus cleared, the forgers poured in from Birmingham numbers of forged acceptances, all of which were discounted to the value of £102,217. The fraud was rendered possible by the absence of a check usual in the United States. There such bills would be sent to the drawer to be initialled, and the forgery would have been at once detected. It was the discovery of this flaw in the banking system which had encouraged the Americans to attempt this crime.

Time was clearly an important factor in the fraud, hence the bills were sent forward in quick succession. Long before they came to maturity the forgers hoped to be well beyond arrest. They had, moreover, sought to destroy all clue. The sums obtained by Bidwell in the name of "Warren" at the Bank of England were lodged at once by drafts to "Horton," another alias, in the Continental Bank. For these cash was obtained in notes; the notes were exchanged by one of the conspirators for gold at the Bank of England, and again the same day a second conspirator exchanged the gold for notes. But just as all promised well, the frauds were detected through the carelessness of the forgers. They had omitted to insert the dates in certain bills. The bills were sent as a matter of form to the drawer to have the date added, and the forgery was at once detected. Noyes was seized without difficulty, as it was a part of the scheme that he should act as the dupe, and remain on the spot in London till all the money was obtained. Through Noyes the rest of the conspirators were eventually apprehended. Very little if any of the ill-gotten proceeds, however, was ever recovered. Large sums, as they were realized, were transmitted to the United States, and invested in various American securities, where probably the money still remains.

The prisoners, who were committed to Newgate for trial, had undoubtedly the command of large funds while there, and would have readily disbursed it to effect their enlargement. A plot was soon discovered, deep laid, and with many ramifications, by which some of the Newgate warders were to be bribed to allow the prisoners to escape from their cells at night. Certain friends of the prisoners were watched, and found to be in communication with these warders, to whom it was said £100 apiece had been given down as the price of their infidelity. Further sums were to have been paid after the escape; and one warder admitted that he was to have £1000 more paid to him, and to be provided with a passage to Australia. The vigilance of the Newgate officials, assisted by the city police, completely frustrated this plot. A second was nevertheless set on foot, in which the plan of action was changed, and the freedom of the prisoners was to be obtained by means of a rescue from the dock during the trial. An increase of policemen on duty sufficed to prevent any attempt of this kind. Nor were these two abortive efforts all that were planned. A year or two after, when the prisoners were undergoing their life sentences of penal servitude, much uneasiness was caused at one of the convict prisons by information that bribery on a large scale was again at work amongst the officials. But extra precautions and close supervision have so far proved effectual, and the prisoners are still in custody after a lapse of ten years.

I propose to end at this point the detailed account of the more prominent criminal cases which lodged their perpetrators in Newgate. The most recent affairs are still too fresh in the public mind to need more than a passing reference. Few of the Newgate notorieties of late years show any marked peculiarities; their crimes follow in the lines of others already found, and often more than once, in the calendars. Violent passions too easily aroused prompted the Frenchwoman Marguerite Dixblanc to murder her mistress, Madame Riel, in Park Lane, as Courvoisier, the Swiss, had been tempted to murder Lord William Russell. Greed in the latter case was a secondary motive; it was the principal incentive with Kate Webster, that fierce and brutal female savage who took the life of her mistress at Richmond. Webster, it may be mentioned here, was one of the worst prisoners ever remembered in Newgate—most violent in temper, and addicted to the most frightful language. Webster's devices for disposing of the body of her victim will call to mind those of Theodore Gardelle, of Good, and Greenacre, and Catherine Hayes. Greed in another form led the Stauntons to make away with Mrs. Patrick Staunton, murdering her with devilish cruelty by slow degrees. The judge, Sir Henry Hawkins, in passing sentence characterized this as a crime more black and hideous than any in the criminal annals of the country. But it was scarcely worse than that of Mrs. Brownrigg, or that of the Meteyards, both of whom did their helpless apprentices to death. It was to effect the rupture of an irksome tie that led Henry Wainwright to murder Harriet Lane deliberately and in cold blood. In this case the tie was unsanctified, but it was not more inconvenient than that which urged Greenacre to a similar crime. In cold-blooded premeditation it rivalled that of the Mannings. As in that case, the grave had been dug long in anticipation, and the chloride of lime purchased to destroy the corpse. Henry Wainwright's attempt to get rid of the body was ingenious, but not original, and the circumstances which led to detection were scarcely novel proofs of the old adage that murder will out. Henry Wainwright's impassioned denial of his crime, even after it had been brought fully home to him, has many parallels in the criminal records. His disclaimer, distinct and detailed on every point, was intended simply for effect. He might swear he was not the murderer, that he never fired a pistol in his life, and that, in spite of the verdict of the jury, "he left the dock with a calm and quiet conscience;" but there was no doubt of his guilt, as the Lord Chief Justice told him, while expressing great regret at his rash assertion. Wainwright's demeanour after sentence has been described in the last chapter. Doubts were long entertained whether Thomas Wainwright, who was convicted as an accessory after the fact, had not really taken an active part in the murder. But a conversation overheard between the two brothers in Newgate satisfactorily exonerated Thomas Wainwright.

Poisoning has still its victims. Christina Edmunds had resort to strychnia, the same lethal drug that Palmer used; her object being first to dispose of the wife of a man for whom she had conceived a guilty passion, then to divert suspicion from herself by throwing it on a confectioner, whose sweetmeats she bought, tampered with, and returned to the shop. The trial of Miss Edmunds was transferred to the Central Criminal Court under Lord Campbell's Act, already referred to. She was found guilty. It will be remembered that she made a statement which led to the empanelling of a jury of matrons, who decided that there was no cause for an arrest of judgment. Kate Webster followed the same course; but these pleas of pregnancy are not common now-a-days. Although sentence of death was passed on Edmunds, it was commuted to penal servitude for life; but she eventually passed into Broadmoor Lunatic Asylum, where she busies herself with water-colour drawing. The still more recent cases of poisoning which have occurred were not connected with Newgate. The mysterious Bravo case, that of Dr. Lamson, and that of Kate Dover unhappily show that society is more than ever at the mercy of the insidious and unscrupulous administration of poisonous drugs.

A case reproducing many of the features of the 'Flowery Land' occurred twelve years later, when the crew of the 'Lennie' mutinied, murdered the captain and mates, sparing the steward only on condition that he would navigate the ship to the Mediterranean. The mutineers were of the same stamp as the crew of the 'Flowery Land'—foreigners, vindictive, reckless, and truculent ruffians, easily moved to murderous rage. The 'Lennie's' men were all Greeks, except one known as French Peter, who was the ringleader, and who had long been an habitual criminal, a reputed murderer, and certainly an inmate more than once of a French *bagne*. Conviction was obtained through the evidence of the steward and two of the least culpable of the crew. In Newgate the 'Lennie' mutineers were extremely well behaved. Resolute, determined-looking men, their courage broke down in confinement. They paid close attention to the counsels of the archimandrite, and died quite penitent. A story is told of one of them, "Big Harry," the wildest and most cut-throat looking of the lot, which proves that he could be grateful for kindness, and was not all bad. He had steadfastly refused to eat meat on some religions scruples, and for the same reason would not touch soup. He was glad, therefore, to get an extra allowance of bread, and to show his gratitude to the warder who procured this privilege for him, he made him a present. It was his own handiwork—a bird pecking at a flower; the whole manufactured while in the condemned cell of the crumb of bread made into paste. The flower had berries also of bread fixed on stems made from the fibre drawn from the stuffing of his mattrass, and the bird's legs were a couple of teeth broken off the prisoner's comb.

Of the lesser criminals, forgers, thieves, swindlers, Newgate continued to receive its full share up to the last. But there were few cases so remarkable as the great ones already recorded. Mr. Bamell Oakley made a rich harvest for a time, and was said at the time of his trial to have obtained as much as £40,000 by false and fraudulent pretences. Messrs. Swindlehurst, Saffery, and Langley cleared a large profit by swindling the Artisans' Dwellings Company; and Madame Rachel passed through Newgate on her way to Millbank convicted of obtaining jewellery under the false pretence of making silly women "beautiful for ever." The greatest *causes célèbre*, however, of recent times were the turf frauds by which the Comtesse de Goncourt was swindled out of large sums in sham sporting speculations. The conviction of the principals in this nefarious transaction, Benson, the two Kurrs, Bale, and Murray, led to strange revelations of dishonest practices amongst the detective police, and was followed by the arraignment and conviction in their turn of Meiklejohn, Druscovich, Palmer, and Froggatt.

NEWGATE REFORMED

M*ovement towards prison reform—Pentonville 'model' prison built—Extension of the movement—Opposing views as to silence and separation—Widely different treatment of criminals in various prisons—Mr. Pearson's committee— His proposed system explained—Attention again attracted to Newgate —Most of the old evils still rampant, and scarcely any enforcement of discipline—Some attempt to exercise supervision, and minor improvements introduced—Scheme of reconstruction by Lord John Russell found impracticable, and Holloway selected for a new city prison— Subsequent reconstruction of Newgate on cellular principle— Committee of House of Lords inquire into whole subject of criminal treatment, and recommend extensive changes, with uniformity of system—Prison Act 1865 embodies most of these recommendations— Finally, an Act passed in 1877 transferring prisons to the Government, and Newgate closed.*

THE time at length approached when a radical and complete change was to come over the old city gaol. It was impossible for Newgate to escape for ever the influences pressing so strongly towards prison reform. Elsewhere the spirit had been more or less active, although not uniformly or always to the same extent. There had been a pause in legislation, except of a permissive kind. The 2nd and 3rd Victoria, cap. 56 (1839) laid it down that individuals *might* be confined separately and apart in single cells. By other acts local authorities were empowered to construct new gaols or hire accommodation in the district; but no steps had been taken in Parliament to enforce a better system of discipline, or to insist upon the construction of prisons on the most approved plan. As regards the first, however, Sir James Graham, when Home Secretary in 1843, had appointed a committee of prison inspectors, presided over by the Under Secretary of State, to draw up rules and dietaries, which were then recommended to and generally adopted by the visiting justices all over the kingdom. As regards the second, the Government had set a good example, and in deciding upon the erection of Pentonville prison had embarked on a considerable expenditure in order to provide a model prison for general imitation. The first stone of Pentonville prison was laid on the 10th April, 1840, by the Marquis of Normanby, then Home Secretary, and the prison, which contained five hundred and twenty cells, was occupied on the 21st December, 1842. This building was a costly affair. The site was uneven, and had to be levelled; moreover, the gross expenditure was increased "partly from its being considered necessary, as it was a national prison, to make a great archway, and to make the character of it more imposing than if it had been situated in the country, and had been an ordinary prison."[127] Up to the 21st December, 1842, with the additions made to that date, the total expenditure amounted to nearly £90,000, or about £180 per cell. On the other hand, it must be admitted that this was an experimental construction, and that too strict a limitation of outlay would have militated seriously against the usefulness of the building. Nor must it be overlooked that this, the first model prison, although obtained at a considerable cost, became actually what its name implied. Pentonville has really been the model on which all subsequent prison construction has been based. All prisons at home and abroad are but variations, of course with the added improvements following longer experience, of the pattern originated by the architectural genius of Sir Joshua Jebb. The internal arrangements of the new model were carefully supervised by a body of distinguished men, among which were many peers, Lord John Russell, Mr. Shaw-Lefevre, the Speaker of the House of Commons, Sir Benjamin Brodie, Major Jebb, R.E., and the two prison inspectors, Messrs. Crawford and Russell, with whose names the reader is already familiar. Major, afterwards Sir Joshua Jebb, was the moving spirit among these commissioners, and he is now generally recognized as the originator of modern prison architecture.

The movement thus laudably initiated by the Government soon spread to the provinces. Some jurisdictions, greatly to their credit, strove at once to follow the lead of the central authority. Within half-a-dozen years no less than fifty-four new prisons were built on the Pentonville plan, others were in progress, and the total number of separate cells provided amounted to eleven thousand odd. This list included Wakefield, Leeds, Kirkdale, Manchester, Birmingham, and Dublin. Liverpool was building a new prison with a thousand cells, the county of Surrey one with seven hundred. The cost in each varied considerably, the general average being from £120 to £130 per cell. At Pentonville the rate was higher, but there the expense had been increased by the site, the difficulty of access, and the admitted necessity of giving architectural importance to this the national model prison.[128] Other jurisdictions were less prompt to recognize their responsibilities, the city of London among the number, as I shall presently show at length. These were either satisfied with a makeshift, and modified existing buildings, without close regard to their suitability, or for a long time did nothing at all. Among the latter were notably the counties of Cheshire, Lincolnshire, Norfolk, Suffolk, Nottinghamshire, the East and North Ridings of Yorkshire. The south and west of England were also very laggard, and many years were still to elapse before the prisons in these parts were properly reconstituted.

Not less remarkable than this diverse interpretation of a manifest duty was the variety of views as regards the discipline to be introduced in these new prisons. The time was one when thoughtful people who concerned themselves closely with social questions were greatly exercised as to the best system of treating the inmates of a gaol. A new and still imperfectly understood science had arisen, the principles of which were debated by disputants of widely opposite opinions with an earnestness that sometimes bordered upon acrimony. One school were strongly in favour of the continuous separation of prisoners, the other supported the theory of labour in association, but under a stringent rule of silence, with isolation only at night. Both systems came to us from the United States. The difference was really more in degree than in principle, and our modern practice has prudently tried to steer between the two extremes, accepting as the best system a judicious combination of both. But about 1850 the two sides were distinctly hostile, and the controversy ran high. High authorities were in favour of continuous separation. Colonel Jebb preferred it; Messrs. Crawford and Whitworth Russell were convinced that the complete isolation of criminals from one another was the true basis of a sound system of prison discipline. Prison chaplains of experience and high repute, such as Messrs. Field, Clay, Kingsmill, Burt, and Osborne, also advocated it. It was claimed for it that it was more deterrent; that in districts where it was the rule, evil-doers especially dreaded coming under its irksome conditions. Another argument was, that it afforded more hope of the reformation of criminals. The system of associated labour in silence had also its warm supporters, who maintained that under this system prisoners were more industrious and more healthy; that their condition was more natural, and approximated more nearly to that of daily life. Better industrial results were obtained from it, and instruction in trades was easier, and prisoners were more likely to leave gaol with the means of earning an honest livelihood if so disposed. The opposing champions were not slow to find faults and flaws in the system they condemned. Separation was injurious to health, mental or physical, said one side; men broke down when subjected to it for more than a certain period, and it was unsafe to fix this limit above twelve months, although some rash advocates were in favour of eighteen months, some indeed of two years. The other side retorted that the system of associated labour was most costly, so many officers being required to maintain the discipline of silence; moreover, it was nearly impossible to prevent communication and mutual contamination.

It is scarcely necessary to follow the controversy further. I have only introduced the subject as showing how little as yet the State was impressed with the necessity for authoritative interference. The legislature was content to let local jurisdictions experimentalize for themselves; with the strange, anomalous result, that a thief or other criminal might be quite differently treated according as he was incarcerated on one side or another of a border line. This variety was often extended to all branches of prison economy. There was an absolute want of uniformity in dietaries; in some prisons it was too liberal, in others too low. The amount of exercise varied from one or two hours daily to half the working day. The cells inhabited by prisoners were of very varying dimensions; some were not sufficiently ventilated, others were warmed artificially, and were unwholesomely close. The use of gas or some other means of lighting might be adopted, but more often was dispensed with. In a great number of prisons no provision was made for the education of prisoners, in some others there was a sufficient staff of schoolmasters and instructors. The discipline also varied greatly, from the severely penal to the culpably lax. The greatest pains might be taken to secure isolation, the prisoners might be supervised and watched at every step, and made liable to punishment for a trifling breach of an irksome code of regulations, or they might herd together or communicate freely as in the old worst days. They might see each other when they liked, and converse *sotto voce*, or make signs; or the chances of recognizing or being recognized were reduced to a minimum by the use of a mask.[129] There was no general rule of employment. Hard labour was often not insisted upon in separate confinement; sometimes it embraced the tread-wheel or the newly-invented instruments known as cranks, which ground air. The alternative between labour or idleness, or the selection of the form of labour, were mere matters of chance, and decided according to the views of the local magistracy. They were approved of and employed at some prisons, at others objected to because they were unproductive, and because the machine was often so imperfect that the amount of effort could not be exactly regulated. Opinions differed greatly with regard to the tread-wheel; some authorities advocated it as a very severe and irksome punishment, which was yet under full control, and might be made to work corn-mills or prove otherwise productive; other authorities as strongly condemned it as brutalizing, unequal in its operation, and altogether a "deplorable invention."

This want of uniformity in prison discipline became ere long an acknowledged evil pressing for some remedy, and the question was once more taken up in the House of Commons. In 1849 Mr. Charles Pearson, M.P., moved for a committee to report upon the best means of securing some uniform system which should be "punitive, reformatory, and self-supporting;" but the session was far advanced, and the matter was relegated to the following year. In 1850 Sir George Grey brought forward a new motion to the same effect, which was promptly carried, with the additional instruction to the committee to suggest any improvements. The latter had reference more especially to a proposal emanating from Mr. Charles Pearson himself. That gentleman had come to the conclusion that the ordinary and hackneyed methods of treatment were practically inefficacious, and that a new system of prison discipline should be introduced. His plan was to devote the whole labour of prisoners sentenced to any term between three months and four years to agriculture. District prisons were to be established for this purpose, each of which would be in the heart of a farm of a thousand acres. The prisoners were to cultivate the land and raise sufficient produce for their own support. Mr. Pearson backed up his recommendations by many sound arguments. Field labour, he urged, and with reason, was a very suitable employment; healthful, easily learnt, and well adapted to the circumstances of unskilled labourers. Such excellent returns might be counted upon, that a margin of profit would be left after the cost of the prisons had been defrayed. The scheme was no doubt fascinating, and in many respects feasible; but Mr. Pearson overlooked some points in which a more practical mind would have foreseen difficulty, and perhaps forecasted failure. In his proposal he dwelt much upon the humanizing effects of healthful open-air toil, anticipating the best results from a system which made earnings, and indeed release, dependent upon the amount of work done. That industry might thus be stimulated and encouraged was probable enough, and later experience has fully proved the advantage of a judicious system of gratuities for labour; but Mr. Pearson hardly considered the converse sufficiently, and omitted the fact that he might have to deal with that persistent idleness which is not an unknown characteristic of the criminal class. The hope of reward might do much, but no system of penal discipline is complete unless it can also count upon the fear of punishment. Mr. Pearson seems to have taken for granted that all prisoners would behave well in his district prisons. On that account he made no provision to insure safe custody, thinking perhaps that prisoners so well disposed would cheerfully remain in gaol of their own accord. But an open farm of a thousand acres would have offered abundant chances of escape, which some at least would have attempted, probably with success. The creation of an expensive staff for supervision, or the still more costly process of walling in the whole farm, would have greatly added to the charges of these establishments.

I have lingered too long perhaps over Mr. Pearson's proposal, but some reference was indispensable to a scheme which marked the growth of public interest in prison affairs, and which was the germ of the new system since admirably developed in the convict prisons of this country. Mr. Pearson and the committee of 1850 have the more claim on our consideration, because, in the inquiry which followed, attention was again attracted to Newgate. The condition of that prison in 1850 may be gathered from the pages of the report. Not much had been done to remedy the old defects; radical improvement was generally considered impossible. The great evil, however, had been sensibly diminished. There was no longer, or at worst but rarely, and for short periods, the same overcrowding. This was obviated by the frequent sessions of the Central Criminal Court, and the utilization of the two subsidiary prisons in Giltspur Street and Southwark. The prison population of Newgate was still subject to great fluctuations, but it seldom rose above two hundred and fifty or three hundred at the most crowded periods, or just before the sessional gaol delivery; and at its lowest it fell sometimes to fifty or sixty. These numbers would have still further decreased, and the gaol would have been almost empty, but for the misdemeanants who were still sent to Newgate at times on long terms of imprisonment, and for the transports, whom the Home Office were often, as of old, slow to remove. The old wards, day rooms and sleeping rooms combined, of which the reader has already heard so much, now seldom contained more than ten or a dozen each. Some sort of decorum was maintained among the occupants in the day-time. Drinking and gaming, the indiscriminate visitation of friends, and the almost unlimited admission of extra food, these more glaring defects had disappeared.

But reformation was only skin deep. Below the surface many of the old evils still rankled. There was as yet no control over the prisoners after locking-up time; this occurred in summer at eight, but in the winter months it took place at dusk, and was often as early as four or five. The prisoners were still left to themselves till next morning's unlocking, and they spent some fourteen or fifteen hours in total darkness, and almost without check or control. Captain Williams, who was the inspector of prisons for the home district in succession to Messrs. Crawford and Russell, stated in evidence that he was visiting Newgate one night, when he heard a great disturbance in one of the day and sleeping rooms, and on entering it found the prisoners engaged in kicking bundles of wood from one end of the ward to the other. Some attempt at supervision was exercised by the night watchman stationed on the leads, who might hear what went on inside. If any disturbance reached his ears, he reported the case to the governor, who next morning visited the ward in fault, and asked for the culprit. The enforcement of discipline depended upon the want of honour among thieves. Unless the guilty prisoner was given up, the whole ward was punished, either by the exclusion of visitors or the deprivation of fire, sharp tests which generally broke down the fidelity of the inmates of the ward to one another. Later on a more efficacious but still imperfect method of supervision was introduced. Iron cages, which are still to be seen in Newgate, were constructed on the landings, ensconced in which warders spent the night, on duty, and alert to watch the sleepers below, and check by remonstrance or threat of punishment all who broke the peace of the prison.

These disciplinary improvements were, however, only slowly and gradually introduced. Other changes affecting the condition and proper treatment of prisoners were not made until the inspector had urged and recommended them. Thus the wards, which, as I have said, were left in complete darkness, were now to be lighted with gas; and after this most salutary addition, the personal superintendence of night officers, as already described, became possible. The rule became general as regards the prison dress; hitherto clothing had been issued only to such as were destitute or in rags, and all classes of prisoners, those for trial, and those sentenced for short terms or long, wore no distinguishing costume, although its use was admitted, not only for cleanliness, but as a badge of condition, and a security against escape. Renewed recommendations to provide employment resulted in the provision of a certain amount of oakum for picking, and one or two men were allowed to mend clothes and make shoes. The rules made by the Secretary of State were hung up in conspicuous parts of the prison; more officers were appointed, as the time of so many of those already on the staff was monopolized by attendance at the Central Criminal Court. Another custom which had led to disorder was abolished; prisoners who had been acquitted were not permitted to return to the prison to show their joy and receive the congratulations of their unfortunate fellows. The Corporation seems to have introduced these salutary changes without hesitation. It was less prompt apparently in dealing with structural alterations and improvements. Well-founded complaints had been made of the want of heating appliances in the gaol. The wards had open fires, but the separate cells were not warmed at all. A scheme for heating the whole prison with hot-water pipes, after the system now generally adopted elsewhere, was considered, and abandoned because of the expense.

As to the entire reconstruction of Newgate, nothing had been done as yet. This, with a scheme for limiting the gaol to untried prisoners, had been urgently recommended by Lord John Russell in 1830. His letter to the Corporation, under date 4th June, is an interesting document, and shows that even at that date the Government contemplated the erection of a model prison. Lord John Russell, commenting upon the offer of the Corporation to improve Newgate, provided it was henceforth used only for untried prisoners, suggested that Newgate should be entirely reconstructed, and the new building adopted as a model. The Corporation had agreed to spend £20,000 on alterations, but £60,000 would suffice to reconstruct. Lord John, with great fairness, admitted that the whole of this burthen could not be imposed upon the city, seeing that since the establishment of the Central Criminal Court, Newgate received prisoners for trial from several counties, and he was therefore prepared to submit to Parliament a proposal that half the cost of reconstruction should be borne by public funds. He forwarded plans prepared by the inspectors of prisons, not for blind adoption, but as a guide. This plan was on the principle of cellular separation, a system, according to Lord John Russell, desirable in all prisons, "but in a metropolitan prison absolutely essential." The Corporation in reply demurred rather to accepting strict separation as a rule, feeling that it approached too nearly to solitary confinement. The court was, however, prepared to consider Lord John Russell's proposal with regard to the cost of rebuilding; but as the plan was "confessedly experimental, for the benefit of the country generally, the amount for which the city should be responsible should be distinctly limited not to exceed a certain sum to be agreed upon." A proviso was also made that the magistrates should continue to exercise full control over the new gaol, "free from any other interference than that of the inspectors on the part of Government."

No doubt wiser counsels prevailed with Lord John Russell, and on a more mature consideration he realized that the limited area of the existing Newgate site, and the costliness of enlarging it, forbade all idea of entirely reconstructing the gaol so as to constitute it a model prison. It would be far better to begin at the beginning, to select a sufficiently spacious piece of ground, and erect a prison which from foundations to roofs should be in conformity with the newest ideas.

The preference given to the Pentonville system destroyed all hopes of a complete reformation of Newgate. But the condition of the great city gaol was evidently considered a reproach by the city authorities, and a year after the opening of the new "model" at Pentonville, a serious effort was made to reconstruct Newgate. In 1845 the Gaol Committee brought forward a definite proposal to purchase ground in the immediate vicinity for the erection of a new gaol. This gaol was nominally to replace the Giltspur Street Compter, the site of which was to be sold to Christ's Hospital, but the intention was of course to embody and absorb old Newgate in the new construction. The proposal made was to purchase some fifty thousand square feet between Newgate, Warwick Lane, and the Sessions House, "the situation having been proved by long experience to be salubrious." But when this suggestion was brought before the court of aldermen, various amendments were proposed. It was urged that the area selected for purchase must be excessively costly to acquire, and still quite inadequate for the city needs. The Home Secretary had laid it down that at least five acres would be indispensable, and such an area it was impossible to obtain within the limits of the city.

Now for the first time the Tuffnell estate in Holloway was mentioned. The Corporation owned lands there covering from nineteen to twenty acres. Why not move the city prison bodily into this more rural spot, with its purer air and greater breathing space?

Eventually Holloway was decided upon as a site for the new city prison. The necessary preliminaries took some time, but the contracts for the new building were completed in 1849, when the works were commenced. The prison was to contain four hundred and four prisoners, and the estimated expenditure was £79,000. It was to accommodate only the convicted prisoners sentenced to terms short of penal servitude, and after its completion the uses of Newgate were narrowed almost entirely to those of a prison of detention. It was intended as far as possible that, except awaiting trial, no prisoner should find himself relegated to Newgate. This principle became more and more generally the rule, although it has never been punctiliously observed. Now and again misdemeanants have found their way into Newgate, and within the last few years one offender against the privileges of the House of Commons.

With the reduction of numbers to be accommodated, there was ample space in Newgate for its reconstruction on the most approved modern lines. In 1857 the erection of a wing or large block of cells was commenced within the original walls of the prison, and upon the north or male side. This block contained one hundred and thirty cells, embracing every modern improvement; it also contained eleven reception cells, six punishment cells, and a couple of cells for condemned criminals. This block was completed in 1859, after which the hitherto unavoidable and long-continued promiscuous association of prisoners came to an end. In 1861 a similar work was undertaken to provide separate cellular accommodation for the female inmates of Newgate, and by the following year forty-seven new cells had been built on the most approved plan. During this reconstruction the female prisoners were lodged in Holloway, and when it was completed, both sides of the prison were brought into harmony with modern ideas. The old buildings were entirely disused, and the whole of the inmates of Newgate were kept constantly in separate confinement.

With the last re-edification of Newgate, a work executed some seven centuries after the first stone of the old gaol was laid, the architectural records of the prison end. Nothing much was done at Newgate in the way of building, outside or in, after 1862. The Act for private executions led to the erection of the gallows shed in the exercising yard, and at the flank of the passage from the condemned cells. The first "glass house," or room in which prisoners could talk in private with their attorneys, but yet be seen by the warder on the watch, had been constructed, and others were subsequently added. But no structural alterations were made from the date first quoted until the time of closing the prison in 1881. But in the interval very comprehensive and, I think it must be admitted, salutary changes were successively introduced into the management of prisons. Newgate naturally shared in any advantages due to these reforms. I propose, therefore, to refer to them in the concluding pages of this work, and thus bring the history of prison discipline down to our own times.

The last inquiry into the condition and management of our gaols and houses of correction was that made by the Lords' Committee in 1863. The inquiry was most searching and complete, and the committee spoke plainly in its report. It animadverted strongly on "the many and wide differences as regards construction, labour, diet, and general discipline" which existed in the various prisons, "leading to an inequality, uncertainty, and inefficiency of punishment productive of the most prejudicial results." The varieties in construction were still very marked. In many prisons the prisoners were still associated, and, from the want of a sufficient number of cells, the principle of separation was still greatly neglected. Yet this principle, as the committee pointed out, "must now be accepted as the foundation of prison discipline," while its rigid maintenance was in its opinion vital to the efficiency of the gaols. Even where cells had been built they were frequently below the standard size, and were therefore not certified for occupation as was required by law. Great numbers were not lighted at night, and were without means by which their inmates could communicate, in case of urgent necessity, with their keepers. Still greater were the differences with regard to employment. The various authorities held widely different opinions as to what constituted hard labour. Here the tread-wheel was in use, there cellular cranks, or "hard-labour machines." Both, however, varied greatly in mechanism and in the amount of energy they called forth, while the former was intended for the congregate labour of a number, and the latter, as its name implies, imposed continuous solitary toil. At other prisons "shot-drill," the lifting and carrying of heavy round shot, was the favourite method of inflicting penal labour. With these differences were others as opposed concerning industrial occupation. The gaol authorities often gave the highest, possibly undue, importance to the value of remunerative employment, and sought to make profitable returns from prisoners' labour the test of prison efficiency. In this view the committee could not coincide, and it was decidedly of opinion that in all short sentences the hard labour of the tread-wheel, crank, and so forth should be the invariable rule.

In dietaries, again, the same wide diversity of practice obtained. The efforts made by Sir James Graham years before to introduce uniformity in this particular had failed of effect. The Secretary of State's suggested scale of diet had seldom been closely followed. In some places the dietary was too full, in others too meagre. Its constituents were not of the most suitable character. More animal food was given than was necessary. Vegetables, especially the potato, that most valuable anti-scorbutic, was too often omitted. In a word, the value of diet as a part of penal discipline was still insufficiently recognized. The prisons were still far from inflicting the three punishments, hard labour, hard fare, and a hard bed, which Sir Joshua Jebb told the committee he considered the proper elements of penal discipline. It is interesting to note here that the committee of 1863 fully endorsed Sir Joshua's recommendations as regards a "hard bed," and recommended that "during short sentences, or the earlier stages of a long confinement, the prisoners should be made to dispense with the use of a mattress, and should sleep on planks." This suggestion was adopted in the Act of 1865, which followed the committee's report, and of which more directly. Clause 92, Schedule I. of that act authorized the use of plank beds, which were adopted in many prisons. They are now the universal rule, introduced, as was erroneously supposed, by the prison commissioners appointed under the Prison Act of 1877. Their origin it will be seen dates back much further than that.

Beds might well be made hard and their use strictly limited. According to this committee of 1863, beds in the smaller and most carelessly conducted prisons formed a large element in the life of a prisoner. In one gaol fifteen hours were spent in bed out of the twenty-four. This was in keeping with other grave defects and omissions. The minor borough prisons were the worst blot on the still dark and imperfect system. They were very numerous, very imperfect in construction and management, and they were very little required. In them, according to the committee, the old objectionable practices were still in full force. There was unrestrained association of untried and convicted, juvenile with adult prisoners, vagrants, misdemeanants, felons. There were dormitories without light, control, or regulation at night, which warders, dreading assault, were afraid to enter after dark, even to check rioting and disturbance. Prisoners still slept two in a bed. In one prison the bedsteads had been removed lest the prisoners should break them up and convert them into weapons of offence. The prison buildings were in many places out of repair; other houses often overlooked them. A single officer was the only custodian and disciplinary authority in the gaol. Complete idleness was tolerated; there was neither penal labour nor light employment. The prisoners inter-communicated freely, and exercised the most injurious, corrupting influences upon one another. The total want of administration was very marked, but in one prison it was such that the prisoners' food was supplied daily from the neighbouring inn, and the innkeeper's bill constituted the only accounts kept. The committee might well suggest the abolition of these gaols, or their amalgamation with the larger county establishments in their immediate neighbourhood. Some idea of the comparative uselessness of these small borough prisons was conveyed by some figures quoted by the committee. In 1862 there were in all one hundred and ninety-three gaols in England and Wales; of these, sixty-three gave admittance during the entire year to less than twenty-five prisoners; twenty-two others received between eleven and twenty-five; fourteen received less than eleven and more than six; while twenty-seven received less than six prisoners, and were in some instances absolutely tenantless.

The result of the recommendation of the committee of 1862 was the Prison Act of 1865, the penultimate of such enactments, many of the provisions of which still remain in force. The main object of this act was to compass that uniformity in discipline and treatment generally which had long been admitted as indispensable, and had never as yet been properly obtained. The legislature was beginning to overcome its disinclination to interfere actively or authoritatively with the local jurisdictions, although still very leniently disposed. However, it now laid down in plain language and with precise details the requirements of a good gaol system. The separation of prisoners in cells duly certified by the inspectors was insisted upon, also their constant employment in labour appropriate to their condition. Hard labour of the first and second class was carefully defined. The former, which consisted principally of the tread-wheel, cranks, capstans, shot-drill, was to be the rule for all convicted prisoners throughout the early stages of their detention; while the latter, which included various forms of industrial employment, was the boon to which willing industry extending over a long period established a certain claim. The infliction of punishment more or less uniform was thus aimed at. On the other hand, new and careful regulations were framed to secure the moral and material well-being of the inmates of the gaols. The law made it imperative that every prison should have a prison chapel, and that daily and Sunday services should be held. The chaplain's duties were enlarged, and the principle of toleration accepted to the extent of securing to all prisoners the ministrations of ministers of their own form of belief. Steps were taken to provide the illiterate with secular instruction. No less close was the care as regards preservation of health. Stringent rules were prescribed for the prison surgeons; every prison was ordered to keep up an infirmary, and the medical supervision was to be strict and continuous. Dietaries were drawn up for adoption on the recommendation of a committee of experts. Baths were provided, ablutions ordered, and all appliances to insure personal cleanliness.

The administration of good government was to be watched over by the local magistracy, certain of whom, styled visiting justices, were elected to inspect the prisons frequently, to examine the prisoners, hear complaints, and check abuses. Under them the governor or gaoler was held strictly responsible.

The books and journals he was to keep were minutely specified, and his constant presence in or near the gaol was insisted upon. His disciplinary powers were defined by the act, and his duties, both in controlling his subordinates and in protecting the prisoners from petty tyranny and oppression, every one of whom he was to see once every twenty-four hours. But discipline was to be maintained if necessary by punishment, while decency and good order were to be insured by the strict prohibition of gambling and drunkenness. The latter was rendered nearly impossible by the penalties imposed on persons bringing spirituous liquors into the gaol. The old custom, so fruitful of the worst evils, of keeping a tap inside the prison was made illegal. So was the employment of prisoners in any position of trust or authority; they were not to be turnkeys or assistant turnkeys, neither wardsman nor yardsman, overseer, monitor, or schoolmaster, nor to be engaged in the service of any officer of the prison.

The Act of 1865 also encouraged and empowered the local authorities to "alter, enlarge, or rebuild" their prisons. They might raise funds for this purpose, provided a certificate for the necessity for the new works was given, either by the recorder, chairman of quarter sessions, or even by a couple of justices. Every facility was promised. The sanction of the Secretary of State would not be withheld if plans and estimates were duly submitted, and they met with the approval of his professional adviser, the surveyor-general of prisons. The funds necessary would be advanced by the Public Works Loan Commissioners, and the interest might be charged against the county or borough rates. Nor were these the only inducements offered. Where local authorities were indisposed to set their prisons in order, or hesitated to embark upon any considerable expenditure to alter or rebuild, they were at liberty to hire suitable cell accommodation from any neighbours who might have it to spare; the only proviso, that no such contract was valid between one jurisdiction and another unless the Secretary of State was satisfied that the prison it was intended to use came up in all respects to modern requirements.

But the act was not limited to permissive legislation. Its provisions and enactments were backed up by certain penalties. The Secretary of State was empowered to deal rather summarily with "inadequate" prisons, in other words, with those in which there was no separation, no proper enforcement of hard labour, no chapel, infirmary, and so forth. He could in the first place withhold the government grant in aid of prison funds by refusing the certificate to the Treasury upon which the allowance was paid. This he might do on the representation of the inspector of prisons, who was bound to report any deficiencies and abuses he might find at his periodical visits. The Secretary of State might go further. Where the local authority had neglected to comply with the provisions of the 1865 Act for four consecutive years, he could close the "inadequate" prison, by declaring it unfit for the reception of prisoners. His order would at the same time specify some neighbouring and more satisfactory prison which the local authority would be compelled to utilize instead, and with the concurrence of the other authority, and on payment. A few provisos governed these rather extensive powers. It was necessary, for instance, to give due notice when the government grant was to be withdrawn, and with the warning a copy of the particular defects and allegations was to be sent to the local authority. The latter too was to be laid before the House of Commons. In the same way, six months' notice was required in cases where the closing of a prison was contemplated; but if these conditions were observed, the Secretary of State could deal sharply enough with the defaulting jurisdictions.

Yet the law was seldom if ever enforced. It was practically

inoperative as regards the penalties for neglect. It was no doubt as irksome and inconvenient to the Secretary of State to avail himself of his powers, as it was difficult to bring home the derelictions of duties and evasion of the acts. Too much was left to the inspectors. It was nearly impossible for them to exercise a very close supervision over the whole of the prisons of the country. There were only two of them, and they could not visit each prison more than once in each year, sometimes not oftener than once in eighteen months. The task imposed upon them, tending as it did to the imposition of a fine upon the local authorities, was not a pleasant one, and it is not strange if they did not very frequently hand up the offenders to the reproof and correction of the Secretary of State. As the almost inevitable consequence, while the more glaring defects in prison management disappeared, matters went on after the 1865 Act much the same as they had done before. Districts differed greatly in the attention they paid to prison affairs. In one part the most praiseworthy activity prevailed, in another there was half-heartedness, even apathy and an almost complete contempt for the provisions of the act.

As the years passed, great want of uniformity continued to prevail throughout the prisons of the United Kingdom. The whole question assumed sufficient importance to become a part of the Government programme when Lord Beaconsfield took office in 1874. The Home Secretary in that administration, Mr. (now Sir Richard) Cross, having applied himself vigorously to the task of reorganizing the whole system, became convinced that no complete reform could be accomplished so long as the prisons were left under the jurisdiction of the local authorities. The Prisons Bill of 1876 contemplated the transfer of the prisons to Government. This bill, reintroduced in 1877, became law that year, after which the whole of the prisons, including Newgate, passed under the more direct control of the State. Since then a strong central authority has laboured steadfastly to compass concentration, to close useless prisons, and to insure that uniformity of system which all thoughtful persons had long admitted to be of paramount importance in the administration of prisons. Three years after the advent of the prison commissioners, it was decided that Newgate was an excessively costly and redundant establishment. It was only filled at the periods when the sessions of the Central Criminal Court were in progress; at others an expensive staff was maintained with little or nothing to do. At a short distance stood another prison of detention, that of Clerkenwell, with spare accommodation sufficient to receive all prisoners who were then committed to Newgate. These arguments were unanswerable. Accordingly, it was ordered by Sir William Harcourt, the present Secretary of State, that Newgate should cease to be used as a regular prison, and it is now, except during sessions or when the gallows is in requisition, practically and for ever closed.

FOOTNOTES TO VOLUME 2

[1] Report of the Committee of the House of Commons on the police of the metropolis, 1816.

[2] Sir James Mackintosh on the state of the criminal law.

[3] Wade, p. 1056.

[4] Evidence of Alderman Harmer before Committee on Capital Punishment, 1819.

[5] A remarkable diminution of forgeries at once followed the abolition of the £1 notes.

[6] See post. chap. vii.

[7] "If Dr. Dodd does not suffer the sentence of the law," said Lord Mansfield to the King in Council, "then the Perreaus have been murdered." The Lord Chief Justice held an opinion in common with most reflecting men of that age, that death for forgery was indispensable to protect commercial credit. Lord Campbell, in his 'Lives of the Lords Chief Justice,' states that he heard a Judge say, after passing the death sentence for forgery, "May you find the mercy above which a due regard to the credit

of the paper currency of this country forbids you to hope for here."

[8] See vol. i. p. 380.

[9] Knapp and Baldwin's 'Newgate Calendar,' i. 160.

[10] See chap. viii. vol. i.

[11] By an act of William and Mary, £40 was offered for the apprehension and conviction of a highwayman; the same sum, by 6 and 7 William III. cap. 17, for conviction of a coiner or clipper; also, by 5 Anne, cap. 31, for conviction of a burglar or housebreaker. Ten pounds was the reward for the conviction of a sheep-stealer, or of a person uttering or paving away counterfeit money, or fabricating spurious copper coins.

[12] Evidence of John Vickery, a Bow Street runner, before committee on the police of the metropolis, 1816.

[13] The sobriquet of Gentleman Harry was also enjoyed by Henry Simms, a highwayman who frequented the Lewisham and Blackheath roads. On one occasion, when travelling into Northamptonshire on a rather fresh horse, a gentleman who was in a post-chaise remarked to him, "Don't ride so hard, sir, or you'll soon ride away all your estate." "Indeed I shall not," replied Simms, "for it lies in several counties," and dismounting, he challenged the gentleman to stand, and robbed him of a hundred and two guineas.

[14] See *ante*, vol. i. p. 187.

[15] See *ante*, p. 29.

[16] See chapter iii., 'Philanthropy in Newgate.'

[17] See *ante*, vol. i. p. 238, where there is an account of how Williams, Wilkes' publisher, was put in the pillory.

[18] Grant's 'Newspaper Press,' vol. i. 172.

[19] *Ibid.* i. 220.

[20] *Ibid.* i. 220.

[21] In March 1805 the sheriffs of London had been committed to Newgate by the House of Commons for gross

partiality in favour of Sir Francis Burdett at the election for Middlesex.

[22] 'State of Prisons in England, Scotland, and Wales,' 1812.

[23] These cabins were partitioned off by a wooden hoarding which went up three parts of the way to the ceiling, and they received all light and air from the top.

[24] See *ante*, vol. i. p. 250.

[25] 'Neild,' p. 425.

[26] *Ibid.*

[27] *Ibid.*

[28] Debtors are still sent to prison (1883) for a fixed term, but only under a warrant of contempt of court. It is in the power of the County Court judge thus to punish all whom he believes can pay, but will not. Nevertheless, numerous cases of hardship still occur. As when a working-man's wife pledges his credit in his absence, makes away with the writs served by the creditor, and ignores judgment obtained. The husband hears first of the affair when arrested for contempt.

[29] The large discretionary powers of these courts created a petty tyranny in a set of standing commissioners.—*Blackstone.*

[30] 'Neild.'

[31] Besides these and other fees paid in prison, there were the charges of the "secondary," who received a shilling per pound for every pound under £100, and sixpence for every pound above that sum. This was called the sheriff's poundage, and often amounted to large sums—as much as £97 odd in one case which is cited by Mr. Neild.

[32] 'Neild,' p. 312.

[33] Neild says in 1803 there were 229 males, 148 females, and 391 children in the gaol.

[34] 1814.

[35] It was so condemned in 1808 on account of its ruinous condition. The debtors were but indifferently lodged, but the

common side felons occupied a horrible den styled the Rat Hole, and the women another called the Mouse Hole.

[36] See *ante*, p. 69.

[37] Mr. John Kirby.

[38] Even the felons were better off for food. See p. 104.

[39] See *ante*, p. 68, *et seq.*

[40] See *ante*, p. 57.

[41] Evidence before Committee of House of Commons, 1814.

[42] See *ante*, p. 72.

[43] One lunatic was kept in the state side upwards of six years. He was described as "sometimes a little dangerous," and generally occupied in a room by himself. There were at this time three or four other lunatics (two of them "dangerous") who went at large in the wards on the common side.

[44] See *ante*, vol. i. cap. v.

[45] Cashman was the only one of the Spafields rioters (1816) who was capitally convicted and executed. Four others who were arraigned with him were acquitted by the jury, to the astonishment of the court. Cashman, who had been a seaman in the Royal Navy, pleaded that he had been to the Admiralty to claim prize-money to the value of £200 on the day of the riot. On his way home, half drunk, he had been persuaded to join the rioters. Cashman's unconcern lasted to the end. As he appeared on the gallows the mob groaned and hissed the Government, and Cashman joined in the outcry until the drop fell.

[46] As to ironing females, see *post*, p. 136.

[47] Visitors were searched at the lodge—the males by a turnkey, the females by a woman retained for the purpose. These officials had orders to strip those they searched if they thought necessary. The examination was seldom of any avail; but on one occasion a wife, who had hopes of compassing her husband's escape, was detected in trying to pass a long rope into the prison. The woman was arrested and committed to Newgate

for trial, where her husband already lay cast for highway robbery.

[48] Petworth Prison, built in 1785, and Gloucester Penitentiary, erected in 1791, were the two first gaols established which provided a separate sleeping cell for every prisoner.

[49] Some interesting details are published by the French Prison Society on this head.

[50] How perfunctory was the performance of his duties by the ordinary may be gathered from the following chapter.

[51] See *post*, p. 491.

[52] 'Dr. Forde's Evidence,' p. 56.

[53] 'Memoirs of Mrs. Fry,' i. 312.

[54] The Philanthropic Society is identical with the Farm School at Redhill, one of our most prosperous and best-managed reformatory schools at the present date. Mr. William Crawfurd, afterwards one of the first inspectors of prisons, was long an active member of the committee during the early days of the Society.

[55] See *ante*, cap. ii.

[56] 'Buxton on Prison Discipline,' 1818.

[57] This was the germ of the Ladies' Committee, which existed down to 1878.

[58] 'Buxton on Prison Discipline,' p. 125.

[59] 'Buxton,' p. 271.

[60] Still in existence, and still deserving of praise.

[61] Stated at length the title is, 'An Inquiry whether crime and misery are produced or prevented by our present system of prison discipline, illustrated by descriptions of various prisons.'

[62] 'Wm. Smith on State of Jails,' 1776, already referred to, vol. i. cap. x.

[63] 19 Charles II. c. 4.

[64] 'Buxton,' p. 23.

[65] In 1823 the society reported that "prisoners for assize at

one county gaol are double ironed on first reception, and thus fettered, are at night chained down in bed, the chain being fixed to the floor of the cell, and fastened to the leg fetters of the prisoners. This chain is of sufficient length to enable the prisoners to raise themselves in bed. The cell is then locked, and he continues thus chained down from seven o'clock in the evening till six o'clock next morning. There were but two gaol deliveries in the county for the year, so a prisoner may continue to be thus treated for from six to eight months, and be then acquitted as innocent." The double irons for the untried varied in weight from ten to fourteen pounds.

[66] Mr. Buxton, while most loudly inveighing against the foul state of most British gaols, fully exonerates the governors. "None of the grievances represented," he says in his preface, "are occasioned by the gaolers; that class of men are often subjected to undistinguished abuse; my experience would furnish me with very different language. Without any exception, I have had reason to approve, and sometimes to applaud, their conduct; and I can truly say that of all the persons with whom I have conversed, they are the most sensible of the evils of our present system of prison discipline."

[67] See *post*, chap. v. The privilege of getting in extra and more luxurious articles of food long survived.

[68] See *ante*, p. 106.

[69] Prisons. 'Edinburgh Review,' Feb. 1822.

[70] See *ante*, p. 139.

[71] The greatest variety existed as to the amount of ascension. In one prison a prisoner had to ascend as much as 17,000 feet daily, in others between 6000 and 7000. Women were put on the tread-wheel in those times.

[72] Dance's Newgate was commenced before Howard's 'State of Prisons' was published, and was very properly condemned as defective by him and others. In the volume from which I am

quoting its defects are fully detailed. Everything was sacrificed to the one idea of safe custody. To secure this, the "airing courts were enclosed by lofty impenetrable buildings, by which the general salubrity and ventilation of the interior became materially diminished." By the arrangement of the courts it was impracticable to preserve a judicious system of separation. No sleeping cells were provided, and, as we know, the prisoners passed the night associated together in crowded rooms. No inspection was possible. On these accounts the Prison Discipline Society were of opinion that Newgate was "particularly objectionable as a model for imitation, ... a remark not deserving the less attention because the exterior of the prison presents a massive and imposing elevation which is calculated to excite impressions in favour of its security and seclusion."

[73] See *ante*, p. 155.

[74] There were still some notorious exceptions. The most extraordinary neglect prevailed in the county prison at Exeter, which was left year after year in its old disgraceful state, overcrowded, filthy, without chaplain, hospital, dietaries, or proper clothing for prisoners.

[75] Just before sessions the total was generally much higher, and reached at times to nearly 500.

[76] See last chapter of this volume.

[77] This is the French and Belgian practice still. In both those countries a portion of the *pécule*, or prisoner's earnings, can be spent in the prison canteen in various luxuries of diet.

[78] The Gaol Acts of 1823-4.

[79] 'Report of P. D. Society, 1827,' p. 37.

[80] It was the Duke of Richmond, himself the chairman of that committee, who had introduced the bill for the purpose.

[81] See *ante*, p. 131.

[82] Mr. Wakefield's abduction of Miss Turner will be found treated at length in chapter viii. His work on the punishment of

death, which deals with Newgate at this time, I shall draw upon largely in the next chapter.

[83] These words were the foundation of the great libel cause of Stockdale *versus* Hansard, which will be remembered as threatening a serious collision between the House of Commons and the administration of the law. Mr. Stockdale, feeling aggrieved at the remarks of the Inspectors of Prisons, brought an action for libel against Messrs. Hansard, who published them. Hansard pleaded justification, and that the report was privileged, being printed by the authority of the House of Commons. Lord Denman, on the bench, dissented, and charged the jury that no such authority could justify a libel, but Hansard obtained a verdict of not guilty. Stockdale then brought a fresh action, and Hansard appealed to the House for protection. A Committee of the House was appointed to inquire into the matter, and it upheld the view that official blue books could not be open to action for libel. This formed the basis of Hansard's defence; but the court would not admit the plea, and cast them in damages. Hansard did not pay, and went on with the publication. A third action was then commenced, on the grounds that the sale of the report was a reiterance of the libel. To this action Hansard would not plead. A fresh declaration was filed by Stockdale, with the damages laid at £50,000; and as Hansard still, under the advice of the House, would not appear, the case again went against him.

Stockdale now sued for his damages in the Sheriffs' Court. The sheriffs, well aware that Messrs. Hansard were backed up by the House of Commons, tried to escape giving a judgment, at least until the House met, but they were ordered by the superior courts to proceed. They accordingly assessed Stockdale's damages at £600, and in liquidation thereof entered into possession of Hansard's premises. The printers once more appealed to the House, which on the first day of the session went into the whole case. On the motion of Lord John Russell, the sheriffs were summoned to the bar of the House for infringing its privileges, and committed to the custody of the sergeant-at-arms. Stockdale was also summoned, cross-examined, and committed, but to Newgate. He, notwithstanding his imprisonment, continued to bring action after action; then his attorneys, through whom they were commenced, were summoned to the bar of the House, and also sent to Newgate. Meanwhile the sergeant-at-arms, under a writ of Habeas Corpus, had to produce the sheriffs at the court of Queen's Bench; but the judges would not release them, holding that they were legally detained. Much dissatisfaction now began to show itself throughout the country, but the House of Commons would not yield an inch on the question of privilege. The subject was debated night after night, and at last, to settle the matter once for all, Lord John Russell introduced a bill specially intended to protect all parliamentary publications, issued by either House, from any proceedings in any court of law. This was passed in due course, and the privileges of Parliament were upheld.

The sheriffs had already been released from custody on grounds of ill-health. An application was made for the enlargement of Stockdale and his attorneys from Newgate on the passing of the bill, but it was at first rejected. Two months later the application was renewed, and being unopposed, the prisoners were set free.

[84] Prisoners' evidence.

[85] In 1833 a sentence of death was passed on a child of nine, who had poked a stick through a patched-up pane of glass in a shop-front, and thrusting his hand through the aperture, had stolen fifteen pieces of paint, worth twopence. This was construed into house-breaking, the principal witness being another child of nine, who "told" because he had not his share of the paint. The boy was not executed.

[86] These Newgate tokens were circular thin pieces of metal of various sizes. The initials or the names of a loving pair were punched upon them, together with a heart or some symbol of affection; sometimes with a motto, such as 'True for ever,' 'Love for life.' The greatest value was attached to these tokens by the criminal classes. Those at large constantly wore them round their necks, and treated them as amulets to preserve them from danger and detection.

[87] Lord John Russell, at that time Home Secretary.

[88] See *ante*, vol. i. cap. vi.

[89] Newgate Calendar.

[90] Catnach's 'Street Literature.'

[91] 'A Book for a Rainy Day,' p. 167.

[92] *Ibid.* p. 171.

[93] See *ante*, p. 127.

[94] Governor Wall had held the rank of colonel in the army when serving at Goree.

[95] 'Picturesque Sketches of London,' by Thomas Miller, 1851.

[96] See *ante*, p. 214.

[97] 'The Punishment of Death in the Metropolis.' E. Gibbon Wakefield, p. 139.

[98] It was the Rev. Peter Fenn.

[99] By 32 Henry VIII. cap. 42 (1540), surgeons were granted four bodies of executed malefactors for "anathomyes," which privilege was extended in the following reign.—Haydn, 'Dict. of Dates,' p. 32.

[100] Sir Baptist Hicks also built Campden House, Kensington. In 1628 he was created Baron Hicks and Viscount Campden, with remainder to his daughter's children. She was the wife of Lord Noel, ancestor of the present Earl of Gainsborough.

[101] 'New Monthly Magazine,' 1855, p. 376.

[102] This murder inspired De Quincey's 'Murder as one of the Fine Arts.'

[103] Dymond, 'The Law on its Trial,' p. 57.

[104] Dymond, 'The Law on its Trial,' p. 194.

[105] That of Roderick Maclean, 1882.

[106] See cap. i. p. 7.

[107] It was said that the dinners he gave were of the most sumptuous and *recherché* description. The story goes, that one of his most chosen friends, who attended him to the scaffold, entreated him, as on the brink of the grave, and unable to take anything out of the world with him, to reveal the secret of where some wonderful curaçoa was obtained, for which Fauntleroy's cellar was famous.

[108] See *ante*, p. 102.

[109] The reader will have perceived from the Inspectors of Prisons first report that this hope was still unfulfilled in 1836, twelve years later.

[110] See chap. ii. p. 129.

[111] For abduction. See *post*, p. 302.

[112] At Liverpool, in 1842, there was a case of abduction, and the well-known case of Mr. Carden and Miss Arbuthnot in Ireland occurred as late as 1854.

[113] See vol. i. p. 178.

[114] But not quite. The Warwick Mail was stopped in 1827, and robbed of £20,000 in bank-notes.

[115] That sound and illustrious lawyer, Sir James Stephen, is of opinion that the receiver of stolen goods is one of the greatest of criminals; and in his recently-published history of the Criminal Law he seriously recommends capital punishment for those who have been repeatedly convicted of the offence.

[116] See *ante*, p. 317.

[117] See *ante*, p. 344.

[118] See *ante*, p. 18.

[119] Erected for night watchman.

[120] *i. e.* sentence.

[121] 'Times,' Nov. 15, 1864.

[122] See *post*, p. 441.

[123] See *ante*, p. 369.

[124] See *ante*, p. 271.

[125] That of Cook, for which he was tried and sentenced to death.

[126] They have since been repeated, but accompanied by more premeditation, in the case of Lefroy, who murdered Mr. Gould in a first-class carriage on the Brighton line in 1881.

[127] Evidence of Lieutenant-Colonel Jebb, Commons' Committee, 1850, ii. 50.

[128] None, however, equalled the enormous expenditure incurred at York, where a prison had been built some years previously, under the auspices of Sydney Smith, at a cost of about £1000 per cell.

[129] Prisoners at first greatly dreaded the mask. Mr. Field, in his book on prison discipline, mentions a prisoner on his way to Reading Gaol, soon after the separate system was introduced, who jumped out of the cart at the gaol door and tried to drown himself, handcuffed as he was. His plea when rescued was that he wished to avoid the mask.

THE END

Printed in Great Britain
by Amazon